The Evolution of Settlement Systems in the Region of Vohemar, Northeast Madagascar

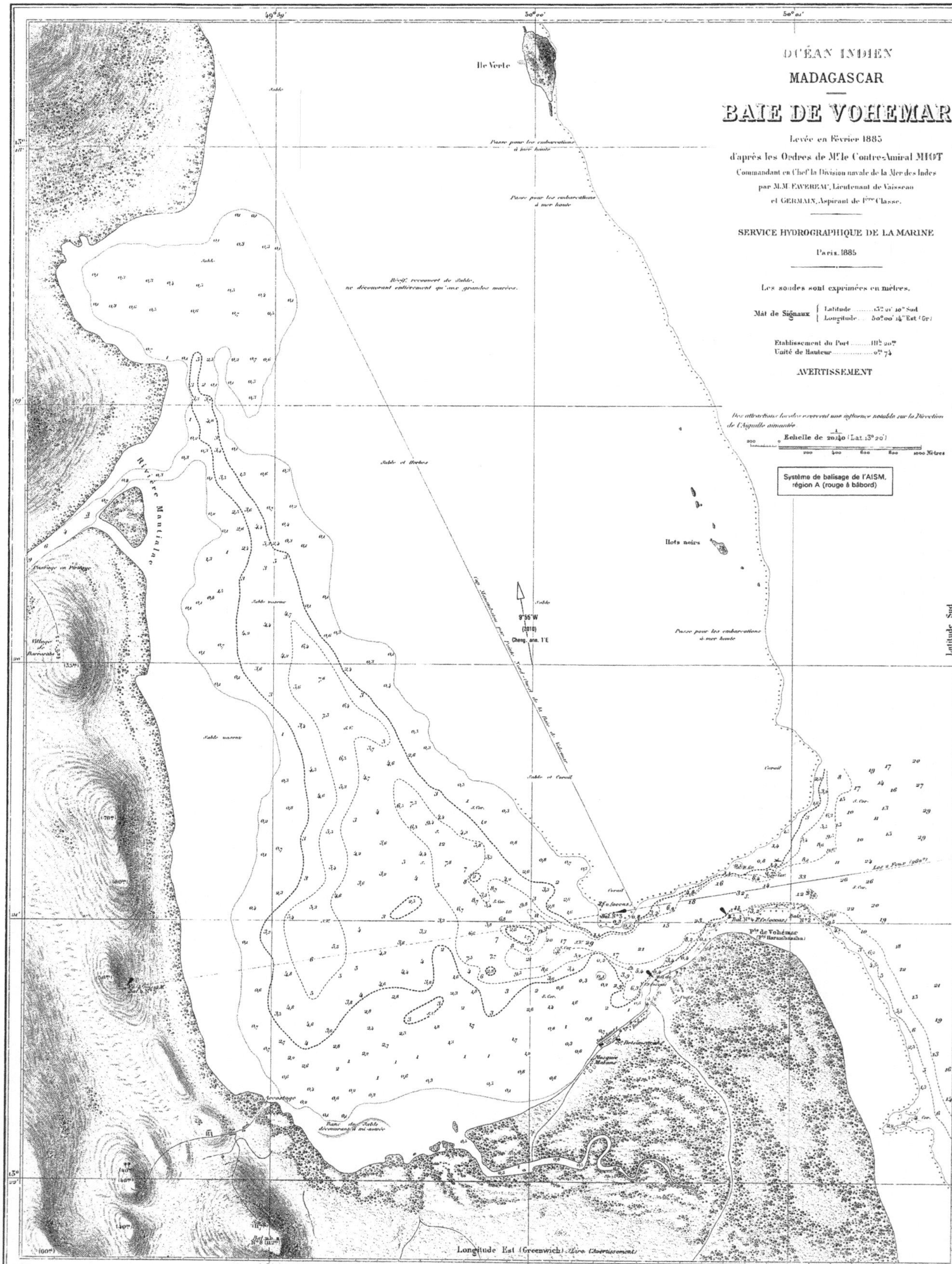

Gravé par A. Grenier. Corr. : 1948-703 à 2001-0343

Écrit par F. Lefèvre.

Édition de Novembre 1936

Memoirs of the Museum of Anthropology
University of Michigan

Number 63

The Evolution of Settlement Systems in the Region of Vohemar, Northeast Madagascar

by Henry T. Wright, Robert E. Dewar,
Chantal Radimilahy, and Lucien M. A. Rakotozafy

Ann Arbor, Michigan
2022

Printed in the United States of America
ISBN 978-1-951538-70-5 (print)
ISBN 978-1-951538-71-2 (ebook)

Cover design by John Klausmeyer

Buy this book at **www.press.umich.edu//search/vohemar**
Browse all of our books at **sites.lsa.umich.edu/archaeology-books**
Visit the Museum website at **lsa.umich.edu/ummaa**

The University of Michigan Museum of Anthropological Archaeology (UMMAA) publishes books on archaeology and anthropology. For permissions, questions, or manuscript queries, contact Museum publications in Ann Arbor, Michigan, by email at umma-pubs@umich.edu.

Library of Congress Cataloging-in-Publication Data

Names: Wright, Henry T. (Henry Tutwiler), 1943- author. | Dewar, Robert E., author. | Radimilahy, Marie de Chantal, author. | Rakotozafy, Lucien M. A., author. | Michigan Publishing (University of Michigan), publisher.
Title: The evolution of settlement systems in the region of Vohémar, Northeast Madagascar / by Henry T. Wright, Robert E. Dewar, Chantal Radimilahy, and Lucien M. A. Rakotozafy.
Other titles: Memoirs of the Museum of Anthropology, University of Michigan ; no. 63.
Description: Ann Arbor : University of Michigan Museum of Anthropological Archaeology, 2022. | Series: Memoirs of the Museum of Anthropology, University of Michigan ; number 63 | Includes bibliographical references (pages175-179). | Summary: Henry T. Wright, Robert E. Dewar, Chantal Radimilahy, and Lucien M. A. Rakotozafy report on the results of a four-year archaeological survey on the northeast coast of Madagascar, near the town of Vohemar. Researchers found evidence of a roughly 600-year-old port site; early estuarine villages of the seventh and eighth centuries; and a rock shelter with microlithic tools.
Identifiers: LCCN 2022021542 (print) | LCCN 2022021543 (ebook) | ISBN 9781951538705 (paperback) | ISBN 9781951538712 (ebook)
Subjects: LCSH: Excavations (Archaeology)--Madagascar--Vohémar. | Land settlement patterns--Madagascar--Vohémar. | Archaeology--Madagascar--Vohémar. | Vohémar (Madagascar)--History. | Vohémar (Madagascar)--Antiquities. | BISAC: SOCIAL SCIENCE / Archaeology | HISTORY / Africa / East
Classification: LCC DT469.M38 V627 2022 (print) | LCC DT469.M38 (ebook) | DDC 969.1/01--dc23/eng/20220506
LC record available at https://lccn.loc.gov/2022021542
LC ebook record available at https://lccn.loc.gov/2022021543

The paper used in this publication meets the requirements of the ANSI Standard Z39.48-1984 (Permanence of Paper).

Table of Contents

Appendices

Acknowledgments

The 2007–2010 fieldwork was made possible through a grant to Robert E. Dewar by the British Institute in Eastern Africa. The Institute des Civlisations/ Musée d'Art et d'Archéologie contributed equipment, vehicles and experienced technicians. The University of Michigan Museum of Anthropology contributed additional funds for travel and radiocarbon dating. For their assistance in the field, we thank Victor Rajanatovo, Jeannot Ramisharison, Jean-Aimé Andriamaherilala, Harisoa Ravoviarimanara, Sylvain Solimora, and Annita Ramanankierana for their hard work in the field. For his advice on local geology, we are indebted to Jean-Aimé Rakotoarisoa. For advice on early maritime issues, we thank Jean-Christian Peyre. Finally, we are indebted to Jeffrey Parsons for his careful critical reading of the entire text, to John Klausmeyer for his excellent maps, plans, and sections, and Elizabeth Noll for her thorough editing.

List of Illustrations

Part I

Background to a Survey in Northeast Madagascar

Chapter 1

Introduction

Madagascar—among the last large land masses to be settled by human communities—is an environmentally diverse mini-continent in the Western Indian Ocean. It manifests almost every known type of environment except arctic tundra and taiga. Madagascar has attracted the interest of scholars sine at least the seventeenth century CE, because of its unique endemic flora and fauna and because the majority of its people and languages show affinities not with nearby Africa, but with distant Southeast Asia. For historians and anthropologists, this poses the questions of whether the diverse people of Madagascar arrived with a homogenous Southeast Asian culture and subsequently adapted to Madagascar's varied landscapes, or whether, in contrast, different people went to different parts of the mini-continent that best suited their prior experience and needs. The four principal authors of this volume have concerned themselves with different aspects of these questions. Dewar has long been interested in early human arrivals and their impact on differing environments. Radimilahy has been equally interested in different human developments in the thorn deserts of the far south, the high central plateau, and the humid forests and coasts of the northwest. Wright has focused on the relatively late development of hierarchical polities and urban economies in various parts of Madagascar. Rakotozafy has studied the human uses of animals throughout Madagascar's history.

Until recently, most scholars thought that Madagascar was first settled less than two millennia ago by people from Southeast Asia with sophisticated outrigger sailing craft, iron technology, and agriculture, who rapidly spread throughout the island (Dewar 2003; Dewar and Wright 1993) transforming its diverse natural ecosystems (Burney 1999). The earliest well-dated occupational site, Lakaton'i Anja, in the Gorge of Andavakoera in the northernmost part of Madagascar, was recognized as a forager campsite in a limestone rock shelter dating as early as AD 400 (Dewar and Rakotovololona 1982). Village and hamlet sites of the eighth to tenth centuries AD were known on the northeast

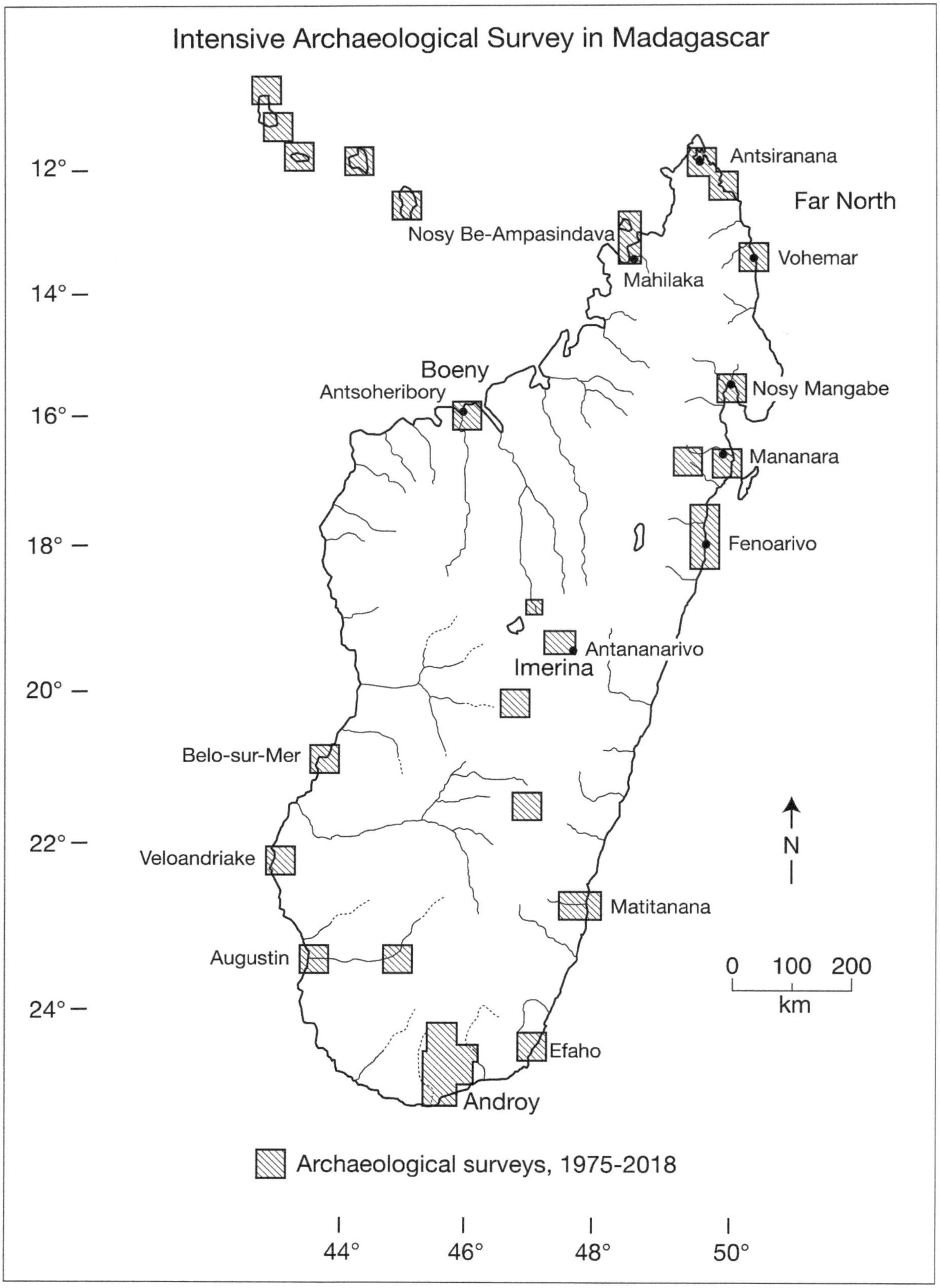

Figure 1.1. Madagascar, showing places and surveyed areas mentioned in the text.

coast and around the Bay of Antongil (Wright and Fanony 1992) and farther south in the valley of the Maningory near Fenoarivo (Dewar et al. 2011). In this monograph we present the evidence of early foragers and early villagers around the Bay of Iharana near modern Vohemar, as well as evidence of the development of the rich seaport of Vohemar (Figure 1.1).

In July 2007 we initiated a survey of the area of Vohemar as one element in Le Projet des Embouchures, a broader study by the Institue des Civilisations/ Musée d'Art et d'Archéologie of the history of settlement and land use changes on the embouchures—a term that includes both the tidal estuaries proper and the bays or sounds into which these flow—of the coasts of Madagascar. Studies previous to ours have focused on the following areas: the west coast; the Bay of St. Augustine and the lower Onilahy Valley on the southwest coast (Radimilahy et al. 2006); the Bay of Boeny and the lower Mahavavy Valley on the central west coast (Matsumoto and Burney 1994; Vérin 1975 I:341–439; Wright et al. 1996); and the Bay of Ampasindava, including the island of Nosibe and the lower Sambirano Valley, on the northwest coast (Radimilahy 1998; Wright and Radimilahy 2005). On the east coast, previous studies have focused on the Valley of the Efaho on the southeast coast (Rakotoarisoa 1998; Wright et al. 1993); the embouchures of the Manambato and Onibe and the area around Fenoarivo (Dewar et al. 2011; Wright and Dewar 2000); the embouchure and middle reaches of the Mananara Valley and adjacent seacoasts south of the Bay of Antongil on the northeast coast (Wright and Dewar 2000; Wright and Fanony 1992); and the Bay of Antseranana (Diego Suarez) and adjacent areas in the far north (Dewar and Rakotovololona 1992).

We hoped to clarify two specific problems in the developing human ecology of the Embouchure of Iharana. First, because the area would be one of the first visited by mariners coming across the Indian Ocean from the northeast, and because it is particularly rich in marine resources (both in the lagoon of Iharana and around the protecting reefs) and in the resources of the mangroves and marshes and of the estuary itself, we predicted we would find evidence of early villages. Our first task was to find and characterize the earliest villages around the Bay of Iharana. Second, because its location profits from winds coming from South and Southeast Asia, because the earliest accounts of European mariners mention a rich town here in the sixteenth century, and because parts of a rich cemetery of the fourteenth to seventeenth centuries had been excavated (Goudebout and Venier 1941b; Schreurs et al. 2011), we predicted we would find this rich town site. Our second task was to find and characterize this town and its predecessors. The first task was quickly accomplished. The second task proved more difficult. Our discovery of evidence of foragers using a stone tool technology was completely unexpected.

Chapter 2

The Vohemar Area in Geographical Perspective

Geology

The Vohemar area flanks the northeast edge of the ancient Archean continental fragment—the core of Madagascar—which was transformed into granites, migmatites, and other rocks by pervasive metamorphic processes during the Paleozoic and Mesozoic eras (Schreurs and Rakotoarisoa 2011). The resistant higher ridges visible today are primarily granite, but many other rocks and minerals occur. Of importance to the early human inhabitants were localized occurrences of chlorite schist, commonly called soapstone, which was worked into vessels and exported (Gaudebout and Vernier 1941a; Mouren et Rouaix 1913; Serneels et al. 2017; Vérin 1986:209–216). Quartz is also common, though not, as far as we know, the clear crystal quartz exported from the Bay of Antongil. Iron oxide nodules, found eroding from iron-rich ultisols in and near marshes, may have been the source of iron ore used by early blacksmiths. Found in alluvial sands from the Loky River in the north to the Manambery River in the south are small particles of gold (Christopher 2004; Lemoine 1906:82).

The coastal areas manifest a complex development of Late Pleistocene and Holocene shoreline features (Rossi 1980:89–123).

- The active first beach extends up to two meters above mean low tide and has evidence of modern occupation.
- The second beach, from two to six meters above high tide—which Battistini (1964) called the Flandrian beach—is articulated with coral platforms about one meter above mean low tide. These have weakly developed soils on light brown sand and evidence of occupation during the past millennium, as well as the eggshells of flightless birds (discussed below). West of this beach are dunes, through which what we term the "old estuary" meanders, emptying

into the Bay of Iharana from the south (we were unable to elicit a local name for the old estuary).

- The third beach, the Karimbolian beach of Battistini (1964), reaches up to 60 meters in altitude above mean low tide near Vohemar and is articulated with coral platforms about three meters above sea level. It has a thick soil development with .80 m or more of leached white A-Horizon. This is well dated in several areas from 80,000 to 150,000 years ago and could have been occupied during any cultural period. This massive beach formation is well defined in the Vohemar area.
- A higher complex of beaches with deeply weathered red sands is also well defined. These beaches, termed Tatsimian by Battistini (1964), must be greater than 150,000 years old, and also could have been occupied during any cultural period.

Climate

The climate of the Vohemar area is relatively warm and humid, with a mean daytime temperature in the austral summer of about 27°C and mean daytime temperature in the austral winter of about 23° C (Rossi 1980:39). During the mid-twentieth century, Vohemar had a mean annual rainfall of 148 cm occurring an average of 184 days a year (Donque 1975:317). The heaviest rains fall in the austral summer months of December through April, with the least rainfall during the month of October. Even the drier months usually have rain on more than ten days (Donque 1975:343.)

Discussion of the mean conditions, however, neglects the more abrupt and often disastrous natural events that can strike human communities in this region. As in many areas of Madagascar, there is a high frequency of tropical cyclones with damaging winds and floods. Between 1960 and 1974 Vohemar was struck by cyclones in January 1962, December 1965, January 1966, December 1968, November 1969, and January 1971 (Donque 1975:243–299.) In addition, this coastline is directly exposed to the southeastern trade winds of the austral winter. Sea conditions in those months are often dangerous for small craft. Anchorages for larger craft are usually dangerously exposed. However, the harbor of Vohemar in the lagoon of the Bay of Iharana, with its massive reefs and sand banks, is relatively well protected and has good fishing and shellfishing opportunities.

Flora and Fauna

By the tenth century, people had been living on the northeast coast for at least three millennia (Dewar et al. 2013). There is little record of the Holocene ecological history of the region from pollen analysis or other techniques, although it is likely, as elsewhere on Madagascar, that there have been significant changes over the twelve millennia since the last glaciation. Today this region is covered with a mosaic of dry and humid forest remnants, brushy secondary growth, grassy pasturelands, dry fields on slopes, irrigated fields on valley bottom, wetlands, and—close to the coast—significant areas of coconut (*Cocos nucifera*) and other introduced cash crops. There are some small areas of surviving coastal forest, such as that at Sahaka, about 30 km north of Vohemar. Several recent biological surveys in this 9222-ha forest show high levels of biodiversity and endemism (Goodman and Wilmé eds. 2006; Safford 2000). The forest is a littoral remnant of the Eastern Lowland Domain. The emergent canopy, which is only 10 to 15 meters in height, is dominated by trees of the Aricardiacae, Panandanacae, Rubiacae, and Sapindacae (Ranaivonasy 2003).

Amongst the fauna of Sahaka, there is also high diversity and endemism. Most wild mammals today are quite small. There are five species of lemurs (*Microcebus rufus*, *Lepilemur* sp., *Eulemur coronatus*, *Propithecus tatersalli*, and *Cheirogaleus* sp.) (Randrianarisoa et al. 1999) and three species of insectivores, including the often-hunted *Tenrec ecaudatus*, the introduced rodent *Rattus rattus* (Raheriasena and Goodman 2006), and two species of bats, including the larger, often-hunted *Pteropus rufus* (Safford 2000). There are also 26 species of reptiles and amphibians, few of which are large enough to eat (Rakotondravony 2006). There is only one larger terrestrial mammal, the bush hog (*Potamochoerus larvatus*), introduced from East Africa. In the past, there were probably other larger species that early human occupants could have hunted, including large flightless birds, the pygmy hippopotamus, and various larger lemurs. The eggshells of a flightless bird were reported by Battistini and Vérin (1972, see also Battistini 1965:139) from the Vohemar area. Our survey has revealed others in sandy beach ridges southeast of modern Vohemar (07-041: S13° 22' 20" / E50° 01' 12") —perhaps the emu-sized *Mullerornis*. How late these may have flourished in the area has not yet been determined.

Traditional Cultural Life

The traditional occupants of the Vohemar think of themselves as belonging to distinct social identities with different histories: the Anjoaty and the Sakalava. People claiming these identities live in nucleated villages and hamlets of small houses raised on poles and covered with split bamboo siding and roofs made of the coconut fronds, all easily reconstructed after one of the region's frequent tropical storms. Families of both identities cultivate gardens, catch fish, and herd cattle. They differ, however, in their ritual responsibilities and performances. The Anjoaty, who claim descent from early settlers, are the guardians of the embouchures, maintain their cemeteries close to the sea, sacrifice cattle standing in the sea near these cemeteries, and bury their dead extended on the right side with heads pointed east and facing north, the position required by Islam. The dead, however, are buried with material offerings, often gender specific—a practice forbidden in Islam (Hurvitz 1986; Appendix D, this volume). The Sakalava, who claim descent from west coast armies that invaded during the seventeenth and early eighteenth centuries, live on both the coasts and the interior and practice rituals of kingship. They bury their dead both in rock clefts and shelters and in stone tombs, in groupings specific to social rank. Unlike the Anjoaty, the Sakalava of the Vohemar area have been neglected by ethnographers.

There is no barrier to marriage between Anjoaty and Sakalava. When one asks people what they are, the answer is often "Anjoaty-Sakalava" or "Sakalava-Anjoaty." Many people have grandparents identified with both groups, and many have ancestors who are Betsimisaraka from farther south on the East Coast, Tsimihety from the northern highlands, Merina from the central highlands, Comorians from the Comoro Archipelago, Makoa from Tanzania, or people from South Asia or Europe. Though both Anjoaty and Sakalava have Islamic elements in their dialects and customs, only recently have some families formally adopted Islam. Other families have adopted Christianity, either Catholicism or one of the many Protestant sects. Many families, however, maintain traditional Malagasy beliefs, and there is much syncretism.

Inland and coastal subsistence practices differed in the following ways.

In the interior, swidden fields were planted in dry rice or manioc, and smaller wetlands and spring seeps were planted in irrigated rice. Bananas and many cash crops such as vanilla and cloves can be easily grown in the interior. Cattle herding is widespread, and pigs, chickens, ducks, and geese can be raised. Hunting of tenrecs, wild pigs, bats, and lemurs is also widespread. Fish can be netted, trapped, or taken with lines in the larger rivers.

Along the coast, there was more raising of coconut and the cultivation of wetlands for a form of irrigated rice, the seed traditionally being broadcast directly onto cultivated marshlands rather than started in nurseries and then transplanted, though irrigated paddies with transplanting techniques are becoming more widely utilized. There was probably less hunting on the coast. However, there was much fishing and collecting of shellfish, particularly from canoes in areas with reefs. Fish are also trapped in the embouchures.

The artifacts of daily life are widely produced. Most men can work wood, though furniture making is a craft of more limited occurrence. Most women make mats and baskets. Anyone can make cords, coconut roofing, or woven bamboo house siding. Local blacksmiths can make knives, hoes, axes, and other tools from scrap steel, and they can repair such tools. We have found no local potters, and people were often surprised to see potsherds. Weaving no longer seems to be practiced in this region, and all cloth is imported.

Chapter 3

Historical Records of the Vohemar Area

It is not our intent to present a systematic summary of the historical traditions or documented history of the Vohemar area. This problem requires work by specialists, and it is important that their oral traditional studies be conducted independently from our archaeological studies. Nevertheless, we wish to alert the reader to the existence of multiple levels of evidence about past inhabitants. Our team collected oral traditions volunteered by local villagers, some of which refer to historical events before the nineteenth century CE. This newly collected traditional evidence is mentioned in Appendices A and D.

Early sporadic mentions of Vohemar tell us about little beyond its existence. Around 1508, Lopez de Siqueira apparently visited a port on the east coast of Madagascar, which was ruled by "Ben-Marra." There was a large bay into which flowed two rivers where one could anchor safely at any time (Allibert 2011a:5). De Barros (1628:III-I-2) mentioned that "Bemaro" was visited by Pedreanes about 1515; he found a prosperous port from which he bought much "amber," by which is probably meant a gum or "copal"—perhaps the incense derived from trees of the genus *Hymenaea* (cf. *Trachylobium),* which is found today on the east coast of Africa and northeast coast of Madagascar (Mabberley 1987:586; Meyer, Todd and Beck 1991).

Flacourt, writing in 1658, provides an overview of the east coast, though neither he nor his agents visited Vohemar. However, he described it as "a land and a coast called Vohémaro (or, on the map of the Portuguese, 'Bonmaro') where there were 'whites' for a long time." There the rice is cultivated "as in Ghallemboule" (the area around modern Fenoarivo Atsinanana) (Flacourt 1995:134). In Ghallemboule, Flacourt describes both the planting of seeds in burned swidden fields and the broadcast of rice seeds into wetlands (Ibid:129–130). In addition, he describes an interview with a goldsmith in Anosy in the southeast of Madagascar, who said that his ancestors were from Vohemar, from whence came both the gold used for ornaments throughout the east coast and the specialists who trained goldsmiths throughout the coast.

The Mauritian trader Nicholas Mayeur visited the area in 1775. He was told that the ancient town of Vohemar had been destroyed by a storm. He also noted two ruined rectangular buildings "south of the Vohémar river" (Mayeur 1912:93–136). The armies of the Merina ruler, Radama I, conquered the region in 1823, and Merina officials and a garrison occupied "Hiarana, Vohimar, or Amboanio" (Raombana 1994:139–130 [897–898]) .

We are fortunate to have the account of the French surgeon and botanist Charles Bernier (1802–1858), director of the Jardin Botanique of La Réunion (Dorr 1997:40–41), who recorded his visit to the far northeast coast about 1834. His nephew Théophile Fleury edited his account after his death. Bernier arrived in the area of the Bay of Diego Suarez in February (Fleury 1886:5 Avril:202) and explored southward, arriving in Vohemar in mid-May. His account, however, goes from south to north, describing each bay or embouchure in some detail. He says that the people of this region in general are called "Antancares" (today "Antankarana")—often confounded with the Sakalava. Among these are several groups of varied origin. From Vohemar north to the Bay of Andravina are the "Hénésouastes" (today usually "Anjoaty"), originally from an island in the Mozambique Channel, whence they fled after many wars with their neighbors. Also present are the "Antondroune" (today "Antandrona"), a "noble caste" allied with the ruling "Zafine volaména" ("Zafivolamena") of the Sakalava. The fisher folk also form a "distinct caste" termed "Vezes" (today "Vezo") concerned with tortoise hunting, but this part of the account may refer to west coast peoples and not to Vohemar. Scattered among these peoples are "Arabes or Antolotches" (the latter now written "Antalaotra"), said by Bernier to be Comorean Muslims who lived around the west coast port of Majunga before its conquest by the English and Merina after 1818 and who concern themselves with trade (Fleury 1886:5 Avril:203–204). Bernier describes village life, particularly the crafts of mat-making and sail-making, the production of pottery by women, and the making and use of outrigger canoes by men (Fleury 1886:5 Avril:208). Bernier made many observations on food production. In earlier times, the indigenous people depended on their herds, on fishing, and on the cultivation of yams (*Dioscorea* sp.). In many places, the soil is rich. Since the 1820s, excellent crops of sugar cane, cloves, potatoes, manioc, and maize—all newly introduced—also have been grown (Fleury 1886; 8 Avril:195 and 19 Avril:226). The common domestic animals are cattle and dogs. Wild pigs were hunted but rarely eaten. Chickens and ducks occur, but geese and turkeys are never seen (Fleury 1886:3 Mai:257–258). Local merchants told him that an average of about 30,000 cows were exported from Vohemar each year (Fleury 1886:19 Avril 8:225). Fishing and the salting of fish and whale meat with locally manufactured salt were common (Fleury 1886:3 Mai:259–260). The taking of tortoises, attended by much ritual, was locally important, but the meat was not usually eaten; the merchants of Vohemar were said to export about 2000 kilograms of tortoise shell each year (Fleury 1886:3 Mai:260–261). Various marine fish, crabs, octopus, and sea anemones, all taken from the reef of Vohemar, are mentioned. Bernier's description of the settlement of Vohemar during the 1830s is brief. The settlement was composed of several distinct villages on a sandy peninsula at the south end of the bay. This area has no fresh water, as local wells produced only brackish water, and the inhabitants brought fresh water from the "Ranofotsy" stream to the west (Fleury 1886:3 Mai:265). The merchants' establishments and the customs office of the Merina government are emplaced in the former village of the locals, who now live in several large villages up to a league (about four kilometers) to the south (Fleury 1886:3 May:264). Several of these are the villages of "Antalotse," one with about 100 houses. In 1824, the Merina ruler Radama I led an army of 4000 men to the far north and left a garrison of 500 troops at Vohemar. At the time of Bernier's visit, the garrison was in the fort of Amboanio (787.7-1398.0), 12 km south of Vohemar and often numbered as few as 150 soldiers. In 1837, the English merchant J. S. Leigh spent 24 days near Vohemar, but noted only that the town was composed of two small villages. He spent most of his time to the northeast, in the lower reaches of the Maintialaka and Manambato rivers (Allibert 1999:91–99).

Given the lack of detail in Bernier's account, we are fortunate to have a map of the Vohemar area from 1885 made by officers of the French Indian Ocean fleet (frontispiece, this volume; Favereau and Germain 1885). The map shows that the settlement had "Indiens" and shops in the northeast part of the town, "Sakalaves" and "Betsmisaraks" in the center, and a mosque near the present congregational mosque amidst the "Makoas" to the southwest (in the center of the present town.) The southwest extent of the twentieth-century town had only a few isolated houses and was otherwise open areas or brush.

In 1883, Vohemar was shelled by French naval forces and the remaining houses were burned. In 1884, the garrison at Ambonio was attacked and taken, with a loss of 200 Malagasy troops (Oliver 1885:172–173). As a result of the treaty ending this war, French customs inspectors were placed in various Malagasy ports. Records of exports from Vohemar recorded by M. Guinet, inspector for the Comptoir Nationale d'Escompte de Paris (CNEP), indicate that from 1886 to 1890, the export of cattle from Vohemar, mostly sent to the Mascarene Islands, varied from 4295 to 6290 animals per year. Exports of other commodities such as hides, horn, tallow, rubber, and copal were few and of irregular value. Imports included rum, wine, manufactured cloth, flour, hardware, glassware, ceramics, and soap (Esoavelomandroso 1979:240–242). It is notable that many of the exports reported by Bernier and Guinet—cattle products, tortoise products, and copal—are important in the old medieval trade system, while others (live cattle and laborers) are primarily products of the demands of the emerging modern world system, with its sugar plantations on the Mascarene Islands and elsewhere.

After the French conquest of 1895, Vohemar became the chief place of a province including much of the northeast coast. In the early years of the colonization, the yearly "Annuaire" reported that the excellent anchorage of the Bay of Iharana was thriving, and many Muslim merchants of South Asian origin had established themselves at Vohemar, as had a number of French planters and merchants, among whom are Henry and Eduard Guinet, probably related to the inspector. Sometime before the 1914, the modern city grid was laid out and the long-established mosque and congregationalist church to the west were matched by a Catholic cathedral to the east. The well-documented twentieth-century history of the town is beyond the concerns of this study.

Chapter 4

Past and Present Archaeological Work

In the area of Vohemar, there have been several previously reported archaeological investigations. They can be grouped into research foci—some were concerned primarily with evidence of the quarrying and working of chlorite schist in the interior southwest, west, and northwest of Vohemar, and others were concerned with cemeteries in the sand dunes just east of Vohemar, close to the sea. These earlier studies merit detailed critical analysis, but we will limit ourselves to a brief overview.

From 1904 to 1917, colonial civil servants stationed at Vohemar catalogued at least 20 major quarries for the removal of chlorite schist and workshops in which to carve vessels. It appears to have been these early scholars who attributed the working of chlorite schist to a group called the Rasikajy without specific citation of a local indigenous tradition. We do not know if this is an ancient tradition or a recent speculation. The Mouren brothers located a number of workshops and with their supervisor, Rouaix, described the details of manufacturing (1913). Later, Paul Gaudebout and Elie Vernier (1941a) revisited many of these and located more sources and workshops. Pierre Vérin also revisited many of these sites and recorded several new ones (Vérin 1975 II:760–ff). The team of Serneels have done an exemplary excavation and dating of a chlorite schist quarry southwest of Vohemar (Serneels et al. 2017).

The first investigator of the tombs east of the modern town was the Postmaster Maurein, who excavated a number of "Musulman tombs" about 1904 (Vérin 1975 II: 766, quoting Van der Sleen). Mouren and Rouaix (1913) conducted further excavations in 1912. Other excavations followed, and in 1941 and 1942, Gaudebout and Vernier directed major and systematic excavations of cemeteries, revealing 571 tombs (1941b). Smaller excavations were undertaken by Charles Poirier in 1948 and by Jacques Millot in 1955. Pierre Vérin (1975:762–844) summarized these efforts and described a range of material from the tombs dating mostly from the fourteenth to sixteenth centuries CE. A final report has yet to be prepared. A recent overview of the earlier work has been prepared by Guido Schreurs, Sandra J.T.M. Evers, Chantal Radimilahy, and Jean-Aimé Rakotoarisoa (Schreurs et al. 2011).

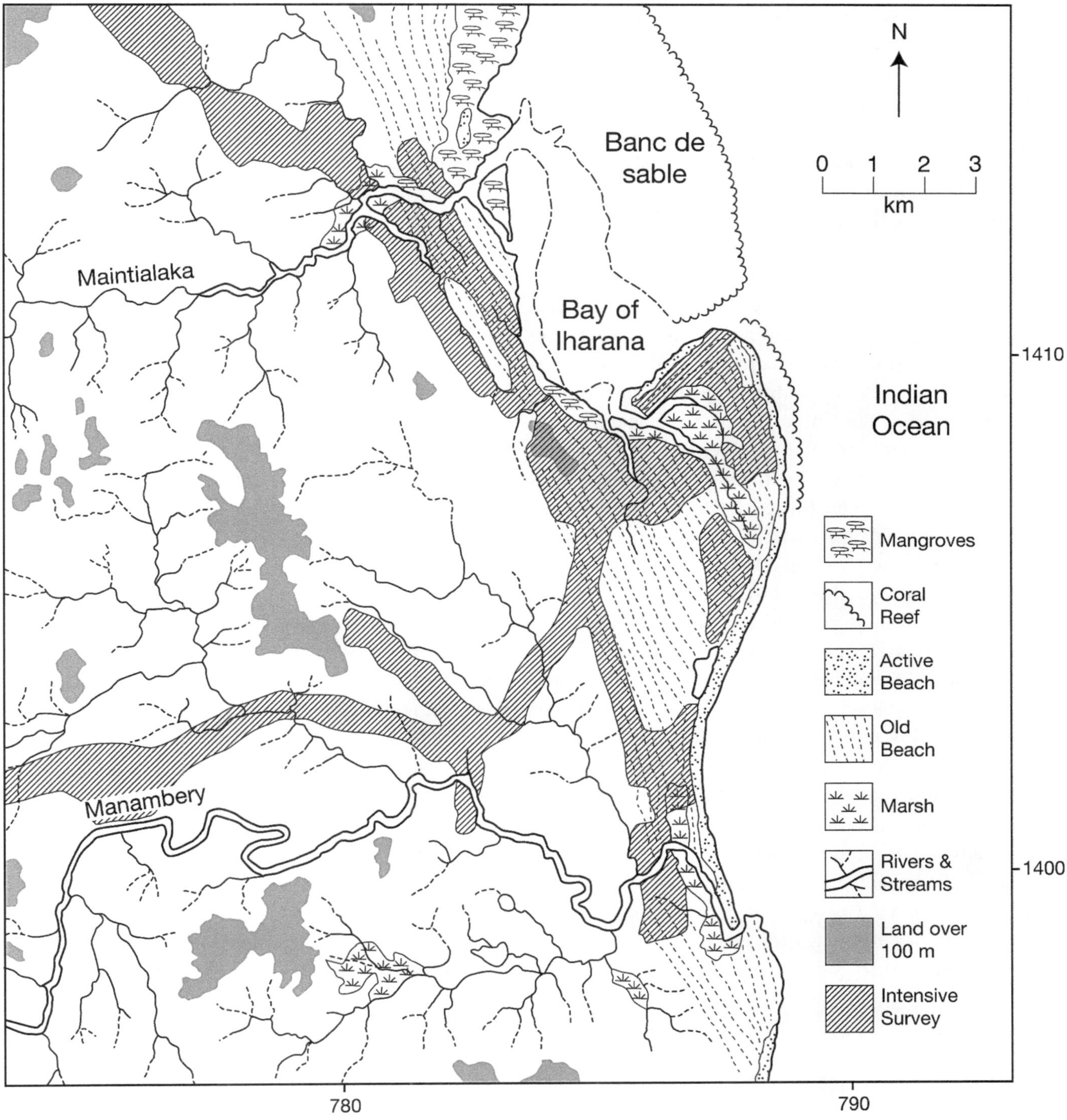

Figure 4.1. Vohemar archaeological survey area, 2007–2014. Coordinates on these and subsequent maps are from the Labordes Grid, used for assigned site numbers in Madagascar.

Our research in the Vohemar area was officially sponsored by the Institut des Civilisations/ Musée d'Art et d'Archéologie of the Université d'Antananarivo, which provided us with equipment, vehicles, and the skills of several technicians and students. The study was carried out under the aegis of the Musée's "Projet des Embouchures," conceived by Dr. Chantal Radimilahy (at the time director of the Institute and the Musée) as a context in which to address both early colonization by farmers and fishermen and the development of commercial ties throughout the Indian Ocean. The project was led by Robert Dewar, then of Cambridge University, and Chantal Radimilahy of the University of Antananarivo Musée d'Art et d'Archéologie. Henry Wright of the University of Michigan Museum of Anthropological Archaeology assisted with the fieldwork, the ceramics, and the drafting of this report. Jean-Aimé Andriamaherilala and Annita Ramanankierana of the University of Antananarivo and Harisoa Ravoviarimanara of the University of Toamasina were valuable team members. Technical assistance was provided by the artist of the Musée, Jeannot Ramisharison, and the master mechanic and chauffeur of the Musée, Victor Razanatovo. Various local officials—most importantly the Mayor M. Jean Claude, the Secretary-General Hector Rahajaona, and the Regional Head Dr. Malaza Ramanamahafahay—were very helpful. Our return visit in 2018 could not have succeeded without the help of Sulivan Rabarison, then Vice Mayor, and Sylvain Solimora, Vohemar regional archaeologist. Finally, little could have been achieved without the help of many interested local fokontany (village) officials and ordinary people in Vohemar and its environs.

Our immediate objective was simply to determine what kinds of archaeological sites, other than the quarries and cemeteries previously reported, could be found in this region of reefs, beaches, estuaries, and hills. From 2007 to 2010, we worked every year from mid-September to late October. There have been shorter visits in subsequent years to finish small areas of survey and work on special problems.

Archaeological survey is not easy in the lush vegetation of Madagascar's east coast, whether it is old growth humid forest, semi-arid thorny forest, or recently cultivated or grazed secondary vegetation. Our teams—walking 10 to 30 meters apart, as best we could—searched the surfaces of sand blows, gardens, fallen trees, paths, villages, and hamlets for potsherds and shell debris. We also talked to many local people. In the end, our intensive survey was limited to the immediate environs of the town of Vohemar and the main roads that were frequently traveled. We recognize that even in the areas "intensively surveyed" there are areas of thick vegetation (Figure 4.1), and we probably have not found all the archaeological sites. As elsewhere on the east coast, we hope to have found at least most types of sites from each period and to have estimates of their sizes, surface features, and available local resources. During 140 days of fieldwork over 7 seasons we recorded 184 collection areas and made 12 small excavations. Clearly contiguous collection areas were grouped into discrete sites. We noted 74 datable occupations on 45 sites, there being many sites with multiple occupations. In the following discussion, sites are identified by metric coordinates based on the Laborde metric grid shown on all official topographic maps of Madagascar. In addition, in the detailed site descriptions in Appendix A, we give their field collection numbers based on the year and a serial number in order of discovery, and by the location of their centers on both the Mercator Longitude and Latitude Grid and on the Universal Transverse Mercator (UTM) Metric Grid. (Some sites were revisited at different times and thus have more than one collection number). The collections—primarily of potsherds but also including stone tools, metal and slag, and animal bone and shells from our excavations, as well as maps and field notes—are all stored at the Institute des Civilizations/ Musée d'Art et d'Archéologie facility in Antananarivo.

Part II

Human Occupation Around the Bay of Iharana

Chapter 5

Introduction to the Survey Evidence

The purpose of this section is to develop and present a ceramic and cultural sequence for the area around Vohemar and the Bay of Iharana. The following chart (Figure 5.1) summarizes the preliminary chronology we have developed. The first column indicates the approximate dates of the beginnings and ends of the six proposed cultural phases. The second lists the phase names. The third indicates the time spans of distinctive wares or fabrics. The fourth and final column shows the development of both open and restricted vessel forms made with the sandy wares. The arrows show that there was a continuous evolution of the most common forms from the Ampasimahavelona Phase, the earliest known phase with ceramics, until the Patrick Phase. Only with the appearance of the latest Ave Maria Phase was there a marked break in ceramic traditions, with the introduction of many new forms.

Concentrations of similar local ceramics define archaeological sites on Madagascar's east coast, and sites dated by such ceramics define the settlement patterns from which we infer economic and social patterns during each chronological phase. Each section of this chapter begins with a narrative of the various small excavations that provided datable local ceramic samples specific to a "phase"—the artifactual indicators thought to mark a social formation for a specific span of time. More excavation details are in Appendix B. The sections of Chapter 6 then continue with a detailed presentation of the ceramics, focusing on manufacturing order: from clay preparation and fabrics to vessel manufacturing techniques, to vessel forms, vessel firing, and decoration. This is a first approximation based on field records. Studies of minerology, statistics measuring form and size, experiments defining firing atmospheres, etc., will require lengthy future laboratory studies. Each section finishes with a brief note on each site dated to that phase. More site details are in Appendix A. In these notes, we generally say whether an occupational site is a hamlet (less than 0.5 ha and with room only for 1 to 3 houses); a small village (0.5 to 3.0 ha with more houses); or a large village (more than 3 ha, but primarily with traces of domestic activity and lacking the evidence of craft specialization or nondomestic architecture such as masonry mosques). Sites with such evidence can be termed towns. These settlement ascriptions are tentative and require confirmation with excavation.

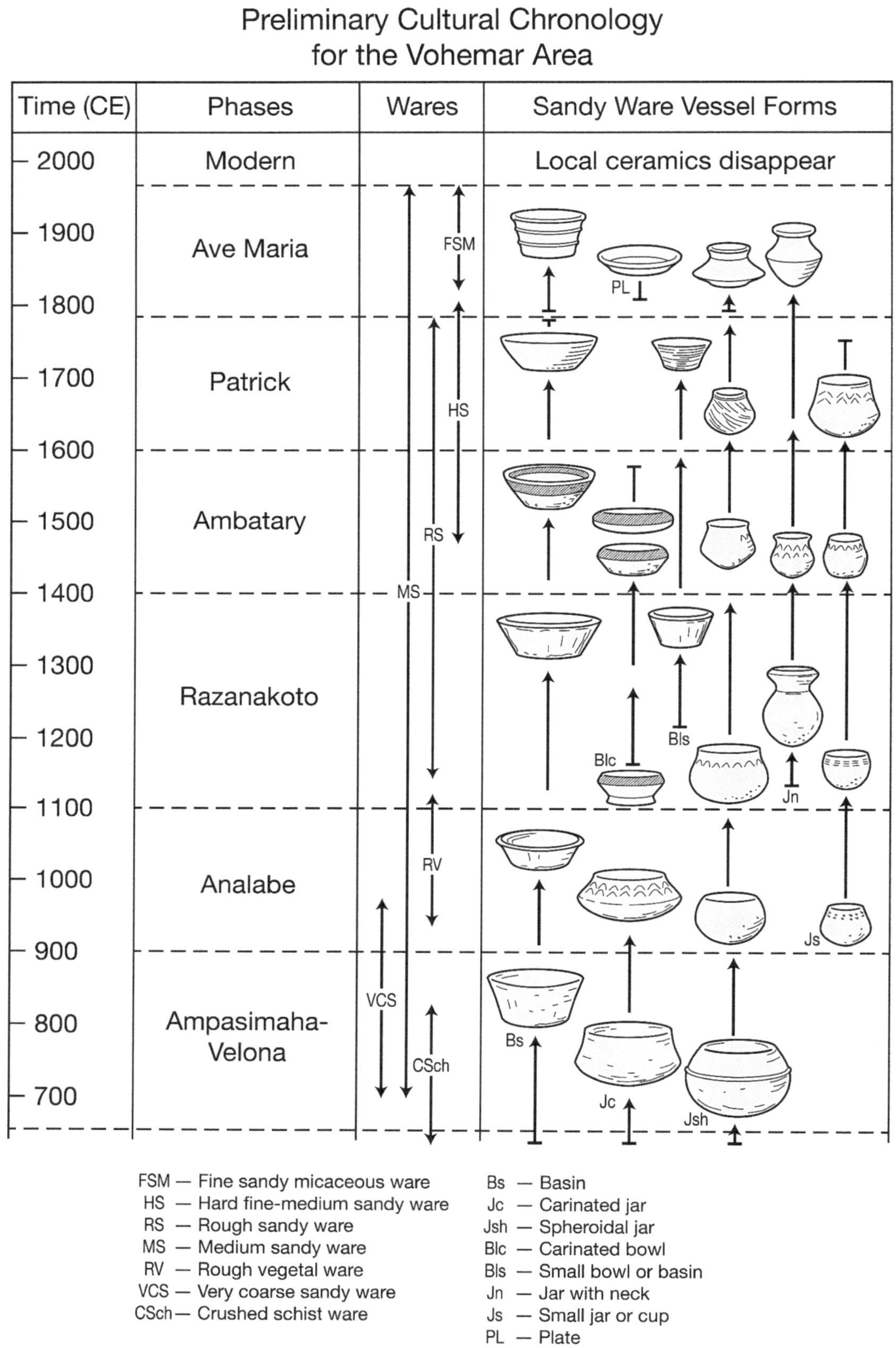

Figure 5.1. Preliminary chronology based on ceramic ware.

Chapter 6

Evidence of Early Foragers in the Iharana Area

Excavations at Ambohiposa Rock Shelter

Near the end of our first season of survey, we discovered a rock shelter overlooking the Bay of Iharana. It is locally known as Ambohiposa: the "village of the fossa," named after the fossa (*Cryptoprocta ferox*), Madagascar's largest native carnivore, whose scats are evident in the shelter. A small test in its floor revealed stratified layers, with tiny fragments of flaked chert. This was the first evidence ever recovered of a stone tool assemblage on Madagascar, and its implications for human impacts on Madagascar's environments were immediately evident. Though this was not our research objective, we diverted some of our resources to make a small excavation in the floor of Ambohiposa in 2007 and two more in 2008. The site is discussed in Appendices A and B, and published elsewhere (Dewar et al. 2013).

Ambohiposa (07-064: Laborde 784.3-1408.1) is situated in the east-facing slope of Ambatomalama, a massif of Mesozoic rocks (including layers of basalt, rhyolite, marl, siltstone, and sandstone) reaching an altitude of 120 m. The shelter is one of several at the base of an outcrop of rhyolite. At 54 m above sea level, it has a view eastward over the Bay of Iharana and the sandy plain to its south. The sheltered area is small, only 6 m from north to south. Today the overhang extends only 1.3 m from the back wall to the drip line, but possible blocks of roof-fall down the slope suggest it was once larger. At most, the shelter could protect only a few people.

Our three excavations were each 0.5 m wide and extended up to 1.30 m from the back of the shelter to the drip line. The southern and central units had similar relatively regular stratigraphies composed of six layers with little evidence of disturbance (Figure 6.1). The northern unit had a compressed stratigraphy, perhaps disturbed.

Each context was excavated and sieved with 3 mm mesh. All sediment except larger natural rocks was carried to Vohemar to be washed through 1 mm screen in the sea, dried, and sorted under magnification. We excavated

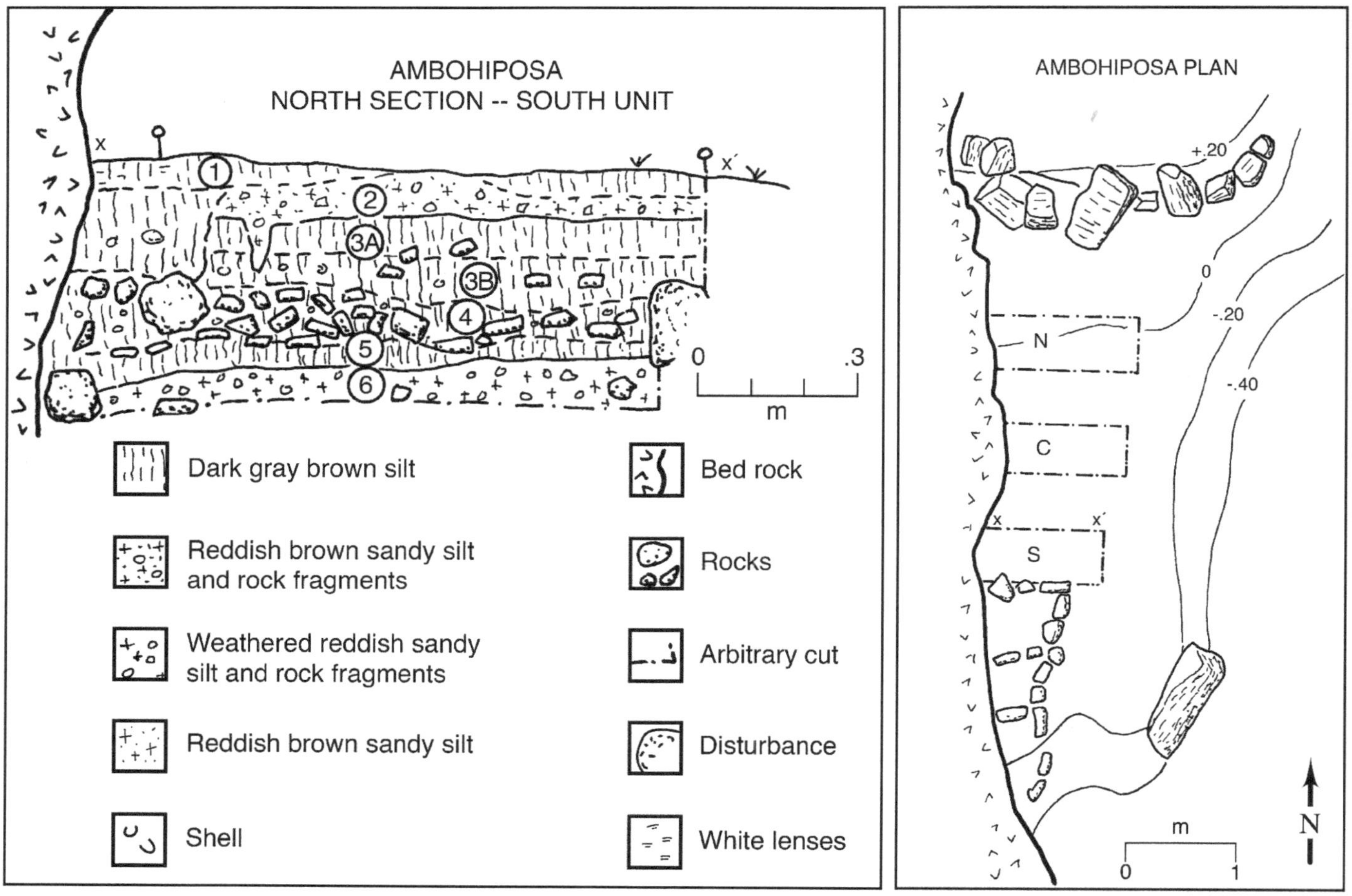

Figure 6.1. Sections and plan of Ambohiposa (787.4-1408.1).

approximately 25% of the area of Layers 3 to 5. The remainder was left for future research.

The Flaked Stone Assemblage from Ambohiposa

A majority of the flaked stone items recovered were of a range of crypto-crystalline silicates we term chert, and a minority were of a volcanic glass we term obsidian (see Appendix B, Table B.2). The chert items can be opaque and gray, tan or brown or translucent and brown in color. The few unmodified pieces are < 2 cm in length. Some of the fragments and flakes have glossy surfaces and pot-lidding attributable to either deliberate heating or accidental burning. The obsidian is opaque and black. Survey in the area of Ambohiposa identified small blocky fragments of opaque brown chert in a gully 80 m north of the shelter, and small rounded pebbles of translucent gray and white agate on the slope of the hill of Ambatomalama 180 m northwest of the shelter. We found few pieces of this agate in our assemblage.

Some Ambohiposa flaked chert items probably result from direct percussion on small amorphous flake cores. Others, however, result from a simple and widely known reduction procedure called bipolar reduction, which is used throughout the world wherever available raw material pieces are small (see White and Thomas 1972 for an ethnographic description of such a procedure in Highland New Guinea, and Shott 1999 for a discussion of archaeological studies). In such cases it is difficult to control the platform, the striking angle, and other variables that allow one to produce pieces useful for tools. The small piece of raw material was placed on a large rock or "anvil" and struck with a smaller rock or "hammer." Both the flakes and the core remnants have flake scars that originate from both the hammer blow and the large stone below. Flakes of useful size and shape were selected and utilized as-is or modified for specialized use. Small flakes or bits of shattered stone were swept aside. The larger remnant pieces of raw material were struck again, and the selection procedure was repeated until only small pieces remained. In our three units, there are no larger chert flake cores or recognizable fragments of such cores. There is, however, a bipolar core remnant of chert (Figure 6.2a) with scars on both faces originated from both ends.

Chert waste recovered by fine-screen washing includes 1833 pieces of blocky shattered chert, weighing a total of 158 grams. Some of the shatter fragments—many of which are very small—could be a product of natural fracture. It is the flakes that have the most interesting implications for past human activity. We recovered 241 flakes (including possible blade fragments) weighing a total of only 14 grams. Most of these are not weathered, and they exhibit bulbs from directed percussion or pressure.

Some of the larger flakes are products of bipolar core reduction. One (Figure 6.2b) has scars on both faces originating from both ends. This flake was utilized on one edge, indicated by very small flakes along the edge, but not otherwise reworked or broken. Others are probably fragments of such flakes. Two modified items are made from crescent-shaped pieces of chert, triangular in cross-section, probably resulting from bipolar reduction (Figure 6.2c, d); neither is systematically retouched, but both have small edge removals emphasizing their crescentic shape. Both have possible mastic traces from hafting.

Some flakes may have been detached from larger blocky or amorphous cores by a direct blow of the hammer stone without an underlying anvil. One nearly complete brown chert flake appears to be a product of conventional flake removal from such a core (Figure 6.2e). The outer surface was guided by a previous flake removal on the left and secondary retouch flakes struck from the right. The inner surface has small secondary flakes and a pot-lid, which removed the platform. Nibbling on the edges could result from binding to a haft and polish on the tip suggests use in cutting or perforating.

Fragments of larger flakes without clear evidence of flakes struck from two directions may have been detached from either bipolar cores or larger blocky or amorphous cores. A brown chert flake (Figure 6.2f) has small flakes removed from its left edge, perhaps from retouch to create a reinforced edge. Two chert flake fragments are notable for their trapezoidal shape. One (Figure 6.2g) is probably the proximal end of a larger flake struck from the weathered surface of a tan chert pebble whose left side was retouched to emphasize the trapezoidal shape. The other (Figure 6.2h) is from the distal end of a flake ending on the weathered surface of a fragment. The upper surface is formed by flakes converging from either side of this flake, and the piece was detached from the proximal end of the original flake by a blow on the ridge where the

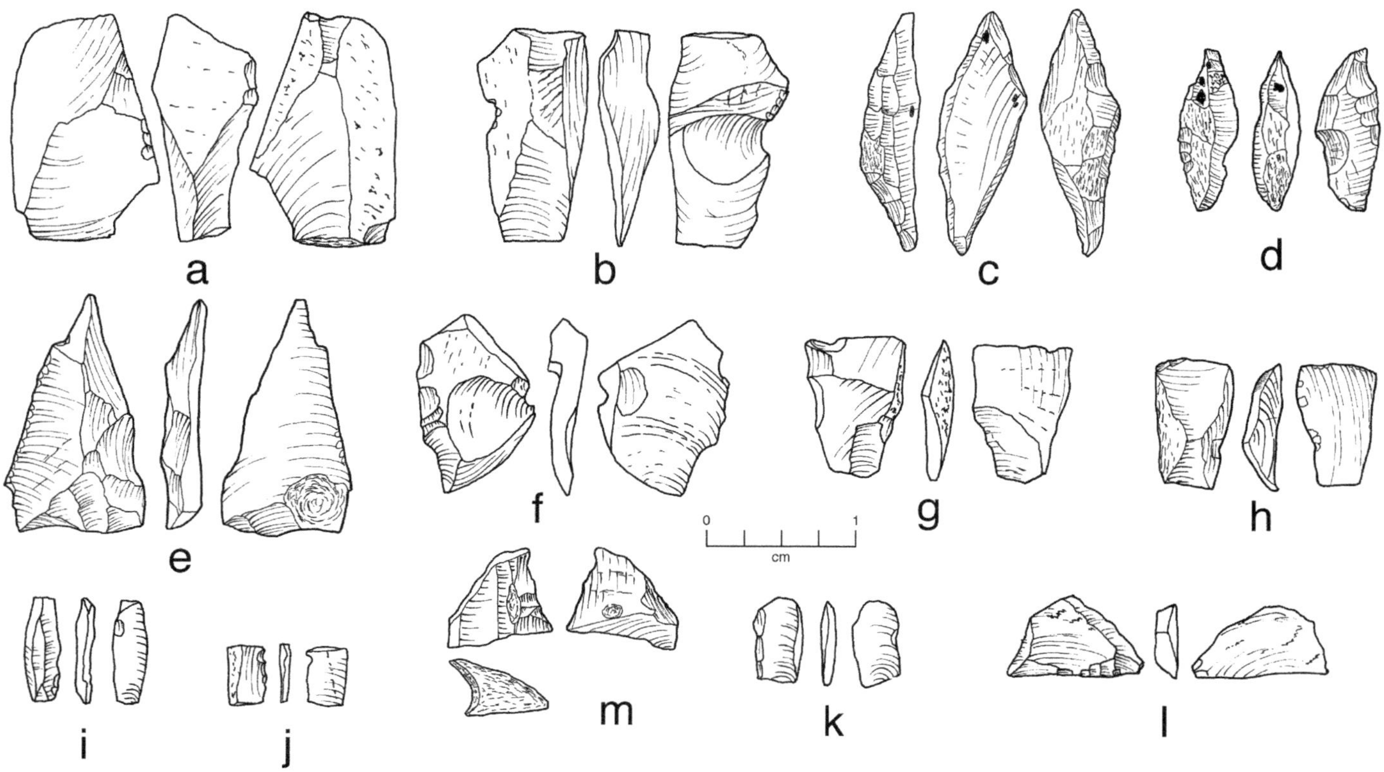
a
b
c
d
e
f
g
h
0 1
cm
i
j
m
k
l

Figure 6.2. Flaked stone items from Ambohiposa. For core fragments, flakes and blades, length (Ln) is measured along the last-used striking axis, width (Wd) is perpendicular to that, and thickness (Thk) is perpendicular to width. For finished crescentic and trapezoidal pieces, length is the longest dimension, and so forth. A "+" indicates that the item is broken and the original dimension was greater.

a. Bipolar core remnant, chert (Central Unit, Layer 2) Ln: 1.62, Wd: 0.97, Thk: 0.72.
b. Bipolar flake, chert (Central Unit, Layer 3) Ln 1.41, Wd: 0.72, Thk: 0.43.
c. Bipolar crescentic flake with retouch, light brown chert (North Unit, Layer 6) Ln: 1.74, Wd: 0.60, Thk: 0.37.
d. Bipolar crescentic flake with retouch, light brown chert (North Unit, Layer 6), Ln:1.18, Wd: 0.41, Th: 0.31.
e. Triangular flake, chert (South Unit, Layer 5) Ln: 1.67, Wd: 0.91, Thk: 0.36.
f. Retouched flake, chert (Central Unit, Layer 4) Ln 1.25, Wd: 0.86, Thk: 0.31.
g. Trapezoidal flake fragment, chert (Central Unit, Layer 4) Ln 0.96, Wd: 0.71, Th 0.23.
h. Trapezoidal flake fragment, chert (South Unit Layer 5) Ln: 0.91, Wd: 0.50,Thk: 0.23.
i. Microblade, chert (Central Unit, Layer 5) Ln 0.74, Wd: 0.18, Thk: 0.12.
j. Segment of microblade core preparation flake, chert (Central Unit, Layer 5) Ln 0.41+, Wd: 0.26, Thk: 0.09.
k. Fragment of microblade core, obsidian (North Unit, Layer 5) Ln: 1.36+, Wd: 1.40+, Thk: 0.81+.
l. Microblade segment, obsidian (Central Unit, Layer 3) Ln 0.60, Wd: 0.35, Thk: 0.11.
m. Small flake, obsidian (Central Unit, Layer 5) Ln 0.53, Wd: 0.89, Thk: 0.16.

converging flakes meet. No additional retouch was needed to create a trapezoidal form.

Finally, there are a few small narrow parallel-sided chert flakes, termed microblades. One chert example (Figure 6.2i) is complete, and the scars on the anterior face show that it was one of a series pressed from a core similar to the obsidian core noted below. Retouch is uncertain. Another medial segment of chert (Figure 6.2j) does not have the characteristic parallel scarring on the anterior face and may be simply an accidental flake from the edge of a small blocky core of chert. Such parallel-sided flakes are often created in shaping a blocky piece into a core and are not true blades.

Obsidian waste recovered by the fine-screen washing procedure includes 1 obsidian microblade core fragment weighing .17 gm and 12 tiny obsidian flake and microblade fragments weighing .55 gm. The fragment of a microblade core of obsidian (Figure 6.2m) has the scars of three microblade removals. The widest of these removals is .38 cm. Retouch from the right side could result from use of the core as a scraper after it was exhausted. Note the pot-lidding, indicating the piece was burned late in its history. A microblade segment of obsidian (Figure 6.2k) is .35 cm wide has possible retouch on the left edge. This it could have been removed from a core similar to the above. An obsidian flake may have utilization on its pointed right side (Figure 6.2*l*).

This is a small sample of tiny items. Nevertheless, there are indications that people created a stone industry here: first, most of the raw materials do not occur near the site and must have been carried in; second, there is evidence of blows detaching a series of flakes from cores; and third, there is evidence of retouch or use on some pieces.

Other Evidence from Ambohiposa

From Layers 3–5 of the North Unit, we recovered two small fragments of pottery, both oxidized to a red color and with 40% coarse angular quartz inclusions. The inclusions and color indicate a date during our Ampasimahavelona or Analabe Phases of the eighth to eleventh centuries AD, discussed below. Note that in the north unit the upper organic layers are thin and compressed, and these could be later sherds deposited after the occupation that left the stone artifacts.

No bones survived in Ambohiposa, Layers 3–6. From the light fraction of a 6.0-liter flotation sample from the South Unit, Layer 3, archaeobotanist Amanda Logan reports three carbonized seeds, probably of the Poaceae or grasses.

Two small fragments of wood charcoal from Layer 5 of the South Excavation were submitted to Beta Analytic for AMS radiocarbon dating. The piece from Layer 5A yielded a calibrated date with a 95% probability of being between Cal AD 1220 and 1385 (see Appendix C for lab numbers and details). The piece from somewhat earlier (Layer 5B) yielded a calibrated date with a 95% probability of being between Cal AD 885 and 1030. These two pieces of charcoal are unlikely to be of the same age, but both date to the time of the early villages in the area, as discussed below. We must keep in mind that during the time of the earlier iron-using villages around Vohemar, swidden gardens could have been cut off and burned on the slope below the rock shelter, and pieces of charcoal could easily have been blown into the shelter long after the occupation that left the stone artifacts but before erosion led to the deposition of reddish sandy-silt Layer 2. We need dates on other materials and with other methods.

In sum, this small and ephemeral foraging camp could date to the same time as the earliest village and could represent hunters using a microlithic flaked stone technology attached to the villages. Alternatively, the sherds and the dated charcoal could result from later visits to the site, and the foragers could have been in the area earlier than the iron-using farmers and cultivators. We need additional dating evidence. In 2008 and subsequent seasons, we searched most of the cliffs around Ambatomalama and elsewhere in the Iharana area, looking for more rock shelters; we also searched exposed sandy areas on hill tops and near water sources, looking for open air sites. Unfortunately, we did not find them. It was only in 2011, when we reopened excavations at Lakaton'i Anja (discovered in the 1980s in the Gorge of Andavakoera in the Montagne des Françaises near Antsiranana in the far north of Madagascar) that we found further evidence of early foragers using flaked stone technologies (Dewar et al. 2013).

Chapter 7

The Ampasimahavelona Phase

Evidence

We first recognized this early cultural phase based on coarse oxidized ceramics. The ceramics were similar to those of a phase previously established on the basis of evidence from the village of Sandrakatsy in the middle Mananara Valley, on the northeast coast, 350 km to the south-southwest of Vohemar (Laborde 739.5-1080.7, S16° 20' 22"/ E49° 36' 49", UTM E 0351915-N 8193010). Though Sandrakatsy was badly eroded, five small excavations exposed several features (Wright and Fanony 1992:25–37), two of which were absolutely dated. Unfortunately, most of the sherds were undecorated body sherds, but a few rim and base fragments indicated open basins with flat bases and closed globular vessels. In 2007, we recognized such ceramics in several surface collections from the Vohemar area, mixed with later material, but were cautious about making any interpretations.

Early in the 2008 season, we found the site of Ampasimahavelona. It lay south of the modern town of Vohemar, on the left or west bank of the old estuary, which flowed north toward the Bay. The site is on two adjacent sandy terrace remnants—one to the northwest ("Avaratra": 08-011: 786.7/1408.2) and one to the southeast ("Atsimo": 08-012: 786.8/1408.1)—each with flat surfaces about 3 m above the surface of the rice paddies, which now fill the old estuary, and 7 m above sea level (Figure 7.1b). (See additional details in Appendices A and B.) There is a trace of a linear depression on the southwest edge of site, perhaps a filled ditch or path. The area of sherd scatter within (e.g., northeast of) this trace is about 1.1 ha. We mapped the site and made surface collections from the two parts. We selected a location in the north part of the site, in an area where coring indicated .50 cm of very dark gray midden, dense with sherds and shell fragments, and placed Unit J, a 1-by-1 m square. We were disappointed to find that the entire deposit was disturbed by manioc cultivation. A posthole in a row of postholes visible in the light reddish-brown sand below contained scraps of a recent plastic fiber sack, and the landowner identified this row as the remains of his house destroyed by a cyclone in the 1990s. There were no undisturbed deposits.

Thinking about the lack of stratified deposits, we realized that we might find site-edge middens on the flanks of the site, close to or even under the rice paddies. We returned in 2009 and cored around the edge of the site, finding a deeply buried shell deposit on the northeast edge. We placed Unit VII, another 1 m square, near the fallow paddy (see Appendix B). Here the cultivated layer of black silty paddy soil was only .23 m thick. Below this was Layer 2, a mottled dark brown silt .04 m thick containing clay nodules. In this layer there was a concentration of large sherds, shells, and fractured rocks, termed Feature 1, in the northwest corner of the square. Below this was Layer 3: to the south, a mottled light brown silt .08 m thick with a few sherds, and to the north, a .12 m thick concentration of sherds and poorly preserved *Terebralia* shells. At the bottom of Layer 3 to the south was a lens of gray silt with small pieces of charcoal, termed Feature 2. Below this was a layer of yellowish-brown silt with a few sherds, a few *Terebralia* shells, and a single fish bone. This was generally about .10 m thick but thickened and dipped steeply toward the northwest corner, reaching a thickness of .30 m, suggesting there is an early pit to the northwest of our square. This rested on an orange sandy clay, which lacked cultural traces.

Two small pieces of wood charcoal from Unit VII were submitted to Beta Analytic Laboratories for AMS accelerator dating.

From Ampasimahavelona Unit VII, Lower Layer 3, Beta 267774 gave an age determination that yields a 95% probability that the date is within the range of AD 885 to 1025.

From Ampasimahavelona Unit VII, Feature 2, Beta 267773 gave an age determination that yields a 95% probability that the date is within the range from AD 885 to 1020, very close to the preceding.

These determinations indicate that the Ampasimahavelona Phase spanned at least the late ninth to early eleventh centuries (see Appendix C for details).

Flotation of samples from Feature 2 and Layer 4 produced more charcoal but no identifiable seeds. There was one small but well-preserved fish spine. This and the relatively good condition of the shell in Layer 4 indicate there is no reason that bone would not be preserved in the lower layers of Ampasimahavelona, Unit VII, had it been present. Also found in the flotation samples were some tiny flakes of stone, most polished and battered, probably from water transport.

In 2013, this site was excavated by the Sealinks team from Oxford University. Their work yielded some Ampasimahavelona phase material, much later Analabe phase material, and some Razanakoto phase material, some associated with burials. A report is in preparation.

Artifacts

Ampasimahavelona yielded a relatively large sample of ceramics and some other items. These allow us to define a significant portion of the preserved material culture of the Ampasimahavelona Phase. The material from other sites of this phase can usually be unambiguously identified based on comparisons with the stratified sample from Ampasimahavelona Unit VII.

A majority of the Ampasimahavelona Phase ceramics from the type site contain substantial proportions of distinctively coarse, gritty inclusions, usually rounded or sub-rounded quartz sand, but sometimes crushed angular quartz, mica, feldspar, or chlorite schist. A minority have lesser amounts of similar particles. From sealed Feature 1 originating in Layer 3, we have nine sherds representing two vessels (out of 42 sherds representing 11 vessels) that have a majority of chlorite schist inclusions. However, from older sealed Feature 2 originating in Layer 4, we have 33 sherds representing 30 vessels, none of which has chlorite schist inclusions. There is no evidence at Ampasimahavelona that schist inclusions were earlier. In general, in the totality of sealed excavated samples from Unit VII, inclusions range from 10% to 40% coarse material. About half are Coarse Ware, with 25% or more coarse angular quartz or sand inclusions, a coarseness rarely noted in the ceramics of later phases. These ceramics are characteristically oxidized. Colors just below the exterior surface range from reddish brown (5YR 4/3) to red (2.5YR 5/6) to yellowish red (5YR 5/6) and few are in the brown or yellowish brown (7.5YR or 10YR) range. These sherds are also relatively thick, ranging from .50 to 1.35 cm, but with almost half being greater than .90 cm in thickness. The remainder of the ceramics of the Ampasimahavelona Phase are Sandy Ware, with a less coarse texture and with 10% to 20% usually medium sand and angular quartz but oxidized with a similar range of colors and thicknesses. The surface collection from the south portion of Ampasimahavelona has similarly very coarse, mostly oxidized, and very thick sherds. However, the surface collection from the north portion of

Figure 7.1. Some Ampasimahavelona Phase sites in the Vohemar area.

Ampasimahavelona and the mixed sample from Unit III are finer: less than a third have more than 25% coarse inclusions and less than a third are thicker than .90 cm. On the basis of clay body, construction, and firing, these suggest a later occupation, perhaps Analabe Phase.

Three simple vessel shapes are attested, each made of both coarser and finer ware.

First are open, out-leaned basins or large bowls with mouth diameters from 24 to 46 cm, with a mode of 28 cm. The rims have simple rounded lips (Figure 7.2e–g; Figure 7.3c, e), thickened rounded lips (Figure 7.2d; Figure 7.3a), horizontal flat lips (Figure 7.2a–c, k–m; Figure 7.3b, f, g, k), an inwardly thickened lip (Figure 7.3i), or an inwardly beveled lip (Figure 7.3j). The last two are represented only by single examples from the surface of the north portion of the site and are typical if not indicative of later occupation. Some of these basins had a flat base (Figure 7.3j).

Second are slightly incurved basins with mouth diameters varying from 25 to 43 cm with a mode of 33 cm. The rims have simple rounded lips (Figure 7.4h, I, l; Figure 7.3c, l) or flattened lips (Figure 7.2k; Figure 7.3c; Figure 7.4o).

Third are restricted globular hole-mouth jars with mouth diameters ranging from 13 to 25 cm, with a mode of 20 cm. The rims have simple rounded lips (Figure 7.4a, b, e, f), thickened rounded lips (Figure 7.4j, k), internally thickened rims (Figure 7.4g–i) and inwardly beveled lips (Figure 7.4c, d). There is one carinated example from the north portion of the site (Figure 7.4m). A few of these jars have imprints below the lip (Figure 7.4a, b), which may be either shell impressions or partly smoothed ring junctures. A jar from the surface of the north portion of the site has the imprints of grass stems below the rim (Figure 7.4h).

Several ceramic feet, square in cross-section, were collected from the surface of Ampasimahavelona (Figure 7.4n, p). We have no evidence of the type of vessel that these feet supported, but they resemble chlorite schist tripod supports known from later carved stone cylindrical vessels found in the region. These ceramic versions may have been made during a later occupation at Ampasimahavelona.

Even a small sample of undecorated body sherds of this phase can easily be recognized because of their coarseness, thickness, and predominately oxidized condition. Basin rims and hole-mouth jar rims with heavily thickened round lips appear to be characteristic of this phase.

Ampasimahavelona ceramics are comparable to other early assemblages from Madagascar's east coast. It would be difficult to differentiate a sample of Sandrakatsy Phase sherds from sites around the Bay of Antongil (Wright and Fanony 1992: Figs. 3, 4) from Ampasimahavelona sherds, as they are similar in coarseness, thickness, and degree of oxidation. The basic open and restricted forms are shared, as are the thickened and flattened lip variants. In addition, both assemblages have a few jars with impressions on the exterior of the rim that may be shell impressions. We are hesitant, however, to equate the two assemblages because the ceramics of Sandrakatsy are known from only a few small, excavated samples from the eponymous site and from Nosy Mangabe near Maroansetra (Vérin 1975:879–889, Figure 370). In addition to coarseness, degree of oxidation, and simple vessel shapes, Ampasimahavelona ceramics share several other features with early assemblages even farther south. Basin rims of both the Middle Marovahiny Phase sites from the mouth of the Matitana River (Griffin 2009: 104, 125) and the Maliovola Phase sites from the Lower Efaho Valley near Tolagnaro dated from the eleventh to the thirteenth centuries AD (Wright et al. 1993) have the impressions of grass stems on the rims of vessels. Also, the ceramics of the earliest phase known in the Matitanana embouchure on the southwest coast, the Early Marovahiny Phase, provisionally dated to the tenth to eleventh centuries AD, are coarse plain oxidized vessels tempered with chlorite schist (Griffin 2009:116).

From the surface collections, there is one vessel rim and a few body sherds of the Rough Ware common on many later sites. These have a typical ropy texture and unsmoothed exteriors. The rim is of an incurved basin with rounded lip (Figure 7.4n). These Rough Ware items were probably left by later occupants.

A few of the vessel fragments from Ampasimahavelona Phase assemblages are from vessels carved from chlorite schist (rather than turned on a lathe). All are from surface collections and may also be from later occupations. These sherds vary in thickness from .80 to 1.40 cm. The few rim sherds are from the south part of Ampasimahavelona. They are from open basins. Two are carved rather than turned on a lathe, but with out-leaned sides and flat lips similar to the ceramic basins (Figure 7.4c, l). Another has horizontal ridges like later wheel-turned basins, but it is too eroded to be certain (not illustrated). There is no indication of handles or feet on these early stone vessels.

From the heavy fraction of the flotation samples in dated Unit VII, we retrieved a few very small pieces of fractured stone:

- From Layer 4 Upper are seven pieces of quartz, all less than .01 gm. Four are fresh splintered fragments of translucent quartz, and three are flakes with battered edges of white quartz.
- From Feature 2 Lower are one fresh quartz flake and 6 rolled and battered flakes, not weighed.
- From Feature 2 Upper are two fresh quartz splintered fragments weighing about .03 gm.
- From Layer 3 Upper is a slightly rolled and battered brown chert flake fragment; weight less than .01 gm.
- From Feature 2 Upper is a rolled and battered coarse reddish chert flake weighing .015 gm.
- From Feature 1 is a fresh flake of basalt with denticulation on two edges; weight .13 gm.

We need to determine whether such tiny quartz and chert items are a natural part of the bed load of the ancient river that flowed into the estuary. If not, they indicate early stone tool use on or near this site. This is not surprising, as there is one translucent quartz blade core from the surface of Ampasimahavelona. The basalt item is likely to be a tool. Interestingly, we recorded no iron slag in these early contexts.

The only food remains recovered in good context are *Terebralia* shells from the mangroves, a conch shell from the bay, and a fish spine, the latter from Unit VII, Feature 2.

Chronology

Coarse ceramic basins and hole-mouth jars generally date to the eighth to twelfth centuries CE elsewhere in Madagascar. Fortunately, as discussed above and in Appendix C, Ampasimahavelona has yielded ^{14}C age determinations, calibrating to the late ninth to early eleventh centuries CE. We suggest that further dating will show that the Ampasimahavelona Phase dates from the eighth to tenth centuries CE.

Ampasimahavelona Settlement

Eight sites produced ceramics of the Ampasimahavelona Phase (see details in Appendix A).

1. Ampasimahavelona (North: (08-011: Laborde 786.7-1408.2: S13° 22' 22"/ 50° 00' 26"), detailed above, is the largest site on the old estuary entering the bay from the south. It is 185 m from southeast to northwest and 90 m wide; we attribute a size of 1.1 ha during the Ampasimahavelona occupation of the eighth to tenth centuries CE. It is on a small peninsula of the same sandy terrace as Amboronana, and rice paddies border it on the northwest, northeast, and southwest (Figure 7.2b). We tentatively classify this as a small Ampasimahavelona village.

In addition to the larger Ampasimahavelona, there are three smaller sites on the old estuary entering the Bay of Iharana from the south.

2. Antsofaly-Andranonana (08-009: Laborde 785.4-1408.5, S13° 22' 13"/ E49° 59' 41") is near the mouth of the estuary, facing north over the Bay of Iharana, 1.4 km west-northwest of Ampasimahavelona. Its dark sandy soil is intensively cultivated for manioc, sweet potatoes, pineapples, and other crops (Figure 7.2a). Three coarse large open basins and bowls with thickened round lips (Figure 7.5b–d) and a jar with similar rim (Figure 7.5h) confirm an Ampasimahavelona occupation. A vessel foot rectangular in section (Figure 7.5k) is later. In contrast to Ampasimahavelona itself, these rims are less coarse, most having medium rather than coarse sand inclusions. Only the foot and the jar rim have angular quartz. This perhaps simply indicates these vessels are locally produced with clay from marshes behind a low-energy beach rather than from the high-energy alluvial contexts farther up the river. These rims and coarse thick sherds occur only in the east part of the site, covering about .35 ha. It is notable that, though this site is adjacent to the mangroves of the estuary and looks north across the Bay of Iharana, there is little of the shell debris we expect on a site oriented toward marine resources, and we suggest it was a hamlet devoted primarily to gardening.

3. Amboronana Atsinanana (08-010: Laborde 786.6-1408.4, S13° 22' 17"/ E 50° 00' 23) is 210 m northwest of Ampasimahavelona on a flat sandy terrace, now a mature coconut grove, on the left or west bank of the estuary (Figure 7.2b). Coarse thick oxidized sherds were found in paths in the coconuts and around some temporary huts, over at least 0.10 ha. Large open basins and bowls (Figure 7.5i, j) and a round rim jar (Figure 7.5n), all with thickened round lips, are definitive of the Ampasimahavelona Phase.

4. Jeunesse et Sport (08-013: Laborde 787.0-1407.9, S13° 22'22"/ E50° 00' 38") is on a sandy ridge near the left or west bank of the estuary, 470 m southeast of

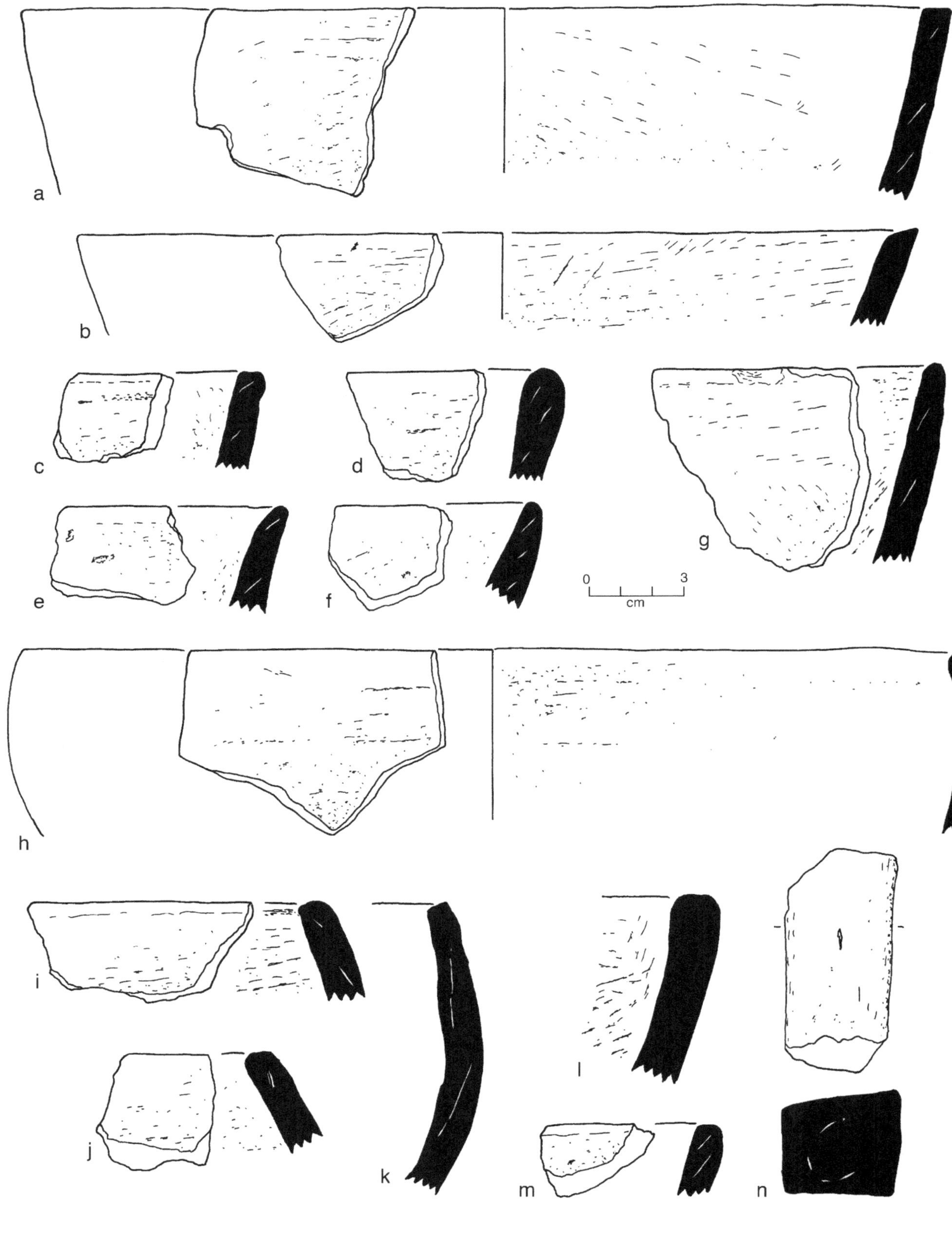
a
b
c
d
g
e
f
0 3
cm
h
i
k
l
j
m
n

Figure 7.2. Ceramics and chlorite schist artifacts from Ampasimahavelona Atsimo (08-012: 786.8-1408.2). Note: Munsell colors were taken on a fresh chip under the outer surface. Abbreviations: Dm = Diameter; Body T = Body thickness 2 cm below lip; Rim T = Rim thickness. All measurements are in centimeters.

a. Basin with flat lip (Ampasimahavelona Atsimo). 25% Medium Sand, Dm 31, Body T: .90, Rim T: 89, Gray (N5) body.
b. Basin with flat lip (Ampasimahavelona Atsimo). Gray chlorite schist, Dm 29, Body T:.90, Rim T:89, Carved, not lathe-turned.
c. Basin with rounded lip (Ampasimahavelona Atsimo). 5% Medium Sand, Dm ca. 28, Body T: 1.00, Rim T: 1.04, Very dark gray (N3) body.
d. Basin with thickened rounded lip (Ampasimahavelona Atsimo). 25% Coarse Sand, Dm ca. 46, Body T: .80, Rim T: .92, Reddish brown (5YR 5/4) body.
e. Basin with tapered lip (Ampasimahavelona Atsimo). 25% Coarse Sand and Crushed Sherd, Dm ca. 24, Body T: 1.00, Rim T: .57, Red (2.5 YR 5/6) body.
f. Basin with rounded lip (Ampasimahavelona Atsimo). 10% Medium Sand, Dm ca. 26, Body T: 1.25, Rim T: .79, Reddish brown (2.5 YR 4/5) body.
g. Basin with rounded lip (Ampasimahavelona Atsimo). 25% Medium Sand and Mica, Dm 33, Body T: .95, Rim T: .89, Grayish brown (10 YR 5/2) body.
h. Incurved basin with rounded lip (Ampasimahavelona Atsimo). 30% Medium Sand, Dm 33, Body T: .93, Rim T: .79, Reddish brown (2.5 YR 4/4) body.
i. Hole-mouth jar with flat lip (Ampasimahavelona Atsimo). 15% Fine Sand and Angular Quartz, Dm 43, Body T: 1.08, Rim T: 1.01, Dark reddish brown (5 YR 3/3) body.
j. Incurved basin with flat lip (Ampasimahavelona Atsimo). 30% Coarse Sand and Angular Quartz, Dm 24, Body T: 1.19, Rim T: 1.04, Reddish brown (2.5 YR 4/3) body.
k. Incurved basin with flat lip (Ampasimahavelona Atsimo). 25% Coarse Sand, Dm ca. 35, Body T: 1.26, Rim T: .78, Reddish brown (7.5YR 5/6) body.
l. Basin rim with flat lip (Ampasimahavelona Atsimo). Green chlorite schist, Dm 30, Body T: 1.41, Rim T: 1.33, Carved, not wheel turned.
m. Basin rim with flat lip (Ampasimahavelona Atsimo). 25% Coarse Sand, Dm 22, Body T: .99, Rim T: .99, Dark red (2.5YR 2.5/6) body.
n. Tripod foot fragment (Ampasimahavelona Atsimo). Probably Analabe or Razanakoto Phase. 20% Coarse Sand, Reddish brown (2.5YR 4/6) body.

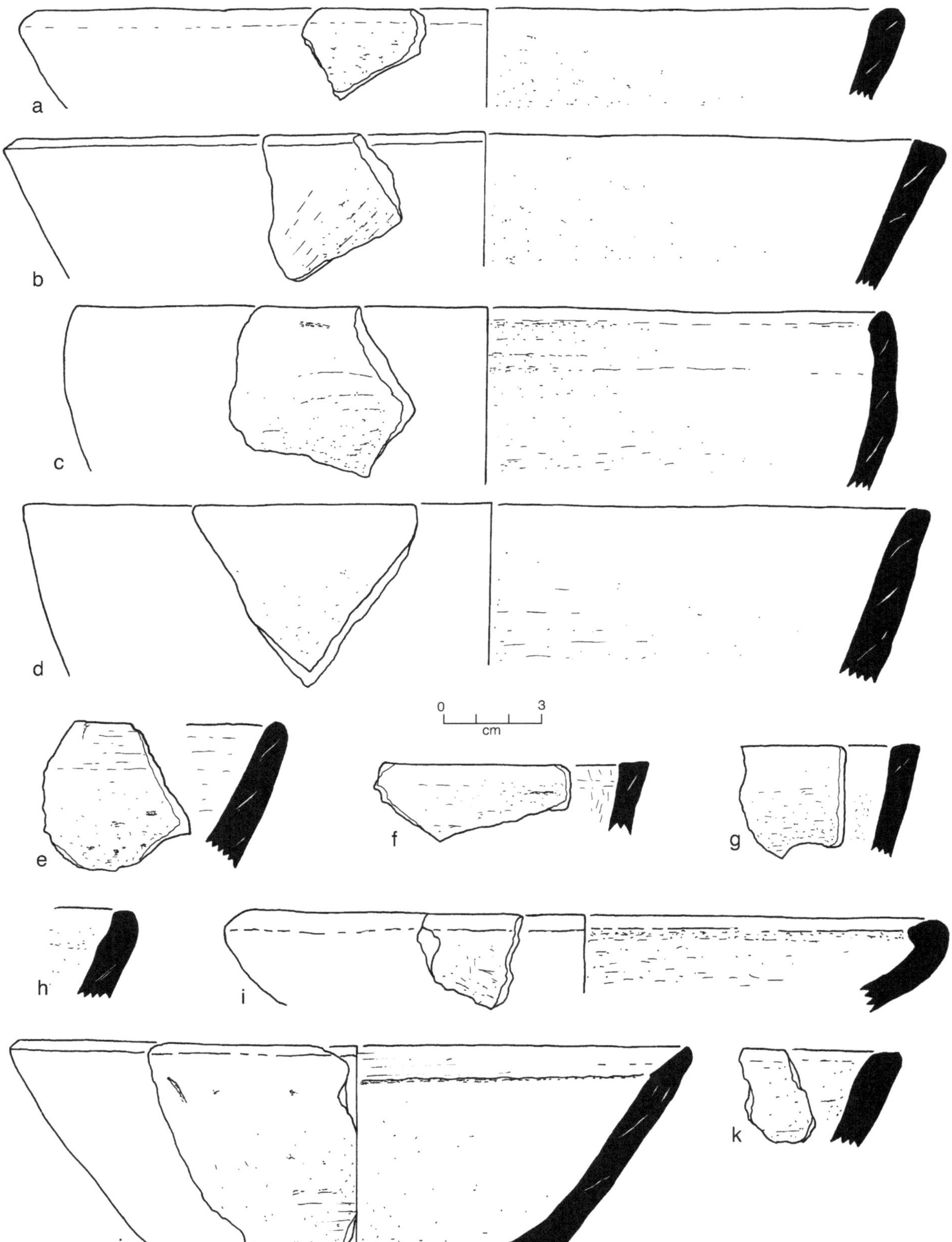
a
b
c
d
0 3
cm
e
f
g
h
i
j
k

Figure 7.3. Open vessels from Ampasimahavelona Avaratra (08-011: 786.7-1408.2). [See note, page 31.]

a. Basin with expanded rim and round lip (Ampasimahavelona Avaratra, Unit VII, Layer 1, Feature 1). 25% Angular Quartz, Dm 28, Body T: .72, Rim T: 93, Yellowish brown (10YR 5/6) body.
b. Basin rim with thickened flat lip (Ampasimahavelona Avaratra, Unit VII, Layer 2, Feature 1). 25% Chlorite Schist and Angular Quartz, Dm 31, Body T: .70, Rim T: 1.05, Reddish brown (5YR 4/5) body.
c. Incurved basin with obliquely flat lip (Ampasimahavelona Avaratra, Unit VII, Layer 2, Feature 1). 25% Angular Quartz, Dm 25, Body T: .72, Rim T: 93, Yellowish brown (10YR 5/6) body.
d. Basin with flattened lip (Ampasimahavelona Avaratra, Unit VII, Layers 4 upper). 25% Coarse Angular Quartz , Dm 28, Body T: 1.05, Rim T: 1.03, Yellowish brown (10YR 5/5) body.
e. Basin with rounded lip (Ampasimahavelona Avaratra, Unit III). 15% Coarse Sand, Angular Quartz, Dm ca. 42, Body T: 1.04, Rim T: .76, Dark reddish brown (5YR 3/2) body.
f. Basin with flat lip (Ampasimahavelona Avaratra, Unit III). 10% Medium Sand, Dm 28, Body T: .76, Rim T: .79, Reddish brown (5YR 4/4) body.
g Basin with flat lip (Ampasimahavelona Avaratra, Unit III). 10% Medium Sand, Dm ca. 36, Body T: .70, Rim T: .76, Red (2.5YR 3/6) body.
h. Basin with rounded lip (Ampasimahavelona Avaratra Unit VII, Layers 3-4, Feature 2). 25% Coarse Angular Quartz Inclusions, Dm 26, Body T: 1.02, Rim T: .98, Yellowish red (5YR 5/6) body.
i. Bowl with internally thickened rim (Ampasimahavelona Avaratra). Probably Analabe Phase. 10% Fine Sand and Angular Quartz, Dm 22, Body T: .80, Rim T: 1.26, Dark red (2.5YR 3/6) body.
j. Bowl with internally beveled rim (Ampasimahavelona Avaratra). 20% Medium Sand, Dm 22, Body T: .93, Rim T: .84, Dark brown (7.5YR 3/3) body.
k. Basin with flat lip (Ampasimahavelona Avaratra). 25% Medium Sand, Dm: ?, Body T: .97, Rim T: 1.05, Reddish brown (5YR 5/4) body.

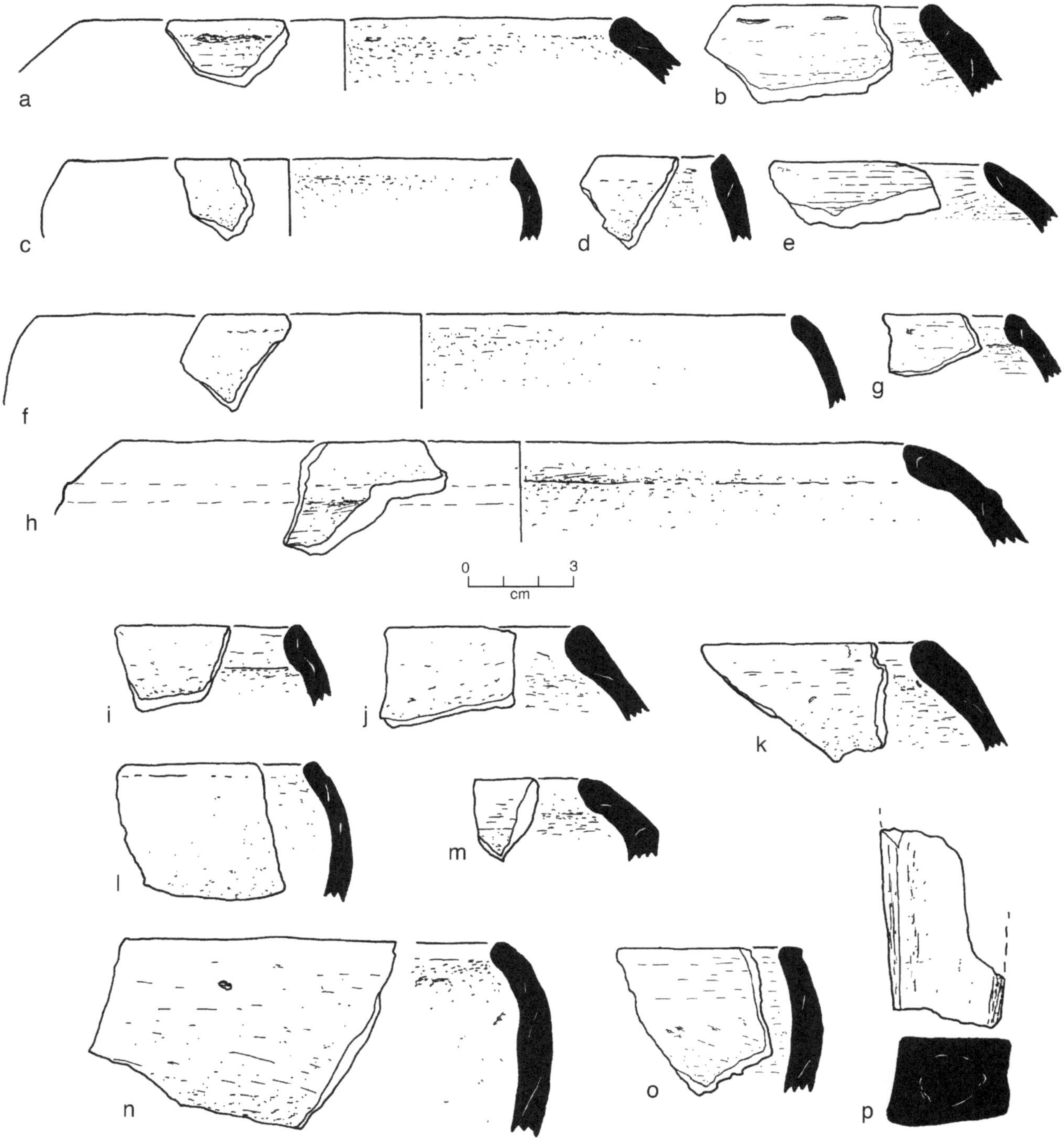
a
b
c
d
e
f
g
h
0
3
cm
i
j
k
l
m
n
o
p

Figure 7.4. Closed vessels from Ampasimahavelona Avaratra (08-011: 786.7-1408.2). [See note, page 31.]

a. Hole-mouth jar with thickened rounded lip (Ampasimahavelona Avaratra, Unit VII, Feature 1). 25% Chlorite schist, Angular Quartz and Mica, Dm 15, Body T: .82, Rim T: 89, Reddish yellow (5YR 4/6) body. Possible imprint below rim.

b. Hole-mouth jar with rounded lip (Ampasimahavelona Avaratra, Unit III). 10% Coarse sand, Dm 23, Body T: .90, Rim T: .88, Dark brown (5YR 4/3) body. Possible imprints below rim.

c. Small hole-mouth jar with inwardly beveled rim (Ampasimahavelona Avaratra, Unit VII, Feature 2). 15% Coarse Angular Quartz, Dm 13, Body T: .59, Rim T: .60, Light yellowish brown (10YR 6/4) body.

d. Small hole-mouth jar with inwardly beveled rim (Ampasimahavelona Avaratra, Unit VII, Feature 1). 20% Angular Quartz, Dm ca. 15, Body T: .77, Rim T: .64, Color not recorded.

e. Hole-mouth jar with rounded lip (Ampasimahavelona Avaratra, Unit III). 10% Medium sand, Angular Quartz, Dm 10, Body T: .90, Rim T: .88, Reddish brown (5YR 4/3) body.

f. Hole-mouth jar with rounded lip (Ampasimahavelona Avaratra, Unit VII Layer 3). 25% Coarse Sand, Angular Quartz, Dm 21, Body T: .62, Rim T: .61, Strong brown (7.5YR 3/6) body.

g. Small hole-mouth jar with interior thickening (Ampasimahavelona Avaratra, Unit III). 10% Medium sand, Dm 16, Body T: .54, Rim T: .61, Reddish brown (5YR 4/4) body.

h. Hole-mouth jar with internal rim thickening (Ampasimahavelona Avaratra). 30% Coarse Sand and Angular Quartz, Dm 28, Body T: .81, Rim T: .93, Black (N 2) body, possible grass imprint below external appliqué ridge.

i. Hole-mouth jar with internal rim thickening (Ampasimahavelona Avaratra, Unit III). ?? % Medium Sand, Dm 26, Body T: .75, Rim T: .91, Reddish yellow (5YR 4/6) body.

j. Hole-mouth jar with thickened rounded lip (Ampasimahavelona Avaratra). 25% Coarse Sand, Dm ca. 28, Body T: .62, Rim T: .98, Dark brown (7.5YR 4/4) body.

k. Hole-mouth jar with thickened rounded lip (Ampasimahavelona Avaratra). 20% Coarse Sand, Dm ca 34, Body T: .71, Rim T: 1.03, Reddish brown (2.5YR 4/3) body.

l. Incurved basin with rounded lip (Ampasimahavelona Avaratra). 20% Medium Sand, Dm 28, Body T: .56, Rim T: .52, Red (2.5YR 4/6) body.

m. Carinated vessel with rounded lip (Ampasimahavelona Avaratra). 15% Coarse Sand, Angular Quartz, Dm ?, Body T: .81, Rim T: .85, Reddish brown (2.5YR 5/5) body.

n. Rough Ware Incurved vessel with rounded lip (Ampasimahavelona Avaratra), 10% Medium Sand, Dm: ?, Body T: .96, Rim T: .65, Red (10R 4/6) body.

o. Incurved basin with flat lip (Ampasimahavelona Avaratra, Unit III). 5% Coarse Sand, Angular Quartz and Feldspar, Dm ca. 40, Body T: 1.03, Rim T: .70, Dark reddish brown (2.5YR 2/2) body.

p. Tripod foot fragment (Ampasimahavelona Avaratra). Probably Analabe or Razanakoto Phase. 30% Coarse Rock, T:3.20 x 2.5, Red (2.5YR 5/6) body.

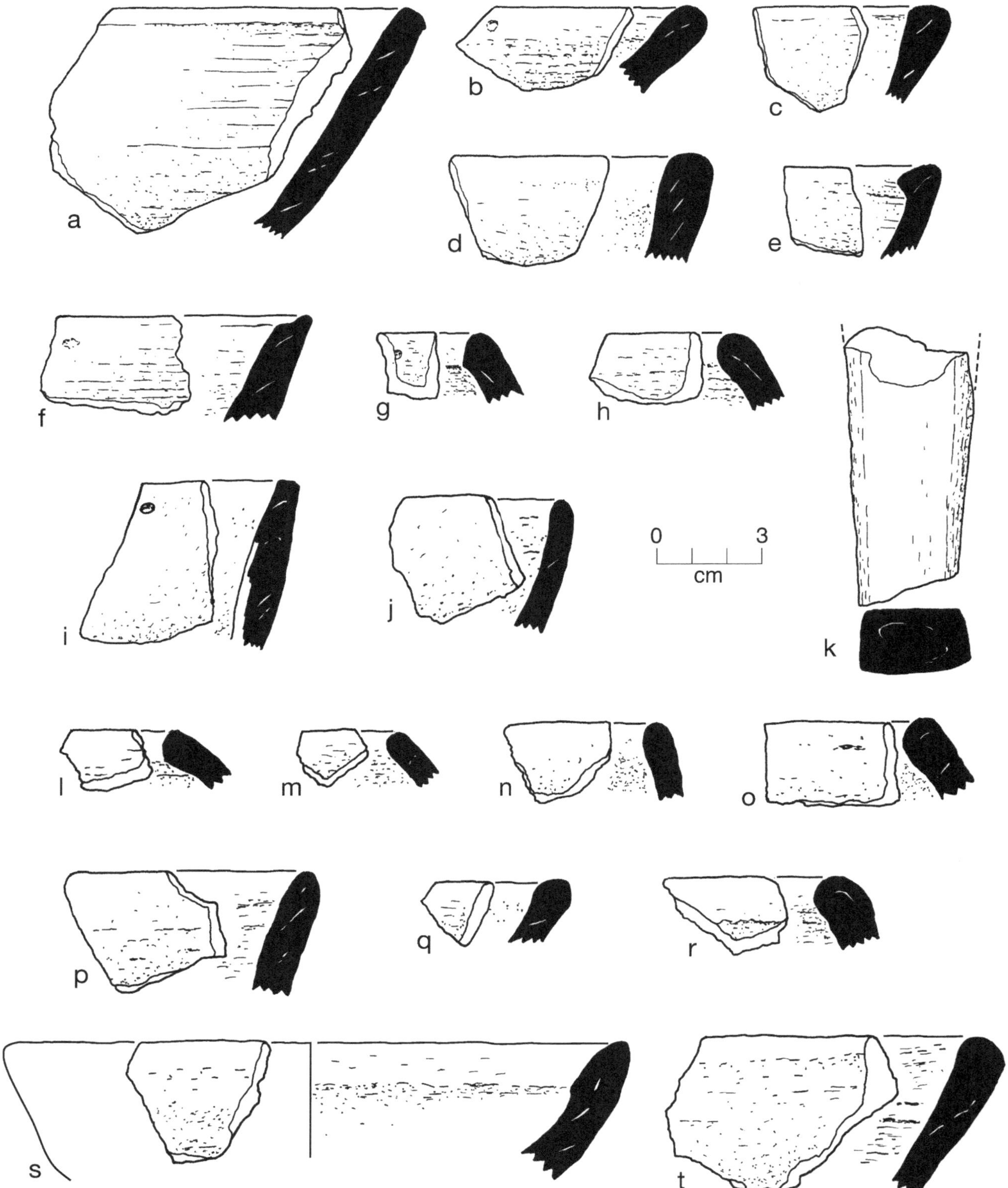
a
b
c
d
e
f
g
h
i
j
0
3
cm
k
l
m
n
o
p
q
r
s
t

Figure 7.5. Ceramics of other Ampasimahavelona Phase sites:
Antsofaly-Andranonana (785.4-1408.5: S13° 22' 13"/ E49° 59' 41"),
Amboronana Atsinanana (786.6-1408.4: S13° 22' 15"/ E50° 00' 30"),
Vohemar-Jovenna (785.8-1409.6: S13° 21' 48"/ E49° 59' 55"),
Jeunesse et Sport (786.9-1407.9: S13° 22' 30"/ E50° 00' 38"),
Maintialaka-Antafiabe (781.8-1413.1: S13° 19' 45"/ E49° 57' 45"),
Maintialaka Southeast (781.9-1412.8: S13° 19' 50"/ E49° 57' 51"),
Maintialaka Southwest (781.5-1411.1: S13° 19' 53"/ E49° 57' 25"). [See note, page 31.]

a. Large bowl with thickened rounded lip (Antsofaly Andranonana: 08-009: 785.4-1408.5). 10% Coarse Sand, Dm ca. 40, Body T: 1.11, Rim T: .72, Reddish brown (2.5YR 4/4) body.
b. Large bowl with thickened rounded lip (Antsofaly Andranonana: Same). 15% Coarse Sand, Dm ca. 34, Body T: .76, Rim T: .79, Reddish brown (2.5YR 4/4) body.
c. Basin with thickened rounded lip (Antsofaly Andranonana: Same). 15% Coarse Sand, Dm 24, Body T: .86, Rim T: 1.29, Strong brown (7.5YR 5/6) body.
d. Basin with thickened rounded rim (Antsofaly Andranonana: Same). 20% Coarse Sand and Angular Quartz, Dm ca. 34, Body T: 1.10, Rim T: 1.55, Strong brown (5YR 5/6) body.
e. Bowl with internally thickened rim (Antsofaly Andranonana: Same). 20% Medium Sand, Dm ?, Body T: .66, Rim T: 1.20, Reddish brown (2.5YR 4/5) body. (Probably Analabe Phase.)
f. Heavy bowl with grooved lip (Antsofaly Andranonana: Same). Crushed Sherds and Coarse Sand, Dm 24, Body T: 1.09, Rim T: .85, Red (2.5YR 6/4) body.
g. Hole-mouth jar with internally beveled lip (Antsofaly Andranonana: Same). 5% Coarse Sand, Dm ?, Body T: 1.15, Rim T: 1.05, Dark brown (7.5YR 3/1) body.
h. Hole-mouth jar with rounded lip (Antsofaly Andranonana: Same). 5% Coarse Sand, Dm ca. 18, Body T: 1.09, Rim T: 1.00, Red (2.5YR 4/6) body.
i. Large bowl with thickened flattened lip (Amboronana: 08-010: 786.6-1408.4). 15% Coarse Sand and Hematite, Dm ?, Side T: .95, Lip T:1.04, Lip T: .79, Reddish gray (5YR 5/2) body.
j. Small bowl with rounded lip (Amboronana: Same). 20% Coarse Sand, Dm 23, Side T: .78, Rim T: .66, Reddish brown (2.5YR 4/5) body.
k. Tripod foot fragment (Antsofaly Andranonana: Same). Probably Analabe or Razanakoto Phase. 10% Medium Sand, T: 3.20 x 2.54, Reddish brown (5YR 5/4) body.
l. Hole-mouth jar with thickened rounded lip (Amboronana: Same). 10% Coarse Sand, Dm 16, Side T: .79, Rim T: .83, Brown (7.5YR 4/3) body.
m. Hole-mouth jar with rounded lip (Amboronana: Same). 10% Medium Sand, Dm ca. 12, Side T: .83, Rim T: .71, Weak red (2.5YR 4/3) body.
n. Incurved jar with thickened rounded lip (Amboronana: Same). 10% Coarse Sand, Dm ca. 30, Side T: .95, .66, Rim T: .90, Red (2.5YR 5/5) body.
o. Hole-mouth jar with thickened rounded lip (Vohemar-Jovenna: 14-023: 786.1-1409.5). 35% Coarse Sand, Dm ca. 28, Side T: 1.03, Rim T: 1.30, Red (10Y 4/5) body.
p. Basin with rounded lip (Jeunesse et Sport: 08-013,787.2-1407.1). 10% Coarse Sand, Crushed sherds?, Feldspar? Dm ca. 46, Side T: 1.02, Rim T: .82, Dark reddish brown (2.5YR 3/4) body.
q. Basin with thickened rounded lip (Jeunesse et Sport: Same). 10% Coarse Sand, Dm ?, Side T: .95, Rim T: 1.11, Reddish brown (5YR 4/4) body.
r. Hole-mouth jar with thickened rounded lip (Maintialaka Southeast: 08-016: 782.2-1412.9). 20% Coarse Sand, Dm ca. 24, Side T: 1.08, Rim T: 1.30, Reddish brown (2.5YR 5/4) body.
s. Heavy small bowl with thickened rounded lip (Maintialaka Southeast: Same). 20% Coarse sand, Dm 20, Side T:1.08, Rim T: 1.25, Reddish brown (5YR 4/5) body.
t. Heavy basin with thickened rounded lip (Maintialaka Southwest: 08-017, 781.5-1412.9). 20% Coarse sand, Dm 32, Side T:1.17, Rim T: 1.44, Reddish brown (2.5YR 4/4) body.

Ampasimahavelona. Coarse oxidized basins (Figure 7.5r) and hole-mouth jar rims with thickened round lips indicate Ampasimahavelona occupation. The sherd scatter is at least 150 m from northwest to southeast and 15 m wide on part of the river terrace, now a sand ridge facing east over the old estuary (Figure 7.2b). The site was perhaps a linear settlement with houses facing the river. It now covers at least 0.15 ha.

Isolated Coarse Sandy Ware thick sherds occur throughout the beaches facing north over the Bay of Iharana from the south, on which the recent town of Vohemar has developed. The one definite Ampasimahavelona Phase occurrence was recorded.

5. Vohemar-Jovenna (Labordes 785.8-1409.6, S13° 21' 47"/ E49° 59' 55"), 1.4 km northwest of Ampasimahavelona, and 890 m northeast of Antsofaly-Andranonana, on the second beach facing north over the harbor and the bay. Construction of a petrol station revealed primarily Razanakoto and Ambatary Phase sherds, but there were some oxidized coarse thick sherds, including a hole-mouth jar with thickened rim (Figure 7.5o), indicating Ampasimahavelona use. This site was at most a small beach camp.

Three sites are on the active estuary of the Maintialaka River entering the Bay of Iharana from the northwest.

6. Maintialaka-Antafiabe (Laborde 781.8-1413.1 : S13° 19' 45"/ E49° 57' 45") is on a flat sandy terrace on the left or north bank of the Maintialaka River, 6m above sea level, now used for sweet potato and manioc gardens (Figure 8.1a). Coarse oxidized sherds are scattered over at least 0.50 ha. One large open bowl with thickened round rim indicates Ampasimahavelona Phase occupation (Figure 7.5t), though the other rims and the occurrence of Rough Ware indicate later occupations, discussed subsequently. This is the largest site known on the Maintialaka estuary. We tentatively classify this site as a small Ampasimahavelona village.

7. Maintialaka Atsimo-Atsinanana (southeast) (Laborde 781.9-1412.8: S13° 19' 50"/ E49° 57' 50") is on a flat sandy area on the right or south bank of the river just behind a high mid-Holocene dune, 400 m from Antafiabe, near the mangroves, about 7 m above sea level (Figure 8.1a). We have no local name for this field. It had been recently cleared for a manioc garden. Coarse oxidized sherds were scattered over at least 0.30 ha. Two rims of vessels made of a coarse, oxidized ware—one large open bowl and the other a round jar rim—both with thickened rims (Figure 7.5s), indicate Ampasimahavelona occupation.

8. Maintialaka Atsimo-Andrefana (southwest) (08-017: Laborde 781.5-1411.1: S13° 19' 51"/ E49° 57' 25") is on a flat sandy terrace on the right bank of the river now a mature coconut grove, 600 m from Antafiabe and about 7 m above sea level (Figure 8.1a). We have no local name. Coarse oxidized sherds are found only around deep pits made to convert wood into charcoal, over at least 0.20 ha, but the full extent of this early material is obscured by later debris. One large basin of very coarse oxidized ware with thickened round rim (Figure 7.5t) indicates Ampasimahavelona occupation.

The Maintialaka sites—one larger and two small—appear to have less material and less dense occupation of this early phase than sites near Vohemar. Perhaps Ampasimahavelona people used the Maintialaka embouchure only sporadically, or perhaps they only occupied this area late in the phase, as population gradually increased. Occupation of this embouchure certainly continued into Analabe and later times.

In contrast, repeated survey of the next embouchure to the south of Vohemar, the Manambery, which today drains directly into the Indian Ocean, has failed to reveal any early sites. There are suggestions of massive erosion and truncating of Holocene beach ridges, perhaps the catastrophic action of cyclones or tsunamis, which destroyed embouchures unprotected by reefs. Whatever the explanation, present evidence suggests that only some estuaries were actively exploited in this early phase.

In sum, the evidence from our soundings and surveys documents the occupants of the Vohemar area during the late eighth to tenth centuries CE. The known sites with Ampasimahavelona Phase ceramics are located on major embouchures (Figure 7.6). Occupied estuaries had one larger site and a few small sites—varying from .20 to 1.1 ha—each a kilometer or less from its nearest neighbor. No other intensively surveyed area on Madagascar's east coast has such a dense spacing of early settlements. Ampasimahavelona itself has evidence of fishing and shellfish collecting. All sites are close to marshes—which could have been used for either root crop or rice cultivation—and sandy terrain suitable for coconuts or yams. Villagers produced a range of ceramic basins and jars, most of Coarse Ware, without elaboration or decoration. There are also few fragments of vessels carved from chlorite schist. There is no iron slag or artifacts, though evidence of iron smelting occurs on contemporary sites to the south (Wright and Fanony 1992). It seems unlikely that either chlorite schist or iron was exported, and there is no evidence of any import of goods.

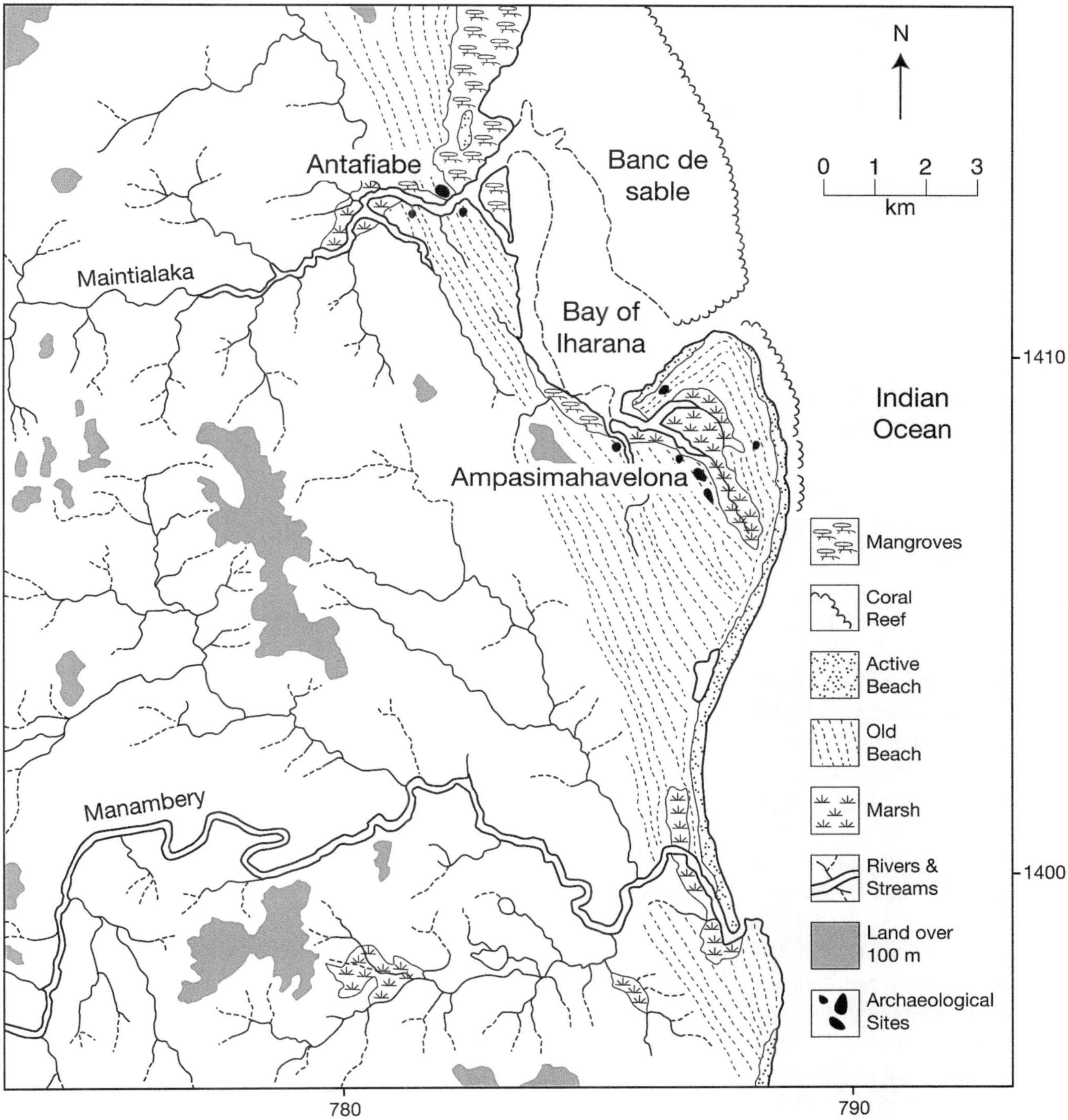

Figure 7.6. Ampasimahavelona Phase settlements.

Chapter 8

The Analabe Phase

Evidence

This proposed cultural unit is defined on the basis of soundings at the site of Analabe-Régis (786.9-1408.7), a large site on the east or right side of the old estuary (Figure 8.1b). We were led to this site by Jean-Yves Régis, a Vohemarian with an interest in archaeology, whose family lives upon and gardens part of the site. We found shells and sherds over an area covering about 5.8 ha. In 2007, we selected an area in a brushy pasture on the south edge of the site next to the wetlands and made a one-meter square excavation (Unit G: 786.9-1408.6) (see Appendix B). The cultivated layer of dark gray sand with charcoal and few sherds was removed as two layers, totaling .13 m thick. Below was Layer 3A, a dark gray sand .04 m thick containing a pavement of Rough Ware sherds and shells. Below this gray sand was Layer 3B, .18 m thick with sherds and shells. Layer 4 is a dark gray sand layer, .11 m thick with many *Terebralia* shells and sherds, many on edge. In this layer there was a concentration of heat-fractured rocks in the northeast corner of the square. At .29 m was a clear interface with Layer 5, mottled light brown silt with few cultural remains below. Below .38 m was gray white sand without cultural traces. Unfortunately, Unit G is near several recent charcoal burning pits, and fearing that samples from these layers would surely contain intrusive recent charcoal, we did not submit any for dating.

In 2008, we made another sounding on the central part of the site (Unit VI: Labordes 786.9-1408.7), revealing a shallow but useful stratigraphy. We removed Layer 1, the modern leaf litter, and Layer 2, a dark gray sand with little cultural material, certainly the cultivated layer. Below this at .20 m below surface was the homogenous black sand of Layer 3A. At .24 m we found the dense sherd pavement of Layer 3B. We removed this sherd pavement and found a lighter gray sand at -.29 m. We took a flotation sample and some sherds for thermoluminescence dating from Layer 3C. There seemed to be a slightly deeper depression with dark gray sand in the southeast corner of the unit, so we took additional samples, but there was little cultural

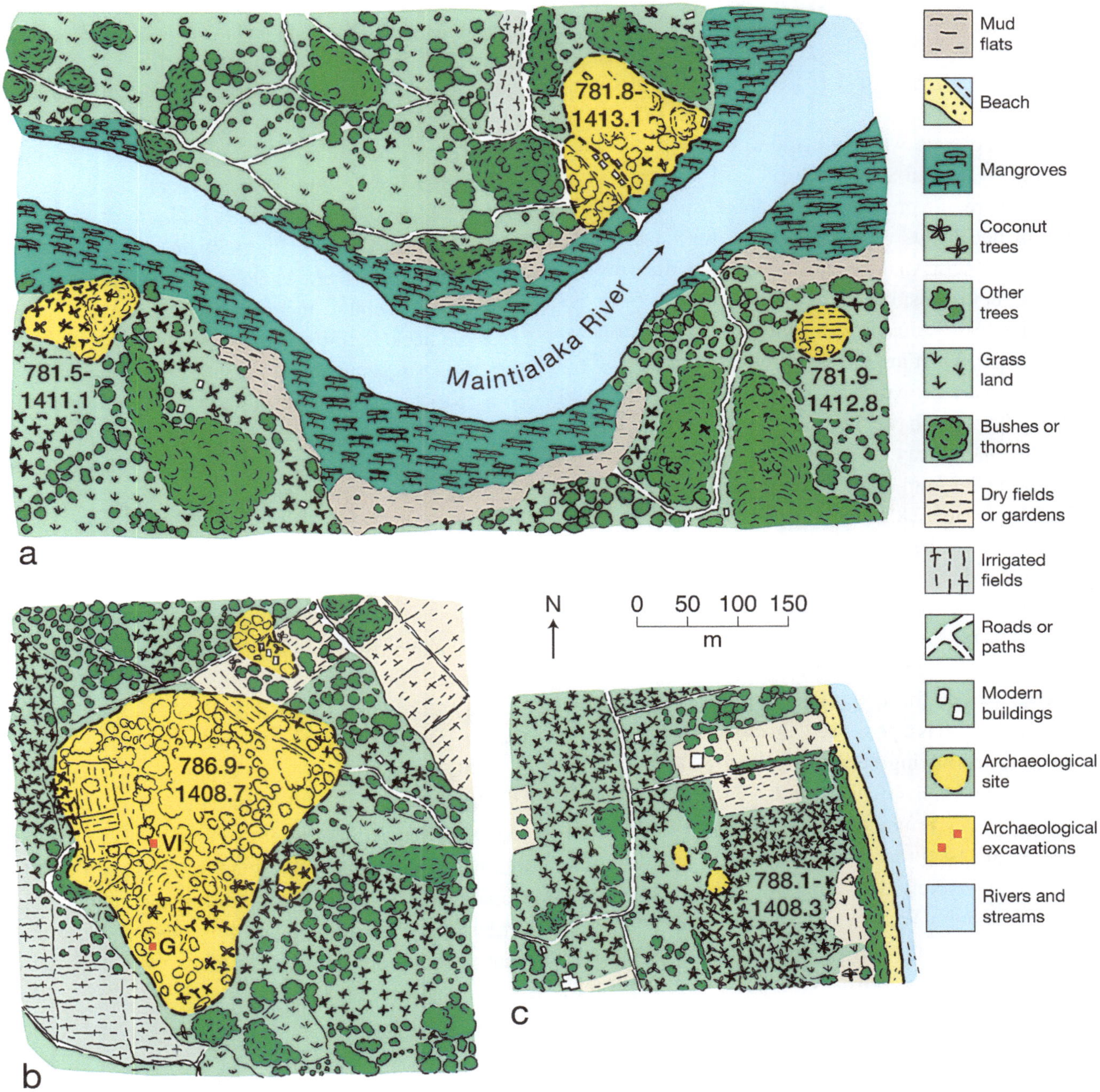

Figure 8.1. Some Analabe Phase sites.

material. The top of Layer 4 at .45 m was a mottled white sand without cultural evidence. Once again, no datable charcoal was recovered.

These two units have similar ceramics. These constitute the type samples for the Analabe Phase.

Artifacts

Two distinct ceramic wares are found on Analabe Phase sites: Rough Ware and Sandy Ware.

Rough Ware, the preponderant ware at Analabe-Régis, is distinguished by its ropy texture and the unsmoothed exterior surfaces. In Analabe sites, the Rough Ware always has vegetal inclusions, but other additions range from 5% medium sand to 30% coarse sand, with additions of crushed granite or shell. Most are oxidized reddish brown (2.5YR 4/4), but some are brown (7.5YR 4/2). Analabe-Régis and related sites have one basic Rough Ware vessel form: a large, deep basin. These vary in diameter—from 22 to 41 cm, with the mode at 37 cm—and have simple rounded (Figure 8.2n), grooved (Figure 8.2o), and outwardly beveled (Figure 8.2p) rims. As will be shown, Rough Ware remains in use at least until the early eighteenth century and is common at some sites, and rare at others. Such expedient ceramics varying in frequency are widely attested in the world and often have been used in specific activities. A common use for coarse open forms throughout the world is for salt manufacture, which is a possibility in northeast Madagascar, such an industry having been observed by Bernier in his journey during 1831 (Fleury 1886: 3 May: 261). This proposal, however, remains untested. Other uses proposed for such rough vessels are as bread pans and yogurt bowls, but both seem unlikely this region. Whatever the activity indicated by Rough Ware, variation in the proportion of such an activity-specific ware cannot be taken to indicate a regular technological or stylistic change in ceramics through time. Fortunately, Analabe Rough Ware has heavy vegetal inclusions, while later Rough Ware has mineral inclusions.

Sandy Ware is gritty but with well-smoothed surfaces. The inclusions in the Sandy Ware sample from Analabe-Régis range from 10% to 30% medium to coarse sand; most have about 15% medium sand. A few sherds have gray (N/3) bodies, probably fired in a reducing atmosphere, but most have been oxidized. Most sherds are brown (7.5YR 3-5/3-6) in color, but some are in the reddish brown to red range (2.5YR-7.5YR 4-6/2-6). The sherds are of medium body thickness, ranging from 0.60 to .90 cm; less than 10% are thicker than .80 cm. A portion of Analabe Sandy Ware body sherds have somewhat finer inclusions and are thinner and somewhat darker than any in the Ampasimahavelona sample. Analabe-Régis and related sites have a range of Sandy Ware vessel forms. Smaller shallow open basins and bowls range in diameter from 18 to 34 cm with a mode at 20 cm; they have round lips with exterior thickening (Figure 8.2c, d), horizontal flat lips (Figure 8.2a, e), or inwardly beveled flat lips (Figure 8.2b). Several have graphite on the lip. Probably the mat-impressed sherds are from the flat bases of such basins (Figure 8.2m). Only one restricted jar form is known from Analabe-Régis and related sites. It is a roughly globular incurved vessel with a hole-mouth, lacking a neck or rim modification, similar to those of the preceding Ampasimahavelona Phase. Rim diameters range from 16 to 24 cm. The rims have either simple rounded lips (Figure 8.2h–j) or flattened lips (Figure 8.2l). One has an incised arcuate decoration (Figure 8.2h) similar to that on a Mahilaka IIb jar (Radimilahy 1998:373).

Among the other artifacts are items of chlorite schist, including a fragment, a plain sherd, and a basin rim. The rim has a horizontal flat lip, a ridge below the rim on the exterior, and a grove on the interior to fit a top (Figure 8.2q). This was probably made on a lathe, but is too weathered to detect the typical scoring. There are also some small basalt flakes.

The 220 liters of sieved deposit from midden Layers 3 and 4 include 68 bones of fish (including head elements as well as vertebrae and spines, indicating the preparation of whole fresh fish); 11 bones of small land tortoises, several perhaps of the endemic genus *Pyxis* found today in southwestern Madagascar; and 7 medium turtle elements, probably marine turtle. Two limb bones of small birds could not be further identified. The only other food remains are many *Terebralia* shells from the mangroves and a few conch shells from the bay.

Chronology

So far we have no direct dating evidence for this phase. No datable imports and no carbon samples in secure context were recovered. Thermoluminescence samples have not yet been dated. Because the Sandy Ware ceramics are technically and stylistically intermediate between the ceramics of Ampasimahavelona phase and the Rajanakoto phases, we tentatively place it between these better-dated phases. If correct, the Analabe Phase probably dates sometime during the tenth and eleventh centuries CE.

Analabe Settlement

Eleven sites produced ceramics attributed to the Analabe Phase. Of these, five, including the large site of Analabe-Régis, are near the old estuary entering the Bay of Iharana from the south.

1. Analabe Atsinanana (07-42: Laborde 788.2-1408.3, S13° 22' 20"/ E50° 01' 13"). This site is composed of a concentration of Analabe Phase ceramics exposed in a grassy area, probably a fallow garden (Figure 8.1c). Just to the northeast is a paleontological site—a concentration of ratite eggshell from a relatively small variety of flightless bird (such as *Mullerornis* sp.) at the foot of the third beach about 6 m above sea level. The four rims—two basins (Figure 8.3a) and two hole-mouth jars (Figure 8.3b)—lack the thickening diagnostic of Ampasimahavelona Phase vessels, and could thus be either Ampasimahavelona or Analabe Phase. We place the site in Analabe Phase because of the small proportion of coarse inclusions, the brown body colors, and the use of Rough Ware. This site, probably one reported decades ago by Battistini and Vérin (1972), merits excavation to verify the age of the ratites and the human occupation and learn whether the ratites were exploited by people.

2. Analabe-Régis (07-43 to 51, Laborde 786.9-1408.7, S13° 22' 19"/ E50° 00' 29"). This large site, for which the approximate center is given here, is on the right or east bank of the old estuary. It covers at least 5.8 ha. It was little cultivated at the time of our visit, and most sherds were found around charcoal burners' pits (Figure 8.1b). Lenses of shell, primarily *Terebralia* from the mangrove swamps, are concentrated on the southeast side on the bank of the estuary. The two small stratigraphic excavations (see Appendix B) revealed shallow deposits with sherd pavements, lenses of shell, and possible post molds. There were three nearby small sites with Analabe Phase ceramics: one to the east (787.6-1408.3: S13° 22' 06"/ E50° 00' 34", UTM E0392750-N8521920), one to the northeast (787.1-1410.5: S13° 22' 02"/ E50° 00' 38", UTM E0392860-N8522035), and one to the north (786.8-1410.5: S13° 21' 58"/ E50° 00' 34", UTM E0392735-N8522165). We suggest these were hamlets affiliated to the larger village. In spite of repeated visits, we found no imported items and no rubble concentrations suggesting stone architecture. Clearly, however, several visits and two soundings give us a limited idea of the complexities of this large ancient settlement.

3. Antsofaly-Andranonana (08-009: Laborde 785.4-1408.5, S13° 22' 13"/ E49° 59' 41"). The west portion of this site, on the beach facing north over the Bay of Iharana (Figure 7.1a), has some Rough Ware as well as an internally thickened bowl rim (Figure 7.5e), indicating Analabe occupation. It covers about 0.35 ha. This site had easy access to the resources of the sandy beaches and terraces and the estuarine mangrove swamps of the old estuary and the Bay beyond. Its location suggests a site focused on resources of the embouchure and sandy areas, but the absence of the usual quantities of marine and estuarine shell suggests it was a hamlet devoted primarily to gardening. However, shell may have been destroyed by the acidic sandy soils.

4. Ambondrona Avaratra-Atsinanana (08-003: 786.4-1408.7, S13° 22' 06"/ E50° 00' 10"). This is a small site on a sand terrace on the southwest or left bank of the old estuary, south of modern Vohemar, now covered by mango trees and grassy pasture (Figure 11.1a). A scatter of Coarse Sandy Ware and Rough Ware sherds over about 0.30 ha were revealed in tree falls and eroded paths. The rims are not specific to phase, but the scarcity of thick coarse sandy sherds and the high proportion of Rough Ware indicates this is not an Ampasimahavelona site. This site would have access to mangroves and to marshlands appropriate for rice or taro fields. There is no shell debris indicating the exploitation of mollusks; they may have been destroyed by the very acidic sandy soils.

5. Vohemar-Jandarma (07-017: 787.0-1409.8, S13° 21' 26"/ E50° 00' 13") is a sherd collection from small gardens near the gendarme compound. Coarse Sandy Ware body sherds are found in other collections from central Vohemar, but only in this area did we find basin (Figure 8.3c) and bowl (Figure 8.3d) rims datable to the Analabe Phase. This settlement, whose size is not known, would have had easy access to the bay.

6. Vohemar-Ave Maria (07-019, 786.8-1410.0, S13° 21' 20" / E 50° 00' 30). In our Unit J, Layer 5, in this predominantly later site, mixed with later Patrick Phase sherds (discussed below), are four Coarse Sandy Ware sherds, including a heavy bowl rim (Figure 12.1d) of

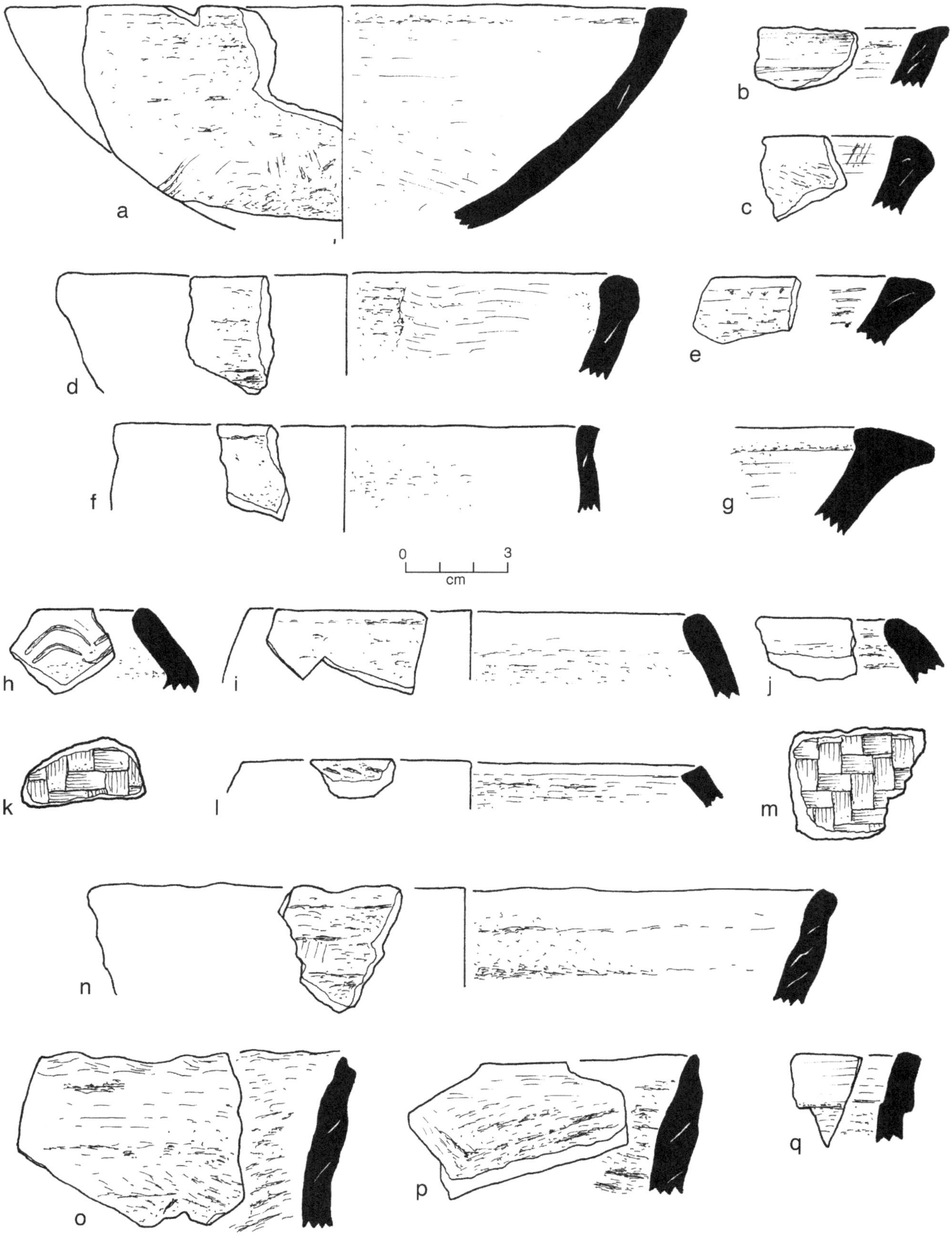
a
b
c
d
e
f
g
0
3
cm
h
i
j
k
l
m
n
o
p
q

Figure 8.2. Analabe Phase ceramics and chlorite schist artifacts of Analabe-Régis (786.8-1410.2). Note: Munsell colors were taken on a fresh chip under the outer surface. Abbreviations: Dm = Diameter; Body T = Body thickness 2 cm below lip; Rim T = Rim thickness. All measurements are in centimeters.

a. Heavy bowl with flat lip (Analabe-Régis, Unit VI, Layer 3B). 10% Coarse sand and vegetal inclusions, Dm 20.5, Body T: .89, Rim T: 1.10, Brown (7.5YR 5/4) body.
b. Basin with flat lip (Analabe-Régis, Unit G, Layer 3B). 10% Angular quartz and medium sand, Dm 22, Body T: .81, Rim T: .72, Reddish brown (5YR 4/3) body.
c. Basin with flat lip (Analabe-Régis, Unit VI, Layer 3A). 15% Medium sand, Dm 28, Body T: .86, Rim T: 1.31, Dark reddish brown (5YR 3/4) body. Trace of graphite on rim.
d. Heavy bowl with externally thickened rim (Analabe-Régis, Unit VI, Layer 3A). 10% Coarse sand, Dm 18, Body T: .69, Rim T: 1.47, Red (2.5YR 4/5) body.
e. Basin with flat lip (Analabe-Régis, Unit G, Layer 3B). 10% Medium sand, Dm 28, Body T: .93, Rim T: 1.24, Dark red (2.5YR 3/6) body.
f. Incurved bowl with flat lip (Analabe-Régis, Unit VI, Layer 3B). 10% Coarse sand, Dm 15, Body T: .70, Rim T: .66 , Brown (7.5YR 5/3) body.
g. Large bowl with interior-exterior thickened rim (Analabe-Régis, Unit VI, Layer 3A), 5% Coarse sand, Dm 33, Side T: .82, Rim T: 2.55, Dark reddish brown (2.5YR 3/4) body. Graphite on rim.
h. Carinated bowl with rounded lip and arcuate incised decoration (Analabe-Régis, Unit G, Layer 3B). 5% Medium sand, Dm ca. 30, Body T: .80, Rim T: .78, Reddish brown (2.5YR 5/4) body. (Radimilahy 1998: Fig.7.4: 15)
i. Incurved bowl with thickened rounded lip (Analabe-Régis, Unit VI, Layer 3A), Dm 15, 20% Medium sand, Dm ca. 15 cm, Body T: .77, Rim T: .80, Dark brown (7.5YR 3/2) body.
j. Hole-mouth jar (Analabe-Régis, Unit G, Layer 3B). 10% Medium sand, Dm ca. 35, Body T: .83, Rim T: .79, Reddish brown (2.5YR 4/4) body.
k. Mat-impressed base fragment (Analabe-Régis, Unit VI, Layer 3A). 15% Medium sand, Base T: 1.21, Reddish brown (2.5YR 4/4) body.
l. Hole-mouth jar (Analabe-Régis, Unit VI, Layer 3A), 5% Medium sand, Dm 14, Body T: .60, Rim T: .68, Red (10YR 5/6) body.
m. Mat-impressed base fragment (Analabe-Régis, Unit VI, Layer 3B). 15% Medium sand, Base T: 1.14, Red (2.5YR 4/6) body.
n. Rough Ware basin with rounded lip (Analabe-Régis, Unit VI, Layer 3A). 5% Coarse sand and vegetal inclusions, Dm ca. 22, Body T: .99, Rim T: .69, Dark reddish brown (2.5YR 3/4) body.
o. Rough Ware basin with grooved lip (Analabe-Régis, Unit VI, Layer 3B). 20% Coarse sand, shell, granite and vegetal inclusions, Dm 39, Body T: .88, Rim T: ca. .79, Dark reddish brown (7.5YR 5/4) body.
p. Rough Ware basin with tapered lip (Analabe-Régis, Unit VI, Layer 3B). 30% Coarse sand, granite, and vegetal inclusions, Dm 41, Body T: .88, Rim T: ca. .59 , Dark red (2.5YR 4/4) body.
q. Basin rim (Analabe-Régis, Unit G, Layer 3B), Gray chlorite schist, Dm ca. 19, Body T: .79, Rim T: .69.

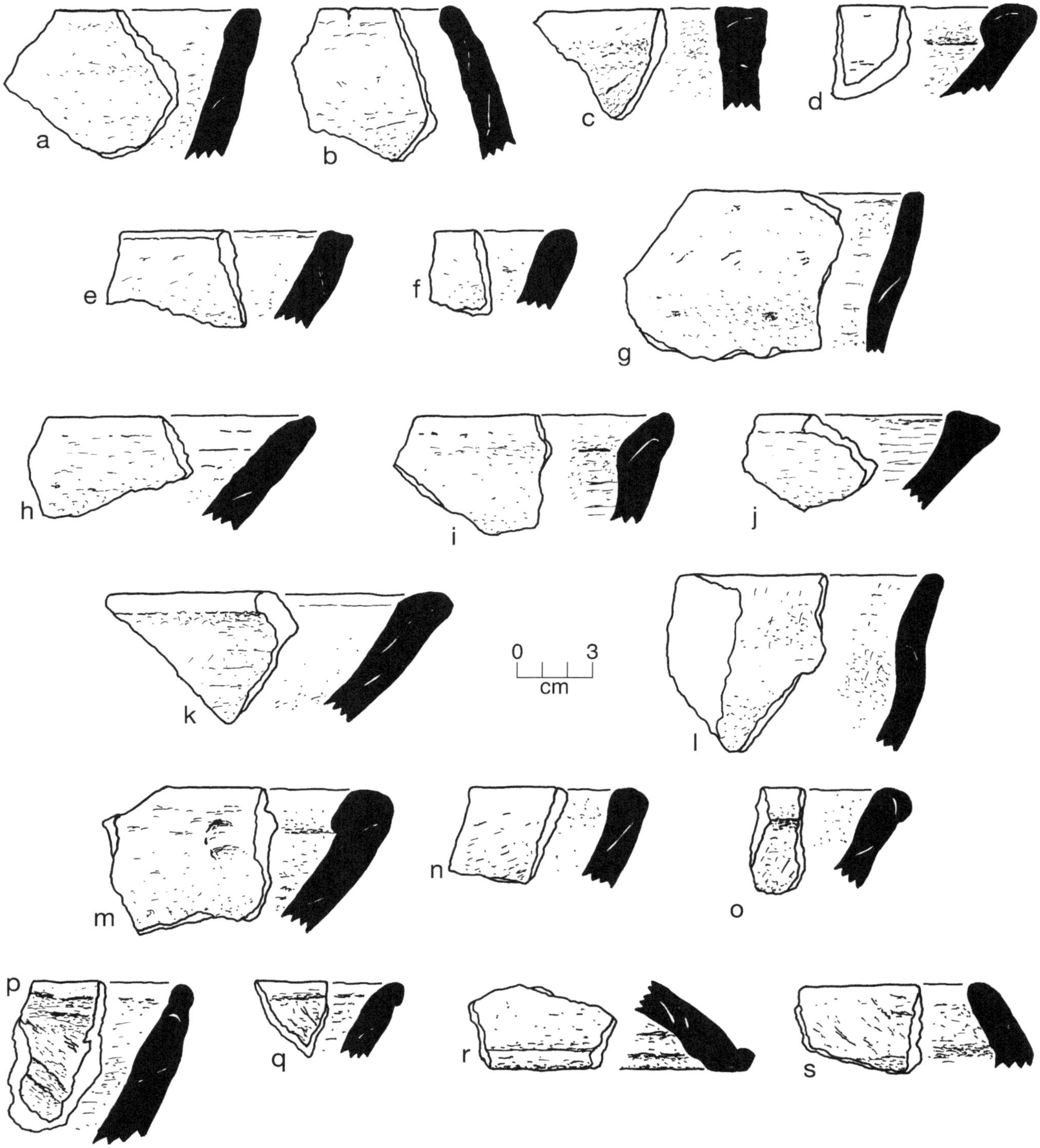
a
b
c
d
e
f
g
h
i
j
k
0 3
cm
l
m
n
o
p
q
r
s

Figure 8.3. Ceramics from other Analabe Phase sites:
Analabe Atsinanana (07-042: 788.2-1408.3, S13° 22' 21"/ E50° 00' 13"),
Vohemar-Jandarma (07-017: 787.0-1409.8, S13° 21' 26"/ E50° 00' 13"),
Jeunesse et Sport (08-013: 787.0-1407.9: S13° 22' 22"/ E50° 00' 38"),
Maintialaka-Antafiambe (08-015: 781.8-1413.1: S13° 19' 45"/ E49° 57' 45"),
Maintialaka Atsimo-Atsinana [SE] (08-016: 781.9-1412.8: S13° 19' 50"/ E49° 57' 52"),
Maintialaka Atsimo-Andrefana [SW] (08-017: 781.5-1411.1: S13° 19' 51"/ E49° 57' 25"),
Andranomasokely Centre (07-029: 787.5-1409.9, S13°21' 36"/ E50° 00' 43").
[See note, page 45.]

a. Basin with rounded lip (Analabe Atsinanana: 07-042, 788.2-1408.3). 15% Coarse sand and angular quartz, Dm ca. 40, Side T: 1.02, Rim T: .81, Reddish brown (5YR 5/4) body.
b. Hole-mouth jar with round lip (Analabe Atsinanana: Same). 20% Coarse sand and angular quartz, Dm 26, Side T: .73, Rim T: .66, Dark brown (7. 5YR 3/2) body.
c. Basin with flat lip (Vohemar-Jandarma: 07-017, 787.0-1409.8). 15% Coarse sand, Dm ca. 35, Side T: .89, Lip T: 1.29, Color not recorded.
d. Bowl with interior rounded thickening (Vohemar-Jandarma: Same). 15% Coarse sand and angular quartz, Dm ?, Side T: .99, Rim T: 1.22, Red (2.5YR 5/6) body.
e. Basin with flattened oblique lip (Jeunesse et Sport: 08-013: 787.0-1407.9). 5% Coarse sand, Dm ca. 48, Side T: 1.05, Lip T: .95, Yellowish red (5YR 3/5) body.
f. Basin with round lip (Jeunesse et Sport: Same). 10% Medium sand, Dm ?, Side T: .90, Lip T: .89, Reddish brown (5YR 5/5) body.
g. Rough Ware basin with round lip (Jeunesse et Sport: Same). 5% Coarse sand, Dm 35, Side T: .71, Lip T: .50, Brown (7.5YR 4/4) body.
h. Rough Ware basin with tapered rim (Maintialaka-Antafiambe: 08-015: 781.8-1413.1). 25% Coarse sand, Dm ca. 40, Side T: 99, Lip T: .91, Yellowish red (5YR 6/6) body.
i. Bowl with internally thickened rim (Maintialaka-Antafiambe: Same). 25% Coarse sand, Dm ca. 24, Side T: .80, Rim T: 1.17, Light reddish brown (5YR 6/5) body.
j. Bowl with externally thickened rim with obliquely flattened lip (Maintialaka-Antafiambe: Same). 25% Coarse sand, Dm ?, Side T: .92, Lip T: 1.41, Brown (7.5YR 4/2) body.
k. Bowl with internally thickened rim (Maintialaka-Antafiambe: Same). 15% Medium sand, Dm ca. 50 (warped), Side T: .87, Lip T: 1.19, Very dark gray (2.5YR 3/1) body.
l. Carinated bowl with rounded lip (Maintialaka-Antafiambe: Same.) 25% Medium sand, mica, and feldspar, Dm ca. 30, Side T: .61, Lip T: .70, Red (10R 5/5) body.
m. Bowl with internal thickening (Maintialaka Atsimo-Andrefana [SW]: 08-016, 781.9-1412.8). 20% Coarse sand, Dm ca. 28, Side T: 1.10, Rim T: 1.30, Red (2.5YR 5/6) body.
n. Basin with flattened lip (Maintialaka Atsimo-Andrefana [SW]). 15% Medium sand, Dm ca. 34, Side T: .83, Lip T: .91, Reddish brown (5YR 5/4) body.
o. Bowl with externally thickened rim (Maintialaka Atsimo-Andrefana[SW]: Same). 20% Coarse sand, Dm ?, Side T: .84, Lip T: 1.15, Dark reddish brown (2.5YR 3/4) body.
p. Rough Ware bowl with tapered rim (Andranomasikely Centre: 07-029: 787.0-1409.5). 5% coarse sand, Dm ?, Side T: 1.14, Lip T: .56, Red (2.5YR 4/6) body.
q. Rough Ware bowl with externally thickened rim (Andranomasikely Centre: Same). 20% Angular quartz and coarse sand, Dm ?, Side T: .74, Lip T: .53, Reddish brown (2.5YR 4/4) body.
r. Rough Ware: possible cover rim (Andranomasikely Centre: Same). 25% Angular quartz and coarse sand, Dm ca. 16, Side T: .85, Lip T: .54, Red (2.5YR 4/5) body.
s. Rough Ware carinated bowl with tapered lip (Andranomasikely Centre: Same). 15% Angular quartz and coarse sand, Dm ca. 20, Side T: .74, Lip T: .68, Red (2.5YR 4/7) body.

Analabe Phase affinity (cf. Figure 8.2d). Coarse sherds are found in several collection areas in the far northeast of Vohemar, but only Ave Maria has yielded a datable rim.

7. Ampasimahavelona Avaratra (08-011: 786.7-1408.1, S13° 22' 20"/ E 50° 00' 25"). In the northwest area, the disturbed deposits have a few Rough Ware sherds. Sandy Ware basin rims with internal (Figure 7.3c) and external (Figure 7.3i) thickening and a tripod foot fragment (Figure 7.4p) indicate continuing Analabe occupation on the old village site (Figure 7.1b.) We attribute an area of .50 ha to the Analabe phase at this site.

8. Jeunesse et Sport (08-013: 787.0-1407.9, S13° 22'22"/ E50° 00' 38") is a sherd scatter southeast of Ampasimahavelona, extending 150 m and covering at least 0.15 ha, on a sand ridge on the left bank of the old embouchure (Figure 7.1b). In addition to Ampasimahavelona occupation, the predominance of medium Sandy Ware brown sherds—including a basin rim (Figure 8.3e), a bowl rim (Figure 8.3f), a mat-impressed base (not illustrated), and a Rough Ware bowl rim (Figure 8.3g)—indicate Analabe occupation. This site had good access to land for both dry farming and irrigated fields.

The three early sites on the estuary of the Maintialaka River continued to be occupied into the Analabe Phase.

9. Maintialaka-Antafiabe (08-015: Laborde 781.8-1413.1 : S13° 19' 45"/ E49° 57' 45"). This site is on a flat sandy terrace on the left or north bank of the river, now sweet potato and manioc gardens (Figure 8.1a). Rough Ware and coarse Sandy Ware oxidized sherds are scattered over at least 0.50 ha. Several bowls with internally (Figure 8.3i, k) and externally (Figure 8.3j) thickened rims, and also Rough Ware sherds, are characteristic of the Analabe Phase. Occupation seems denser and was perhaps larger than that of the Ampasimahavelona Phase.

10. Maintialaka Atsimo-Atsinanana (southeast) (08-16: Laborde 781.9-1412.8: S13° 19' 50"/ E49° 57' 50") is on a flat sandy terrace on the right or south bank of the river, just behind the high mid-Holocene dune and near the mangroves (Figure 8.1a). Coarse oxidized sherds are scattered over at least 0.30 ha. A Rough Ware bowl with internally thickened rounded rim (Figure 7.5s) suggests Analabe Phase occupation.

11. Maintialaka Atsimo-Andrefana (southwest) (08-017: Laborde 781.5-1411.1: S13° 19' 51"/ E49° 57' 25") is on a flat sandy terrace on the right or south bank of the river, now a mature coconut grove (Figure 8.1a). Coarse sherds are found only around deep pits made for charcoal burning. These pits extend over at least 0.20 ha, but the full extent of this early material cannot be estimated. Bowls with internally (Figure 8.3n) and externally (Figure 8.3m) thickened rims and a bowl of coarse Sandy Ware with externally thickened round rim (Figure 8.3o) indicate Analabe occupation.

The evidence from our soundings and surface surveys documents the occupants of the Vohemar area during the Analabe Phase, which we currently believe to be of the tenth to eleventh centuries. The distribution of settlement is similar to that of the Ampasimahavelona Phase. The known sites with Analabe Phase ceramics are located near the coast on substantial embouchures (Figure 8.4). Each estuary has one larger village site and a number of small hamlet sites. All sites are close to areas of marshy ground, which could have been used for either root crops or rice cultivation. These people produced a range of ceramic jars, predominantly a simple hole-mouth form made of Sandy Ware, and bowls and basins on both Rough Ware and Sandy Ware. The most striking change from earlier times was the emergence of Analabe-Régis, a large settlement of more than five hectares across the old estuary to the northeast of Ampasimahavelona, which appears have shrunk to hamlet size. This large settlement has much Rough Ware, which must indicate a special, albeit yet unspecified, activity. Surprisingly, there is no evidence of imported goods. A slag fragment indicates some iron work, and rare chlorite schist fragments indicate finishing of stone vessels, but both activities may have been for local purposes. If there is no evidence of participation in the Indian Ocean trade network, then the emergence of a larger settlement on the Bay of Iharana must have been related to local factors.

This contrasts strongly with contemporary material recovered by the team of Vincent Serneels (2017) at Benavony, a large port site about 180 km south of Vohemar. Here there is massive evidence of iron working and the finishing of chlorite schist vessels, as well as the imports of quantities of early sgraffito ceramics, as well as glass, probably from the Persian Gulf (Serneels et al. 2017). The local ceramics are now being studied in detail by Nelas Fanny Sabe.

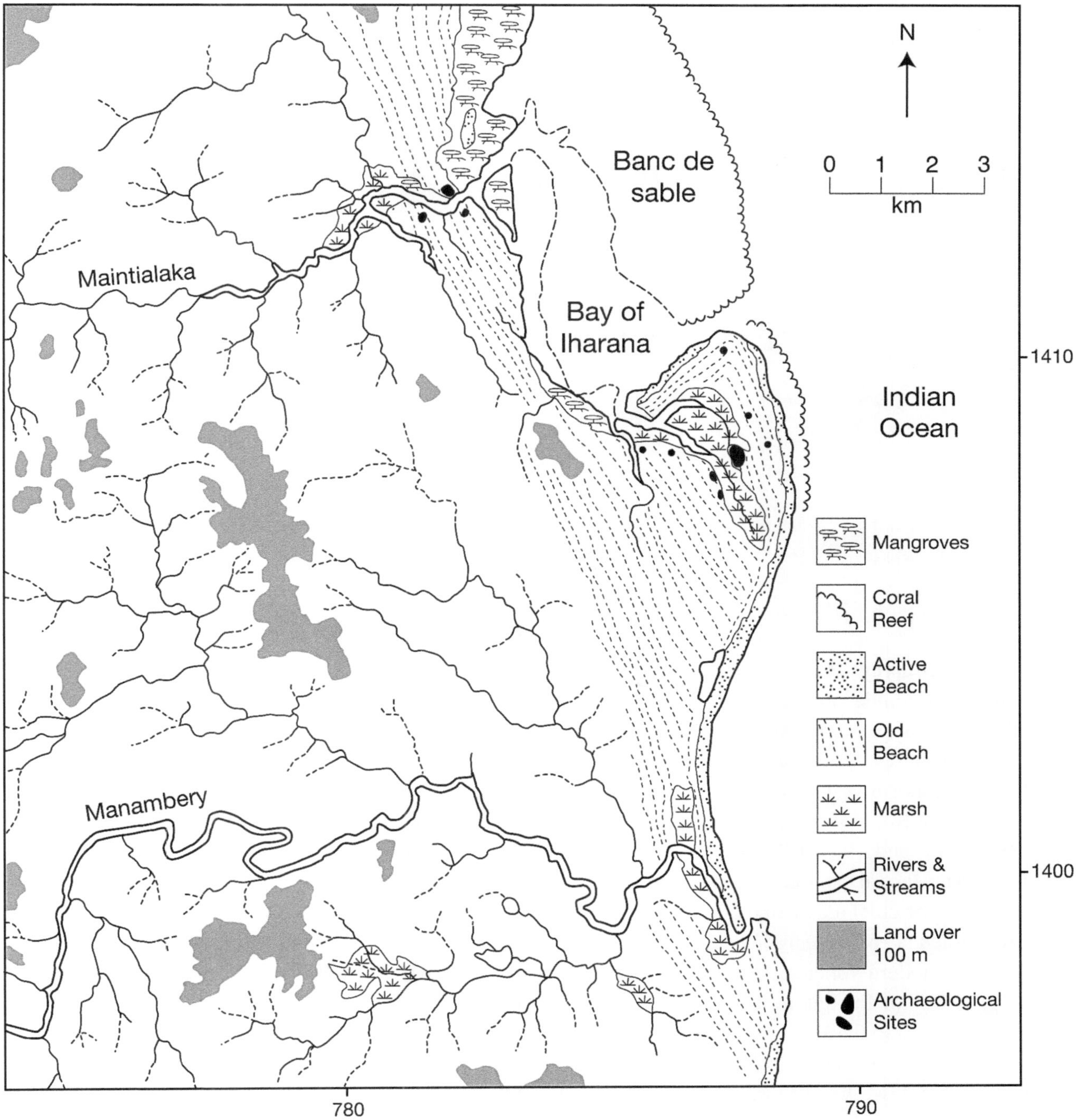

Figure 8.4. Analabe Phase settlements.

Chapter 9

The Razanakoto Phase

Evidence

During our initial surveys in 2007, we noted a number of sherds with forms and decorations like those of the well-dated Mahilaka Phase, the prosperous period of occupation (late eleventh to fourteenth centuries) at the great port of Mahilaka on the northwest coast of Madagascar, only 180 km south-southwest of Vohemar (Radimilahy 1998; Wright, Radimilahy and Allibert 2005). However, we found no site with a substantial sample of such sherds. Early in our 2008 season, the chief technician of the Musée, Victor Razanatovo, noted sherds in gardens and carparks in the northeast end of modern Vohemar, along the deep channel connecting the Bay of Iharana to the Indian Ocean. The site appeared limited to the second beach ridge southeast of the channel, no more than 20 m wide. We could trace sherds from the southwest end of the site northeastwards 60 m along this second beach, but the site certainly extends northeastward under the garage of the Hotel "Baie d'Iharana," where we could not survey, perhaps another 140 m (Figure 9.1a). We mapped the accessible part of the site carefully, talked with the various landowners, and found local sherds similar to Mahilaka, a sherd of imported Persian Gulf sgraffito (also well-known from Mahilaka and datable to the late eleventh to early fourteenth centuries CE) (Figure 9.2o), and a sherd of monochrome green glazed ware, dated from the early thirteenth to the fifteenth centuries CE. We cored widely and found an area of deeper deposits in the vegetable garden of M. Paul Razanakoto.

We excavated a one-meter square in this deeper deposit (see Appendix B), first removing Layer 1: .25 m of cultivated mottled gray sand, rich in recent bottle fragments, plastic items, metal items, etc. This revealed the top of Layer 2A, a dark gray sand layer with earlier Sandy Ware sherds and only one modern beer bottle fragment. At .33 m, we found Layer 2B—black sand with flat-lying early sherds, shell, coral fragments, and iron slag. This midden layer was removed, and at .40 m we found the top of transitional Layer 3, a mottled gray sand with fewer sherds, mammal and fish bone, iron slag, and some rounded coral fragments. As we troweled downward, the mottled sand became lighter, and an intrusive feature with a gray sand fill was defined in the center of the square. This divided into three discrete smaller disturbances, indicating it was the mold of a tree stump. The few sherds and bones from Layer 3B were in this disturbance. Two smaller

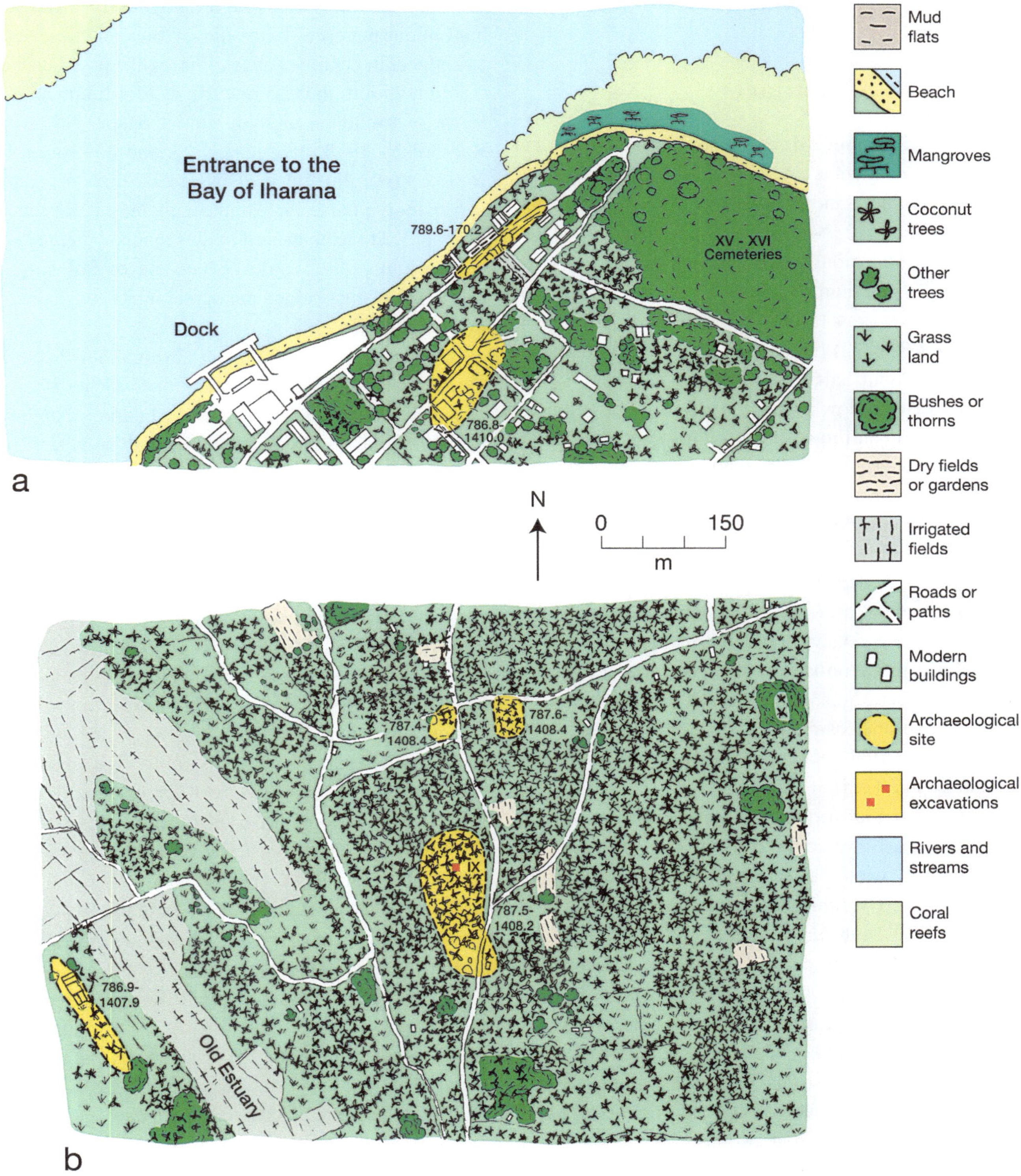

Figure 9.1. Some Razanakoto Phase sites.

disturbances from 2B, probably postholes, were noted in the southeast and southwest sections (see Appendix B for further details).

Artifacts

The samples of ceramics from the stratified deposits and the surface of the Razanakoto site is small but distinctive. Most have medium sandy inclusions. These range from 10% medium sand to 25% medium sand and angular quartz, but the coarser inclusions and mica do occur. Most sherds have about 15% medium to coarse sand. About half of the sherds have dark gray (5YR-7.5YR 3/1) to dark brown (7.5YR-10YR 3-4/1-2) bodies probably fired in reducing atmospheres. About half have oxidized exteriors. A few sherds have red to yellowish red (2.5YR-5YR 5/5-6) colors, but most are reddish brown or light brown (7.5YR-10YR 4/5-3/5). The sherds are of medium thickness, ranging from 0.40 to .90 cm with a mode of .77 cm. We found only one sherd of Rough Ware at the Razanakoto site. Perhaps the range of activities undertaken at the part of the site we studied rarely included the use of these expedient vessels.

The Razanakoto assemblage includes open bowls and basins with simple rims with predominantly flattened lips (Figure 9.2b, e, g; Radimilahy 1998: Figs. 7.b,c,g) and some rounded lips (Figure 9.2a, f; Radimilahy 1998: Figs 7.1:21; 7.2:21). There is one basin with a tapered rim (Figure 9.2d) and one with external thickening (Figure 9.2e). Diameters vary from 20 to 30 cm.

Two restricted jar forms are known from Razanakoto and related sites. More common is the rim of a spherical or "hole-mouth" vessel lacking a neck, familiar from the preceding phases. The rims are slightly tapered with rounded or flattened lips. Both plain examples (Figure 9.2j) and examples with round or rectangular punctates (Figure 9.2h, k; Radimilahy 1998: Figs 7.3:20; 7.4:17, 25) are known. The less common restricted form is an everted neck jar (Figure 9.2m; Radimilahy 1998: Figs 7: 7.1:6, 7.4: 4,7,18), though the flattened lip linear horizontal incising are unprecedented until later. There are also several shoulder fragments, either from such jars or from small carinated bowls, one with oblique incising (Figure 9.2h; Radimilahy 1998: Figs 7.1:6, 7.3:11, 7.4:21) and punctates and one with heavy wavy incising (Figure 9.2i; Radimilahy 1998: Figs 7.4: 4,26). The small number of diagnostic sherds from Razanakoto makes comparison with Mahilaka difficult, but the broad relation to well-dated Mahilaka are clear. One illustrated everted jar on a distinctly hard sandy fabric, a surface find, has oblique patterned burnishing, typical of the seventeenth to eighteenth century Patrick Phase (discussed below).

In addition, there is one tripod foot fragment, similar to those found on chlorite schist basins (Figure 9.2n; Radimilahy 1998: cf. Fig 7.1: 3), and one rough handle for a top (not illustrated). Both are oxidized red and have surprisingly coarse inclusions. This may be because they were added to leather-hard bodies that had already shrunk; coarse inclusions would reduce the overall amount of shrinkage of such added parts, and thus reduce the chance they would break off.

In general, a collection of Razanakoto Phase Sandy Ware sherds is finer and darker than earlier body sherd samples. Jars tend to be coarser and darker than bowls or basins. Bodies are thinner. Rims of both bowls and jars are commonly flattened rather than rounded, but internal and external rim thickenings are both rare.

There are a number of chlorite schist sherds in Razanakoto Phase surface samples from the Vohemar area. Most examples appear to have been finished on a lathe, creating horizontal ridging and cut marks. The few rims are from out-leaned basins with flattened lips. No foot or top fragments have been found on the occupational sites.

Chlorite schist body sherds and fragments were sometimes reworked as net weights. We have recorded a small oval weight from Layer 3 at the Razanakoto site, a drilled sherd fragment (Figure 9.2p). Another drilled sherd (Figure 9.2q) is perhaps part of a weight. An ovoid piece of chlorite schist with crossed grooves to facilitate tying a cord around it (Figure 9.2r) is also probably a weight. These are surface finds. Iron slag, probably from forging or repairing iron tools rather than smelting, occurs in midden Layers 2B and 3 in our sounding.

Sieving of Layers 2 and 3 at the Razanakoto site yielded only a few *Anadara* shells, indicating exploitation of the sandy beaches of the Bay, five fish bones, and ten mammal bones. This sample has not yet been studied in detail.

While the Razanakoto Site surface and excavation samples allowed us to tentatively define the cultural assemblage of the twelfth to fourteenth centuries CE, it was a small sample and eventually led us to challenging problems and unexpected solutions. Initially, we supplemented the Razanakoto evidence with related material from a site termed Analabe Centre (07-032: 787.5-1408.2), from which we had a large ceramic sample from a wind-deflated disturbed excavation unit (termed Unit D; not discussed in Appendix B.) When, however, our ceramic analysis of all Vohemar survey sites was completed in 2014, we found a new problem. Analabe Centre was immediately to the south of a group of coconut groves, covering more than 3.8 ha, which we had not been allowed to survey during the 2007–2014 seasons. Was Analabe Centre an isolated hamlet or was it the southern portion of a much larger twelfth to thirteenth century CE site? In fact, we had found no larger Razanakoto Phase sites in other surveyed areas, and we needed to know not only the dates of sites in this unsurveyed area but what kinds of sites they might be. Were they smaller or larger villages sites with purely domestic debris or did they also have the evidence of specialized craft production and social differentiation that typify a town?

A special return visit to Vohemar to survey and test the unexamined tract was planned for October 2018. The cooperation of Vohemar authorities was sought, and proved essential, as discussed in Appendices A and B. In brief, we established that collection area 07-032 extended northwest without interruption into collection area 18-002, named Analabe-Zafindravao after the landowner. The site as a whole is termed Analabe Centre (787.5-1408.2). The sounding in Analabe-Zafindravao (Unit IX) yielded another small stratified artifact sample. The deeper layers have a majority of ceramics with 5% fine to 20% medium sand; a few others have coarser rounded quartz inclusions. Most sherds have about 10%–15% medium sand. About half of the sherds have gray bodies, probably from firing in reducing atmospheres. About half have oxidized exteriors. Rims indicate most vessels were deep open bowls (Figure 9.5a–c: cf. Radimilahy 1998 Fig 7.1:18–19) and basins (Figure 9.5d) most with flat lips. A minority of the vessels were restricted spherical (Figure 9.5i–k) or everted jars (Figure 9.5n). Most jars were plain, but surface collections from Analabe-Zafindravao also have fragments with dentate impressions (Figure 9.5i,l; Radimilahy 1998 Figs 7.1:8, 7.4:7,11,32), wavy incising (Figure 9.5n; Radimilahy 1998 Fig 7.1:4, 7.2:7), wavy combing (Figure 9.5r; Radimilahy 1998 Fig 7.4:6), and linear imprints (Figure 9.5j, m, q: Radimilahy 1998 Fig 7.1:7, 10, 7.2:5, 7.3: 14, 7.4:17). The collection is thus similar to those from Mahilaka as well as nearby Razanakoto. It appears to be a typical domestic assemblage, with a majority of open forms.

It is interesting that Unit IX revealed only level midden layers and a shallow pit, with no evidence of sandy floor traces or postholes. The faunal remains are predominantly of mollusks from the mangroves, with only a small and diverse scatter of mollusks from the Banc du Sable. Bone is scarce, primarily platey head parts of fish, indicating whole fish consumption at Analabe Centre. Thus, the features and faunal remains from this single square reinforce the ceramic indications of a modest domestic occupation. We recovered no flotation samples for the study of floral remains. More soundings would be useful.

Neither surface collections nor the soundings yielded any scraps of iron slag. Similarly there are fragments of lathe-finished chlorite schist basins (Figure 9.5s), but no small fragments from the process of the lathe-finishing the rough chlorite schist preforms brought from the quarries. Conversely, the 2018 research at Analabe-Zafindravao yielded no additional evidence of imports brought from the Near East or from Southeast Asia.

The surface of Analabe-Zafindravao and the uppermost layer in Unit IX yielded a few sherds of the hard sandy ware, often scraped in various ways (Figure 9.5y–a'). In 2007, this ware was shown to be characteristic of the seventeenth- to eighteenth-century Patrick Phase. The large Patrick site is only 430 m south of Analabe-Zafindravao, and the sherds probably mark a brief Patrick Phase reoccupation.

Chronology

The rectangular punctates and wavy incising on closed forms are known from a number of other ceramic assemblages in northern Madagascar. For example, Mahilaka, a town of the eleventh to fourteenth centuries CE on the northwest coast (Radimilahy 1998); Lakaton'ny Akanga, a hunting camp of the thirteenth to fourteenth centuries CE near Ramena on the Bay of Antsiranana in the far north (Dewar 1996); and Tafiantsirebika, a coastal village of the twelfth to fourteenth centuries near Irodo on the northeast coast (Vérin 1975: 710–742, Fig. 305). These parallels support a twelfth to fourteenth century span for the Razanakoto Phase, also indicated by the imported sgraffito and monochrome sherds found on the surface.

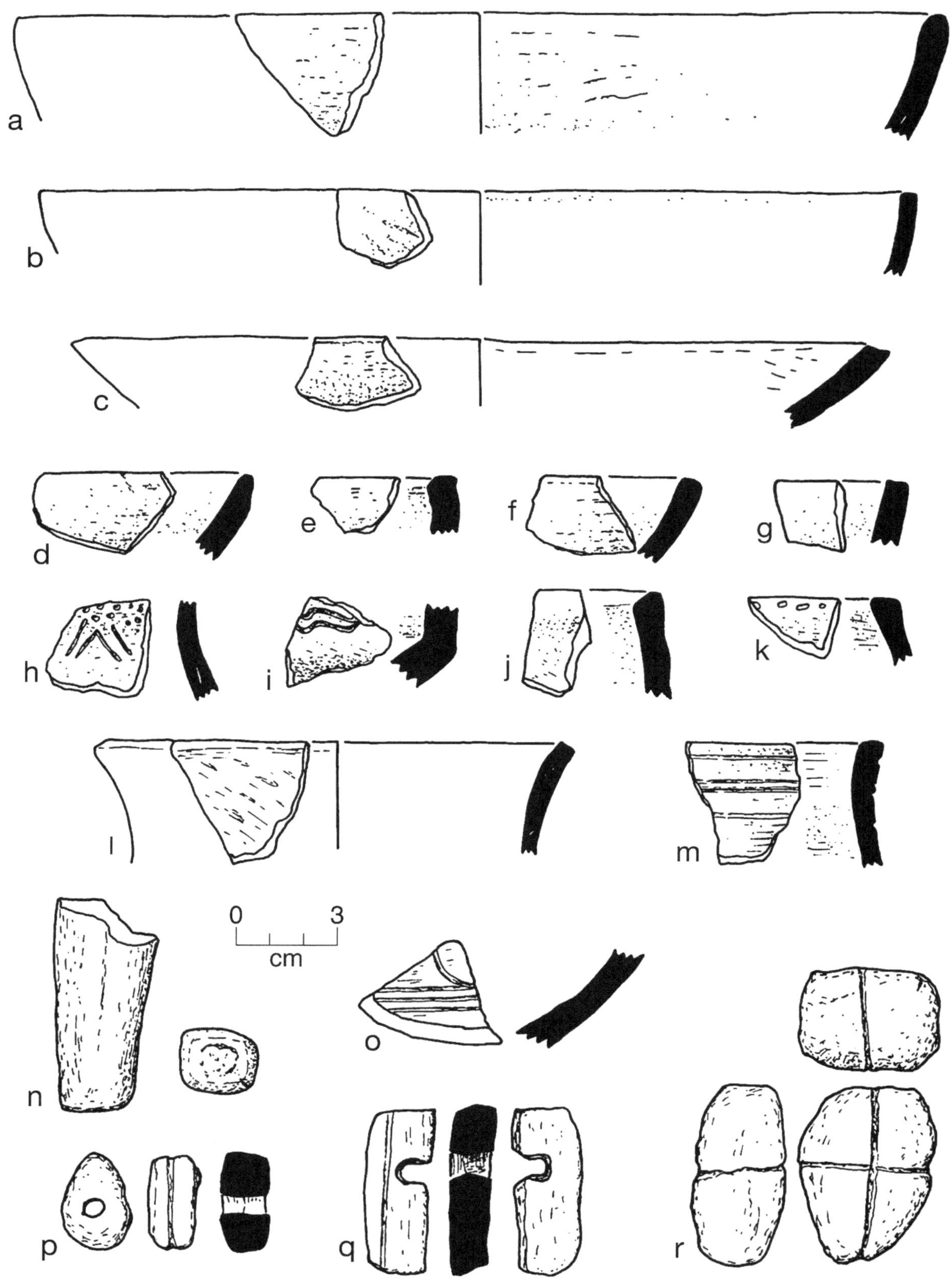
a
b
c
d
e
f
g
h
i
j
k
l
m
0
3
cm
n
o
p
q
r

Figure 9.2. Razanakoto Phase ceramics and chlorite schist items of the Razanakoto site (786.9-1410.2).
Note: Munsell colors were taken on a fresh chip under the outer surface. Abbreviations: Dm = Diameter; Body T = Body thickness 2 cm below lip; Rim T = Rim thickness. All measurements are in centimeters.

a. Basin with round lip (Razanakoto Surface). 5% Medium sand, Dm 28, Body T: .82, Rim T: .77, Reddish brown (5YR 4/3) body.
b. Basin with flat lip (Razanakoto Surface). 10% Fine sand, Dm 26, Body T: .63, Rim T: .42, Dark brown (10YR 3/3) body.
c. Large shallow bowl with flat lip (Razanakoto Surface). 15% Medium sand, Dm 25, Body T: .62, Rim T: .62, Dark brown (7.5YR 4/4) body.
d. Bowl with rounded lip (Razanakoto, Unit I Layer 2A). 10% Medium sand and mica, Dm 23, Body T: .74, Rim T: .57, Yellowish red (5YR 5/6) body.
e. Incurved basin with externally thickened rim (Razanakoto, Unit I, Layer 2B). 15% Medium sand and angular quartz, Dm ca. 30, Body T: .87, Rim T: .85, Reddish yellow (7.5YR 6/5) body.
f. Bowl with rounded lip (Razanakoto, Unit I Layer 2B). 15% Medium sand, Dm ca. 20, Body T: .63, Rim T: .74, Dark brown (7.5YR 4/1) body.
g. Basin with flat lip (Razanakoto, Unit I, Layer 3A). 10% Medium sand, mica, and angular quartz. Dm ca. 24, Body T: .78, Rim T: .68, Yellowish red (5YR 5/6) body.
h. Everted jar shoulder with round punctates and chevron incising (Razanakoto Surface).10% Medium sand, Dm ?, Neck T: .55, Color not recorded.
i. Vessel carination with wavy incising (Razanakoto , Unit I, Layer 1). 15% Medium sand, Dm 29, Shoulder T: .77, Very dark brown (10YR 2/2) body.
j. Possible jar rim with inwardly beveled lip (Razanakoto, Unit I, Layer 3A). Perhaps Analabe Phase. 30% Coarse sand and angular quartz, Dm ca. 16, Body T: .75, Rim T: .81, Dark brown (7.5YR 3/1) body.
k. Jar rim with flat lip and rectangular punctates (Razanakoto, Unit I, Layer 1). 10% Medium sand, Dm?, Body T: .77, Rim T: .75, Very dark grayish brown (10YR 3/2) body.
l. Everted jar rim with flat lip and oblique patterned burnish (Razanakoto Surface), 25% Medium sand, Dm 14, Neck T: .60, Rim T: .55, Reddish brown (2.5YR 4/5) body (Patrick Phase).
m. Everted jar rim with flat lip (Razanakoto, Unit I, Layer 2B). 15% Medium sand, Dm 17, Neck T: .48, Rim T: .68, Very dark gray (10YR 3/1) body. Horizontal incised lines similar to chlorite schist vessels.
n. Foot fragment (Razanakoto Surface) 30% Coarse sand and angular quartz. Th: 3.20 x 2.54, Reddish brown (5YR 5/4) body.
o. Base of sgraffito bowl with interior incisions and glaze (Razanakoto Surface). No visible inclusions. Body T: .62, Light red (2.5YR 6/6) body, Pale green (2.5G 6/5) glaze.
p. Perforated weight. (Razanakoto, Unit I, Layer 3A), Grayish-green chlorite schist.
q. Perforated sherd. (Razanakoto Surface), Grayish-red chlorite schist.
r. Incised weight. (Razanakoto Surface), chlorite schist.

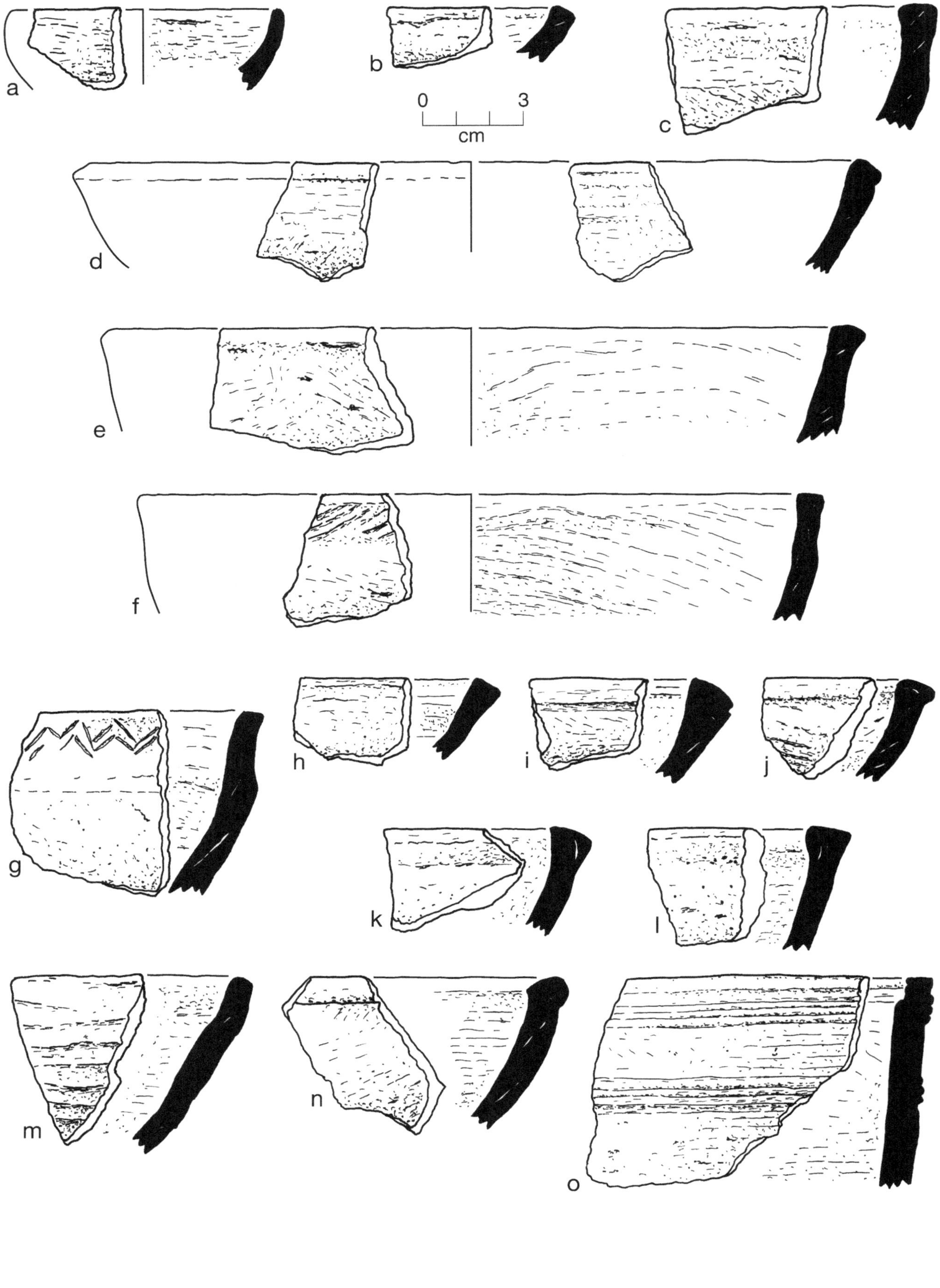
a
b
c
0
3
cm
d
e
f
g
h
i
j
k
l
m
n
o

Figure 9.3. Open vessels and chlorite schist rims from other Razanakoto Phase sites:
Analabe Centre (07-32: 787.5-1408.2, S13° 22' 23"/ E50° 00' 54"),
Analabe Avaratra-Andrefana [NW] (07-033, 787.6-1408.3, S13° 22' 19"/ E50° 00' 52"),
Andranomasikely Atsimo (08-14, 787.2-1409.0, S13° 22' 05"/ E50° 00' 48"),
Ampasin'Analabe (07-055: 788.4-1407.4, S13° 22' 38"/ E50° 01'18").
[See note, page 55.]

a. Small bowl with rounded lip (Analabe Centre: 07-032: 788.2-1407.5, Unit D). 10% Angular quartz and coarse sand, Dm 8, Body T .55, Lip T .38, Dark reddish brown (7.5YR 3/4) body.

b. Small bowl with oblique flattened lip (Analabe Centre: Same). 5% Medium sand and angular quartz, Dm 14, Body T .60, Lip T .61, Very dark gray (N 3) body.

c. Large bowl with flattened lip (Analabe Centre: Same). 10% Medium sand and angular quartz, Dm 28, Body T .92, Lip T .94, Color not recorded.

d. Large bowl with oblique flattened lip (Analabe Centre: Same). 15% Angular quartz and medium sand, Dm 24, Body T .60, Lip T .72 , Dark brown (7.5YR 3/4) body.

e. Large bowl with oblique flattened lip (Analabe Centre: Same). 15% Medium sand, Dm 22, Body T .81, Lip T 1.06, Red (2.5YR 4/4) body. Interior scraped.

f. Large bowl with flattened lip (Analabe Centre: Same). 15% Medium sand, Dm 20, Body T .56 Lip T .74, Brown (5YR 4/4) body. Interior and exterior scraped.

g. Carinated bowl with oblique flattened lip, Zigzag incising (Analabe Centre: Same). 35% Coarse sand, angular quartz, feldspar, Dm 21, Body T .81, Lip T .55 , Red (2.5YR 4/3) body.

h. Small bowl with oblique flattened lip (Analabe Avaratra-Andrefana [NW] 07-033: 788.6-1408.3). 5% Fine sand, Dm 17, Body T .54, Lip T .62, Brown (7.5YR 4/2) body.

i. Small bowl with oblique flattened lip (Analabe Avaratra-Andrefana [NW] Same). 20% Medium sand, Dm 19, Body T .47, Lip T 1.25, Brown (7.5YR 4/2) body. Exterior lip groove.

j. Large bowl with oblique flattened, exterior thickened lip (Analabe Avaratra-Andrefana [NW]: Same). 20% Medium sand, Dm ca 50, Body T .75, Lip T 1.16, Reddish gray (5YR 5/2) body.

k. Large bowl with obliquely flattened, exterior thickened, lip (Andranomasikely Atsimo: 08-014: 787.2-1409.0). 15% Medium sand, Dm 30, Body T .80, Lip T 1.37, Reddish brown (2.5YR 5/5) body, Trace red slip.

l. Large bowl with obliquely flattened, interior thickened lip (Andranomasikely Atsimo: Same). 10% Medium sand, Dm 34, Body T .76, Lip T 1.31, Weak red (5YR 4/3) body, Trace interior red slip.

m. Rough Ware bowl with rounded lip (Analabe Avaratra-Andrefana [NW] 07-033: 787.6-1408.3). 15% Medium sand and feldspar, Dm ca 28, Body T .74, Lip T .61, Brown (7.5YR 3/2) body.

n. Bowl with flattened lip and external rim thickening (Ampasin'Analabe: 07-055, 788.2-1407.4). 20% Coarse sand and angular quartz, Dm 20, Side T .81, Lip T 1.01, Reddish brown (5YR 5/4) body, Trace interior and exterior red slip.

o. Chlorite schist basin (Analabe 07-032: 787.2-1408.3). Green chlorite schist, Dm 28, Side T .77, Lip T: .58.

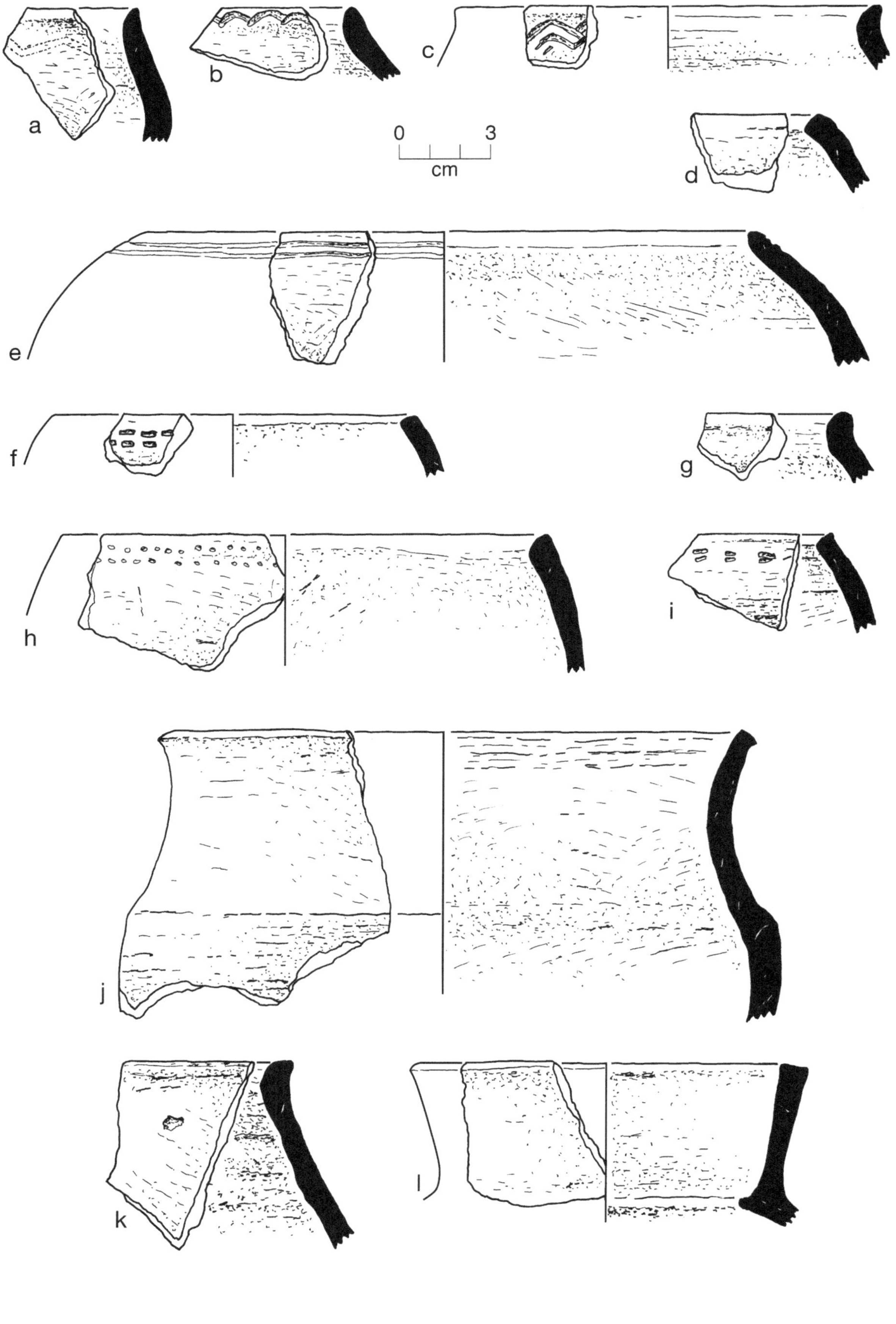
a
b
c
d
0
3
cm
e
f
g
h
i
j
k
l

Figure 9.4. Closed vessels from other Razanakoto Phase sites.
Vohemar-Bifa (07-011: 786.8-1410.2, S13° 21' 12"/ E50° 00' 32"),
Andranomasikely Atsimo (08-14, 787.2-1409.0, S13° 22' 05"/ E50° 00' 48"),
Analabe Centre (07-32 = 07-039: 787.5-1408.2, S13° 22' 23"/ E50° 00' 54"),
Analabe Avaratra-Andrefana [NW] (07-033, 787.6-1408.3, S13° 22' 19"/ E50° 00' 52"),
Ampasin'Analabe (07-055: 788.4-1407.4, S13° 22' 38"/ E50° 01'18").

[See note, page 55.]

a. Inverted jar with zigzag comb impressions (Vohemar-Bifa: 07-011: 786.8-1410.0). 5% Medium sand and coral, Dm ca 26, Side T .69, Rim T .68, Red (2.5YR 4/6) body. Light burnish.
b. Inverted jar with arcuate incising (Vohemar-Bifa: Same). 5% Medium sand, coral, Dm 20, Side T .69, Lip T .82, Red (2.5YR 4/6) body.
c. Inverted jar with arcuate incising (Andranomasikely Atsimo: 08-014: 787.2-1409.0). 20% Medium sand, Dm 17, Side T .66, T .69, Rim T .75, Color not recorded.
d. Hole-mouth jar (Andranomasikely Atsimo: Same). 20% Medium sand and angular quartz, Dm 20, Side T .90, Lip T .85, Dark gray (10YR 2/2) body.
e. Hole-mouth jar with horizontal incised lines (Analabe Centre: 07-32: 787.3-1408.2). 15% Medium sand, Dm 20, Side T .75, Lip T .49, Reddish brown (2.5YR 4/5) body.
f. Hole-mouth jar with rectangular punctates (Analabe Centre: Same). 10% Medium sand and angular quartz, Dm 12, Side T .48, Lip T .49, Black (N 2) body.
g. Inverted jar (Analabe Centre: Same). 10% Medium sand and angular quartz, Dm 17, Side T .66, Rim T .70, Black (N 2) body.
h. Hole-mouth jar with small round punctates (Analabe Centre: 07-39 (=07-32) 787.2-1408.3). 10% Angular quartz, basalt, and mica, Dm 18, Side T .67, Rim T .67, Reddish brown (5YR 5/4) body.
i. Hole-mouth jar with double rectangular punctates (Analabe Centre: 07-32: 787.3-1408.2). 10% Fine sand, Dm 20, Side T .49, Lip T .53, Very dark gray (7.5YR 3/1) body.
j. Everted neck jar (Analabe Centre: Same). 20% Medium sand, Dm 19, Side T .61, Neck T .67, Brown (7.5YR 5/4) body.
k. Rough Ware jar (Analabe Avaratra-Andrefana [NW]: 07-033: 782.6-1408.3). 10% Medium sand, granite, mica, Dm 17, Side T .69, Rim T: .86, Reddish yellow (2.5YR 5/5) body.
l. Straight neck jar (Ampasin'Analabe: 08-55, 788.2-1407.4). 10% Medium sand, Dm 13, Neck T .58, Lip T .96, Light reddish brown (10YR 6/4) body.

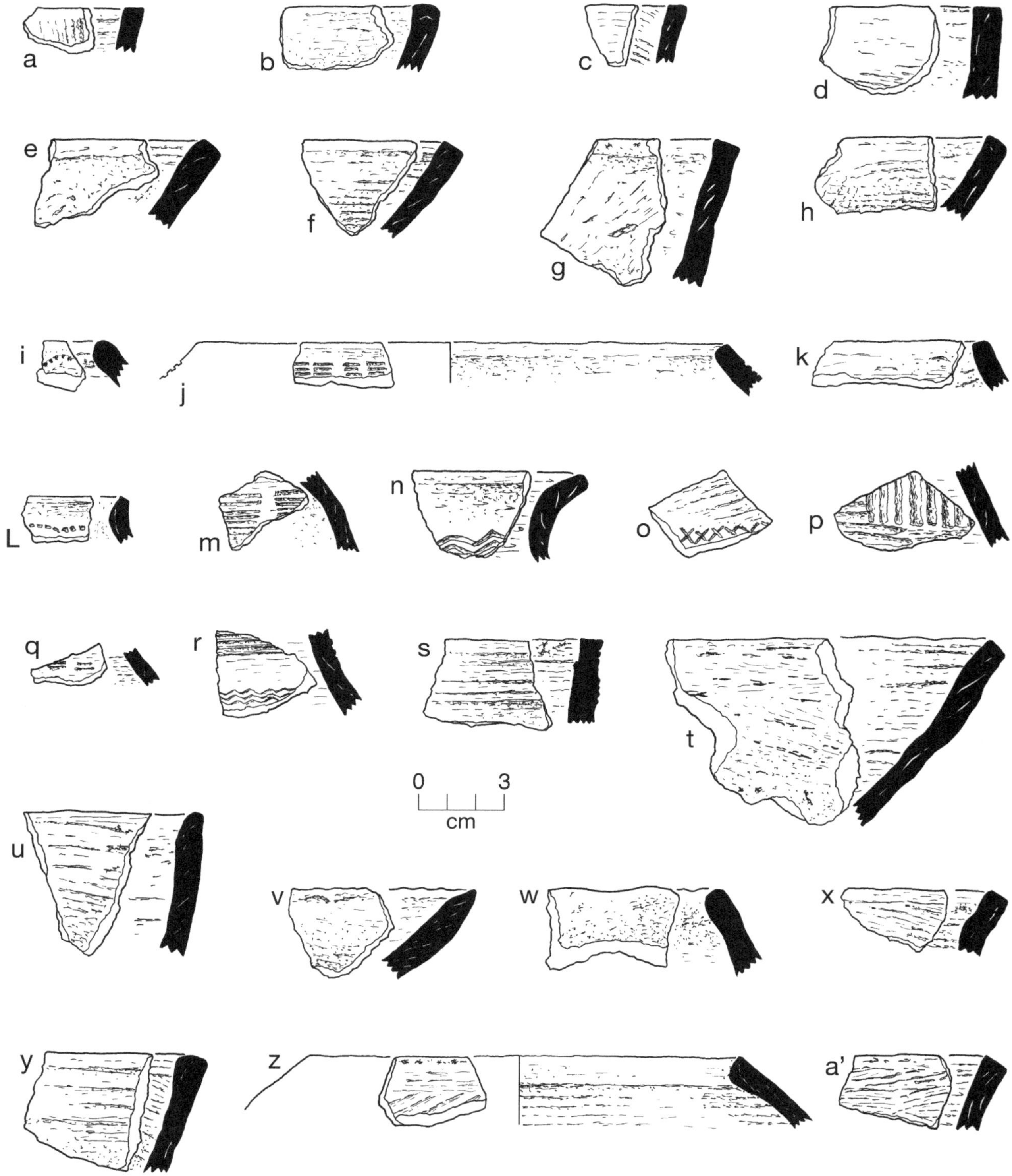
a
b
c
d
e
f
g
h
i
j
k
L
m
n
o
p
q
r
s
t
0 3
cm
u
v
w
x
y
z
a’

Figure 9.5. Razanakoto Phase ceramics and chlorite schist artifacts of the Analabe-Zafindravao area (786.9-1410.2) collected or excavated in 2018. [See note, page 55.]

Medium Sandy Ware: a–r

a. Bowl with flat lip (Analabe-Zafindravao Unit IX: Layer 2A). 5% Medium sand, Dm ?, Body T: .72, Rim T: .74, Red (2.5YR 4/6) body.
b. Bowl with flat lip (Analabe-Zafindravao Unit IX: Layer 1). 15% Medium sand, Dm 21, Body T: .91, Rim T: .94, Dark brown (2.5YR 5/6) body.
c. Bowl with flat lip (Analabe-Zafindravao Unit IX: Layer 1). 10% Medium sand, Dm ?, Body T: .60, Rim T: .76, Light yellowish brown (10YR 6/4) body.
d. Basin with flat lip (Analabe-Zafindravao: Surface). 10% Medium sand, Dm 31?, Body T: .97, Rim T: .99, Brown (10YR 5/3) body.
e. Basin with externally thickened rim (Analabe-Zafindravao Surface). 5% Medium sand, Dm ca. 25, Body T: .77, Rim T: 1.06, Reddish brown (10YR 4/4) body.
f. Bowl with oblique lip (Analabe-Zafindravao Surface). 10% Fine sand, Dm ca. 26, Body T: .66, Rim T: .91 Very dark gray (2.5YR 3/1) body, interior-exterior scraped.
g. Basin with oblique thickened lip (Analabe-Zafindravao Surface). 15% Medium sand, Dm ca. 25 W, Body T: .76, Rim T: .1.01, Very dark gray (2.5YR 3/1) body. Rough surfaces. Trace exterior red slip.
h. Everted jar shoulder with round punctates and chevron incising (Analabe-Zafindravao Surface). 10% Medium sand, Dm ca 27, Body T: .73, Rim T: .87, Brown (7.5YR 4/4). Exterior roughly scraped, trace exterior red slip.
i. Spherical jar rim with rounded lip and shell imprints (Analabe-Zafindravao Unit IX: Layer 1). 5% Medium sand, Dm?, Body T: .92?, Rim T: .96, Red (2.5YR 5/5) body.
j. Spherical jar rim with rounded lip and linear imprints (Analabe-Zafindravao Surface). 5% Fine sand, Dm ca. 19, Body T: .72?, Rim T: .70, Reddish brown (5YR 5/4) body.
k. Plain spherical jar rim with rounded lip (Analabe-Zafindravao Surface). 5% Fine sand, Dm ca. 29 W, Body T: .45?, Rim T: .89, Reddish brown (2.5YR 4/4) body.
l. Spherical jar rim with flat lip and oblong imprints (Analabe-Zafindravao Unit IX: Layer 1). 5% Medium sand, Dm?, Body T: ., Rim T: .76, (2.5YR 5/6) body.
m. Vessel shoulder with linear imprints (Analabe-Zafindravao Unit IX: Layer 1). 10% Medium sand and mica, Dm ?, Shoulder T: .53 , Red(2.5YR 5/26 body. [Mahilaka Radimilahy 1998: Fig 7.3, Fig 7.4:34; Antsoheribory: Vérin 1975: Figs 158 top row, 164 third row, 166 second row].
n. Everted jar rim with flat lip and wavy incising on neck (Analabe-Zafindravao Surface). 10% Medium sand, Dm 19, Neck T: .41, Rim T: .88, Black (10YR 2/1) body.
o. Jar shoulder with incised cross-hatch decoration (Analabe-Zafindravao Surface). 10% Fine sand, Interior damaged, Body T?, Reddish brown (5YR 4/3) body.
p. Jar shoulder with broad incising (Analabe-Zafindravao Surface). 5% Fine sand and mica, Dm ?, Body T .70, Reddish brown (7.5YR 5/4) body.
q. Jar shoulder with linear imprints (Analabe-Zafindravao Surface). 5% Medium sand, Dm ?, Body T .55, Reddish brown (5YR 5/5) body.
r. Carinated jar shoulder with horizontal and fine wavy combing (Analabe-Zafindravao Unit IX: Layer 1). 5% Fine sand, Shoulder T .58, Brown (7.5YR 4/2) body.

Carved stone vessel: s

s. Chlorite schist basin rim. (Analabe 07-030 [=07-032]: 787.2-1408.3) Gray chlorite schist, Dm 29, Side T .92, Lip T: .74. Interior inset height: .90.

Rough Ware: t–x

t. Basin rim with oblique flattened lip (Analabe-Zafindravao Surface). 20% Medium sand and hematite, Dm 25, Side T ca .75, Lip T: 1.16, Brown (7.5 YR 4/4) body.
u. Basin rim with tapered lip (Analabe-Zafindravao Surface). 20% Medium sand and mica, Dm ca 25, Side T ca .83, Rim T: .92, Brown (7.5 YR 5/4) body.
v. Top or Plate rim with tapered lip (Analabe-Zafindravao Surface). 15% Coarse crushed rock and chlorite schist, Dm 15, Side T .77, Rim T: .80, Reddish brown (2.5 YR 4/4) body.
w. Spherical jar rim with rounded rim and flattened lip (Analabe-Zafindravao Surface). 15% Coarse sand, Dm 22, Side T .89, Rim T .90, Light yellowish brown (10YR 6/4) body.
x. Everted jar rim with oblique flattened lip (Analabe-Zafindravao Surface). 20% Medium sand and hematite, Dm ca. 20, Neck T .90, Lip T .90, Brown (7.5 YR 4/4) body.

Hard Fine-Medium Sandy Ware of the Patrick Phase: y–a'

y. Basin rim with thickened rounded lip (Analabe-Zafindravao Surface). 20% Fine sand. Dm 30, Side T: .68, Rim T: 1.02, Dark brown (10YR 3/3) body. Interior oblique scraping.
z. Spherical jar rim with internally thickened rim (Analabe-Zafindravao Surface). 15% Fine sand. Dm 16, Shoulder T: .79, Rim T: 82, Brown (5YR 5/4) body. Interior horizontal scraping, Exterior oblique scraping. Note lip wear.
a'. Everted jar rim with oblique flattened lip (Analabe-Zafindravao Surface). 15% Fine sand, Dm 25, Neck T: .75, Lip T:.88, Brown (5YR 5/3) body. Interior-exterior scraping, interior and lip burnish.

Razanakoto Settlement

Ceramics similar to those of the Razanakoto assemblage have been found on a number of sites.

1. **Analabe Centre** (07-32 [including area 07-034] and 18-002 [including area 18-003 and 004] : Laborde 787.5-1408.2, S13° 22' 23"/ E50° 00' 54"; 18-002-004: Labordes 787.9-1408.3, S13° 22' 24"/ E50° 00' 53"). This site covers at least 2.0 ha in the central part of the former old growth coastal forest of Analabe, in an area of undulating sand ridges now covered with coconut groves, manioc gardens, and a few houses (Figure 9.1b). The site appears to have been partly deflated. For example, Unit D (not in Appendix B), a one-meter square to the south, produced a large sample of displaced sherds in the uppermost .10 m. Most are of a medium sandy fabric, half oxidized and half reduced. Predominant are open bowls, most with flattened lips, mostly plain (Figure 9.3b–h), and one carinated bowl with zigzag incising (Figure 9.3g). There are hole-mouth jars with out-turned tapered rims (Fig.9.4g), others with rectangular punctates on the rim (Figure 9.4f, i), and another with small round punctates (Figure 9.4h). There is also an everted rim jar (Figure 9.4j). A little Rough Ware was noted. From this area of the site, we recovered several sherds of a vessel with a fine soft reddish fabric and a blue-on-white glaze. At first we were puzzled by this import, but similar ceramics are reported from the ninth to tenth century Belitung shipwreck northwest of Sumatra (Flecker et al. 2010), and identical sherds have been observed on twelfth- to thirteenth-century Dvaravati sites in Thailand (author's observation). In addition to ceramic vessels, we found a few fragments of lathe-turned chlorite schist vessels, including a basin rim (Figure 9.3o). In contrast to the deflated areas in the south, Unit IX, in the north-central area of this site, had preserved stratified midden layers. (See Appendix B for stratigraphic details and above discussion for the ceramics.) The ceramics and the few preserved faunal elements from this excavation were ordinary domestic debris. There was no evidence of craft production or of social differentiation. Evidence of export and import are minimal. We classify this largest of the Razanakoto Phase settlements as a large village.

2. **Razanakoto** (Laborde 786.9-1410.2, S13° 21' 11"/ E50° 00' 33") was probably a beach site stretching at least 150 m from southwest to northeast, and only 30 m wide, covering at least .45 ha (Figure 9.1a; see Appendix B for stratigraphic details and above discussion for the ceramics). Coring and testing in gardens and the administrative complex to the southwest revealed no early remains. It is likely that the site extends southward onto a higher beach (Vohemar-Bifa: 07-012, 786.8/ 1410.2), which is better protected from storms, but we are not certain. It is notable that several imported Persian Gulf ceramic fragments were recorded from the surface of this site.

3. **Vohemar-Jovenna** (Labordes 785.8-1409.6, S13° 21' 47"/ E 49° 59' 55"). In 2008 in the southwest end of town, we found sandy oxidized sherds near the market, in an area scraped for the then new "Jovenna" petrol station (08-06). In 2014, we revisited this site and collected a larger sample around a recent pit (14-023: Laborde 785.8-1409.7, S13° 21' 68"/ E49° 59' 55", UTM E0391570-N8522480), including an internally thickened rim bowl rim and two hole-mouth jar rims with arcuate incising (not illustrated). Farther southwest, coring and testing in the Vohemar Hospital compound (08-007: 786.1-1409.5, S13° 21' 47"/ E49° 59' 50", UTM E0391575-N8522502) and surface survey nearby (08-008: 785.9-1409.4, S13° 21' 49"/ E49° 59' 52", UTM E0391489-N8522248) yielded little, except a red slipped bowl rim with oblique flat thickened lip and the fragment of a chlorite schist basin top. While it is possible that there was a 1600 m long village close to the Bay, perhaps damaged by catastrophic erosion from cyclones or tsunamis as well as by modern urban construction, a series of small sites seems better supported by current evidence. We envision the Razanakoto Site and perhaps similar sites hidden by modern Vohemar to have had a row of structures, work areas, and beached canoes, facing north and west toward the Bay of Iharana.

4. **Andranomasikely Atsimo** (08-014, Laborde 787.2-1409.0 S13° 22' 05"/ E 50° 01' 18") is a small site on a sandy terrace the east or right bank of the old embouchure. At the time of our survey it was covered by sand blowouts, coconut groves, and modest residences overlooking rice paddies. In a sand blow, we recorded a concentration of ceramics covering about .14 ha, but the site may well have been larger. Among the large sample of mostly oxidized medium sandy sherds are bowl rims with thickened lips flattened obliquely and covered with red slips (Figure 9.3k, l) and an inverted jar with wavy incising (Figure 9.4c), all with parallels to the Razanakoto site itself and to Mahilaka. We tentatively classify this as the site of a hamlet.

5. **Analabe Avaratra** (07-033, Laborde 787.6-1408.3: S13° 22' 19"/ E50° 00' 52") is a part of a site deflated to expose a dense sherd pavement about 15 by 10 m, resting

on clean sand. Our 2007 soundings A and B (not discussed in Appendix B) revealed only deflated deposits. It may continue to the north and west into grassy pasture and with scattered mango and coconut trees (Figure 9.1b). Re-examination in 2018 shows it does not continue south into an area of mature coconut plantation. Among a large sample of oxidized medium Sandy Ware sherds are bowl rims with obliquely flattened lips (Figure 9.3h, i) and another bowl with externally thickened rim (Figure 9.3j). There is also a round lip bowl (Figure 9.3m) and an out-turned jar rim with an internally thickened rim on Rough Ware (Figure 9.4k). We tentatively identify this as a Razanakoto Phase hamlet.

6. **Andranomasikely Centre** (07-029, Laborde 787.5-1409.9, S13° 21' 36"/ E50° 00' 43"). This possible ceramic production site in an area of undulating sand ridges has Rough Ware sherds in a dense concentration about 6 m in diameter. This Rough Ware has majorities of quartz rather than vegetal inclusions, and the rims are tapered (Figure 8.3p, s) or externally thickened (Figure 8.3q). One may be the rim of a cover (Figure 8.3r). Rough Ware could date to any phase from the tenth century Analabe to the seventeenth to eighteenth century Patrick Phase, but we discuss this site with the Razanakoto Phase because, although Rough Ware with quartz inclusions is typical of Razanakoto to Patrick Phases, the few Sandy Ware body sherds have none of hard burnished sherds typical of Ambatary and Patrick times. Also, this site is close to the large Razanakoto site at Analabe Centre. At the time this site was in use, it may have been in a good location for collecting fuel for firing pottery. This clearly a very small specialized activity site.

7. **Ampasin' Analabe** (07-055: Laborde 788.4-1407.4, S13° 22' 38"/ E50° 01'18"). This is a long diffuse sherd scatter extending about 200 m from north to south and 30 m wide in blowouts on the second beach, covering about 0.50 ha, not far from the surf of the Indian Ocean and a fringing reef. Amongst the medium sandy, oxidized sherds were a bowl with externally thickened rim and flattened lip (Figure 9.3n) and a straight-necked jar with flattened lip (Figure 9.4*l*), which indicate a Razanakoto Phase occupation. A few items were either exported or imported in Razanakoto times: some chlorite schist fragments, a piece of crystal quartz, and a single piece of sgraffito. We envision this as a settlement similar to the Razanakoto site, with a row of structures, work areas, and beached canoes, but facing east toward the Indian Ocean rather than toward the Bay of Iharana.

The Razanakoto settlement evidence indicates a single large centrally located village at Analabe Centre, surrounded by small hamlets along the old embouchure and in the sandy rolling terrain between the embouchure and the sea, and with at least two somewhat larger linear settlements along the beaches of the Indian Ocean and the Bay of Iharana (Figure 9.6). One could argue that the transregional dominance of the port of Mahilaka (Radimilahy 1998) suppressed the growth of larger settlements on the far northeast coast. One jar shoulder from Analabe-Zafindravao has thick parallel incising (Figure 9.5p) that is otherwise unknown in northeastern Madagascar, but is attested from northwest coast sites of the thirteenth to eighteenth centuries (Radimilahy 1998: Fig. 7.4.5–7.4.16; Wright, Radimilahy and Allibert 2005: Fig. 10b, g, i). This is perhaps an indication of the movement of pots or potters within Madagascar. Some known Razanakoto sites, though modest in size, have examples of Persian Gulf sgraffito and green monochrome, which suggest a connection to the same network as that of the contemporary large trade entrepot of Mahilaka on the northwest coast. One possible Thai sherd suggests a connection with Southeast Asia. It must be emphasized that these are isolated surface finds concentrated on the known beach sites. None of the soundings on Razanakoto sites have yielded imported sherds in a controlled context, and the small amounts noted do not approach the rich assemblages from major ports such as Mahilaka (Radimilahy 1998) and Benavony (Serneels et al. 2017). It is likely that from this period, if not before, the Iharana region, with its rich chlorite schist resources, was involved in the exchange of carved stone vessels for the exotic manufactures of southwest and southeast Asia, whether directly or via other coastal ports of Madagascar. There is, however, so far no evidence of working areas where chlorite schist vessels were finished on the lathe at any of our Razanakoto sites. Finally, there is no evidence at present of tap slags that would indicate that iron bloom was smelted on Razanakoto sites; there are only vesicular slags, suggesting forging or tool repair. Iron may not have been exported from the Vohemar area during this period. Farther south, however, major smelting sites have been reported inland from Sambava, 110 km south of Vohemar with dates between 1220 and 1390 cal CE (Clist 1995), and from the large embouchure site of Benavony, 125 km south of Vohemar with dates between 700 and 1400 cal CE (Serneels et al. 2017: 116). Perhaps specialized iron smelting sites will be found in the largely unsurveyed interior near Vohemar, but there is no evidence at present.

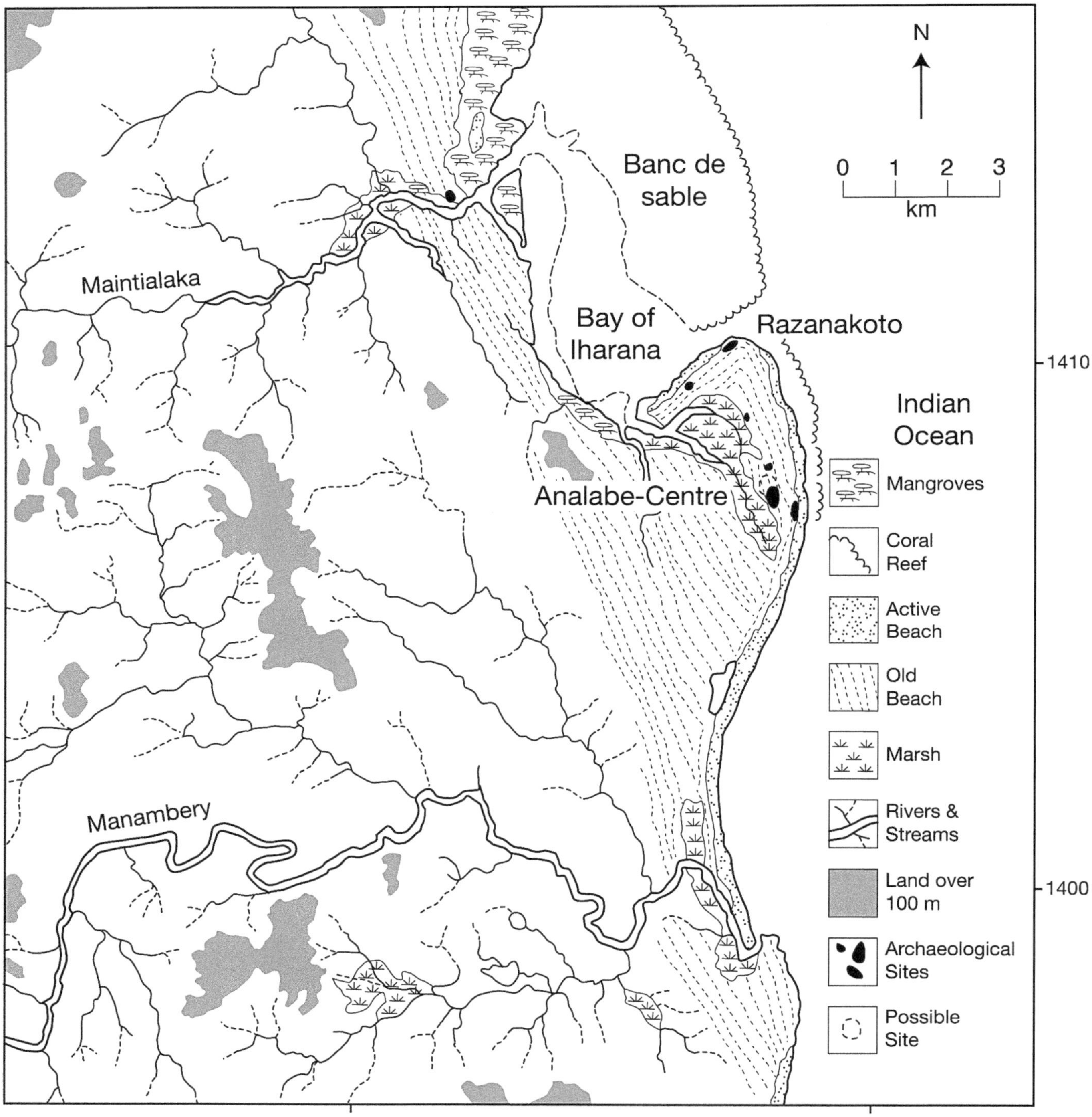

Figure 9.6. Razanakoto Phase settlements.

Chapter 10

The Ambatary Phase

Evidence

By the end of our second season in October 2008, we had not found any definite sites, much less a major occupational site of the fifteenth to sixteenth centuries AD, the major period of use for the rich cemeteries of Vohemar (Schreurs et al. 2011; Vernier and Millot 1971). We had already tested various points in the extant town of Vohemar without finding any remains between the fourteenth century and the late nineteenth century CE. We had surveyed most areas around the old embouchure. We resurveyed the west shore of the bay without success. Thinking that a town site might have been overwhelmed by the sea, we searched the southern end of the Banc de Sable north of the channel into the Bay of Iharana during a low tide. Similar sites eroded by the sea on the coast of East Africa have sherds of porcelain offshore, but we found nothing ancient in the shallow water. In mapping out our collections and soundings around Vohemar, we realized that we had good coverage of the northeast area around Razanakoto and Ave Maria and the southeast area around the Regional Hospital, but for the approximately 15 hectares in between, we had only the disappointing sounding at the former Ecole Bambino (07-06: 786.4-409.8, S13° 21' 29.2"/ E 50° 00' 13.3"; see Appendix B for further details), which showed that the earlier deposits close to the bay were damaged by storm surges. Late in the season, resurveying in the northeast edge of this unstudied area of Vohemar, we noticed in several places hard sandy sherds with distinctive red or orange burnished slips, some with wavy combing similar to ceramics from the fifteenth to sixteenth century Mamoko Phase on the northwest coast (Vérin 1975:639–672; Wright, Radimilahy and Allibert 2005).

Looking for datable deposits with such ceramics, we started at the northeast side of Vohemar and worked southwestwards with our bucket auger, coring in a number of places, finding only shallow and disturbed deposits until we reached the neighborhood called Ambatary (after an artillery battery placed on a mound of sand in 1942 by French troops expecting a British invasion). We cored this mound and found 1.20 m of stratified deposits. Several local people assured us that the entire mound had been built by the soldiers, but sediment from the bucket auger used in coring indicated that there are items of twentieth-century plastic, glass and iron only in the upper .25 m of the mound fill. We inferred that the mound is primarily precolonial. Because of the evidence of surficial disturbance, the samples from Layers 1 and 2 are listed in Appendix A, but not included in our analysis.

Our one-meter square at Ambatary was located in a neglected garden for manioc, papayas, and coconut (see Appendix B: Unit VIII: 09-012: Laborde 786.6-1409.8, S13° 30' 28.5"/ E50° 00' 23.9", UTM E0392435-N8523060). We first removed a layer of homogenous dark gray sand .20 m thick. We then removed Layers 2 and 3, predominantly dark gray sand with light gray and brown lenses. At the top of Layer 4, about .70 m below surface, the deposit became predominantly brown sand with dark and light gray lenses with more sherds, shells, and chlorite schist fragments. All of these layers and lenses are probably debris loaded into baskets around domestic compounds and dumped on a neighborhood trash heap. Such trash heaps are known from the sixteenth to early eighteenth century town site of Antsoheribory on the Bay of Boeny (Vérin 1975:342, 377–439; Wright et al. 1996:62, 63). The top of Layer 5, at .94 meters below surface, was a hard black granular sand floor without visible sherds or shells, but Layer 5A below had many shells, bones, and sherds, including an imported Chinese blue-and-white porcelain cup rim of late fourteenth or early fifteenth century date. A thin gray sand floor below had no artifacts, but Layer 5B below was a midden with sherds, charcoal, shell, and well-preserved bone. Below 1.12 m, we removed 0.10 m thick red-brown transitional Layer 6 with sparse cultural material. Below that was a reddish layer with few cultural traces. From the base of the excavation at 1.40 m, we cored down through very light brown sand and coral fragments without traces of human occupation to 2.00 m below the surface.

A charcoal fragment from Ambatary Unit VIII, Layer 5B, indicates a 95% probability of a date between AD 1290 to 1410 (see Appendix C).

Artifacts

We are fortunate to have large samples of artifacts from the well-stratified deposits in Unit VIII at Ambatary. Most ceramics are of a hard Sandy Ware. The inclusions in the sherds range from 5% to 25% fine to coarse sand, but most sherds have about 15% medium sand. The sherds are well-fired and relatively hard. A majority of the vessels are oxidized; most are reddish brown (2.5-5YR 3/2 to 5/4), but some are red (2.5YR 5/6) and one is reddish-yellow (5YR 6/6) in color. A quarter of the vessels have dark gray (5YR 3/1) to dark grayish brown (10YR 4/2) bodies probably fired in reducing atmospheres. Gray sherds with fugitive red slips are a notable minority. The sherds are of medium thickness. Most bodies range from .60 to .96 cm with a mode of .85 cm, with only 10%—usually heavy bowls—being thicker than .90 cm.

Open forms are composed primarily of two distinctive types.

First, there are bowls with heavy rims created by pressing a strip of clay inside the rim to create an internal thickening on the inside of the rim (Figure 10.1c–f). These range from 24 to 33 cm in diameter. The clay has 20% to 25% of medium sand inclusions, the heaviest proportions known in Ambatary ceramics. The surfaces sometimes have a carefully smoothed red slip, and in most cases the lips are burnished. These may be functional replacements for the large basins common in earlier assemblages.

Second are bowls with in-turned rims, made by adding a clay strip to the lip (Figure 10.1g–i). These range from 22 to 28 cm in diameter. Medium sand inclusions range from 15 to 20%. Some are red slipped and some have burnished rims. These have few precedents in ceramics from earlier phases. Similar bowls are, however, well known from eleventh to fourteenth century AD Mahilaka on the northwest coast, contemporary in part with our Razanakoto Phase. Perhaps by chance we have not found these in our small excavated Razanakoto sample. Alternatively, perhaps we do not have these because it is only when Mahilaka and the surrounding settlements are abandoned, about AD 1400, and Vohemar grows substantially during the Ambatary Phase, that this form is brought to the far northeast.

In addition, there are a few unique open forms. There is a shallow bowl or plate with a flat lip (Figure 10.1a). Also, there is a basin rim with thickened rounded lip (Figure 10.1b), the only later bowl that might be mistaken for the diagnostic Ampasimahavelona basin rim. However, rather than heavy coarse sand inclusions, it has typical Ambatary Phase medium sand inclusions. There is also one small incurved bowl with externally thickened rim (Figure 10.1q).

Restricted Sandy Ware forms are also distinctive. Most have flattened, inwardly beveled lips.

There are a few globular vessels with hole mouths, so common earlier (Figure 10.1j–k). However, both of these are lightly burnished and one has arcuate impressions below the rim, perhaps the imprints of a bivalve shell edge (Figure 10.1j). There is also a similar vessel with a larger diameter, properly an incurved bowl or basin (Figure 10.1p).

More common are in-turned forms, probably from carinated vessels (Figure 10.1*l–n*). The earliest example has a burnished red slip (Figure 10.1*l*). The other two illustrated examples have similar fine inclusions, similar reduced firing, and similar bold incising. These are both in the upper Ambatary layers. Perhaps they are the work of a single potter. In any event, these vessels presage the typical jars of the succeeding Patrick Phase.

A unique restricted vessel has an external rim thickening (Figure 10.1o), similar to those of the sixteenth to seventeenth century Serenambe Phase of the Bay of Antongil and the central east coast farther south (Dewar and Wright 2000: Fig. 3e). However, rather than the characteristic Serenambe impressed decoration, it has oblique burnish.

In general, a sample of Ambatary Phase Sandy Ware sherds are hard with fine to medium inclusions, similar to Razanakoto phase sherds, except for some large heavy bowls, which are coarser. Most are oxidized red in color, some also with red slips, the few reduced sherds being from jars rather than open bowls. Bodies are somewhat thicker. Rims of both bowls and jars are commonly flattened rather than rounded. Both internal and external rim thickenings are widely used. Many vessels are burnished, at least on the lip, and oblique pattern burnishing is diagnostic.

We found 10% to 20% Rough Ware sherds in the nine sieved Ambatary samples. As at other sites, the clay has a ropy texture and the exteriors are unfinished, but in contrast to earlier Rough Ware, inclusions of angular quartz were more common and sand, vegetal fragments, and other inclusions were not noted. Both open (Figure 10.1s) and closed (Figure 10.1r) forms occur. These have internally thickened rims, but rounded and flattened variants also occur.

There are many chlorite schist fragments in the Ambatary Phase samples from Ambatary Unit VIII, particularly in Layers 4 and 5, but most are small, perhaps the detritus of finishing the rough cut vessels brought from the quarries. There are very few body sherds, and diagnostic vessel parts are restricted to a single top fragment. There are many small iron slag fragments and a few small flat pieces of iron scale, particularly in Layer 5. It seems likely that among the activities in the Ambatary area were such crafts as the finishing of chlorite schist vessels and the forging of iron. There are also some basalt flakes, perhaps the debris from blocks trimmed by masons. If so, we have indirect evidence of architecture with masonry elements somewhere in the town.

Animal remains are common in Ambatary Unit VIII (see Appendix E). Shell and bone is well preserved and diverse. The shell is mostly *Terebralia* from the mangroves and *Anadara* from the sandy shores of the bay. Today, the former is used for fish bait and both are used in stews. In 180 liters sieved from Layer 5, there are 4546 bones, representing all parts of small to large marine fish. There are 68 large mammal bones, mostly limb fragments but with a rib and a few teeth, all probably domestic *Bos*. Bones of smaller mammals include 12 domestic *Ovis* or *Capra,* a few hunted *Potamochoerus* and *Tenrec,* and a few commensal *Rattus* and *Mus.* The bones of birds include three of domestic chickens and 17 of hunted ducks. Reptiles include 58 marine turtle carapace fragments and eight terrestrial tortoise elements. Surprisingly, the flotation samples taken to recover plant remains produced only wood charcoal. We had expected burnt rice grains—as rice was widely cultivated in Madagascar at this time—and burnt coconut shell.

Chronology

Similarities to fifteenth and sixteenth century CE Mamoko Phase ceramics of the northwest coast are supported by the recovery of the late fourteenth to early fifteenth century early Ming blue and white porcelain cup fragment and by the late thirteenth to early sixteenth century radiocarbon age determination (see Appendix C), both from Layer 5 at Ambatary. Keeping in mind that porcelain is likely to have been used for some time before it was broken and lost, and radiocarbon dates on charcoal are often on wood tissue laid down long before the tree was burned, the suggested date of the fifteenth to sixteenth centuries for Ambatary seems reasonable.

Ambatary Phase Settlement

The sites with sherds of the Ambatary Phase indicate a marked organizational change.

1. Ambatary Phase Vohemar, a major town and international port of the region during this phase, can be

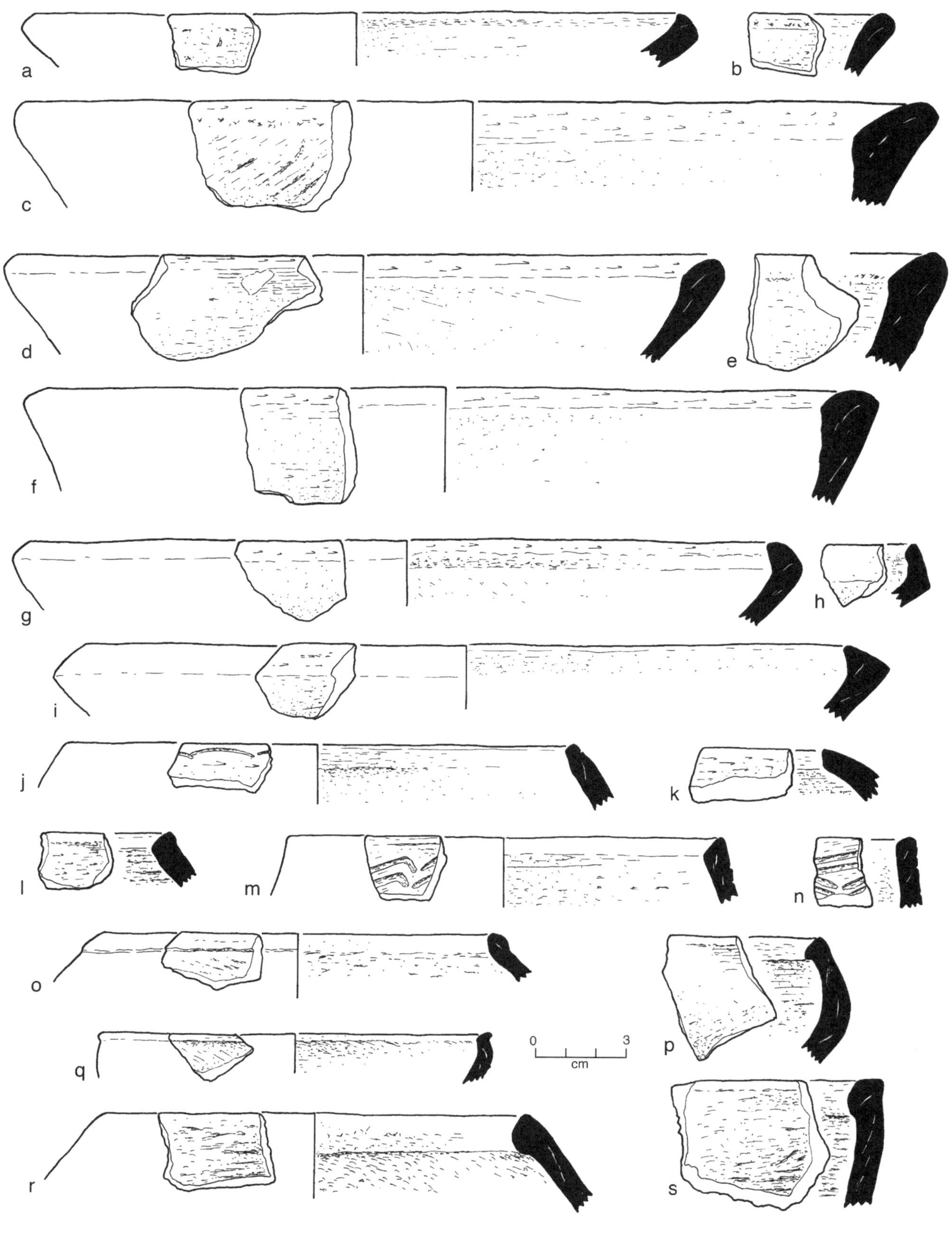
a
b
c
d
e
f
g
h
i
j
k
l
m
n
o
p
q
r
s
0
3
cm

Figure 10.1. Ceramics of the Ambatary Unit VIII: Vohemar-Ambatary (09-012: 786.6-1409.8, S13° 30' 28.5"/ E50° 00' 23.9", UTM 392435-8523060).
Note: Munsell colors were taken on a fresh chip under the outer surface. Abbreviations: Dm = Diameter; Body T = Body thickness 2 cm below lip; Rim T = Rim thickness. All measurements are in centimeters.

a. Heavy bowl with externally beveled rim (Ambatary, Layer 5B). 15% Medium sand, Dm 33, Body T: .82, Rim T: .97, Brown (5YR 5/4) body, Lip abraded.
b. Bowl with thickened rounded lip. (Ambatary, Layer 5A) 10% Medium sand, Dm 26, Body T: .61, Rim T: .85, Brown (5YR 5/5) body, Lip abraded.
c. Heavy bowl with internally thickened rim (Ambatary, Layer 5B). 25% Coarse sand, Dm 33, Body T: .82, Rim T: .97, Reddish brown (2.5YR 4/4) body, Lip burnished.
d. Heavy bowl with internally thickened rim (Ambatary, Layer 5A). 25% Medium sand and mica. Dm 24, Body T: .63, Rim T: .1.26 , Reddish brown (5YR 5/4) body, Lip burnished.
e. Heavy bowl with internally thickened rim (Ambatary, Layer 5A). 25% Medium sand, Dm ?, Body T: 1.38, Rim T: .1.26, Dark reddish brown (5YR 3/2) body.
f. Heavy bowl with internally thickened rim (Ambatary, Layer 5B). 20% Fine sand and mica, Dm 33, Body T: .96, Rim T: 1.23, Reddish brown (2.5YR 5/4) body, Red (10R 4/5) micaceous slip. Lip burnished.
g. Heavy bowl with internally thickened rim (Ambatary, Layer 5B). 20% Coarse sand, Dm 26, Body T: .68, Rim T: 1.43, Weak red (2.5YR 4/3) body. Lip burnished.
h. Small bowl with in-turned rim (Ambatary, Layer 5B). 15% Coarse sand, Dm ca. 20, Body T: .60, Rim T: .49, Reddish yellow (5YR 6/6) body, Red (10R 4/5) slip.
i. Heavy bowl with internally thickened rim (Ambatary, Layer 6). 15% Medium sand, Dm 28, Body T: .92, Rim T: 2.08, Red (2.5YR 5/6) body.
j. Hole-mouth jar with flat lip, burnished and with possible shell imprints (Ambatary, Layer 5B). 5% Angular quartz and coarse sand, Dm: 16, Body T: .70, Rim T: .59, Very dark gray (10YR 3/1) body.
k. Hole-mouth jar with flat lip, burnished rim (Ambatary, Layer 4A). 5% Medium sand, Dm: 20, Body T: .98, Rim T: .75, Reddish brown (2.5YR 5/5) body. Burnished exterior.
l. Hole-mouth jar with flat lip, burnished rim (Ambatary, Layer 5B). 10% Medium sand, Dm: 22, Body T: .85, Rim T: .86, Red (2.5YR 5/6) body. Red slip and burnished exterior.
m. Hole-mouth jar or carinated bowl with inwardly beveled lip (Ambatary, Layer 3C). 5% Medium sand, Dm: 16, Body T: .70, Rim T: .81, Dark grayish brown (10YR 4/2) body, Bold arcuate incised exterior.
n. Hole-mouth jar with flat lip (Ambatary, Layer 4A). 5% Medium sand, Dm: ?, Body T: .62, Rim T: .77, Dark grayish brown (10YR 4/2) body, Bold incised exterior chevron.
o. Hole-mouth jar with externally thickened rim (Ambatary, Layer 5B). 10% Angular quartz and medium sand, Dm:13, Body T: .79, Rim T: .68, Strong brown (7.5YR- 5/6) body, Burnished exterior.
p. Inwardly curved bowl with internally thickened rim (Ambatary, Layer 3-4). 10% Medium sand, Dm: ca. 28, Body T: .68, Rim T: .57, Dark red (2.5YR 3/5) body.
q. Small inwardly curved bowl with externally thickened rim (Ambatary, Layer 4B). 10% Medium sand, Dm: 13, Body T: .68, Rim T: .57, Very dark gray (5YR 3/1) body.
r. Rough Ware hole-mouth jar with internally thickened lip (Ambatary, Layer 5B). 30% Coarse angular quartz, Dm 14, Body T: .81, Rim T: 1.06 , Red [?] (7.5YR 5/6) body.
s. Rough Ware Basin with internally thickened lip (Ambatary, Layer 3A). 30% Angular quartz, limestone, and medium sand, Dm 32, Body T: .87, Rim T: 1.05, Color not recorded.

mapped based upon the distinctive red burnished fine sandy sherds, often with heavy rims. It extended from the area of **Vohemar-Stade** (Figure 10.2f–g) on the northeast (07-013: 786.7-1410.0: S13° 21' 19"/ E50° 00' 29"), southwest at least 800 m to at least the **Bureau de Poste** (14-020: 786.5-1409.7, S13° 21' 32"/ E50° 00' 16"), where there were a few red burnished fine Sandy Ware sherds. The width went from the second beach southeastwards for about 200 m, with a total area of at least 13 ha. Within this area, the only definite constructed feature is the trash heap at **Ambatary** itself (09-012: 786.6-1409.8, S13° 21' 28.5"/ E50° 00' 23.9"), the mound that provides the controlled samples defining this phase. The northeastern limit of dense Ambatary settlement is near the Stadium and the Gendarmerie (**Vohemar-Stade**: 07-024: 786.9-1409.8, S13° 21' 21"/ E50° 00' 31"; **Vohemar-Zandarma:** 07-017, 786.8-1409.8, S13° 21' 23"/ E50° 00' 30"). Here we found a range of characteristic sherds with a minority of reduced gray sherds with red slip, including a heavy bowl with internal thickening (Figure 10.2n), an internally flattened ledge rim bowl (Figure 10.2o), and a heavy everted jar with flat lip and arcuate incisions (Figure 10.2m). Not far southeast of Ambatary (**Vohemar-Grandidier**: 14-019: Laborde 786.7-1409.8, S13° 21'30"/ E50° 00' 25"), construction in 2009 cut a midden deposit that yielded red burnished sandy sherds, including a heavy incurved bowl with flattened lip (Figure 10.2j) and two out-turned hole-mouth jars (Figure 10.2k, l), one plain and one with wavy incising. The ruined stone walls noted by Mayeur in 1775—perhaps the remains of buildings such as mosques or palatial residences—were near the southwest edge of the site, but there is no indication of a surrounding town wall in any account or in the extant archaeological evidence. Indeed, both our scattering of collections and our coring suggest that the fifteenth to sixteenth century sherd density diminished gradually rather than abruptly at its edges. A test excavation at the former **Ecole Bambino** (07-06, 08-08: Laborde 786.4-1409.8, S13° 21' 30"/ E50° 00' 18"), northeast of the present Congregational Mosque near the beach, is provocative. Under a dense layer of twentieth-century trash .30 m thick we found a layer of gray beach sand with a fine laminar structure suggesting a storm surge. This yielded a small number of medium to coarse Sandy Ware sherds, mostly oxidized, several with burnished red surfaces typical of Ambatary ceramics. One of these was a nondiagnostic everted jar rim, three were chlorite schist sherds, one a top rim, and one had been worked into a small net weight. All items were rolled, apparently by wave action. Bambino indicates the area close to the Bay was only casually inhabited, perhaps by fishermen, perhaps making the town less visible from the Bay and perhaps providing protection from storm damage. Indications of a storm surge after the period of Vohemar's great prosperity confirms Nicholas Mayeur's report (Mayeur [1775] 1912; Corby and Mayeur 2011:18) of a local tradition that the port had been destroyed by storms. However difficult, more excavation is needed on the site of fifteenth to sixteenth century Vohemar, and any excavations for new constructions in the modern town should be carefully monitored.

2. Amboronana Avaratra-Atsinanana (northeast) (08:004: Laborde 786.4-1408.7, S13° 22' 06"/ E50° 00' 10") is a small site on a sandy terrace on the west or left bank of the old embouchure. It covers .2 ha. It is mostly pasture and mango trees, but there is an eroded area on the north, exposing a shell midden with many sherds of medium to fine Sandy Ware oxidized to a reddish color. The sample includes a plain bowl (Figure 10.2p), a flat lip basin (Figure 10.2q), two internally flattened ledge rim bowls (Figure 10.2r, s), and hole-mouth jars with slightly thickened lips (Figure 10.2u, v). This site is only 400 meters south of the south edge of the Ambatary Phase town site of Vohemar across the estuary. While the raison d'être of the site may have been the rice paddies to its east, it is also possible that when there was less sediment in the estuary it was possible to pass by canoe between Vohemar-Ambatary and Amboronana. This site was excavated by the Sealinks team in 2013, but the material has not yet been studied.

3. Analabe Marie Claude Atsinanana (07-57: 787.8-1407.7 and 07-58: 787.8-1407.8) yielded two Ambatary basin rims (Figure 10.2t, w) amidst Patrick Phase assemblages. Probably there was a small Ambatary site on the northeast edge of the large later Patrick Phase site discussed in the next section, but the area had just been bulldozed and visibility was poor. The sherds are scattered over at least .40 ha; it could have been larger.

4. Ambanimanasy (14-024: Laborde 771.2-1418.9, S13° 16' 43"/ E49° 51' 54") is a small linear ridge-top village 17 km northeast of Vohemar and 4 km south of the Manambato River, on the route toward the northwest and far northern coasts. It was found surveying ridges and terraces searching unsuccessfully for a chlorite schist source reported in the area. The area today has some hamlets with gardens but is devoted primarily to cattle herding. It is marked by an eroded midden on the slope of its west edge. The flat grassy ridge top, probably the village area, extends 90 meters from south-southwest to north-northeast and was about 30 m wide, about .25 ha. It overlooks the perennial Ambanimanasy stream to the west. A heavy bowl rim (Figure 10.2x) and two hole-mouth jar rims (Figure 10.2y, z) are of the Ambatary phase; a thinner hole-mouth jar with horizontal burnishing (Figure 10.2a') may indicate occupation continuing into Patrick Phase times. Though a source is nearby, no items of chlorite schist were found. Given its location, this small village is likely to have been involved in the herding of cattle. In 1837, Leigh described the area as rich in cattle (Allibert 1999), and we have seen thousands of cattle, driven from the northwest coast, pasturing here, grazing and waiting for a cattle transport ship to reach Vohemar. This is the only occupational site so far found in the interior.

Though it was not the object of our survey, we did examine a few localities where chlorite schist was mined. We focused on an area southwest of Vohemar and north of the Middle Manambery Valley, where several sources had been reported, and where we found a particularly knowledgeable local guide, M. Bemanzira Christian. All of these quarry sites had been visited by earlier researchers, who had doubtless picked up much surface material.

5. Ambovon'y Rasikajy, the Well of the Rasikajy (09-010: Laborde 765.6-1399.0, S13° 27' 33"/ E49° 48' 46") is about 24 km west-southwest of Vohemar. In this area, the early twentieth-century investigators found many chlorite schist quarries (Gaudebout and Vernier 1941a; Mouren and Rouaix 1913) and carefully studied the manufacturing technique. Our soundings near Vohemar show that chlorite schist was carved into simple open vessels from earliest times, but during the Analabe, Rajanakoto, and Ambatary Phases—that is, from the eleventh until the sixteenth century AD—it was finished on a lathe in the coastal villages and towns to make cylindrical vessels with tripod feet and tops for such vessels. The quarries were not a major objective of our research, but we did study a few such sites. We place our discussion here because, though the lathe carving tradition starts in Analabe times, the material we see on the surface around these quarries should date from just before their abandonment in Ambatary times. This quarry has not been excavated, and no ceramics or other datable material provide an independent date of the use of Ambovon'y Rasikajy. The Rasikajy were a people identified in oral traditions as the carvers of chlorite schist vessels. An elder of Marosely (S13° 36' 13"/ E 49° 47' 42"), 2.25 km northwest of Ambovon'y Rasikajy, a recently founded Sakalava village, recounted the tradition of the area: that the Rasikajy were small people who camped in the forest and mined the soft stone. Mouren and Rouaix (1913) and subsequent scholars elaborated the local traditions they heard, also ascribing the term Rasikajy to the inhabitants of the coastal settlements who finished the carving of the vessels and made them available to maritime traders. However, this does not seem to be the local tradition near the quarries. Mouren and Rouaix probably reported this site under the rubric of "Sous Groupe 1" of "Groupe 2." The quarry is a pit oriented north-northwest by south-southeast, about 22 m long and 16 m wide (Figure 10.3, left). The pit is partially refilled, but it is still about four meters deep. Two bedrock outcrops of granular gray-green chlorite schist are visible in the side of the pit, one with traces of the removal of a cylindrical mass, probably a pre-form for a vessel. Surrounding the pit is an oval ring of debris carried out of the pit, in places still two to three meters high and covered by thorny acacia and brushy vegetation. At the foot of this oval and on the surrounding flat are many fragments of chlorite schist broken in the process of manufacture and discarded. Careful survey in the area revealed no occupational sites with datable ceramics. The recognizable forms noted at Ambovon'y Rasikajy are unfinished tripod vessels and unfinished tops. The unfinished vessels are represented by fragments of cylinders shaped by picks in which the planned location of the three legs has been incised. Some cylinders were broken as the intervening stone was being removed to isolate the legs. There are also fragments of roughed-out vessel shapes in which the legs were successfully freed from the matrix, but the form was broken as the stone in the interior of the vessel body was being removed (Figure 10.4c, d). Apparently, if the basic form was successfully shaped with picks, the vessel was carried from the quarry to a village or a town like Vohemar, where it was fit onto a large wooden shaft that was rotated as a lathe so that the vessel could be finished with chisels. The unfinished tops are represented by conical forms shaped with picks (Figure 10.4a, b). Apparently these were discarded when the top handle at the apex of the cone was broken off. If top forms were successfully finished with picks, they too would be carried away to be finished on a lathe.

6. Madirobe (14-029: 767.8-1396.3, S13° 29' 02.5"/ E49° 49' 40") is on the southwest flank of the mountain of Manirirano, 24 km southwest of Vohemar and 3.2 km southeast of Ambovon'y Rasikajy. Mouren and Rouaix (1913) probably reported this site and others under the rubric of Ankorimpa Sud, shown on their map as Sous Groupe 1. It is a complex of quarry pits and dumps oriented

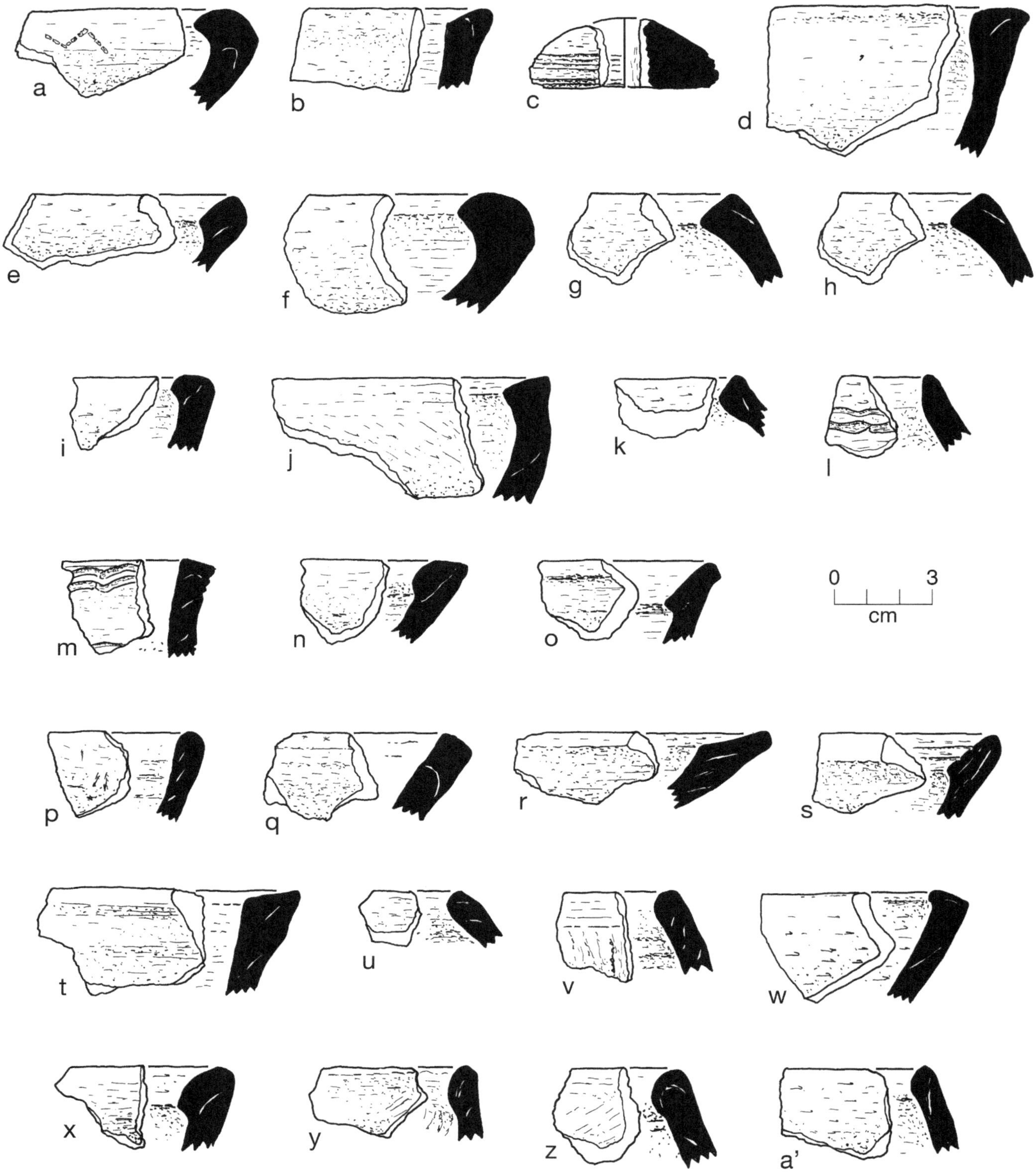
a
b
c
d
e
f
g
h
i
j
k
l
m
n
o
0
3
cm
p
q
r
s
t
u
v
w
x
y
z
a’

Figure 10.2. Ceramics and chlorite schist items from various Ambatary Phase sites:
Vohemar-Cimetière: (07-005: 787.0-1409.9, S13° 21' 24"/ E50° 00' 38"),
Vohemar-Ambatary (09-012: 786.6-1409.8, S13° 30' 28"/ E50° 00' 24"),
Vohemar-Ave Maria Atsinanana (07-013: 786.8-1410.0, S13° 21'19"/ E50° 00' 29"),
Vohemar-Tribunal (07-015: 786.7-1408.7, S13° 21' 17" / E 50° 00' 28),
Vohemar-Stade (07-024: 786.8-1409.8, S13° 21' 20" / E 50° 00' 31"),
Vohemar-Grandidier (14-019, 786.7-1409.8, S13° 22' 30"/ E 50° 00' 25"),
Vohemar-Zandarma: 07-017, 787.0-1409.8, S13° 22' 30"/ E 50° 00' 25),
Amboronana Avaratra-Atsinanana (NE) (08:004: 786.4-1408.7, S13° 22' 06"/ E50° 00' 10"),
Analabe Marie-Claude Avaratra (07-035: 787.7-1407.8, S13° 22' 39"/ E50° 00' 57"
Ambanimanasy (14-024: 772.2-1418.9, S13° 16' 43"/ E49° 51' 54").
[See note, page 69.]

a. Large incurved bowl with heavy rim and dentate zigzag (Vohemar-Cimetière: 07-005: 787.1-1409.9). 5% Medium sand, Dm 40, Side T .92, Rim T 1.50 , Reddish brown (2.5YR5/5) body.
b. Large basin with flattened lip and externally thickened rim (Vohemar-Cimetière: same). 10% Medium sand, Dm 38, Side T .1.35, Rim T 1.90, Weak red (10R 4/4) body.
c. Chlorite-schist spindle whorl (Vohemar-Ambatary surface: 09-012: 786.6-1409.8). Dm: ca 5.80 cm, Thickness 2.10 cm, Estimated weight 94 gm.
d. Large bowl with heavy internally thickened rim (Vohemar-Ave Maria Andrefana: 07-0013: 786.7-1410.0). 5% Medium sand, Dm ca 40, Side T 1.15, Rim T 1.56, Gray (5YR 5/1) body.
e. Bowl with internally thickened rim (Vohemar-Tribunal: 07-015: 786.9-1410.1). Dm 22, Side T .62, Rim T 1.31, Dark reddish gray (5YR 4/2) body.
f. Incurved bowl with heavy rim (Vohemar-Stade: 07-024: 786.9-1410.0). 5% Medium sand and angular quartz, Dm 26, Side T .1.06, Rim T 1.94, Reddish brown (2.5YR5/5) body.
g. Hole-mouth jar with internally beveled flat lip (Vohemar-Stade: Same). 15% Medium sand, Dm: ca 22, Side T: .95, Lip T: .1.35, Reddish brown (5YR 4/4) body. Burnished exterior.
h. Hole-mouth jar with internally beveled flat lip (Vohemar-Tribunal: 07-015: 786.9-1410.1). 10% Medium sand, Dm ?, Neck T: .60, Lip T .67, Reddish brown (5YR 5/4) body.
i. Bowl with internally thickened rim (Vohemar-Stade (07-024: 786.9-1410.0). 10% Medium sand, Dm ca 22, Side T .78, Rim T 1.15, Gray (N 4) body. Interior and exterior burnish.
j. Bowl with internally flattened rim (Vohemar-Grandidier: 14-019, 786.7-1409.8). 15% Medium sand, Dm 25, Side T .94, Lip T 1.36, Red (5YR 5/6) body. Interior and exterior burnish.
k. Hole-mouth with internally thickened rim (Vohemar-Grandidier: Same). 10% Fine sand, Dm ca 36, Side T .79, Rim T .96, Dark Red (2.5YR 3/4) body. Exterior burnish.
l. Hole-mouth with tapered rim and wavy incising (Vohemar-Grandidier: Same). 10% Medium sand, Dm ? , Side T .80, Lip T .55, Reddish brown (5YR 5/3) body. Exterior burnish.
m. Everted jar with wavy incising (Vohemar-Zandarma: 07-017, 786.8-1409.8). 5% Medium sand, Dm 21, Neck T: .84, Lip .T 84, Light olive brown (2.5YR 5/5) body, Trace red slip.
n. Bowl with internally thickened rim (Vohemar-Zandarma: Same). 20% Medium sand, Dm 22, Side T .60, Rim T 1.12, Olive brown (2.5YR 4/4) body.
o. Bowl with internal ledge rim (Vohemar-Zandarma: Same). 10% Medium sand, Dm ca 40, Side T .75, Rim T 1.05, Ledge width 1.75, Olive gray (5YR 3/2) body, Trace weak red (10R 4/4) slip.
p. Bowl with rounded lip (Amboronana Avaratra-Atsinanana (northeast): 08-004: 786.4-1408.7). 15% Medium sand, Dm ca 20 [warped], Side T: .69, Lip .T 79, Weak red (7.5YR 4/3) body.
q. Large basin with beveled flattened lip (Amboronana Avaratra-Atsinanana (northeast): Same). 15%, Medium sand, Dm ca 30, Side T .96, Rim T 1.20, Reddish brown (2.5YR 4/4) body.
r. Bowl with internal ledge rim (Amboronana Avaratra-Atsinanana (northeast): Same). 10% Medium sand, Dm 24, Side T .73, Rim T 1.20, Ledge width 2.18, Dark yellowish brown (10YR 4/4) body. (These bowls do not occur in Ambatary Unit VIII, but the ware is unmistakably Ambatary.)
s. Bowl with incised internal ledge rim (Amboronana Avaratra-Atsinanana (northeast): Same). 5% Medium sand, Dm ca 25, Side T .75, Rim T 1.15, Ledge width 1.80, Red (2.5YR 4/6) body. (See previous comment.)
t. Large basin with internally beveled flattened lip (Analabe Marie-Claude Atsinanana: 07-057: 787.8-1407.6). 10% Coarse sand, Dm 37, Side T .86, Lip T 1.75, Weak red (2.5YR 4/3) body.
u. Hole-mouth jar with rounded lip (Amboronana Avaratra-Atsinanana (northeast): 08-004: 786.4-1408.7). 15% Medium sand, Dm ?, Side T .77, Rim T .84, Reddish brown ? (5YR 4/3) body.
v. Hole-mouth jar with rounded lip (Amboronana Avaratra-Atsinanana (northeast): Same). 15% Medium sand, Dm ca 16, Side T .85, Lip T .93, Dark brown [?] 10YR 5/2 [?] body.
w. Heavy bowl with internally thickened rim (Analabe Marie-Claude Atsinanana: 07-058: 778.8-1407.8). 5% Medium sand, Dm 27, Side T .72, Rim T 1.20, Reddish brown (5YR 5/5) body. Burnished exterior and interior.
x. Large bowl with internal thickened rim (Ambanimanasy (14-024: 771.5 -1418.9). 20% Fine sand, Dm ?, Side T .83, Rim T 1.40, Yellowish brown [?] (7.5YR 5/5) body. Burnished lip.
y. Hole-mouth jar or carinated bowl with rounded lip (Ambanimanasy: Same). 15% Medium sand, Dm 26, Side T .75, Rim T .92, Red (2.5YR 4/4) body.
z. Hole-mouth jar with internal thickened rim (Ambanimanasy: Same). 20% Medium sand, Dm ?, Side T .84, Rim T 1.16, Yellowish brown [?] (7.5YR 5/4) body. Burnished lip.
a'. Hole-mouth jar with internal thickened rim: (Ambanimanasy: Same). 10% [?] Medium sand, Dm 18, Side T .79, Rim T .87, Light red [?] (2.5YR 5/4) body. Burnished exterior.

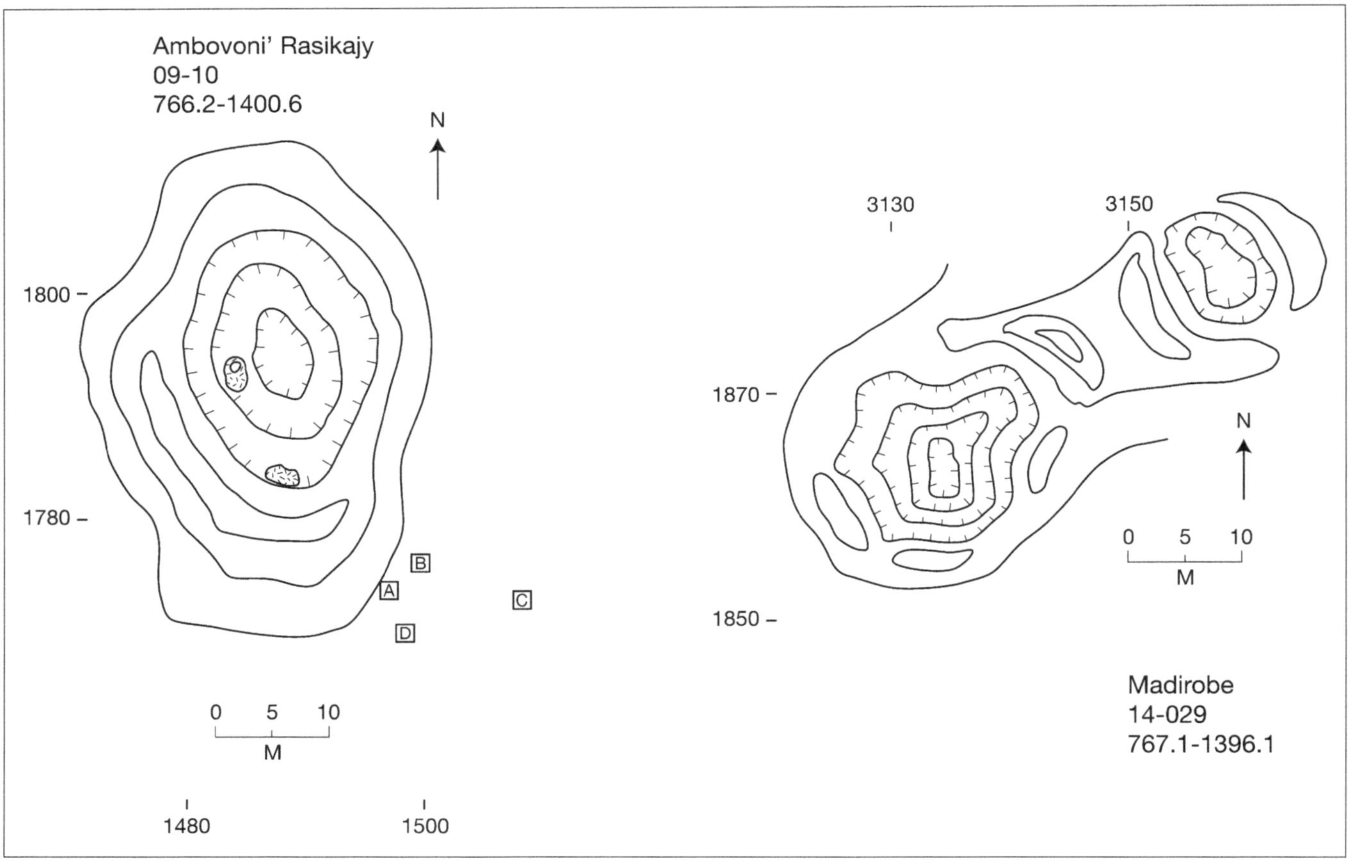

Figure 10.3. Chlorite schist quarry sites.

northeast-southwest, totaling 50 m long and 16 m wide (Figure 10.3, site on the right). Rock fragments on the debris piles are a coarse gray chlorite schist. There are few recognizable pieces of unfinished vessels on the surface, perhaps because many visitors over the past century have removed samples. We did not take another collection of chlorite schist fragments.

The northeast pit is smaller and more eroded—10 m from northwest to southeast, 7 m wide, and refilled to about 2 m in depth. There are two arcs of debris about 1.5 m high, one to the northeast and one to south west.

The southwest pit is irregular, about 17 m in diameter and about 4 m deep. There are three small debris piles to the east, south, and west and a large arc of debris about 3 m high to the northeast. These debris piles are less eroded and the pit is deeper. It is probably younger than the northeast pit.

Between the two pits and under arcs of debris, there may well be an even older pit completely filled with later debris. A test excavation could quickly determine if this is so.

Unfortunately, we arrived at Madirobe late in the day and could not search the wider area for occupational sites with datable ceramics. We had hoped to return, undertake additional survey, and make few small excavations to recover charcoal to date the beginning and end of mining at Madirobe. Unfortunately, this was not possible.

En route to Madirobe, we stopped at a location 1.8 km southeast of the quarry, called by our guide the "Lieu de culte de Madirobe" (14-030: 768.8-1395.8, S13° 29' 17.4"/ E49° 49' 47.5"). This recent site was centered on a rectangular arrangement of quartz cobbles about two meters square. Beside this was a wooden post on which cow skulls has been skewered. A few meters away was a collection of

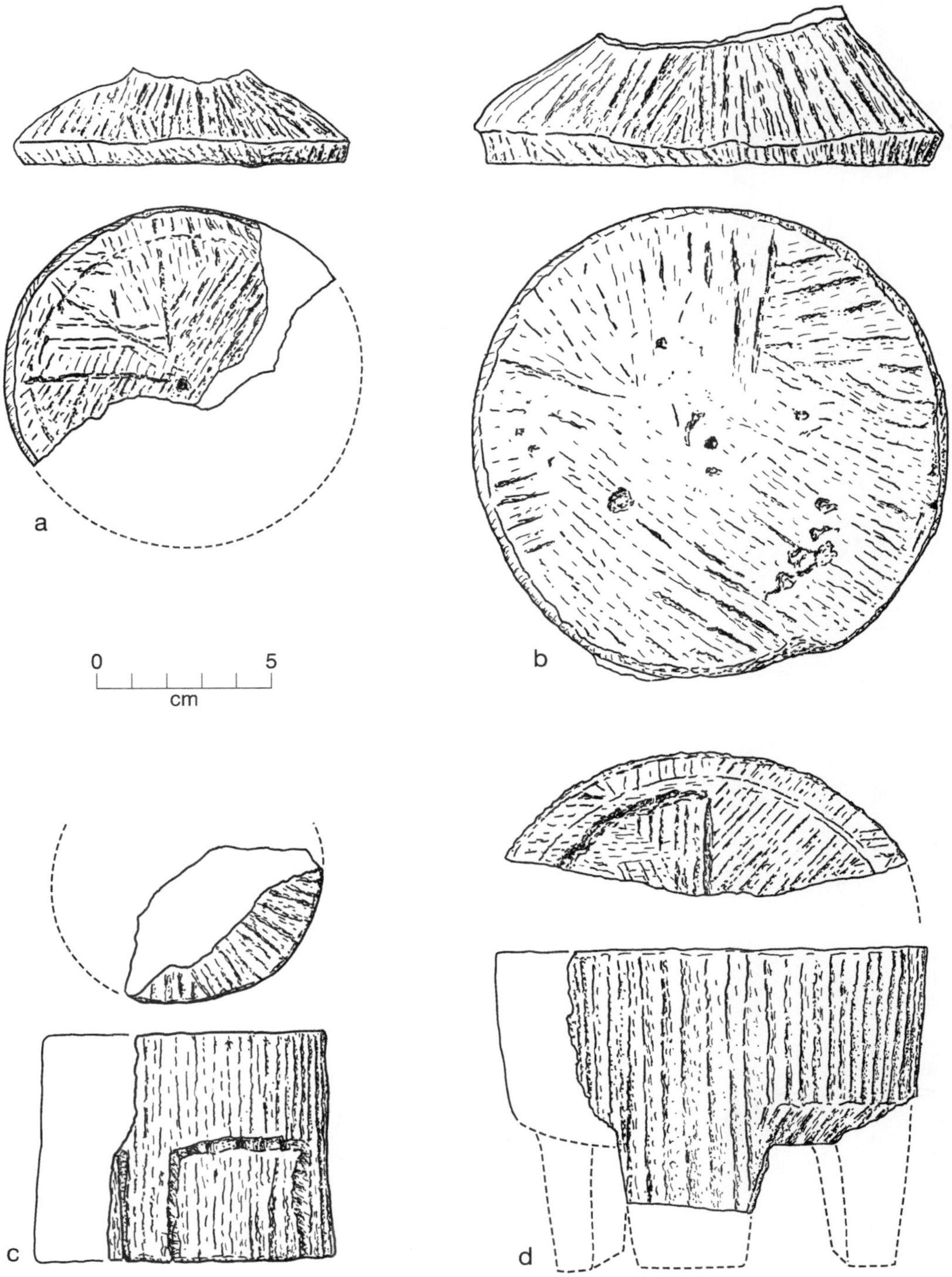

Figure 10.4. Unfinished chlorite schist items from Ambovon'i Rasikajy (09-010: Laborde 766.2-1400.6). Capital letters in the descriptions below correspond to the letters in squares on the previous illustration, Figure 10.3, marking locations. a. Small top (D), Gray chlorite schist, Dm 20.0, apparently broken while outlining top handle. b. Large top (B), Gray chlorite schist, Dm 27.0, apparently broken while outlining top handle. c. Small basin (A), Greenish-gray chlorite schist, Dm 13.5, Height 13.2, Leg Wd 2.5, apparently broken while outlining area between legs to be removed. d. Large basin (C), Bluish-gray chlorite schist, Dm 24.0, Height 13.0+ [ca. 19.0]. Leg Wd 7.6, Leg Thickness 2.5, apparently broken while outlining interior area to be removed.

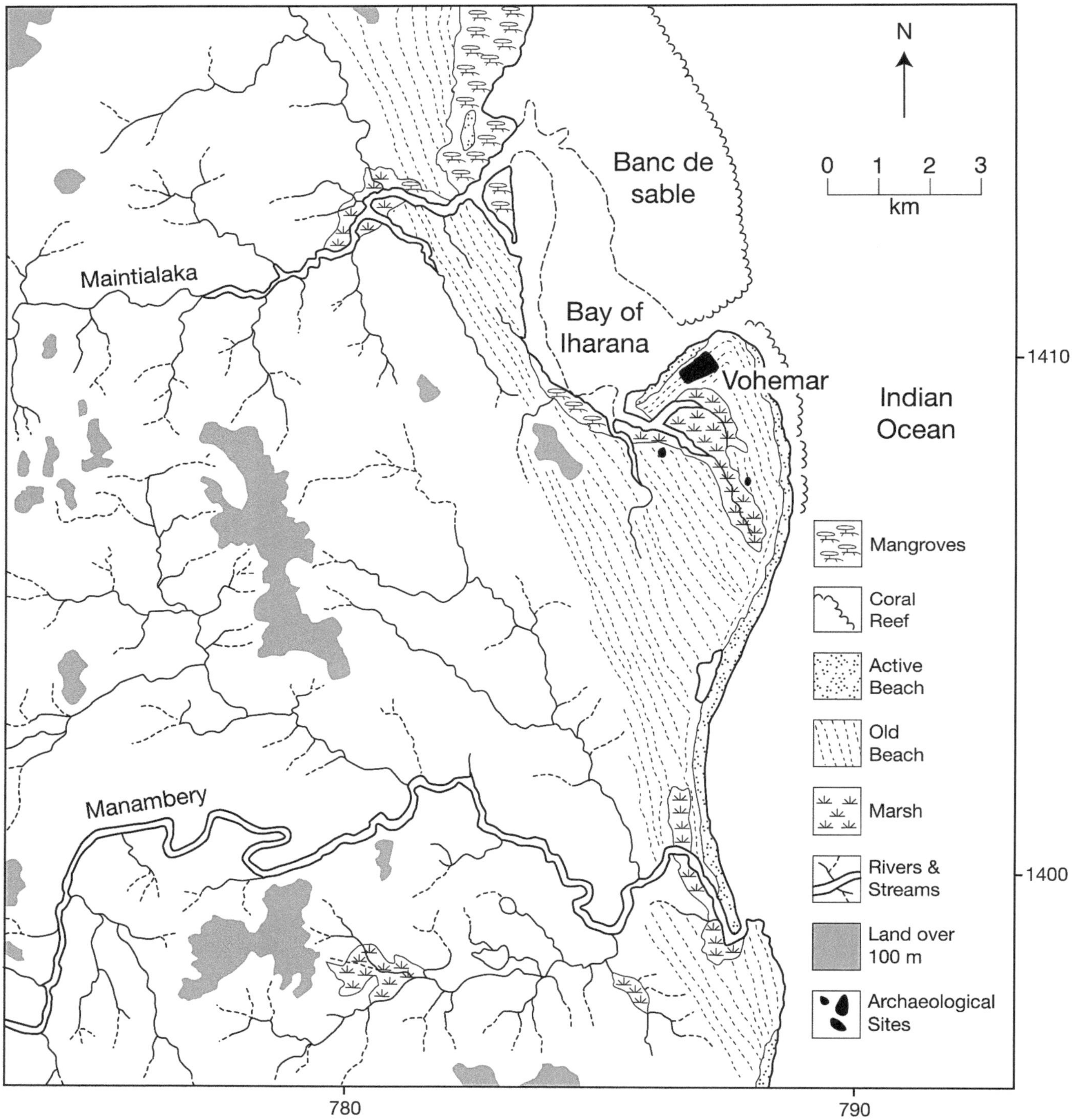

Figure 10.5. Ambatary Phase Settlement.

unfinished basin fragments, and nearby was a collection of unfinished tops. We were told these had been brought from the Madirobe quarry. However, this location is only 350 meters north of the left bank of the Manambery River and it is possible the basin and top fragments were from a nearby workshop or occupational site. Further survey is needed here.

The chlorite schist quarries discussed above are only two among the scores known in northeast Madagascar. There are doubtless many more that have not yet been discovered. We cannot begin to assess the economics of the exchange in chlorite schist until we have a reliable assessment of the number of quarries, the time during which they were exploited, and the volume of material removed. Since there is no question of surveying all of Madagascar's northeast, this will require survey of a statistically rigorous sample of tracts. Excavations in a sample of quarries in these tracts will have to be made to provide both estimates of how much chlorite schist was removed and carried to the workshops, and samples for radiocarbon or OSL dating to establish when quarrying became widespread and when it ended. The problem of curating and storing the recovered quarry debris in museums would be immense, and the funds and trained scientific staff are not available at present. In time, this research will be done, and—combined with parallel studies of iron, crystal, gold, sea turtle scutes, tree gums, and other traded commodities—the results will document Madagascar's contributions to the economy of the Western Indian Ocean.

In sum, Ambatary Phase settlement is focused on the large port site of Vohemar itself. At more than 13 hectares, it was the largest settlement known in the Iharana area before modern times. (Even if it was larger than we think, it could not be as large as the earlier port on the northwest coast, which we know as Mahilaka, with at least 45 ha within its walls.) Alas, we know little about this important town, as our efforts to make additional excavations in other parts of the Ambatary town did not succeed. Analysis of a large faunal sample (see Appendix E) shows that, as before, fishing was the predominant source of protein, but there is some use of domestic mammals and fowl and some hunting. The evidence from Ambatary Unit VIII—the modest sand floors of houses, the predominance of fish in the bone assemblage, the lack of evidence of rice consumption, evidence of such modest crafts as the finishing of chlorite schist items and the recycling of iron tools (perhaps tools for working chlorite schist), and the rarity of imported items—indicate this was a quartier of ordinary townspeople. It is likely that excavations in other quartiers of Ambatary Phase Vohemar will yield the remains of masonry buildings with cement floors; food remains, including more cattle and the remains of rice; the evidence of workshops and storehouses for the exports to distant lands; and a greater diversity and quantity of imported valuables, well represented in the wealthier graves of cemeteries east of Vohemar, which were excavated early in the twentieth century. Broader excavations may also yield early mosques and schools, the marks of literate Islamic society. At first it may seem surprising that we found relatively little evidence of nearby villages dependent on Ambatary Phase Vohemar in our surveys. We are certain of only one small hamlet (**Amboronana Avaratra-Atsinanana:** 786.4-1408.7) to the south of the town over the old estuary (Figure 10.5) and one possible herding outpost in the interior far to the northwest of the town (**Ambanimanasy**: 772.2-1414.9). We found no evidence of Ambatary occupation along either the Manambery embouchure to the south or the Maintialaka embouchure to the north. It seems likely that most of those who produced the rice and other crops for the town lived in the town. Whether this was a largely self-contained city-state or, in contrast, was an urban center with subsidiary towns, perhaps associated with a regional state, will be learned when survey is undertaken to the north around the Manambato embouchure and to the south around the Fanambana embouchure.

Chapter 11

The Patrick Phase

Evidence

The first weeks of survey in 2007 revealed many occupational traces within and near modern Vohemar, and a cluster of sites several kilometers to the south in an area of sandy Holocene beaches and dunes called Analabe, or the Big Forest, today primarily groves of coconut. We were told that this had been an old growth coastal forest protected by tradition until 1972, when it was damaged by a cyclone. After, it was divided among farmers. Our survey recorded several sites marked by concentrations of twelfth to fourteenth century ceramics in blowouts, but test excavations revealed that the deposits in such locations were shallow and disturbed. Consequently, we searched for an area undisturbed by the wind. We found such a location in the coconut grove of M. Patrick (07-062: Laborde 787.7-1407.5, S13° 22' 41"/ E50° 00' 56", UTM E0393395-N8520835) (Figure 11.1b). We excavated a one-meter square termed Unit H, hoping to find undisturbed material. In fact, what we found is of the seventeenth to early eighteenth centuries CE, an interesting local assemblage unknown before.

We first removed Layer 1, a thin humus layer, and Layer 2, .15 m of cultivated gray sand with fresh charcoal fragments. This revealed the top of Layer 3: .16 m of dark gray sand with flat-lying sherds and thin sand lenses perhaps marking house floors. This layer was removed, revealing the top of transitional Layer 4, a mottled gray sand with fewer sherds. We removed .14 m of mottled sand and revealed the top of Layer 5, a reddish sand with no cultural remains. Five features intrusive from Layer 3 became clearer. In the northwest corner is a large shallow pit with many sherds, and in the south section there is a small shallow pit with a few sherds. In the center of the square and in the east section are three small deep intrusions .18 to .20 m in diameter, perhaps postholes. These indicate past structures, but one would have to clean a substantially larger area to determine what types of structures were built here.

A small sample of Patrick Phase remains were also found in Layers 5 and 3b of our Unit J sounding at an Ave Maria residence in Vohemar (07-019: Laborde 786.8-1410.0), discussed in detail below. The former is a gray sand layer with lenses of light sand and charcoal only .09 m thick. It had a small sample of ceramics, of which a few

Figure 11.1. Some Patrick Phase sites.

are Coarse Sandy Ware—perhaps of Analabe Phase affinity discussed above. A majority, however, are representative of the Patrick Phase, including 23 Medium Sandy Ware sherds, some burnished, including two hole-mouth thickened jar rims (Figure 12.1b, c) and three Rough Ware sherds, including a thickened rim bowl (Figure 12.1a) of Patrick affinity (cf. Figure 11.3o). While the coarse ware suggests some earlier occupation, these other sherds can be ascribed to the Patrick Phase. Later Layers 3a and 2 provide the evidence for our provisional late eighteenth to nineteenth century Ave Maria phase, discussed in the next section.

Artifacts

We have a relatively large and coherent sample of ceramics from the well-stratified deposits in Unit H at Analabe-Patrick. Most are medium to fine Sandy Ware. The inclusions in the sherds range from 5% fine sand to 20% medium to coarse sand and some angular quartz or mica, but most sherds have 10–15% medium sand. A majority of the vessels were oxidized; most are reddish brown (2.5-5YR 3/2 to 5/4), but some are dark brown (7.5YR 4/2) and some are red (10R-2.5YR 5/3-4) in color. One vessel has a dark gray (7.5YR 3/1) body, probably deliberately reduced. The sherds are of medium thickness, most bodies ranging from 0.44 to .92 cm with a mode of .68 cm.

Open forms are varied. There are open bowls with simple rounded rims (Figure 11.2a), slightly thickened rounded rims (Figure 11.2b), and slightly out-curved bowls with external rim thickening (Figure 11.2c). These have distinct horizontal or oblique scraping on the interior and exterior. In contrast are larger bowls or basins with flat lips (Figure 11.2d, e). It could be argued that these heavy basins were remnant earlier sherds. However, one has horizontal scraping and one has horizontal burnishing like other Patrick Phase vessels, and it seems more likely that the large basins were occasionally made and used in the Vohemar area until relatively recent times. Finally, there is one small flat lip bowl with small punctates below the rim (Figure 11.2f).

Restricted Sandy Ware jar forms predominate and are distinctive. Most have out-curved upper bodies and inwardly thickened rims or tapered lips. Most of these have horizontal or oblique scraping or burnishing (Figure 11.2h–j), but one had bold chevron incising (Figure 11.2g). Similar bold incising is known from the preceding Ambatary Phase (Figure 10.1m, n). In contrast are two small hole-mouth jars with simple rounded rims (Figure 11.2k, l). Both have interior horizontal scraping, and one (Figure 11.2k) had horizontal burnish, a mode of surface treatment characteristic of Analabe-Patrick.

We found less than 5% Rough Ware in the contexts of Analabe-Patrick Unit H. As at other sites, the clay has a ropy texture and the exteriors are unfinished, but inclusions of angular quartz were more common. Here, neither sand nor vegetal fragments nor other inclusions were noted. Open forms with rounded (Figure 11.2m, o), tapered (Figure 11.2n), and internally thickened rims occur (Figure 11.2q), as do closed forms with incurved (Figure 11.2r) and out-curved (Figure 11.2s) rims with rounded lips.

A sample of Patrick Phase Sandy Ware sherds are relatively fine, similar to Ambatary sherds, though angular quartz and inclusions seem more common. Most are oxidized red in color, the few reduced sherds being mostly from jars. Bodies are much thinner. Vessels other than the basins range from .44 to .90, with a mode of .67 cm. The lips of bowls are rounded, while those of basins are flattened. The slightly out-curved rims of the globular jars have internal rim thickenings and tapered lips. Most vessels have patterned scraping or burnishing on the upper exterior, and many have scraping on the interior. About a third of the body sherds are burnished or scraped.

In addition to ceramic vessels, there is one roughly spherical perforated ceramic item (Figure 11.2p). Such ceramic artifacts are used as net weights on the northwest coast. Another was found in a possible Patrick Phase context at Ave Maria (Figure 12.1e).

There are no chlorite schist fragments, sherds, or weights from this sounding. Iron working is represented by one slag fragment.

Examination of two flotation samples from Patrick Unit H by Amanda Logan yielded one carbonized seed of the *Andropogoneae*, perhaps a small sorghum seed, and two small grass seeds, probably weedy forms. The other food remains recovered from 230 liters of sieved deposit from house floors and fills of Layers 3 and 4 include 25 bones of fish (including head elements as well as vertebrae and spines, indicating the preparation of whole fresh fish), some bones of marine turtle, the shells of *Anadara*, a bivalve found in the sandy shorelines of the bay, and one large mammal limb fragment, perhaps *Bos*. In contrast, from Ave Maria Unit J, Layer 5, in the 54 liters sieved, there were 112 bones of marine fish, very few of head parts (suggesting the consumption of cleaned and perhaps dried or salted fish), one mammal limb fragment, perhaps *Bos,* and a few *Anadara* shells.

Chronology

We know from the stratigraphy at the Ave Maria site in Vohemar, discussed below, that burnished Patrick sherds and rims of a characteristic pattern are stratified below early nineteenth-century remains. In addition, the one Chinese blue-and-white porcelain sherd found in Layer 3 at Analabe-Patrick dates to the late seventeenth or early eighteenth century. Furthermore, the Patrick Phase jar forms and burnished surface treatments have prototypes in Ambatary ceramics of the fifteenth to sixteenth centuries. We can date the Patrick Phase to the seventeenth and eighteenth centuries, without giving precise dates for its beginning or end.

Patrick Settlement

1. Patrick Phase Vohemar. As noted above, a single diagnostic pattern burnished jar rim (Figure 9.2*l*) was found on the surface of **Razanakoto** (08-002: 786.9-1410.2, S13° 21' 10"/ E50° 00' 33") and at **Vohemar-Ave Maria Atsinanana** (14-08: 786.8-1410.0: S13° 21' 17"/ E50° 00' 34"). In the course of excavation, several burnished sherds were found in Layers 5 to 3a of Unit J at **Vohemar-Ave Maria** (07-019: 786.8-1410.0, S13° 21' 18"/ E50° 00' 30", UTM E0392600-N8523385), stratified under nineteenth- and twentieth-century layers. These included a heavy bowl (Figure 10.2x) and two hole-mouth jar rims (Figure 10.2y, z). Around the present **Vohemar-Jandarma** (07-017: Laborde 787.0-1409.8, S13° 21' 26"/ E50° 00' 13") we found several Patrick Phase fine-medium burnished Sandy Ware sherds, including a zigzag incised jar rim (Figure 11.3a) and an arcuate incised jar rim (Figure 11.3b). At **Vohemar-Ecole St. Joseph** (07-018: 786.8-1409.9, S13° 21' 17"/ 50° 00' 31") there is a large sample of fine-medium burnished Sandy Ware sherds, including a hole-mouth jar and everted jar and shoulder with wavy combing (not illustrated). The southwesternmost known occurrence of burnished fine to medium Sandy Ware sherds is at **Bureau de Poste** (14-020: 786.5-1409.7, S13° 22' 32"/ E50° 00' 16"). In no case did we find a dense seventeenth- to eighteenth-century occupational area, but it seems that the northeast half of modern Vohemar is an area of widespread Patrick Phase occupation, about 700 m (from northeast to southwest) by 150 m, covering at least 9 ha. The low density of material could result from masking by the debris of the modern town, but it is also possible that there was only a brief occupation or series of brief occupations, perhaps brief because of the danger to seaside sites from raids by pirates or slavers during this time.

2. Analabe Avaratra (07-031: Laborde 787.4-1408.3, S13° 22' 19"/ E50° 00' 55"). This small site is in an area of sand ridges, now mature coconut trees, but formerly forested, southeast of the large, earlier Analabe-Régis site. It is about 680 m north of the large village site at Analabe-Patrick. A sparse scatter of sherds is visible in an area only 30 m in diameter or about 0.10 ha, though it may continue to the east and north where there were no exposures. Puzzled by the many sherds from a single large Southeast Asian jar, we cored and tested carefully. This revealed only shallow deposits with a low density of ceramics. The surface collection contains a range of burnished hole-mouth (Figure 11.3f, g, j) and out-curved jars (Figure 11.3h, i), and an everted carinated jar (Figure 11.3k), all on relatively fine ware, some with incised or punctate designs. In addition, there are a number of sherds from the bottom of a large stoneware jar with olive-green glaze, probably a storage jar from the sixteenth to seventeenth century from East or Southeast Asia, of the form called "Martaban." Unfortunately, none of the diagnostic rims, handles, or appliqué decorations common on these jars was found. The low density suggests that this site was only briefly occupied. Alternatively, perhaps it was a ritual site and not an ordinary residential site.

3. Analabe-Ilôt (07-050; Laborde 786.9-1408.3, S13° 22' 19"/ E50° 00' 31") This small site, located on a sandy knoll in the old embouchure, 920 m northeast of the large village site at Analabe-Patrick, is surrounded by marshy areas and rice paddies. The site is about 70 m long from southwest to northeast, and 40 m wide, covering only 0.2 ha. A canal, no longer in use, defines its northeast and southeast sides, and at least four footpaths on raised causeways meet at this site. The dense sherd cover is largely of medium to fine sandy fabrics with burnished surfaces, including a basin (Figure 11.3e), thickened-rim open bowls (Figure 11.3n, o) and carinated bowls (Figure 11.3p, q). In addition, this is the only Patrick site that has yielded diagnostic fragments of chlorite schist vessels—a basin rim (Figure 11.3*l*) and the rim of a top (Figure 11.3m)—that could indicate continued use of such vessels; or they could be earlier pieces resulting from unrecognized Razanakoto or Ambatary activity on the locality or collected in Patrick times to make net weights.

4. Analabe-Patrick (07-062: 788.0-1407.7, S13° 22'41"/ E50° 00' 56.00, UTM E0393395-N8520835) including

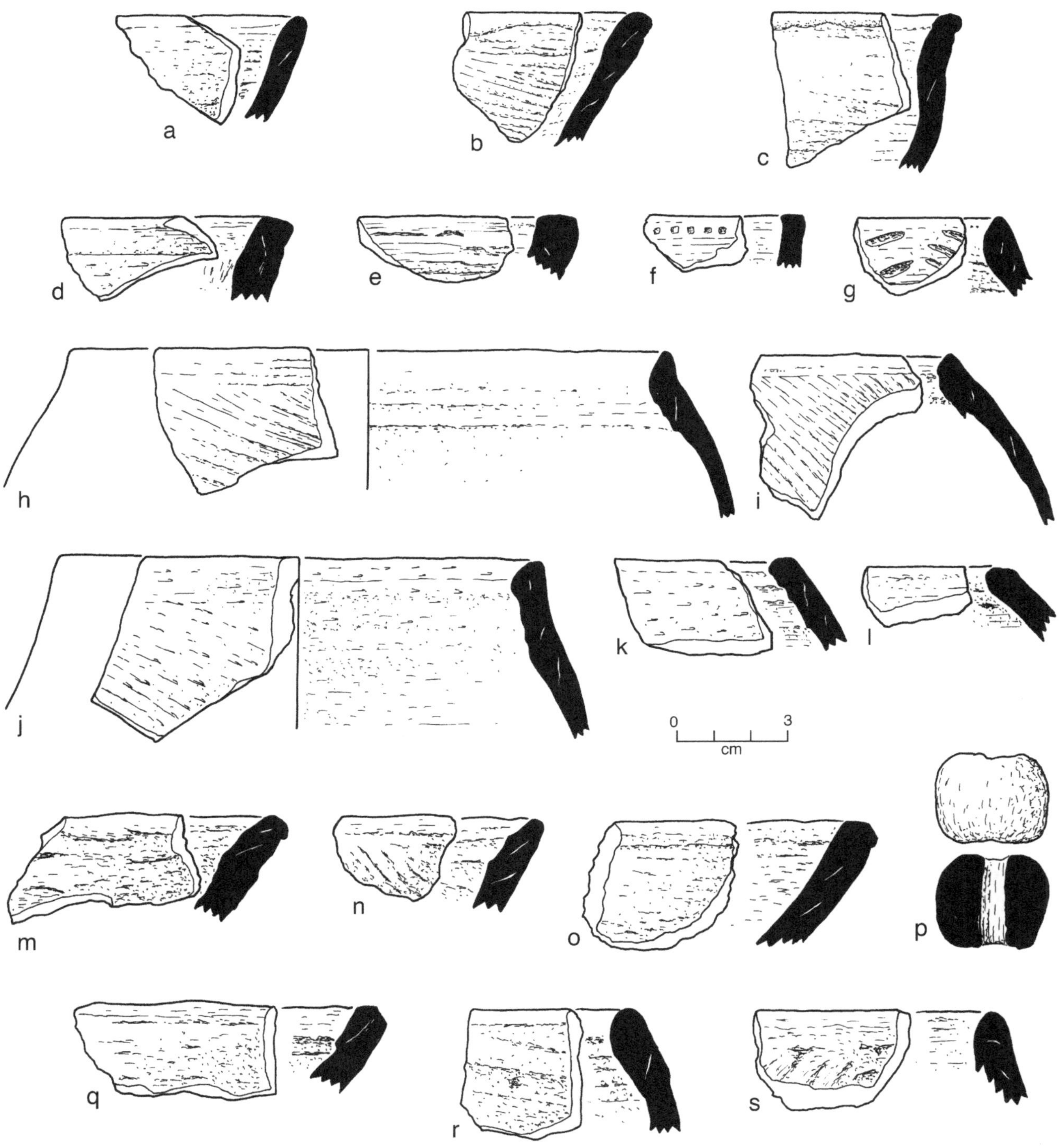
a
b
c
d
e
f
g
h
i
j
k
l
0 3
cm
m
n
o
p
q
r
s

Figure 11.2. Ceramics of the Analabe-Patrick Site, Unit H (07-062: 787.7-1407.5, S13° 12' 41"/ E50° 00' 56")
Note: Munsell colors were taken on a fresh chip under the outer surface. Abbreviations: Dm = Diameter; Body T = Body thickness 2 cm below lip; Rim T = Rim thickness. All measurements are in centimeters.

a. Bowl with rounded lip (Analabe-Patrick, Unit H, Layer 3A). 10% Fine sand and angular quartz, Dm 17, Body T: .72, Rim T: .78, Dark brown (7.5YR 4/2) body.
b. Bowl with thickened rounded lip, oblique exterior scraping (Analabe-Patrick, Unit H, Layer 2). % Medium sand and mica, Dm 18, Body T: .66, Rim T: .93, Reddish brown (5YR 5/3) body.
c. Carinated bowl with rounded lip (Analabe-Patrick, Unit H, Layer 2). 10% Medium sand and mica, Dm 25, Body T: .63, Rim T: .76, Weak red (2.5YR 5/3) body.
d. Heavy basin with flat lip, exterior burnish (Analabe-Patrick, Unit H, Layer 3B). 15% Coarse sand, Dm: 24, Body T: 1.10, Rim T: .94, Very dusky red (2.5YR 2.5/2) body.
e. Heavy basin with flat lip, exterior scraping (Analabe-Patrick, Unit H, Layer 4). 20% Coarse sand, Dm: 32, Body T: 1.06+, Rim T: 1.15, Dark reddish brown (2.5YR 2.5/2) body.
f. Small vessel with small rectangular punctuates (Analabe-Patrick, Unit H, Layer 2). 10% Medium sand and mica, Dm: 13, Body T: .44, Rim T: .62, color not recorded.
g. Hole-mouth jar with inwardly beveled rim, bold chevron incising (Analabe-Patrick, Unit H, Layer 3B). 20% Medium sand and Angular quartz, Dm ca. 25, Body T: .77, Rim T: 1.11, Dark brown (7.5YR 4/2) body.
h. Hole-mouth jar with inwardly thickened rim, oblique scraping (Analabe-Patrick, Unit H, Layer 2). 15% Medium sand and angular quartz, Dm: 16, Body T: .68, Rim T: .80, Weak Red (10R 5/4) body.
i. Hole-mouth jar with inwardly thickened rim, oblique scraping (Analabe-Patrick, Unit H, Layer 4). 15% Coarse sand, Dm: 16, Body T: .65+, Rim T: .94, Very Dark gray (7.5YR 3/1) body.
j. Hole-mouth jar with inwardly thickened rim, burnished exterior and interior (Analabe-Patrick, Unit H, Layer 3A). 15% Medium sand and mica, Dm: 13, Body T: .90, Rim T: .86, Reddish brown (2.5YR 4/4) body.
k. Hole-mouth jar with rounded rim, horizontal burnish, scraped interior (Analabe-Patrick, Unit H, Layer 2). 15% Medium sand and mica, Dm: 12, Body T: .69, Rim T: .93, Reddish brown (5YR 4/3) body.
l. Hole-mouth jar with rounded rim, scraped interior (Analabe-Patrick, Unit H, Layer 4).15% Coarse sand, Dm: 16, Body T: .67, Rim T: .81, Dark reddish gray (5YR 4/2) body.
m. Rough Ware bowl with rounded rim (Analabe-Patrick, Unit H, Layer 2). 20% Coarse sand, Dm: ca. 30, Body T: .77, Rim T: .79, Reddish brown (5YR 5/5) body.
n. Rough Ware bowl with rounded rim (Analabe-Patrick, Unit H, Layer 4). 15% Coarse sand, Dm: 18, Body T: .87, Rim T: .88, Reddish brown (5YR 6/4) body.
o. Rough Ware bowl with externally thickened rim (Analabe-Patrick, Unit H, Layer 3A). 40% Coarse sand and angular quartz, Dm ca. 38, Body T: 1.01, Rim T: .98, Light yellowish brown (10YR 6/4) body.
p. Spherical spindle whorl or net weight (Analabe-Patrick, Unit H, Layer 3B). 5% Coarse medium sand, Dm: 3.1, Ht: 2.6, Light red (2.5YR 7/6) body.
q. Rough Ware bowl with interior thickening and flattened lip (Analabe-Patrick, Unit H, Layer 4). 20% Coarse sand, Dm: 31, Body T: .84, Rim T: 1.02, Strong brown (7.5YR 4/6) body.
r. Rough Ware hole-mouth jar with thickened round lip (Analabe-Patrick, Unit H, Layer 4). 15% Medium sand and angular quartz, Dm 22, Body T: .84, Rim T: 1.17, Reddish brown (2.5YR 4/4) body, Interior scraped.
s. Rough Ware out-curved jar with round lip (Analabe-Patrick, Unit H, Layer 2). 15% Coarse sand, Dm ca. 28, Body T:?, Rim T: ..83, Very dark gray (7.5YR 3/1) body.

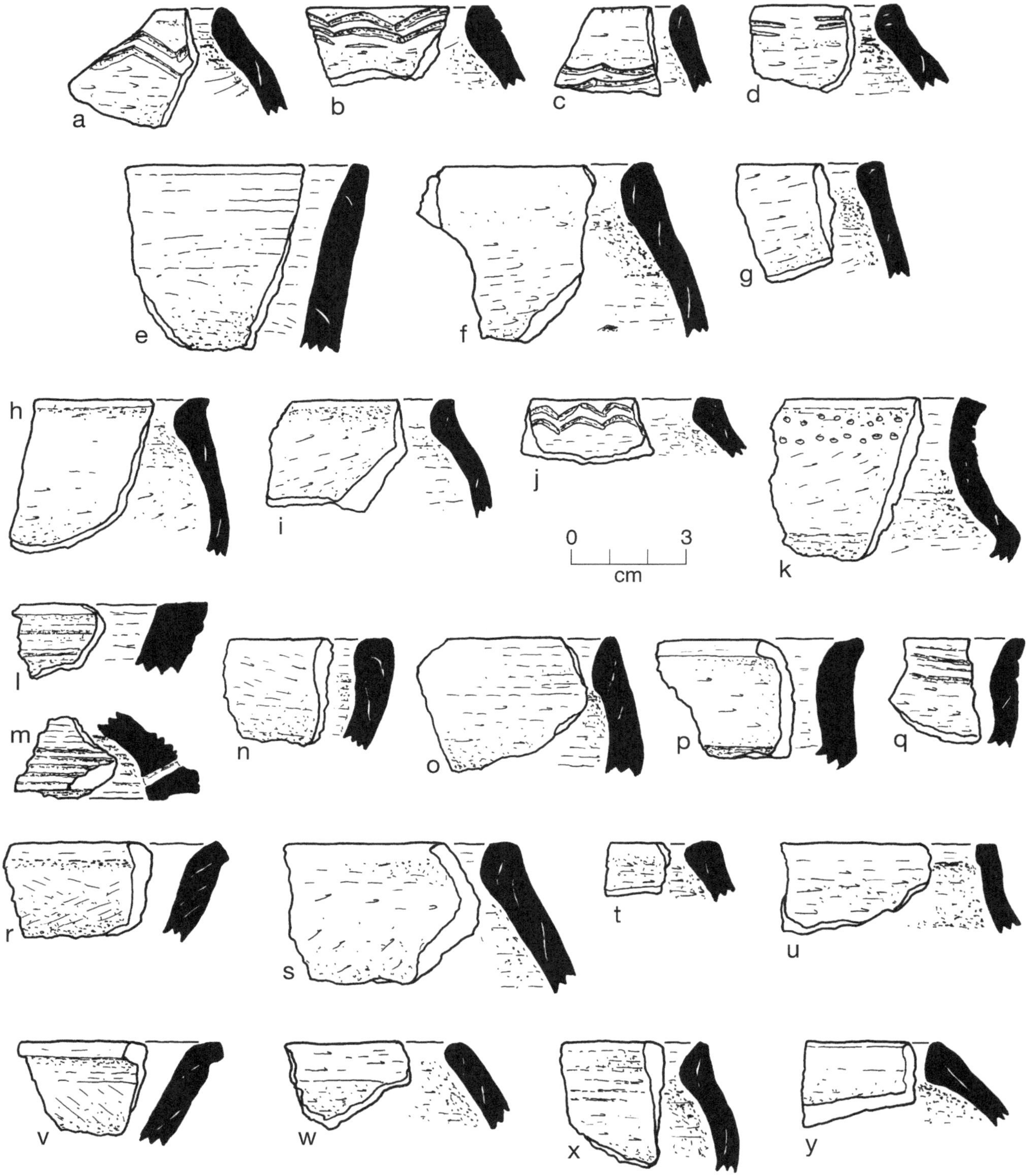
a
b
c
d
e
f
g
h
i
j
k
0
3
cm
l
m
n
o
p
q
r
s
t
u
v
w
x
y

Figure 11.3. Ceramics of other Patrick Phase sites:
Vohemar-Jandarma (07-017: Laborde 786.8-1409.8, S13° 21' 23"/ E50° 00' 30")
Ave-Maria Atsinanana (14-018: Laborde 786.8-1410.0, S13° 21' 17"/ E50° 00' 34")
Analabe-Ilôt (07-050: Laborde 786.9-1408.3, S13° 22' 19"/ E50° 00' 31")
Analabe Avaratra (07-031: Laborde 787.4-1408.3, S13° 22' 19"/ E50° 00' 55")
Analabe Atsimo-Atsinanana (SE): 07-056: Laborde 788.2-1407.6, S13° 22' 41"/ E50° 01' 05")
Ampasin'Analabe (07-055: 788.4-1407.4, S13° 22' 38"/ E50° 01' 18")
Analabe Marie-Claude Atsinanana (07-057: 787.8-1409.8, S13° 22'39"/ E50° 00' 57")
[See note, page 83.]

a. Hole-mouth jar with zigzag incising (Vohemar-Jandarma: 07-017: 786.8-1409.8). 10% Fine sand, Dm ca 30, Side T .64, Rim T .65, Very dark grayish brown (10YR 3/2) body, Red (10R 4/5) slip. Burnished exterior.
b. Hole-mouth jar rim with arcuate incising (Vohemar-Jandarma: Same). 10% Medium sand, Dm 23, Side T .66, Rim T .66, Reddish brown (5YR 4/3) body. Burnished exterior.
c. Hole-mouth jar rim with zigzag incising (Ave Maria-Atsinanana:14-018: 786.8-1410.0). 10% Medium sand, Dm 28, Side T .66, Rim T .53, Red (10R 5/5) body. Burnished exterior.
d. Hole-mouth jar with comb incising (Ave Maria-Atsinanana: Same).10% Medium sand and angular quartz, Dm 26, Side T .81, Rim T .40, Very dark gray (7.5YR 3/1) body. Burnished exterior.
e. Large basin with rounded rim (Analabe-Ilôt: 07-050; 786.9-1408.3). 15% Medium sand and mica, Dm 36, Side T .83, Lip T .68, Dark reddish brown (2.5YR 3/4) body. Exterior scraped.
f. Hole-mouth jar (Analabe Avaratra (07-031: 787.4-1408.3). 20% Medium sand, Dm 19, Side T .90, Rim T l.16, Colors not recorded. Oblique burnished exterior and interior.
g. Hole-mouth jar (Analabe Avaratra: Same). 10% Fine sand, Dm 23, Side T .64, Rim T .79, Colors not recorded. Oblique burnished exterior.
h. Inverted jar with internally thickened rim (Analabe Avaratra: Same). 20% Fine sand, Dm 15, Side T .60, Rim T .78, Colors not recorded. Burnished exterior.
i. Inverted jar with internally thickened rim (Analabe Avaratra: Same). 15% Medium sand, Dm 22, Side T .67, Rim T .74, Colors not recorded. Oblique burnished exterior.
j. Hole-mouth jar with arcuate incising (Analabe Avaratra: Same). 5% Medium sand and angular quartz, Dm 26, Side T .48, Rim T .82, Colors not recorded.
k. Inverted jar with small round punctates (Analabe Avaratra: Same). 15% Fine sand, Dm 13, Side T .70, Rim T .65, Colors not recorded. Oblique burnished exterior.
l. Chlorite schist basin rim (Analabe-Ilôt: 07-050, 786.9-1408.3). Dm ?, Side T 1.11, Lip T 1.29.
m. Chlorite schist top rim (Analabe-Ilôt: Same). Dm ?, Side T .65, Lip T 1.43.
n. Bowl with thickened rounded rim (Analabe-Ilôt: Same). 5% Angular quartz, Dm 12, Side T .71, Rim T 1.00, Dark brown (7.5YR 4/2) body. Exterior scraped.
o. Incurved bowl with internally thickened rim (Analabe-Ilôt: Same). 10% Medium sand, Dm 19, Side T .95, Rim T 1.00, Red (2.5YR 4/6) body. Exterior and interior burnished.
p. Carinated bowl with tapered rim (Analabe-Ilôt: Same). Trace of medium sand. Dm 24, Side T .89, Lip T .75, Red (2.5YR 4/6) body. Exterior and interior burnished.
q. Carinated bowl with combing (Analabe-Ilôt: Same). 5% Angular quartz and medium sand, Dm 22, Side T .63, Lip T: 66, Lip T .47, Reddish brown (5YR 4/3) body. Exterior burnished.
r. Bowl with everted flattened lip (Analabe Atsimo-Atsinanana (SE): 07-056: 788.2-1407.6). 20% Fine sand, Dm 22, Side T .63, Lip T: 66, Lip T .47, Dark yellowish brown (10YR 4/4) body.
s. Hole-mouth jar with internally thickened rim (Analabe Atsimo-Atsinanana (SE): Same). 15% Fine sand and mica, Dm 23, Side T .74, Rim T 1.12, Light red (2.5YR 6/4) body. Oblique burnished exterior.
t. Hole-mouth jar with internally thickened rim (Analabe Atsimo-Atsinanana (SE): Same). 15% Fine sand, Dm ?, Side T .51, Rim T .96, Grayish brown (10YR 5/2) body. Interior and exterior burnish.
u. Carinated bowl or hole-mouth jar (Ampasin'i Analabe (07-055: 788.4-1407.7). Trace fine sand and coral, Dm ?, Warped, Side T .59, Lip T .59, Dark grayish brown (10YR 3/2). Interior and exterior burnish.
v. Bowl with everted flattened lip (Analabe Marie-Claude Atsinanana: 07-057; 787.8-1407.7). 10% Medium sand, Dm 22, Side T .63, Lip T: 66, Lip T .47, Brown (7.5YR 5/62) body.
w. Hole-mouth jar with rounded lip (Analabe Marie-Claude Atsinanana: Same). 10% Fine sand and round quartz, Dm 16, Side T .72, Lip T .61, Very dark gray (7.5YR 3/1). Interior and exterior burnish.
x. Inverted jar with interior thickened tapered rim (Analabe Marie-Claude Atsinanana: Same). 10% Fine sand, Dm 20, Side T .50, Rim T .89, Light reddish brown (10YR 6/4), Exterior burnish.
y. Inverted jar with interior thickened beveled rim (Analabe Marie-Claude Atsinanana: Same). 10% Fine sand, Dm 20, Side T .62, Lip T 1.01, Brown (10YR 5/3) body.

Analabe-Patrick Avaratra (07-059, 787.6-1407.8, S13° 22' 38"/ E50° 00' 52", UTM E0393295-N8520945), **Analabe Marie-Claude Avaratra** (07-035: 788.7-1407.8, S13° 22' 42"/E50° 00' 59", UTM E0393410-N8520920) and **Analabe Marie-Claude Atsinanana** (07-057,058: 787.8-1407.7, S13° 22' 39"/E50° 00' 57", UTM E0393440-N852885). This substantial site is located on the right or east bank of the old embouchure, with good access to localities for the cultivation of rice and other crops, forest resources, and pasture. In addition to the excavated material described above, several surface collections of fine Sandy Ware, often with pattern burnishing, were found. Of these, one—**Analabe Marie-Claude Avaratra** (07-035)—yielded some Rough Ware and medium Sandy Ware hole-mouth jars with internally thickened rims and pattern burnish (not illustrated.) In addition, there was a small jar shoulder with interior brown glaze and exterior mottled light and dark brown glaze, probably Bahla Ware imported from Oman in the seventeenth to nineteenth centuries (Whitcomb 1975). Another—**Analabe Marie-Claude Atsinanana** (07-057,058)—yielded both a bowl with out-turned flattened rim (Figure 11.3v) and burnished hole-mouth jars, one plain (Figure 11.3w) and two with internally thickened rims (Figure 11.3x, y) on fine-medium Sandy Ware fabric. This largest of the Patrick Phase villages extends about 220 m (northwest to southeast) by 180 m, covering about 3.8 ha. West of this site are four small lakes in an expanded part of the old embouchure, perhaps the remnants of a larger artificial lake enclosed by a possible dam to the north. Detailed study of these features might date the use of controlled canal irrigation for rice paddies. Pollen analysis would be useful.

5. Mahabo Atsinanana (07-060: 787.3-1407.2, S13° 22' 39"/ E50° 01' 42", E0392990-N8520925). This is a small site 400 m west of Analabe-Patrick, on the opposite side of the old estuary. The ceramic sample is primarily medium Sandy Ware, a majority with pattern burnish, including both hole-mouth jars and flat-rim bowls (none illustrated). These appear to be exclusively of the Patrick Phase. The path from the Analabe-Patrick complex to this small site is on a substantial artificial bank, which may have created a reservoir to its south, providing water for the paddies of the old estuary to the north. Only geological coring or test excavations can determine if this is a Patrick Phase feature or a more recent construction.

6. Analabe Atsimo-Atsinanana (southeast) (07-056: 788.2-1407.6, S13° 22' 41"/ E50° 01' 05") is a small hamlet site about 40 m in diameter, about 0.13 ha, 250 m east of Analabe-Patrick. It has a dense scatter of Patrick Phase sherds. Diagnostic rims of burnished hole-mouth jars (Figure 11.3s, t) and bowls (Figure 11.3r), both on fine fabrics, were found. This was perhaps a single isolated residential unit.

7. Ampasin'Analabe (07-055: 788.4-1407.5, S13° 23' 45"/ E50° 01'19"). A few Patrick sherds were found on the site of this Razanakoto Phase beach site, of which one jar rim is illustrated (Figure 11.3u), perhaps indicating no more than occasional use as a canoe landing or fishing spot.

8. Lac Verte (11-028: ca 787.5-1403.7, S13° 24' 55"/ E50° 00' 25"). Because this is a sacred place for both Anjoaty and Sakalava, it was never possible for us to examine the site ourselves. Fortunately, a Vohemarian friend made a small collection of large body sherds for us. All were a hard medium Sandy Ware, one with pattern burnishing, unquestionably of the Patrick Phase. We do not have an exact location and cannot estimate the size of the site. We provisionally show it as a small village on Figure 11.4. It is important to study this site in the future.

Given the sites recorded, we can say that the Patrick major settlements and their subsidiaries are in locations similar to those of the Analabe and Razanakoto Phases. The Ambatary Phase port site covered by modern Vohemar, with its rich evidence of participation in the Indian Ocean trade network, was partially abandoned. Some settlement continued in the center and northeast end of the old (and modern) town. A new focus of settlement is the large village to the south, centered on the coconut grove of M. Patrick. Our one sounding there had evidence of scattered postholes and the debris of domestic activity, such as sherds and food remains, primarily from fishing and shellfish collecting. There is only one piece of slag and none of the chlorite schist scrap we would expect from production for export. We found four imported sherds, three of late Chinese blue-and-white porcelain and one possible Omani stoneware. The limited evidence of export and import parallels that from the earlier large Analabe-Régis village. There were four possible small subsidiary hamlets within a kilometer of this large village, two in the Holocene sand ridges between the ocean and the old embouchure and two on sandy knolls in the wetlands that dominate the old embouchure (Figure 11.4). Doubtless there would be more in areas farther south, where we were unable to survey. We found no evidence of Patrick occupation along either the Manambery River to the south or the Maintialaka River to the north. The settlement pattern and the few remains of food consumption and craft production imply a local focus for people of the Patrick Phase.

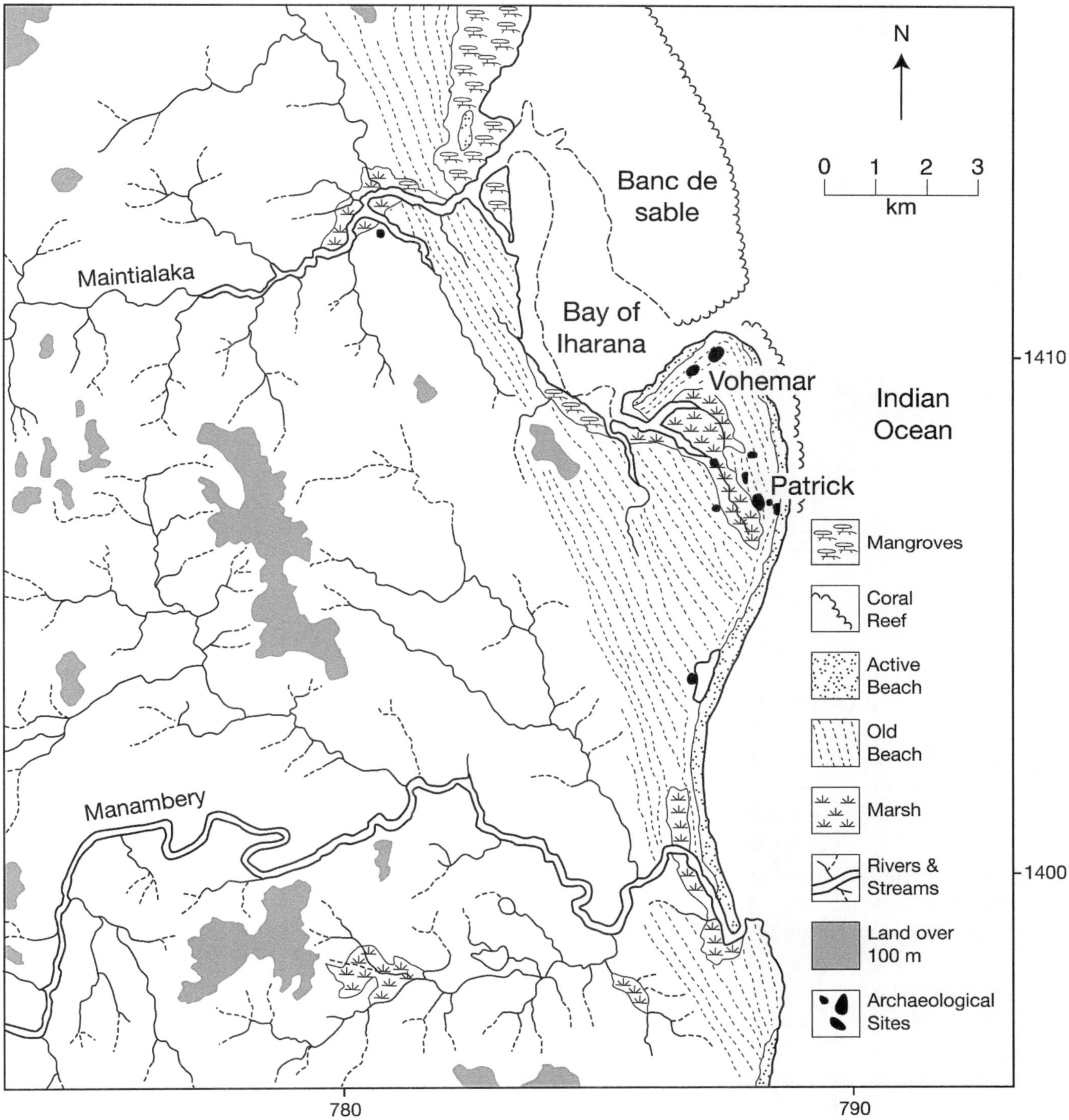

Figure 11.4. Patrick Phase settlements.

Chapter 12

The Ave Maria Phase

Evidence

Late in the 2007 season, after the Analabe-Patrick excavation, we decided to search for a site in which later material stratified above Patrick Phase layers could establish an end-date for the Patrick Phase and provide evidence of succeeding occupations. We selected an area of the northeast portion of modern Vohemar, where early maps indicated "Sakalave" settlement. After coring widely on the third beach, we selected a location in the compound of the Soeurs Catholiques d'Ave Maria, where there was almost a meter of cultural stratigraphy (**Vohemar-Ave Maria**: (07-019: Laborde 786.8-1410.0, S13° 21' 18.1"/ E50° 00' 29.5"). The Mother Superior gave us permission to make an excavation in their private garden (see details in Appendix B).

We first removed two layers of homogenous gray sand. Layer 1 had twentieth-century plastic, glass, iron, and ceramics. Layer 2 was similar, but distinguished by lenses of brown sand, with similar modern material and some locally made sherds and iron slag. Layer 3A, from .30 to .40 in depth, is a gray-brown sand with much slag. Originating from Layer 3A were two parallel trenches oriented roughly north-south. The western trench averages .24 m wide and .40 m deep and has possible post molds .75 m apart; the eastern trench averages .20 m wide and .29 m deep and has definite post molds about .48 m apart in its base. One of these was .15 m in diameter and had a flat base. This is a wall trench, probably for a post and beam building. The western trench is less certain. The fill of the wall trenches was black sand with much slag and some local sherds; in the west trench, there was one sherd of imported white glazed, white bodied ware, discussed below. The trenches cut from Layer 3a into the top of Layer 5 and have a mixture of sherds. Layer 3b is .15 m thick, also a gray-brown sand grading into a brown sand below, has few sherds and little slag. Layer 4 below is .20 m thick and is gray with lenses of brown sand and has little cultural material. Layer 5 is a gray sand with lenses of light sand and some charcoal, shell, and bone, as well as Patrick Phase sherds detailed in the previous section. It is not the density we see in village refuse deposits, so this is either the edge of a site or a garden to which some village debris was brought to improve the sandy soil. Below this is Layer 6, a thick gray sand with some light sand lenses and very little cultural material. At its base, resting on clean reddish beach sand, are white lenses, probably siliceous ash left from the burning of herbaceous vegetation.

Artifacts

The sample from the upper Layers 2 and 3 of our Ave Maria sounding is tiny, but it is all we have and we can use it to at the least provisionally characterize an Ave Maria Phase.

A majority of the sherds are Medium Sandy Ware and a minority are Fine Sandy Ware with 10% or less of fine sand. The inclusions in the sherds range from 5% to 20% fine to medium sand and some angular quartz or mica inclusions, but most sherds have 10% to 15% medium sand. A majority of the vessels were oxidized, varying from red (2.5 YR 5/7) to reddish brown (5YR 3/2 to 5/3) to brown (5YR-7.5YR 4-5/3-4) in color. Some vessels have grayish brown (7.5YR 5/2-3) bodies, probably deliberately reduced, sometimes with black surface coatings. The sherds are of medium thickness, the measured bodies ranging from 0.45 to .85 cm with a mode of .62 cm.

The open forms include flat lip bowls, some plain (Figure 12.1i) and some with incisions (Figure 12.1m). The latter resembles chlorite schist bowls. Also notable are carinated forms with everted rims and rounded—often slightly thickened—lips, some with zigzag incising (Figure 12.1k, l), some with arcuate incisions (Figure 12.1n). The latter example is burnished. The open forms appear to differ from their Patrick Phase predecessors.

The closed forms include hole-mouth jars with rounded (Figure 12.1h) or internally thickened lips (Figure 12.1f). The latter is burnished and is similar to Patrick jars.

Because of the small size of the excavated sample, we have few criteria for recognizing sites occupied in the late eighteenth to nineteenth centuries. We ascribe Ave Maria Phase occupation to sites that have sherds of reduced Sandy Ware with fine sand and mica inclusions, often with burnished black surfaces. The one recognizable shape is a strongly carinated vessel with everted rim. However distinctive it may be, dating based on one vessel type is questionable.

One ceramic feature—the thin reduced fine ware with wavy-combed surface treatment that characterizes the entire west coast as far north as the Bay of Ampasindava, where they are common during the seventeenth to eighteenth century Amporoha Phase (Wright, Radimilahy and Allibert 2005: Figure 10b, g, i)—is not found in Vohemar or elsewhere, except for one sherd from a coring sample from **Vohemar-Hôpital** (08-008: 785.6-1409.4: S13° 21' 49"/ E 49° 59" 58"), the supposed Makoa quartier of nineteenth-century Vohemar. If confirmed, this would indicate that the craft patterns of the West Coast Sakalava had some, albeit limited, impact on Vohemar.

Chlorite schist is represented by an amorphous fragment and an ovoid perforated piece, perhaps a pendant or weight (Figure 12.1j). There is no indication that chlorite schist was used to fashion vessels during this period.

In addition to the iron slag mentioned above, several pieces of flat iron sheet were found in Layer 3A. Surprisingly, there were no nails or pins. There was, however, a fragment of a sandstone sharpening stone (*vato asaina*), which would have been used to sharpen iron tools, also in Layer 3A. In spite of careful searching of both screened and floated samples, no glass pieces—neither vessel fragments nor beads—were found.

Our flotation samples from the west wall trench produced no seeds. Sieving of 140 liters of sediment from Layer 3 and the wall trenches yielded 211 marine fishbones, two marine turtle bones, a duck and two possible chicken bones, a bat wing fragment, a lemur phalange not identifiable to species, and 10 large mammal bones, perhaps *Bos*.

Chronology

Ave Maria sherds are found in Unit J, Layers 3A and 3B, at Vohemar-Ave Maria, stratified above Patrick Phase material in Layer 5, as discussed above. These sherds were associated in a Layer 3A feature with a European white-glazed white ware sherd, probably an early nineteenth-century sherd from Stoke-on-Trent in Staffordshire, U.K. The transition from Patrick to Ave Maria probably took place in the mid eighteenth century. On one site, Amboronanana-Dieudonné (07-053: 785.8-1408.5, S13° 22'10"/ E 49° 59' 57"), Ave

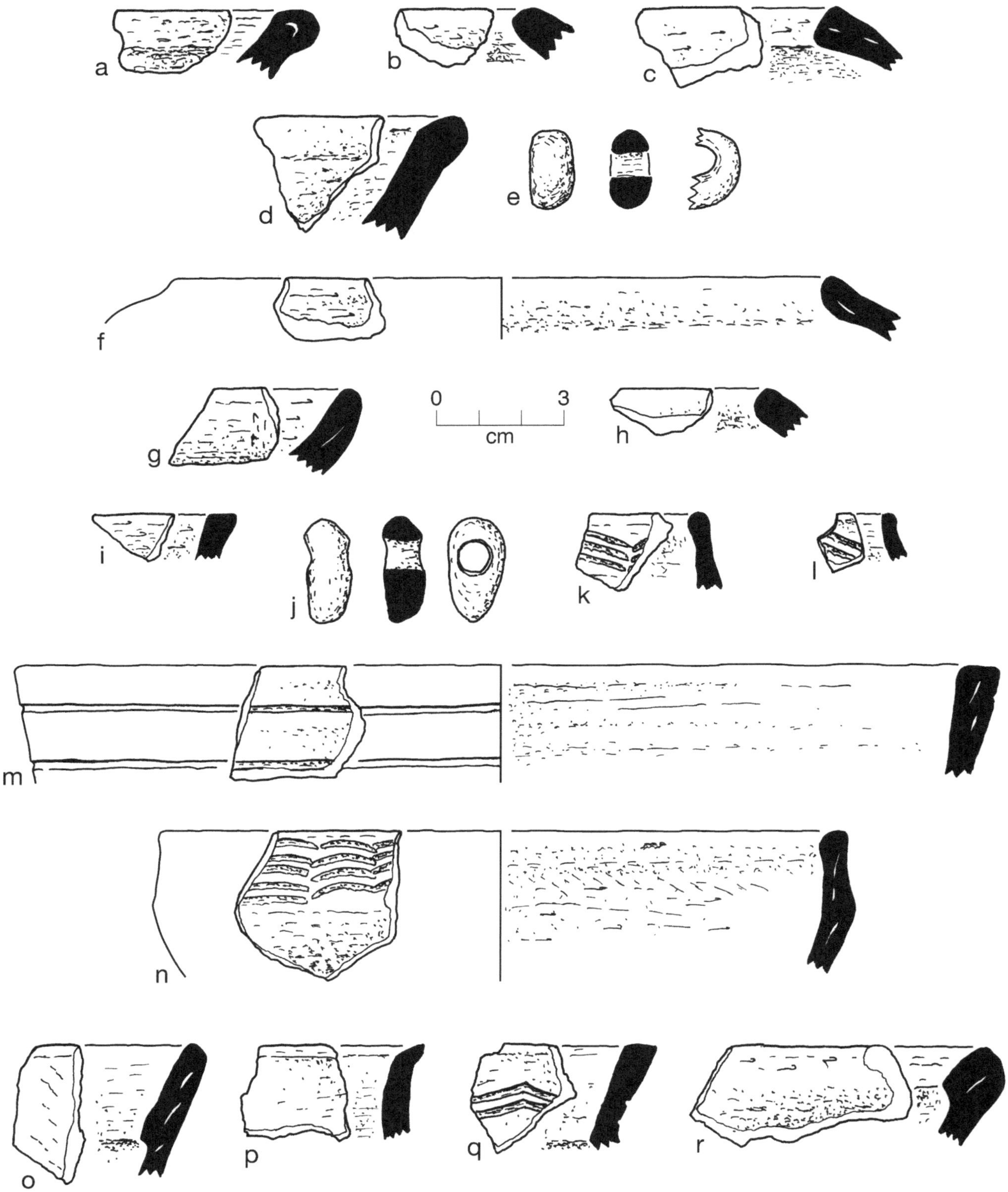
a
b
c
d
e
f
0 3
cm
g
h
i
j
k
l
m
n
o
p
q
r

Figure 12.1. Artifacts from Ave Maria and other sites:
Vohemar-Ave Maria (07-019: 786.8-1410.0, S13° 21' 18"/ E50° 00' 29", UTM E0392650-S85234635),
Amboronana-Dieudonné (07-053: 785.8-1408.5, S13° 22'10"/E 49° 59' 57", UTM E0391630-S8521800),
Vohemar-Tribunal (07-015: 786.8-1410.1, S13° 21' 16"/ E50° 00' 29", UTM E0392570-S8523455).
Note: Munsell colors were taken on a fresh chip under the outer surface. Abbreviations: Dm = Diameter; Body T = Body thickness 2 cm below lip; Rim T = Rim thickness. All measurements are in centimeters.

a. Rough Ware bowl with exterior thickening and flattened lip (Ave Maria Unit J, Layer 5). 30% Coarse sand and angular quartz, Dm: 27, Body T: .75, Rim T: 1.15, Red (2.5YR 5/5) body.
b. Hole-mouth jar with rounded lip (Ave Maria Unit J, Layer 5). 15% Coarse sand, Dm 18, Side T: 1.05, Rim T: .86. Interior and exterior burnish.
c. Hole-mouth jar with thickened lip (Ave Maria Unit J, Layer 5). 20% Coarse sand, Dm ca 34, Side T: .77, Rim T: .1.04, Reddish brown (5YR 4/4) body. Interior and exterior burnish, Exterior carbon residue.
d. Heavy bowl with out-turned rim (Ave Maria, Unit J, Layer 5). 40% Coarse sand, angular quartz, feldspar, Dm 26, Side T 95, Rim T .88, Dark reddish brown (5YR 3/3) body. Burnished exterior.
e. Ceramic bead or weight (Ave Maria, Unit J, Layers 4-5 section cleaning). 10% Fine sand and angular quartz, Dm 1.87, T: 1.27, Hole Dm .79, (2.5 YR 3/2) body (phase uncertain).
f. Hole-mouth jar with internally thickened rim (Ave Maria, Unit J, Layer 3B, East trench). 20 % Fine sand, Dm 15, Side T: .70, Rim T:.81, Brown (7.5YR 5/4) body. Exterior burnish.
g. Heavy bowl with rounded rim (Ave Maria, Unit J, Layer 3B, West trench). 15% Medium sand, Dm ca 18, Side T .99, Rim T .77, Dark reddish brown (5YR 3/2) body. Burnished interior.
h. Hole-mouth jar with rounded rim (Ave Maria, Unit J, Layer 3B, West trench). 15% Coarse sand, Dm ca 26, Side T 97, Rim T .73, Red (2.5YR 5/5) body.
i. Bowl with flat rim (Ave Maria, Unit J, Layer 3B, East trench). 10 % Medium sand, Dm ?, Side T .70, Rim T .77, Brown (7.5YR 5/3) body. Burnished interior and exterior.
j. Pendant or weight (Ave Maria, Unit J, Layer 3B). Coarse green chlorite schist, Length 2.47, Width 1.49, Thickness 1.14, Hole Dm .79. No drill marks.
k. Carinated bowl rim with zigzag incising (Ave Maria, Unit J, Layer 3). 15% Medium sand and angular quartz, Dm ca. 22, Side T .57, Rim T .58, Reddish brown (5YR 4/3) body.
l. Carinated bowl or everted jar rim with incising (Ave Maria, Unit J, Layer 3A). 10% Medium sand, Dm ?, Side T .51+, Rim T .44, Brown (7.5YR 5/3) body.
m. Bowl with flat lip and incising (Ave Maria, Unit J, Layer 3A). 10% Coarse sand, Dm 23, Side T .85, Lip T 1.01, Brown (7.5YR 5/2) body.
n. Carinated bowl with rounded lip and arcuate incising (Ave Maria, Unit J, Layer 3A). 15% Medium sand, Dm: 17, Side T .66, Neck T .45, Rim T .54, Red (2.5YR 5/7) body. Burnished interior and exterior.
o. Bowl with internally thickened ledge rim (Amboronana Dieudonné: 07-053) 5% Medium sand, Dm ?, Side T .62, Ledge T .75, Rim T .53, Very dark gray (5YR 3/) body.
p. Everted jar neck (Amboronana Dieudonné: 07-053). 10% Fine sand, mica, Dm 12, Neck T .65, Lip T .40, Very dark brown (7.5YR 3/2) body. Very dark gray (10YR 3/1) reduced surface.
q. Carinated bowl or everted neck jar with arcuate incisions (Vohemar-Tribunal: 07-015). 10% Fine sand, Dm ?, Neck T .60, Lip T .67, Reddish brown (5YR 5/4) body.
r. Bowl with internally thickened rim (Vohemar-Tribunal: 07-015). 5% Medium sand, Dm 22, Side T .62, Rim T 1.31, Dark reddish gray (5YR 5/2) body. Burnish on lip.

Maria reduced Fine Sandy sherds were found with both an East Coast bowl rim dated to the late nineteenth to early twentieth century and imported early twentieth-century European glazed sherds. Local Vohemarians have no tradition of making pottery. When shown sherds, they assert that these vessels were made in Ambilobe on the northwest coast, where burnished, carinated vessels similar to Ave Maria vessels are still made. We suggest that ceramics ceased to be made in Vohemar in the early twentieth century, if not before.

Ave Maria Settlement

Through the nineteenth century, Vohemar regained its predominant position in the area (Figure 12.2). Settlement sites with Ave Maria ceramics are as follows:

1. Maintialaka-Antafiabe Andrefana (08-015: Laborde 781.8-1413.1, S13° 19' 44"/ E49° 57' 45", UTM E0387882-N 8526230) is a village site first occupied in Ampasimahavelona and Analabe Phase times. It is still occupied today. On the 2010 satellite image, there were seven houses in an area of 0.2 ha. The early ceramics were scattered in the gardens to the east of the modern village. Under and west of the modern village is a dense concentration of predominantly reduced medium to fine Sandy Ware ceramics covering about .45 ha. The villagers conserve an iron cannonball. This was probably the landing through which Bernier passed on his explorations to the northwest of Vohemar in 1834 (Fleury 1886), but unfortunately, he provides little description. The 1885 map appears to show five houses here (Favereau and Germain 1885).

2. Maintialaka-Southwest (08-017: 781.5-1411.1, S13° 19' 53"/ E49° 57' 25", UTM E0387050-N 8526050) was also an Ampasimahavelona and Analabe site. However, medium to fine Sandy Ware sherds, often reduced, indicate Ave Maria Phase. Late sherds were found over an area of 140 m (east to west) by 40 m, with area of about 0.6 ha, seemingly larger than the earlier occupied area. There is a shell concentration on the northeast edge near the river.

3. Imaiky (08-021: 783.2-1410.8, S13° 20' 40"/ E49° 58' 25", UTM E0388790-N8524505) is a location on the west slope of the high sand dunes overlooking the west side of the Bay of Iharana. About 110 meters from the shore and 20 m above sea level, we found a scatter of shell debris along a path running from the coast westward, about 30 m long with a reduced Fine Sandy Ware sherd. The north-south dimension of this site is unknown, but it is probably a relatively small site of less than a hectare. The village no longer exists at this point; the name is taken from the 1961 FTM 1/100,000 map.

4. Ave Maria Phase Vohemar was the major center in the region. Reduced thin Fine Sandy Ware occurs not only in the iron-working area around the Ave Maria residence (07-019: 786.8-1410.0, S13° 21' 18.1"/ E50° 00' 29.5"), but throughout modern Vohemar. At **Vohemar-Hôpital** (08-008: 785.6-1409.4, S13° 21' 50"/ E 49° 60" 00") coring revealed predominantly reduced Fine Sandy Ware sherds in one location. At **Vohemar-Cimetière** (07-005, 021: 787.1-1409.9, S13° 21' 24"/ E50° 00' 38") there are a few reduced plain fine Sandy Ware sherds. There is also reduced thin Fine Sandy Ware at the **Bureau de Poste** (14-020: 786.5-1409.7, S13° 21' 30"/ E50° 00' 15"). These scattered occurrences suggest dispersed settlements over an area of perhaps 5 ha. The late nineteenth-century map shows that the present congregational mosque already existed in the space between the Sakalava and Makoa neighborhoods (Favereau and Germain 1885).

5. Ambararatra (07-052: 784.0-1409.0, S13° 21' 58"/ E49° 58' 55"). This small site is located near where several small perennial streams draining the massif of Ambatomalana enter the southwest corner of the Bay of Iharana. The site measures 50 m (southwest to southeast) by 30 m and covers 0.14 ha. It is 2.1 km west-southwest of the mosque of Vohemar. The site is near the road toward the Manambato River and Ambilobe. The stream mouth today contains rich rice paddies, and the location has easy access to the dense mangroves fringing the Bay and to the resources of the Bay itself. The small sherd collection has mostly Medium Sandy Ware, which could be earlier, but several reduced Fine Sandy Ware sherds indicate Ave Maria occupation. There are no diagnostic rims. The site has two structures today and could have had a line of two or three structures when occupied. No structures are shown here on the Favereau and Germain (1885) map of the Bay of Vohemar, but the stream mouth is marked as an "accostage" or landing, and there are eight houses inland north of the stream, where we have found a few nondiagnostic sherds.

6. Amboronananana-Dieudonné (07-053: 785.8-1408.5, S13° 22'10"/ E 49° 59' 57") is a tiny site is on the south or right bank of the old estuary, about 0.9 km south-

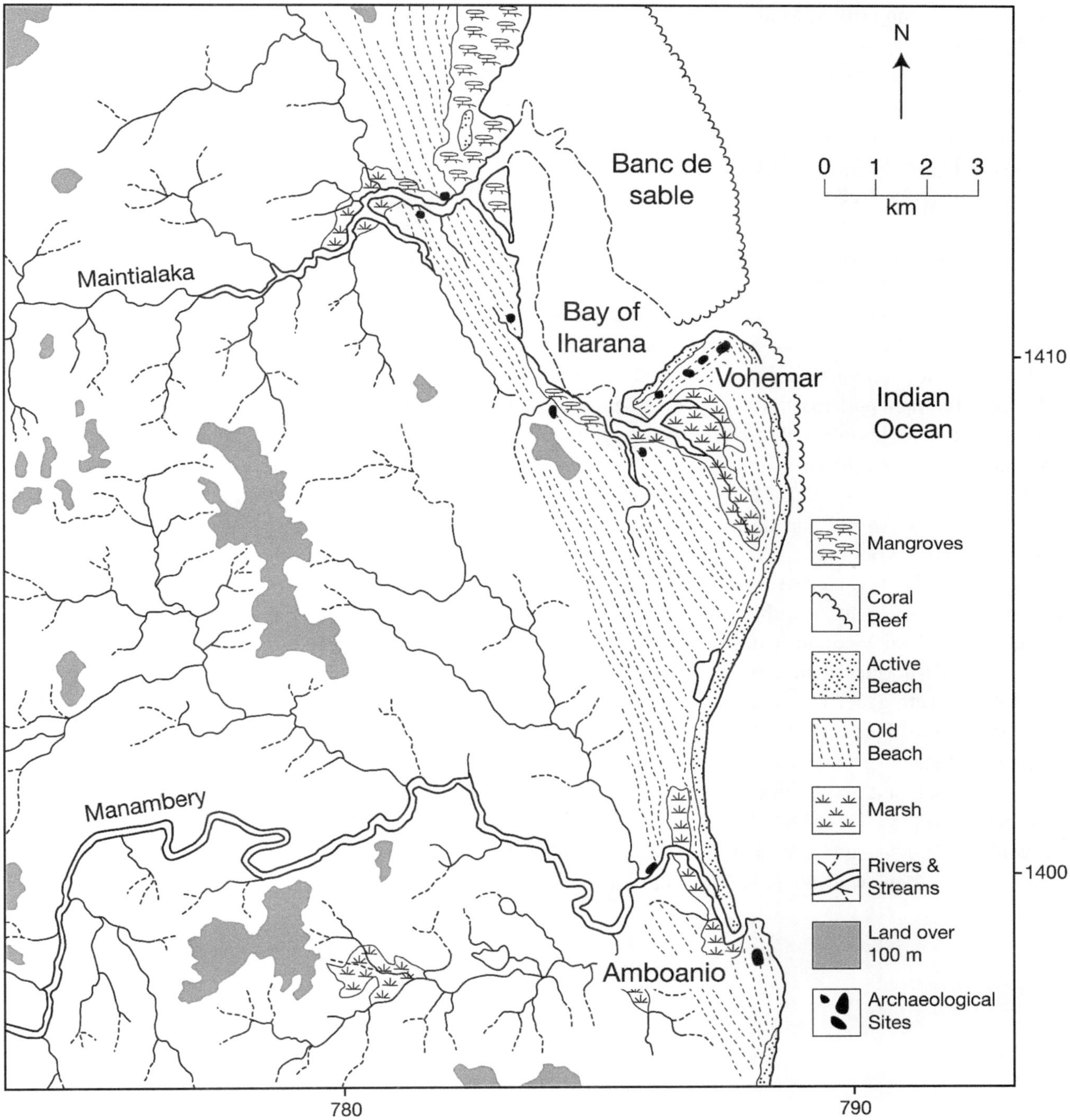

Figure 12.2. Proposed Ave Maria Phase settlements.

southwest of the mosque of Vohemar. It is 45 m from north to south by 25 m, covering about 0.11 ha of a sandy knoll, with rice paddies to the west, north, and east. A substantial sherd scatter, exposed by the recent construction of a new house, contained a majority of Medium Sandy Ware, most oxidized, and a few Rough Ware sherds, some of which are earlier. A substantial minority of the sherds are fine Sandy Ware, about half of which are reduced. Diagnostic among these are the rim of a reduced Fine Ware everted jar with flattened rim (Figure 12.1p), typical of Ave Maria sites in the far northeast near Irodo, and a reduced Sandy Ware bowl with undecorated interior ledge rim (Figure 12.1o). This last is associated with late nineteenth/early twentieth century European imports in the Mananara Valley south of the Bay of Antongil (Wright and Fanony 1992: Fig. 11r, s), and there are such sherds on this site. This indicates that Ave Maria ceramics were used as late as the early colonial period. This settlement perhaps had only one residence, but two structures may be shown in this location on the map of Favereau and Germain (1885).

7. Analamangabe (08-020: 785.9-1400.4: S13° 26' 37"/ E49° 59' 59"). An old and deeply entrenched track comes south from Vohemar, passes Antanambao and Marobengy, goes down to a crossing over the Manambery River, then continues south to Amboanio. Beside the road, we found one reduced Medium Sandy Ware sherd. About 270 m to the east-northeast, farmers report seeing many sherds while cultivating their rice paddies, and we found two similar sherds there. This is probably an Ave Maria Phase site taking advantage of extensive opportunities to build paddies, cut timber, and graze cattle in this area.

8. Amboanio (787.7-1398.0: S13° 28' 03"/ E50° 01' 00'), a parallelogram-shaped fort on a high sand dune outside the limits of our survey, was the main Merina garrison and seat of the local Merina governors from 1820 until about 1890. The satellite image indicates it was small, its ditches measuring about 110 m northeast-southwest and 70 m northwest-southeast, surrounding about .5 ha. According to Bernier (Fleury 1886), in about 1834 the external ditch was about two meters deep, and the stockade within was about two meters high. Cannons were emplaced on each corner. There were residential hamlets nearby. The fort has a thick grass cover, and our one visit yielded few sherds. Clearly, this key site merits further archaeological study.

In sum, during the time of Merina domination and the beginning of French colonization, the port of Vohemar remained diminished in size, in use primarily for the export of cattle to Mauritius and La Réunion and the import of manufactured goods. The construction of the modern town has damaged the underlying archaeological deposits. However, it seems that Ave Maria settlement within the bounds of the earlier town was dispersed in several discrete villages, as is described in nineteenth-century accounts. As in Ambatary times, there are only a few known hamlet sites. Two are close to the larger settlement—both near rice paddies and canoe landings—and to the northwest along on the route north-westward toward the village of Mahasoa on the Manambato River. The route continues on to Daraina, the long-exploited source of placer gold in the headwaters of the Mahakolana River, and on to the town of Ambilobe on the lower Mahavavy River on the northwest coast. This route must have been important, both for late nineteenth-century Merina defenses against the French in the Bay of Diego Suarez and for trade. This road is important today for truck and minibus traffic, and for the driving of cattle from the northwest coast to the modern abattoir and port at Vohemar. Three other hamlets are farther north, one close to the bay at Imaiky and two in the Maintialaka embouchure.

Chapter 13

Cultural Development in the Vohemar Area

The Vohemar survey has been the most difficult of all the surveys we have undertaken in Madagascar. At the time of our fieldwork, we had only 1/100,000 maps, GPS coordinates were often not stable, and we did not have satellite images until our final visits to the area, so it was difficult to record the exact locations of sites. From the perspective of field methods, the survey of areas of relatively dense housing in the modern town was time-consuming, and some landowners simply refused to allow examination of their tracts, which is unusual in Madagascar. However, the most serious difficulties were encountered in analyzing the ceramics and precisely dating the sites. The Vohemarian ceramic tradition is conservative, with slow changes in techniques of fabrication through time. Decorations are rare in all periods and some of the motifs found were used for long spans of time. For example, the arcuate incised motif appeared in the Analabe Phase at least by the eleventh century (Figure 8.2h) and was used until ceramics ceased to be made locally in the Ave Maria Phase (Figure 12.1n), a span of a millennium. This motif is rare in other areas, and it is possible that it had a local emblematic significance in the Vohemar area. Whatever the explanation of the conservatism of decorative motifs in Vohemar, these motifs do little to help us to build a ceramic sequence. In spite of the difficulties, we have built a working sequence based on evidence from sealed and variously dated deposits. However, we emphasize that it is still tentative. One reason we have illustrated so many ceramics is so that, as the sequence is improved, future readers can revise our ascriptions and dating of sites. The following discussion of the general implications of our evidence is based upon this tentative Iharana sequence.

The discovery of the rock shelter of Ambohiposa (784.3-1408.1), with evidence of foragers using stone tools, challenges long-held understandings of the early settlement of Madagascar. This is an example of the discovery of something completely unexpected in the course of fieldwork, a relatively common event in disciplines such as archaeology. Few food remains were preserved, but the chert and obsidian microlithic assemblage includes retouched pointed pieces and chisel-shaped elements elsewhere thought to be arrow tips. We infer a small group of foragers hunting and gathering on the slopes of Ambatomalama.

Radiocarbon dates and the occurrence of oxidized Coarse Sandy Ware sherds suggests this occupation dates to the time of the early villages. However, evidence from Lakaton'i Anja on the Bay of Antsiranana in the far north (Dewar et al. 2013) indicates that foragers using a microlithic technology were established in the far north of Madagascar before 2000 BCE. Three millennia of hunting and gathering may well have had impacts on Madagascar's ecosystems, driving some species to extinction and introducing exotic species such as the African bush pig *(Potamochoerus larvatus)* and the Guinea fowl *(Numidia meleagris)*. We can envision foragers watching the arrival of villagers in sailing canoes with cargoes of domestic animals, rice, iron tools, and ceramics, but we need more evidence to even begin to characterize either early forager impacts on Madagascar's ecosystems or interactions between different populations with different ways of life on Madagascar.

The earliest phase of village life known on the coasts of Madagascar, the eighth to tenth centuries CE, is what we have termed the Ampasimahavelona Phase in the Iharana area. This phase is represented by small village and hamlet sites on the lower estuaries of rivers entering the Bay of Iharana. Given the ecology of estuaries and lagoons, Dewar and Radimilahy predicted the occurrence of such settlements in our original research proposal. (This is an example of the discovery, during fieldwork, of the existence of something previously predicted given theoretical concerns. It is thus a case of the evaluation of an existential proposition with evidence, rather than the evaluation of an explanatory hypothesis, albeit that the term "hypothesis" is frequently misused for such existential propositions.) The villagers used simple undecorated ceramic basins, bowls, and spherical jars and basins made from local chlorite schist. From the larger village of Ampasimahavelona (786.7-1408.1), we have evidence of fishing and shell fishing, but little evidence of animal exploitation or gardening. However, we know that cattle (*Bos* sp.) (Allibert, Argant and Argant 1990) and Asian rice *(Oryza sativa)* (Crowther et al. 2016) were in use on the nearby Comoro Islands. It is likely that such early husbandry will be documented in Madagascar. The Ampasimahavelona Phase evidence supports the proposition that the juxtaposition of rich reef, bay, estuary, and riverine resources would attract early settlement. Most Ampasimahavelona sites develop into communities of the Analabe Phase of the eleventh and twelfth centuries with similar hamlets and small villages, but also a notably larger village on both of the inhabited estuaries. However, these larger villages have not yielded evidence of increased social complexity. During these centuries of early village development, there is little evidence of participation in Indian Ocean trade networks.

During the late twelfth or thirteenth centuries CE, the settlements of the Iharana area were reorganized, and there is evidence of new cultural interactions. Given our knowledge of other parts of northern Madagascar and the Comoros, we expected to define these phases, and we expected the evidence of them to be critical in evaluating hypotheses regarding the emergence of trading ports. This is an example of the testing of explanatory propositions with the evidence recorded during fieldwork. During the Razanakoto Phase of the twelfth to fourteenth centuries, densely occupied hamlet sites formed near the embouchures and linear villages on beaches faced reefs of the Bay and the Ocean. The local tradition of basins and spherical jars continued, but in-turned bowls and inverted jars appear, the former with red slips and the latter with incised and impressed designs. These new ceramic features are similar to ceramics of the eleventh to the fourteenth centuries from the port town of Mahilaka and related towns on the Comoros. Lathe-turned chlorite schist basins and tops, some perhaps made in Vohemar, were transported to Mahilaka, the Comoros, and the east coast of Africa (Radimilahy 1998). In return, glazed ceramics from the Persian Gulf and some glazed stone wares and porcelains from East Asia reached the Iharana area. However, neither earlier archaeological projects, nor our intensive surveys, have revealed a larger town near the Bay of Iharana that could have served as a point of exchange of local for imported commodities.

Two contrasting hypotheses might explain this seeming absence. The first hypothesis was suggested by Pierre Vérin (1975, 1986). Inferring from the scarcity of material earlier than the fourteenth century in the collections from the earlier excavations of the cemetery that there was no larger twelfth to thirteenth century town, he proposed that the growth of a twelfth to thirteenth century town on the shores of the Bay of Iharana had been stifled by the growth of Mahilaka, 150 km away on the northwest coast. He remarked that Mahilaka has easier access to the East Coast of Africa and the Middle East beyond, whereas Vohemar has easier access to Southeast Asia and China beyond. The possibilities of direct Southeast Asian and Chinese contact with Vohemar is supported by the preponderance of ceramics imported from those regions in the cemetery. If Vérin's hypothesis—focused on the dynamics of the Indian Ocean trade networks—is correct, from the twelfth and thirteenth centuries CE we would find only the remains of smaller settlements with limited traces of exported and imported commodities in the Vohemar region. Only after the decline of Mahilaka, about CE 1400, would Vohemar be able to take advantage of its excellent harbor on the lagoon and its estuaries, and, perhaps with the aid of refugees from Mahilaka, grow into a thriving point of exchange. The obvious contrasting hypothesis is that Vohemar, in its rich estuarine environment far from Mahilaka, developed slowly from its Analabe roots, and expanded when Mahilaka diminished, for whatever reasons. If this null hypothesis—focused on local ecological dynamics—is true, we had somehow missed the main Rajanakoto Phase settlement during our surveys. Fortunately, we were able to return to Vohemar in 2018 and survey areas neglected in earlier seasons. The most likely location for a larger settlement, Analabe Centre (787.5-1408.2), was a large twelfth to thirteenth century village of about two hectares. While relatively large, it appears to have been local in orientation, lacking evidence of social complexity or significant involvement in the long-range Indian Ocean trade. This evidence appears to support Vérin's hypothesis of local decline in the shadow of Mahilaka and negates the contrasting hypothesis of steady local growth.

In the late fourteenth or early fifteenth century, with the decline of Mahilaka, Vohemar emerged as a large and prosperous port. This has long been known from both sixteenth- and seventeenth-century documents and from knowledge of the nearby cemeteries. However, the exact location of the actual town was unclear. Our survey examined many locations without success, but finally found direct evidence of a fourteenth- to sixteenth-century town in the Ambatary quarter of the modern town (786.6-1409.8). This is an example of the discovery during fieldwork of the existence of something predicted by historical evidence. It is thus another case of the evaluation of an existential proposition with evidence, rather than the evaluation of an explanatory hypothesis. During the Ambatary Phase of the fifteenth and sixteenth centuries, the region was dominated by this new settlement, which covered at least 13 ha (directly under the heart of the modern town) in an optimal location vis-à-vis the deepwater anchorage in the Bay of Iharana, where previously there were only beach camps and villages. There were a few nearby hamlets associated with areas that today are major rice paddies. The syncretic ceramic traditions of the Razanakoto Phase continue, but with innovations such as higher-temperature ceramic firing and the use of larger, heavier vessels in each shape class. The trade connections also flourished, with continuing production and export of chlorite schist basins. Durable imports included predominantly Chinese blue-and-white porcelain, with limited Iberian and Near Eastern imports.

In the seventeenth and early eighteenth centuries, during the Patrick Phase, Vohemar town diminished in size, perhaps breaking into several adjacent villages, and a new large village flourished to the south (787.8-1407.5). There seems to have been a return to a pattern of large villages surrounded by hamlets, as first noted in the Analabe Phase. As in that earlier phase, the settlements of the Iharana area are local in focus. This was probably a consequence of new political and economic conditions in the Indian Ocean. The Portuguese and Dutch had taken control of long-distance trade; the Islamized traders remained as local agents (Newitt 1978). By the end of the seventeenth century, the Omanis had taken control of the East Coast of Africa, and European pirates were becoming established in Madagascar (Bialuschewski 2005). It is not surprising that the major Patrick Phase settlement was inland, hidden from threats coming across the sea. The reduced flow of imported pottery to the villages of the Vohemar area manifests these changes. Some Chinese blue-and-white porcelain was still imported, and we have a possible sherd of an Omani ware.

In the late eighteenth century, during the provisional Ave Maria Phase, the remnants of old Vohemar had clearly disintegrated into several villages scattered across the ruins. One of these had a blacksmith's workshop (786.8-1410.0). Documents indicate that during the eighteenth century, Sakalava nobles from the northwest coast had established themselves in the Iharana area. By the mid nineteenth century several other ethnic groups were represented. There was a customs post, a detachment of Merina soldiers, and the installations of merchants and cattle exporters. The main Merina garrison and the local governor were at Amboanio, a parallelogram-shaped fort on a high sand dune 13 km south of Vohemar, outside the limits of our intensive survey. Other than Vohemar and Amboanio, there were only hamlets in the area. The only identified imported item is a white glazed sherd, probably of English manufacture.

It is possible to make a tentative measure of changing population during this long and dynamic history. By measuring the known sites of each phase and adding their areas, we can—given a number of assumptions—make a rough proxy of the minimal settled population of the phase. We recognize that even in the intensively surveyed area around Vohemar, some sites remain unknown, hidden under thick vegetation or urban trash, so this is a minimal estimate. We assume that residential density, and thus population density, remained roughly constant during the millennium under consideration and thus settled area can be used as a proxy for population, even though we know that larger settlements are often denser than smaller settlements. We assume that all sites were occupied during the entire time span of each phase, even though we know that settlements could have been moved during the span of a phase. With more complete survey and better knowledge of architecture in each phase, we could make much better estimates (Dewar 1991, 2007), but this is a task for the future. Plotting our rough estimates against time (Figure 13.1), we see that there was an initial slow growth in settlement during the ninth to eleventh centuries CE, seen primarily in the larger size of the central villages. There was a drop in settled area in the twelfth to thirteenth centuries, perhaps to about half of what was occupied before. During the fourteenth century there was at least a rapid tripling of settled area as the large port town of Vohemar emerged, perhaps because of the movement of refugees from Mahilaka. During the seventeenth and early eighteenth centuries, the port diminished in size, but a new large village developed to the south, and overall settled area remained high. In the later eighteenth and nineteenth centuries, however, settlement appears to have diminished.

Though the samples of food remains we were able to collect are relatively few and mostly small, we can provide an outline of relations between early Vohemarians and the natural environment of the Iharana area (see Appendix D). We found so few plant remains that we can say little, other than that settlement locations suggest that both irrigated and rain-fed fields were exploited. Of the earlier sites, only the large central village of Analabe-Régis, dated to about CE 1000, has yielded a useful sample of animal remains. These are primarily marine fish, shellfish, and turtles. There are few bones of hunted small terrestrial tortoises and birds. There are no domesticates. The next oldest sample is a large one from the Ambatary locality of the early town of Vohemar, dated to about CE 1400. This also has a range of marine fish, shellfish, and turtles. There are, however, the remains of domestic cow, probably of sheep or goat, and of chicken. Small lemurs, birds (especially ducks), and terrestrial tortoises were hunted. The Analabe-Patrick locality, dated to about 1700 CE, also has the same range of marine remains and a single probable cow bone. The later layers of the Vohemar-Ave Maria locality, dated to about 1800, have the usual suite of marine fish, shellfish, and turtle; domestic cows and chickens; and a few remains of hunted birds, bats, and perhaps terrestrial tortoises. In brief, around the Bay of Iharana, marine sources probably provided most of people's daily meat, with relatively little hunting. Sometime before 1400, domestic cattle and fowl were added to the repertoire.

We can cautiously propose some correlations between this archaeological sequence and the traditional histories preserved in oral traditions. Before the traumas of colonization, the most recent historical transformation remembered was the arrival of Sakalava warriors and their ruling princes. These claimed affiliation with the ruling Zafivolafotsy deme of the Antankarana, and thus are referred to as Antankarana rather than Sakalava in some accounts. Emigrants from East Africa, referred to as Makua and often viewed as dependents of the Sakalava rulers, were certainly in Vohemar by the mid nineteenth century. Hurvitz demonstrated that some of the named ancestors of the ruling Sakalava lineages in the Vohemar area were encountered by the French trader Mayeur in 1775, and it is reasonable to propose that they arrived earlier in the eighteenth century (Hurvitz 1980:19, 98–103). This would correlate with the transition from the Patrick Phase to the Ave Maria Phase. The preceding major transformation emphasized in the traditions was the arrival of the Anjoaty on the northeast coast. For this, the archaeology allows three possibilities. Most recently, they could have arrived at the time of the rapid expansion of the early port of Vohemar in the late fourteenth century. Somewhat earlier, they could have arrived at the time of the expansion of Indian Ocean trade connections at the beginning of the Razanakoto Phase in the twelfth century. At both of these junctures, we have evidence of close relations with the northwest coast port

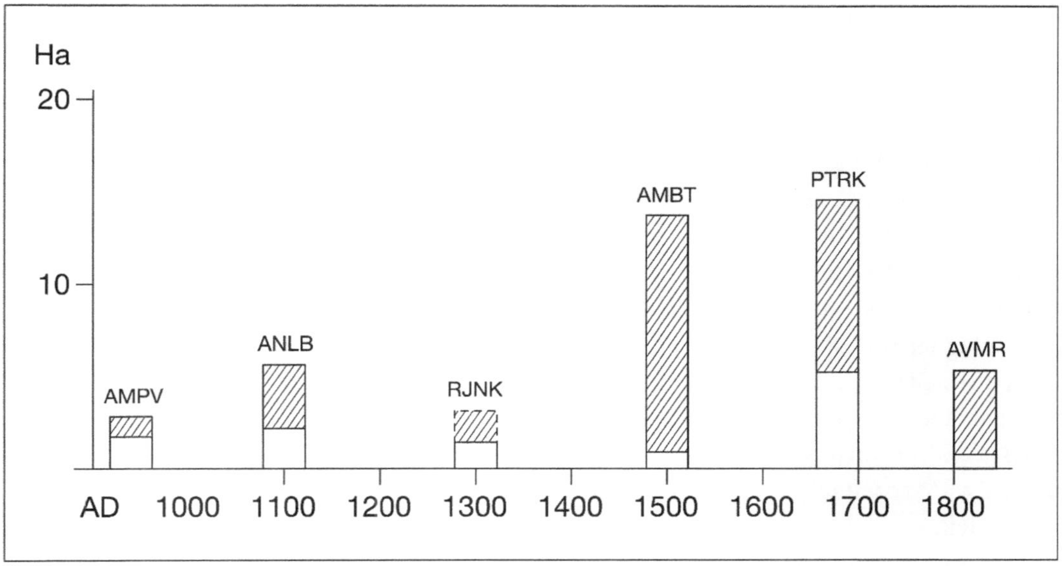

Figure 13.1. Minimal settlement area through time in the Iharana area. The hatched portion of each bar represents the area included in large settlements.

of Mahilaka. Finally, the Anjoaty could have arrived at the time of the first appearance of villages, at the beginning of the Ampasimahavelona Phase, during the eighth or ninth century. It is wise to keep in mind that the ethnogenesis of the Anjoaty has been a long process, and that the historical traditions of the Anjoaty arrival could be a palimpsest of memories of all of these archaeologically attested events. Publication of the work of David Hurvitz and the collection and study of more historical traditions, where possible in the language of the traditionalists, is imperative.

Our initial survey raises many possibilities for future archaeological research in the broader Vohemar region.

First and foremost, resurvey is important, not only to fill in gaps in survey coverage from 2007 to 2014, but to see what has been revealed by cultivation and construction in areas obscured by vegetation during our earlier visits.

Second, the intensively surveyed area should be expanded, both westward into the interior to study more chlorite schist sources and to locate more occupational sites like Ambanimanasy (771.5-1418.9: S13° 16' 47"/ E49° 51' 48"), and northward and southward around the embouchures of the Fahamabana to the south and the Manambato and the Bay of Loky to the north. We would like to know if all embouchures have early occupation during the eighth to eleventh centuries, or only those entering bays and lagoons. Also, we would like to know if, during the twelfth to sixteenth centuries, the embouchures to the north and south developed smaller towns subsidiary to Vohemar, or only villages. We have initiated intensive surveys around some of these, but none is sufficiently comprehensive to allow answers to such questions.

Third, the fourteenth- to fifteenth-century town of Vohemar is in desperate need of urban archaeology. It is not easy to excavate remains under living towns, but the people of modern Vohemar are interested in knowing more and in having a town museum, for both local students and for visitors. At present the town is mostly of wood construction, often on concrete slabs, but there are many courtyards and gardens where excavations would be possible. As more masonry buildings with deep footings are constructed, archaeological opportunities will rapidly diminish, so time is of the essence. In addition to work on the port site under the modern town, excavations on its predecessors are needed, particularly the known large tenth to eleventh century settlement of Analabe-Régis (786.9-1408.7, S13° 22' 05"/ E50° 00' 30"), which has hardly been tested.

Fourth, paleoecological studies are needed, including influx studies of ancient pollen and spores, charcoal studies, stable isotope studies, and perhaps bulk DNA studies (Grealy et al. 2016). The nearest studied locality on the east coast is near Tolagnaro, 1300 km southwards (Virah-Sawmy et al. 2009, 2010). There are not as many appropriate marshes and lakes near the Bay of Iharana as along the coast to the south, but several promising localities exist in the old estuary southeast of Ampasimahavelona (786.7-1408.2) toward Analabe-Patrick.

Fifth, local studies of interaction between early settlers and Madagascar's extinct megafauna are needed. The sites with the early Coarse Ware pottery and the eggshell fragments of a small ratite, perhaps *Mullerornis*—one near Vohemar (788.2-1408.3: S13° 22' 21"/ E50° 01' 13", discussed above) and one on the east side of the Bay of Loky (753.0-1475.3: S12° 46' 07.8"/ E49° 41' 12.6, not yet reported)—need work by specialized teams, similar to the study conducted at Talaky by Parker Pearson et al. (2010) and at Andolonomby/Ambolisatra by MacPhee and Burney (1991; Burney 1993) and by Virah-Sawmy and colleagues (2016).

Like most archaeological projects, the Vohemar survey yielded unexpected discoveries and ambiguous results. However, it provides a first approximation of the development and decline of a port and the region around it on the northeast coast. This tentative developmental overview parallels those available for the west coast ports of Mahilaka (Radimilahy 1998; Wright, Radimilahy, and Allibert 2005) and Boeny (Vérin 1975, 1986; Wright et al. 1996). These three are only a fraction of the many port towns that must have arisen, flourished, and disappeared between the tenth century and the seventeenth. Much more fieldwork will be needed if we are to have a range of cases spanning the economic, political, and conceptual variability we are only beginning to comprehend. Only with such a range of cases can we test basic hypotheses about a range of processes from local to ocean-spanning transregional in scale, and work towards synthetic models in which multiple processes interact in uniquely constituted local geographies. We can only hope that such research can be initiated before a majority these varied sites are transformed by modern coastal development and climate change.

Appendices

Appendix A

A Catalogue of Sites in the Vohemar Area

by Henry T. Wright and Robert Dewar

Note: The coordinates are the center of the site, unless otherwise specified. All Mercator and UTM coordinates have been checked with Google Earth. All UTMs are in Zone 39 L. UTM coordinates are rounded to the nearest 5 meters. The site numbers are based on Madagascar's local Labordes Grid, which is found on all maps. Each specifies one hectare of terrain, as estimated from the 1:100,000 Institute Géographique National Topographic Map of 1962. Given the scale of this map, there are possible errors of up to 150 m in the Labordes numbers.

Site 765.6-1399.0
Site name: Ambovon'i Rasikajy
Field number: 09-010
Coordinates:
Mercator: S13° 27' 33" / E 49° 48' 46"
UTM: E 0371620-S 8511880
Notebook references: HTW **09**:34–40, 96–97; **14**:34
Illustrations: Figs. 10.3 left, 10.4
Length: NE-SW, Area: .07 ha, Elevation ASL: 49 m
Land use at time of survey: Mosaic of pasture and brush
Ceramics: None
Other items: Chlorite schist—broken cylinders, fragments of tripod legs, and tops
Comments: This is a traditional name for this quarry pit. It is cut into a yellow sandy silt clay with quartz fragments. As in all of the larger pits we examined, vessels had been roughed out with a pick. Those we illustrate in Chapter 10 had been broken during this process. Those that were successfully rough-cut were presumably taken back to settlements for lathe-finishing. During three visits to Ambovon'i Rasikajy, we surveyed widely, looking for datable ceramics, without success.

Site 766.8-1397.1
Site name: Andamoty Northeast
Field number: 14-028
Coordinates:
Mercator: S13° 28' 39" / E49° 49' 01"
UTM: E 0372015-S 8509555
Notebook references: HTW **14**:35
Illustrations: None
Length: 30 m NE-SW, Width: 20 m, Area: 01 ha, Elevation ASL: 94 m
Land use at time of survey: Pasture
Ceramics: None
Other items: Chlorite schist—fragments of tops

Comments: Between the northwest and southeast quarry pits, the path—about 340 m distance—is marked by at least four discarded unfinished tops, and there are more tops fragments around the large quarry pit. This suggests a focus on tops in some pits. However, it would be more sensible to make the tops and the tripod vessel in the same place, to be certain that they were the same size and could be made to fit well. It seems more likely that recent visitors removed tripod vessel fragments from this site.

Site 766.9-1396.8
Site name: Andamoty Southwest
Field number: 14-027
Coordinates:
Mercator: S13° 28' 47.6"/E49° 49' 06.4"
UTM: E 0372110-S 8509480
Notebook references: HTW **14**: 35
Illustrations: None
Length: 7 m E-W, Width: 4 m, Area: 01 ha, Elevation ASL: 84 m
Land use at time of survey: Pasture (brush and tamarind trees)
Ceramics: None
Other items: Chlorite schist—fragments of very coarse material
Comments: The pit is small, only 7 m by 6 m and about a meter deep. There is a rough paving of coarse chlorite schist fragments in its bottom, perhaps signaling that the pit is not worth further effort at exploitation.

Site 767.8-1396.3
Site name: Madirobe
Field number: 14-029
Coordinates:
Mercator: S13° 29' 02.5"/ E49° 49' 40"
UTM: E 0373125-S 8509065
Notebook references: HTW **14**:37–38
Illustrations: Fig 10.3 right
Length: 50 m NE-SW, Width: 16 m, Area: 07 ha, Elevation ASL: 60 m
Land use at time of survey: Mosaic of pasture and brush
Ceramics: None
Other items: Chlorite schist—fragments of tops and tripod vessels, rough fragments
Comments: This site is on a ridge to the southwest of the mountain of Maintirano. It is a complex array of quarry pits. The most recent, to the southwest, is 16 m NE-SW, by 15 m wide, and still about 4 m deep. The surrounding spoil piles are up to 3 m high. An older pit to the northeast is about 11 m NW-SE by 8 m wide and 2 m deep. The surrounding spoil piles are about 1.5 m high. Between these two, it is possible that the spoil heaps cover a third, even older, pit. We did not have time to either note the types of chlorite schist fragments or search for ceramics. Soundings in and under the spoil piles would provide samples of debris and perhaps in situ charcoal for radiocarbon dates.

Site 768.0-1395.8
Site name: Madirobe 'Lieu de Culte'
Field number: 14-030
Coordinates:
Mercator: S13° 29' 17.4"/ E49° 49' 4"
UTM: E 037370-S 8508825
Notebook references: HTW **14**:37–38
Illustrations: None
Length: 50 m NE-SW, Width: 16 m, Area: ca .01 ha, Elevation ASL: 55 m
Land use at time of survey: Dense brush
Ceramics: None
Other items: Chlorite schist—unfinished tops, unfinished tripod vessels
Comments: Focused on a roughly rectangular platform of quartz cobbles, about 2 m E-W by 1.5 m. Next to this was a wooden post on which had been skewered several cow skulls. A few meters eastward was a small pile of near-complete tripod vessels, and a bit farther was another small pile of nearly complete tops. We were told that these were brought here from the quarry of Madirobe, only 560 m to the NW. We had no map or image with us when we visited the Madirobe area, and we only later realized that the "Lieu de Culte" was on a terrace close to the Manambery River, just north of an ideal location for a village or base camp for the chlorite schist miners. This area in particular needs further examination.

Site 772.2-1418.9
Site name: Ambanimanasy
Field number: 14-024
Coordinates:
Mercator: S13° 16' 43" / E 49° 51' 54"
UTM: E 0377070-S 8531830
Notebook references: HTW **14**:33–34, 85

Illustrations: Fig. 10.2x–a'
Length: 60 m NE-SW, Width: 15+ m, Area: .2+ ha, Elevation ASL: 36 m
Land use at time of survey: Grassland with scattered bushes and mango trees
Ceramics: Badly weathered sherds on eroded slope midden
Coarse Sandy Ware:
Oxidized: 1 medium plain body
Medium Sandy Ware:
Oxidized:
5 thick plain bodies
15 medium plain bodies
2 heavy hole-mouth jar rims, inner rim thickening (Abtry)
1 spheroidal or hole-mouth jar rim, inner rim thickening (burnished) (Ptrk)
1 heavy bowl, internally thickened rim (Abtry)
Reduced:
1 thick plain body
1 medium plain body
Other items: Though close to the Ambanimanasy chlorite schist source, we found no traces of this material.
Comments: This is a linear site, but on a ridge rather than a beach, overlooking the perennial Ambanimanasy stream to the northwest, from which the site takes its name. Any houses must have been on the flat ridge top, but the grass cover is thick, and nothing was visible there. The ceramics were found in an eroded slope midden northeast of this flat ridge top, a brownish silt with quartz fragments. A number of definite Ambatary Phase rims occur, but only one possible Patrick Phase rim, so this later occupation may be minor. The area is devoted to cattle herding today. Excavations to search for house features and evidence of economic practices are needed.

Site 781.5-1411.1
Site name: Maintialaka Atsimo-Andrefana [SW]
Field number: 08-017
Coordinates:
Mercator: S13° 19' 53" / E 49° 57' 25"
UTM: E 0387080-S8526025
Notebook references: HTW **08**:35, 46; **12**:62
Illustrations: Figs. 7.5t, 8.1, 8.3n, o
Length: 50 m NW-SE, Width: 40 m, Area: .40+ ha, Elevation ASL: 18 m
Land use at time of survey: Mature coconut grove
Ceramics:
Coarse Sandy Ware:
Oxidized:
10 thick plain bodies
5 medium plain bodies
1 thickened round lip basin rim (Ampv)
2 spheroidal or hole-mouth jar rims
Reduced:
1 thick plain body
1 medium plain body
Medium Sandy Ware:
Oxidized:
2 medium plain bodies
1 round lip bowl rim
Reduced:
2 medium plain bodies
Rough Ware:
Oxidized: 3 thick rough bodies
Fine Micaceous ware:
Oxidized: 2 medium plain bodies
Reduced: 4 medium plain bodies
Comments: Site on a sandy terrace on the right bank and about 5 m above the Maintialaka River. Recent pits for making charcoal show .20 m of dark brown sand, with a yellowish white sand below. The coarse sherds appeared to be in the deeper light sand and were only noted in the NE part of the site, covering at least .20 ha. These probably mark an Ampasimahavelona Phase hamlet. Fine micaceous reduced sherds and shell fragments were found in the upper dark sand throughout the site, indicating an Ave Maria Phase village.

Site 781.8-1413.1
Site name: Maintialaka-Antafiambe [NE]
Field number: 08-015
Coordinates:
Mercator: S13° 19' 45" / E 49° 57' 45"
UTM: E 0387610-S 8526270
Notebook references: HTW **08**:34, 49, **12**:62
Illustrations: Figs. 8.1, 8.3h–l
Length: 90 m NE-SW, Width: 70 m, Area: .50 ha, Elevation ASL: 10 m
Land use at time of survey: Mature manioc gardens, mango trees, houses of a small village
Ceramics:
Coarse Sandy Ware:

Oxidized:
21 thick plain bodies (Ampv)
11 medium plain bodies
1 incurved, interior beveled-lip basin rim (Anlb-Rznk)
1 thick tapered rim basin (Ampv)
Reduced:
1 thick plain body
1 medium plain body
Medium Sandy Ware:
Oxidized:
16 medium plain bodies
1 rounded lip bowl rim
1 thickened, flattened bowl rim (Anlb-Rznk)
Reduced:
6 medium plain bodies
1 exterior thickened lip bowl (Rznk-Abtry)
Rough Ware:
Oxidized:
7 thick plain body (Anlb-Ptrk)
11 medium plain body (Anlb-Ptrk)
1 tapered basin rim (Anlb-Ptrk)
1 thickened round lip basin rim (Anlb-Ptrk)
Fine red Karana Ware:
1 thin body (Modern)
1 rim (Modern)

Other items: M. Bezara, a village elder, has an iron cannonball found near the village.

Comments: This site is sparse sherd scatter on a sandy terrace on the left bank of the Maintialaka River. The name was briefly noted by Leigh in 1838 (Allibert 1999). The sediment is a brown sand. Ampasimahavelona, Analabe, and Razanakoto Phase sherds are scattered over at least 0.50 ha. Though seemingly low in density, this scatter marks a long-lived early village. The fine reduced micaceous sherds (not counted or illustrated) in the present village and to its southwest cover an area of about .40 h., marking a small Ave Maria Phase village. This site, the largest in the Maintialaka embouchure, merits further study.

Site 781.9-1412.8
Site name: Maintialaka Atsimo-Atsinanana [SE]
Field number: 08-016
Coordinates:
Mercator: S13° 19' 50" / E 49° 57" 52'
UTM: E 0387835-S8526045

Notebook references: HTW **08**:35, 46; **12**:62
Illustrations: Figs. 7.5s, 8.1, 8.3m
Length: 24 m NE-SW, Width: 15 m, Area: .30 ha, Elevation ASL: 15 m
Land use at time of survey: Freshly burned garden, being prepared for manioc
Ceramics:
Coarse Sandy Ware:
Oxidized:
6 thick plain bodies (Ampv)
3 medium plain bodies
1 thickened round lip basin rim (Ampv)
1 tapered lip basin rim
Reduced:
1 thick plain body
1 medium plain body
Medium Sandy Ware:
Reduced: 1 medium plain body

Comments: Site on a sandy terrace on the right bank and about 5 m above the embouchure of the Maintialaka River. The surface soil is a yellowish sand. There is no evidence of debris other than ceramics. The sherd concentration probably marks an Ampasimahavelona Phase hamlet.

Site 783.2-1410.8
Site Name: Imaiky
Field number: 08-021
Coordinates:
Mercator: S13° 20' 40"/ E 49° 58' 25"
UTM: E0388790-S 8524505

Notebook references: HTW **08**:53
Illustrations: None
Length: N.A., Width: 30 m E-W, Elevation ASL: ca. 20 m
Land use at time of survey: thorny brush
Ceramics:
Fine Sandy Ware:
Reduced: 1 medium plain body (Ave Maria or modern)

Comments: This was probably a linear site overlooking the Bay of Iharana to the east, transected by an old path in which shell debris and a sherd were exposed. We know its width but not its length. This village is shown as a small linear village on the 1962 map from which we have taken the site name. At the time of our visit, the nearest settlement was a village 0.3 km NNE on the shore of the Bay. We found no one to tell us its current name.

Site 783.9-1410.2
Site name: Ambararatra
Field number: 07-052
Coordinates:
Mercator: S13° 21' 58"/ E49° 59' 55"
UTM: E 0389770-S 8522140
Notebook references: HTW **07**:36, **12**:71
Illustrations: None
Length: 50 NW-SE, Width: 30m, Area: .15 ha, Elevation ASL: 8 m
Land use at time of survey: Thorny brush, manioc garden to north, open court around house, scattered mango and coconut trees.
Ceramics:
Coarse Sandy Ware:
Oxidized: 1 thick plain body (Ampv-Anlb)
Medium Sandy Ware:
Oxidized:
5 medium plain bodies
1 thin plain body
Reduced:
2 medium plain bodies
1 round lip bowl rim, interior scraping (Ptrk-Ave Maria)
Fine Sandy Ware:
Reduced: 1 medium graphite-coated body (Ave Maria)
Imported Ware:
White glazed ware: 1 medium body (early 20th c)
Comments: This local name appears on the 1961 map and thus has been used since at least the mid-20th century. A coarse sherd suggests early use and one bowl rim could be Patrick Phase, but the reduced fine ware sherd indicates Ave Maria Phase. The low-density linear sherd scatter suggests a line of a few houses on the sandy ridge, overlooking a stream with rice paddies and the mangroves. The 1885 Favereau and Germain map shows no houses here, and the name "Barraratra" designates a village on a high sand dune 3.5 km NNW of this site, where we found no traces.

Site 784.3-1408.1
Site name: Ambohiposa
Field number: 07-064
Coordinates:
Mercator: S13° 22' 32"/ E 49° 59' 06"
UTM: E 0390085-S 8521190
Notebook references: HTW **07**:25–26, 48–52; **08**:40–43, 69, 83
Illustrations: Figs. 6.2 and 6.3
Length: 4.0m N-S, Width: 1.2 m, Area: 4.8 m^2, Elevation ASL: 54 m
Land use at time of survey: Thorny brush
Other features: There is a scatter of scats of a carnivore, perhaps the fossa (*Cryptoprocta ferox*), after which the shelter is named. In the south end of this shelter is a low heap of rodent bones, largely from the invasive black rat (*Rattus rattus*) and a few from the Madagascan pygmy shrew (*Suncus madagascariensis*), all probably recently eaten by owls (*Tyto alba*) (Goodman, personal communication). This heap obscures a roughly rectangular arrangement of stones, perhaps the remnants of a tomb. About 30 meters to the south is another rock shelter, which was filled with recent coffins.
Ceramics (Both from our North Unit, mixed Layer 3):
Coarse Sandy Ware:
Oxidized: 2 medium
Other items (All from our three small excavations; see Appendix B):
Chert: 241 flakes, 1 microblade, 2 crescents, 2 trapezoids, 1 piercer, 1 scraper
Obsidian: 11 flakes, 3 microblades, and 1 microblade core fragment
Comments: This small rock shelter in the Mesozoic outcrop of Ambatomalama is in a cliff facing east across the southeast of the Bay of Iharana and the sandy beach and dune remnants to its south. The name was given by M. Bemisy, the mayor of Andranonana. Three small stratigraphic soundings in 2007–2008 removed about 25% of the deposit in the shelter. These revealed a humus and a layer of reddish silt and rock fragments sealing three layers of gray sediment with rock fragments, and scattered stone flakes and charcoal. Below these layers is a reddish clayey silt with rounded rock fragments. There was no preserved ancient bone or shell. All deposits were washed through a 1 mm screen and the remnants sorted under magnification. Two AMS dates span the 9th to 12th cs. AD, but the date of the stone tools could be earlier. (See Appendix C.) This is the first evidence of a stone tool industry in Madagascar.
References: Dewar, Radimilahy, Wright, Jacobs, Kelly and Berna 2013:12583–12585, Sup 1–3; Dewar, Radimilahy, and Wright 2015.

Site 785.4-1408.5
Site name: Antsofaly-Andranonana
Field number: 08-009
Coordinates:
Mercator: S13° 22' 13"/ E 49° 59' 41"
UTM: E 0391130-S 8521720
Notebook references: **08**:12, 27, 58–59; **12**:56,59
Illustrations: Figs. 7.1a, 7.5a–h
Length: 80 m E-W, Width: 40 m, Area: .35 ha, Elevation ASL: 3 m
Land use at time of survey: Manioc garden, coconuts, and mango trees
Ceramics:
Coarse Sandy Ware:
Oxidized:
12 thick plain bodies (Ampv)
11 medium plain bodies
1 round lip bowl rim (Ampv-Anlb)
2 thickened round lip bowl rims (Ampv)
1 thickened flat lip basin rim (Ampv-Anlb)
1 internally thickened rim bowl (Anlb)
Reduced: 1 thick plain body
Medium Sandy Ware:
Oxidized:
2 thick plain body
12 medium plain bodies
1 round lip bowl rim (Ampv-Anlb)
1 square section vessel leg (Anlb)
Reduced: 1 thick plain body
Rough Ware:
Oxidized: 7 medium plain bodies
Reduced:
2 medium plain bodies
4 round lip basin rims (Anlb-Ptrk)
1 flat lip basin rim (Anlb-Ptrk)
Comments: This small site faces north over mangroves and the south part of the Bay of Iharana. It is on a low terrace, probably an ancient beach. The soil is a dark brown sand. In spite of its littoral location, it has little or no marine shell. The owner, the late M. Bezano—a "Silamo ny Anguja" (a "Muslim of Anjouan" in the Comoros)—had saved large sherds for us. In our notes, we termed this the "Bezano site," but were later given the above-noted local name. The prevalence of very coarse Sandy Ware, oxidized and often thick ceramics, plus the thickened, rounded basin rim, indicate this was an Ampasimahavelona Phase hamlet. The occurrence of finer sherds, internally thickened bowl rims (Fig. 7.5e), a square leg (Fig. 7.5k), and Rough Ware indicate occupation continued into the Analabe Phase or even the Rajanokoto Phase.

Site 785.6-1409.4
Site name: Vohemar-Hôpital
Field number: 08-008
Coordinates:
Mercator: S13° 21' 50"/ E 49° 60" 00"
UTM: E 0391475-S 8522450
Notebook references: HTW **08**:23; **12**:55
Illustrations: None
Length: 80+ m E-W, Width: 25 m, Area: .20 ha, Elevation ASL: 5 m
Land use at time of survey: driveways, hospital buildings, mango and coconut trees, and sand
Ceramics:
Medium Sandy Ware:
Oxidized: 5 medium plain bodies
Reduced:
2 medium plain bodies
1 flat base fragment, black slip
Fine Sandy Ware:
Oxidized:
5 medium plain bodies
2 medium red-slipped bodies
1 medium combed body
1 shallow bowl rim with oblique flattened lip, brown slip
Reduced:
1 medium plain body (Ave Maria)
2 medium black slip bodies (Ave Maria)
Fine ("Karana") Ware:
Oxidized: 1 thin red-slipped body (Modern)
Comments: We hoped this tract might yield evidence of the 14th–16th century town hidden beneath the modern town. The hospital authorities welcomed our work, and we cored widely between the hospital buildings, but found little. The cores revealed .30 m of gray sand, in which Fine Sandy Ware sherds and a Karana Ware sherd were found, underlain by pale brown sand in which a few Medium Sandy Ware oxidized sherds were noted. Traces earlier than modern times are ephemeral; the hospital tract must be southwest of the early town.

Site 785.8-1409.6
Site name: Vohemar-Jovenna
Field numbers: 08-05, 14-023
Coordinates:
Mercator: S13° 21' 47"/ E 49° 59' 55"
UTM: E 0391565-S 852280
Notebook references: HTW **08**:12, 33; **14**:84
Illustrations: Fig. 7.5o
Length: 30+ m NW-SE, Width: 25+ m, Area: .06 + ha, Elevation ASL: 3 m
Land use at time of survey: Sand lot, industrial dump, with dense housing to the SE, NW, and NE
Ceramics:
Coarse Sandy Ware:
Oxidized:
3 thickened rounded hole-mouth jar rim (Ampv)*
Medium Sandy Ware:
Oxidized:
3 medium plain bodies
1 medium red slipped body (Abtry ?)
1 heavy round lip basin (Ampv-Anlb)
1 medium carinated side, burnished, horizontal incising (Ptrk?)
Reduced:
2 medium plain bodies
1 interior thickened lip, burnished (Abtry)
1 spheroidal or hole-mouth jar rim, burnished, arcuate incised (Ptrk)
Fine Sandy Ware:
Oxidized: 1 spheroidal or hole-mouth jar rim, burnished, arcuate incised (Ptrk)
Rough Ware:
Oxidized: 1 medium body (Anlb-Ptrk)
Comments: This is an irregular sherd scatter of unknown size between the Jovenna station and the modern beach. Sherds were noted in and just below a gray sand humus, but sherds have doubtless been displaced by storms and construction. The occurrence of Coarse Sandy Ware sherds, oxidized and often thick, plus the thickened, rounded jar rim (Fig. 7.5o), indicates this was an ephemeral site in Ampasimahavelona times, with occupation continuing into later phases. It was perhaps simply a place where canoes were beached.

Site 785.8-1408.5
Site name: Amboronana-Dieudonné
Field number: 07-053
Coordinates:
Mercator: S13° 22' 09" / E 49° 59' 57"
UTM: E 0391625-S 8521975
Notebook references: HTW **07**:37**, 12**:71–72
Illustrations: Figs. 11.2a, 12.1o, p
Length: 45 m N-S, Width: 25 m, Area: .10 ha, Elevation ASL: 7 m
Land use at time of survey: Cleaned house lot without vegetation
Ceramics:
Medium Sandy Ware:
Oxidized:
19 medium plain bodies
2 round lip bowl rims
9 everted jar rims (Ptrk)
1 flat, interior thickened, bowl rim (Ave Maria)*
Reduced:
1 medium plain body
2 round lip bowl rims
Fine Sandy Micaceous Ware:
Oxidized:12 medium body
Reduced:
12 medium body (Ave Maria)
1 everted jar rim, flat lip *
Rough Ware:
Oxidized:
2 medium rough bodies
1 tapered basin rim
Imported Ware:
1 blue glazed white ware: "Willow" transfer print (late 19th/early 20th c)
1 white glazed white ware ring base fragment (late 19th/early 20th c)
1 brown glaze cup rim (Modern)
Comments: "Amboronana" refer to the large western suburb of Vohemar. M. Dieudonné is the owner, having recently built his house here. The site is on a terrace on the left bank of the old embouchure. The soil is a light brown sandy silt. It was a very recent hamlet.

Site 785.9-1400.4
Site name: Analamangabe
Field number: 08-020
Coordinates:
Mercator: S13° 26' 37" / E49° 59' 59"
UTM: E 0391860-S 8513535
Notebook references: HTW **08:**44
Illustrations: None
Length: ca. 90 ENE-WSW, Width: ca 35 m, Area: ca. .30 ha, Elevation ASL: 11 m
Land use at time of survey: Cultivated rice paddies, pasture, and (to the north) mature gallery forest
Ceramics:
Fine Sandy Ware:
Reduced: 3 medium body (Ave Maria)
Comments: The name refers to the forest remnant just to the north. The site is on the alluvial terrace of the left bank of the Manambery River. The soil is a brown sandy silt. Here, two paths coming from Vohemar meet: one to the west, on the ancient red sand of the Tatsimian beaches, and one to the east, on the high dunes above the Karimbolian beaches. Bernier passed through here in 1834 (Fleury 1885 III: 266) and noted a village with the "chef" and traders just above the crossing of the Manambery River. The terrace extends over at least 270 m, but the farmers' descriptions suggest sherds are concentrated in a smaller area to the east, for which dimensions are given above. The sediment is a brown silt. The site may have been a small village. To the south of the ford, this path crosses more padis, then zigzags up the slopes and continues to the Merina fort of Amboanio (787.7-1398.0). The lower Manambery was difficult for us to reach. It needs additional survey.

Site 786.4–1409.8
Site name: Vohemar-Ecole Bambino
Field number: 07-006, 08-008
Coordinates:
Mercator: S13° 21' 29.2"/ E 50° 00' 13.3"
UTM: E 0392110-S 8523045
Notebook references: HTW **08**:27–28; **12**:54–55
Illustrations: None
Length: ca 50 m NW-SE, Width: ca 40 m, Area: ca .20 ha, Elevation ASL: 4 m
Land use at time of survey: courtyard between abandoned school buildings and houses
Ceramics: (From initial 2007 surface collection)
Coarse Sandy Ware:
Oxidized: 3 medium plain bodies
Medium Sandy Ware:
Oxidized:
23 medium plain bodies
1 thin plain body
1 spheroidal or hole-mouth jar rims (burnished) (Ptrk)
Reduced:
8 medium plain bodies
3 thin plain bodies
1 shoulder of carinated vessel (burnished)(Ptrk)
3 plain appliqué bodies
Fine Sandy Ware:
Oxidized:
4 medium plain bodies
2 thin plain bodies
Reduced:
4 medium plain bodies
3 thin plain bodies (Ave Maria)
1 thin plain body, interior red slip!
1 small spheroidal or hole-mouth jar rim (burnished)(Ptrk)
Rough Ware:
Reduced: 1 tapered lip basin rim (Anlb-Ptrk)
Fine red slip (Karana) Ware:
1 thin body (late 19th-20th centuries, Modern)
Imported Wares:
White glazed White Ware: 1 medium plain body (Modern)
1 medium body with green transfer print (Modern)
1 medium body with floral motif (Modern)
Comments: The name is that of a Jardin des Enfants closed in 2007, so though it is a local name, it is likely the be soon forgotten by local residents. This site is under dense modern buildings, the courtyard having a thick surficial layer of plastic and other trash, so the dimensions of the modern city block centered on the Bambino sounding are given as the site area. Ambatary Phase sherds from the deepest layer of our small sounding are abraded by wave action and are in a deposit of finely stratified sand, indicating storm damage (see Appendix B). Artifact density is low. One chlorite schist sherd was in the process of being drilled and carved to be a fish net or line weight, suggesting that Ambatary use of this area was for maintaining canoes and nets rather than for habitation. The initial surface collection, in contrast, has much Patrick

Phase, perhaps some Ave Maria Phase, and much modern material.

Site 786.4-1408.7
Site name: Amboronana Avaratra-Atsinanana [NE]
Field numbers: 08-003 and 08-004
Coordinates: The site as a whole is given the coordinates of the denser northeastern area:

Mercator: S13° 22' 08"/ E 50° 00' 10"
UTM: E 0392405-S 8521620

Notebook references: HTW **08**:22; **12**:61
Illustrations: Figs. 10.2p–s, 11.1a
Length: 80 m NNE-SSW, Width: 30 m, Area: .24 ha, Elevation ASL: 6 m
Land use at time of survey: pasture, manioc garden, mango trees

08-003

From the southerly area, recorded in the field as collection area 08-003, we have a sample with few diagnostic sherds.

Mercator: S13° 22' 08"/ E 50° 00' 10"
UTM: E 0391912-S 8521855

Ceramics:
- Coarse Sandy Ware:
  - Oxidized:
    - 5 thick plain bodies (Ampv-Anlb)
    - 21 medium plain bodies
    - 1 round lip bowl rim
  - Reduced:
    - 1 thick plain body (Ampv-Anlb)
    - 3 medium plain bodies
- Medium Sandy Ware:
  - Oxidized:
    - 9 medium plain bodies
    - 1 thickened round lip bowl (Ampv-Anlb)
  - Reduced:
    - 4 medium plain bodies
    - 1 medium exterior combed body
    - 1 slipped shoulder, interior combed
- Rough Ware:
  - Oxidized:
    - 2 thick rough bodies (Anlb-Ptrk)
    - 10 medium rough bodies (Anlb-Ptrk)
  - Reduced:
    - 1 medium rough body (Anlb-Ptrk)
    - 1 round lip basin (Anlb-Ptrk)

Comments: This part of the site is on a terrace facing east over the embayment of the old estuary, now rice paddies, perhaps formerly marsh. The soil is a yellowish sandy silt. This small southern collection had a strong early representation—probably Analabe Phase, given the range of Rough Ware sherds and the lack of anything definitely later.

08-004

From the northerly area, recorded as collection area 08-004, we have a larger collection. In 2013, the Sealinks team excavated here, but study of their collection has not yet been possible.

Mercator: S13° 22' 06"/ E 50° 00' 06"
UTM: E 0391910-S 8521910

Ceramics:
- Coarse Sandy Ware:
  - Oxidized: 1 thick plain body (Ampv)
  - Reduced: 4 medium plain bodies
- Medium Sandy Ware:
  - Oxidized:
    - 15 medium plain bodies
    - 2 medium grooved bodies
    - 1 heavy flat lip basin rim (Ambtry)
    - 6 round lip bowl rim
    - 1 thickened round lip bowl rim (Ampv-Anlb)
    - 2 shallow bowls, interior ledge rims (Ambtry)
    - 1 burnished jar shoulder (Ptrk)
  - Reduced:
    - 5 medium plain bodies
    - 1 rounded lip bowl
    - 1 rounded thickened lip bowl
    - 1 spheroidal hole-mouth jar, internally thickened rounded rim (Ptrk?)
    - 1 heavy hole-mouth jar, rounded rim, exterior combed (Ambtry)

Comments: This site is on a terrace facing north over the embayment of the old estuary—now rice paddies, but formerly mangroves. The soil is similar to the southern area. There are only a few possibly early sherds in this north part of the area, but early occupation is perhaps masked by later deposits. The heavy bowl and hole-mouth jar rims and the ledge rim bowls are Ambatary Phase. Some of the sherds may be Patrick Phase, but scarcity of burnished sherds is puzzling. It is possible that this part of the site is the focus of later occupation, because the site was a canoe landing for people crossing the embouchure to or from the large Ambatary town.

Site 786.5-1409.7
Site name: Vohemar-Bureau de Poste
Field number: 14-020
Coordinates:

Mercator: S13° 21' 30"/ E 50° 00' 15"
UTM: E 0392185-S 8522970

Notebook references: None
Illustrations: None
Length: 120 m NE-SW, Width: 40 m, Area: .48 ha, Elevation ASL: 7 m
Land use at time of survey: Government buildings, sheds, mango trees
Ceramics: In the dripline of the post office building, we retrieved a few Medium Sandy oxidized and reduced sherds, of which two had burnished reddish-orange slips that indicated Ambatary Phase occupation. There were also some Fine Sandy reduced medium sherds, probably from Ave Maria occupation We have neither drawings nor statistics for these sherds.
Comments: These few sherds indicate that the Ambatary town extended at least this far to the southwest. Satellite images indicate several large gardens north of the Bureau de Poste, where perhaps excavation would yield useful stratification.

Site 786.6-1408.4
Site name: Ambondronana Atsinanana
Field number: 08-010
Coordinates:

Mercator: S13° 22' 15"/ E 50° 00' 25"
UTM: E 0392410-S 8521575

Notebook references: HTW **08**:26; **12**:56–57
Illustrations: Fig. 7.5o
Length: 70 m NW-SE, Width: 25 m, Area: .20 ha, Elevation ASL: 7 m
Land use at time of survey: brush, coconut, mango trees, small field house
Ceramics:
Coarse Sandy Ware:
Oxidized:
6 thick plain bodies (Ampv)
8 medium plain bodies (Ampv-Anlb)
1 flat lip basin (Ampv-Anlb)
1 possible lug handle fragment (Ampv)
1 thickened round lip bowl (Ampv)
1 thickened flat lip bowl (Ampv)
2 round lip bowls (Ampv-Anlb
Reduced:
1 thick plain body (Ampv)
1 medium plain body (Ampv-Anlb)
Medium Sandy Ware:
Oxidized:
6 thick plain bodies (Ampv-Anlb)
21 medium plain bodies
1 thickened rounded basin rim (Ampv)
Reduced:
2 medium plain bodies
1 spheroidal or hole-mouth jar rim (Ampv-Anlb)
Rough Ware:
Oxidized: 3 medium body (Anlb-Ptrk)

Comments: This small sherd scatter is on a terrace facing east across the old estuary. Today it is an area of rich rice paddies. Thick vegetation prevented assessment of the soil. The high proportions of coarse and oxidized sherds and the thickened rims on basins and hole-mouth jars indicate this was an Ampasimahavelona Phase hamlet. The Rough Ware sherds indicate occupation continues into the succeeding Analabe Phase (10th–11th c).

Site 786.6-1409.8
Site Name: Ambatary
Field number: 09-011
Coordinates:

Mercator: S13° 21' 30"/ E50° 00' 24"
UTM: E 0392425-S 8523070

Notebook references: HTW **09:**42–45, 50–51, 81–85
Illustrations: Figs. 10.1, 10.2c
Length: 45 m NE-SW, Width: 40 m, Area: ca 13 ha, Elevation ASL: 8 m
Land use at time of survey: Brush, manioc, scattered houses with bananas and coconuts
Ceramics (From surface of Unit VIII):
Coarse Sandy Ware:
Oxidized: 1 thick plain body (Ampv)
Reduced: 1 thick plain body
Medium Sandy Ware:
Oxidized:
3 medium plain bodies
1 medium red slipped body

1 round lip basin
1 medium carinated bowl, burnished (Ptrk)
Reduced:
2 medium plain bodies
1 interior thickened lip bowl rim, burnished(Abtry)
1 spheroidal or hole-mouth jar rim, burnished, arcuate incised (Ptrk)
Fine Sandy Ware:
Oxidized: 1 medium body
Rough Ware:
Oxidized: 1 medium body (Anlb-Ptrk)
Other items: Chlorite schist—part of a large hemispheroidal spindle whorl (Fig. 10.2c)
Comments: We were drawn to this locality by the presence of a mound on the higher sand ridge that forms the center of Vohemar. Excavation showed that this mound was composed of more than a meter of lenses of trash, mostly from the fifteenth century (see Appendices B and C). The mound extended under the street to the west and north, and under the location of a modern house to the northeast. It was at least 35 m NE-SW by 25 m. Several inhabitants of the quartier assured us that the site name came from an artillery battery placed by French troops in 1941–1942. We collected an area comprising about one quarter of a city block, defined by the grid emplaced after 1895, long after the early town was abandoned. Most of the ceramics have a hard sandy body and lightly burnished red or orange surface and are definitive of the Ambatary Phase.

Site 786.7-1408.1
Site name: Ampasimahavelona
Field number: 08-011, 08-012
Coordinates:
Northwest (08-11):
Mercator: S13° 22' 20"/ E 50° 00' 25"
UTM: E 0392490-S 8521415
Southeast (08-12):
Mercator: S13° 22' 25"/ E 50° 00' 30"
UTM: E 0392565-S 8521335
Notebook references: HTW **08**:26, 28–30, 38–39, 47–48, 69, 83; **09**:27–25; **12**:63–64
Illustrations: Figs. 7.1b, 7.2–7.4
Length: 185 m NW-SE, Width: 90 m, Area: 1.1 ha, Elevation ASL: 7 m
Land use at time of survey: houses and manioc gardens with banana and mango trees
Other features: Possible trace of a ditch or path on southwest edge of the site

Ceramics (2008 collections, North Area):
Coarse Sandy Ware:
Oxidized:
13 thick plain bodies (Ampv) (3 Applq)
22 medium plain bodies (1 Applq)
2 thickened rounded lip basin rims (Apmv)
1 incurved flat lip basin rim
3 tripod leg fragments, square section (Anlb-Rznk)
3 lug fragments (Ampv)
2 flat base fragments
Reduced:
3 thick plain bodies
7 medium plain bodies (2 Applq)
1 spheroidal or hole-mouth, rounded lip jar rim 1 (Applq)
Medium Sandy Ware:
Oxidized:
5 thick plain bodies
22 medium plain bodies
5 round lip bowl rims
1 internally thickened bowl rim (Anlb-Rznk)
1 spheroidal or hole-mouth, rounded-lip jar rim (Ampv)
Reduced:
1 thick plain body
1 medium plain body
Rough Ware:
Oxidized:
1 thick plain body (Anlb-Ptrk)
4 medium plain bodies (Anlb-Ptrk)
1 tapered rim basin rim (Anlb-Ptrk)
1 flat rim basin rim (Anlb-Ptrk)
Other:
Fine green chlorite schist
3 carved body fragments (Ampv)
3 lathe-turned body fragments (Anlb-Abtry)
Crystal quartz: 1 possible blade core

Ceramics (2008 collections, South Area):
Coarse Sandy Ware:
Oxidized:
8 thick plain bodies (Ampv)
13 medium plain bodies

4 tapered rim basin rims
11 thickened rounded lip basin rims (Apmv)
2 incurved flat lip basin rims
1 rounded lip bowl rim
1 ring base fragment (Anlb-Rznk)
3 tripod leg fragments, square section (Anlb-Rznk)
1 tripod foot fragment, oval section (Rznk)
1 flat base fragment
Reduced:
1 thick plain body
1 medium plain body
1 internally thickened bowl rim (Anlb-Rznk)
1 spheroidal or hole-mouth, rounded lip jar rim
Medium Sandy Ware:
Oxidized:
2 thick plain bodies
2 medium plain bodies
2 round lip bowl rim
1 flat base fragment
Reduced:
1 thick plain body
1 medium plain body
Rough Ware:
Oxidized:
2 medium plain bodies (Anlb-Ptrk)
1 tapered rim basin rim (Anlb-Ptrk)
2 flat rim basin rims (Anlb-Ptrk)
Other:
Fine green chlorite schist
1 carved body fragment (Ampv)
1 lathe-turned body fragment (Anlb-Abtry)
2 carved flat basin rims (Ampv)
1 lathe-turned grooved basin rim (Anlb-Abtry)
Quartz: 1 flake

Comments: This site is located on an eroded terrace facing northeast toward the old estuary—today rice paddies. The name was given by the owner, the late M. Frederique, and is not known outside his family. The site's deep dark brown silty sand is disturbed by cultivation. The collections reported above are surface finds from 2008 and samples from our soundings (see Appendix B) or from the 2013 Sealinks excavations. AMS dates from the deepest of our 2009 sounding indicate the earliest Ampasimahavelona Phase dates between the late 9th to early 11th centuries AD (see Appendix C). Note that some Ampasimahavelona Phase basin and jar sherds have plain appliqué on the exterior, an attribute found locally only at this site, though also known from 9th–11th c assemblages from the eastern highlands (Gabler 2005) and the central east coast (Rakotoarisoa et al. 2008). Occupation continued into the Analabe Phase. The Sealinks excavations found Razanakoto Phase (12th–13th c) burials on the south part of the site (Pomerantz 2017).

Site 786.7-1409.8
Site name: Vohemar-Grandidier
Field numbers: 09-008, 14-019
Coordinates:
Mercator: S13° 21' 30" / E 50° 00' 25"
UTM: E 0392480-S 8523040
Notebook references: HTW **09**:29–31, **14**:83
Illustrations: Fig. 10.2j–l
Length: 120 m NE-SW, Width: 70 m, Area: .9 ha, Elevation ASL: 7 m
Land use at time of survey: houses, gardens, coconut trees
Ceramics:
Medium Sandy Ware:
Oxidized:
1 medium plain body
2 medium burnished bodies (Abtry-Ptrk)
1 medium broad incised body
1 medium body, interior red slip (Abtry-Ptrk)
1 thickened round lip bowl (Ptrk)
1 heavy shallow in-turned bowl, flat, inwardly beveled rim (Ambtry)
1 spheroidal or hole-mouth jar, wavy incised (burnished) (Ptrk)
1 spheroidal or hole-mouth jar, internally thickened lip (burnished) (Ptrk)
Reduced:
2 medium black-coated bodies (Ave Maria)
1 ring base fragment
Fine Red-slipped (Karana) Ware:
Oxidized: 1 medium body (Modern)

Comments: Wall construction in 2009 cut into dark brown sand and midden deposits with red-burnished sandy sherds, including a heavy incurved bowl with flattened lip (Fig. 10.2j), certainly Ambatary Phase, and two out-turned hole-mouth jars, one plain and one with wavy incising (Fig. 10.2k, l)—perhaps Patrick Phase. A reduced sherd with black coating is probably Ave Maria. The deposits northwest of Rue Grandidier are 35 to 40 cm deep, while those to the southeast thin out to 20 to 30 cm deep and have few sherds.

Site 786.8-1409.9
Site name: Vohemar-Ecole St. Joseph
Field number: 07-018
Coordinates:
Mercator: S13° 21' 20" / E 50° 00' 25"
UTM: E 0392435-S 8523290
Notebook references: HTW **12:**97–98
Illustrations: None
Length: 70 m NE-SW, Width: 65 m, Area: .46 ha, Elevation ASL: 8 m
Land use at time of survey: Secondary school yard and buildings
Ceramics (2007 collection)
Coarse Sandy Ware:
Oxidized: 1 medium plain body
Reduced: 1 thick plain body (Ampv-Anlb)
Medium Sandy Ware:
Oxidized:
32 medium plain bodies (6 burnished) (Ptrk)
1 crude bowl with interior thickened rim
1 round lip basin
1 round lip basin with incised zigzag (Ambtry)
1 carinated bowl with externally thickened lip (burnished) (Ptrk)
1 carination with incised zigzag (burnished) (Ambtry)
1 spheroidal or hole-mouth jar rim
Reduced:
12 medium plain bodies (7 burnished)
3 thin plain bodies (burnished) (Ptrk)
1 carination with wavy incised (Ptrk)
3 spheroidal or hole-mouth jar rims (burnished) (Ptrk)
1 everted neck jar rim (burnished) (Ptrk)
1 flat base fragment (burnished) (Ptrk)
Fine red-slipped (Karana) Ware:
Oxidized: 5 medium bodies (Ave Maria-Modern)
Imported Wares:
White-glazed White Ware, plain: 1 medium body (Modern)
Floral motif: 1 medium body (Early 20th c)
Yellow-glazed Fine Tan Ware: 1 medium body (Modern)
Brown-glazed stone ware, White interior glaze: 1 medium body (Modern)
Comments: This site is located on the higher recent beach facing northwest over the Bay of Iharana and the Banc de Sable. The surface sediment is a light brown sand. As often in Vohemar, there are a few coarse sherds, which may be early. There is definite Ambatary and much Patrick Phase in our sherd collection. Since there are no traces in the administrative area to the east until one reaches the neighborhood of Ave Maria, this may be the northern extremity of the Ambatary town. This area—west of Ecole St. Joseph and the nearby cathedral—has much open space, and perhaps here archaeologists can find evidence of the transition from Ambatary to Patrick Phase material culture. There is little evidence of Ave Maria Phase here—perhaps another indication that the earlier town had become disjunct neighborhoods with empty spaces between.

Site 786.7-1410.1
Site name: Vohemar-Tribunal
Field number: 07-015
Coordinates:
Mercator: S13° 21' 15" / E 50° 00' 30"
UTM: E 0392550-S 8523410
Notebook references: HTW **12**
Illustrations: Fig. 10.2e, h
Length: 45 m NE-SW, Width: 40 m, Area: ca .18 ha, Elevation ASL: 7 m
Land use at time of survey: Collection from eroded area near the Tribunal
Ceramics (2007 collection):
Coarse Sandy Ware:
Oxidized: 1 thick plain body (Ampv?)
Reduced: 1 thick plain body
Medium Sandy Ware:
Oxidized:
3 medium plain bodies
1 medium red slipped body
1 round lip basin
1 medium carinated bowl, burnished (Ptrk)
Reduced:
2 medium plain bodies
1 interior thickened lip bowl rim, burnished(Abtry)
1 spheroidal or hole-mouth jar rim, burnished, arcuate incised (Ptrk)
Fine Sandy Ware:
Oxidized: 1 medium body
Rough Ware:
Oxidized: 1 medium body (Anlb-Ptrk)

Comments: The Tribunal is a well-known locality in Vohemar. The 2007 collection is small, and the site was covered with grass in later years. This locality sits on the higher beach facing northwest across the Bay of Iharana and the Banc de Sable. The surface soil is a light brown sand. The thick sherds suggest some early occupation, and there is one diagnostic Ambatary sherd; only Patrick Phase occupation is certain.

Site 786.8-1409.8
Site name: Vohemar-Zandarma
Field number: 07-017
Coordinates:

Mercator: S13° 21' 25"/ E 50° 00' 30"
UTM: E 0392605-S 8522325

Notebook references: HTW **12**:96–97
Illustrations: Figs. 8.3c, d, 10.2m–o, 11.3a, b
Length: 140 m NE-SW, Width: 90 m, Area: 1.26 ha, Elevation ASL: 7 m
Land use at time of survey: Rows of barracks and small houses for police families, as well as parking areas and areas of thorny brush. Also scattered coconut trees.
Ceramics:
Coarse Sandy Ware:
- Oxidized: 1 internally thickened rim basin (Anlb)
- Reduced: 1 heavy flat lip basin (Apmv-Anlb)

Medium Sandy Ware:
- Oxidized:
  - 3 thick plain bodies
  - 21 medium plain bodies (1 burnished)
  - 1 round lip bowl rim
  - 1 flat lip bowl
  - 1 hole-mouth jar
- Reduced:
  - 1 thick plain body
  - 6 medium plain bodies (3 burnished)
  - 1 flat lip basin
  - 1 round lip bowl rim
  - 1 internally thickened bowl rim
  - 1 ledge rim bowl, red slip (Abtry)
  - 2 combed carinations (2 burnished) (Abtry)
  - 1 internally thickened rim bowl rim (burnished) (Abtry)
  - 1 flat lip carinated bowl, arcuate incising (Abtry)
  - 2 plain spheroidal or hole-mouth jars
  - 1 spheroidal or hole-mouth, internally thickened jar rim, arcuate incising (burnished) (Ptrk)
  - 1 spheroidal or hole-mouth, internally thickened jar rim, zigzag incised (burnished) (Ptrk)

Comments: This collection is selected for rim sherds. In 2007, the local children helped with collecting; in 2009, during the resurvey of Vohemar town, access to this block was denied. This location is on low dunes facing north toward the Bay of Iharana. The soil is a brown sand. The coarse bowls suggest there were Analabe field camps or hamlets in this area. The hard sandy wares of the Ambatary and Patrick Phases, often red-slipped or burnished, are more common, suggesting this was a part of the Ambatary town that continued to be occupied in Patrick Phase times.

Site 786.9-1409.8
Site name: Vohemar-Stade
Field number: 07-024
Coordinates:

Mercator: S13° 21' 20" / E 50° 00' 31"
UTM: E 0392660-N 8523315

Notebook references: HTW **09**:4; **12**:100
Illustrations: Fig. 10.2f, g
Length: 80 m NE-SW, Width: 30 m, Area: .24 ha, Elevation ASL: 6 m
Land use at time of survey: Damaged grassy field, weeds
Ceramics:
- Coarse Sandy Ware:
  - Oxidized: 1 thick round lip basin rim (Ampv-Anlb)
- Medium Sandy Ware:
  - Oxidized:
    - 1 thick plain body
    - 32 medium plain bodies
    - 2 thin plain bodies
    - 1 heavy shallow bowl, incurved thickened round lip (burnished) (Abtry)
    - 1 heavy deep bowl, internally thickened round lip (burnished) (Abtry)
    - 1 spheroidal or hole-mouth jar, internally beveled flat lip (burnished) (Abtry)
  - Reduced: 2 medium plain bodies
- Fine Red-slipped (Karana) Ware:
  - Oxidized: 1 medium body (Modern)

Imported Wares:
- White glazed ware, painted floral design (Modern)

Comments: The northeastern limit of dense Ambatary

settlement is on the northwest side of the Stadium. This is an area of brown sand. Coring indicates only a shallow depth. A few sherds suggest early occupation, but the diagnostic rims are Ambatary Phase.

Site 786.8-1410.0
Site Name: Vohemar-Ave Maria
Field numbers: 07-015, 08-019
Coordinates:

Mercator: S13° 21' 20" / E 50° 00' 30
UTM: E 0392600-S 8523390

Notebook references: HTW **07:**43–47, **08:**73–75, **012:**95
Illustrations: Fig 12.1a–n
Length: 65 m NE-SW, Width: 45 m, Area: .30 ha, Elevation ASL: 7 m
Land use at time of survey: Large buildings, including the nunnery and a school; gardens; garbage disposal pits; and a grove of mango trees
Ceramics (2007 surface collection from manioc garden to west, toward the VOH radio bureau):

- Coarse Sandy Ware:
  - Oxidized: 1 thick plain body (Ampv)
  - Reduced: 1 thick plain body
- Medium Sandy Ware:
  - Oxidized:
    - 3 medium plain bodies
    - 1 medium red slipped body
    - 1 round lip basin
    - 1 medium carinated bowl, burnished (Ptrk)
  - Reduced:
    - 2 medium plain bodies
    - 1 interior thickened lip bowl rim, burnished (Abtry)
    - 1 spheroidal or hole-mouth jar rim, burnished, arcuate incised (Ptrk)
- Fine Sandy Ware:
  - Oxidized: 1 medium body (Ave Maria)
  - Reduced: ??
- Rough Ware:
  - Oxidized: 1 medium body (Anlb-Ptrk)

Comments: This site on the same higher beach as is Ambatary (786.6-1409.8). Because of modern streets, industrial buildings, and dense weeds, we cannot know the full extent of this site without more excavation. It would have faced northwestward over the channel entering the bay and the reef of the Banc de Sable. The excavation here (see Appendix B) has earlier layers—perhaps on the periphery or in the gardens of an Analabe or Razanakoto village—and later layers from the Ambatary or Patrick village. It was intensively used in Ave Maria times as a forging and smithing area.

Site 786.8-1410.0
Site name: Vohemar-Ave Maria Antsinanana
Field numbers: 07-013, 14-018
Coordinates:

Mercator: S 13° 21' 15" / E 50° 00' 30"
UTM: E 0392650-S 85234635

Notebook references: HTW **12:**93 **14:**83
Illustrations: Fig. 11.3c, d
Length: 60 m NW-SE, Width: 50 m, Area: .30 ha, Elevation ASL: 7 m
Land use at time of survey: In 2007, an abandoned manioc garden; by 2009, a pasture
Ceramics (2007 collection):

- Medium Sandy Ware:
  - Oxidized:
    - 7 medium plain bodies
    - 2 thin plain bodies (burnished) (Ptrk)
    - 1 round lip bowl rim
    - 2 spheroidal or hole-mouth jar rims
    - 1 square tripod foot fragment (Rzkt)
  - Reduced:
    - 1 thick plain body
    - 2 medium plain bodies (burnished) (Ptrk)
    - 1 thin plain body (burnished) (Ptrk-Ave Maria)

Ceramics (2014 collection):

- Medium Sandy Ware:
  - Oxidized:
    - 2 medium plain bodies
    - 4 thin plain bodies (burnished) (Ptrk)
    - 1 carinated jar rim, burnished, wavy incised(Ptrk)*
    - 1 spheroidal or hole-mouth jar rim, plain
  - Reduced:
    - 1 medium plain body
    - 1 spheroidal or hole-mouth jar rim, combed(Rzkt?)*

Comments: This collection area, immediately east of the Ave Maria compound, was named by our team. Most sherds were in the dripline around a large building, perhaps a former school. The tripod foot fragment and hole-mouth jars suggest some Razanakoto Phase occupation. The burnished sherds indicate Patrick Phase occupation, and the thin reduced burnished sherd may be Ave Maria Phase.

Site 786.8-1410.2
Site name: Vohemar-Bifa
Field number: 07-011
Coordinates:

Mercator: S13° 21' 10" / E 50° 00' 35"
UTM: E 0392700-S 8523580

Notebook references: HTW **08**:19, **12**:92–93
Illustrations: Fig. 9.4a, b
Length: 30+ m NE-SW, Width: 25+ m, Area: .07+ ha, Elevation ASL: 7 m
Land use at time of survey: Garden, house, mango and coconut trees
Ceramics:

Medium Sandy Ware:

Oxidized:

12 medium plain bodies (1 burnished) (Ptrk)
2 round lip bowls
1 everted jar rim, arcuate incised on rim (Rznk)
1 everted jar rim, double dentate zigzag on rim (light brnsh) (Rznk or Ptrk?)

Reduced:

8 medium plain bodies (1 burnished) (Ptrk)
1 thin plain body (1 burnished) (Ptrk)
1 spheroidal or hole-mouth jar rim

Comments: This is probably an extension of the Razanakoto site (see below) to the high beach on the southeast and also a Patrick Phase site—the one from whence came the Patrick Phase jar rim from the Razanakoto site. We named the site after the owner, Mme. Bifa, a prominent citizen. Because of modern streets, housing, and dense weeds, we cannot determine the full extent of this site without excavation. It would have faced northwestward over the channel entering the bay and the reef of the Banc de Sable. The predominance of sherds with medium sandy inclusions, the high proportion of reduced firing, and the everted jar with incising indicate Razanakoto Phase occupation. The burnished sherds and perhaps the jar with dentate decoration indicate Patrick Phase occupation. In both phases, this area would probably have been part of a larger village.

Site 786.9-1408.7
Site name: Analabe-Régis
Field numbers: 43 to 51
Coordinates:

Mercator: S13° 22' 05" / E 50° 00' 30"
UTM: E 0392695-S 8521990

Notebook references: HTW **07**:31, 34–35; **08**:45, 50–52, 77–78
Illustrations: Figs. 8.1b, 8.2
Length: 435 m N-S, Width: 255 m, Area: 5.8 ha, Elevation ASL: 7 m
Land use at time of survey: Brush, mango trees, coconut groves, garden plots for manioc
Ceramics and other items: The scattered surface finds from various parts of Analabe-Régis were not drawn and measured. Counts of the excavated material from our two soundings (illustrated in Figure 8.2) are given in Appendix B.
Comments: This large site is on a low sandy peninsula extending from the right bank of the old estuary northwest into the embayment at the mouth of this estuary. There were marshes on the NE, NW, and SW sides of the peninsula—today these are mostly rice paddies. The sediment is composed of dark brown to gray sand with much shell, mostly *Terebralia* from the mangroves in the estuary, and sherd pavements. The predominant ceramics are handmade bowls or basins of Rough Ware. The other ceramics are mostly similar to Ampasimahavelona ceramics but tend to have finer sand inclusions and thinner walls and are more often reduced. In addition to the simple bowls and basins and the spheroidal (or hole-mouth) jars familiar from Ampasimahavelona, there are bowls with various flattened and interior and exterior thickened rims and carinated bowls. Surface treatments include incising, the impressions of mats, and graphite applied to the rims of bowls. Incising, the application of graphite, and other rim modifications are shared with Mahilaka assemblages found on the northwest coast. Repeated visits to Analabe failed to yield imported ceramics, in contrast to ports like Mahilaka (Radimilahy 1998). So even though Analabe-Régis was the largest site and near an excellent anchorage, it seems to have had little involvement with Indian Ocean trade networks.

Site 786.8-1408.3
Site name: Analabe-Ilôt
Field number: 07-050
Coordinates:

Mercator: S13° 22' 20"/ E 50° 00' 30"
UTM: E 0392655-S 8521510

Notebook references: HTW **07**:29–30, **12**:69–70
Illustrations: Fig. 11.3e, l–q
Length: 70 m NE-SW, Width: 40 m, Area: 0.20 ha, Elevation ASL: 4 m

Land use at time of survey: Paths, coconut trees, grassy pasture
Ceramics:
Coarse Sandy Ware:
Oxidized:
2 thick plain bodies (Ampv-Anlb)
11 medium plain bodies
1 flat lip bowl rim
Reduced:
2 medium plain bodies
Medium Sandy Ware:
Oxidized:
3 thick plain bodies
27 medium plain bodies
2 round lip basin rim (Anlb)
1 flat lip basin rim
1 round lip bowl rim
2 flat lip bowl rims (Ptrk)
1 medium carinated bowl, burnished (Ptrk)
1 spheroidal or hole-mouth, interior thickened jar rim (burnished) (Ptrk)
Reduced:
1 thick plain body
5 medium plain bodies
1 round lip bowl rim
1 everted tapered bowl rim, exterior scraped (Ptrk)
1 round lip bowl (Anlb-Ptrk)
2 thickened lip bowl rims, burnished (Abtry-Ptrk)
1 low ring base fragment
Rough Ware:
Oxidized:
1 round lip basin rim (Anlb-Ptrk)
1 flat lip basin rim (Anlb-Ptrk)
1 tapered lip basin rim (Anlb-Ptrk)
Reduced:
1 thick rough body (Anlb-Ptrk)
1 medium rough body (Anlb-Ptrk)

Other items:
Fine green chlorite schist
1 lathe-turned basin rim
1 lathe-turned top rim
Comments: This name was used by the discoverer of the site, Jean-Yves Régis. This small site has a dense sherd scatter and a ditch and bank to the northeast and southeast. Examination of the images suggests this is the remnant of a canal rather than any kind of fortification. The coarse thick sherds and basin rim suggest early occupation, perhaps Analabe. The collection was studied before the characteristic fabrics and surface colors of Ambatary ceramics were recognized, but one heavy bowl rim suggests some Ambatary occupation, to which the chlorite schist vessels fragments may be ascribed. However, most of the sherds have the burnishing and rim forms of the Patrick Phase.

Site 786.9-1410.2
Site name: Razanakoto
Field numbers: 07-014, 08-002
Coordinates:
Mercator: S13° 21' 15"/ E 50° 00' 35"
UTM: E 0392695-S 8523635
Notebook references: HTW **08**:17–21
Illustrations: Fig. 9.2
Length: 60+ m NE-SW, Width: 30 m, Area: .2+ ha, Elevation ASL: 6 m
Land use at time of survey: gardens, houses, mango and coconut trees, and a large workshop and garage.

Ceramics: (2008 collection, Tract 14)
Coarse Sandy Ware:
Oxidized:
2 rectangular foot fragments (Rzkt)
1 cover handle (Rzkt)
1 tripod foot fragment
Medium Sandy Ware:
Oxidized:
5 thick plain bodies (all brnshd)
34 medium plain bodies
1 flat lip bowl rim
1 everted jar rim, brnshd (Ptrk)
Reduced:
1 thick plain body
21 medium plain bodies
1 flat lip basin rim
1 shallow bowl rim (Rzkt)
1 spheroidal or hole-mouth jar rim
2 everted jar rims
Fine Sandy/ Micaceous Ware:
Oxidized:1 thin plain body
Reduced: 2 thin plain bodies (Ave Maria)
Rough Ware:
Oxidized: 1 thick body (Anlb-Ptrk)

Reduced: 2 medium bodies (Anlb-Ptrk)

Imported Wares:

1 scraffiato bowl side with interior pale green glaze

1 thick body with matte green monochrome glaze

1 modern white glazed body

Comments: The northeast part of the site, southeast of the Relais Baie d'Iharana and in its parking area, is listed as 07-014. The southwest part of the site—in the garden of M. Razanakoto, where our sounding was located—is listed as 08-002 (see Appendix B). This was a linear site on what had been the second beach, the first beach having been obscured by the building of the seawalls and modern hotels. The site faced northwest over the channel, providing access to the port of Vohemar toward the Banc de Sable. The northeast end of the Razanakoto Phase site is disturbed by the parking area, but probably extended for 150 m along the beach and 30 m inland. If so, it covered about .45 ha. The location and form indicate a site good for beaching fishing canoes, a conjecture supported by the discovery of net weights in our sounding (see Appendix B). However, postholes in our sounding indicate there were also houses or other structures suggesting residential use. Our small ceramic samples—predominantly oxidized, of medium thickness and medium texture—include simple and carinated bowls, deep bowls or pots with legs, shallow plates, and spheroidal and everted neck jars with punctate, oblique, and curvilinear incised designs. These are similar to the pottery of the twelfth to fourteenth centuries from Mahilaka. We tentatively use evidence from the sounding (see Appendix B) to define the Razanakoto Phase of the twelfth to early fourteenth centuries. There are also traces of the Ambatary and Ave Maria Phases.

Site 787.0-1407.9
Site name: Jeunesse et Sport
Field number: 08-013
Coordinates:

Mercator: S13° 22' 22"/ E 50° 00' 38"

UTM: E 0392393-S 8521140

Notebook references: HTW **08**:84, **12**:58–59

Illustrations: Figs. 7.1b, 7.5q, r, 8.3e–g

Length: 150 m NW-SE, Width: 15 m, Area: .15 ha, Elevation ASL: 5 m

Land use at time of survey: Manioc gardens, ruined sports center to north

Ceramics:

Coarse Sandy Ware:

Oxidized:

3 thick plain bodies (Ampv)

12 medium plain bodies (Ampv-Anlb)

4 round lip rims (Apmv-Anlb)

1 thickened round lip basin rim (Apmv)

1 heavy flat lip basin rim (Apmv-Anlb)

1 flat plain base (Apmv-Anlb)

1 flat mat-impressed base (Anlb)

Reduced:

2 medium plain bodies

1 heavy flat lip basin rim (Apmv-Anlb)

Medium Sandy Ware:

Oxidized:

2 medium plain bodies

2 heavy round lip basin rims (Apmv-Anlb)

2 heavy flat lip basin rims (Apmv-Anlb)

1 rounded lip bowl rim (Anlb-Ptrk)

1 spheroidal or hole-mouth jar rim (Anlb)

Rough Ware:

Oxidized: 1 hole-mouth jar rim (Anlb-Ptrk)

Reduced:

1 medium body (Anlb-Ptrk)

1 flat lip bin rim (Anlb-Ptrk)

Comments: This site is on a linear ridge, perhaps a levee formation, on the left bank of the old estuary, overlooking rice paddies. The predominance of Coarse Sandy Ware, oxidized and often thick, plus the thickened, rounded jar rim, indicates this was an Ampasimahavelona Phase hamlet. The small hole-mouth jar and the Rough Ware indicate probable Analabe occupation as well. The site seems to have been a small linear hamlet.

Site 787.0-1409.9
Site name: Vohemar-Cimetière
Field number: 07-005
Coordinates:

Mercator: S13° 21' 25" / E 50° 00' 40"

UTM: E 0392860-S 8523210

Notebook references: HTW **12**:90–91

Illustrations: Fig. 10.2a, b

Length: 100 m NW-SE, Width: 70 m, Area: .70 ha, Elevation ASL: 7 m

Land use at time of survey: tombs surrounded by mango trees and a few houses

Ceramics:
Coarse Sandy Ware:
Oxidized: 2 thick plain bodies (Ampv-Anlb)
Reduced: 3 thick plain body (Ampv-Anlb)
Medium Sandy Ware:
Oxidized:
13 medium plain bodies
1 thin plain body
1 round lip basin
1 heavy basin, interior thickened rim (Abtry)*
1 shallow bowl, incurved thickened rim, rounded lip, with dentate zigzag motif (Rzkt-Abtry)*
1 hole-mouth jar rim
Reduced:
2 medium plain bodies
1 thin plain body
1 jar shoulder with double incised zigzag (Rzkt-Abtry)
1 small spheroidal or hole-mouth jar rim
Fine red slipped (Karana) Ware: 1 thin body
Imported wares:
1 modern white glazed body
1 modern stoneware bottle neck

Comments: This is an area of light brown sediment with a low density of sherds of the Razanakoto, Ambatary, and later phases. It is separated from the continuous deep middens of the Ambatary Phase town by an area without traces. This was perhaps an isolated Razanakoto hamlet or small village, which later became a satellite of the Ambatary Phase town of Vohemar.

Site 787.2-1409.0
Site name: Andranomasikely Atsimo
Field number: 08-014
Coordinates:
Mercator: S13° 22' 00" / E 50° 00' 50"
UTM: E 0393160-S 8522080
Notebook references: HTW **08**:24–25; **09:**110, **12:**60
Illustrations: Figs. 9.3k, l, 9.4c, d
Length: 60 m N-S, Width: 30 m, Area: .14+ ha, Elevation ASL: 5 m
Land use at time of survey: Sand blow, houses, coconut groves
Ceramics:
Coarse Sandy Ware:
Oxidized:
19 medium plain bodies
1 everted jar rim, arcuate incising (Rzkt)
Reduced:
4 medium plain bodies
1 flat lip basin rim
Medium Sandy Ware:
Oxidized:
3 medium plain bodies
1 internally thickened flattened bowl rim, red slip (Rzkt)
Reduced:
1 medium plain body
1 internally thickened flattened bowl rim, red slip (Rzkt)
Rough Ware:
Oxidized:
11 medium rough bodies (Anlb-Ptrk)
3 round lip basin rims (Anlb-Ptrk)
2 tapered rim basins (Anlb-Ptrk)

Comments: This small compact site with a dense accumulation of sherds marks a hamlet overlooking (to the west) a small marsh ideal for rice paddies (a branch of the embayment of the old estuary) and toward the abandoned large village site of Analabe-Régis. The diagnostic ceramics—the red slipped bowls with internally thickened flattened rims and the arcuate incised jar—all have close parallels from Mahilaka and Razanakoto.

Site 787.3-1407.2
Site name: Mahabo Atsinanana
Field number: 07-060
Coordinates:
Mercator: S13° 22' 40"/ E 50° 01' 40"
UTM: E 0392985-S 8520910
Notebook references: HTW **12:**78
Illustrations: None
Length: ca. 70 m NW-SE, Width: ca. 30 m, Area: ca. 0.20 ha, Elevation ASL: 6 m
Land use at time of survey: thorny brush, sand blow
Ceramics:
Medium Sandy Ware:
Oxidized:
5 medium plain bodies
2 thin plain bodies (burnished)
2 spheroidal or hole-mouth jar rim with internal thickening (1 burnished) (Ptrk)

Reduced:
3 medium plain bodies (2 burnished)
4 thin plain bodies (3 burnished)
2 flat lip bowl rims (burnished) (Ptrk)
1 carinated bowl, round lip
Rough Ware:
Reduced: 1 round lip basin (Anlb-Ptrk)
Imported wares:
White glazed white ware: 1 body (Modern)
Other items:
Fine green chlorite schist
1 lathe-turned basin rim
2 medium bodies
Comments: The high sand ridge west of this site—the modern cemetery for many Vohemar families—is called Mahabo. The name Mahabo Atsinanana was given by our team. It was not carefully measured or mapped, but the sand ridge on which it sits is small, and the site cannot be much bigger than the dimensions given above. This site is on the left bank of the old embouchure at the west end of the causeway crossing the old embouchure, which we believe also functioned as a dam that maintained a reservoir for irrigating the paddies in the old embouchure to the north. The ceramics seem to be mostly Patrick Phase. We infer this was a hamlet or small village.

Site 787.4-1408.4
Site name: Analabe Avaratra
Field number: 07-033
Coordinates:
Mercator: S13° 22' 20" / E 50° 00' 50"
UTM: E 0393235-S 8521595
Notebook references: HTW **07**:27, 28, **12**:66; **15**:74,75
Illustrations: Figs. 9.3h–j, m, 9.4k
Length: 60 m in diameter, Area: .28 ha, Elevation ASL: 9 m
Land use at time of survey: Sand blows, grassy pastures, and scattered mango trees; mature coconut grove to the NW and SE
Other features: Sherd pavement 20 m N-S x 15 m exposed in sand blow to SW
Ceramics (2007 collection selected for rims):
Medium Sandy Ware:
Oxidized:
5 round lip bowl rims
1 round lip, externally thickened bowl rim (Rznk)
1 round lip, internally thickened bowl rim (Rznk)
1 spheroidal or hole-mouth, internally thickened rim jar, fine wavy combing (Rznk)
1 everted jar, internally thickened rim (Rznk)
Reduced:
6 round lip bowl rims
3 round lip, externally thickened bowl rims (Rznk)
3 flat lip bowl rims (Rznk)
1 oblique flat lip bowl rim (Rznk)
Rough Ware:
Oxidized: 1 spheroidal or hole-mouth internally thickened lip jar rim (Anlb-Ptrk)
Reduced:
1 round lip basin (Anlb-Ptrk)
1 spheroidal, rounded lip jar rim (Anlb-Ptrk)
Comments: This site is on low dunes 240 m ENE of the old estuary. The predominant medium sandy, medium thickness, reduced sherds; the bowl and hole-mouth jar rim variants; and the wavy combing are all typical of Razanakoto Phase assemblages. We are unsure whether this was an isolated Razanakoto hamlet or perhaps a satellite of Analabe Centre to the south, separated from it by 160 m of land with little occupation evidence.

Site 787.5-1403.7
Site name: Andranotsara/ Lac Vert
Field number: 11-028
Coordinates:
Mercator: S13° 25' / E 50° 00' 25"
UTM: E 0392580-S 8516075
Notebook references: HTW **14**:7, **18:**14
Illustrations: None
Length: ? Width: ?. Area: ?. ha. Elevation ASL: 6 m
Land use at time of survey: Grass-covered ancient dunes
Ceramics:
Medium Sandy Ware:
Oxidized: 2 medium plain bodies
Reduced:
1 medium plain body (linear burnish) (Ptrk)
1 medium plain body (scraped)
Comments: The lake is often green from algal blooms, thus its name. This is the site of annual rituals by both Anjoaty and Sakalava groups. We have only a small collection made by the Vohemarian engineer Vevé Norbert Richard Olivier. The site is located near the south end of the lake, between the active beach on the east and the high Karimbolian dunes on the west. Veve reports that sherds were found in the lake

at low tide. The burnished sherd indicates Patrick Phase occupation, but we do not know either the exact location or size of the site.

Site 787.5-1408.2
Site name: Analabe Centre
Field numbers: 07-030, 07-032, 07-034, 18-002
Coordinates:

Mercator: S 13° 22' 25" / E 50° 00' 55"
UTM: E 0393325-S 8521340

Notebook references: HTW **07**:10, 21–22, 27, 28; **12**:66; **14**:21–24; **15**:75; **18**:13–22
Illustrations: Figs. 9.3a–h, 9.4e–j
Length: 210+ m N-S, Width:120+ m, Area: 2.0+ ha, Elevation ASL: 9 m
Land use at time of survey: Sand blows to the SE and mature coconut groves to SW, center, and north
Ceramics (2007 collection, Tract 032):
Medium Sandy Ware:
Oxidized:
6 thick plain bodies
20 medium plain bodies
8 bowl rims, round lips
1 round lip, externally thickened bowl rim (Rznk)
1 round lip, internally thickened bowl rim (Rznk)
1 round lip, carinated deep bowl rim with double zigzag incising (Rznk)
1 small hole-mouth jar rim, interior thickened lip (Rznk)
1 spheroidal or hole-mouth jar rim, tapered lip, horizontal incised (Rznk)
1 spheroidal or hole-mouth jar rim, tapered lip, small round punctates (Rznk?)
1 everted jar neck, rounded, externally thickened lip, combed lower body (Rznk)
1 everted jar neck, tapered lip, fine wavy combing on neck (Rznk)
Reduced:
1 thick plain body
19 medium plain bodies
1 round lip bowl rim
1 bowl rim, obliquely flattened lip (Rznk)
3 spheroidal or hole-mouth jar rims, round lips
Rough Ware:
Reduced: 1 bowl rim, flat lip inwardly beveled (Anlb-Ptrk)

Other items:
Gray chlorite schist:
1 lathe-turned basin rim (Anlb-Ptrk)
1 lathe-turned body (Anlb-Ptrk)
Coarse green chlorite schist:
1 lathe-turned basin rim (Anlb-Ptrk)
Sandstone:
1 sharpening stone fragment

Ceramics (2018 collection, Tract 002):
Coarse Sandy Ware:
Oxidized:
2 thick plain bodies
1 medium plain body
1 spheroidal or hole-mouth jar rim, round lip
Reduced: 1 thick plain body
Medium Sandy Ware:
Oxidized:
6 thick plain bodies
72 medium plain bodies
3 bowl rims, round lips
1 round lip, externally thickened bowl rim (Rznk)
1 round lip, internally thickened bowl rim (Rznk).
1 spheroidal or hole-mouth jar rim, flat lip, linear punctates (Rznk)
1 spheroidal or hole-mouth jar shoulder, linear punctates (Rznk)
1 everted jar shoulder, cross-hatch incising (Rznk)
1 jar shoulder, unique channeled decoration
Reduced:
2 thick plain bodies
21 medium plain bodies
1 medium scraped body
1 medium black polished body
1 round lip bowl rim
1 bowl rim, obliquely flattened lip (Rznk)
1 everted jar neck, rounded, externally thickened lip, double wavy incised on neck (Rznk)
Hard Sandy Ware:
[Body sherds not separated from above] [Ptrk]
Oxidized:
1 spheroidal or hole-mouth jar rim, internally thickened lip, exterior brnsd
1 everted jar rim, flat lip, exterior scraped, interior brnsd

Reduced: 1 deep bowl rim, int thickened flat lip, exterior brnsd

Rough Ware:

Oxidized:

5 thick bodies

14 medium bodies

1 flat base fragment

8 basin rims, round lip

1 basin rims, flat lip

Reduced:

2 thick bodies

21 medium bodies

1 bowl rim, flat lip inwardly beveled (Anlb-Ptrk)

Other items:

Gray chlorite schist:

1 lathe-turned basin rim (Anlb-Ptrk)

1 lathe-turned body (Anlb-Ptrk)

Coarse green chlorite schist:

1 flat perforated piece: a net weight?

Comments: This site was first visited in the beginning of the 2007 survey season. It is in an area of dunes and sand blow-outs 250 m east-northeast of the old estuary, covered by a mature coconut grove. The landowner did not permit access to the main part of the site, so the 2007 collections are from 07-032 (**787.5-1408.2**) to the south. Soundings C and D, located here, indicated no surviving depth of deposit, probably because of wind deflation. The exposed soil in the sand blow is a light gray sand. Sandy Ware sherds are of medium thickness and largely reduced. The bowl and hole-mouth jar rim variants, and decoration such as wavy combing, punctates, and incising are all typical of Razanakoto Phase assemblages.

We returned in 2018 to determine the date and size of sites in the area north of 07-032, which we could not enter previously. During two days of delicate negotiations by the Adjuant Mayor of Vohemar, M. Sulivan Rabarivelo, and local archaeologist M. Sylvain Velomora, it was possible to examine most of the formerly closed area. We learned that the area termed 07-032 only continues north and west into the coconut grove of Mme. Zafindravao. We termed this collection area 18-002/3/4 and named it Analabe-Zafindravao. The ceramics were predominantly Razanakoto Phase, as listed above (indicating 12th–13th century CE occupation) with a small minority of distinctive bowl and jar rims of the burnished Hard Sandy Ware of the Patrick Phase (indicating a limited 17th–18th century CE reoccupation). After more negotiations with Mme. Zafindravao, we cored from northeast to southwest across her tract and selected a location for excavation Unit IX with less evidence of wind deflation and better stratigraphy (see Appendix B).

Neither the surface collections nor this excavation yielded evidence of other than ordinary domestic life. Specifically, there was no evidence of craft activities such as iron smelting or the production of chlorite schist vessels. Nor was there any evidence of architecture more elaborate than post-and-beam construction, such as basalt or coal block fragments. We therefore classify Razanokoto Phase Analabe Centre as a large village. The total area covered by the site is probably larger that given above, because the southern edge is poorly defined.

Site 787.5-1409.9
Site name: Andranomasikely Centre
Field number: 07-029
Coordinates:

Mercator: S13° 21' 35"/ E 50° 00' 40"

UTM: E 0392990-S 8522835

Notebook references: HTW **07**:21, 27; **12:**103

Illustrations: Fig. 8.3p–s

Length: 6+ m in diameter, Area: ca .01 ha, Elevation ASL: 8 m

Land use at time of survey: Sandy area with houses and coconut and mango trees

Ceramics:

Medium Sandy Ware:

Oxidized:

1 thick worn body

3 medium plain bodies

Reduced:

3 medium plain bodies

2 spheroidal or hole-mouth jar rims

Rough Ware:

Oxidized:

2 thick rough bodies (Anlb-Ptrk)

30 medium rough bodies (Anlb-Ptrk)

4 round lip basin rims (Anlb-Ptrk)

1 flat lip basin rim (Anlb-Ptrk)

3 tapered rim basin rims (Anlb-Ptrk)

2 spheroidal or hole-mouth jar rims (Anlb-Ptrk)

Reduced:

1 thick rough body (Anlb-Ptrk)

2 medium rough bodies (Anlb-Ptrk)
1 round lip basin rim (Anlb-Ptrk)

Comments: The site name was given by our team; we were unable to elicit a local name. This site is on low dunes in the Andranomasikely suburb of southeast Vohemar. The site is composed of at least three dense clusters of Rough Ware sherds, each less than two meters in diameter, all within an area not six meters in diameter. We interpret these clusters as firing areas, to which unfired Rough Ware bowls could be brought and fired with the wood of the dry coastal forest trees that once covered these dunes. While Rough Ware was used from Analabe to Patrick times, the fragments from this site have quartz inclusions, which is typical of Razanakoto to Patrick Phase samples, in contrast to Analabe Phase vegetally tempered Rough Ware. Since the hard Sandy Ware burnished sherds typical of the Ambatary to Patrick Phases are absent, this workshop site is likely to be of the Razanakoto Phase.

Site 787.6-1408.4
Site name: Analabe Avaratra-Atsinanana
Field number: 07-031
Coordinates:
Mercator: S13° 22' 20" / E50° 00' 55"
UTM: E 0393340-S 8521530
Notebook references: HTW **07**:32–33; **12**:104–105
Illustrations: Fig. 11.3f–k
Length: 50 m NE-SW, Width: 40 m, Area: ca 0.16 ha, Elevation ASL: 9 m
Land use at time of survey: Mature coconut grove
Ceramics:
Coarse Sandy Ware:
Oxidized:
1 thick plain body (Ampv)
5 medium plain bodies
1 round lip basin rim
Reduced:
1 medium plain body
1 round lip basin rim
1 spheroidal or hole-mouth jar rounded rim
Medium Sandy Ware:
Oxidized:
8 thick plain sherds
30 medium plain bodies (22 burnished) (Ptrk)
11 thin plain bodies (9 burnished) (Ptrk)
3 everted lip, interior thickened jar rims (burnished)(Ptrk)
3 spheroidal or hole-mouth jar rims (brnshd) (Ptrk)
Reduced:
11 medium plain bodies (6 burnished) (Ptrk)
5 thin plain bodies (burnished) (Ptrk)
1 carination fragment
2 round lip bowls
6 spheroidal or hole-mouth jar rims
1 carinated everted jar rim, small round punctates (burnished) (Ptrk)
1 everted exterior thickened jar rim, arcuate incised (Ptrk)
Imported Ware:
16 fragments of one green-glazed stoneware Martaban jar base (16th–17th c)

Comments: Note that this name was given by our team; we were unable to elicit a local name other than Analabe. The owners were Régis and Jeannot. The careful surface collection was made by Jean-Yves Régis. We measured in 9 cores, then excavated and sieved two .50 x .50 tests, establishing that the cultural deposit on this site was nowhere more than .32 m deep. Each test produced only a few tiny sherd fragments. The surface sample has some very coarse sherds, mostly of medium thickness, indicating some earlier occupation, perhaps Analabe Phase. However, the great majority of sherds are of the Patrick Phase. It is notable that most rims are of jars and there are none of the typical flat lip bowls. The low sherd density in screened units indicates a brief occupation. The preponderance of jars suggests a specialized activity.

Site 787.7-1398.0
Site Name: Amboanio
Field number: 07-002
Coordinates:
Mercator: S13° 28' 05" / E 50° 01' 00"
UTM: E 0393600-S 8521010
Notebook references: HTW **12**:89
Illustrations: None
Length: 110 m NE-SW, Width: 70 m, Area: 0.52 ha, Elevation ASL: 95 m
Land use at time of survey: Heavy grass cover, brush and trees in ditches north and west of the site, unused church.
Ceramics (2007 collection):
Coarse Sandy Ware:

Oxidized: 1 thick plain body (?)
Medium Sandy Ware:
Oxidized: 1 medium plain body
Reduced:
7 medium plain bodies
1 thin plain body (Ave Maria)
Fine Sandy Ware:
Oxidized:
1 medium body
2 thin plain bodies
Reduced:
5 medium bodies
1 thin plain body (Ave Maria)
3 carinated shoulders (Ave Maria)
Imported wares:
Industrial tile 1 fragment (very modern)
White Glazed White Ware:
Floral decoration: 8 medium bodies (late 19th–early 20th c)
Speckled decoration: 1 medium body (Modern)

Other items:
Glass:
1 green cylindrical molded bottle body (19th–20th c)
3 clear cylindrical molded bottle bodies (Modern)
Coarse gray chlorite schist:
1 carved crude cup or crucible?
Crystal quartz:
1 fragment

Comments: This is a typical Merina coastal fortification, located 700 m from and 95 m above the sea. The measurements are taken from satellite images and the 1834 description of Bernier (Fleury 1886 III:266–267). The fort was taken by French troops in 1885 (Oliver 1885:244). Local people at the time of the survey said the church was in use until recently. Vérin (1975) has shown that Floral Ware was made in Sarguemine in Alsace and imported to Madagascar from about 1895 to 1920. The tile and clear bottles are probably twentieth century.

Site 787.8-1407.5
Site Name: Analabe-Patrick
Field numbers: 07-57, 07-62
Coordinates:
Mercator: S13° 22' 41"/ E50° 00' 56"
UTM: E0393405-N8520844

Notebook references: HTW **07**:28, 39–42; **12**:69–72, 76; **15**:80
Illustrations: Figs. 11.1b, 11.2
Length: 285 m NW-SE, Width: 160 m, Area: ca 3.80 ha, Elevation ASL: 7 m
Land use at time of survey: Coconut groves ranging from newly planted to mature to neglected

Ceramics: This large site was collected as six different areas, defined by fields. The tract of M. Patrick, a mature coconut grove termed collection area 07-62, had a thick grass cover presenting few surface exposures. The excavated sample, which allows us to define the 17th–18th century Patrick Phase, is detailed in Appendix B. Four of the nearby tracts yielded useful surface collections.

From the north-central portion of this large site, termed **Analabe Marie-Claude Avaratra** (07-035: 788.7-1407.8, S13° 22' 40"/E50° 01' 00", UTM: E 0393760-S 8520845), we have few sherds. We are indebted to Mme Marie-Claude Ah-toe for permission to survey this area. The site had been leveled with a bulldozer, and our collection was hasty and biased toward rim sherds.

Ceramics:
Medium Sandy Ware:
Oxidized:
1 thick plain body
5 medium plain bodies
2 thin plain bodies
2 round lip bowl rims
1 heavy hole-mouth jar rim (Ambtry?)
1 spheroidal or hole-mouth jar rim (burnished) (Ptrk)
Reduced:
1 medium plain body
2 spherical or hole-mouth jar rim (1 burnished) (Ptrk)
1 out-turned jar rim (burnished) (Ptrk)
Rough Ware:
Oxidized:
1 medium body (Anlb-Ptrk)
1 round lip bowl rim (Anlb-Ptrk)
1 tapered lip bowl rim (Anlb-Ptrk)
Imported ware:
Omani Bahla Ware: 1 jar shoulder (17th–18th c)

From collection area 07-57, the southeast portion of this large site, termed **Analabe Marie-Claude Atsinanana**

(07-057: 787.8-1407.7, S13° 22' 39"/E50° 00' 57", UTM: E 0393440-S 852885) we have the following collection.

Ceramics:
- Coarse Sandy Ware:
  - Oxidized:
    - 4 thick plain bodies (Ampv)
    - 4 medium plain bodies
    - 1 round lip bowl rim
    - 1 basin with internally thickened rim, flat lip (Ambtry)
  - Reduced: 1 medium plain body
- Medium Sandy Ware:
  - Oxidized:
    - 19 thick plain bodies
    - 10 medium plain bodies
    - 4 round lip basin rims
    - 4 flat lip bowl rims (Ptrk)
    - 5 spheroidal or hole-mouth jar rims
  - Reduced:
    - 7 medium plain bodies
    - 1 thin plain body
    - 4 round lip bowl rims
    - 1 ledge rim bowl
    - 1 flat lip bowl
    - 3 spheroidal or hole-mouth jar rims (1 burnished) (Ptrk)
- Fine Sandy Ware:
  - Oxidized:
    - 5 medium plain bodies
    - 2 flat lip bowl rims (Ptrk)
    - 5 spheroidal or hole-mouth jar rims (3 brnshd)(Ptrk)
  - Reduced:
    - 7 medium plain bodies
    - 1 thin plain body
    - 1 flat lip bowl (Ptrk)
    - 1 spheroidal or hole-mouth jar rim (brnshd) (Ptrk)
- Rough Ware:
  - Oxidized:
    - 2 round lip basin rims (Anlb-Ptrk)
    - 1 thickened lip basin rim (Anlb-Ptrk)

Other items:
- Mica schist: 2 sharpening stone fragments

Comments: There are a few possible early items, perhaps Analabe Phase, and one Ambatary basin rim, but the majority of the ceramics are Patrick Phase.

From the northeastern portion of this large site, termed **Analabe Marie-Claude Avaratra-Atsinanana** (07-058: 787.8-1407.8. S13° 22' 40"/E50° 00' 60", UTM: E 0393505-S 8520850), we have the following collection, also biased toward rim sherds.

Ceramics:
- Medium Sandy Ware:
  - Oxidized:
    - 4 medium plain bodies
    - 1 flat lip basin rim
    - 2 round lip bowl rims (burnished)
    - 1 heavy in-turned bowl rim, flattened lip (Abtry)
    - 1 round lip basin
    - 4 spherical or hole-mouth jar rims
    - 1 round handle or foot fragment
  - Reduced:
    - 3 medium plain body (1 burnished) (Ptrk)
    - 1 thin plain body (burnished)
    - 1 everted neck, flat lip, jar rim (burnished) (Ptrk)
- Fine Sandy Ware:
  - Oxidized:
    - 1 spheroidal or hole-mouth jar
    - 2 everted jar rims
  - Reduced:
    - 1 medium plain body (burnished)
    - 1 everted neck flat lip jar rim: punctates, zigzag incising (burnished) (Ambtry-Ptrk)
    - 1 heavy carinated bowl rim, flattened lip (burnished) (Ptrk)
- Rough Ware:
  - Oxidized: 1 round lip bowl rim (Anlb-Ptrk)
  - Reduced:
    - 1 medium rough bodies (Anlb-Ptrk)
    - 2 round lip bowl rims (Anlb-Ptrk)
- Imported wares:
  - Chinese blue-and-white:
    - 1 medium body (early 17th c)
    - 1 medium body (late 17th–early 18th c)

Other items:
- Fine green chlorite schist:
  - 1 lathe-turned body
  - 1 unfinished lathe-turned top fragment
- Green blown glass:
  - 1 conical bottle neck fragment (17th–early 18th c)
  - 1 cylindrical body fragment (18th c)

From the northwestern portion of this large site, termed **Analabe-Patrick Avaratra-Andrefana [NW],** (07-059, **787.6-1407.8,** S13° 22' 38"/ E50° 00' 55", UTM: E 0393310-S 8520940), we have the following small collection.

Ceramics:
- Coarse Sandy Ware:
  - Oxidized: 2 medium plain bodies
  - Reduced: 1 medium plain bodies
- Medium Sandy Ware:
  - Oxidized:
    - 11 medium plain bodies
    - 2 flat lip bowl rims (1 burnished) (Ptrk)
    - 2 spheroidal or hole-mouth jar rims
  - Reduced: 1 flat lip basin rim (burnished) (Ptrk)
- Fine Sandy Ware:
  - Reduced:
    - 2 medium plain bodies (burnished) (Ptrk)
    - 2 thin plain bodies (burnished) (Ptrk, Ave Maria?)
- Rough Ware:
  - Oxidized:
    - 2 medium rough bodies (Anlb-Ptrk)
    - 2 heavy round lip bowls (Anlb-Ptrk)
- Other items:
  - Mica schist: 2 sharpening stone fragments

Comments: The locally used names for this large site are Analabe-Patrick and Analabe Marie-Claude. This site is situated on right bank of the old embouchure, adjacent to a possible reservoir and area with rich rice paddies. The few Ambatary Phase sherds appear to be an oval concentration on the east edge of the site, oriented NNW-SSE, with the dune or beach ridges in the area (now obscured as a result of land leveling for coconut cultivation) covering about .40 ha. The Patrick Phase occupation covers the entire site, an area of at least 3.80 ha. Our single small excavation revealed a sequence of Patrick Phase middens and sand floors with associated postholes and pits. We saw no evidence of special buildings or craft areas in our surface examination. We classify this settlement as a large village.

Site 788.2-1408.3
Site name: Analabe Atsinanana
Field number: 07-042
Coordinates:
Mercator: S13° 22' 20" / E 50° 01' 15"
UTM: E 0393920-S 8521530

Notebook references: HTW **07**:29; **13**:102; **18**:22
Illustrations: Figs. 8.1c, 8.3a–b
Length: 15+ m N-S, Width: 08+ m, Area: 0.1+ ha, Elevation ASL: 7 m
Land use at time of survey: thorns, sand blows, mature coconut grove

Ceramics (2007 collection):
- Coarse Sandy Ware:
  - Oxidized:
    - 1 thick plain body (Ampv-Anlb)
    - 7 medium plain bodies
  - Reduced:
    - 1 spheroidal or hole-mouth, thicknd round lip jar rim (Ampv-Anlb)*
- Medium Sandy Ware:
  - Oxidized:
    - 2 medium plain bodies
    - 1 round lip basin rim (Ampv)*
- Rough Ware:
  - Oxidized:1 thick body (Anlb-Ptrk)
  - Reduced: 2 medium bodies (Anlb-Ptrk)

Ceramics (2018 collection):
- Coarse Sandy Ware:
  - Oxidized:
    - 2 thick plain body (Ampv-Anlb)
    - 5 medium plain bodies
  - Reduced:
    - 1 spheroidal or hole-mouth, round lip jar rim
- Medium Sandy Ware:
  - Oxidized:
    - 1 jar shoulder with wavy incised line (Anlb)
- Rough Ware:
  - Reduced: 1 round lip basin rim

Comments: This name was given by our team; we were unable to elicit a local name. This site is small scatter of sherds located between the second and third beaches, which are now about 170 meters west of the active first beach of the Indian Ocean. The site may be larger, extending south and east into a coconut grove with dense ground cover. The Rough Ware, the predominance of sherds of medium thickness, and the absence of thickened rounded rims suggested in 2007 that this was an Analabe Phase site, but the sample was small. A revisit in 2018 confirms this ascription. About 20 m southwest of this site, on the lower slope of the third beach, is a scatter of ratite eggshell (07-041: S13° 22' 20" / E 50° 01' 14", UTM: E 0393930-S

8521460). Eggshell from this site is thinner and smaller in girth than *Aepyornis* eggshell and is perhaps from the eggs of a smaller ratite, such as *Mullerornis*. Ratite eggshell was noted from this area by Vérin and Battistini (Pierre Vérin P.C.).The exact relation between the eggshell and the Analabe ceramics and the use of this site can only be established with excavation and absolute dating.

Site 788.2-1407.6
Site name: Analabe Atsimo-Atsinanana [southeast]
Field number: 07-056
Coordinates:

Mercator: S13° 22' 40"/ E 50° 01' 05"
UTM: E 0393725-S 8520930

Notebook references: HTW **07**:39, **12**:74–75
Illustrations: Figs. 11.1b, 11.3r–t
Diameter: ca 40 m, Area: 0.13 ha, Elevation ASL: 8 m
Land use at time of survey: Thorny brush, sand blows
Ceramics:
Fine Sandy Ware:
Oxidized:
14 medium bodies (3 burnished) (Ptrk)
1 thin plain body
3 spheroidal or hole-mouth jar rims
Reduced:
5 medium bodies (3 burnished) (Ptrk)
1 flat rim basin (burnished) (Ptrk)
1 thickened round lip bowl rim (burnished)(Ptrk)
2 hole-mouth jar rims (1 burnished) (Ptrk)
Rough Ware:
Oxidized:
2 medium body (Anlb-Ptrk)
1 round lip basin (Anlb-Ptrk)
1 spheroidal or hole-mouth jar (Anlb-Ptrk)

Comments: Note that this name was given by our team; we were unable to elicit a local name. Fine hard fabrics with burnishing, interior thickened jar rims, and Rough Ware indicate Patrick Phase occupation of this small, dense site. It was probably a small farming hamlet.

Site 788.4-1407.4
Site name: Ampasin'i Analabe
Field number: 07-055
Coordinates:

Mercator: S13° 22' 40" / E 50° 01' 20"
UTM E 0394090-S 8520905

Notebook references: HTW **07**:38; **12**:72–73
Illustrations: Figs. 9.3n, 9.4*l*
Length: ca 200 m N-S, Width: 30 m, Area: .50 ha, Elevation ASL: 5 m
Land use at time of survey. Beach dunes, thorny weeds
Ceramics:
Coarse Sandy Ware:
Oxidized:
4 thick plain bodies (Ampv)
11 medium plain bodies
Reduced:
1 medium plain body
Medium Sandy Ware:
Oxidized:
2 thick plain bodies
19 medium plain bodies
2 thin plain bodies
3 round lip bowls
1 flat lip, externally thickened, shallow bowl rim, traces of exterior red slip (Rzkt)
1 high everted straight neck jar (Rznk?)
1 flat base fragment
1 square foot fragment (Rznk)
1 oval foot fragment
Reduced:
10 medium plain bodies
2 thin plain bodies
2 round lip basin rims
1 round lip bowl
2 spheroidal or hole-mouth jar rims
1 flat base fragment
Rough Ware:
Oxidized: 2 medium rough bodies (Anlb-Ptrk)
Hematitic/ Coralline Ware:
Oxidized: 2 medium plain bodies.
Hard Fine Sandy Ware:
Reduced:
1 medium burnished body (Ptrk)
1 flat lip, carinated bowl rim (burnished) (Ptrk)
Imported ceramics:
Fine Tan Ware: Sgraffito bowl fragment with olive green glaze (11th–13th c)
Other items:
Fine green chlorite schist: 1 carved body
Crystal quartz: 1 fragment (89 gm)

Comments: Note that this name was also given by our team; we were unable to elicit a local name. This linear site faces east toward the Indian Ocean. Only a near-shore reef and the crest of the first beach protects people here from the constant wind and surf. The sea is increasingly cutting into the land. It is likely that the site deposits have been damaged by storms. The carved (rather than lathe-turned) chlorite schist and coarse thick sherds suggest earlier occupations, perhaps Ampasimahavelona or Analabe. However, most of the Medium Sandy Ware sherds and bowl and jar rims indicate Razanakoto Phase use. In addition to the beaching of canoes and reef fishing, it seems likely that Malagasy natural resources—e.g., crystal and chlorite schist—were taken out to oceangoing ships, and imports such as glazed ceramics were received. There are also traces of Patrick Phase use. The sherds with hematite and coral inclusions are notably rare in the northeast, but common elsewhere.

Appendix B

Stratigraphic Excavations in the Vohemar Area

by Henry T. Wright

In previous surveys we learned that it is wise to excavate small soundings when possible. Because many parts of Madagascar are developing rapidly, a site may be gone or badly damaged the next time archaeologists are able to visit. All of our soundings, except those at the rock shelter site of Ambohiposa, were one meter square. Squares excavated in 2007 were identified by capital letters; in later seasons, they were designated by Roman numerals. The sediment of all contexts except the uppermost disturbed contexts were sieved in 3-mm screen. The evidence from such soundings is, at the least, useful simply in characterizing the extent and depth of site deposits. More important, it is essential for providing stratigraphically discrete, sieved, and volume-controlled samples to better define assemblages and cultural phases. If we are lucky and find charred remains in secure contexts (which can be radiocarbon-dated) or imported items (the dates of which are known), these small excavations can contribute to establishing an absolute chronology. We have also floated defined volumes of deposits in water, in hopes of finding charred plant parts of economic significance. Unfortunately, and to our surprise and disappointment, we found few such charred plant materials, but in the heavy fractions of flotation samples, we have found mollusk, fish, reptile, bird, and mammal remains, which provide evidence of environments and economic pursuits (see Appendix D).

In this appendix, we provide the details of those excavations that produced useful evidence. If the sounding found badly disturbed deposits, or was otherwise uninformative, the mention is brief. Each entry has a site description that recapitulates some of the information detailed in Appendix A; this is followed by the dimensions of the excavation, the date it was initiated, and names of those who excavated the unit. Next, excavated contexts are presented in a table followed by a discussion that emphasizes the inferred depositional processes. This is keyed to a figure with plans and a section. Finally, the major recovered material classes are presented in a table followed by a discussion that emphasizes the activities implied by these finds. As there are relatively few soundings, we have not put them in site number order as in the site catalogue (Appendix A). Rather, they are in chronological order from oldest to youngest—that is, in the order Ambohiposa, Ampasimahavelona, Analabe

-Régis, Razanakoto, Ambatary, Patrick, and Ave Maria. The reader will note that these key sites have inspired the names given to the cultural phases.

Ambohiposa (784.3-1408.1): South, Central, and North Excavation Units

This site is a small rock shelter with stone tools, the excavations of which have been described in detail in a previous and easily available publication (Dewar et al. 2013). We here summarize the data presented in the supplementary materials for that article, as these supplements are only available online. The tiny rock shelter was discovered late on the day of 5 October 2007 by Henry Wright, while the rest of the team were recording oral histories in the neighborhood of Amboronanana, the western suburb of Vohemar. A notable feature of the shelter is a heap of recent rodent bones left by owls, comprised exclusively of the remains of mouse (*Mus musculus*), black rat (*Rattus rattus*), and Asian house shrew (*Suncus murinus*). The heap almost completely covers a roughly rectangular array of rocks, perhaps the remnant of a tomb. Thinking that these recent bones might indicate preserved bone in older layers, indicating earlier ecological conditions, a small sediment sample was taken from what was later termed Layer 3. This was washed in 1-mm mesh and left to dry overnight. The following morning the residue was sorted under magnification. To our surprise, though we found no bone, we did find two chert flakes and one obsidian flake.

Later, on 10 October 2007, we returned and placed a small rectangular excavation extending 1.30 m from the back of the shelter to the dripline and .50 m in width, termed Unit K in the field notes, but published as the "Central Unit." On 8 October 2008, we returned and placed two parallel .50 by 1.00+ m units, one .50 m to the north and one .50 m to the south of the first season's unit. The "North Unit," originally termed Unit III, had a thin and compressed organic layer. At first we thought this was upper organic Layer 1 from the previous year's unit, but we continued down below the level of the deepest red silt year of the previous year, and realized that the upper organic layer must be Layers 3 to 5 compressed together. The "South Unit," originally termed Unit IV, was similar to the Central Unit of 2007, but had thicker and better-defined organic layers. These were somewhat disturbed close to the back wall of the shelter, probably by rodents. This report presents a synthetic stratigraphy for all three units, here termed South, Central, and North. Within each unit, different layers had slightly different volumes because the back of the shelter was irregular, and some layers contained large rocks, whose approximate volumes were subtracted from the volume excavated to better approximate the volume screened, as recorded in Table B.1. At various times, Robert Dewar, Chantal Radimilahy, Henry Wright, Harisoa Ravoviarimanara, and M. Bemisy, the mayor of Amboronanana, helped in the excavations.

The deposits were excavated in natural stratigraphic layers (Table B.1). Each context was sieved in 3-mm screen. The larger rock fragments were examined for evidence of use, then discarded. Possible chert, bone, and charcoal fragments were saved separately, and everything remaining was carried to Vohemar to be washed through 1-mm screen in the sea, dried, and sorted under magnification. We excavated approximately 25% of the area of Layers 3 to 5. Average thicknesses are estimated from the sections. Sediment samples from Layers 3 and 5 in the South Unit were floated in fresh water. The water was poured through a fine cloth strainer in search of carbonized seeds. The heavy material left in the bucket was washed through a 1-mm sieve, dried, and sorted as usual, but presented separately in Table B.2.

Sediment samples from Ambohiposa were studied by Paul Goldberg and Francesco Berna at Boston University. They have established that a major component of silty material found in all levels is kaolinite, which is forming on the hilltop above and could have been washed over the cliff. A minor component is quartz, which could have been from the bedrock or introduced by wind or water.

We suggest the following depositional history. A period of the deposition of kaolinitic sediment with rock fragments from the shelter walls and roof ended with intense weathering and iron oxide deposition, creating Layer 6. This was followed by the deposition of three layers of dark kaolinitic sediment with organic remains such as charcoal and flaked stone items. The lowest of these was well preserved; the middle layer was primarily small fragments of rock; and the uppermost seemed disturbed. These organic sediments are sealed under Layer 2, a thin layer of reddish sediment, probably washed from above relatively recently. Layer 1 is the layer of recent leaf litter.

Table B.1. Deposits in the excavation units at Ambohiposa.

Layer	Thickness	Sediment description	Munsell color	Comments
(1)	.03 m	Brownish silt, angular rock fragments	NA	Recent leaf litter
(2)	.10 m	Reddish silt and angular rock fragments	7.5YR 4/3	Slope wash
(3)	.11 m	Dark brown fine silt with a few small rock fragments	10YR 3/2	Charcoal, flakes
(4)	.15 m	Brown silt with many angular or flat rock fragments	NA	Charcoal, flakes
(5)	.05 m	Gray brown silt with a few small rock fragments	NA	Charcoal, flakes
(6) upper	.04 m	Reddish silt with rounded pebbles	7.5YR 3/4	Oxidized slope wash
(6) lower	.05+ m	Reddish silt with subangular rock fragments	7.5YR 3/4	Oxidized slope wash

This description refers to the South and Central Units, which had almost identical stratification (Figure B.2, Table B.1). In these, the oxidized reddish silt (Layer 6) appears to be highly weathered and is probably much older. Organic Layer 5 to 3 had brief occupations by people using stone tools. The dated charcoal fragments are from the deepest part of Layer 5 (see Appendix C). These are sealed by a reddish silt with rock fragments, probably washed in from the hilltop above the rock shelter. In the North Unit, Layer 2 was not present and Layers 3–5 were compressed into a single layer. Worried that we had not yet reached Layers 3–5, we cut deeply into Layer 6, finding a few flaked stone items in its uppermost spit, but no traces of deeper occupation.

Most of the chert debris is smaller blocky pieces (Table B.2), thought to be the shatter remnants left over from the bipolar smashing of small chert cores. These are most dense in the lower layers of the Central Unit. Small chert flakes are most dense in the lower layers of the Central and South Units. Rare chert implements and tools are found in all units throughout Layers 3 to 5. Foraging activities are represented by possible projectile elements of chert or obsidian. Maintenance activities are represented by cutting, scraping, and piercing tools of chert. Rare obsidian items are mostly in the lower layers of the Central Unit. We infer that Ambohiposa was visited several times by foragers who made fires and repaired projectiles and other items, perhaps while avoiding rainy weather or staying overnight.

Ampasimahavelona (786.7-1408.1): Excavation Unit VII

This site, and several others of the same phase, were discovered on September 28, 2008, when the survey team made its first sweep down the left or west bank of the old estuary. The resemblance of many of the surface finds from Ampasimahavelona to early ceramics from Sandrakatsy (Wright and Fanony 1992) and Nosy Mangabe (Vérin 1975:II: 879–889), both in the area of the Bay of Antongil to the south, indicated that this site had an early occupation. It was the richest early site we found, and we hoped it would yield datable material in context.

On October 6, 2008, after exchanging "high-fives" with the site owner, M. Frédéric, a retired employee of the Mobil Oil Co, we cored widely with a hand auger. We selected a location in the center of the north part of the site, where coring indicated .50 cm of dark gray midden, dense with sherds and shell fragments. There we placed Unit V, a one meter square. (Labordes 786.7-1408.1, Mercator S13° 22' 21.5/ E50° 00' 26.1", UTM Zone 39 L E0392518 -N8521449.) We were disappointed to find that the entire deposit was disturbed by manioc cultivation. One posthole in a row of postholes visible in the light reddish brown sand below contained scraps of a plastic fiber sack. M. Frédéric identified these posts as the remains of his house, which was destroyed by a cyclone in about 1992. In the sand we

Table B.2. Densities and mean sizes of stone items from Ambohiposa (page 1).

Context	Volume	Coarse flakes	Chert scatter	Chert flakes	Obsidian flakes	Other
South Unit						
3a	16.5L	12	66	9	-	1 core fragment
		1.4 g	3.2 g	.2 g	-	
		.12g	.01g	.02g	-	
3b	26L	19	21	3	-	
		2.7 g	1.70 g	.2 g	-	
		.14g	.08g	.02g	-	
3b float	6L	53	30	3	-	1 blade fragment
		14.1 g	1.28 g	.01 g	-	1 notched flake fragment
		.26g	.04g	.02g	-	
4 E	10L	61	48	4	-	
		0.41 g	2.80 g	.22 g	-	
		.01g	.06g	.05g	-	
4 W	14L	22	99	18	-	1 microblade
		0.30 g	5.38 g	0.47 g	-	
		.13g	.05g	.03g	-	
5 W float	3.8L	32	316	87	-	1 core fragment
		9.09 g	3.20 g	5.45 g	-	1 retouched flake
		.29g	.10g	.06g	-	2 medial blade segments 1 used blade fragment
6	12L	67	47	7	-	
		4.66 g	2.78 g	0.13 g	-	
		.29g	.06g	.02g	-	
Central Unit (K)						
3	53L	18	11	3	0.7	1 microblade segment
		5.4 g	.3 g	.3 g	-	
		.29g	.11g	.09g	-	
4	75L	34	31	2	-	1 trapeze
		9.7 g	7.0 g	.1 g	-	
		.41g	.22g	.05g	-	
5	27L	49	48	8	1.5	1 microblade
		4.7 g	5.9 g	.8 g	.3 g	
		.09g	.12g	.10g	-	
6 up	22L	35	39	6	2.3	1 microblade segment
		1.5 g	2.0 g	.1 g	.1 g	
		.04g	.05g	.02g	-	
6 lo	27L	19	15	1	-	
		1.3 g	.7 g	.2 g	-	
		.06g	.04g	.17g	-	

Table B.2. Densities and mean sizes of stone items from Ambohiposa (page 2).*

Context	Volume	Coarse flakes	Chert scatter	Chert flakes	Obsidian flakes	Other
North Unit (IV)						
3-5	16L	112	106	10	-	1 obsidian microblade core fragment
		31.02 g	8.92 g	0.14 g	-	
		.39g	.08g	.01g	-	
6 up east	30L	18	30	2	-	
		6.81 g	2.85 g	0.19 g	-	
		.39g	.09g	.11g	-	
6 up west	34L	75	91	6	-	2 retouched bipolar flakes
		10.8 g	4.12 g	0.26 g	-	
		.14g	.05g	.04g	-	
6 mid east	10L	28	25	2	-	
		4.63 g	1.28 g	0.18 g	-	
		.16g	.05g	.04g	-	
6 mid west	12L	38	47	3	1	
		10.24 g	2.62 g	0.17 g	.19g	
		.28g	.06g	.05g	.23g	
6 lo	19L	97	45	14	1	
		11.69 g	2.04 g	0.46 g	.01g	
		.12g	.04g	.03g	.01g	

*Note: This table presents the counts of individual items per 10 liter unit and their total weight in grams per 10 liter volume, followed by their mean weights.

could see two faint gray areas, perhaps shallow pits, but they contained no ceramics or other remains. Everything else was disturbed. We had a screened sample of mixed ceramics, but there were no datable imported items or organic samples that we might use for radiocarbon dating. We present neither plans, sections nor statistics on this mixed unit.

Back in the U.S. during the austral summer, we discussed the lack of sealed deposits. We realized that it was more likely that in situ deposits would survive on the flanks of the site, close to or even under the paddies, rather than on the heavily cultivated terrace surfaces. We returned on October 23, 2009, and cored around the edge of the site and in the rice paddies, finding a deeply buried shell deposit on the northeast edge. On October 26, we placed Unit VII, another one meter square, near the promising core at the edge of the fallow paddy (Labordes 786.7-1408.1, Mercator S13° 22' 21.4/ E50° 00' 26.8). The excavators were Robert Dewar, Henry Wright, Victor Razanatovo and M. Frédéric. The following stratigraphy was recorded (Figure B.1, Table B.3).

The deeper deposits had the consistency of cement; we excavated only the west half of the square. The oldest deposit revealed at Ampasimahavelona was a yellowish brown sandy clay without cultural evidence, termed Layer 5, probably a levee of the river that ran into the old estuary. Above this, we removed three ill-defined deposits, termed Layers 4 to 2, varying from a yellow-brown sandy silt below to a mottled dark silt above, each with some coarse plain sherds and shell fragments. There are several cultural features in this compressed deposit. The oldest is in the northeast corner, where a cut from the base of Layer 4 dips steeply to the west. This is doubtless a pit, most of which is beyond the west section, awaiting future excavation. It was not given a

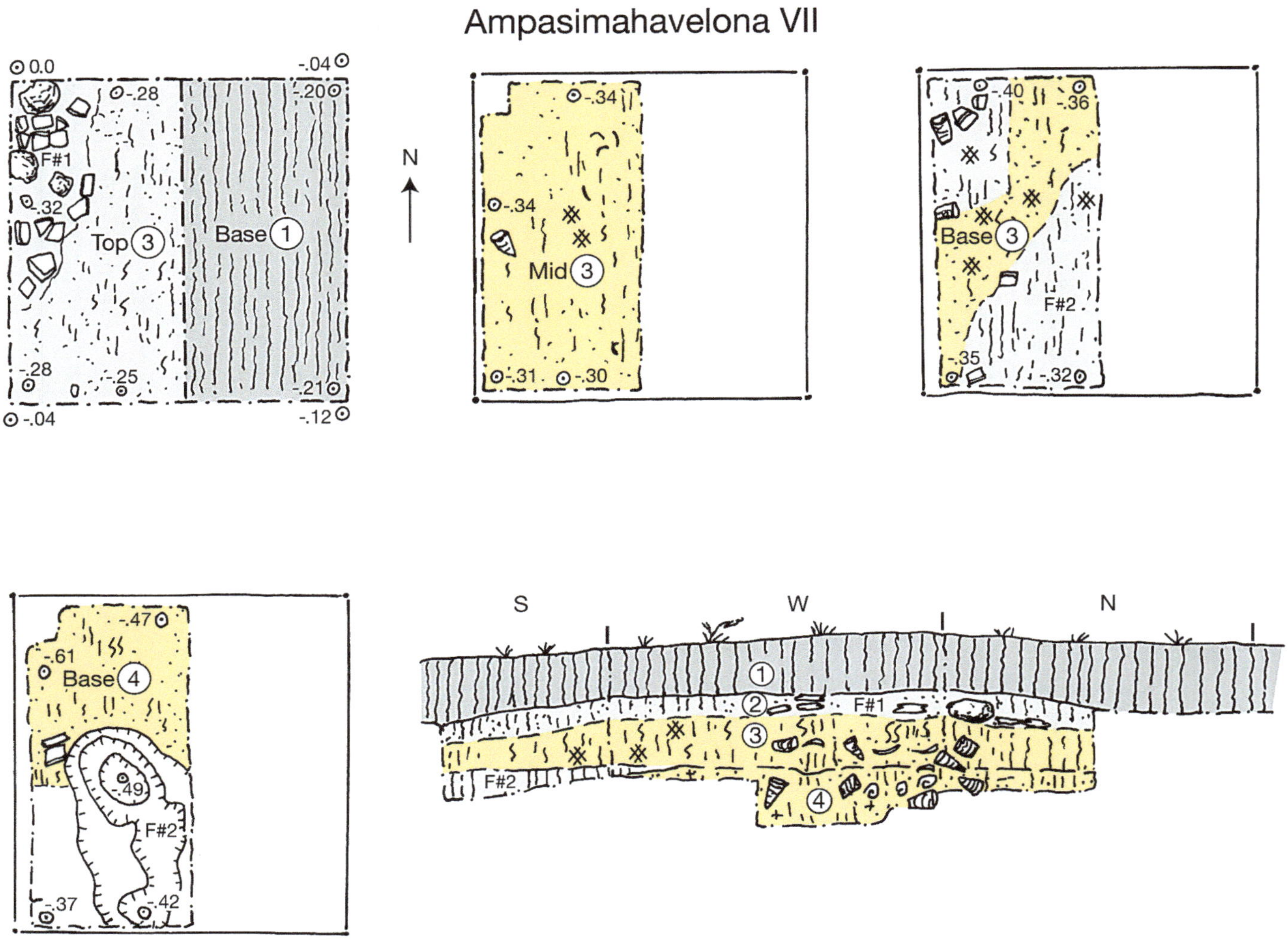

Figure B.1. Plans and sections from Ampasimahavelona Excavation Unit VII.

Table B.3. Deposits in Excavation Unit VII at Ampasimahavelona.

Context	Mean thickness	Estimated volume	Composition	Comment
Layer (1)	.23 m	.2300 m^3	Black silt	AP Horizon
Layer (2)	.04 m	.0108 m^3	Mottled dark brown and silt	Midden: some shell, sherds
Feature 1	.04 m	.0046 m^3	Mottled dark brown silt	Pit: Large sherds, shells, rocks
Layer (3)	.08 m	.0340 m^3	Light grayish brown sandy silt (2.5Y 3/2)	Midden: some shell, sherds
Feature 2	.06 m	.0046 m^3	Dark gray sandy silt (2.5Y 3/1)	Shallow pit: charcoal, sherds
Layer (4)	.15 m	.0304 m^3	Yellowish brown sandy silt (2.5Y 4/4)	AL Horizon: Terrace sediment
Layer (5)	-	-	Yellow brown sandy clay (10YR 5/4)	B Horizon: Terrace sediment

Table B.4. Artifacts from the deeper contexts of Excavation VII at Ampasimahavelona.

Context	Coarse Sandy Ware					Sandy Ware		Cracked rock	Shell	
	Oxidized			Reduced		Oxidized	Reduced			
	Thick	Medium	Rim	Other	Medium	Medium	Medium		*Terebralia*	Other
Feature 1	1	22	5 h-m* 2 bowl	5 basin	1	4	-	4	1	-
Layer (3) upper	-	2	-	-	1	2	-	-	-	-
Layer (3) lower	3	7	1 bowl	-	3	-	2	9	7	-
Feature 2 upper	5	7	-	-	-	1	-	-	-	-
Feature 2 lower	7	12	1	-	4	-	-	2	2	1 conch
Layer (4) upper	3	1	1	2 basin	-	-	1	4	14	1 turbo
Layer (4) upper	3	-	-	-	-	1 lug?	-	-	-	-

*h-m = hole-mouth

feature number. At the bottom of Layer 3, to the south, was a lens of gray sandy silt with small pieces of charcoal and coarse plain sherds (Feature 2). No features were recognized in Layer 3, but in Layer 2 in the northeast corner there is a concentration of large coarse oxidized basin and jar sherds and cracked rocks (Feature 1). We thought that this was simply a load of trash dumped on the edge of the site, but it is directly above the possible pit in Layer 4 and it is possible that a deep pit we did not detect in Layer 3 was dug from Layer 2 down into Layer 5. If so, most of this possible pit is unexcavated. Finally, there is the recently cultivated layer of disturbed black silt, termed Layer 1.

Two small pieces of wood charcoal from the deepest contexts of Unit VII were submitted for accelerator dating. They yielded almost identical radiocarbon age determinations with a 95% probability that the date is within the range from AD 885 to 1025 (see Appendix C for technical details). These determinations indicate that the early occupation of Ampasimahavelona falls within the late ninth to early eleventh centuries.

Flotation of samples from Feature 2 and Layer 4 produced more charcoal, but no identifiable seeds. However, there was one small but well-preserved fish spine. This and the relatively good condition of the shell in Layer 4 indicate there is no reason that bone would not be preserved in the lower layers of Unit VII, had it been present. Also found in heavy residues from the flotation samples were some tiny flakes of quartz and chert, most slightly polished, probably from water transport. We have not determined whether such tiny chert items are a natural part of the bed load of the ancient river that flowed into the old estuary, or whether they indicate early stone tool use on or near this site.

The frequencies of items from the earlier sieved samples are in Table B.4. Some layers were excavated in two spits, here designated "upper" and "lower."

There are several interesting patterns in this table. First, most sherds are in features. Second, some cracked rock is in designated features, while the other contexts with much rock are directly under Feature 1, supporting the idea that they too are in a feature. This is perhaps rock cracked in steam cooking, a common type of cooking among foragers everywhere. Finally, the estuarine and marine shell is also concentrated below Feature 1, further supporting the idea that Feature 1 continues downward.

Analabe-Régis (Site 786.9-1408.7): Unit G and Unit VI

During our first survey season of 2007, we moved south and east of Vohemar into an area on the right bank of the old former estuary. This area, called Analabe or "the big forest," had been a protected tract of coastal forest until 1972, when the forest was badly damaged by a cyclone. The forest was not allowed to regenerate; instead it was divided into small tracts, which were sold to farmers, most of whom chose to plant coconuts. This creates a problem for archaeologists, because the ground around coconuts develops a thick, coarse grass cover, and the ground surface with the sherds and shells that mark coastal archaeological sites is rarely visible. Nonetheless we found many sites in the area, of which Analabe-Régis seems to be the largest. Over much of the site, the coconuts had died without replacement, and the ground was covered with thick and often thorny brush, some of which had been cleared and cultivated for manioc.

On October 2, 2007, we selected an area in a pasture on the south edge of the site next to the wetlands, where charcoal burning pits had exposed some sherds. We laid out a one-meter square excavation (Unit G: Labordes 786.9-1408.6, Mercator S13° 22' 09"/ E50° 00' 29", UTM Zone 39 L E0392589-N852134). The excavators were Robert Dewar, Henry Wright, Jean-Yves Régis, and Jean-Aimé Andriamaherilala. The following stratigraphy was defined (Table B.5, Figure B.2).

The rocks in the northeast corner of Layer 4 should have been defined as a feature and better described; it is only noted that the rocks were "burned." Unfortunately, Unit G is near several recent charcoal burning pits, and the samples from these layers could contain recent intrusive charcoal, so we did not submit any for dating.

The items found in this unit are given in Table B.6.

Worried by the small sample of Sandy Ware diagnostic sherds from Unit G, we returned to Analabe-Régis on October 15, 2008, to make another sounding in the central part of the site (Unit VI: Labordes 786.9-1408.7: S13° 22' 04.4"/ E50° 00' 32.6", UTM 0392694.7-8521962.2). The excavators were Henry Wright, Harisoa Ravoviarimanara, and Jean-Yves Régis. This revealed a well-defined stratigraphy similar to Unit G, but with more diagnostic sherds than the first unit. The contexts are as follows (Table B.7, Figure B.3).

The two units have similarities, probably a result of common archaeogeological processes. Before occupation,

Table B.5. Deposits in Excavation Unit G at Analabe-Régis.

Context	Mean thickness	Estimated volume	Composition	Comment
Layer (1)	.04 m	.04 m^3	Dark brown humic sand and litter	AP Horizon, few sherds
Layer (2)	.09 m	.09 m^3	Dark brown humic sand	AP Horizon, some sherds
Layer (3a)	.04 m	.04 m^3	Dark gray sand, sherds, and shell	Pavement of Rough Ware sherds
Layer (3b)	.15 m	.15 m^3	Gray sand with sherds and shell	Midden layer, sherds on edge
Layer (4)	.11 m	.11 m^3	Dark gray sandy silt; rocks in NE	Midden layer, many shells and sherds
Layer (5)	.08 m	.08 m^3	Mottled gray, brown sand	Former Ah Horizon, few sherds
Layer (6)	-	-	Grayish white sand	AL Horizon, no cultural traces

Table B.6. Artifacts from the contexts of Excavation Unit G at Analabe-Régis.

Context	Sandy Ware						Rough Ware						Other
	Oxidized			Reduced			Oxidized			Reduced			
	Thick	Med.	Other	Thick	Med.	Other	Thick	Med.	Rims	Thick	Med.	Rims	
Layer (1)	-	2	-	-	1	1 jar	-	9	1 basin	-	-	-	1 thb bottle chip*
Layer (2)	3	25	-	-	4	-	5	78	8 basin	1	11	-	-
Layer (3)	17	98	6 bowl	4	7	1 basin 1 jar	89	17	28 basin	1	33	1 basin	1 c-s basin rim* 14 cracked rocks 11 *Terebralia*
Layer (4)	5	48	5 bowl 2 jar 2 base fragments	3	8	3 bowl	17	152	24 basin 1 jar	3	21	-	6 *Terebralia* 2 conch
Layer (5)	-	3	-	2	-	1 basin	-	4	1 basin	-	1	-	-

*thb = Three Horses Beer (a brand introduced in the 1940s and still popular); c-s = chlorite schist

Table B.7. Deposits in Excavation Unit VI at Analabe-Régis.

Context	Mean thickness	Estimated volume	Composition	Comment
Layer (1)	.03 m	.03 m^3	Dark brown humic sand and roots	Loose surface litter, few sherds
Layer (2)	.09 m	.09 m^3	Dark gray sand	AP Horizon, few sherds
Layer (3a)	.04 m	.04 m^3	Compact dark gray sand	Midden, many sherds
Layer (3b)	.05 m	.05 m^3	Dark gray sand with sherds and shell	Sherd pavement, many sherds
Layer (3c)	.11 m	.11 m^3	Dark gray	Former Ah Horizon, few sherds
Layer (4a)	.07 m	.07 m^3	Mottled dark and light gray sand	Transition, very few sherds
Layer (4b)	-	-	Grayish yellow white sand	AL Horizon, no cultural traces

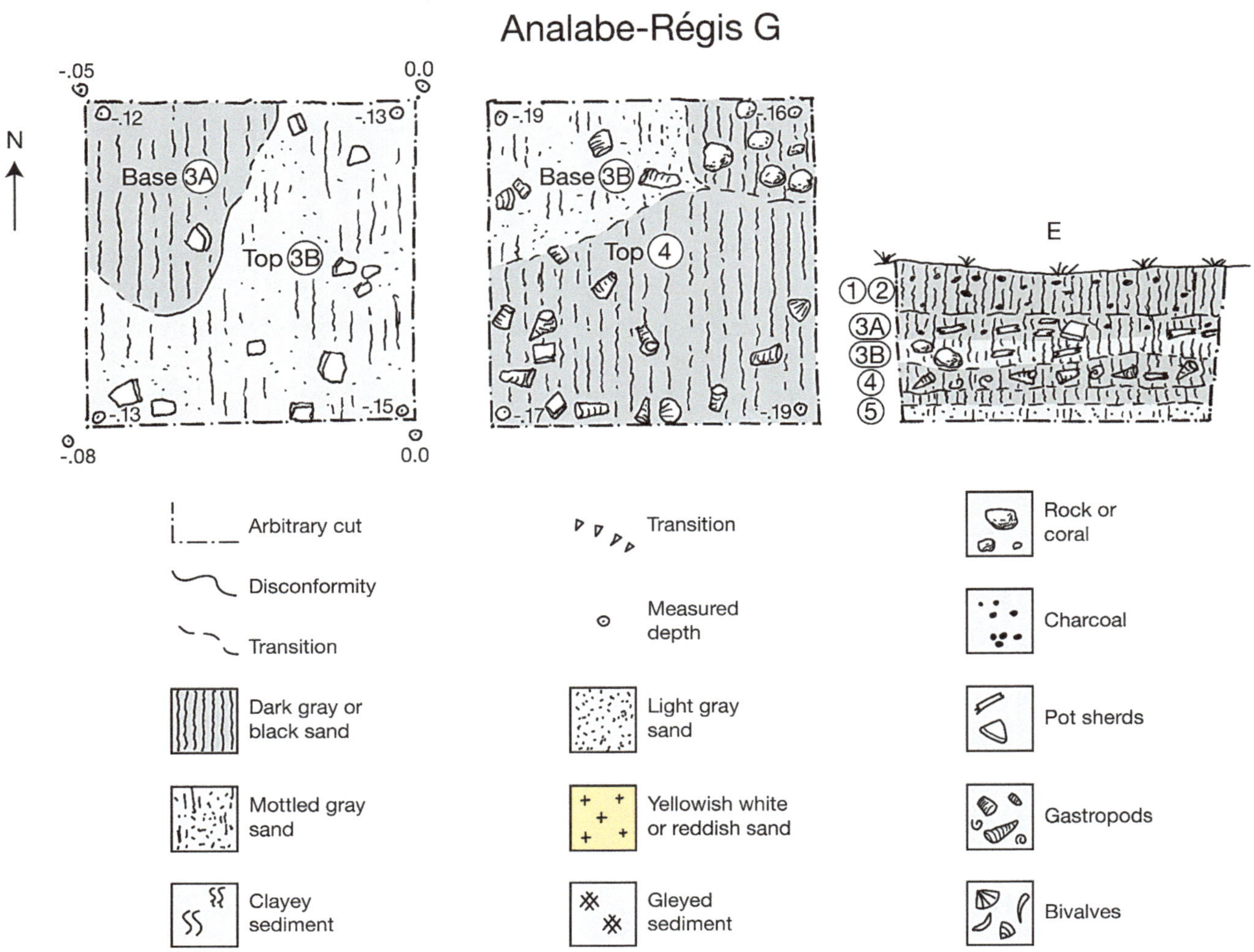

Figure B.2. Plans and sections of Analabe-Régis Excavation Unit G and key to appendix figure symbols.

both units developed deep leached AL horizons and a relatively intact humic AH horizons. That the latter is intact indicates that occupation over the site's large (approximately 5 ha.) area was of low intensity. Both units have similar dark organic middens, both with notable pavements of pottery fragments. The sherds composing the pavements are mostly from Rough Ware basins. Their presence may indicate that whatever special use these basins had was widely performed in the community or, alternatively, that secondary recycling of vessels fragments broken somewhere else were widely used for architectural purposes. Finally, both units end with a deep deposit of sand with relatively few cultural traces. The sherds found there were probably brought up by animal burrowing, by cultivating manioc or yams, or by tree falls during cyclones. We suggest that after abandonment, there was much exposed sand near the site, and this was carried in by the wind, sealing the middens. This sand was subsequently cultivated.

In Table B.8, we list items found in these contexts.

The two units generally have similar ceramic types, which constitute the type samples for our Analabe Phase. They differ, however, in several ways attributable to human activities. For example, Unit G, on the periphery of the site, adjacent to the former embayment, has copious evidence of the processing of estuarine resources such as *Terebralia* shell, but Unit VI, near the center of the site, has less. Also, Unit G has no evidence of post structures, while Unit VI has possible post molds originating from Layer 3c and penetrating into Layer 4. Finally, there are differences in the Sandy Ware, thought to be for domestic storage, cooking

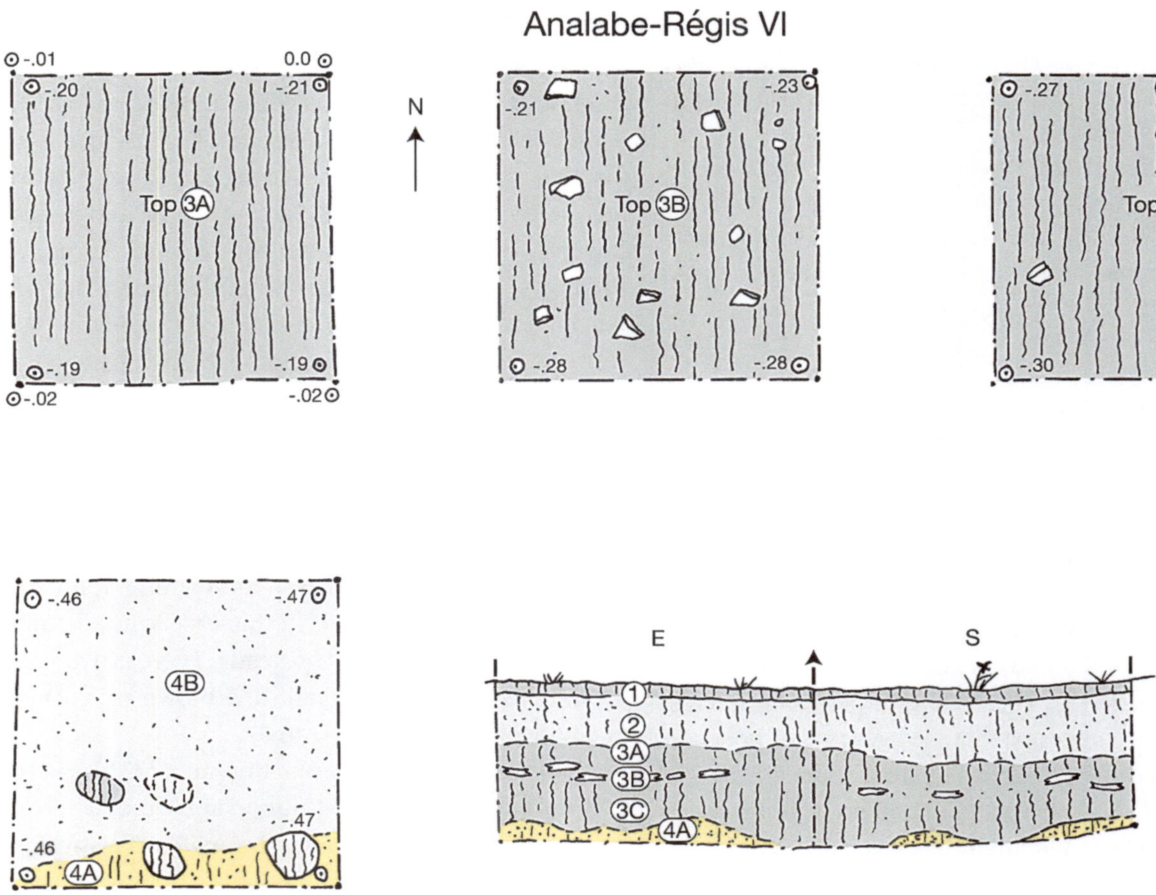

Figure B.3. Plans and sections of Analabe-Régis Unit VI.

Table B.8. Artifacts from the contexts of Excavation Unit VI at Analabe-Régis.

Context	Sandy Ware						Rough Ware						Other
	Oxidized			Reduced			Oxidized			Reduced			
	Thick	Med.	Other	Thick	Med.	Rim	Thick	Med.	Other	Thick	Med.	Other	
Layer (2)	-	19	1 flat-rim bowl	1	3	1 sm bowl	7	2	4 basin	-	-	-	-
Layer (3a)	12	57	8 bowl	-	-	-	53	72	11 basin	1	3	-	1 *Terebralia* 1 c-s thin body 1 agate pebble
Layer (3b)	5	36	1 bowl 1 h-m	-	2	-	48	37	7 basin	-	-	-	7 *Terebralia* 6 cracked rock 1 c-s fragment 2 sm basalt flakes
Layer (3c)	2	6	1 h-m	-	1	1 bowl	8	6	1 basin	-	2	-	3 *Terebralia*
Layer (4a)	-	8	1 bowl	-	1	-	6	4	2 basin	-	1	-	1 *Terebralia*

h-m = hole-mouth, c-s = chlorite schist

and serving. In the central area, small bowls thought to be for food serving are more common relative to jars than on the periphery. However, samples are small. Clearly more excavation is needed to recover both more structural remains and more domestic debris.

The occurrence of agate merits comment. Agate occurs naturally on the south slope of Ambatomalama, a Mesozoic outcrop 3.3 km west of Analabe. This piece is unworked, but agate can be made into beads, and natural agate could have been traded.

Razanakoto (786.9-1410.2): Unit I (i)*

**Editor's note: this is the alphabetical i, not the Roman numeral one.*

During our first season, we found a few sherds in mixed collections that were very similar in form and decoration to ceramics of the eleventh to fourteenth centuries from the large port of Mahilaka on Madagascar's northwest coast (Radimilahy 1998). These were of particular interest because it has been suggested that the later port of Vohemar might have been settled by refugees from Mahilaka (Vérin 1975: 85–106, P.C.). However, we found no well-preserved site where a sealed sample might be excavated in order the characterize this period. In fact, our residence in Vohemar—the Sol y Mar Hotel and Bistro—was very close to such a site. In 2008, Victor Razanatovo found Mahilaka-like sherds in a parking area. Coring revealed a deeper deposit in the swale behind the second beach in the garden of Paul Razanakoto. We excavated a one-meter square in this deeper deposit (08-002, Labordes 787.9-1410.2, Mercator S13° 21' 10.5"/ E50° 00' 32.9", UTM Zone 39L E0392688.8-N8523621.5). The excavators were Robert Dewar, Henry Wright, Harisoa Ravoviarimanara, and Victor Razanatovo. The stratigraphy was as follows (see Table B.9, Figure B.4).

Layer 4 is a natural sand deposit. Layer 3 was a mottled sand, except for an intrusive feature with a gray sand fill definable in the center of the square. This divided into three discrete smaller disturbances, indicating the feature was the mold of a tree stump. The few sherds and bones from Layer 3 were in this disturbance. Because charcoal found in Layers 2b and 3 could be from this modern disturbance, we did not submit any for dating. Originating in Layer 2b were two smaller disturbances, perhaps postholes, noted in the southeast and southwest sections. Layer 2a was an earlier cultivated deposit. Layer 1 is a recent cultivated deposit with plastic bags, glass, etc. Originating from this is a pit, visible in the south section, filled with plastic and other twentieth-century debris.

This is a typical northeast coast stratigraphy. There is an underlying beach sand, in this case with no surviving evidence of Holocene soil horizons. There is a thin midden layer, and there is additional sand blown or washed over this midden, recently cultivated.

This small sample from this unit (Table B.10) has predominantly reduced thinner and finer sherds. The predominance of bowls versus jars marks this as a domestic assemblage. The complete absence of Rough Ware, common on other Razanakoto sites as well as earlier and later sites, is striking. It is also notable that the ceramics in the surface collection from this site are predominantly oxidized, as are those in surface collections from some other sites of this phase. It may be that the surface sherds have been burned in brush fires, only being oxidized in recent times. It is also possible that with more excavation, the Razanakoto Phase will be divided into an earlier phase with more reduced

Table B.9. Deposits in Excavation Unit I at Razanakoto.

Context	Mean thickness	Estimated volume	Composition	Comment
Layer (1)	.24 m	.250 m^3	Mottled gray sand	AP: Bottles, plastic, metal items, etc
Layer (2a)	.11 m	.075 m^3	Lighter mottled gray sand	AP: Some sherds
Layer (2b)	.12 m	.080 m^3	Black organic sand, coral fragments	Midden: sherds, shell, bone
Layer (3)	.05 m	.045 m^3	Mottled gray sand, coral fragments	Transition
Layer (4)	-	-	Yellow white sand	Beach sand, no cultural traces

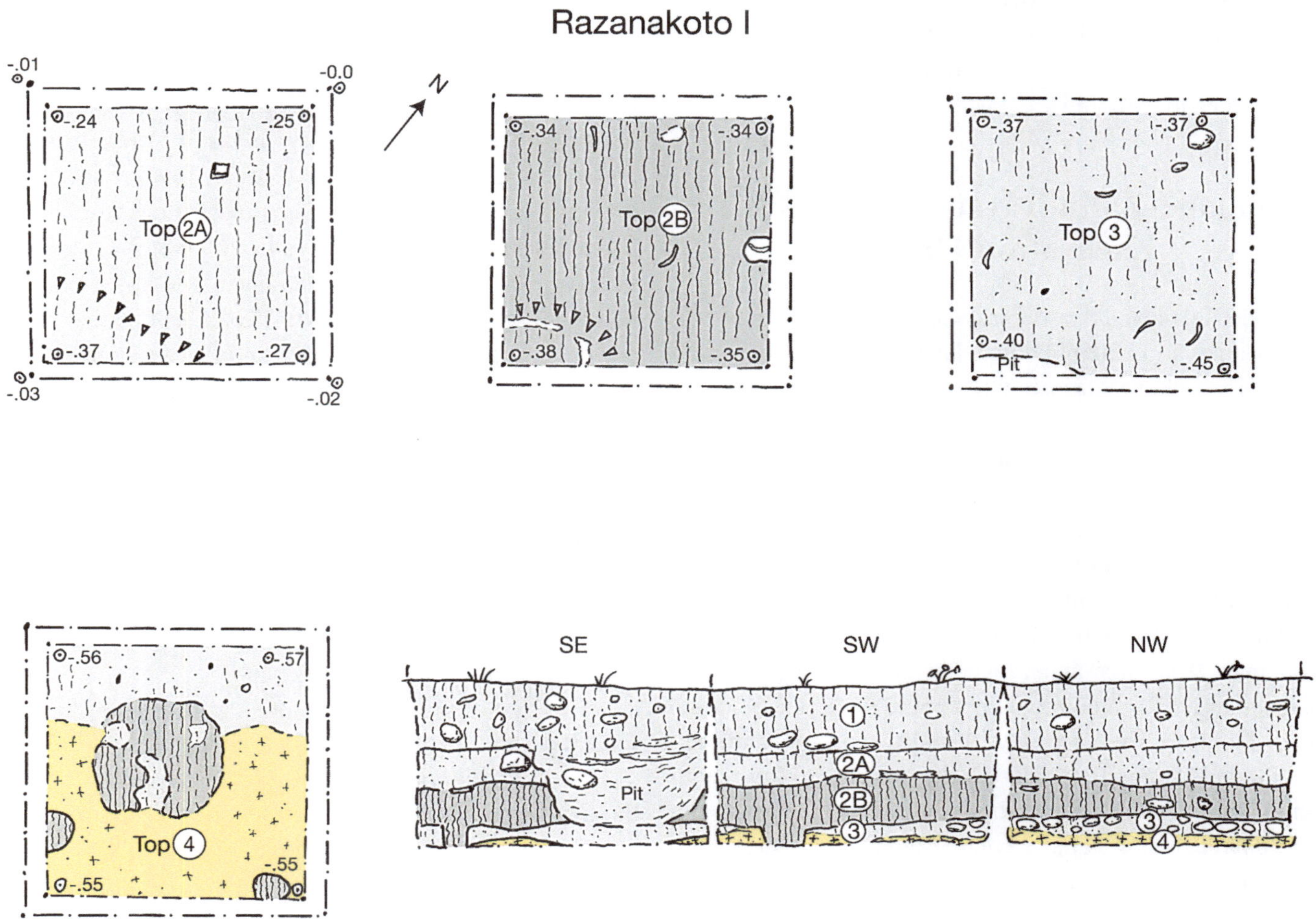

Figure B.4. Plans and sections from Razanakoto Unit I.

Table B.10. Items from the sieved contexts of Excavation I at Razanakoto.

Context	Sandy Ware						Bone		Other
	Oxidized			Reduced					
	Thick	Med.	Other	Med.	Thin	Rim	Fish	Mammal	
Layer (2a)	3	17	1 bowl 1 jar	22	3	-	2	1	1 modern glass
Layer (2b)	-	17	2 bowl	17	3	1 bowl 1 jar	-	-	2 slag 1 daub
Layer (3)	-	7	2 bowl	12	-	1 jar	4	4	1 c-s weight
Layer (4)	-	-	-	3	-	-	4	-	1 slag

c-s = chlorite schist

pottery and a later phase with more oxidized pottery. The possible postholes and burned daub indicate the presence of structures, and the iron slag indicates at least iron forging, so this site had residential and craft activities and was not merely a canoe landing.

Analabe-Zafindravao (787.5-1408.2): Excavation Unit IX

We hoped 2014 would be our last season of survey. However, during analysis in 2016, I noted that there was no larger site of the Razanakoto Phase, but there was an unsurveyed tract of about 5.0 ha., around which were situated several smaller Razanakoto Phase sites. On the one hand, it seemed possible that there would have been a gradual development of scale and complexity of human settlement around the Bay of Iharana, and therefore there would be a Razanakoto Phase center intermediate in size between tenth- to eleventh-century Analabe-Régis and fifteenth- to sixteenth-century Vohemar. If so, this unsurveyed tract would be the only place a larger Razanakoto center could have been. On the other hand, Pierre Vérin (P.C.) and Chantal Radimilahy (1998) had proposed that during the eleventh to fourteenth centuries CE, the great northwest coast port of Mahilaka would have so dominated northern Madagascar that smaller competing ports would have withered. We needed to test these competing proposals. Examination of the 2016 satellite images showed that the house of the landowner who did not allow survey in 2007 was gone, and that the coconut groves were being divided into small parcels. The threat of destruction gave further impetus to a return to Vohemar to survey this unexamined tract. The details of our return and our negotiations are given in Appendix A.

After we established that 2007 collection areas 07-032 and 034 and the 2018 collection areas 18-002 to 18-004 formed a continuous artifact scatter—a single site—covering more than 2.0 ha., we cored the central portion with the permission of landowner Mme. Zafindravao, looking for area less damaged by the wind. The sand was dry and coring was difficult. The midden layers were thin, but we did find areas with some deposits protected from the ravages of the wind. We excavated a one-meter square in this protected deposit (18-002, Labordes 787.9-1410.3, Mercator S13° 21' 10.5"/ E50° 00' 32.9", UTM Zone 39L E0393292.0-N8521363.2). The excavators were Henry Wright, Annita Ramankierana, and Sylvain Velomora. The stratigraphy was as follows.

Layer 4 (Figure B.5) is a natural sand deposit with a brownish tint, indicating the beginning of iron accumulation in a Middle Holocene B horizon. Layer 3 was mottled sand, with distinct white and nearly black mottles, probably created by insect burrowing through black humic sand into the white leached zone. The few artifacts from Layers 3 and 4 were probably intrusive from Layer 2. Originating in Layer 2b was a small disturbance, perhaps a small pit noted in north section. Unfortunately it had neither sherds nor datable charcoal. Layers 2a and 2b are interpreted as midden deposits. Layer 1B is a disturbed humic sand and Layer 1A is the remains of higher, later layers deflated by the wind.

These deposits begin as a typical northeast coast stratigraphy (Table B.11). There is an underlying beach sand, in this case without evident soil horizons. There are thin midden deposits resting on these. There was, however, no additional sand over this midden protecting the deposits, and they were damaged by the wind.

Two issues merit discussion: the first regarding site formation, the second regarding activities.

First, considering the densities of the ceramics from the deposits in Unit IX (Table B.12), note that relatively undisturbed Layer 2a has about 20 sherds per 10-liter volume, while uppermost Layer 1 has about 40 sherds per 10-liter volume. If the two deposits originally had a similar density of sherds, this indicates that this part of Analabe Centre has lost at least 7 centimeters of sand matrix to deflation. Thus the deposits remaining below were protected by a sherd pavement rather than a thick layer of sand, as at Analabe-Régis, Razanakoto, and Patrick. This may explain why organics such as shell and bone were uncommon at Analabe Centre and why features such as small pits and post molds were poorly preserved.

Second, turning to the details of the ceramics from this unit: they are predominantly reduced, thinner, and finer sherds contrasting with those from Analabe-Régis. They are similar to those from the collections from area 07-032 and from the Razanakoto site itself. The predominance of bowls versus jars marks this as a domestic assemblage. The occurrence of Rough Ware, common on other Razanakoto sites as well as earlier and later sites, may indicate the pursuit of special activities. There is no indication that the small samples from these thin Razanakoto deposits imply any differences

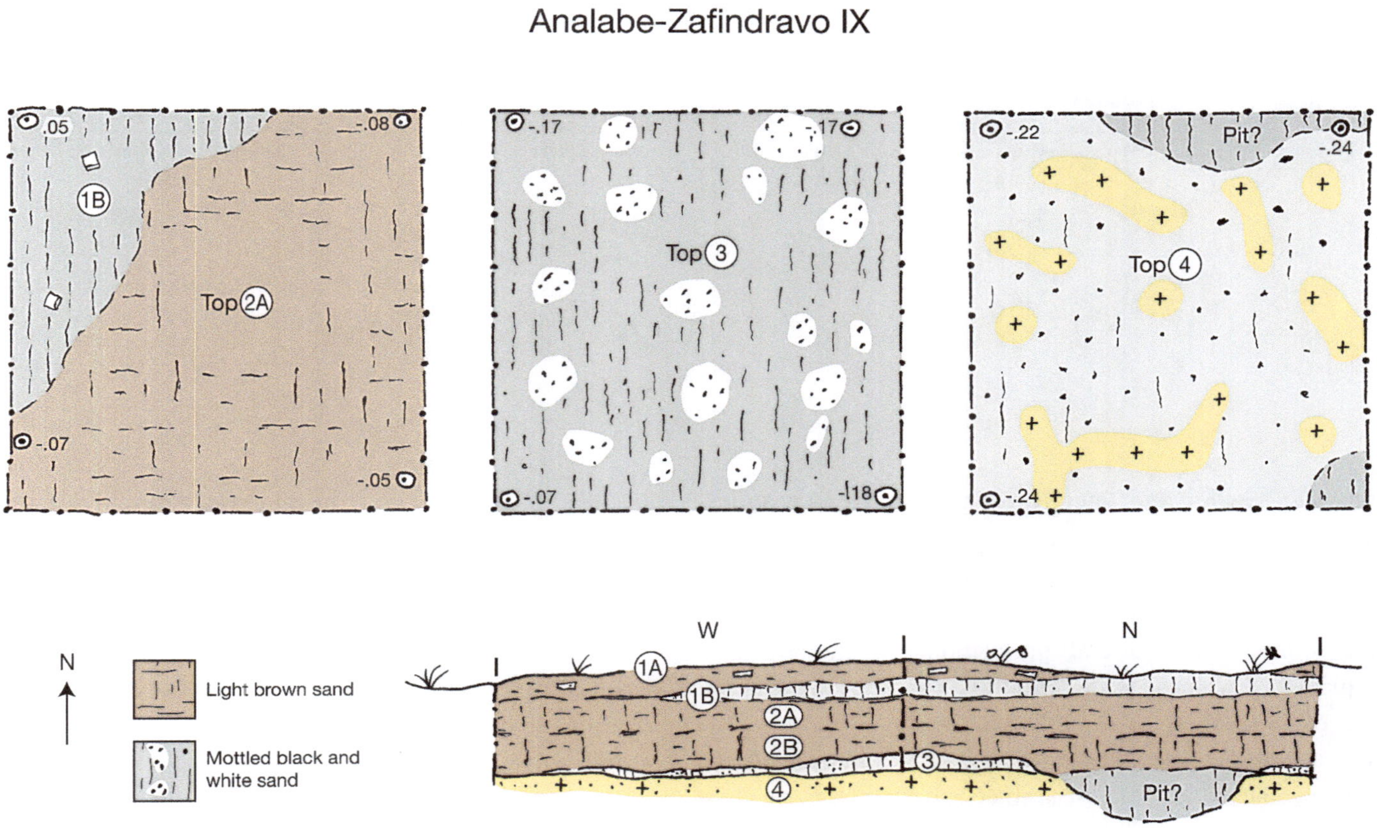

Figure B.5. Plans and sections of Analabe-Zafindravao, Unit IX.

Table B.11. Deposits in Excavation Unit IX at Analabe-Zafindravao.

Context	Mean thickness	Estimated volume	Composition	Comment
Layer (1a)	.07 m	.070 m^3	Dark gray sand	Bottles, plastic, metal items, etc
Layer (1b)	.05 m	.040 m^3	Black sand	AH and L soil horizons mixed by bioturbation
Layer (2a)	.05 m	.050 m^3	Mottled light and dark brown sand	Midden: sherds, shell, bone
Layer (2b)	.05 m	.048 m^3	Mottled light and dark brown sand	Midden: sherds, shell, bone
Layer (3)	.06 m	.055 m^3	Mottled dark gray and white sand	AH and AL horizons mixed by bioturbation
Layer (4)	-	-	Light grayish brown sand	B Horizon, no cultural traces

Table B.12. Artifacts from the sieved contexts of Excavation Unit IX at Analabe-Zafindravao.

Context	Sandy Ware						Hard Sandy Ware Burnished	Rough Ware			Bone		Shell	
	Oxidized			Reduced				Oxidized						
	Thick	Med.	Other	Med.	Thin	Rim		Thick	Med.	Rim	Fish	Mammal	*Terebralia*	Other
Layer (1)	14	133	4 bowl 3 jar	1	138	4 bowl 4 jar	3 jar	2	5	2 basin	2	4	5	48
Layer (2a)	4	62	1 bowl 1 jar	-	49	3 bowl 1 jar	-	-	2	3 basin	1	1	2	43
Layer (2b)	-	2	-	1	13	1 bowl	-	-	1	1 basin	-	-	1	2
Layer (3)	-	5	-	-	2	-	-	-	1	-	-	6	-	6

between earlier and later Razanakoto phase ceramics. While the pottery does seem essentially domestic, there is no additional support, in the form of possible postholes and burned daub, for the presence of domestic structures. There is also no evidence of craft production or of the receipt of typical Indian Ocean trade ceramics, in contrast to the beach site of Razanakoto, a short distance to the north. As far as we can tell, Analabe-Zafindravao has neither the size nor the supra-domestic activities of a center, and so the evidence best conforms to the second proposal, that there was no center during Razanakoto times.

Vohemar-Bambino (786.4-1409.8): Excavation Unit II

Bambino is located in the central area of modern Vohemar, about 245 m northeast of the main mosque. This unit was placed in the play area of the abandoned school in hopes of finding evidence of the fourteenth- to sixteenth-century CE town of Vohemar. The earliest cultural deposit of Layer 4B appears to be a seaside work area of the Ambatary Phase. There is no deposit between the fifteenth- to sixteenth-century Ambatary deposit and the dense twentieth-century deposits. Probably most seventeenth- to nineteenth-century deposits were removed by wave action or by land leveling after 1895 to lay out the street grid and building lots for the early colonial town of Vohemar.

This excavation was not very useful, and we do not show plans and sections. The presence of laminated deposits in Layer 4b, however, may be an indication of a tsunami, rather than simply a normal cyclone, during or after the Ambatary Phase (Tables B.13, B.14). This may relate to a local tradition, recorded by Mayeur (1912) during his visit in 1775, that the town of foreigners, which existed before at Vohemar, was destroyed by a storm. These deposits need examination by a geologist experienced in tsunami impact.

Vohemar-Ambatary (786.6-1409.8): Excavation Unit VIII

As discussed in the main text, we expected to easily find a large site of the fifteenth and sixteenth centuries CE, mentioned in sixteenth-century texts and implied by the 1942–1955 cemetery excavations. This phase, however, was the last to be defined. It required a deliberate search to find evidence of a large town of this period under the buildings and debris of the modern town.

Our search led us to a distinctive mound with surface sherds of the fifteenth and sixteenth centuries. With the permission of the owner, M. Albert Razafindrakoto, we cored this mound and found more than a meter of deposits. We immediately decided to attempt a stratigraphic excavation.

Our one-meter square was located in a garden for manioc, papayas, and coconuts (Unit VIII: 09-012: Labordes 786.6-1409.8, Mercator S13° 30' 28.5"/ E50° 00' 23.9", UTM E0392433.8-N8523064.6). The square was oriented to the corner points in hopes of transecting any dip of the strata to the southwest. Alas, the strata were more

Table B.13. Deposits in Excavation Unit II at Vohemar-Bambino.

Context	Mean thickness	Estimated volume	Composition	Comment
Layer (1)	.18 m	.18 m^3	Black sand	AP: 20th c. glass, plastic, metal items, etc
Layer (2)	.12 m	.75 m^3	Gray sand	AP: 20th c. glass, bone, plastic, metal items, European ceramics, etc
Layer (3)	.25+ m	.13+ m^3	Lenses of black and gray sand	Pit fill: Early 20th c. trash
Layer (4a)	.05 m	.03 m^3	Dark gray sand lenses	AH: Possible humus remnant
Layer (4b)	.24 m	.05 m^3	Light brown sand, finely laminated	Wave-washed beach sand: some sherds, rolled coral fragments
Layer (5)	-	-	Light brown sand	Beach sand: no cultural traces

Table B.14. Artifacts from the sieved Layer 4b context of Excavation Unit II at Vohemar-Bambino.

Context	Ceramics (rolled)			Other
	Medium Sandy Ware		Fine Sandy Ware	Chlorite Schist
	Oxidized	Reduced	Oxidized	
Layer (4b)	2 medium plain bodies 3 medium body, burnished orange slip (Ambatary) 1 bowl, round lip, internally thickened	1 medium plain body 1 interior thickened lip bowl rim, burnished orange slip (Ambatary) 1 hole-mouth jar rim, burnished, arcuate incised (Patrick)	1 medium body	1 coarse red body 1 coarse gray lathe-turned basin rim (Analabe-Ambatary) 1 fine gray lathe-turned body, drilled hole (Analabe-Ambatary)

complicated! The excavators were Robert Dewar, Henry Wright, Victor Razanatovo, and Harisoa Ravoviarimanara. The stratigraphy is as follows.

The deepest deposit tested (Figure B.6, Table B.15) is the reddish-brown sand of Layer 7, which had few cultural traces. From the bottom of the excavation, at 1.40 m below surface, we cored downward through very light brown beach sand and coral fragments to 2.00 m. below surface and found no traces of older occupation. Above Layer 7, we removed red-brown transitional Layer 6 with some cultural material. It is possible that Layers 6 and 7 are a disturbed Holocene B-horizon with some iron accumulation. If so, the overlying leached A-Horizon is no longer visible. Above this is the well-defined Layer 5b midden, with copious amounts of ceramics, fish and mammal bone, slag, and chlorite schist fragments. Mixed with ordinary Ambatary sherds in the midden of Layer 5b and scattered in later layers were a few sherds of oxidized thick, plain Coarse Sandy Ware, typical of the Ampasimahavelona or Analabe phases, suggesting that there had been earlier deposits in situ, but that the intensity of the initial fifteenth-century occupation has mixed up all traces of these earlier deposits. The early midden of Layer 5b produced a charcoal fragment with a 95% probability of a date from AD 1290 to 1410 (see Appendix C), as well as the rim of a Chinese blue-and-white porcelain cup of the late fourteenth or early fifteenth centuries. The area was then leveled off and a light gray sand floor, on which was the hard black sand floor deposit of Layer 5a, with many sherds, chlorite schist fragments, bits of iron slag, and organic items. This floor may be related to several possible postholes on the southeast side of the unit, visible in section. Subsequent to the building and use of this structure, the use of this area changed radically. In Layer 4, from .93 to .70 m below surface, the deposits became predominantly brown sand with dark and light gray lenses with some sherds, shells, and chlorite schist fragments. In Layer 3, from .70 to .27 m below surface, the deposits are predominantly dark gray sand with lenses of light gray and brown sand and similar artifacts. These layers and lenses are probably debris swept into baskets around domestic compounds and dumped on a neighborhood trash heap, just as ladies in the neighborhood assiduously did every day when we were working. The fact that these trash deposits are mostly a lighter sand in the beginning, and become darker through time, is perhaps a testimony to the creation of an urban environment with more organic debris. However, there may have been times when the dump had other uses. A possible posthole—visible in the southeast section and the successive plans of the tops of Layers 3b, 3c, and 3d—originates in Layer 3a from a point near a larger light sand lens, perhaps a remnant of a floor, visible in the southwest section. Above these trash deposits is the disturbed dark gray sand of Layers 1 and 2, filled with the debris of twentieth-century Vohemar, from which was cut a large posthole with pieces of plastic in it, visible in the northwest section. This may be the only trace of the artillery battery of 1942.

In Tables B.16a, B.16b, and B.16.c, we enumerate the artifacts found in these contexts. Unsieved Layer 1 is not included, but the sieved portion of Layer 2 is included, even though it has evidence of modern disturbance.

We note that in spite of the large volume excavated and the many well-made sherds, there are only a few rims from Unit VIII. They are predominantly large bowls, suggesting—as does the well-preserved faunal material (see Appendix E)—that the deposits we have sampled at Ambatary are domestic trash left by cooking and serving. Perhaps useful from a chronological perspective, the occurrence of thin reduced sherds in the lower Layers 5 and 6 is intriguing. Such ceramics are common in the Central Highlands during the fifteenth to seventeenth centuries. Perhaps some of the potters in Vohemar during the earlier subphase of the Ambatary Phase were trained in the highlands. In contrast, the occurrence of boldly incised sherds in the Layers 3 and 4 (Figure 10.1 m,n), may be a local innovation in ceramic decoration, which marks a later subphase of the Ambatary Phase.

Were we to follow hallowed past procedures focused on the building of chronologies, we would convert the sherd frequencies into proportions within each layer and search for shifts from the older lowest layers to the high more recent layers. Such procedures tacitly assume the archaeological record is a direct representation of styles created by artisans. In fact, between the ancient work of the artisans and recent work of archaeologists, many other processes affect the occurrence of artifacts. Such processual effects are particularly complicated on urban sites such as fifteenth- to sixteenth-century Vohemar. To account for such processes, we use both the counts of items and their weights. In contrast to excavations made during the 2007 and 2008 seasons, many common classes of material from Ambatary Unit VIII have been weighed as well as counted. The postmaster in the Vohemar post office was so kind as

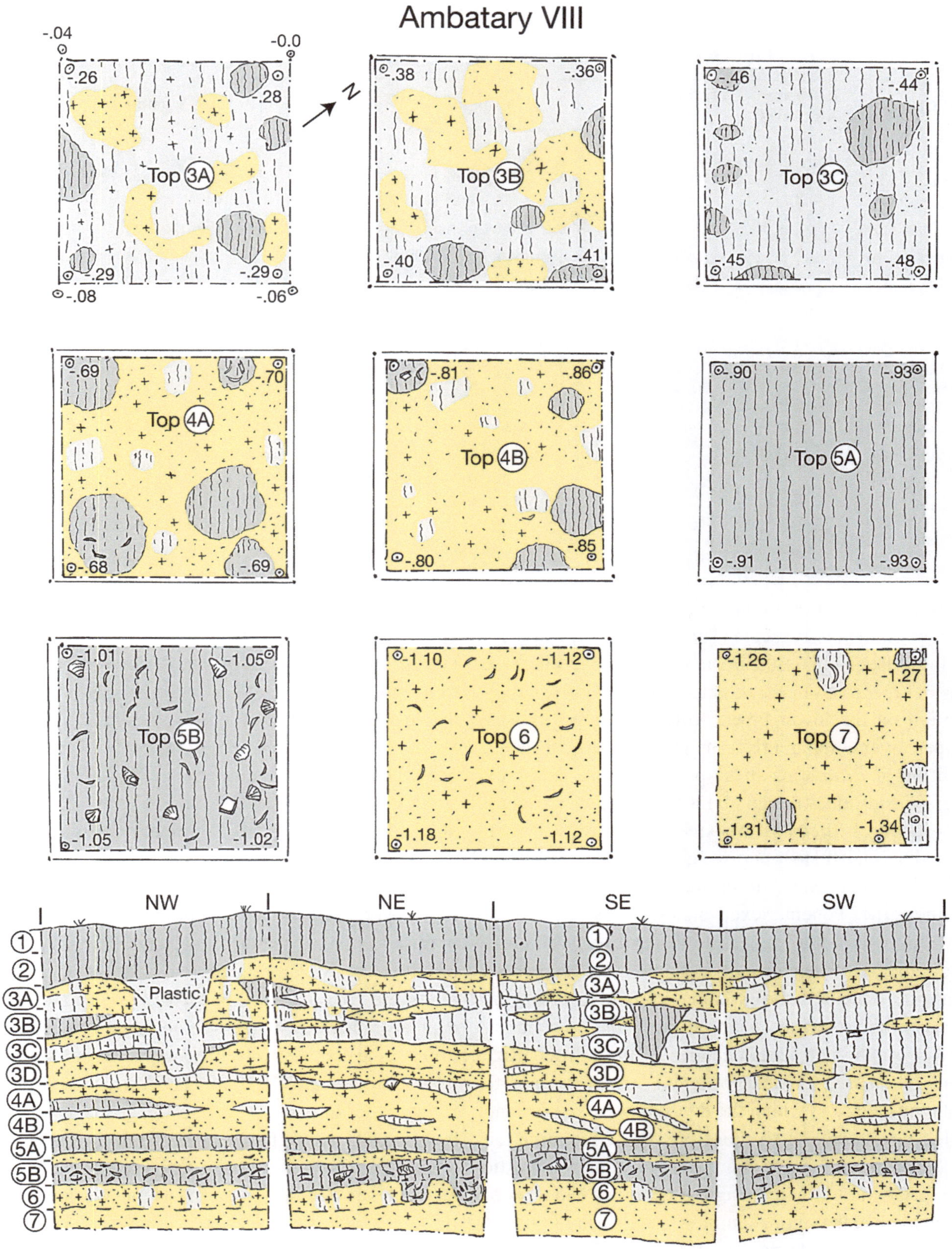

Figure B.6. Plans and sections of Vohemar-Ambatary, Unit VIII.

Table B.15. Deposits in Excavation Unit VIII at Vohemar-Ambatary.

Context	Mean thickness	Estimated volume	Composition	Comment
Layer (1)	.12 m	.120 m^3	Dark gray sand	Disturbed surface sand: modern trash
Layer (2)	.14 m	.140 m^3	Dark gray sand	Recently cultivated sand: few sherds
Layer (3a)	.12 m	.120 m^3	Mottled dark gray and brown sand	Possible surface: some sherds, slag
Layer (3b)	.10 m	.098 m^3	Mottled light gray and brown sand	Loads of trash: some sherds
Layer (3c)	.12 m	.115 m^3	Mottled dark and light gray sand	Loads of trash: some sherds
Layer (3d)	.10 m	.094 m^3	Mottled light gray sand	Possible surface: some sherds, slag
Layer (4a)	.11 m	.100 m^3	Mottled gray-brown sand	Loads of trash: some sherds
Layer (4b)	.12 m	.101 m^3	Mottled gray-brown sand	Loads of trash: some sherds
Layer (5a)	.11 m	.090 m^3	Hard black sand, gray sand below	Floors
Layer (5b)	.11 m	.081 m^3	Dark grayish brown sand with shell	Midden: many sherds, bones
Layer (6)	.10 m	.071 m^3	Reddish brown sand with shell	Mixed transitional layer: some sherds
Layer (7)	.12+ m	-	Light reddish brown sand	Beach sand: No cultural traces

to allow us to weigh the common classes of items from each layer on his metric scale. This was done specifically to facilitate the estimation of mean size of artifacts in these classes in order to compare possible primary or secondary deposition on the lower layers to tertiary deposition in the upper layers, apparently a neighborhood trash heap. In addition to evaluating these proposals, we learned a number of additional things about town life in a modest neighborhood of fifteenth- to sixteenth-century Vohemar. In general, it is useful to report weights as well as counts on all controlled samples, but unfortunately we were unable to weigh the earlier Vohemar excavated samples.

In Figure B.7, the upper graph represents changes through time in the densities of artifact classes (expressed as items per 10 liter volume), which we take to represent the frequency of the activities that produced them. In contrast, the lower graph represents changes in the average size of items (expressed as mean weights), which we take to indicate the degree to which the deposits were moved and trampled upon, leading to more breakage. Examination of the upper graphs shows that the frequency of domestic activities leading to the breakage of ceramics and discard of mammal bone was more common in the earlier middens and floors of Layer 5. The crafts of finishing chlorite schist vessels and repairing iron tools were also pursued in the Ambatary neighborhood in the time of earlier Layer 6 and 5, after which there is little working of chlorite schist in this neighborhood. There is a later minor increase in iron tool repair at the time of Layers 3a and 3b, when post holes and sand floors indicate some domestic occupation on the trash heap. Such areas have been occupied by the very poor and the homeless since the time of the first cities. This suggests that even the poorest inhabitants of Vohemar were able to repair iron tools. Examination of the lower graph shows that the samples from lowest layers, 5b and 6, are less trampled, but the floor deposits of 5a and the lowest trash layer (Layer 4) are comminuted from the movement of trash from place to place and from trampling. Some parts of Layer 3 show less reduction in fragment size, indicating that these are composed partly of primary and secondary deposits rather than purely tertiary trash. Note that a rise in iron forging debris density is accompanied by a rise in its size. Also note the lack of mammal bone, which may result from the activities of dogs and the destruction of bone in general by soil acids. All of these should be further tested with the additional excavation of the early layers, which are now hidden by modern Vohemar. In general, we now think that it is useful to report the excavated volumes and item weights as well as the counts for all controlled samples. Unfortunately, we were unable to weigh the earlier Vohemar collections.

Table B.16a. Ceramics in the contexts of Excavation Unit VIII at Vohemar-Ambatary.

Context	Coarse Ware			Sandy Ware										Rough Ware		
	Oxidized			Oxidized					Reduced					Oxidized		
	Thick	**Med.**	**Other**	**Thick**	**Med.**	**Thin**	**Other**	**Rim**	**Thick**	**Med.**	**Thin**	**Other**	**Rim**	**Thick**	**Med.**	**Rim**
Layer (2)	1	-	-	6	8	-	-	1 basin 1 bowl	-	2	-	-	-	-	3	-
Layer (3a)	-	1	1 base	5	14	-	-	1 bowl	-	6	-	1 brn	1 bowl	2	2	-
Layer (3b)	-	-	1 foot?	4	10	-	2 brn	1 bowl	-	2	-	-	-	1	1	1 bowl
Layer (3c)	-	-	-	2	7	-	1 rdsl 1 incs	1 jar	1	4	-	-	-	-	3	-
Layer (3d)	-	3	-	2	20	-		1 bowl	-	1	-	-	-	4	9	-
Layer (4a)	1	-	-	4	61	-	1 pnc 1 incs	1 bowl 2 h-m	-	7	-	-	1 h-m	1	2	-
Layer (4b)	-	-	-	2	19	2	-	1 basin 1 jar	-	8	2	-	-	-	4	-
Layer (5a)	-	1	-	5	111	35	2 cmb	2 bowl	-	83	26	-	-	-	23	-
Layer (5b)	2	1	1 basin	7	53	2	1 rdsl	3 bowl	5	26	2	3 brn	-	3	11	1 basin
Layer (6)	1	-	-	2	15	4	-	3 bowl	-	4	3	-	-	-	4	-

Abbreviations: brn = burnished, cmb = combed, h-m = hole-mouth, incs = incised, pnc = punctate, rdsl = red slip.
These are field identifications, counts and weights. A more detailed study of the bone is presented in Appendix E.

Table B.16b. Artifacts in the contexts of Excavation Unit VIII at Vohemar-Ambatary: Other materials.

Context	Chlorite schist		Rough stone			Iron			Shell		Bone**				
	Fragment	**Other**	**Cracked rock**	**Basalt**	**Other**	**Slag**	**Sheet**	**Nails**	***Terebralia* bases**	***Anadara* fragments**	**Large mammal**	**Medium mammal**	**Fish**		**Other**
													Vert	**Spine**	
Layer (2)	8	2 body	1	2 pebbles	1 quartz flake	1	1	2	2	3	1 frg	4 frg	-	-	4 eggshell
Layer (3a)	2	-	-	2 pebbles	-	5	3	1	-	-	3 frg	-	2	-	-
Layer (3b)	1	-	6	1 flake	-	1	3	1	2	2	1 spltr	1 *Capra* mtpd	1	3	-
Layer (3c)	1	-	2	1 flake	-	1	-	-	-	4	4 spltr	6 spltr	2	3	1 bird 1 tortoise
Layer (3d)	3	-	-	2 flakes	-	12	-	-	12	13	1 lumbar	5 spltr	2	5	-
Layer (4a)	94	-	2	2 flakes	-	3	1	-	7	7	1 phalanx 1 rib	3 frg	3	6	1 tortoise
Layer (4b)	38	-	-	-	-	-	-	-	1	2	-	1 frg	3	1	-
Layer (5a)	108	2 body	-	2 flakes	-	19	3 sm	-	6	5	16	27	110	90	3 bird 1 tortoise
Layer (5b)	35	2 top frg	-	1 flake	-	20	2 sm	-	87	19	2	8	1030	210	7 bird 38 tortoise
Layer (6)	8	1 weight?	-	-	-	2	-	-	3	3	1	2	NA	NA	3 tortoise

Abbreviations: frg = fragment, mtpd = metapodial, vert = vertebra. These are field identifications, counts and weights.
A more detailed study of the bone is presented in Appendix E.

Table B.16c. Select counts and weights from Excavation Unit VIII at Vohemar-Ambatary.

Context	Volume (dcl)	Sandy Ware								Rough Ware oxidized				Chlorite schist				Iron Slag and Scale				Large-medium mammal bone			
		Oxidized				Reduced																			
		Count	Weight (gm)	Weight (dcl)	Mean weight	Count	Weight (gm)	Weight (dcl)	Mean weight	Count	Weight (gm)	Weight (dcl)	Mean weight	Count	Weight (gm)	Weight (dcl)	Mean weight	Count	Weight (gm)	Weight (dcl)	Mean weight	Count	Weight (gm)	Weight (dcl)	Mean weight
Layer (3a)	11.64	20	86	7.4	1.4	8	12	1.0	1.5	2	2	.2	1.0	2	NA	-	-	8	76	6.5	9.5	3	5	-	-
Layer (3b)	6.50	18	90	13.8	5.0	2	5	-	-	3	33	5.1	.1	1	NA	-	-	4	18	2.7	4.5	2	4	-	-
Layer (3c)	12.88	11	58	4.5	5.3	5	24	1.9	4.8	3	9	-	-	1	NA	-	-	1	1	-	-	10	NA	-	-
Layer (3d)	8.64	25	97	11.2	3.9	1	5	-	-	13	65	7.5	5.0	3	NA	-	-	12	19	2.2	1.6	6	40	4.6	6.7
Layer (4a)	12.32	69	203	16.4	2.9	8	17	1.4	2.1	3	19	1.5	6.3	94	39	3.2	.4	4	10	-	-	8	13	1.1	1.6
Layer (4b)	7.66	24	49	6.4	2.0	10	25	3.3	2.5	4	8	1.0	2.0	38	17	2.2	.4	1	2	-	-	1	NA	-	-
Layer (5a)	9.13	155	550	60.2	3.5	109	183	20.0	1.7	23	69	7.6	3.0	338	104	11.4	.3	22	140	15.3	6.4	43	130	14.2	3.0
Layer (5b)	8.70	68	520	59.8	7.6	32	177	20.3	5.2	15	96	11.0	6.4	35	55	6.3	1.6	22	113	14.0	5.1	10	171	19.6	17.1
Layer (6)	8.10	24	146	18.0	6.1	7	27	3.3	3.9	4	38	4.7	9.2	8	8	1.0	1.0	2	4	-	-	3	75	9.3	25.0

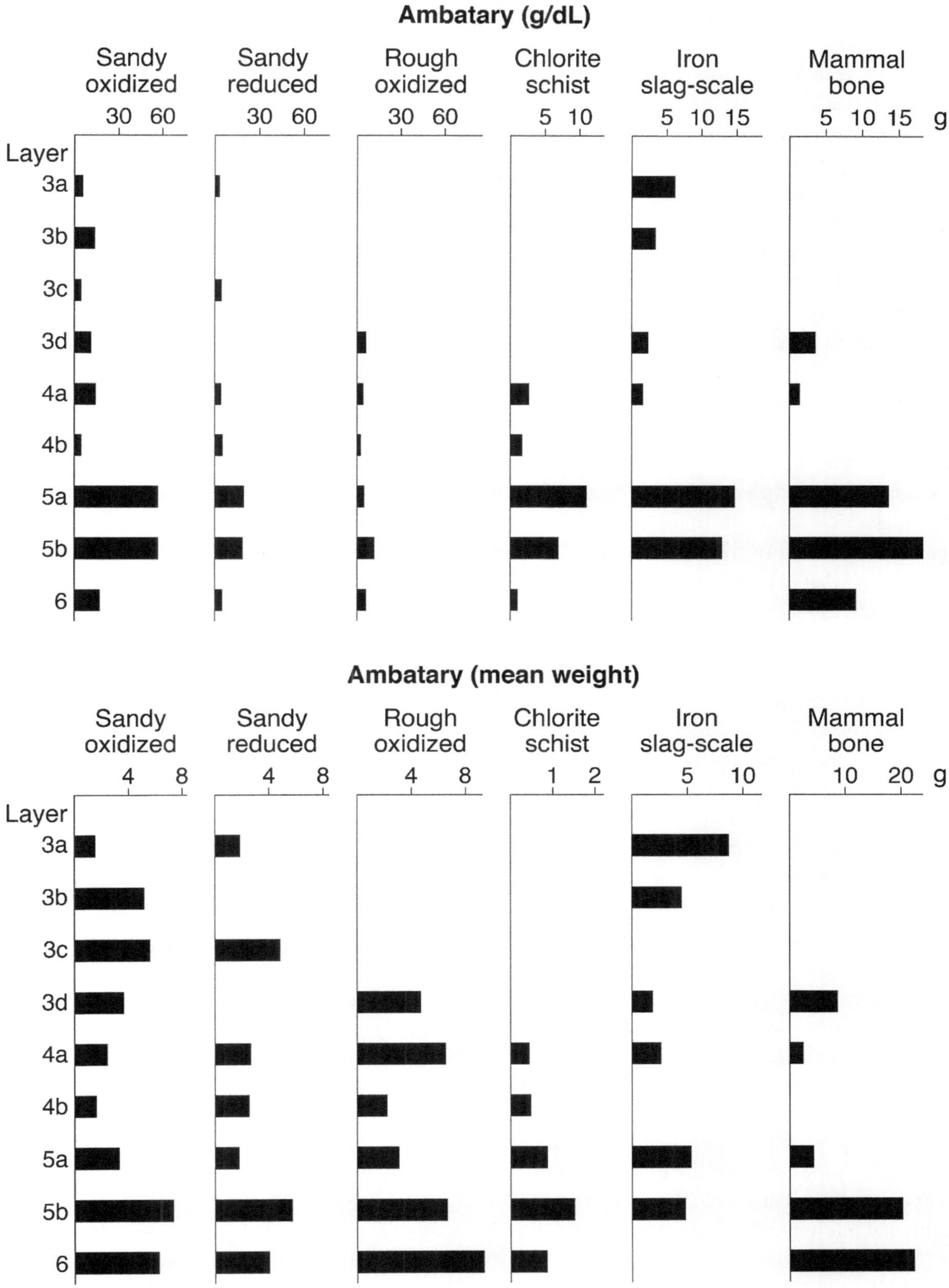

Figure B.7. Changes in densities and average size of items from Ambatary.

Analabe-Patrick (787.8-1407.5): Unit H

In 2007 the survey team working south on the right bank of the old estuary located sites with pottery similar to Mahilaka in the center of Analabe (**787.5-1408.2**). Testing showed that these sites were badly scoured by the wind, and the surviving sherd scatters were no more than .10 m deep. We found a less-disturbed location farther south in the coconut grove of M. Patrick (07-062: Laborde 787.7-1407.5, Mercator S13° 22' 41"/ E50° 00' 56", UTM E0393408.6.6-N8520829.2). We excavated a one-meter square (termed Unit H), hoping to find undisturbed twelfth to fourteenth-century material. To our surprise, what we found is of the seventeenth to early eighteenth centuries CE. We surveyed a one-meter square on October 6, 2017. The excavators were Robert Dewar, Jean-Aimé Andriamaherilala, and Victor Razanatovo. Henry Wright, though ill, recorded plans and sections. The deposits recorded at the Patrick site are as follows.

The earliest layer visible in Unit H (Figure B.8, Table B.17) is the top of what is termed Layer 5, a reddish sand with no cultural traces—certainly the B Horizon, a zone of iron oxide accumulation, which had formed on the Holocene beach. Above this is transitional Layer 4, a mottled gray sand with few sherds, probably the remnants of a light gray leached AL Horizon and a dark gray humic AH Horizon, disturbed by the Patrick Phase occupation. Above is Layer 3, .16 m of dark gray sand with flat-lying sherds and thin sand lenses, perhaps house floors. We were afraid the charcoal in upper Layer 3 was intrusive from the forest clearing in 1972 and did not submit any for radiocarbon dating. However, a sherd of a blue-and-white porcelain bowl of the late seventeenth or early eighteenth century was found in the base of Layer 3, indicating a late date for the Patrick Phase.

Five features, cut from Layer 3 into deeper deposits, are identified by letter codes on the plans and sections.

Northwest (NW): In the northwest corner is a pit about 1.20 m in diameter and at least .30 m deep, with light and dark gray sand lenses and many sherds, first noted in mid Layer 3. This may have been a borrow pit for sand for floors.

Central (Cn): In the center of the unit is a small deep pit .20 m in diameter and at least .28 m deep with a dark gray sand fill and a few sherds, first noted in mid Layer 3. Perhaps a large posthole.

Northeast (NE): In the east section is a small irregular pit .22 cm N-S and .18 cm deep, with dark gray sand fill, first noted in mid Layer 3. Perhaps this is a large posthole mostly in the adjacent square. South of this there is a smaller shallow pit, .12 m in diameter and .08 m deep, with gray sand fill, first visible at the base of Layer 3. Its use is unknown. No artifacts were recorded from either of these features.

South center (SC): In the center of the south section is a small pit .35 m in diameter, cut from lower Layer 3. It yielded cracked rock, charcoal, sherds and *Terebralia* shell. It was perhaps used as a hearth.

Southeast (SE): In the southeast corner is a small deep pit .35 in diameter and at least .19 m deep, first visible at the base Layer 3. In the dark gray sand fill of the pit are a few sherds and a piece of coral. Its use is unknown.

Above is Layer 2: about .15 m of homogenous gray sand with fresh charcoal fragments and many sherds. This is probably a cultivated soil that disturbed the midden, formed after the destruction of the protected forest during the 1970s. Finally, a thin layer of dark sand with humus, termed Layer 1, formed recently.

This site has a normal soil profile of the sort that has developed on many of our sites. The thickness of the cultural layers, the density and diversity of features such as small or large pits and possible postholes, and the occurrence of thin isolated patches of sand—probably the damaged remnants of house floors—at different levels within Layer 3 all argue for a relatively long Patrick Phase occupation at the Patrick site.

Table B.18 lists the occurrence of artifacts, primarily ceramics, in the successive layers and features found in Unit H. The feature samples are from the feature fills at the depth of Layer 4, though they all originated in Layer 3, as noted above. The general material from Layer 4 is either from feature edges or from initial occupation before structures and pits were placed in this part of the Patrick site.

The substantial sample of sherds from Patrick Unit H, whether relatively coarse or relatively fine, are hard and compact, like Ambatary ceramics. However, they tend to be thinner. Many of the vessels have linear burnishing, often at oblique angles—a characteristic of the Patrick Phase. Rough Ware occurs but is a small minority in these loci. Inspection of this table shows that bowls are more common than jars, as is typical of domestic ceramics throughout the long ceramic tradition in the Vohemar area. Sherd density is greater in later Layers 2 and 3a and in features cut from these later layers. This is presumably a function of the accumulation of sherds on the surface of the settlement through the relatively long Patrick Phase occupation. As noted in the main text, there are few chlorite schist items, basalt flakes, or fragments of iron or slag.

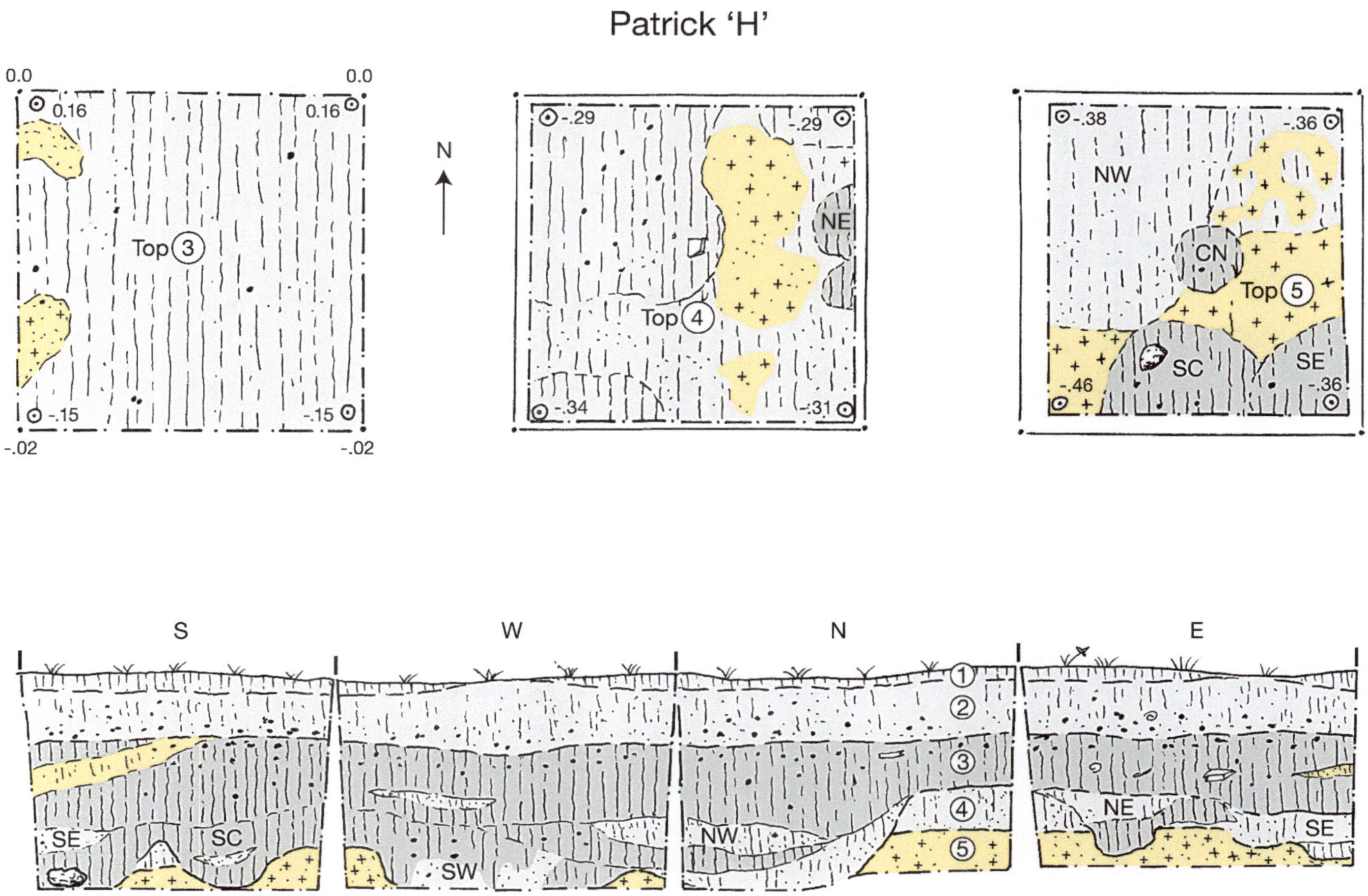

Figure B.8. Plans and sections of Analabe-Patrick, Unit H.

Table B.17. Deposits in Excavation Unit H at Analabe-Patrick.

Context	Mean thickness	Estimated volume	Composition	Comment
Layer (1)	.04 m	.040 m^3	Gray sand and leaf litter	AH Horizon: Modern humus, roots
Layer (2)	.11 m	.110 m^3	Light gray sand and charcoal	AP Horizon: Cultivated layer, sherds
Layer (3)	.15 m	.140 m^3	Black organic sand, charcoal	Midden: Sherds, shell, bone
Layer (4)	.07 m	.059 m^3	Light gray sand with dark lenses	AL Horizon: Leached sand cut by pits
Layer (5)	-	-	Reddish sand	B Horizon: no cultural traces

Table B.18. Artifacts in the contexts of Excavation Unit H at Analabe-Patrick.

Context		Coarse Ware			Sandy Ware				Rough Ware			Shell
		Thick	Med.	Other	Thick	Med.	Thin	Rim	Thick	Med.	Rim	(*Terebralia*)
Layer (1)	oxidized	4	4	-	1	16 (6 brn)	12 (5 brn)	1 jar	-	-	-	-
	reduced	-	3	-	-	4 (1 brn)	11 (2 brn)	2 jar	-	-	-	-
Layer (2)	oxidized	4	13	1 bowl	2	113 (23 brn)	-	4 bowl 4 jar	2	1	1 bowl	16
	reduced	1	1	1 bowl	1	31 (16 brn)	17 (12 brn)	1 bowl 1 jar	1	1	2 bowl	-
Layer (3a)	oxidized	3	9	2 bowl	1	30 (7 brn)	11 (4 brn)	2 bowl	-	1	1 bowl	3
	reduced	-	4	2 bowl	-	35 (13 brn)	7 (5 brn)	2 bowl 2 jar	-	1	-	-
Layer (3b)	oxidized	3	5	-	1	19 (3 brn)	3 (2 brn)	2 bowl	-	5	1 bowl	5
	reduced	-	5	-	1	35 (14 brn)	6 (4 brn)	2 jar	-	1	-	-
Layer (4 General)	oxidized	2	2	-	1	24 (5 brn)	7 (1 brn)	1 bowl 1 jar	1	2	2 bowl	6
	reduced	-	-	-	-	22 (8 brn)	6 (4 brn)	1 jar	-	1	2 bowl	-
Layer (4 NW)	oxidized	1	-	-	-	14 (3 brn)	3	1 bowl	-	-	-	-
	reduced	2	2	-	-	9 (5 brn)	4	3 bowl 1 jar	-	2	-	-
Layer (4 Cn)	oxidized	-	-	-	-	4	-	-	-	-	-	-
	reduced	-	-	-	1	3 (1 brn)	-	-	1	1	-	-
Layer (4 SC)	oxidized	-	2	-	1	12 (5 brn)	1 brn	-	-	-	-	5
	reduced	-	-	-	2	4	2	-	-	1	-	-
Layer (4 SE)	oxidized	-	-	-	-	2	2	-	-	-	-	1
	reduced	-	-	-	-	3	1	-	-	1	-	-
Layer (5)	oxidized	-	-	-	-	-	-	-	-	-	-	-
	reduced	-	-	-	-	-	-	-	-	-	-	-

Abbreviation: brn = burnished

Ave Maria (786.8-1410.0): Excavation Unit J

One of the tasks we undertook in our first season was the characterization of the latest phase of ceramic development in the Vohemar area. No indigenous ceramics were seen in the local markets, and we found no villagers making ceramics in the villages we visited in 2007 and 2008. In many areas of northern Madagascar where we had previously worked, indigenous potting ceased in the last years of the nineteenth century or the first years of the twentieth. The 1885 map of Lieutenant Favereau and Midshipman Germain (see inside cover, this volume) gave us important clues regarding where we might find stratified nineteenth-century deposits. At that time, Vohemar was several discrete villages. Near the mosque in the densely occupied center of the present town were neighborhoods with "Makoas," "Betsimisaraks," and "Sakalaves." Farther northeast, where the Catholic cathedral and schools now stand, were the residences of "Indiens." Our sounding in this area at the Ecole Bambino locality (07-008) revealed twentieth-century deposits resting directly on laminated sand with a few Ambatary sherds. In what is today the northeastern suburbs of Vohemar, "magasins," an "abattoir," a "puit," and a scattering of residences were mapped. Today, this area has many open areas where we could make corings and soundings, and we thought we would have a good chance to find local ceramics in association with datable nineteenth-century imports. After coring in various open spots, we selected a locus with deep stratigraphy in the garden of the Soeurs Catholiques d'Ave Maria (07-015: Labordes 786.8-1410.0, Mercator S13° 21'

Table B.19. Deposits in Excavation Unit J at Ave Maria.

Context	Mean thickness	Estimated volume	Composition	Comment
Layer (1)	.21 m	.210 m^3	Loose dark gray sand	AP Horizon: Cultivated layer
Layer (2)	.09 m	.090 m^3	Homogenous dark gray sand	Midden: Much slag, some sherds
Layer (3a)	.10 m	.092 m^3	Mottled gray sand	Midden: Many sherds, shell, bone
Layer (3b)	.15 m	.081 m^3	Brown sand cut by wall trenches	Transition: Few sherds, shell
Layer (4)	.12 m	.076 m^3	Mottled gray sand cut by posts	Dune?: Few sherds
Layer (5)	.10 m	.058 m^3	Mottled gray sand, charcoal	Midden?: Some sherds, bone, shell
Layer (6)	.25 m	.135 m^3	Light gray sand, light lenses	Cultivated?: Few sherds, some shell
Layer (7)	-	-	Reddish sand, ash lenses on top	B Horizon: No cultural traces

18"/ E50° 00' 30", UTM 39L E 0392599.9-S 8523385.0). With the blessings of the sisters, on October 8, 2007 we began excavation of a one-meter square oriented with sides to the cardinal directions. The excavators were Robert Dewar, Henry Wright, Victor Razanatovo, and Jean-Aimé Andriamaherilala.

Table B.19 and Figure B.9 show the stratigraphy of Unit J. This is a complex deposit, and it merits detailed archaeogeological study, a kind of study we have not been able to do. The deepest deposit is a clean reddish beach sand termed Layer 7, probably a B-horizon with iron accumulation similar to those at Ampasimahavelona and Patrick. On top of this are white lenses, perhaps siliceous ash left from the initial burning of the herbaceous vegetation of the dry coastal forest. Above this is Layer 6, a thick gray sand with some light sand lenses and a few coarse thick sherds. This may be a cultivated layer. Layer 5 is a gray sand with lenses of light sand containing some charcoal, shell, and bone, as well as Ambatary and Patrick Phase sherds discussed in the main text. It is not the density we see in domestic refuse deposits, so this is the edge of a site or a garden to which some village debris was brought to improve the sandy soil. Layer 4 above this is gray sand with lenses of brown sand and has little cultural material. It may have been blown in by the wind between phases of occupation. Layer 3B is .15 m thick, also a gray-brown sand grading into a brown sand below, and has some sherds and a little slag. Layer 3A, from .30 to .40 in depth, is a gray-brown sand with many sherds and much slag, the refuse of an iron working area.

Originating from Layer 3A are two parallel features, apparently trenches oriented roughly north-south. The northwestern trench averages .24 m wide and .40 m deep and has possible post molds .75 meters apart; the southeastern trench averages .20 m wide and .29 m deep and has definite post molds about .48 m apart in its base. One of these was .15 m in diameter and had a flat base. This is a wall trench, probably for a post-and-beam building with vegetal roof and siding. The northwestern trench is less certain. There was an isolated post mold about .16 m in diameter west of the trenches. The fill of the trenches was black sand with much slag and some sherds; in the west trench, there was also a sherd of imported white glazed, white bodied ware, probably an early nineteenth-century import from Europe. The trenches cut through Layer 4 and into the top of Layer 5 and can be expected to have a mixture of sherds from various phases.

Finally, late in the sequence were two layers of homogenous gray sand. Layer 2 was similar to Layer 3a, with lenses of brown sand, with some modern material and some locally made sherds and iron slag. Layer 1 was similar but homogenous, and had much twentieth-century plastic, modern glass, modern iron, and ceramics.

It was disappointing that Ave Maria Unit J yielded only small numbers of items in most of its contexts (Table B.19). The reason for this was perhaps that none of the layers were ordinary domestic deposits (with many sherds), such as those we found at Patrick, Ambatary, Analabe Centre and other even earlier sites. As discussed

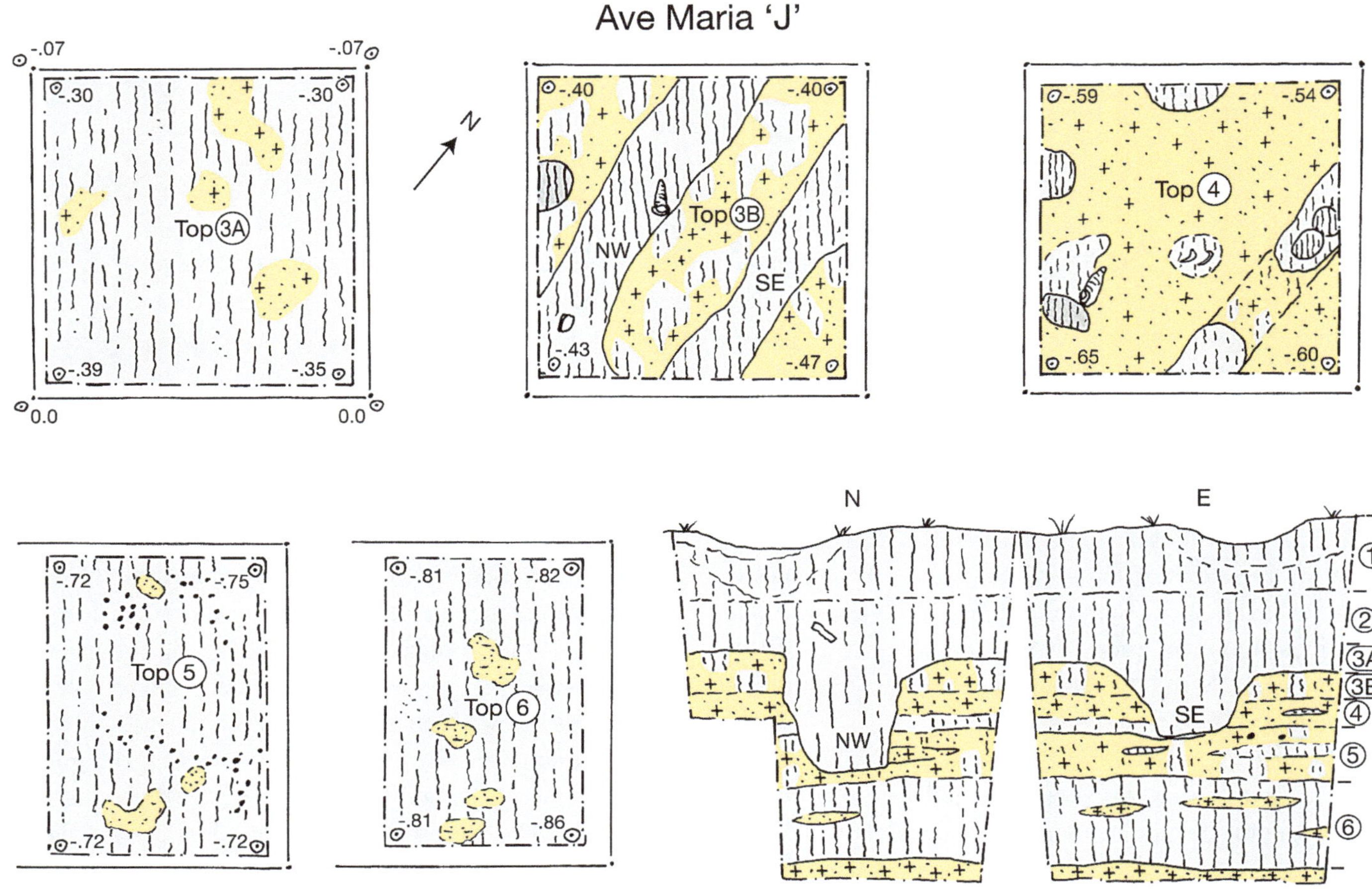

Figure B.9. Plans and sections from Ave Maria, Unit J.

above, earlier Layers 6 to 3b appear to have been site margin or garden deposits, while later Layers 3a and 2 and associated features are rich with the debris of iron-working. We always hoped there would be an opportunity to open other units in a nearby area with more domestic contexts, but this was not possible.

Table B.20 lists the artifacts in the successive layers and features found in Unit J.

The sherds from Layer 6 are few, but their thickness and coarse inclusions are like the ceramics of Ampasimahavelona and Analabe-Régis. The presence of many more shells than sherds—*Anadara* from nearby sandy beaches and *Terebralia* from the mangroves of the embouchure—may indicate a deliberate effort to decrease the acidity of a sandy garden soil. The debris from Layer 5, though sparse, are similar to the domestic midden inventories of sherd, shell, and bone. Several of the rims have close parallels with those from Ambatary, but several sherds have the patterned burnishing typical of the Patrick assemblage. These could represent either a transitional assemblage between Ambatary and Patrick or a mixture of material brought in to improve the fertility of a garden. The debris from Layers 4 and 3b is too sparse to permit any inference beyond what is said above based on sediment alone. The debris from Layer 3a and features cut from it into Layers 3b, 4, and 5 are dominated by iron slag, much of it with flow marks suggesting these are "tap slags" from iron smelting. Technical studies of these slags are needed. The ceramics, particularly those from the southeast trench, have interior thickened jar rims and a flattened bowl rim identical to those in the Patrick

Table B.20. Items in the contexts of Excavation Unit J at Ave Maria.

Context		Coarse Ware		Rough Ware			Medium Sandy Ware				Fine Ware			Other
		Thick	Med.	Thick	Med.	Rim	Thick	Med.	Thin	Rim	Med.	Thin	Rim	
Layer (3a)	oxidized	-	1	-	-	-	1	25 (2 rdsl and 2 incs)	2	1 jar (incs) 1 bowl (rdsl incs)	-	-	-	c-s: 4 frg slag: 54 1 *Andara*
	reduced	-	-	-	-	-	-	18	11	1 bowl (incs)	2	-	-	
Layer (3a NW)	oxidized	-	-	-	-	-	-	12	1	2 jar	-	-	-	slag: 71+ 2 *Terebralia*
	reduced	-	-	-	-	-	-	7	3	1 bowl 1 jar	3	-	-	
Layer (3a SE)	oxidized	-	-	-	-	-	-	6	1	1 bowl (brn)	-	-	1 jar	slag: 20
	reduced	-	-	-	-	-	-	2	2	-	-	1	-	
Layer (3b)	oxidized	-	-	-	1	-	-	1	-	-	-	-	-	c-s: 1 frg 1 sm wt slag: 3
	reduced	-	-	-	-	-	-	1	-	-	-	-	-	
Layer (4)	oxidized	-	-	-	-	-	-	1	-	1 base	-	-	-	1 ceramic bead
	reduced	-	-	-	-	-	-	-	-	-	-	-	-	
Layer (5)	oxidized	4	-	1	1	1 basin	-	8	-	1 bowl (brn)	-	-	-	c-s: 2 med 5 *Andara*
	reduced	-	-	-	-	-	-	9 (2 brn)	2	1 bowl (brn) 1 jar (brn)	-	-	-	
Layer (6)	oxidized	-	-	-	1	-	-	2	-	-	-	-	-	slag: 1 5 *Andara* 14 *Terebralia*
	reduced	-	-	-	-	-	-	1	-	-	-	-	-	

Abbreviations: brn = burnished, c-s = chlorite schist, frg = fragment, incs = incised, rdsl = red slip.

assemblage, but every context also has the fine reduced thin sherds, which appear to be typical of the latest occupation of the Vohemar area, provisionally termed the Ave Maria Phase. Rims from other sites show that these are from vessels with thin flared necks (e.g., Figure 12.1), probably from carinated bowls or jars.

Retrospect on the Stratigraphic Excavations in the Vohemar Area

The allocation of time to actual field survey (walking over terrain and mapping surface traces) versus time to excavation (in the Vohemar case, the relatively small soundings designed to define stratigraphies and date surface assemblages) is always a problematic decision. Fortunately, we had three full seasons of several weeks each, as well as several follow-up visits to Vohemar, and we could correct some of our misjudgments by doing more survey here or making another sounding there. As it stands, most of our phases are well defined and well dated, though we would do more soundings on sites of the Razanakoto and the Ave Maria phases if possible. The Vohemar program as a whole lays the foundations for major work in the future—both surveys in adjacent areas and extensive excavations on key locations in and near Vohemar. Such future programs are discussed at the end of the main text.

Appendix C

Absolute Dates from Sites in the Vohemar Area

by Henry T. Wright

All samples were dated by Beta Analytic with AMS radiocarbon dating. Pretreatment involved cleaning with acid, alkali, and acid again. The lab reports no special problems with any of these determinations. Calibration was based on the Southern Hemisphere Calibration (Hogg et al. 2013). We thank Dr. Murray Tammers and Mr. Darden Hood for their prompt and professional help. Calibrations were done with the OxCal platform.

Ambohiposa (784.3-1408.1)

Two small fragments of wood charcoal from Layer 5 of the South Excavation were submitted.

Beta–251454: 750 +/- 40 BP. $^{13}C/\ ^{12}C$ ratio -24.5 o/oo. Calibrated date: 760 +/- 40 BP. This piece, from the latest portion of Layer 5, yielded a calibrated date with a 95% probability of dating between Cal CE 1220 to 1385.

Beta–251455: 1120 +/- 40 BP. $^{13}C/\ ^{12}C$ ratio -25.5 o/oo. Calibrated date: 1110 +/- 40 BP. This piece, from somewhat earlier Layer 5B, yielded a calibrated date with a 95% probability of being between Cal CE 885 and 1130.

Comment: These two pieces of charcoal are unlikely to be of the same age. Both date to the time of the early villages from Ampasimahavelona to Rajanakoto times. There are two very sandy, oxidized sherds of the earliest phases from poorly stratified North Unit, but not from the well stratified Central and South Units. If these samples date the use of microlithic technologies at Ambohiposa, then these technologies continued to be used for foraging when the earlier agricultural and fishing villages with ceramic and iron technologies were flourishing. See further discussion in the main text.

Ampasimahavelona (786.9-1408.1)

Two small pieces of wood charcoal from the earliest layers of Unit VII were submitted.

Beta–267774: 1130 +/- 40 BP. $^{13}C/^{12}C$ ratio of -25.0 o/oo. Required no correction. This piece, from Lower Layer 3, yielded a calibrated date with a 95% probability that the date is between CE 885 and 1025.

Beta–267773 1180 +/- 40 BP. $^{13}C/^{12}C$ ratio of -27.2 o/oo yielded a calibrated date of 1140 +/- 40 BP. This piece, from Unit VII, Feature 2, is calibrated with a 95% probability that the date is between CE 885 to 1020, very close to the preceding.

Comment: These determinations suggest that the Ampasimahavelona Phase spanned at least the late ninth to early eleventh centuries. This is conformable with other dates from sites with similar ceramics elsewhere in northeast Madagascar, as discussed in the main text.

Ambatary (786.6-1409.8)

A piece of charcoal from Ambatary Unit VIII was submitted.

Beta–267775: 620 +/- 40 BP. $^{13}C/^{12}C$ ratio of -25.6 o/oo. Calibrated date 610 +/- 40 BP. This piece, from Layer 5B, yields a calibrated date indicating a 95% probability that the date is between AD 1290 to 1410.

Comment: A Chinese blue-and-white porcelain teacup rim from this layer has been dated to the late fourteenth century. The totality of evidence indicates that the Ambatary Phase spanned at least the late fourteenth and fifteenth centuries of the common era.

Appendix D

Research on Oral Traditions in the Vohemar Area

by Chantal Radimilahy

Throughout Madagascar, there are many traditions of early peoples. They were perhaps already present before the mid first millennium CE, when language evidence indicates the Malagasy speakers arrived (Adelaar 2016). For example, on the southeast coast, the Kimosy are believed to have been ancestors of some of the Tanosy (Rakotoarisoa 2013), while in the central and southern highlands, the Vazimba were ancestors whose tombs, shrines, and descendant groups are widely recognized (Berg 1977; Callet 1912:7–9, 442–446). In other parts of Madagascar, myths mentions such groups as the Gola, the Mikimiky, and the Fonoka. Who were these people? Where are their descendants? Research has yet to clarify the traditions of these peoples.

While our work from 2007 until 2010 on the far northeast coast of Madagascar was focused primarily on archaeological research, we made every effort to seek out indigenous people knowledgeable about local traditions. The following is a brief summary of the results of this research on traditions and customs of the area of Vohemar. Vohemar is a modern market town, a seaport, and the governmental subcenter for an area comprising 8200 square kilometers: about one-third of the modern administrative region of SAVA in northern Madagascar. Some derive the toponym Vohemar from Vohimarina (vohitra marina, lit. "city of justice" or perhaps "city in a flat place"), a name said to have been given by King Radama I during his expedition to this region in 1822, because the population welcomed him instead of resisting. However, the name Vohemaro was used by Etienne de Flacourt in the mid-seventeenth century, and Portuguese maps and texts of the sixteenth century refer to Boamaro or Bemaro, which could be an earlier version of the name (see Chapter 2). Another toponym that designates Vohemar and the area of reefs and rocky hills around it is Iharana ("at the rocks"). Nicolas Mayeur, the Mauritian trader, when reporting his visit of 1775, may be rendering this term when he refers to Iharambazaha (perhaps Tsirang-bazaha or Tsiragnam-bazaha, which he translates as the "Port of the Whites") (Mayeur 1912).

Social and cultural aspects

Traditions recorded in Vohemar suggest that the first inhabitants of the region were the Antavaratra (inhabitants of the North) and the Antiharana (inhabitants of the rocks). These people may have descendants elsewhere, but no groups in the Vohemar area use these names today. The contemporary population of Vohemar is affiliated primarily with such autochtonous groups as Tsimihety, Betsimisaraka, Sakalava, Makoa, Hova, Antaimoro, Anjoany, Betsileo, Sihanaka, but especially the Anjoaty. We also see a mix of groups: people often refer to themselves as the Sakalava-Anjoaty or Betsimisaraka-Anjoaty or Sakalava-Hova. The latter, however, are few in number. There are also a few newcomers from Europe, South Asia, and the East.

Who are the Anjoaty, so important around Vohemar, but whose name is not found on the too well-known and unfortunately much misused map of Madagascar's ethnic groups? According to the traditions collected from the Mpijôro (the guardians of the tradition in Vohemar), the term Anjoaty has developed from the earlier term Onjatsy, still used to the south. The Onjatsy of the southeastern part of Madagascar, who dwell among the Antemoro, say they are relatives of those from the north. They are said to be descended from Arabs, whose way of life was fishing. Their country of origin, Djoati, is said to have given the name of the Onjoaty group, but the original "village" was Hadzaz, on the Red Sea. The latter name is identical with the Hejaz, the broader area in which Mecca is located. The Onjoatsy are said to be Ishmaelites descended from Abraham and his Egyptian wife Hagara, Ishmael's mother. During their travels, from Djoati onwards, the ancestors sometimes endured natural disasters and storms, including the flooding of Muzombi or Mojomby, a mythical island perhaps near the Red Sea, which they had to leave. Their journey continued along the east coast of Africa, then via the Comoros to Madagascar. Traditions specify that during storms and to avoid the shipwreck, it was decided to throw overboard all heavy objects, then the old people, and finally the children. The Makoa slaves threw their children into the sea, but their masters the Anjoaty did not. The Makoa occupy the northeastern part of the city of Vohemar, where all these refugees landed after passing through the northwest coast: Ampasindava Bay, Ambilobe, Bobaomby, and finally Iharana. Ambavan' Iharana (lit. "at the mouth of Iharana"), which is northeast of the town, on the edge of the sandy coastal plain, was chosen by the Anjoaty for their burial place. This place serves as a place of pilgrimage for descendants who come from all over Madagascar to attend the *Jôro vangy tany manintsy* ("ritual for visiting the cold land," e.g., the necropolis) every three years. This ritual consists of requesting blessings from the ancestors, then sacrificing zebu in the sea to remember the ancestors buried in this place along the seashore, and consuming the meat at feasts. The most recent ritual was performed in October 2018. Some Anjoaty have ritual responsibilities, such as those with the *masimbava* (the "holy mouth")—they can perform miracles (such as carrying water in woven baskets) thanks to their holiness. As noted in Chapter 2, most rural Anjoaty are cultivators of rice, fruits, and spices, and herders of cattle, like most people of the Vohemar region, while those who live in towns have every kind of occupation, from craftsmen and merchants to teachers and officials.

Among the former inhabitants of the Vohemar area are the Rasikajy, thought to be *mpihavy* (that is, newcomers, in the sense that they are not natives). The term Rasikajy has been interpreted in many ways; a few examples will suffice. It could be a phrase in Malagasy, *Ra-tsy-kajo*, meaning "the ones who are not tired." Perhaps it was derived from the Segeju, the name of a group now living in the Africa coastal hinterlands near the present border of Tanzania and Kenya, some of whom were known as stone workers (cf. Allibert 1988:115, 2011:151). Also, it has been said to be a name derived from Sikajy (name of the Portuguese coin), but this name would have to be given after the late fifteenth century, when the Portuguese first reached the Indian Ocean. Villagers living near the chlorite schist quarries southwest of Vohemar in the upper Manamberna Valley have traditions of the Rasikajy as small people skilled in mining and carving chlorite schist, locally termed *vaton-dRasikajy* (see Chapter 10). This report of the small size of these people, however, is in contradiction to what is said in other traditions, since the Rasikajy are also linked to traditions of "giants," whose actions are said to account for unusual natural features all up and down the eastern coast of Madagascar (cf. Dewar, Radimilahy, Darsot, and Wright 2011:681). Tradition attributes to the Rasikajy the quarries, which contained the remnants of many containers and tops broken in manufacture as well as graceful finished pieces, especially the tripod pots and incense burners. Vessels of this material have also been found in sites of the so-called Swahili period (eleventh to fifteenth century BC) in the

Comoros or on the east coast of Africa. The excavators of the necropolis of the fourteenth to sixteenth centuries CE near Vohemar, in which were found tombs with very rich funerary offerings, many of chlorite schist, were told that these were the graves of the Rasikajy. We have not found anyone in Vohemar who claims Rasikajy descent, but some Vohemarian informants have suggested that descendants of the Rasikajy might be found 30 km to the north-northwest of Vohemar, around the coastal forest of Sahaka. However, there are no outcrops of chlorite schist there; the way of life is now oriented towards fishing and agriculture.

For the other population groups that have emigrated from distant parts of Madagascar, in addition to their names, some information on their regions of origin is provided by their taboos or *fady*, their household rituals, or their funerals.

The Betsimisaraka Anjoaty have *fadys* forbidding the eating of pork, eel, and lemurs. In much of Madagascar, it has been accepted that inside houses, the place in which one receives blessings from the ancestors is the northeast corner. However, among this group, the sacred place is rather the south side or the southeast corner. Similarly, the place of honor in the house for men is in the south, and for women in the north—the opposite of other Malagasy communities.

The Makoa Morimo may not eat *Sokatra* turtles, and have their sacred place in the west side of the house. Unlike Betsimisaraka and Anjoaty, or Sakalava Anjoaty, during rituals they drink *toaka* (rum) or *sora* (a fermented drink obtained from the *satrana* palm), and also *Betsa* (fermented mead) made from honey or sugar cane.

The Anjoaty and the Sakalava share one well-known ritual site at Andranotsara, also called Lac Vert or Green Lake (see Appendix A), because the water is green from algae. Located six kilometers due south of modern Vohemar, Andranotsara is separated from the nearby ocean by a sandbank. According to oral traditions, the area was inhabited by Rasikajy, but is inhabited today by Sakalava Anjoaty. In this area, potable water is difficult to find, as is recounted in the following traditional story. One day, an Antemoro ("diviner"), tired from a long journey, arrived here. He asked for water to drink, but only a mother of three children granted his request. The man then told her to leave because he intended to cast a spell during the night, bringing a flood of water inundating the entire village. Only the woman with her children and her mother-in-law were saved. The people who refused his request were turned into crocodiles. The descendants of those who were saved can now be found in Antanambaon'ny Ankirikiriky (in a neighborhood near the zebu market mentioned below). We were unable to witness any of the ceremonies held at Andranotsara.

Both the Anjoaty and Sakalava Anjoaty also share cultural customs practiced by Muslims in the Near East and East Africa, such as a *fady* against the eating of pork or customs regarding the placement of bodies in burials. Perhaps they brought these from their regions of origin. The people of the northern coasts of Madagascar have been in contact with Muslim world for more than a millennium. Glazed ceramics from Basra appear as early as the ninth century CE on the northeast coast (Dewar and Wright 1993:429–430; Verin 1975:879–889). There are remains of mosques at Mahilaka (Radimilahy 1998) showing the existence of Islamic congregations as early as the twelfth century. However, the extent of Muslim influence is not as great as one might think; in recent centuries, few people have subscribed to Quranic doctrines, though many continue some of its traditional practices. At present, in the Vohemar area, more than half the population is Christian (mostly Catholic, Protestant, or Anglican) and about a third of the population is Muslim (either Sunni, including both people of Arabian or Comorian descent plus some Anjoaty and Sakalava who have recently converted; or Shia, mostly of South Asian descent). Various new religious movements, often called "sects," attract more and more people (perhaps 10%). There are also some followers of Hinduism. Even if people adhere to one of these introduced religions, most still follow traditional religious ideas and practices (such as belief in ancestors manifested in funerary rituals), or other daily practices, such an orienting houses or using traditional "supernatural" protections.

Economic Aspects

Traditionally, economic life on the northeast coast revolves around cattle breeding and cultivation. The Vohemar region is rich in good pasturage for cattle. Also, to the southwest, on the great plain that extends towards Andrafainkona, is the rice granary of this area. However, poor roads isolate rural villages and it is difficult to get products out to markets, as in many other regions of Madagascar.

The area northeast of the city is more involved in extensive cattle and goat breeding and coconut cultivation, as well as the production of seafood for local consumption.

However, some fish is salted or frozen and shipped further south to Sambava or Andapa. In the northwest, the population is involved in cattle, pig, and poultry breeding. There is also some irrigated rice cultivation, the harvesting of vanilla and other spices, and the cultivation of vegetables and tubers such as cassava.

The more fertile and better-watered south is focused on the growing rice and maize. Since there are fewer cattle wandering around, the culture is extensive—i.e., without fences. There is also much pig and poultry breeding. Rice, vanilla, coffee, cloves, letchis (lychees), and tubers are the common crops. Depending on the topographical situation, rice can be cultivated in either irrigated paddies or in dry-farmed, "slash-and-burn" fields. During the contemporary period, and no doubt long before, cattle have often been exchanged among the local districts. Two days of the week are important for the economic activities of the local population. Monday is the day of the market for zebu, located eight kilometers south of the city, at Antanambaon'ny Ankirikiriky on the Vohemar-Sambava road. Wednesday is day of the market in Vohemar itself for other commodities.

Within the city of Vohemar are the activities found in any capital of the world—namely trade, education, medicine, and various political and administrative duties. Among the traditional crafts practiced in the town (as well as in the villages), are the weaving of mats, the making of canoes for fishing, the forging of iron to make and repair metal tools, the making of leather, and shaping of stone for house construction.

Since its foundation, Vohemar has been an important trading port. Towards the beginning of the twentieth century, ships from Mumbai filled with English cotton, Russian oil, and diverse goods made in India arrived regularly in the ports of northern Madagascar. From the east coast of Africa, sailing dhows unloaded numerous products. During the later twentieth century, the merchants of Vohemar exported cattle, coffee, cloves, copra, and especially vanilla.

Concluding Note

Our research in Vohemar spanned a difficult period for its citizens. The world economic crisis diminished imports to occasional visits by tankers bearing fuel, and exports to longstanding commodities such as cattle and vanilla. However, the export of frozen beef has replaced that of live cattle. Tourism, so promising for Madagascar's future, diminished. Many young people left for work in other parts of Madagascar and in other countries, connecting to their families only by such new electronic means as Skype and Facebook.

Often, during our enquiries into oral traditions, the elderly would complain about the danger to traditional rituals and social life posed by the development of technology, rapid urbanization, and the exodus of the young to distant larger cities. Still, it is not too late to record surviving traditions, particularly in the more isolated villages, and further research on the oral traditions will resolve many of the problems raised in this appendix.

Appendix E

Analysis of Osteological Remains Recovered from the Site of Vohemar-Ambatary

by Lucien Marie Aimé Rakotozafy

Institut de Civilisations - Musée d'Art et d'Archéologie, Université d'Antananarivo

The environment and the area of study

Research on the early peopling of the northern regions of Madagascar has accelerated in recent years, and the area of Vohemar has an important place in this research. The archaeological data provides indications of the first human arrivals (Dewar et al. 2013), of cultural activities, and of the relations between human populations and their environments (this volume). These data, especially those of the osteological remains, provide information that can determine the inter-relations between these populations and the animals that they have encountered in the natural environment (or which they themselves have introduced). This analysis focuses on the well-preserved osteological specimens from the excavations of the site of Ambatary within the fourteenth- to sixteenth-century town of Vohemar. Their identification shows the former faunistic associations of the area, which facilitate the definition of the natural history in this region of the island of Madagascar.

The port town of Vohemar is mentioned in the earliest Portuguese texts and the rich cemetery of the fourteenth to sixteenth centuries has been known since the 1940s (Vernier et al.), but the actual site of town was only located by our survey project in 2009. It is hidden by dense housing of the twentieth century and by such twenty-first century trash as iron scrap, plastic bags, water bottles, cement and brick fragments, and automobile tires. However, our 2009 fieldwork yielded distinctive ceramics indicating the remains of the fourteenth- to sixteenth-century town covered at least 13 ha. One of our corings revealed a deep stratigraphy and we expanded it into our Unit VIII (See main text and Appendix B). This excavation revealed two layers of floors and secondary middens, overlain by four layers of lenses of debris and tertiary middens, thought to be composed of basket loads of daily sweepings. The lower layers have well-preserved faunal material, while the upper layer have poorer organic preservation. In addition, we should keep in mind, as noted in the main text, that the evidence of architecture and material goods indicates that Unit VIII documents a neighborhood of modest town dwellers, and that when excavations are done elsewhere, we may find deposits discarded by wealthier households which had access to more cattle and other foods rare at Ambatary.

Systematic study

Based on the evidence from Unit VIII recovered in 2009 (see Appendix B), the paleofauna is constituted of a majority of vertebrates (Table E.1), but with a substantial minority of invertebrates (Table E.2).

Among the vertebrates, at Ambatary we collected the remains of mammals, birds, reptiles, and fish. There are animals of small or medium size introduced by people, such as domestic cattle *(Bos* sp.), sheep (*Ovis aries*), and chickens (*Gallus gallus*). There are also introduced wild animals such as the African Bush Pig (*Potamochoerus larvatus),* which somehow crossed the Mozambique Channel. Other local wild animals also hunted include a medium sized lemur, the *sifaka* (*Propithecus* sp.), a large tenrec (*Tenrec ecaudatus*), and several wild ducks (*Spatula* (previously *Anas*) *hottentota* and *Sarkidiornis melanotos*). Beyond these, different species of turtles and fish complete the list of animals exploited. There is more emphasis on sea turtles, which were perhaps taken while fishing for marine fish. Both boney fishes (Osteichthyes) and cartilaginous fishes (Chondrichthyans) were caught.

Among the invertebrates, there are many mollusks, among which we have recognized a number of gastropods and several bivalves. Two are more common.

Most common is the well-known mangrove whelk, *Terebralia* (formerly *Pyrazus) palustris,* a gastropod, locally called *norogana*, which can be seen today clustering around the roots of mangroves at low tide in the estuaries. Sakalava men use this mollusk for fish bait, and its discarded shells are dense around canoe landings, but they say they do not eat it, as it is forbidden for Moslems. Women, however, say it makes an excellent soup, which the men eat with gusto. Because they are so visible and therefore easily gathered, these gastropods are affected by intensive human exploitation, and show a diminution in size through time (Figure E.1).

Less common is the arc clam, *Anadara (Arca)* cf. *similis*, locally called *kodiva*, a less visible bivalve which buries itself in sandy beaches. Women and children collect it from the lagoon and ocean beaches when the tide is out. We did not elicit a specific recipe, but have no doubt that this too makes an excellent soup.

Zooarchaeological study

One must take note of the evidence of the traces left by human activity on several of the archaeological faunal remains. Among others, the remains of *Bos* sp. from Layer 5A, on the one hand show a trace of a cut from a sharp tool on a femur fragment, and on the other hand , a burned surface. Among the remains of sheep (*Ovis aries*) found in Layer 4, a fragment of long bone exhibits the trace of the cut of a sharp tool. An epiphysis of a young individual confirms the activity of sheep herding in the area.

The recovery of fragment of eggshell of an extinct ratite (cf. *Mullerornis*) in uppermost Layer 3 raises the possibility of the use of this species in the human diet. If this was not a piece of sub-fossil eggshell collected in the nearby dunes (see Appendix A, Site 788.2-1408.3), it may be the latest evidence of the existence of this extinct species. At the least, the presence of this eggshell fragment confirms the distribution of this genus in the far north of Madagascar.

The great quantity of fish remains of different sizes, apparently some of the same group and others of different groups, show the human deposition of food debris after different meals by the population of the site. Such a richness of fish would have provided the ancient population with an inestimable resource of animal protein. The diversity of these marine species can be attributed to the biological diversity of the bay and the reefs.

Biostratigraphic study

The long sequence of cultural strata allows us to follow the development of the quantities of animals utilized in the human diet at Ambatary (Figure E.2).

At first view, the occurrence through time has a stratigraphic distribution indicating respectively at the beginning and end with modest quantities of bone, interrupted by an intermediate part with a great quantity of bone expressing a flourishing not only of hunting, fishing,

Table E.1. Groups of vertebrates recorded in the site of Vohemar-Ambatary, Unit VIII.

Biological Groups		**Families - Subfamilies**	**Genera and Species**
Mammals	Primates	Indriidae	*Propithecus* sp.
	Artiodactyla	Bovidae – Bovinae	*Bos* sp.
	Artiodactyla	Bovidae – Caprinae	cf. *Ovis aries*
	Artiodactyla	Bovidae – Caprinae	*Capra/Ovis*
	Artiodactyla	Suidae – Potamochoerinae	cf. *Potamochoerus larvatus*
	Carnivora	Unknown	Indeterminate (of small size)
	Chiroptera	Pteropodidae	cf. *Pteropus rufus*
	Rodentia	Muridae	cf. *Rattus* sp.
	Rodentia	Muridae	cf. *Mus* sp.
	Afrosoricida	Tenrecidae	*Tenrec ecaudatus*
	Afrosoricida	Tenrecidae	Indeterminate (of size smaller than *T. ecaudatus*)
	Afroscoricida	Indeterminate	(of very small size)
Birds	Ratites	Aepyornithidae – Mullerornitinae	cf. *Mullerornis* sp.
	Anseriformes	Anatidae – Anatinae	cf. *Sarkidiornis melanotos*
	Anseriformes	Anatidae – Anatinae	*Anas* cf. *hottentota*
	Anseriformes	Anatidae – Anatinae	cf. *Anas* sp.
	Galliformes	Phasianidae	cf. *Gallus gallus*
Reptiles	Chelonia	Testudinidae (Turtle)	sp.1 (Indeterminate large species)
	Chelonia	Testudinidae (Turtle)	sp.2 (Indeterminate medium species)
	Chelonia	Testudinidae (Turtle)	sp.3 (Indeterminate small species)
Fish	Chondrichthyans-Selachians	Selachians	sp.1 (Indeterminate species of shark)
	Chondrichthyans-Selachians	Selachians	sp.2 (Indeterminate species of shark)
	Chondrichthyans-Selachians	Selachians	sp.3 (Indeterminate species of shark)
	Osteichthyes	Large marine fish	spp. (Numerous indeterminate species)
	Osteichthyes	Medium marine fish	spp. (Numerous indeterminate species)
	Osteichthyes	Small marine fish	spp. (Numerous indeterminate species)

Table E.2. Groups of invertebrates recorded in the site of Vohemar-Ambatary, Unit VIII.

Biological Groups		**Families**	**Genera and Species**
Molluscs	Gasteropods	Potamididae	*Terebralia palustris*
	Gasteropods	Small marine gasteropods	Indeterminate small species
	cf. Gasteropods	Of small size	Indeterminate species
	Gasteropods	Indeterminate	Species of microscopic size
	Lamellibranche	Ostreidae	Species of small size of bivalve (oyster)
Cnidaires	Hydrozoans	Indeterminate family of sea urchin	Indeterminate small species
Protozoaire	Anthozoan	Indeterminate family of coral	sp.1 (Indeterminate species)
Protozoaire	Anthozoan	Indeterminate family of coral	sp.2 (Indeterminate species)

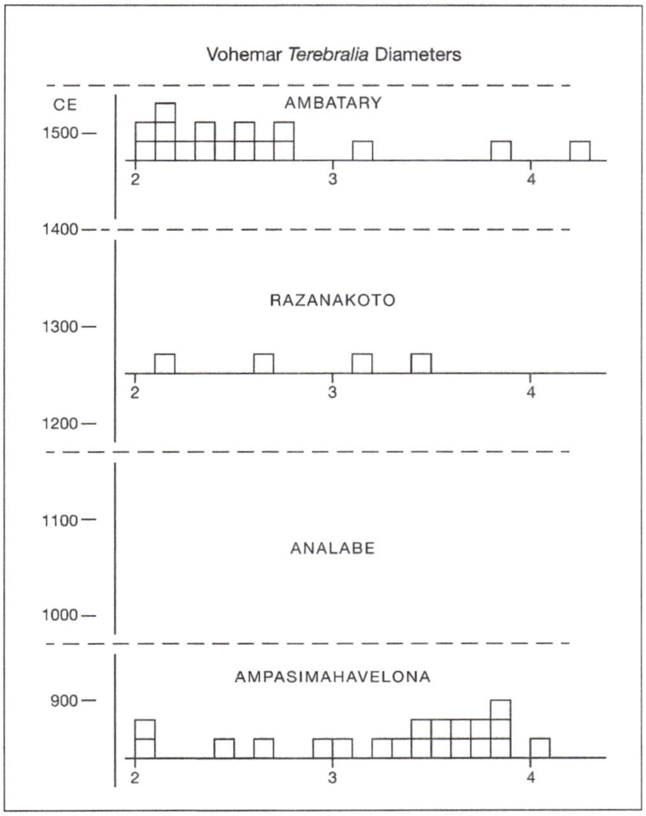

Figure E.1. Vohemar *Terebralia* diameters.

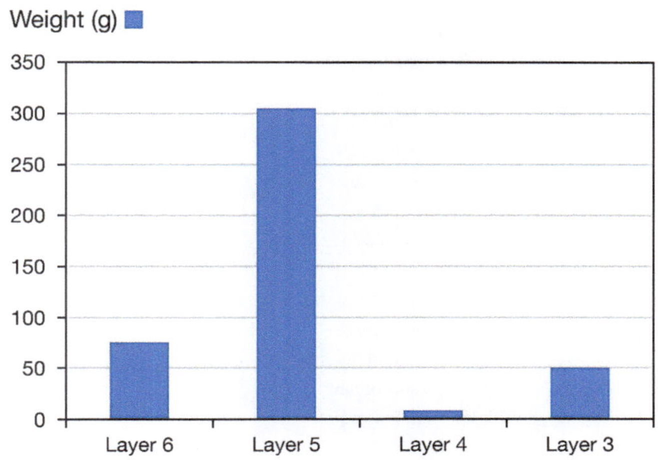

Figure E.2. Changing total bone weight through time in Ambatary VIII.

and herding, but also of the increase in human inhabitants. However, we must keep in mind that some of the diminution in bone in the upper layers may result from geological weathering and other taphonomic processes.

For each species considered, the distribution in time is as follows.

If the minimum number of individuals (MNI) of each taxon gives us no more than a qualitative aspect of the recovered bone that is of the species that coexisted together with people or who appeared in the environment in the course of human occupation in the area, then the number of identified specimens (NISP) permits us, in contrast, to follow changes in their importance in the course of daily activities. Above all, the list shows, on the one hand, the development of the mode of subsistence of the people at Ambatary, and on the other hand, the mode of acquisition differed in terms of human activity—sometimes hunting, sometimes fishing or collecting marine molluscs such as gastropods and clams, and at other times raising domestic animals.

In fact, even at the beginning of human settlement at Ambatary, there was already a predominance of the products of the estuaries, the lagoon, and the sea—notably the different species of marine turtles and molluscs, including estuarine gastropods such as *Terebralia* and lagoonal bivalves such as *Anadara* or *Ostrea*.

At the time of population increase in the fourteenth-century town, there were only small changes in human activities. There was growth in the taking of fish ranging from small to large, including species of both boney fish (Osteichthyans) and cartilagenous fish. The raising of domestic animals had increased, including cow (*Bos* sp.), sheep (*Ovis aries*) and fowl, especially chickens (*Gallus*

Table E.3. Change in the quantities of remains by faunal taxon.

Taxa counted	Number of identified specimens (NISP)			
	Layer 6 (lowest layer)	Layer 5 (low layer)	Layer 4 (intermediate layer)	Layer 3 (upper layer)
Propithecus	1	-	-	5
Bos sp.	-	68	17	36
Ovis aries	-	12	-	-
Indeterminate bovids	1	350	-	-
Potamochoerus larvatus	-	3	-	2
Indeterminate carnivores	1	-	-	-
cf. *Rattus* sp.	-	2	-	-
cf. *Mus* sp.	-	3	-	-
Tenrec ecaudatus	-	1	-	-
Smaller tenrecs	2	-	-	-
Small indeterminate mammals	-	12	-	-
cf. *Mullerornis* sp.	-	-	-	1
Anas cf. *hottentota*	-	13	-	-
Anas sp.	-	4	-	-
cf. *Sarkidiornis melenatos*	-	-	-	1
Gallus gallus	-	3	-	-
Phasianidae/Anatidae	-	-	1	-
Small marine turtle	1	30	-	4
Marine turtle of medium size	1	24	-	-
Large marine turtle	1	16	-	14
Eight species of boney fish	78	4 546	-	-
Various species of shark	3	-	-	-
Various small oysters (Ostreidae)	-	-	-	1
Various gasteropods	4	56	-	5
Small sea urchin (Cnidaria)	1	42	-	-
Various species of coral	-	3	-	-

gallus). At the same time, hunting activities favored by the increase in human population begin to occupy the daily lives of the ancient inhabitants of the town. One notes the hunting of small mammals such as the tenrec (*Tenrec ecaudatus*), wild ducks such as the teal (*Spatula hottentota*) and others. The occurrence of species commensal with humans, including rodents such as *Mus* sp. and *Rattus* sp. in Layer 5, confirm the existence of a growing human population.

However, in the higher intermediate Layer 4, the deposit is poor in osteological specimens, other than the existence of *Bos* sp. elements and a few bird elements, either *Gallus gallus* or *Anas* sp. The cause of this restriction in activity can be explained in several ways; a diminution in the availability of wild species, or a specialization on herding among the humans whose debris is represented in Layer 4 are both possibilities.

In the uppermost sampled layer (intermediate Layer 3), there is a diversity of hunting activity, but with a very low intensity.

Environmental analysis

This analysis is concerned with the interaction in the past between people and their environments. After their arrival in the Iharana region, people hunted existing wild species in the region of the site, from which we can infer the environments they exploited. Thus, the hunting of *Propithecus* sp. would indicate the use of dense forests, the hunting of *Spatula hottentota* would indicate the use of freshwater marshlands, and the taking of various fish, turtles, and molluscs would indicate exploitation of the reefs

Table E.4. Faunal elements identified from the Site of Ambatary, Unit VIII, 2009 (page 1).

Layer	Biological class	Family	Taxon	Elements	NISP	MNI	Weight (grams)
Layer 3A							6
	Mammalia	Bovidae	cf. *Bos*	Fragment of spongy epiphysis	1	1	
	Mammalia	Bovidae	cf. *Bos*	Fragment of central bone (burnt)	1	1	
	Mammalia	Bovidae	cf. *Bos*	Fragments of burnt rib, limbs	3	1	
	Aves (Birds)	Ratite - Aepyornithidae	cf. *Mullerornis*	Fragment of egg shell (thickness = 2 mm)	1	1	
	Reptilia	Chelonia	Small turtle	Dorsal carapace	3	1	
	Osteichthyes	Indeterminate	Large species	2 different globular teeth, 2 fragments of skull, 1 spine	3	2	
	Osteichthyes	Indeterminate	Small species	Vertebra	1	1	
	Invertebrates (Mollusks)	Gasteropod	Several small species	Shell fragments	3	2	
	Invertebrates (Mollusks)	Lamellibranche	Bivalve species of small size	Fragment of valve of whitish color	1	1	
Layer 3B							8
	Mammalia	Bovidae	*Bos* sp.	Fragment of burnt periosteum	1	1	
	Mammalia	Bovidae	*Bos* sp.	Fragment of distal condyle of canon bone	1	1	
	Mammalia	Indeterminate	Unknown	Fragments of limbs and skulls	1	1	
	Aves (Birds)	Anseriformes	cf. *Sarkidiornis*	Cervical vertebra, more or less altered	1	1	
	Osteichthyes	Indeterminate	Marine fish of medium size	Mandible with alveolar teeth	1	1	
	Osteichthyes	Indeterminate	Marine fish of large size	Vertebra, spine	2	1	
	Vertebrates	Indeterminate	Unknown	Small fragments of burned bone	10	indet.	
Layer 3C							16
	Mammalia	Indeterminate	cf. *Potamochoerus* sp.	Proximal part of a metapodial, epiphysis of a limb bone	2	1	
	Mammalia	Lemuriformes (Indriidae)	cf. *Propithecus*	Small fragments of limb, 1 burnt	5	1	
	Mammalia	Mixed	Medium size	Small fragments of bone			
	Reptilia	Chelonia	Small turtle	Fragment of burnt carapace (8.5 mm in length)	1	1	
	Osteichthyes	Indeterminate	Fish of medium size	Fragments of vertebrae (2 cm and 3 cm in diameter)	2	1	
Layer 3D							14
	Mammalia	Bovidae	cf. *Bos*	Fragment of burnt periosteum	1	2	
	Mammalia	Bovidae	Indeterminate	Fragments of periosteum	6	indet.	
	Osteichthyes	Indeterminate	Large species	Fragment of vertebral disc (3 mm thick; 1, 3 mm in diameter)	1	2	
	Osteichthyes	Indeterminate	Small species	Mandible, spines	4	3	
	Invertebrates	Gasteropode	Small species	Fragment of opaque white shell	2	indet.	
Layer 4A							7
	Mammalia	Bovidae	cf. *Bos*	Periosteum of limb bone	15	1	7
	Mammalia	Bovidae	*Bos* sp.	An articular limb bone (burnt)	1	1	
	Mammalia	Bovidae	*Bos* sp.	Fragment of molar (enamel)	1	1	
	Aves	Phasianidae / Anatidae ?	Indeterminate	Fragment of periosteum of a long bone	1	1	
	Reptilia	Chelonia	Turtle of medium size	Dorsal shell	3	1	
	Osteichthyes	Indeterminate	Indeterminate small species	Vertebra	1	1	
	Osteichthyes	Indeterminate	Indeterminate medium species	Fragment of skull	1	1	

Table E.4. Faunal elements identified from the Site of Ambatary, Unit VIII, 2009 (page 2).

Layer	Biological class	Family	Taxon	Elements	NISP	MNI	Weight (grams)
Layer 5A							126
	Mammalia	Artiodactyla	cf. *Bos*	Fragment of bone, fragment of skull, fragment of rib, 12 fragments of periosteum, of which 4 are burnt	16	1	
	Mammalia	Artiodactyla	cf. *Ovis aries*	Fragment of lower molar, fragment of limb bone with sharp cut mark, 1 epiphysis (unfused)	4	1	
	Mammalia	Artiodactyla	cf. *Potamochoerus larvatus*	3 fragments of limb bone (1 tibia metaphysis, 2 subproximal femurs), 20 fragments of limb bone	3		
	Mammalia	Tenrecidae	cf. *Tenrec ecaudatus*	1 medial rib	1	1	
	Aves (Birds)	Anseriformes	*Anas* cf. *hottentota*	subproximal coracoid, 1 medial radius, 1 distal condyle of tibio-tarsus, 1 phalange, fragments of limb bones	13	1	
	Reptilia	Chelonia	At least three species of turtle: small, medium, large	Dorsal and ventral carapace fragments, mandible fragments, ischium: specifically costal shell (10 mm thick, 23 mm long, dorsal side 16 mm thick) (very small, small, medium, large), mandible 16 mm long, dental plate: 4 mm in height, some fragments burnt	28	4	
	Fish	Indeterminate	More than 6 species of fish	110 vertebrae, 90 spines, mandibles, teeth; NB: criteria of classification type of teeth	270	6	
	Vertebrates	Mixed	Mixed	Many fragments of fish bone	Nbx	indet.	
	Invertebrates	Gasteropod	Unknown	2 fragments of crushed shell	2	2	
5A (flotation)	Mammalia	Indeterminate	Unknown	50 fragments of bone	Nbx	?	
5A (flotation)	Fish	Indeterminate	Unknown	10 fragments of bone, 2 vertebrae	12	indet.	
Layer 5B (fine screen)							180
	Mammalia	Artiodactyla	*Bos sp.*	Fragment of possible femur with trace of cut mark from sharp tool, periosteum, some burned	2	1	
	Mammalia	Artiodactyla	cf. Caprinae	2 fragments of periosteum of femur, part of caudal vertebra, fragment of head of proximal condyle of femur (unfused), 3 fragments of limb bone (unfused)	8	1	
	Mammalia	Rodentia	cf. *Rattus rattus*	Fragment of axis, right part; fragment of proximal condyle of ulna	2	1	
	Mammalia	Rodentia	Size of *Mus*	Proximal femur, mandible with 3 molars	3	1	
	Mammalia	Indeterminate micromammals	Unknown	Fragments of periosteum	12	indet.	
	Aves (Birds)	Galliformes	cf. *Gallus gallus*	Right scapula, 2 phalanges from foot	3	1	
	Aves (Birds)	Anseriformes	cf. *Anas*	Fragments of tarso-matatarsus with articulating condyle (unfused), proximal right coracoid, periosteum of limb bone	4	1	
	Reptilia	Chelonia	Medium species	Left femur (36 mm long), 3 marginal carapace fragments, 8 ventral carapace fragments, 1 dorsal (costal) carapace fragment	13	1	
	Reptilia	Chelonia	Very small species	Subdistal part of femur, fragment of ischium, 35 fragments of carapaces (dorsal 1.5 mm thick, ventral, and marginal)	35	1	
	Fish	Indeterminate	Various species	Spines, several fragments of maxilla, teeth	210	+ 7	
	Fish	Indeterminate	More than 8 species, given the forms of the mandibles	Cranial bones, mandibles (some with teeth), several burnt	228	Nbx	
	Fish	Indeterminate	Different species	Vertebrae of various sizes	1030	Nbx	
	Fish	Indeterminate	Different species	A mixture of various fish bones	3000	Nbx	
	Mammalia	Indeterminate	Mixed	Various fragments of periosteum and unknown bones	100	Nbx	
	Invertebrates (Mollusks)	Gasteropod	Very small species	More or less complete: 5 mm long (opaque white)	1	1	

Table E.4. Faunal elements identified from the Site of Ambatary, Unit VIII, 2009 (page 3).

Layer	Biological class	Family	Taxon	Elements	NISP	MNI	Weight (grams)
Layer 5B (continued)							
	Invertebrates (Mollusks)	Gasteropod	Different species	Fragments of shell	Nbx	+1	
	Invertebrates	Cnidaria	Species of small sea urchin	Shell and spines	Nbx	1	
	Invertebrates	Coral	Different species	Coral of various forms (tubular, amorphous)	3	1	
Layer 6							
	Mammalia	Artiodactyla	Indeterminate	Various fragments of bone: periosteum, spongey bone	1	8	
	Mammalia	Small Afrosoricida	Indeterminate small species	Phalange (thin)	1	1	
	Mammalia	Carnivora	Indeterminate small species	Fragment of metapodial (short but robust)	1	1	
	Mammalia	Chiroptera (Pteropodidae)	cf. *Pteropus*	Fragment of subproximal femur, 2 teeth	1	1	
	Mammalia	Afrosoricida	Tenrecidae (smaller than *T. ecaudatus*)	Mandible	1	1	
	Reptilia	Chelonia	3 species of turtle (small, medium, large size)	Shell fragments: some dorsal (2.5 mm thick), 3 ventral, 1 burnt ischium, 1 skull fragment with orbit, 1 fragment of shell edge	3	7	
	Fish	Chondrichtes	cf. shark species	Shark teeth	1	1	
	Fish	Indeterminate	6 species	Mandibles with teeth of different forms and various other bones	Nbx	Nbx	
	Fish	Indeterminate	Unknown large species	1 cheek bone (maxillary)	1	1	
	Fish	Indeterminate	Unknown species	Numerous fish bones	Nbx	1480	
	Invertebrates (Mollusks)	Gastropod	4 species (from medium to microscopic)	Several shells	4	5	
	Invertebrates	Coral	Species 1	Small fragment	1	1	
	Invertebrates	Coral	Species 2	Small fragment	1	1	
	Invertebrates	Cnidaria	Species of sea urchin	5 fragments of shell	1	1	

Nbx.: numerous (individuals) ; indet.: A number of indeterminate individuals ; + : more than.

and lagoons. During their period of growth, people engaged in some hunting, but fishing became more important. One can well ask if this change in activities was caused by new conditions leading to an increased abundance of marine products, or rather was caused by a reduction in the number of terrestrial species in the environmental milieu. Moreover, the two conditions seem to have coexisted, given that the introduction of the rat (*Rattus* sp.) and the house mouse (*Mus* sp.), both invasive species, could have led indirectly to a change in the natural milieu of endemic rodents. One can equally explain this change by the fact that the activities of fishing and the hunting of marine species, specifically sea turtles, could coexist with herding activities, this being parallel to the reduction of wild terrestrial species in the natural environment.

At the end of the occupation of the early town of Vohemar in the sixteenth century, there is abrupt diminution in the evidence of all activities concerning the exploitation of the fauna except for a limited persistence in the herding of cattle (*Bos* sp.), the hunting of the African bush pig (*Potamochoerus larvatus*) (a species introduced at an unknown time, which has become completely naturalized in Madagascar), and the hunting of certain species of sea turtle. If this is not a simple result of greater weathering of the uppermost deposits, one could explain the decreased faunal exploitation as a result of the diminution in the size of the human population and of its impact on the natural environment.

The importance of this study

Historical importance

Excavations done in the Ambatary neighborhood of fourteenth- to sixteenth-century Vohemar revealed the debris of modest households, whose residents consumed mostly fish and only occasionally cattle and hunted game. When other neighborhoods are excavated, we may find deposits discarded by wealthier households, which had access to more cattle and other foods rare at Ambatary. The biostratigraphic analysis shows the initial population of the fifteenth-century neighborhood hunted and fished and introduced domestic animals such as chickens, cows, and sheep into the environment. However, there is evidence of a change through time with less hunting to more fishing and herding of domestic cattle during the sixteenth century.

Biological and environmental interest

Various remains of vertebrates and invertebrates were collected at Ambatary site. Among the vertebrates there are animals of small or medium size, in one hand, introduced by people, such as chickens, sheep, and cows. In contrast, introduced wild animals such as the African bush pig and other still-extant wild animals—including a lemur, several species of tenrecs, and several species of wild ducks—were hunted. Different species of turtles and fish (boney fishes and cartilaginous fishes) were found, but these require additional study. These animal remains allow us to determine the interrelations between the human populations of Ambatary and the animals that they found in the local natural environment or which they themselves have introduced. This site also has evidence of distribution the extinct giant flightless ratites in the far north of Madagascar.

Conclusion

This study allows us to assess the subsistence bases of human settlement in fifteenth- to sixteenth-century Vohemar and the impact of human exploitation on biodiversity. Further sampling with rigorous sieving and flotation to recover remains from different parts of the town and further taxonomic identifications and quantification will allow a more precise assessment of human exploitation and its impact on the local environment.

Bibliography

Adelaar, Alexander
2016. A linguist's perspective on the settlement history of Madagascar. *NUSA* 61:69–88.

Allibert, Claude
1988. Les contacts entre l'Arabie, le Golfe persique, l'Afrique orientale et Madagascar: confrontation des documents écrits, des traditions orales et des données archéologiques récentes. In: *L'Arabie et ses mers bordières. I. Itinéraires et voisinages.* Séminaire de recherche 1985–1986. Lyon: Maison de l'Orient et de la Méditerranée Jean Pouilloux, 1988. pp. 111–126. (*Travaux de la Maison de l'Orient*, 16).

1999. Le Journal du J. S. Leigh (1836–1840) à bord du "Kite". *Etudes Océan Indien* 27–28:61–170.

2011. Reflexions autour de Vohémar. *Etudes Océan Indien* 46–47:149–160.

Allibert, Claude, Alain Argant, and Jaqueline Argant
1990. Le site de Dembéni (Mayotte, Archipel des Comores). *Etudes Océan Indien* 11:63–172.

Battistini, René
1964. *Étude géomorphologique de l'extrême sud de Madagascar*. Vol. 1. Paris: Éditions Cujas.

1965. Le Quaternaire littoral de l'extrême nord de Madagascar. *Bulletin de l'Association Française pour l'étude du Quaternaire* 2/2:133–144.

Battistini, René, and Pierre Vérin
1972. Man and the environment in Madagascar. In *Biogeography and ecology in Madagascar,* edited by René Battistini and G. Richard-Vindard, pp. 311–337. Springer, Netherlands.

Berg, Gerald M.
1977. The Myth of Racial Strife and Merina Kinglists: The Transformation of Texts. *History in Africa* 4:1–30.

Bialuschewski, Arne
2005. Pirates, slavers, and the indigenous population in Madagascar, c. 1690–1715. *The International Journal of African Historical Studies* 38/3:401–425.

Burney, David A.
1993. Late Holocene environmental changes in arid southwestern Madagascar. *Quaternary Research* 40:98–106.

1999. Rate, patterns, and processes of landscape transformation and extinction in Madagascar. In *Extinctions in Near Time: Causes, Contexts and Consequences*, edited by Ross D. E. MacPhee, pp. 145–164. New York: Plenum.

Callet, François
1974. *Histoire des Rois.* (Traduction G.-S. Chapus and E. Ratsimba.) Editions de la Librairie de Madagascar.

Clist, Bernard-Oliver
1995. New field data on the ancient iron metallurgy of Madagascar. *Nyame Akuma* 43:23–27.

Corby, Lt. Le Sieur de and Nicolas Mayeur
2011. Description des côtes nord de Madagascar par Corby et Mayeur à la fin du XVIIIe siècle. *Études Océan Indien* 46–47:17–24.

Christopher, Peter A.
2004. *Technical Report on Proposed Exploration for the A5 (Andavakoera) Project, Madagascar, Africa.* Vancouver, BC: Peter Christopher and Associates.

Crowther, Alison, Leilani Lucas, Richard Helm, Mark Horton, Ceri Shipton, Sarah Walshaw Matthew Pawlowicz, Chantal Radimilahy, Henry Wright, Katerina Douka, Llorenç Picornell-Gelabert, Dorian Q. Fuller, and Nicole L. Boivin
2016. Ancient crops provide first archaeological signature of the westward Austronesian expansion. *Proceedings of the National Academy of Sciences* 113(24):6635–6640.

De Barros, João
1628. *Da Asia,* Terceira Decado, Captula I, Folia 2. Lisboã: Imp. Per Jorge Rodriguez.

Dewar, Robert Earle
1991. Incorporating variation in occupation span into settlement pattern analysis. *American Antiquity* 56(4):604–620.

1996. The archaeology of the early colonization of Madagascar. In *The Indian Ocean in Antiquity*, edited by Julian Reade, pp 471–486. London: Kegan Paul and the British Museum.

2003. Relationship between Human Ecological Pressure and the Vertebrate Extinctions. In *The Natural History of Madagascar*, edited by Steven M. Goodman and Jonathan P. Benstead, pp. 119–122. Chicago and London: University of Chicago Press.

2007. Processual Assessment of Population Change in Western Avaradrano. In *Early State Formation in Central Madagascar: An Archaeological Survey of Western Avaradrano.* Museum of Anthropology Memoir No. 43, edited by Henry T. Wright, pp. 101–103. Ann Arbor: University of Michigan Museum of Anthropology.

Dewar, Robert E., Chantal Radimilahy, Léon Darsot Rasolofomampianina, and Henry T. Wright
2011. Early Settlement in the Region of Fenoarivo Atsinanana. In *Civilisations des Mondes Insulaires*, edited by Chantal Radimilahy and Narivelo Rajanarimanana, pp. 677–740. Paris: Karthala.

Dewar, Robert E. and Solo Hilarion Rakotovololona
1992. La chasse aux subfossiles: Les preuves du XIeme siècle au XIIIeme siécle. *Taloha* 11:4–15.

Dewar, Robert E. and Henry T. Wright
1993 The Culture History of Madagascar. *Journal of World Prehistory* 7:417–466.

2000. Northeast Madagascar in the XVth and XVIIth Centuries In *L'extraordinaire et le quotidien: Variations anthropologiques,* edited by Claude Allibert and Narivelo Rajaonarimanana, pp 287–311. Paris: Karthala.

Dewar, Robert E., Chantal Radimilahy, Henry T. Wright, Zenobia Jacobs, Gwendolyn O. Kelly and Francesco Berna
2013. Stone tools and foraging in northern Madagascar challenge Holocene extinction models. *Proceedings of the National Academy of Sciences* 110(31):12583–12588.

Dewar, Robert E., Chantal Radimilahy, Henry T. Wright
2015. Campements de cueilleurs-chasseurs dans l'extrême nord de Madagascar: travaux préliminaires à Ambohiposa et Lakaton'i Anja. *Taloha* 21:1–28.

Donque, Gérald
1975. *Contribution géographique à l'étude de climate de Madagascar*. Antananarivo: Imprimeries des Arts Graphiques.

Dorr, Laurence J.
1997. *Plant collectors in Madagascar and the Comoro Islands.* London: Royal Botanic Gardens, Kew.

Esoavelomandroso, Mannasé
1979. *Le Province orientale du "Royaume du Madagascar" à la fin du XIXe Siècle (1882–1895).* Antananarivo: Imprimerie F.T.M.

Favereau, Lt. Charles-Eugéne and Midshipman Germain
1885. *Baie de Vohémar*. Paris: Service Hydrographique de la Marine.

Flacourt, Etiénne de
(1658)1995. *Histoire de la Grand Isle Madagascar.* Edited by Claude Allibert. Paris: INALCO and Karthala.

Flecker, Michael
2010. A Ninth-Century Arab or Indian Shipwreck in Indonesia: The First Archaeological Evidence of Direct Trade with China. In *Shipwrecked: Tang Treasures and Monsoon Winds*, edited by Regina Krahl, John Guy, J. Keith Wilson, and Julian Raby, pp. 100–119. Washington, DC: Smithsonian Institution Press.

Fleury, Théophile
1886. Quelque Notes sur le Nord de Madagascar, d'après le manuscript du Dr. Charles Joseph Alphonse Bernier. *Bulletin de la Société de Géographie Commerciale de Bordeaux,* Communications: 5 and 9 April, 3 and 10 May de 1886.

Gabler, Sigrid C.
2005. *Iron furnaces and future kings: Craft Specialization and the Emergence of Political Power in Central Madagascar. University of Michigan Dissertation.* Ann Arbor: ProQuest Dissertations and Theses.

Gaudebout, Pierre and Elie Vernier
1941a. Notes à le suite d'une enquete sur les objects e pierre de la Région de Vohémar. *Bulletin de l'Académie Malgache*, Nouvelle Série, Tome XIV:91–99.

1941b. Notes sur une campagne de fouilles à Vohémar <<Mission RASIKAJY 1941>> *Bulletin de l'Académie Malgache*, Nouvelle Série, Tome XIV:100–120.

Goodman, Steven M. and Luciénne Wilmé, editors
2006. *Inventaires de la faune et de la flore du nord de Madagascar dans la région Loky-Manambato, Analamerana et Andavakoera.* Recherches pour le developpement, Série Sciences Biologiques No. 23. Antananarivo: Ministère de l'Education Nationale et de la Racherches Scientifique.

Grandidier, Alfred, J. Charles-Roux, C. Delhorbe, H. Froidevaux, and Guillame Grandidier
1903. *Collection des ouvrages anciens concernant Madagascar.* Paris: Comité de Madagascar.

Grealy, Alicia, Kristina Douglass, James Haile, Chriselle Bruwer, Charlotte Gough, and Michael Bunce
2016. Tropical ancient DNA from bulk archaeological fish bone reveals the subsistence practices of a historic coastal community in southwest Madagascar. *Journal of Archaeological Science* 75:82–88.

Griffin, William
2009. *The Matitanana Archaeological Project: Culture History and Social Complexity in the Seven Rivers Region of Southeastern Madagascar.* Doctoral dissertation in anthropology, University of Michigan, Ann Arbor.

Hogg, Alan G., Quan Hua, Paul G. Blackwell, Mu Niu, Caitlin E. Buck, Thomas P. Guilderson, Timothy J. Heaton, Jonathan G.Palmer, Paula J. Reimer, Ron W.Reimer, Christian S.M.Turney, and Susan R.H. Zimmerman.
2013. SHCal13 Southern Hemisphere calibration, 0–50,000 years cal BP. *Radiocarbon* 55(2):1–15.

Horton, Mark Chatwin
1996. *Shanga: The archaeology of a Muslim trading community on the coast of East Africa.* Memoir 14. Nairobi: British Institute in Eastern Africa.

Hurvitz, David Jay
1979. Anjoaty Cattle Ear-marks. In *Madagascar in History*, edited by Raymond Kent, pp. XX–YYU. Albany, CA: Foundation for Malagasay Studies.

1980. *A Record of Anjoaty History in Vohemar, Madagascar.* Docotral dissertation in anthropology, Princeton University, Princeton, NJ.

1986. The "Anjoaty" and Embouchures in Madagascar. In *Madagascar: Society and History*, edited by Conrad Kottak, Aiden Southall, and Pierre Vérin, pp 107–120. Durham, North Carolina: Academic Press of North Carolina.

Lemoine, Paul
1906. *Etudes Géologiques dans le Nord de Madagascar*. Paris: A.Hermann.

Levat, Ėdouard David
1912. *Richesses Minérales de Madagascar*. Paris: H. Dunod and E. Pinat.

Mabberly, David J.
1997. *The Plant Book: A portable dictionary of the vascular plants*. Cambridge, UK: Cambridge University Press.

MacPhee, Ross, and David A. Burney
1991. Dating of modified femora of extinct dwarf Hippopotamus from southern Madagascar: Implications for constraining human coloization and vertebrate extinction events. *Journal of Archaeological Science* 18:695–706.

Matsumoto, Katsumi, and David A. Burney
1994. Late Holocene environments at Lake Mitsinjo, northwestern Madagascar. *The Holocene* 4/1:16–24.

Mayeur, Nicholas
1912. Voyage dans le nord de Madagascar, au cap d'Ambre et à quelques iles du Nord-Ouest. *Bulletin de l'Académie Malgache*, Tome X:93–136.

Meyer, Carol, J. M. Todd, and Kurt Beck
1991. From Zanzibar to Zagros: a copal pendant from Eshnunna. *Journal of Near Eastern Studies* 50/4:289–298.

Mouren [cf.Maurein, Albert]. et Rouaix, R.
1913. Industrie ancienne des objets de Vohémar. *Bulletin de l'Académie Malgache,* Tome XII, 2eme partie:3–12.

Newitt, Malyn
1978. The southern Swahili coast in the first century of European expansion. *Azania* 13/1:111–126.

Oliver, Samuel Pasfield
1885. *The True Story of the French Dispute in Madagascar.* London: T. Fisher Unwin.

Parker Pearson, Mike , Karen Godden, Ramilisonina, Retsihasetse, Jean-Luc Schwenninger, George Huertebize, Chantal Radimilahy and Helen Smith, with contributions by Irene de Luis, David Barker, Seth Priestman, Lucien Rakotozafy, Bako Rasoarifetra, Alan Vince, Zöe Crossland and Brian Boyd
2010. *Pastoralists, warriors and colonists: the archaeology of southern Madagascar*, B.A.R. 2139, Oxford, UK: Archaeopress.

Pomerantz, Sol
2017. *The Prehistory of Madagascar: Microbotanical and ArchaeologicalEvidence from Coastal and Highland Sites.* Thesis submitted in fulfilment of the requirements for the degree of Doctor of Philosophy in Archaeological Science. St. Hughs College, Oxford University.

Radimilahy, Marie de Chantal
1998. *Mahilaka, an Archaeological Investigation of an Early Town in Northwestern Madagascar*. Studies in African Archaeology 15. Uppsala: Department of Archaeology and Ancient History.

Radimilahy, Chantal, Barthélémy Manjakahery, and Lucien MA Rakotozafy
2006. Archaeology of St Augustine's Bay, Lower and Middle Onilahy Valley. *Studies in the African Past* 5:60–94.

Raheriasena, Martin and Steven Goodman
2006. Les petits mammifères non-volant dans l'extreme Nord de Madagascar (Loky-Manambato, Analamerana et Andavakoera). In *Inventaires de la faune et de la flore du nord de Madagascar dans la région Loky-Manambato, Analamerana et Andavakoera*, edited by Goodman and Wilmé, pp. 175–230. Antananarivo: Ministère de l'Education Nationale et de la Racherches Scientifique.

Rakotoarisoa, Jean Aimé
1998. *Mille ans d'occupation humaine dans le Sud-Est de Madagascar :Anosy, une ile au milieu des terre.* Paris, France: Éditions L'Harmattan.

Rakotoarisoa, Jean Aimé, editor
2013. *De l'Ivongo au Manangoro*. Toamasina (Madagascar): Imp. Ambatovy.

Rakotondravony, Hery A.
2006. Patterns de la diversité des reptiles et amphibiens de la region de Loky-Manambato. In *Inventaires de la faune et de la flore du nord de Madagascar dans la région Loky-Manambato, Analamerana et Andavakoera*, edited by Goodman and Wilmé, pp. 109–147. Antananarivo: Ministère de l'Education Nationale et de la Racherches Scientifique.

Raombana [Sole name]
1994. *Histories II,* edited by Simon Ayache. Anstirabe: Imprimerie Catholique.

Ranaivonasy, J
2003. Aires prioritaires pour la conservation des plantes. *Ravintsara* 1(5):14–15.

Randrianarisoa, P.M., A. A. Rasamison, and Lucien Rakotozafy
1999. Les lémuriens de la région de Daraina: foret de Bekaraoka et foret de Sahaka. *Lemur News* 4:19–21.

Rossi, Georges
1980. *L'Extreme-nord de Madagascar*. Aix-en-Provence: Édisud.

Safford, R. J., editor
2000. *Etude environmentale et écologique du lac Sakaha, Madagascar.* London: Royal Holloway Institute for Enviromental Research, University of London.

Schreurs, Guido, and Jean-Aimé Rakotoarisoa
2011. The archaeological site at Vohemar in a regional geographical and geological context. *Études Océan Indien* 46–47.

Schreurs, Guido, Sandra J.T.M. Evers, Chantal Radimilahy and Jean-Aimé Rakotoarisoa
2011. The Rasikajy civilization in northeast Madagascar: a pre-European Chinese community? *Études Océan Indien* 46–47: 107–132.

Serneels,Vincent, Mélissa Morel, Christoph Nitsche, Chantal Radimilahy, Jean-Aimé Rakotoarisoa, Bako Rasoarifetra, Guido Schreurs
2017. *Pierre at Fer à Madagascar: Vestiges sidérurgiques de Benavony et de la Rivière Matavy*. SLSA Jahresbericht–Rapport annuel–Annual report.

Shott, Michael J.
1999. On Bipolar Reduction and Splintered Pieces. *North American Archaeologist* 20, 3:217–238.

Vérin, Pierre
1975. *Les Echelles anciennes du commerce sur les cotes nords de Madagascar*. Lille: Service de Reproduction des These.

1986. *The History of Civilisation in Madagascar*. Rotterdam, New York: Balkema.

Vernier, Elie
1942–1943. Les Rasikijy dans la Presqu'ile Masoala. *Bulletin de l'Académie Malgache*, N.S. XXV: 187–191.

Vernier, Elie and Jacques Millot
1971. *Archéologie Malgache, Comptoirs Musulmans*. Paris: Musée de L'Homme.

Virah-Sawmy, Malika, Katherine J.Willis, and Lindsey Gillson
2009. Threshold response of Madagascar's littoral forest to sea-level rise. *Global Ecology and Biogeography* 18: 98–110.

2010. Evidence for drought and forest declines during the recent megafaunal extinctions in Madagascar. *Journal of Biogeography* 37/3:509–519.

Virah-Sawmy, Malika, Lindsey Gillson, Charlie J. Gardner, Atholl Anderson, Geoffrey Clark, and Simon Haberle
2016. A landscape vulnerability framework for identifying integrated conservation and adaptation pathways to climate change: the case of Madagascar's spiny forest. *Landscape Ecology* 31:637–654.

Whitcomb, Donald S.
1975. The archaeology of Oman: a preliminary discussion of the Islamic periods. *Journal of Oman Studies* 1:123–157.

White, J. Peter and David Hurst Thomas
1972. What Mean These Stones? Ethno-taxonomic models and archaeological interpretations in the New Guinea Highlands. In *Models in Archaeology*, edited by David L.Clarke, pp 275–308. London, Den Haag: Methuen.

Wright, Henry T., editor
2007. *Early State Formation in Central Madagascar: An Archaeological Survey of Western Avaradrano.* Museum of Anthropology Memoir No. 43. Ann Arbor: University of Michigan Museum of Anthropology.

Wright, Henry T. and Fulgence Fanony
1992. L'évolution des systèmes d'occupation des sols dans la vallée. de la rivière Mananara au Nord-Est de Madagascar. *Taloha* 11:16–64.

Wright Henry T., Chantal Radimilahy, and Claude Allibert
2005. L'évolution des systems d'installation dans la baie d'Ampasindava et à Nosy-Be. *Taloha* 14–15:300–354.

Wright, Henry T., Jean-Aimé Rakotoarisoa, Georges Heurtebize, and Pierre Vérin
1993. The Evolution of Settlement System in the Efaho River Valley: A preliminary report on archaeological reconnaissances of 1983–86. *Indo-Pacific Prehistory Association Bulletin* 12: 2–20

Wright, Henry T., Pierre Vérin, Ramilisonina, David Burney, Lida P. Burney, and Katsumi Matsumoto
1996. The Evolution of Settlement Systems in the Bay of Boeny and the Mahavavy River Valley, northwestern Madagascar. *Azania* 31:37–73.

L. Michael Hall, Ph.D.
Originally presented in the small book with the title, *Make It So!* (2002)
Copyright pending at the Library of Congress, Washington DC.
ISBN: 1-890001-35-X — 978 189 000 1353

Published by: **NSP —*Neuro-Semantics Publications***
P.O. Box 8
Clifton, CO. 81520-0008 USA
(970) 523-7877

Printed by: **Action Printing**
Jerry Kucera, Owner
516 Fruitvale Court, Unit C
Grand Junction, CO. 81504
(970) 434-7701

Neuro-Semantics® is the trademark name for the model, patterns, and society of Neuro-Semantics. ISNS stands for the International Society of Neuro-Semantics. For more than 4000 pages of free information, see the web sites:

www.neurosemantics.com
www.neuro-semantics-trainings.com
www.meta-coaching.org
www.self-actualizing.org
www.nlp-video.com

ACHIEVING PEAK PERFORMANCE

PREFACE

Are you ready and willing to commit yourself to achieving peak performances in your life? If you are, then I want to welcome you to a Neuro-Semantic adventure that you'll experience via this book. Welcome to this journey of discovery and intense activity!

> "Adventure . . . journey . . . intense activity?" I thought I was just buying a book I could leisurely read for some mindless distraction, something to do at the airport, on the beach, or while waiting at the mall."

If that's your motivation and intention then immediately put this book back on the shelf. The escape literature of romance novels and sci-fi books are two aisles over. This book will be a waste of your money and time and probably only serve as a torture to your peace of mind.

You're still here? You are ready for a life-transforming experience of an adventurous journey into what's possible for you to achieve? Good. You're ready to be awakened, challenged, and engaged in ways that will take you out of your comfort zone? To be stretched beyond what you thought possible? Excellent. Have I got a series of experiences for you!

I have written *Achieving Peak Performance* to be the most experiential book I've ever written. I've written it to offer you as much as possible a personal journey into the unleashing of your potentials. It is not as personal or intimate as having a personal coach work with you, but it is the next best thing. What will that mean for you as you read?

- It will mean that there will be an *Action Plan* for you to interact with and act on within each chapter. Sometimes there will be an exercise to do; sometimes a series of actions to engage in with others.

- It will mean that there are lots and lots of *Patterns* within the chapters, patterns that you can use to create new states of mind-and-emotion to enhance your resourcefulness and develop your capabilities for peak performance.

- It will mean that there are *processes* for you to engage in to expand your self-awareness as you set new frames and/or suspend old frames.

Because this is a Neuro-Semantic book, I often refer to many of the other models within NLP and Neuro-Semanitcs. These models include the following:

- The Meta-Model of language
- The Model of Meta-Programs
- Cinematic Features of our Mental Movies (Meta-Modalities)
- The Meta-States Model
- The Matrix Model
- The Axis of Change
- The Self-Actualization Quadrants

I have written the text so that you'll learn enough about these models as you progress through the book. For more about them, refer to Appendix A which provides a short description of each.

This book also is the fifth in the series of Meta-Coaching.

Volume I: Coaching Change (Axes of Change) (2004)
Volume II: Coaching Conversations (2002)
Volume III: Unleashed: Guide to Self-Actualization (2007)
Volume IV: Self-Actualization Psychology (2008)
Volume V: Achieving Peak Performance (2009)
Volume VI: Unleashing Leadership: Self-Actualizing Leaders and Companies (2009)
Volume VII: The Crucible (2010)
Volume VIII: Benchmarking Intangibles

A Special Recognition to **Adrian Beardley** of Tasmania Australia—a friend, a Neuro-Semantic trainer, a Coach, and a man with a vision that was only exceeded by the size of his heart. As this book goes to print in May, 2009, Adrian died after a bout with cancer. Adrian created most of the diagrams in this book and will be remembered by the many lives he touched.

Those who contributed to proof-reading the text of this book and who identified the scores of grammatical mistakes and mis-spellings that I graced the manuscript with include *Sue Anderson* (Australia), *Brand Coetzee* (South Africa), *Douglas Cartwright* (England), and *Diya Welland* (New Zealand). Thank them with a peak performance hug when you see them.

Chapter 1

PERFORMANCE

AT A HIGHER LEVEL

The bottom line to achieving success in any area or field is performance. It is action—*effective action* that makes a difference, that is, that produces the *results* that you desire.

- Can you do (get yourself to do) what you want to do?
- How well can you perform that task?
- Can you take effective action to achieve your goals and turn your dreams into reality?

In this, knowing *what* to do and *how* to do it is not sufficient for success. It is only when you can get yourself to *act* on your knowledge that you experience the knowledge as "power"—the power that makes a difference in your life. Knowledge only becomes powerful as you express the information in effective actions. So the bottom line is *action*—intelligent, informed, and wise actions.

Yet even effective action is not the final step if you want to be truly successful. Getting yourself to act is one thing, organizing those actions so that they are regular, systematic, dependable, consistent, and intuitive is quite another thing. Only then can you count on yourself for being able to consistently perform. And this introduces the idea of "installing" what you know so deeply and thoroughly in your body that what you know becomes *embodied.* Then, with embodiment you experience an unconscious competence where your effective actions are part and parcel of your identity and style. There you have them within you at an unconscious level so you perform them intuitively. Would you like that? Isn't that the kind of integrated learning that you are after? Isn't that the vision for a high quality of consistent performance?

Consistent Performance?

> "I would like to get that idea *inside* me so that it's really mine."
> "Jim has such a great personal charm when it comes to negotiating, I wish I could do it like he does!"
> "I don't know where Brenda learned to stand up for herself so firmly and in a way that doesn't offend. She has it so well ingrained inside her that I don't think it's possible for anyone to run over her."

If you have ever entertained these kinds of hopes, dreams, wishes, or desires, then you know what it is to want something thoroughly incorporated within your personality. When something gets inside you so deeply, so thoroughly, so completely, and so fully that it's just the way you operate, just the way you "are," you can say that the acquisition of the desired ideas, beliefs, skills, understandings, etc. is now *embodied or installed in your personality.*

> *Knowing what's right isn't the hard part, the hard part is doing what's right.*

The *installation* metaphor comes from how we install items in our homes or offices and how we officially install someone into a role or position in a group, business, or political position. Today we install new software programs into our computer, and we also un-install old programs. Installation describes the process of how we put something inside of something else. In the context of learning, we talk about having learned something, perhaps a procedure, a new way of doing things and we may say, "That idea is well installed. I have it." Or, we may say the reverse, "I've learned that, but I just don't have it installed yet."

This means that you can learn something and know it *intellectually* and yet not have it available to you *experientially.* Consider some of the learnings, knowledge, skills, and models that you "know" conceptually and which are also thoroughly installed within you. Make a list of them (see the Action Plan at the end of this chapter). For instance, is riding a bike a learned skill that is thoroughly installed in your neurology? How about typing? Knowing how to behave in a restaurant? Driving on the motorway?

When I made my list of installed programs that are so much a part of my sense of being, I listed numerous things that I had once memorized. As I recalled poetry, pledges, biblical passages, quotations, etc., I realized that this "knowledge" is now so ingrained inside that I could *not* forget them. That would be like forgetting the alphabet or the numerals.

I never open up a book and go, "Opps! I forgot the alphabet again. Let me see, 'A b c d e f g . . .'" I do that sometimes with some foreign languages (e.g., Koine Greek and ancient Hebrew), but not English. It's like some people who are masterful phobics and who never go, "Damn it! I forgot to be afraid in that elevator."

Skills can become so ingrained, so internalized, so much a part of who you are, how you experience yourself, how you move through the world that we say that the learnings or knowledge is completely yours and intuitively governs the quality of your performance. As a Neuro-Semanticist, I am absolutely fascinated in *how* that happens.

- What are the processes involved in installing an idea or knowledge or skills?
- How does abstract knowledge get inside so that it becomes a person's operational programs?
- What learnings, teachings, training mechanisms are involved in effective installation?
- What patterns of installation can you use, learn, or develop?
- What beliefs, values, and decisions enable you to more effectively incorporate in your body what you know in your mind?

An Idea Whose Time Has Come

The idea of *translating great ideas and newest knowledge into muscle memory* so that it is thoroughly installed within you and automatically governs your performances is an idea whose time has come. That's because installing what you know reduces the knowing-doing gap. And when you close the knowing-doing gap, you increase your effectiveness, efficiency, and productiveness. By installing your learnings so that they become truly *yours,* you are able to actually *do and achieve* what you know. Performance at this level then enhances life in a thousand ways.

Why is this idea of accelerating your skills of implementation an idea whose time has come? Because today with the pace of change, new technology, and the world as a global community, you need to be able to incorporate your learnings at a greater speed. You need the ability to implement those models and skills while the moment is hot. And with the pace of change, you need this more than ever before. You also need to be able to *unlearn* old skills and release old models so that you can flexibly adjust as things change.

With the ever-increasing rate of information acceleration, even more important than that knowledge, is your ability to act on it, to put it to use, to take the next step in development, to learn from that, and to integrate it so that you can actually improve your performance. And that is what this book is all about.

Implementing for Enhanced Performance

I have written *Achieving Peak Performance* for everyone interested in improving his or her skills and ability to accelerate the competency learning process. What does this entail? This means identifying the critical success performances in your area of interest, developing a robust strategy, playing to your strengths, modeling best practices, refining and developing your performances, eliminating every interference, using every process that enables you to fully embody the performance, streamlining the "flow" state where you are at your best, and enjoying the benefits of your peak performances. Ah, that's a lot!

Who is Achieving Peak Performance for? I've written this primarily for leaders, managers, trainers, coaches, and consultants—people who work with improving performance. I've also written it for anyone interested in closing the knowing-doing gap and being able to produce one's best. My background in psychology and experience as a psychotherapist, trainer, consultant, and coach has led me to realize that the bottom line of success is the quality and consistence of one's performances. Knowing what to do and feeling good about yourself and others as you do it is simply not sufficient. You must know how to translate what you know into actual performance. At the level of companies and groups, we must become oriented to implementing. We must become competent in making things happen in creating a performance culture.

- *How* do we get these new skills and patterns installed into our own behaviors?
- *How* can we translate these great patterns to others so that they are installed in their behaviors?

- *How* does the installation process work?
- *What* are the mechanisms involved?
- *How* can I become masterful in *installing* training objectives into participants so that they are authentically embodied?
- How can I take my performance to ever higher levels of excellence?

> The idea of *translating our great ideas and newest knowledge into muscle memory* so that it is thoroughly *installed within us* so that we can quickly act on it is an idea whose time has come.

We know that performance will improve very little if all we do is read, think, talk, reflect, and meditate. It will improve, but the improvement will be minimal. To improve the quality and quantity of performance significantly and to raise it to new levels requires *doing*. It requires taking effective action and this means practicing, experimenting, refining, using feedback, learning more, testing, etc.

The Neuro-Semantics of Performance

If you are new to Neuro-Semantics, this field is first and foremost about two phenomena: *performance and meaning*. In previous writings, I have focused mostly on meaning or semantics. You can find this in *Meta-States, Mind-Lines, Winning the Inner Game,* and *The Matrix Model.* We are semantic in our nature because meaning is not given, we have to create it. Without instinctual programs informing us about what a thing is, how it works, what it's for, what we're to do, etc., we have to find and create meaning. That makes us meaning-makers and we create meaning in multiple ways, at multiple levels, and in multiple dimensions.

We are also *neurological* beings. We learn and incorporate our learnings in our physiology and nervous systems (in our body) which is why we are by nature, neuro-semantic. The ideas, as the meanings that we find and create, are learned in our brain and throughout our entire body. That's why we have the phenomenon that we call "muscle memory." The neuro-pathways that run our brain-and-body activate the motor cortex that sends commands throughout the rest of the body so that we can learn and "know" things in our body.

Because of this dual interplay of meaning and performance, Neuro-Semantics studies, explores, models, and then replicates through training, consulting, and coaching *the best meanings that we can invent* so that we can perform them in our body. We also look at every performance as expressing, manifesting, and making-real some meaning. Every skill, behavior, action, competency, experience, and state is actualizing some meaning. The question is always, "What meaning?" "What knowledge are you actualizing in your actions?"

This positions Neuro-Semantics to be about *enriching your performances with the best and most robust meanings.* Performance that's not driven, motivated, and informed by the highest and best meanings will be mediocre, average, even insipid performance. Via Neuro-Semantics, we explore how to update old meanings that we are still performing, releasing meanings that are not appropriate, even toxic to us, and undoing the meaning-making process.

In all of this, Neuro-Semantics distinguishes itself for being able to get results, to raise the quality of performance, and to actually install new patterns.

> *Knowing is not enough; we must apply.*
> *Willing is not enough; we must do.*
> Goethe

What explains this? Part of the explanation is due to our constant focus on mind-body-emotion as a holistic system. We refuse the trap of separating mind from body, but work with these as variables of the system. To do this we use the holistic term—*state.* That's because we know that mind-and-body operate synergistically as a dynamic mental and emotional state. We explain it also by the self-reflexivity inherent in the Meta-States Model. This is what empowers us to be able to apply knowledge and insight to ourselves. This enables "walking our talk" which increases our power of congruency.

With this focus on performing meaning and enriching the meaning of our performances, Neuro-Semantics has a natural affinity to implementation. This is where many disciplines and models fail. They have great ideas, but lack practical ways for incorporating great ideas. They have cutting-edge models and knowledge, but lack methodology for implementing that knowledge. And because performing your meanings, adding rich meanings to your performances, and eliminating all non-productive performances describes the heart pulse of Neuro-Semantics, the focus here will be on the translation from mind to body.

With the acceleration of information, your abilities to assimilate and integrate what you know can easily be swamped. You need a frame of mind that empowers you to both understand and use information so that you are constantly taking effective action to make your dreams come true.

So, are you ready to implement knowledge and turn it into skill, competency, performance, and results? Are you up for the challenge of closing your knowing-doing gap by incorporating concepts, beliefs, decisions, and meaning as you embody and integrate then within you so that they become your way of being in the world? If so, this is the book for you!

Accelerating Performance with Meta-States

In this book, you will learn to work with your states and meta-states to accelerate the quality of your effective actions. To accomplish that we will extensively use the Meta-States Model. You will find that almost every pattern in this work is a meta-stating pattern. If this is a new model for you, then here is a quick description of the *meta-stating process.* We begin with a primary state, that is, a state of mind-and-body that is *about* some stimulus "out there" in the world. Primary states are direct, immediate, and highly kinesthetic.

- "I *fear* the way that dog is barking at me."
- "I'm so *angry* at him for the way he put me down."
- "I really *enjoyed* the play tonight."

Figure 1:1

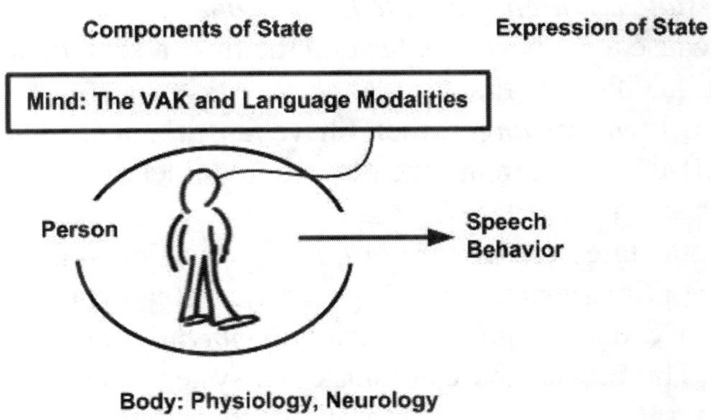

A meta-state arises when you respond to your response.

- "I *hate* it when I become so afraid of things."
- "I feel *ashamed* of getting angry about his response."
- "I *love* having *fun* at the play."

Now the stimulus which sets off the second state is not "out there." The stimulus is now your own thinking-and-feeling. You are *responding* to your first response. You are *reflecting back onto* yourself with more thoughts and feelings. This creates a meta-state.

Figure 1:2

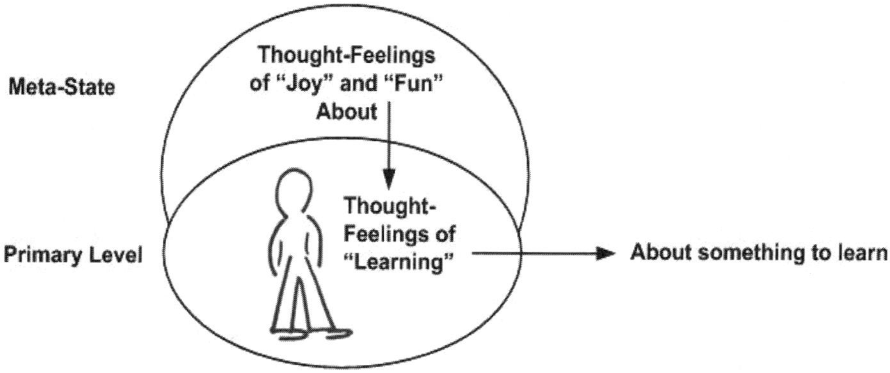

A meta-state is a higher state to the first one. It is about the first one. And because it is *above and beyond* the first, it sets the frame for the first. It qualifies the first.

If I *fear* my *anger,* then I have *fearful* anger.
If I enjoy learning, then I have *joyful* learning.

With meta-states you *texture or qualify* your first states. In a meta-state, the primary state doesn't go away, instead you *transcend and include* it within a higher state. You *embed* the first state within a higher. This creates more complex and systemic states.

In healthy and high self-esteem, I think and feel *value, worth, and importance* about myself as a human being. I think "my value is unconditional, it is not conditioned upon looks, money, degrees, status, or anything else." This high level concept is an abstract understanding or belief about human beings and human nature. That means every meta-state is at the same time, a belief, an understanding, an abstraction, a concept, decision, intention, etc.

What is the process for building up meta-states? *It is to apply one state to another state.* So in creating self-esteem, you *access* several states, acceptance, appreciation, and then awe or esteem. You think about something that causes you to feel and experience "acceptance," "appreciation," and "awe." Once you access that, you then *reflect* that feeling state *back* onto your thoughts-and-feelings about yourself as a person. By *transcending* your everyday sense of self with *awe* and *including* it inside of a sense of awe, you bring the state of awe to yourself. When you do that with *appreciation*, you create self-appreciation. When you do that with *acceptance,* you create self-acceptance.

The *meta-stating process* involves accessing and applying one state to another. If the state you access isn't strong enough or intense enough, you amplify it so that you have enough neurological energy to apply back to yourself. After you apply one mental-emotional state to another, then you give it a chance to integrate. This allows the *transcending and including* or the *embedding* process. So you appropriate the higher state to the lower state. We can do this with a question:

> Feeling this *respect of persons* fully as you feel angry and that some value is violated, how does *that* transform your experience of anger?

We can do it with a suggestion or direction:

> As you *feel* that sense of *unconditionality* as when you look at a newborn infant and know that the baby doesn't have to prove anything, but is infinitely valuable and precious and loveable and you *feel that fully*, notice what happens when you hold that feeling and apply it to yourself . . . knowing you began as a newborn infant and have grown to the person you are today and that deep inside at your core is an *unconditionally valuable person* and as you feel that, would that make a difference if you lived your life from this perspective? What if you *feel this fully* and use it as your core of worth? How does that transform things?

In *meta-stating* you are setting up one state of thought, emotion, or body as a higher frame to another thought, state, or experience. While there are lots of ways to do that, you are essentially creating a meta-relationship between the layers of your thoughts. Or to express it more dynamically, you are layering more and more resourceful thoughts and feelings upon your previous thinking and emoting. As such, the higher thoughts and feelings as states are being set as the higher frames that run the show. So in the end, in meta-stating you create a self-organizing system, a matrix of frames that defines and governs your subjective reality.

There are five steps then in the basic meta-stating process:
1) *Access* the state that you want to set in a meta-relationship.
2) *Amplify* the state so it has sufficient neurological energy.
3) *Apply* to the referent state or experience.
4) *Appropriate* the higher to the lower into the relevant contexts.
5) *Analyze* the end result to make sure it is ecological, realistic, productive, enhancing, empowering, and congruent with values.

Figure 1:3

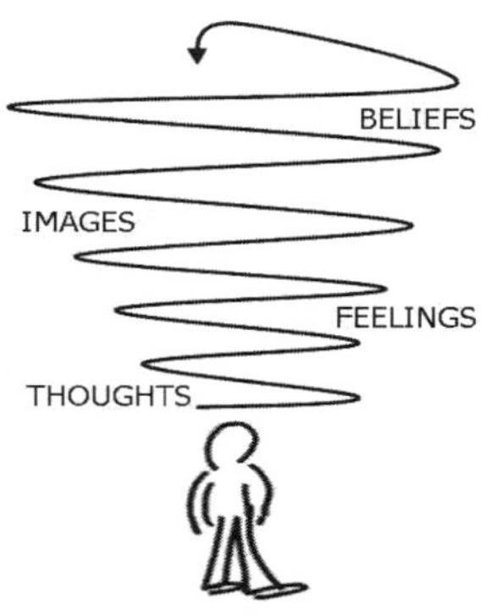

Action Plan

1) Make a list of the things you *know* intellectually which are also completely embodied in your neurology. Writing this list will achieve several objectives: you'll give yourself evidence from your own experience that you can and do translate ideas into neurological patterns.

2) Make a list of things that you know intellectually but are *not* fully incorporated within you yet. Beside each one, gauge the degree to which it is now embodied. Gauge from 0 (not at all) to 10 (totally). Date your entry and update it from time to time.

Chapter 2

CLOSING THE KNOWING-DOING GAP

For most of us, there is far too much of a gap between knowing and doing. We *know* more than we do. Isn't that true for you? Isn't it true that you know a great deal more than you *do?*

- We *know* more about healthy eating and exercising than we put into practice.
- We know more about listening, being patient, validating, being affirmative, and other relationship skills than we do, especially when we're under pressure and feel stress.
- We know more about business, selling, and marketing than we do.
- We know more about learning, accelerating our learning than we practice.

Our performance in dozens of areas consistently falls short of our knowledge. If you were to measure your level of actual performance against your level of knowledge, would you discover that you, like most of us, are constantly under-performing? You over-know and under-perform. This is normal and, for the most part, as it should be. Well, to a degree. And that's the point. The problem is not that there is a gap. That's inevitable. The problem is *how much of a gap is there* and what you are doing to close the gap. Sometimes the lag in the transfer of knowledge to action becomes too much of a gap, it becomes a gulf.

- To what degree are you able to fully perform what you know?
- Is the gap between what you know and what you do too much? How do you know?
- How big is the gap?
- How much of a gap can you endure?
- What causes or contributes to your knowing-doing gap?
- What are you doing about closing the gap?
- How successful are you in closing the gap?
- How mindful are you when you are doing that?

Let what's in the Mind be in the Muscles

I first became aware of the *knowing-doing gap* when I was involved in my original research for the Wealth Creation training that I created as a Neuro-Semantics approach. As I studied the literature of the field, almost everything was written in terms of *principles*— concepts, abstraction, vague truths like "laws of wealth," "rules for becoming wealthy," etc. These statements generalized the basic knowledge of the field into summary declarations, but were not useful for actually *doing* anything about it. The ideas are brilliant:

- Spend less than you make.
- Save a little with every paycheck; pay yourself first.
- Think and grow rich.
- Do what you love and the money will follow.
- Use your passion to add value to a specific market.

> *"The truth of the matter is that you always know the right thing to do. The hard part is doing it."*
> General Norman Scwarzkopf

As I read the literature of the field and came across wonderful insights, I would think, "That's a great idea!" "Yes, a truly inspiring idea. If only I could get myself to practice that." "What would I actually do to perform that idea?"

A little later I was reading about the importance of building up capital for investment. Author after author repeated that the beginning stage of any wealth building system involves capital, but that you won't ever get money to work for you if you don't have some capital to work with. Then as I was reflecting on the point, I found myself saying it aloud.

> "Capital is built by saving a small percentage of one's income on a regular basis."

In doing this, I accidently expressed one of the great wealth creation principles, a simple yet profound one. It was not profound because it takes a rocket scientist to figure it out! Such were the thoughts in the back of my mind as I repeated the insightful statement out loud. And that quiet meta-comment *about* the great idea brought an insight to the front of my awareness.

> "Hey, I already *know* this. But am I acting on it? Am I actually using and implementing this knowledge? No, not really. I am not a serious saver. I *know* I should be. I *know* it is important. It is one of my values. But am I doing it in a committed way? No. Why not? What is stopping me from *doing* what I *know?* What is stopping the performance?"

> "Perhaps the most valuable result of all education
> is the ability to make yourself
> do the thing you have to do when it ought to be done,
> whether you like it or not.
> It is *the first lesson* that ought to be learned;
> and however early a man's training begins,
> it is probably *the last lesson* that he learns thoroughly."
> Thomas Huxley

The *knowing* was already in place, what stopped it from activating my motor programs so that I could actually *use* that knowledge and turn that knowledge into power? What was creating the knowing-doing gap? "Maybe I don't believe it?" I thought.

> "No, but I do. I do believe it."

"But do I really?" I wondered? So speaking out loud again, I used the words,

> "I believe that capital is built by saving a small percentage of my income on a regular basis."

Now in saying that it *felt different* from saying the previous statement. It felt more personal. It felt strong, more inside me. It felt like it was more in my muscles and not only in my mind. So I said it again, and again. As I did I began imagining that I was saying it to someone, or a group, and doing so in a way that was fully congruent and believable. And as I did, the words began to change. The words become even more personal and *the feeling* of the statement began to feel more integrated in my body.

> "I believe that capital is built by saving a small percentage of my income on a regular basis."
> "I believe that I can build capital by saving a small percentage of my income on a regular basis."
> "I believe I will build capital as I save at least a small percentage of my income every week."

It was funny how saying these words seemed to make the ideas more vivid in my mind and more real within my neurology. But then again, that's what a belief is. Unlike a general idea or principle, a belief is a command to the nervous system. I also knew that repetition activates neurology and runs neuro-pathways and so I repeated the belief statement several more times. It was at that point that I finally heard myself use the term "will" as in, "I will build capital . . ." Suddenly I realized that I was now uttering something more and different from just a belief, now I was issuing forth a *decision.* It was at that moment that I consciously turned the statement into a volitional statement of choice. I was creating a direction and a pathway for my future in my mind.

> "From this day forward I will build capital as I save at least 10% of my income every week."

Saying it definitely evoked even more feelings. So I tried it on with different phrases indicating that the idea was of my own personal choice and volition:

> "From this day forward I choose to build capital for my own personal wealth building plan as I save at least 10% of my income every week."
> "From this day forward I will refuse to put off building capital for my own personal wealth building plan and I will save at least 10% of my income every week."

Saying this involved even more of my feelings and neurology. It then dawned on me what I was doing. I was turning an abstract *principle* into a *belief* into a *decision* and into actual neurological *feelings*. So I wondered, What am I feeling?

> "Planning my wealth creation plan by building capital for investment by saving a little bit every week makes me feel a little anxious about things . . . and excited . . . and curious . . . and hopeful . . . and confident . . . "

At first, the emotional awareness came slowly. But then as I got into it, the feelings began to rush in, and as they did I felt a neurological push from within to *do* something. Ah, I had activated some of my motor programs. Now activating motor programs by playing to our emotions is a common process in Neuro-Semantics and NLP. Aware of this I also realized that I had asked a pretty wimpy question. I had merely asked, "What was I feeling?" I could do better than that. So using the "as if frame," I asked, "If I fully believed in this and fully and completely made this decision, what would I be feeling then?" Then I continued to speak out loud:

> "I'd be feeling excited about the possibilities of saving, building capital and investing. I'd been feeling charged up and juiced about taking charge of my life, my money, my budgeting. I'd feel positively proactive."

Talk about a surge in the neurological energy as emotions were activated within my body! Talk about activating motor programs. Motor programs were now definitely being activated! Now I felt as if it was time to act. Time to do something. And that naturally led to the next question, "So what is one thing I could do today that would really give some reality to this idea?"

> "Well, I could write this down as my weekly goal."

And what is one other thing I could do?

> "I could ask a friend to hold me accountable to this by giving him permission to ask me about it."

With this, I suddenly I realized that what I was doing was *moving the principle of a great idea down the levels of my mind-body system.* How did I do that? I started by recognizing a great idea, or concept, of some piece of knowledge in my head and I then slowly transformed that knowledge so that it took the form of a *belief,* then of a *decision,* a *feeling,* and finally into an *action,* into a muscular response. It was in this way that the bare-bones of *the Mind-to-Muscle Pattern* was given birth. Since then I have used the pattern to mind-to-muscle all kinds of great ideas in my head so that they become muscle memory in my body—my way of being in the world.

The Mind-to-Muscle Pattern

The Mind-to-Muscle pattern utilizes the power of language to represent step-by-step the levels of the mind that offers you a bridge from a concept down to belief, decision, state, and finally to action. But the process doesn't end there. You can next begin cycling through the process over and over. This time going up the levels as well as back down. Feeding back new information to the higher levels and feeding forward energy and organization into your body. This taps into and utilizes the power of repetition to habituate a new way of operating. As a neuro-semantic pattern, you activate more and more of the body by bringing a conceptual state (idea or principle) down and translating it into other words you enable it to operate holistically throughout all of the levels. That's why the linguistic phrases almost always change as you *bring the idea down* and let it be fully embodied in your neurology.

And by looping back up and adding in other meta-levels (identification, expectation, pleasure, outcome, intentionality, etc.), you can set up a spiraling of the mind so that it embeds the everyday actions inside of multiple frames of meaning.

Figure 2:1

Spiraling of thoughts and emotions moving up and up higher and higher and then back down into the body

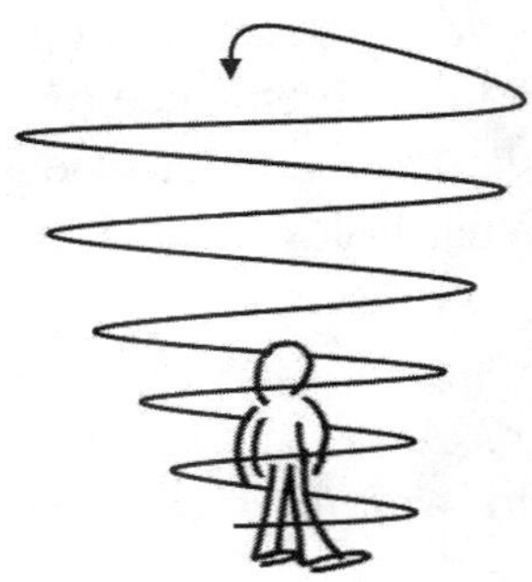

How We Extend the Gap between Knowing-Doing

When your mind is filled with great ideas, you have *conceptual knowledge*. Most of us know lots of truly great and inspiring ideas, ideas that are transformative, awe-inspiring, and fabulous. In those moments when we spend time with such ideas, we live in a very different world. We feel inspired and enraptured. Then we come back to reality. And more often than not, we leave the life transforming ideas in the world of mind without bringing them back with us to our everyday realities (Figure 2:2).

Figure 2:2

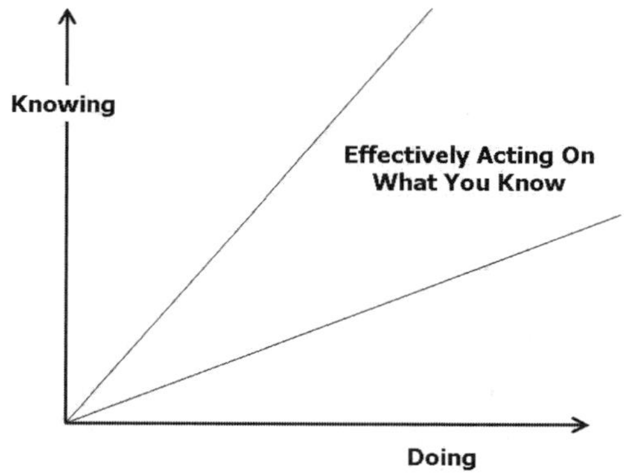

Why do we do this? Why do we not enrich our lives with these ideas? It seems so obvious that great ideas, insightful plans and intentions, and larger level perspectives ought to be transferred into our everyday thinking in order to enhance our performance. So what prevents us from translating them into neurological patterns for guiding our actions? What holds us back from letting such *in-form* our way of being in the world?

The answer? *Actually there are lots of things that can hold us back and interfere with the transference.*

One deceptive thing that interferes is confusing actual action with mental substitutions that only give the impression of action. For example, we often confuse a pre-action like *planning* with the action of performance of that plan. After all, it does seem like you have *done* something when you have planned, especially if you act to write out a plan. But that's the trick. You have not. You're not into the actual performance yet, just the prelude to it. We have only *planned* to take action. This does not de-value planning. Not at all. Planning is critical. Yet it is just a step toward actually doing something and is not performance itself.

Other things that extend the gap between knowing and doing have to do with the inhibitions that fear creates. We become afraid and so we feel inhibited from taking acting. We freeze. We become paralyzed with hesitations and inaction. We *know* but we cannot do. Another frame is getting in the way. The fear evokes a higher frame *about* the knowing. Somewhere in the back of your mind is a fear frame, "Danger. Too risky. Avoid." Fear as a frame increases the distance between what you know and what you do.

People who suffer from this one typically become suckers for another deception. They think, "If only I knew more!" So they buy another book, attend another training, sign up for another course, consult with another coach, etc. But this also broadens the knowing-doing gap. As they are learning more, *they are still not doing*. And because our problem is not in the realm of knowing, the solution will not be in learning more. The problem is fear and all of the inhibitions that fear creates within us. The problem is that your emotion has you and you are refusing to face the fear and *just do* what you know would make a positive difference in your life.

Then there are the taboos that forbid and prevent you from taking action. These are the structures, or lack of structures, that increase the gap—systems that don't allow the translation from knowing to doing. Do you have a structure set up for acting on your knowledge about exercise, fitness, eating right, saving money, etc.? You don't? Then no wonder the gap keeps widening between knowing and doing! And finally there are more personal things like failing to be action oriented, excuses, creating meta-states of procrastination, perfectionism, etc.

Business consultants Jeffrey Pfeffer and Robert Sutton (2000) have written about the attitudes that increase the gap in their book *The Knowing-Doing Gap: How Smart Companies Turn Knowledge into Action*. The following identifies their list of factors that widen the knowing-doing gap:

Pseudo-actions deceptions:

1) Framing knowing as sufficient for success.
2) Framing talking (meetings, committees, reports, etc.) as action.
3) Framing measuring things as action or performance.
4) Framing making a decision as the same as taking action.
5) Framing planning as the same as action.

Clogging the gap by giving into the inhibitions of fear:

1) Fearing complexity, lack of clarity about what specifically to do.
2) Fearing risk, mistakes, errors, and imperfection.
3) Fearing competition, focusing on what others are doing and trying to get ahead.
4) Fearing the new, the different, the unpredictable, falling back on precedence (standard operating procedures) and so mindlessly defaulting to what you've always done.

Taboos that prevent and forbid action:

"Don't make a fool of yourself."
"Don't risk making a mistake, it's too dangerous."
"Don't be imperfect."
"Don't act unless you have full guarantee of success."

Lack of structure for action:

No structure for following up.
No structure for rewarding learning from mistakes.
No structure for rewarding risk taking.

Personal items predisposing you from taking action:

Not being action-oriented, being inactive and passive.
Making excuses and letting excuses stop you.
Discounting small actions as insignificant or "nothing."

Deceived by Pseudo-Actions

Question: When is an *action* not really an "action?"

Answer: When the action does not actually lead to the required performance.

Many people extend the knowing-doing gap by thinking that studying, reading, and learning *alone* is sufficient. It is not. Yet another book, workshop, training, or tape set will not *in itself* change anything. You will only fill your head with more knowledge. It may very well be the best knowledge in the field. Yet, if you do not *act* on it, you will get the same result as if you had learned nothing. Waiting until you "know it all," or have an "expert knowledge level" is a perfectionistic deception that creates personal ineffectiveness. You have to get out there and make mistakes that you can learn from.

Yet, *fear of making a mistake* is yet another way you widen the knowing-doing gap. Many people fully know what to do yet won't act because they fear messing up, making a mistake, risking failure, etc. So they excuse themselves from the most basic form of learning, "trial and error" learning. The solution is to do something. Experiment. See what happens. Did it work or not? If it did not, then take the "or not" in a matter-of-fact way. It's just information, just feedback. No big deal.

If you want to really worsen the knowing-doing gap and make the gap larger, scare yourself with horror stories about the terribleness of making a mistake. That will fill your mind-and-body full of fear and dread and terror of risking a mistake. Do that and you will prevent things in your mind from getting into your muscles.

Confusing *talk* with *doing* is another major way that you can fill your head with more and more and simultaneously weaken your performance muscles from actually doing anything.

> "Well, we convened a meeting and talked about it!"
>
> "Of course, we did something, we formed a committee to discuss the problem, we even passed a resolution."
>
> "Do something about it? We definitely did something, we spent $20,000 on this report about it!"

To these responses, the best response in my opinion is, "Duh?!" *Talk is not doing.* Talk can prepare you for performance. Talk may empower you to formulate your plans and motivate you, but talk in and of itself is not performance. Companies that have a culture of talking about things can get so off-target with this. They can become highly skilled in creating great overheads, awesome Power-Point presentations, memorable pieces of literature (the Report), and then really believe that they are *doing* something about a problem. But they are not. Jeffrey Pfeffer and Robert Sutton (2000) write about this attitude:

> "The purpose of the sessions wasn't really to learn from other parts of the organization. Instead, the agenda was to impress your colleagues with the quality of the presentation you were giving. We're not in the business of making over-heads! This firm is just one of many we have seen in which leaders act as if having something in their mission or values statement meant that it must be true." (p. 40)

Nor is measuring the same as actual performance. The U.S. Post Office is a great example of measuring things and assuming that "measuring" is actually doing something that makes a difference. I have a friend who is a supervisor who measures the feet of mail that has to be sorted each day. Then from time to time she actually has to follow the delivery people (the mail men and women) on their routes to measure how long it takes them, how they park their vehicle, how many feet from one place to another, etc. She knows that none of this matters in the long run. She knows that none of this provides better service to the customers. She knows that none of it improves the quality of the business. So why do they do this? It is forced regulation to satisfy Union rules so that the employees will not have to work too hard and so that they will be sufficiently compensated.

Why does the Post Office engage in this wasteful and mindless behavior? To satisfy regulations. They also do it because it is easier to measure time, space, weight, volume, and other tangible things than the intangible things that really count: sense of responsibility, friendliness, helpfulness, attitude, cooperation, willingness to pitch in and help even if its not your project, etc.

To make things worse, most of the things that really count are intangible and are a hundred times more difficult to measure. We certainly can't measure them in the same way we measure feet of mail. The Benchmarking model and process that I will later introduce for evaluating performance offers one way to measure subjective states and experiences that are inherently intangible. With the Benchmarking Model, we can figure out a way so that they can be measured, yet not with the same kind of precision or ease.

At this point another fear arises, the fear of complexity. Because systems of interactive parts are complex and involve multiple contributing causes, we often become inhibited in action, confused about what to do. The solution for this is to turn our abstract philosophical language into action-oriented language. We call this process *denominalizing*. By denominalizing language, we are able to create sensory-based descriptions that leads to greater clarity and precision about what to do. This is what we will explore when we get to benchmarking performance.

Because Neuro-Semantics is about performing the highest and best meanings, we are dedicated to closing the knowing-doing gap. That's

> **** Jargon Alert! ****
>
> *De-nominalizing*
>
> *Name* something and you *nominalize* it. This works fine for things and objects. But it sucks when you do this to processes. So for processes nominalized and treated as if they are things, we need to de-nominalize. We do this by finding the *verb* hidden within the term and recover the actual process.

why we have identified and develop a great many patterns for translating knowledge into life changing performances. These processes allow you to develop a frame of mind that makes embodying knowledge part of your "way of being in the world." As you find knowledge that makes a difference, knowledge that maps a piece of expertise, you are able to *incorporate* it so that it *informs* the motor programs of your neurology. It becomes what you *do*. No more excuses, you just get things done. No more inertia, no more procrastination, no more taking counsel of irrational fears—just effective action.

- What knowledge do you have that has tremendous potential just waiting to be released?
- Would you like to release what you know so that it becomes the engine in your performances?
- Would you like to experience yourself as an efficient person who takes effective action?

The future does not lie in the hands of those who think, plan, imagine, dream, and hope, but don't do. It lies in the hands and feet of those who act on their reflections. Are you ready to join that future? Then it is all about the skills of transforming knowledge into action, of taking today's level of performance to the next level.

Transforming Knowledge into Action

You have heard that "knowledge is power." By itself, however, that statement is deceptively incomplete. Knowledge that you cannot or do not use, act on, and implement is not power. In fact, knowledge that you don't act on will eventually become antiquated and stale. It can even degenerate into an incompetent arrogance where a person talks boldly all the while being incompetent in performance. As such, it is "mere" knowledge—it is castrated knowledge. That's because it doesn't improve performance. Do we need more of that kind of knowledge? I don't think so. What we need is dynamic knowledge.

We need the true power of applied and implemented knowledge. We need embodied knowledge that is part and parcel of our neurology and that's available for real-time performance.

Because we're dealing in this discussion with two different phenomena, *knowing* and *doing*, we can separate them in our language. Yet you do so to your detriment. Knowing *without* doing creates a dampening, even a deadening, effect in your lives, your bodies, and your neurology. It can even effect knowledge by making what you know un-dynamic: academic data that strokes your ego without enhancing your competency. When you confuse knowing with doing, thinking that by talking about something you know, you have done something, the deception turns you into a great arm-chair critic without increasing your performance.

Given this, our purpose in this book is to close the knowing-doing gap with Neuro-Semantic patterns by which you can create, enhance, and evolve performance until you achieve your very best performance. If you often defeat your best knowledge, understanding, intentions, values, hopes, dreams, and visions by sacrificing *performance* to wanting more knowledge, the patterns here will give you the ability to turn that around. And when you do, that will improve your learning efficiency, your actual productivity, and your confidence in transforming your world.

Embodying for Behavioral Competence

There's been a good bit of talk about installation in recent years among trainers, coaches, and educators. Many now realize that *if we don't incorporate and embody learnings and skills, the learnings will only be "intellectual" and conceptual and not part of actual behavioral competence.* To come out of a training or coaching session without the drive and determination to take action weakens and undermines whatever you have learned. It is in *doing* that you test and experience the inner truth of an idea.

- Does it actually work?
- Can you actually increase your productivity by using this process?
- Does this actually improve your performance?

Knowing your talk, and being able to *talk* your talk, is only the beginning. Next comes the ability to *walk* your talk. Without walking your talk you are in a tenuous position, are you not? Left in this position, you become "armchair quarterbacks," critiquing others for mistakes, but never getting into the game yourself. This will make you incongruent so that your development and effectiveness will deteriorate.

There's a reason for that. It's because we are neuro-semantic beings. The *meanings* (semantics) that we create in our thoughts, ideas, beliefs, understandings, intentions, metaphors, etc. inevitably are processed within our neurology as we process information with our nervous systems, brain, brain stem, and our entire body. The meanings that we create conceptually then become the signals that we send to our body and the commands that we send to our nervous system. What results from this? Emotions, inner sensations and awarenesses, an urge to act, move, and do, and skills and competencies.

As neuro-semantic beings, we inevitably metabolize our ideas and meanings. It is also the source of our psycho-somatic experiences. This is the source of all of our emotions. An emotion, after all, is a *felt meaning*. It is the way your body registers the meanings that you process in your mind. In Neuro-Semantics, we describe emotions as the difference felt in the body between what you have mapped about the world and what you experience in the world. This map / territory difference enables you to *feel* it so you can then respond appropriately, either changing or updating your map or improving and enhancing your performance or skills.

This suggests something of incredible importance. It highlights the fact that you are always *embody-ing* what you think, believe, represent, understand, decide, and so on in your mind. *Embodiment* is what you are designed to do with information. The word *information* reveals this. What does information do within you but *form* you on the inside? The word *incorporate* also speaks about this. *Corpus* is "body" and so *in-corporate* speaks about how you put ideas and meanings into your body.

Our focus in Neuro-Semantics is on the processes for incorporating, embodying, and installing of skills in order to build up competencies. The reputation that we have developed in this area has arisen because of the many patterns that we have developed for implementation. These began with the patterns that we regularly present in the *Accessing Personal Genius* and *Living Genius* introduction trainings to Meta-States:

- *Mind-to-Muscle Pattern* for taking great ideas and translating them into muscle.
- *The Excuse Blow-Out Pattern* for separating silly excuses from legitimate reasons and refusing to tolerate excuses to excellence.
- *Meta-Yes-ing and Meta-No-ing* pattern for refusing or blowing-out limiting beliefs and creating empowering belief as well as solidify frames at multiple levels.
- *Meta-Alignment Pattern* for refining skills and embedding them in contexts of congruency.
- *Accessing Personal Genius Pattern* for commissioning your inner executive to decisively set the boundaries for a piece of excellence and be able to step in and out of a state of "flow" at will.
- *Dancing With Dragons Pattern* for slaying and/or taming "dragon" or unresourceful states to eliminate the toxic ideas and beliefs that sabotage your best responses.
- *Unleashing Potentials Pattern* for self-actualizing as you synergize your meanings and performance using the Self-Actualization Quadrants.
- *Super-Charging Attitude Pattern* for meta-stating and texturing layers of mental and emotional resources to create robustly vibrant attitudes.
- *The Efficiency Pattern* for developing a good relationship to the idea of efficiency and bringing the art of efficiency into needed areas of life.

What is the bottom line? *Embody-ing knowledge closes the knowing-doing gap.* Rather than continuously filling your mind with more and more great ideas without developing the skills for bridging the knowing-doing gap, you focus on the skills and competencies of putting knowledge into action. You can then enhance your performance in all of its dimensions.

I began by saying that the bottom line of all success is performance. Yet that's not exactly accurate. There's another piece to now add to that. Performance is certainly the tangible and objective result that indicates knowledge, understanding, skill, and competency. Yet performance alone is not enough—*performance must be meaningful.* Perform anything for a period of time that you don't find meaningful —significant, valuable, and important—and the performance will suffer. What you do must make sense and provide a sense of significance.

> *Put your Creed into your Deed*
> Ralph Waldo Emerson
>
> *"We know too much and are convinced of too little"*

That's why Neuro-Semantics simultaneously involves both sides. We focus equally on *performing* meaning, getting ourselves to perform the meanings (ideas, beliefs, understandings, decisions, intentions, etc.) that we have mapped out in our mind as our inner game. And we equally focus on *enriching* our performances *with robust and vital meanings.* Further, we also embody toxic and non-enhancing ideas, principles, and beliefs.

Next Stop: The Mind-to-Muscle Pattern

Are you ready to get down to business? Great. When you turn the page, you will find the central Neuro-Semantic pattern for coaching your whole mind-body system to feel, own, and experience a great idea. Let's go.

THE MIND-TO-MUSCLE PATTERN

The *Mind-to-Muscle pattern* is the best and most dynamic pattern for embodying, incorporating, and installing great ideas into the body. As a meta-stating pattern, it will enable you to turn highly informative, insightful, and valued principles into neurological patterns that you feel in your body. The design of this pattern is essentially *to coach your body how to feel great ideas* so that you can embody your ideas.

You do this when you learn to type on a keyboard. The original learning may take a considerable amount of time and trouble in order to get the muscle patterns and coordination deeply imprinted into your muscles. Yet by practicing and training, *the learnings become incorporated into the very fabric of the muscles themselves.* It becomes muscle memory. Then the muscles "know." Your conscious awarenesses drop away as the learnings become incorporated or embodied. The same holds true for expertise, excellence, and mastery in all other fields, from sports, mathematics, teaching, to surgery, selling, and public relations.

In this you begin with a *principle*—a concept, understanding, awareness, belief, etc., and then you translate it into *muscle.* I have found this especially true in our modeling projects regarding resilience, leadership, wealth building, selling excellence, learning, etc.

This pattern creates transformation by moving up and down the various levels of mind so that you map from your understandings about something from the lowest descriptive levels to the highest conceptual levels and back down again.

There are two cautions before you run the pattern:

1) First, do not use a goal for this pattern.

A "goal" is something that you want to do, achieve, or experience. As such it is a primary state experience, not a high level concept in your mind. This pattern is for principles and concepts, not goals. Goals will emerge in the *action step* of the pattern thereby allowing you to create a pathway for step by step action steps into your future. So carefully examine your idea so that you do not use a goal with this pattern. For goals, use the *Well-Formed Outcome* pattern which you can find in *Sourcebook of Magic*, Volume I or *Coaching Conversations.*

2) Second, be sure you start with a solid, accurate, and ecological principle.

You will *not* be checking ecology on the way down through the mind-body system as you run this pattern, only at the end. If the idea or principle feels strange, weird, uncomfortable ... let it be. Those are just feelings. Do not check ecology during the process. The design here is to start with an ecological principle and then *coach your body how to feel it.* If it is new and different, your current system may not like it. So be it.

Start with a general principle. A general principle will be a concept or abstraction that you can find again and again in the literature that governs that area. That's because every field has its general principles. In health and fitness there are general principles like "health is a function of eating and exercising moderately."

I have included most of the language that I use when I demonstrate this pattern or use it with a person. Because *repetition* and *rehearsal* plays such an important role in solidifying this and making the translation more and more real, continue to process through the steps again and again, calibrating to the person and really getting some strong neurological responses. The stronger responses you obtain, the more likely you will assist the person in making the mind-to-muscle translation and setting the principle as a frame. Dance with the feed-*back* and feed-*forward* loops in the last step, changing and varying them as needed.

You will notice that I have some provocation questions throughout the process. I use these to get a person to *fight for* and *defend* the idea and expressions . . . as this activates the person to become more involved in the process, it strengthens the translation. You'll need lots of rapport and respect to be able to pull that off. The more you genuinely care about the person, the better.

As you run the pattern, you can increase your effectiveness if you keep your eyes and ears open to notice the natural gestures and movements of the person. People will be demonstrating their natural "anchors" for the five basic states (principles, beliefs, decisions, emotions, actions). Watch and listen for them.

The bullet points provide the specific questions you can use as you assist someone in coaching that person through the process. In fact, the pattern is written for a facilitator to use in coaching a person through the process.

The Pattern:

1) Identify a desired principle for incorporation into your muscles.

The principle could be a concept, idea, belief, understanding, value, piece of knowledge, secret, law, paradigm, model, presupposition, etc. Any mental awareness will work. It could be a set of competencies that make up a skill. Pick out something that you want to incorporate into the very fabric of your muscles.

Specify the concept or principle by stating it, or even better, writing it down in a clear, succinct, and compelling way. Describe your theory or theoretical understanding in a paragraph or two. *"I understand . . . I conceptualize . . ." "Intellectually, I know that ..."*

Beginning with the principle, after the initial "I" there will be no other personal pronouns but the statement will be stated generally and abstractly. "I understand that wealth is created by saving a little every week." Not: "I understand that I will create wealth by saving a little every week."

- Do you have any great inspiring ideas that you want to commission your body to feel and act on?
- What idea inspires you that you would like to "feel" in your body and let become a program for your way of being in the world?
- What concept or principle do you want to put into your neurology and commission to run your programs?
- What is your conceptual understanding of this?
- What do you know or understand or believe about this that you want to set as a frame in your mind?

2) Describe the principle as a belief.

Now use the semantic environment, *"I believe . . ."* and complete this sentence by rephrasing the concept and understanding as a personal declaration of a belief.

- Do you believe this? Would you like to believe it?
- You believe what specifically?
- You believe *that?* Really? [These questions are designed to turn the concept into a personalized belief. Expect the language that the person uses to change and shift until the person finds "the right words" that work for him or her.]
- You don't sound very convincing. If you did believe that in the fullest way possible for you to believe something, if you really did—what would that sound like? Say "I believe . . ." and make it sound really convincing.
- If you really, really believed that, would that make a big difference in your life?
- As you state the concept as a belief saying, *"I believe ... "*, notice what you feel. Now state it as if you *really did believe it* and again notice the emotions that arise.

3) Reformat the belief as a decision.

Once the belief is stated in a way that sounds powerful, convincing and is stated very succinctly so that it feels compelling, reformulate the personal belief so that it takes the form of a personal decision. To do this, finish the following semantic environment, *"I will . . ."* Describe the belief now as a specific decision regarding something that you will do. *"I am going to ..." "From this day forward, I promise to ..."*

- Are you going to do it? Would you like to live by that belief? [Yes.] You would? [Yes.] Really? [Yes.]

- Will you act on this and make it your program for acting?
- Are you ready to state it as a decision? Great. Go ahead and finish this statement, *"From this day forward, I will . . ."* Or, *"I want . . . I choose . . . it is time to . . ."*
- You will do what?
- You really will do this? You're not just pulling my leg or telling me that?

4) Rephrase the belief-decision as a state or experience.

As you have expressed this great idea as a belief and a decision, what have you felt? What emotions have arisen? And *if* you were to fully experience this concept—> belief—> decision as an emotional state, and felt it even more fully, what will you be feeling and experiencing? Use the semantic environment, *"I feel . . ."* Or *"I experience . . ."*

- It sounds like you really believe that . . . and I think you actually are going to do those things to make it happen . . . so how does all of that make you feel? "I feel . . ."
- So what are you experiencing?
- What would you feel if you were fully believing this empowering belief and decision and living them?
- Be with those emotions . . . let them grow and extend.

> [It does *not* matter at this point whether the emotion is positive or negative. What is important is that you *feel moved* (you experience an e-motion) that activates your body and creates *a motion to act on* what you are feeling.]

5) State the actions you will take to express the great idea.

This time finish the following semantic sentence stem,

> *"The one thing that I will do today as an expression of this concept, belief, decision, and state is . . ."*

Doing this will enable you to begin to formulate specific actions that will enable you to execute your principles.

- So what one thing will you do today to make this happen?
- You will do that? Really? What else will you do?
- And what one thing will you do tomorrow? And the day after that?

6) Step into the action and repeatedly move to the next meta-level.

As you fully imagine carrying out the one action that you will do today . . . seeing what you will see, hearing what you will hear, and feeling what you will feel as you do it . . . now move up through the levels . . . into *the state* from which this action emerges, naming the state and experiencing it fully, owning *the decision,* affirming *the belief* with a powerful *"Yes!"* as you do, and stepping up even higher in your mind into a full awareness of your reasons, understandings, concepts, and *principles* that drive this way of being in the world ... and as you step into that place fully, now bring it back down again through belief, decision, state, and action . . . noticing how it transforms everything even more and creates an even greater sense of empowerment.

Repeat this several times, future pacing as you do.

- Why will you do this?
- And you've decided on this?
- Is that really what you have finally decided to do?
- And what idea or principle governs this?
- And you will do this?
- How do you feel about all of this?
- Will it affect your identity? It will? How?

Afterword

After you have run this pattern, you have several more *levels* that you can utilize to solidify and install even further.

7) Identify with the principle for self-definition and identity .

- As you experience this new principle in your mind-and-body, and imagine moving through life with it, does it affect how you define yourself? Does it affect your identity? Would you want it to?

- [If yes:] Then go ahead and notice how this transforms and enriches your own self-definitions . . . and see *the you,* experience *the you,* feel *the you* . . . who lives by this principle . . . who operates by this principle incorporated into your neurology.

8) Check for the ecology of the principle.

- Now as you imagine living with this dynamic and wonderful principle in your muscles, in your eyes, in your voice, in your very body . . . Does this serve you well?
- Does it enhance your life, your skills, your expertise?
- Does it empower you as a person and enable you to be more powerful in this area of interest?
- Does it fit with your values and your visions?

9) Enrich the pattern with other meta-levels.

- With this what can you now expect? What expectations will enrich this even further?
- What is your intention in doing this? Do you have any other intentions? What's your highest intention?
- How much permission do you now have for this?

    [Use the Meta-Questions in Appendix A for more options.]

10) Confirm and get the person to fight for it.

- So you like this? [Yes]
- Really? You really do? [Yes]
- I don't think you need this or deserve this! [Yes I do!]
- This is just an exercise and not real; you can't have this! [I will to!]
- I'm going to take this away from you! [No, you won't!]

Alternatives for the Mind-to-Muscle Pattern

Over the years I've been experimenting with alternative ways of running the *Mind-to-Muscle pattern.* Here are a few of them.

Spatial anchoring. A spatial anchor refers to the actual space that you use in accessing the various states inherent in the pattern. As a mime will "anchor" space by his or her movements and gestures, giving us the sense of walls, doors, windows, falling, etc., so where we stand and how we stand can "trigger" or anchor a mind-body state that we can then use. Here you will set up five spaces, one for Principle, Belief, Decision, State (Feeling), and Action.

Begin the pattern by asking:

> "What idea, concept, or principle do you have and believe in that's *so well integrated into you* that it is truly *your way of being in the world*? Are there any principles like that? Perhaps it is, 'Do to others as you want them to do to you?' Or, 'Don't judge until you've walked in another person's shoes?'"

When the person identifies a principle *already fully embodied,* then access that principle and state as fully as possible by asking lots of questions about it, supporting and validating the person as you do. Then invite the person to stand up and step in a space in the physical room or location where you are. You might even mark it on the floor. This space will be an anchor for the *principle.* Ask lots of questions about it. What's the principle? Is this important to you? How is this important to you? Then ask, "Do you believe in it?" When the person says yes, invite him or her to take one small step away from the *principle space* and into the *belief space.* Repeat this and create a *decision space,* a *feeling or experience space,* and finally into the *action space.*

Doing this creates *a felt template* in the person's neurology for translating an idea into muscle. Now run the Mind-to-Muscle Pattern stepping the person from the principle space all the way through the spaces and finishing in the action space. As you do you can set an "anchor" by holding the person's arm and walking with him or her, and/or setting a visual or auditory anchor as you go.

> [If *anchoring* is new to you, see *Sourcebook of Magic* or almost any introduction to NLP, *User's Manual of the Brain, Volume I.*]

Sliding Anchor. One of the easiest and most effective "anchors" that we can set is that of touch. This is especially true when we touch in unique ways while eliciting and amplifying a particular state of mind-and-emotion. When we touch the skin of a person's arm and set up a continuum so that on one end is the feeling of *aversion* and on the other end is the feeling of *attraction,* and then *slide* our hand along the continuum, we can trigger or anchor the experience of *degrees of* along that continuum. This is known as a sliding anchor. Here you will use a touch at various points: head-to-shoulder, bicep, elbow, forearm, and hand for the five spaces.

With the Mind-to-Muscle pattern, I begin by asking for a person's arm. "May I have your arm for a moment?" When the person hands me his or her arm (!), I test by using my two fingers next to my thumb and touching for *abstraction to action.* I will then use my two fingers (index and middle) and trace a "line" along the arm anywhere from the shoulder to the hand. The language I use as I speak to this is:

> "Where would you like *abstraction* to be and *action*? Typically people like to experience *action here*[1] at the hand [touching the back of the hand] indicating taking action and *doing* what they know. And typically, most people imagine that their higher ideas, principles, concepts, and more abstract understandings are all the way up *here*[2] [touching the elbow, back of the bicept, or shoulder]. If this *here*[2] is a principle that

you want to get into your muscles and actions at this level [*here*[1]], does this structure make sense to you?"

All of that is to set up the sliding anchor from principle to action. I then like to identify a principle already in muscle-memory and use it to set the sliding anchor (as in the Spatial Anchoring setup). Once I have a template on the arm, then I can run the Mind-to-Muscle pattern using it.

Procedural Knowledge
The kind of knowledge that you can put into muscle memory is procedural knowledge. So to get your neurology to incorporate it, you have to create a step-by-step procedure for how to act on the knowledge. When you do this, you can then train and condition your neurology to feel what you know. This is obvious when you think about driving a car, typing, tying a shoe string, etc.

Action Plan

- Run the Mind-to-Muscle pattern on something that you have already fully embodied. What do you "know" that's now dropped into muscle memory? Driving a car? Riding a bike? Take that "knowing" and back up from Action to State to Decision to Belief to Principle. Then move forward. This will set up a strong template pattern for you.

- Run the Mind-to-Muscle pattern on some basic principles such as the following: Wealth is created by saving a little every week. Health is a function of moderate eating and exercising. Rapport is enriched by using people's names and asking about their day.

- Identify five principles that would transform your life and begin to run the Mind-to-Muscle pattern on these, repeating it every day for a week.

Chapter 3

GETTING YOURSELF TO TAKE EFFECTIVE ACTION

After an exciting and transformative training, some of the questions that I frequently hear are these:

> "This has been great stuff, but now *how* can I get myself to practice these new skills so they become fully mine?"
> "How can I transfer what I've learned here back home or to my work place?"

Most of us don't want to learn new things or invest in training to never use what we learn and discover. We want to turn our knowledge into skills that we can use to improve the quality of our performance and of our lives. We want to use what we've learned to get ourselves to take effective action in our everyday lives.

As you consider the idea of "getting yourself to take action," do you immediately realize that this describes a meta-state structure? Do you see and recognize that the statement has several levels within it? To make sure you do, let's now pull apart the meta-levels.

- The primary state here is that of *taking action.*
- Then there is your sense of yourself as an actor, participant, and the response-able person who takes that action.
- Then above that sense of self is the meta-level response you make *to* yourself as you *get* yourself to feel motivated and organized to do what you know and want to do.

Figure 3:1
The Meta-Levels of Getting Ourselves to Take Action

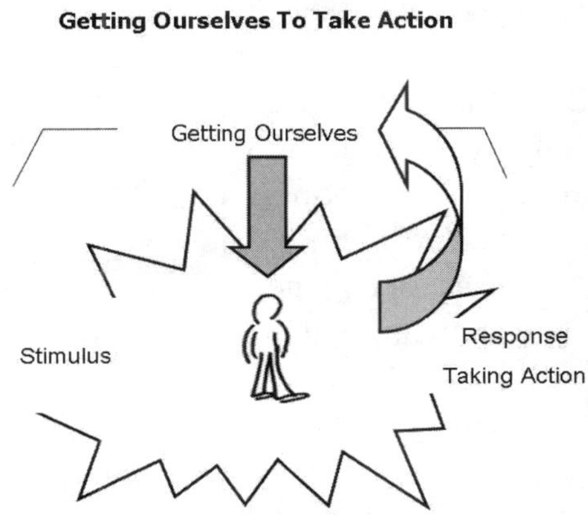

As I have modeled numerous domains of knowledge and skill, from sales, persuasion, fitness, health, wealth building, leadership, etc., it's clear that there is no lack of knowledge of great ideas and principles in these fields. There is also a tremendous volume of ideas filling library shelves and bookstores—ideas that could very well make revolutionary changes in your life. And what you can't find there, is readily available for anyone who will get online and google for the desired information. In all of this, there is a whole world of great ideas giving you wonderful maps for navigating things. The problem is not the lack of great ideas, inspiring ideas, knowledge, models, or principles. The problem is not the lack of information. The problem lies in *the skill and ability to put what we know into action.* There are great ideas—if only we would act on them!

The Question
For over a decade I have begun my Wealth Creation trainings by asking some very focused questions:

> "Does anybody here know anything about finances, budgeting, saving, entrepreneurship, sales, relationships, business, etc. that if you would only *do* on a regular basis would make a significant difference in your life? Does anybody know even *one thing?* Raise your hands if you do."

And *everybody* raises their hands. Everyone!

> "Is there anyone here who doesn't know *one thing* that could improve your life? Is there anyone here who *acts on* every single thing you know, and does so regularly and consistently? Is there anyone like that?"

> *"Make it so!"*
> Captain Jean-Luc Picard,
> Federation Star Ship *Enterprise*

All hands go down on that one. I have never seen one hand go up on the second set of questions. *We all know more than we do.* Of course, this describes the nature of thinking human beings and, in itself, is a good thing.

"Good?" How? It's good because *we can think without doing*. And that, in turn, serves as the basis by which we can *plan* our responses. In thinking and talking we can *plan* a response. We can step back from our first thoughts and feelings and evaluate whether we should act on them. This gives us the sense of choice and from choice, control. And *control* is the foundation for being responsible and being able to use our responses as powers to influence the world of things and people. We are not fated as animals to merely *react. We can respond from choice according to our values, visions, and higher purposes.*

So the ability to think without acting lies at the heart of what makes us uniquely human and responsible and able to run our own brains. We don't want to lose or weaken that power. Problems arise when we think and think and think and think and continue to do so without ever getting around to acting. Reflecting endlessly without acting—that is the problem. This problem shows up as procrastination, inaction, fearful inability to take a risk, caught in mental loops going round and round without being able to exit and take effective action.

This very human power of thinking and feeling about your responses is a meta-state structure that you have to control or it will control you. And when it controls you, then you end up sabotaging your learnings, your best intentions, your highest values and frames. It is this very structure that allows the models of Neuro-Semantics to bridge the knowing-doing gap and to create a set of patterns for managing the levels of mind.

> "Iron rusts from disuse;
> stagnant water loses its purity . . .
> even so does *inaction* sap the vigor of the mind."
> Leonard da Vinci

What does it take then for you to get yourself to take effective action?

1) *A thoughtful analysis of your situation.* First, open your eyes and senses to assess your current situation. As you diagnose your present state, you will be thinking about it in order to more thoroughly know it.

2) *An equally mindful choice about what you want.* Assess your talents, gifts, predispositions, and the environment in order to decide on a direction and some goals. Identify your desired outcome state. What do you want?

3) *The creation of a plan.* Invent a process or strategy for moving from where you are to where you want to get. Create a well-formed outcome plan for getting there—an inner game of what to do, how, when, etc.

4) *An accessing of the required resources.* Access the resources you'll need for your journey. Identify the first thing to do, the next thing, etc. This details the action steps of the plan which begins to make the outer game vividly real.

5) *A flexible awareness of emerging results.* Create an openness to your situation at each moment, constantly checking out what's happening, what's working, how well it's working, what's not working, what you need in order to make it work, etc. This opens up feedback loops so that you can stay current and flexible in moving forward.

That's what it takes for you to get yourself into action. Yet there is yet another action to consider before you jump into the fray of developing new skills and competencies. You need to ask the talent questions.

- "Is this a talent that I have?"
- "Do I have an aptitude for this?"

While you can learn and develop skills in almost anything, it is unlikely that you will become a top performer in an area outside of your talents and strengths. That's why it's important to play to your strengths. Excellence in any performance is impossible without the basic disposition and capacity—what we call "talent." You can get by in areas wherein you lack aptitude and talent if you learn and develop sufficient skills. But you can only become great in the areas of your natural gifts and strengths. That's why it's critical that you identify your strengths. Then you can begin to learn about them, discipline yourself in those areas, focus on developing those competencies, and add plenty of passion to your aptitudes.

Talent Search (S.W.O.T. Analysis)

The SWOT questions are designed to enable you to begin your *talent search.* Use these to explore your strengths and weaknesses and to begin to identify your untapped potentials. Use the following questions to explore your strengths, talents, and capacities and the skills that you could develop from your talents, your weaknesses and hurts (which also may be a place of rich potentials and possibilities), and the threats and opportunities before you.

***Strengths**: Advantages*

What are your talents, strengths, and capacities?
What are your core competencies?
What advantages do you have in terms of your innate gifts?
What competencies and proven skills do you have?
What do you uniquely offer?
What expertise have you developed over the years?
What expertise do you bring into your performance from other areas?
What are your passions and interests? What do you love doing?
What supporting skills do you need for top performance?

***Weaknesses:** Dis-advantages*

What are your weaknesses?
How have you been (or are) hurt in some way by life?
What traumas or dramas have you been through?
What critical skills are you deficient in?
What skills do you need to develop to be fully effective?
Are there any "fatal flaws" that need to be addressed?

[A fatal flaw is a weakness in an area that makes it nearly impossible for people to approach their potential: lack of discipline, lack of talent, poor attitude, inability to get along, etc. A fatal flaw is an action, attitude, or way of interacting that you can derail yourself from your best.]

Threats:

What threats do you sense blocking your path?
What factors might impact negatively on you and your situation?
What changes might be threatening or upsetting?
What are some of the stresses and stressors that you face?
What risks or fears do you sense lie in your pathway?
What things undermine your resourcefulness?

Opportunities:

What opportunities do you see before you?
What circumstances could you use as an opportunity?
What problems or needs do you have a passion to address?
What opportunities could you create or activate?
What opportunities do you want and long for?

Taking the Talent Search to a Higher Level

After you have engaged in the basic SWOT analysis, move up to do a complete *Meta-SWOT.* This idea was first identified and developed by Denis Bridoux (*Mentoring and Coaching,* 2003) involves using *the Meta-Questions* (Appendix A) to explore the higher dimensions of your inner and outer situation. To do this, simply explore any specific strength, weakness, threat, or opportunity.

- What do you believe about that?
- What does it mean to you?
- What memories are associated with it?
- What imaginations?
- How do you evaluate it?

While talent is a great head start to excellence, it is no guarantee. Talent is only potential. For it to become a reality, you have to train and develop the talent so it becomes an actual skill. Because there's a lot of talented people who are not using their gifts, we must add plenty of *attitude to the aptitudes* that we have innately within.

Do You Have a Strategy?

Within and above every performance is a strategy. The strategy is the inner know-how regarding how to engage in the performance.

The strategy is the inner formula that specifies what to do, in what order, in what way, with what style, etc. Doing something as simple as spelling accurately involves a strategy as does getting out of bed in the morning with a sense of zestful energy and anticipation. These are generally very simple strategies. Even engaging in unproductive, toxic, and unhealthy psychological behaviors involves a strategy. There's a strategy in depression, in schizophrenia, in keeping a resentment alive for years.

There's also strategies for leadership, management, delegation, negotiation, creativity, innovation, writing a best seller, selling a big ticket item, entrepreneuring, dating, staying in love, defusing a hothead, starting a business, running a marathon, winning at tennis, coaching an executive, and a million other things.

This realization brings us to the first questions regarding any behavioral performance:

- Do you know what to do?
- Do you have a strategy?
- Is the strategy a winning strategy, ecological, flexible, and well-designed to the outcome?
- Do you have a strategy for learning it, refining it, and taking the performance to the next level?
- Do you know *the critical success variables* that make the performance effective and relevant?
- Do you know how to get a strategy, or to elicit a winning strategy, from a top performer?
- Are you capable of learning and enhancing the strategy?
- Do your talents and predispositions enable you play to your strengths with the strategy or will you be playing to your weaknesses?

I first learned strategy elicitation, unpacking, designing, and installation in my studies of NLP. Robert Dilts' book, *NLP: The Study of the Structure of Subjectivity* (1980) is the best book on the subject. After developing the Meta-States model, I wrote a second book on the subject integrating the meta-levels into strategy work, *NLP Going Meta* (2004). I have also developed several training manuals for modeling: Neuro-Semantic Modeling, Cultural Modeling, Matrix Training, and so on.

Strategy Elicitation

Suppose you want the recipe of a delicious dish. What do you need in order to create that delicious dish? You need specific information about the elements to use, the amounts, the order for mixing them together, temperature, etc. The same thing holds with regard to detecting and using the structure of subjective experiences to create experiences of excellence. The following offers the basic pattern for eliciting a strategy from another person.

The Pattern:

1) Begin by establishing a positive frame for rapport.

> "You do that very well! Would you teach me how to do that? Suppose I lived your life for a day, how would I do this?"

2) Access the state.

> The person needs to fully and congruently associate with the skill or state. To fully elicit their strategy, you may want to take the person back to the place where the behavior naturally occurs. This lets the context, with its natural anchors (i.e., sitting at typewriter) elicit the response. Or we can elicit the state by reproducing a portion of the context (i.e., tonality, gestures, playacting, etc.).

3) Intensify the state.

> In elicitation, you will want to amplify and intensify the state. Doing this helps because the more of the state you evoke, the more of the experience you will have to work with. This will also enable you to more fully access the state.

4) Explore the how.

> "How do you do this?"

If the person has conscious awareness of their strategy, they will tell you. At least they will tell you their thoughts and beliefs about it. If not, look for them to demonstrate it behaviorally. Eliciting a strategy primarily entails techniques of probing questions by which you evoke a person to carry out a task (actually or in thought) which requires the activation of the strategy.

- Have you ever experienced a time when you really felt motivated to do something?
- When did you last feel naturally and powerfully motivated?
- How do you experience the state of feeling exceptionally

creative?

- Have you ever gotten into a situation where you felt very creative?

Typically, accessing questions involves a person recalling an experience.

- What did it feel like?
- How did you do it?
- When do you feel best able to do it?
- What do you need in order to do it?
- What happens as you do it?
- When did that last occur?

Such questioning encourages a person to internally access the representations and steps within their memory which contains "the deep structure" of the framework of the experience. This *trans-derivational search* (from Transformational Grammar) describes how we "go inside" to search for the referents of our thoughts. Such referents make up our referent system by which we relate and understand things. We all engage in these search processes to make sense of things, to deal with stimuli, and to re-create our states and experiences. The process of strategy elicitation involves using the trans-derivational search process to assist someone to go back through their constructs to recover how they have uniquely structured the experience, that is, created their maps.

With the Meta-States Model, we use a different metaphor. Instead of thinking about "going in" and "down" to the deep structure (the depth metaphor), *we use the height metaphor.* Conceptually, we talk about "going in" and *up* to the meta-levels or frames that structure our referents. Instead of "deep structure" we talk about the frame structure of mind. We talk about the levels or layers that we use in the referencing process. We talk about "going in" to access our frame-of-reference, and the entire system of embedded frames within frames. This enables us to identify all of the contextual frames or the meta-level frames as higher level "thoughts"—categories, classifications, abstractions, beliefs, paradigms, etc. When we put all of these layers of frames together, we have matrix of frames that describes and governs the person's inner subjective reality.

5) Calibrate from an uptime state.

Strategy detection and elicitation necessitates that you become fully alert and open to the person's external cues. This enables you to effectively calibrate to the state as we watch the person demonstrate the strategy. Due to the mind-body connection, *people will typically demonstrate* as they talk about problems, outcomes, or experiences. So as you become attentive to such "instant replays," you can note how a person cycles through the sequence of representations that leads to the experience.

6) Ask the person to exaggerate.

If you do not get the strategy through questioning, invite the person to exaggerate some small portion of the strategy. Exaggerating one step in a strategy may also access other representations linked to it as a synesthesia.

7) Stay meta to the content.

Since a strategy operates as a purely formal structure, you have to "go meta" to the structuring process to notice it. This will prevent you from getting caught up in the content, that is, the story and all that's involved in the content—where it came from, what we believe caused it, etc.

Strategy Delivery

After the discovery and elicitation of a strategy comes a pattern. *A pattern* is designed to facilitate the discovery, creation, or experience of a strategy. As such, in every pattern there will be numerous processes which you will use repeatedly. These processes are the critical success factors which are needed for all of the performance patterns in Neuro-Semantics and NLP. You already experienced them in the Mind-to-Muscle pattern and because you will encounter them again and again as you seek to embody the ideas, with a strategy, I have made the following explicit here.

1) Planning to implement

Every pattern essentially facilitates the development of the *inner game* in your mind of *what* to do, when, with whom, how, etc. Generally, when you have a good game plan for what to do, you're ready to begin. So within most of the patterns there will be steps for specific planning or the development of action steps for doing something.

- What plans do you have to put this into practice?
- When will you do this?

- Where? In what contexts? With whom?
- How will you do this?

2) Taking interest and getting involved
In order for a pattern to work and to become part of your new inner game for performance, you have to become engaged in it. The more the engagement, the more likely you will succeed with the pattern. This makes your ability to engage yourself, or someone else, an important part of the process.

As an aside, did you know that the word "interest" speaks about the power of total engagement? In *interest* you put yourself *into* something, you get inside ("*in*") it and even "exist" ("*est*") inside of it. How about that? Taking interest in something is a skill, it is something that you *do*. Given that, how skilled are you at "taking interest" in something? To totally put yourself into something? What enables you to put yourself more fully into something?

We all naturally take interest in things that change, move, are dramatic, etc. Yet how skilled are you in taking interest in things that you would be tempted to call "boring?"

- How do you put yourself *into* something that's new or different?
- How can you put more of your neurology into it? More of your mind? More of your emotions?
- What do you have to eliminate in order to "take interest?" Stress, pressure, anxiety, self-doubt, etc.?

Ellen Langer, Ph.D., *Mindfulness*, describes the nature of involvement as noticing something new. *How do you get involved?* What is the nature of being involved? It is noticing, noticing more things, new things, and becoming aware of new distinctions.

> "Tasks aren't good or bad; tasks are nothing. You want to impose a framework on it to make it good or bad; then behavior that is consistent with that frame will unfold. . . . the way to get involved, just notice more things." (General Semantics Bulletin, p. 40)

Langer's research involved studying people as they aged and found that asking or inviting people to notice a particular thing elicited for those persons more of a sense of engagement and got them more involved in their own lives. Consequently they remembered more and enjoyed more.

> "Mindfulness is a process—a way of taking in and using information that sets you up to be able to reinterpret that information virtually endlessly, rather than be trapped by it." (p. 41)

- How engaged are you in a performance or a pattern?
- How much more interest, passion, engagement can you bring to your presentation of it?

3) Amplification or sizzling of meanings

A key to installing and embodying an idea is intensity. This is what you are going after when you are engaging and *interest-ing* yourself in the pattern and the outcome. So how do you *intensify* something? How do you turn up the passion, interest, and make it more and more compelling?

How do you *amplify* your experience, or someone else's experience, when you facilitate the process? Amplification of a state, thought, belief, etc. refers to giving the ideas, knowledge, and skills an enriched sense of meaning so that it sizzles, so that you feel like drooling when you consider it. Anytime you take your ideas and skills and amplify them so that they really affect you emotionally, you make the subject more memorable and give it more power in your neurology.

- Do I or they need more intensity?
- Am I using words that amplify and intensify the process?
- Does my voice and gestures help or hinder in intensifying?
- How can I put more passion into my elicitation?

4) Somatizing

You have the ability to make ideas *somatic* ("body," *soma*). As you can *see* and *detect* frames of mind in the way people walk, talk, act, respond, hold themselves, etc.—you can also plant and set frames by using physiology and movement. If you would be cheerful, said William James, then "act cheerfully." Eventually the emotions will catch up and you will actually begin to feel cheerful. Ideas can carry emotional charges, some more than others. And you can *juice* them up.

- How much is your body (or the other's body) involved?
- How much does the body need to be involved to embody the idea?
- What part of the body is not involved as it could be?
- Are you coaching your body to feel the idea?

5) Teasing and Playing

Because your mind-body-emotion system is designed to move toward pleasure and away from pain, when you don't frame and present something as fun and enjoyable, full of pleasure, then it becomes more difficult and even unpleasant to embody. Conversely, when you reframe it as fun—watch out! Suddenly things become much easier. The process may even become "a piece of cake." It is when you think of something as fun—you easily enter into it and become good at it. So the more you can add fun, playfulness, teasing, jesting, etc. to the installation processes— the better.

Play is fun for many reasons—the emotional intensity, the engagement, the mindfulness. Playing allows you to enjoy the learning and thereby makes it more difficult to forget.

- Are you making the pattern fun and enjoyable?
- Are you having fun using the pattern or experiencing the pattern?
- How can you make it more fun?
- How can you tease yourself or another about this?

6) Layering of Frames

You do not just think, you think about your thinking. You don't just feel, you feel about your feelings. Ah, yes, meta-states again! The meta-levels of your thinking-and-feeling, that you *reflexively* apply back to yourself, layer upon layer, level upon level, enable you to create layers of frames.

So when you use questions and meta-questions, you can not only *explore* a belief, you can *set* and *reset* multiple frames at the same time, and sometimes quite covertly. Some questions will deframe and fragment, some will invite the construction of a more positive and useful way of framing, and others will solidify that frame as a new belief.

When you layer one frame upon another frame, make sure that they are all aligned toward eliciting the same state or experience. With our conscious mind you can only track so far in keeping so much in awareness. This allows you to use the very "weight" (speaking metaphorically) of the frames to work in a presuppositional way. As you set more layers, you just *assume* the lower layers *and take them for granted.* The layering causes the mind to start assuming and accepting the earlier frames as consciousness shifts to other things. Typically you only need the "weight" of five or six frames before you accept the first frames without question. At that point, they slide right on in. [See *Winning the Inner Game,* 2006, for a whole book about frames.]

In the layering of frames, gestalt states emerge from the neuro-semantic system of your mind-body. If all of the frames are focused in the same direction, then you experience higher and more intense energy all in a straight and focused way. If, however, you have some frames eliciting one thing, and at another level other frames creating other focus, disorientation, trance, paradox, confusion, and many other meta-muddled phenomena can occur.

- Are you effectively layering states and frames in the presentation of the pattern?
- What frames-by-implication are you setting?
- Are these layers of frame making things easier or more difficult?
- What higher frames will solidify or loosen things?

7) Future Pacing

We end almost every pattern by future pacing in order to establish a sense of direction into our future with the pattern as a way of thinking, feeling, and orienting ourselves in the world. In *future pacing* you put ideas and responses that you have imagined into your sense of the future to prepare yourself to see and think that way of operating in your future. This provides a valuable way of incorporating the pattern.

- Have you invited yourself, or the other person, to imagine a future context where thinking and feeling in this new way will be critical?
- How effectively are you inviting this consideration?
- How good of a test is it for the activation of the pattern?
- Are you checking the ecology of the pattern and new inner game?
- Have you run an quality control check?

8) Provoking

At the end of most patterns I usually include some kind of provoking to stir up the person and get him or her to really own and fight for whatever insights, decisions, or transformations experienced. Now lots of people relate provoking to being mean or irritating or annoying, so we have to engage in compassionate provoking. *Compassionate provoking* facilitates and coaches a person to take the new learnings and meanings and integrate them into his or her own mind-body system. In this, it is an integration process that allows each person to customize the pattern.

When you do this, your attitude within and behind the provoking is absolutely crucial. If the person knows that you genuinely care about and respect him or her, if they know that you really do have their best interests at heart, then they will accept the provoking and will use it to support the process. If, however, you are sarcastic, arrogant, insulting, dis-respectful, etc., the provoking will not work to help with the integration, but in fact be counterproductive.

How does this work? In provoking, take anything and everything that could possibly be a reason or excuse for not integrating the pattern or engaging in the performance, and use it to question the person in a provoking way. This will facilitate within the person the ability to build the kind of robust internal maps empowering him or her to handle that objection in the future.

Provoking a response is like wrestling with a person's intention, motivation, and matrix of frames to try it, to put it to the test, to let it grow and develop so that it is stronger and more robust.

When you provoke in a humorous way, you add some humor, laughter, and playfulness to it. Again, this facilitates the provoking to be received and recognized for what it is—*respectful, honoring of the person, and intended to build up the person.* Humorous provoking adds a touch of lightness as well and thereby reduces the seriousness that can so easily slip into things. Of course, the humor here is respectful humor and not aggressive humor that makes jokes at the person's expense.

Provoking a person to inwardly fight for what they want and to push away everything that gets in their way or could get in their way "sharpens their ego-strength." Wrestling with them in this way invites them to create their own answers and solutions and so solidifies a new understanding, belief, decision, or frame making it more and more their own.

How do you do this provoking? If you haven't seen it in person or via a video or DVD, then here's a list of possibilities.

- "So you like that, do you?
- And I suppose you want to keep that with you?
- But you'd be too dangerous with that . . . I don't think we should let you keep that?
- No, you can't. I'm going to take it away from you.
- You can't remember that! You can? Nah! You won't!
- There's not a single thing that you can do to keep that in your mind!
- You'd like to have this when you're at work?
- But there has to be lots of things in the back of your mind objecting to this, right?
- You can answer any objection that arises? No, you can't!
- Is this yours? No, it's mine. I gave it to you. You can't have it.
- They will think you're on drugs!
- They might laugh at you! And that would be really terrible! Right?
- But you're just saying these things, it's not really real.
- It's just a pattern and you don't really want this, do you?
- Well, you might want it, but you don't really feel it.
- You have not really made images in your mind that translates this into your mind.
- No, you can't have this, the world's not ready for you!"

The Strategic Nature of Patterns

Every performance requires know-how or a strategy. If you don't know how to lose weight, eat sensibly, negotiate a raise, handle a strong-willed child, keep yourself up when your hopes crash to the ground, stay resilient when life knocks you down, etc., then you need a strategy. You need a strategy for *how* to engage that activity to create an important performance. You need a pattern that will give you a step-by-step process for learning the critical distinctions.

Do you know *how* to take criticism well and to use it constructively? Do you know *how* to motivate yourself? The blunt fact is—if you don't have a strategy for a particular goal or performance—you won't be able to do it. Do you have a process for resolving conflicts respectfully? Do you have the understanding and skills for gathering high quality information when someone speaks in vague and abstract terms? Do you have a clear image for speaking affirmatively and showing affection with those you love? If not, you may simply need to learn or invent the strategy that will enable you to pull it off.

You develop your strategies through your experiences, learning, and discoveries. In such learning you add the requisite distinctions to your awareness so that you refine your strategy for achieving a given performance. When you learn, you organize and sequence your sensory and abstract representations in a way so that you create your desired skills. As you construct these strategies, you describe them in terms of *what* they do—their *function.* That is, you build up these strategies to achieve certain outcomes. All of the patterns in this chapter and the ones that follow are about *developing capability and competence* for performance.

* NEW BEHAVIOR GENERATOR

The *New Behavior Generator* pattern offers you a way to creatively imagine and design a new behavioral response and a complete performance script. Use it to begin to expand your choices and development.

The Pattern:

1) Identify a performance or expertise that you want.

What specific outcome do you want to achieve or experience? For example, do you want to be more assertive? Do you want to handle conflict positively? Do you want to accelerate your learning? Do you want to develop mastery in writing? Do you want to innovate a new development?

2) Access and anchor the critical components of this expertise.

What are the key elements or components of this response?
Have you ever experienced some part or facet of these elements, even to a small degree?
When was that, where, what was that like?
Access any past experiences when you did some part of it and then relive that situation in order to experience those desired aspects in all representational systems.
Anchor each component piece of this new behavior.

3) Create a full scenario in your imagination.

What is it like when you create a detailed set of images of yourself engaging in this new behavior?
Can you see yourself doing it?

Keep editing your inner movie of this desired behavior until you can set back and observe the entire sequence as you would a documentary show.

4) Run a check on the ecology, reality, and quality of it.

Are you fully aligned with engaging in this behavior?
Is there any part of you that objects to this new behavior?
Is it ecological for your health, relationships, work, etc. if you were to make this movie a reality?
Check in all representational systems for any sense of objection.

5) Check and satisfy any objections.

What is the objection and what does it say that you need?
How will this affect you as you re-edit your movie?
What resource or resources do you need to add to your strategy?
Is there any objection left when you run another ecological check?

[Continue this process until there are no objections.]

6) Step into the movie to fully experience it.

If you're ready to treat yourself to a new behavioral flexibility, then step inside the images so you can then go through the sequences from an inside view.
As you experience yourself successfully engaging in the new behaviors, what can you use for a strong self-anchor for this state and feeling?

7) Commission your inner executive to take ownership of this performance.

Will the part of your mind that makes decisions analyze the movie that you have created and pull from it the essential ingredients of the process you want to have within?
Will this part of your mind take ownership to run your neurology for making this expression more real to you?
Will it take responsibility to enable you to do this performance exquisitely and easily whenever it needs to be done?

8) Future pace.

As you now imagine taking this new behavior into your future, are you fully aligned with this?
Any other considerations so that this new response is completely appropriate?

* SKILL DEVELOPMENT FOR PROFESSIONAL DEVELOPMENT

This pattern utilizes the three process matrices of meaning, intention, and state of the Matrix Model and the five content matrices. The three processes come from cognitive-behavioral psychology while the five content matrices come from developmental psychology. For more about *the Matrix Model,* see the book by that title, also Appendices C and D.

The Pattern:

1) Identify a skill that you want to develop.

What skill do you want to develop for your professional development?
What skill would take you to the next level of experience and development?
What performance do you want to excel at?

2) Create a Matrix of frames about that skill.

1) Intention:

What skill do you want to develop?
Why is this important to you?
What is your first level intention in doing this?
What are your highest intentions for this?

2) Meaning:

What does it mean to you?
What else could it mean to you?
What does this skill development and performance mean to you?
What do you believe about it?
What frames of mind and attitudes do you need?
What is higher than that?

3) States:

What states do you need to pull this off?
What feeling states best support this?
What are the best states of those who are experts in this?

4) Power (Resources)

What other resources do you need?
Do you have talent for this?
Is this playing to your strength?
Do you have a natural predisposition for this?

5) Self:

Who would you have to be to fully own this skill?
Who will you be when you have this skill well developed?
What adjustments in your self-definition do you need to make?

6) Others:

Who would be a wonderful mirror to give you feedback as you develop this skill?
Who will support you in this endeavor?
Who will be your mentor and/or coach?
Who would you like to appoint as someone to hold you accountable for developing this new skill or taking your skills to the next level?

1) Intention (again):

How committed are you to this?
How much more committed do you need to be?
What would do that for you?
Are you going to develop this skill? Will you?
How much better will you become at it this month? This year?
What will you do tomorrow? When will you begin?

7) World:

What domain does this skill or performance occur within?
What do you believe about this field?
What's your attitude about this field?
How passionate and committed are you to making a difference?

* REPRESENTATIONAL CLARITY

While you start with knowing *what* to do, that's not the end of the story about your knowledge. There is also the question of *how clearly* do you know what to do and how clearly do you represent it. Without representational clarity of what you know, you may be operating from a vague, unclear, fuzzy, even confusing map. If so, that lack of clarity may undermine your ability to act.

Clarity refers to having all of the essential elements of a process and being able to represent the action in your mind as if it were a movie. Such clarity endows you with tremendous power. In clarity lies the power of sending clean and discreet messages to your mind-body-emotion system. It gives you the power to know precisely what you want and what distinctions to make along the way. Clarity in this sense enables you to more fully install patterns so that the knowledge becomes skills.

Use the raw material of *representation* (the see-hear-feel sensory-based maps) along with words to take charge of the frame setting process. Since *vividness* facilitates the installation process, use words more elegantly, dramatically and vividly to captivate your consciousness.

The power of expressiveness lies in painting vivid and dramatic word pictures for yourself and others. Develop word pictures that grab attention so powerfully that it will not let a mind go until it does its bidding. What images, words, sounds, and sensations grab you and pull you so close that you can't avoid its presence? To grab attention compellingly, rivet every bit of attention on a dramatic scenario. Make it memorable, dramatic, and unforgettable by using emotion-laden terms to conjure up new possibilities. For more about this, see the book, *MovieMind* (2002).

The Pattern:

1) Identify a wonderful, dynamic, exciting idea.

What idea would you like to install within yourself as your frame of mind?

If it is a NLP presupposition, which one really inspires you?

What exciting idea pulls on you and compels you to make it yours?

As you state it, and find words to express it, how much does even this put you into state?

1b) Identify a desired performance.

What competency (skill, behavior, performance) do you want to develop or take it to a new level?
What would this look or sound like if you described it as a movie?
How well can you see it now, in your mind, from beginning to end?

2) Step into a state of playful outrageousness.

Have you ever been playful? I mean outrageously playful?
As you recall the feeling of being playful in an outrageous way from a memory or imagination, something that invites you to be a bit of outlandish, notice what happens when you use this state to express the great idea. How does that feel?

3) Sensationalize the idea or competency as a sensory movie.

What can you do to make the idea dramatic, vivid, and wild?
What moves you to feel that it has become an internal *sensorama land* for you?
As you re-write the idea, do so until it becomes refined and honed more and more compellingly attractive and just notice what happens to you.
How else can you load the expression of the idea with the qualities and features that make it more sensational, memorable, powerful, etc.?
As you play with it by finding the voice, gestures, movements, etc. that give expression to the frame, what expressions work to really juice it up?

4) Appreciatively enjoy and have fun with the dramatization.

Do you appreciatively enjoy the idea?
Do you have a lot of fun just thinking about how dramatic the idea now seems to you?
How could you add more fun to it?

5) Say a powerful "Yes!" to it.

As you confirm it repeatedly with a bigger and bigger *Yes,* just how much are drooling?

6) Future pace.

As you stick it as a compelling idea into your future, and imagine running into it and then through it, what is that like?

* META-STATING OWNERSHIP

> *"Change imposed is change opposed."*

Once you know *what* to do, you have to take ownership of it so that you build up a robust sense of *response-ableness* about it. Have you done that? Do you feel that this is your responsibility and that you *own* that responsibility?

Unless you "own" your responses of thoughts, feelings, choices, actions, etc. as your own, all implementation, embodiment, and skill development will be most difficult, if not impossible. You also have to train others to "own" their powers so that they can fully commit themselves to their choices.

Ownership arises when you invest your ego in something. You do that by opening your ego-boundaries and bringing that person, object, or experience into your internal world and making it yours. You can then say, "Mine!" In so owning and personalizing you begin to incorporate what you know and somatically acknowledge what you value and want. The design of this pattern is to use your powers of ownership to take true control of your response-powers so you can make things happen.

This pattern enables us to recognize and own our core "powers" or functions. By meta-stating our core powers, and owning them, we can create the foundation for *personal empowerment* and then the more complex states of responsibility, proactivity, initiative, and risk-taking.

The Pattern:

1) Access a full experience of your four central powers.

Have you ever felt in control and empowered?

What has enabled you to experience the sense of power, control, or capability?

As you step back into that experience, how much are you there again?

Now with this in mind, notice your two private inner powers and how you experience them in that context.

Thinking: representing, believing, valuing, understanding, reasoning, etc.

Emoting: feeling, somatizing, valuing, etc.

You also have two public or outer powers by which you can effect yourself and the world. Notice how you used these powers in that event.

Speaking: languaging, using and manipulating symbols, asserting, etc.

Behaving: acting, responding, relating, etc.

Just notice and enjoy and appreciate these powers as you access them fully from that memory. Access them so that you feel these powers now and set a frame in your mind that accepts and owns them. Use your hands to mime these *powers* in your own personal space to create your *Circle of Power* and influence and responsibility.

How fully are you experiencing your powers?

2) Access and amplify a sense of "ownership"

What can you say *"Mine!"* to fully so that every fiber in your body knows that it is yours?

Has there ever been a time when you said *"Mine!'* that fully?

Recall that time and allow yourself to experience it fully.

Feel it when you strongly sense that something is yours, when every fiber in your being says, *"Mine!"*

Keep it small and simple: "My hand!" "My eye." "My cat." "My toothbrush."

Have you found a *"Mine!"* that is clearly yours in a positive way?

How much do you feel that ownership when you say *"Mine!"*?

3) Amplify your ownership states until your neurology radiates.

As you amplify your sense of ownership and say, "This is my *zone* of power. I am totally responsible for my *responses* of mind, emotion, speech and behavior . . ."

What do you notice that transforms things?

How does that feel?

4) Access the states of acceptance and appreciation of "mine!"

What small and simple reference gives you the feeling of

acceptance?
What do you feel when you welcomed and acknowledged something? (Menu: a rainy day, the traffic)
As you apply this feeling to that which you *own,* how does that feel?
What do you easily and naturally appreciate?
What happens when you feel appreciation about your ownership?

5) Apply your personal empowerment.

Where do you need a greater sense of your personal empowerment?
As you consider the skills and competencies that you are developing, are there any contexts where you need to feel, experience, and utilize your powers?
Are there any contexts or situations that have, in the past, created or sense of dis-empowerment?
Feeling fully your personal powers, and holding that awareness, open up a scene of dis-empowerment in your mind but only at a rate and speed that your sense of empowerment grows— and notice how this transforms that imagination and/or that old memory.

6) Future pace to embody.

Imagine in the weeks and months to come, moving through the world with this frame of mind about your zone of response . . . power . . . Do you like that? Just notice how it will transforms things as it allows you to fully claim your mind, heart, voice, and response powers.

* SETTING RESPONSIBILITY TO/FOR FRAMES

Knowing what to do and how to take ownership in doing it is one thing, knowing the boundaries of where it's appropriate and where it is not is another. This is where the *to/for* distinction comes in. *To/For* is the distinction between what you are responsibility *for* and who you are responsible *to*. This distinction critically maps out two very different concepts and experiences. The word *for* maps things about "accountability" and the preposition *to* maps "relationship."

For: You are responsible *for* yourself— what you say and do, the structures and frames that you set up. You are responsible **for** how you interact, treat people, the spirit and atmosphere that you set, etc. But, you are *not* responsible ***for*** how another person thinks, feels, talks, or acts. They are responsible ***for*** that.

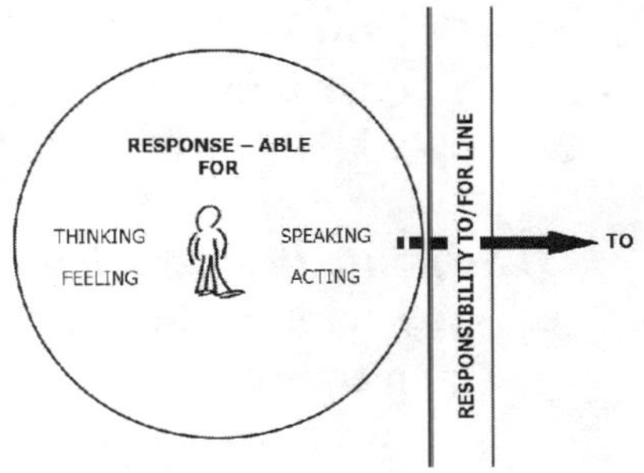

To: Yet you may be responsible *to* them . . . to them as clients, friends, participants, as learners, as colleagues, as human beings, etc. If you are in relationship to them, you may have accepted that there are things that you will give *to* them in exchange for what you want them to give *to* you.

Separating out and stepping into a state of clarity about this *Responsibility To/For Distinction* empowers you in relating in a healthy way, not creating sick and dependent relationships, or getting off on the "power" or "authority" that comes along with being out in front as a leader.

The Pattern:

1) Access your power zone.

Access, acknowledge, and appreciate your four neuro-linguistic powers of thinking-emoting, speaking and behaving. Step into your power zone and own it fully as you bring "ownership" as expressed in "Mine!" to your zone of power. (The Meta-Stating Ownership Pattern).

2) Distinguish between For and To.

Try on the following lines and notice the degree to which they fit and settle well inside you.

> "I am able to respond (response-able) *for* my thinking, emoting, speaking and behaving. I own and acknowledge my ability to make such responses. They are mine and I will not hold anyone else responsible *for* these powers."
>
> "I am **not** able to respond (response-able) *for* the thinking, emoting, speaking, or behaving of anyone else! I cannot and will not assume any ownership over their power zone. It belongs to them. I acknowledge that, appreciate that, and will honor that."

How well do these belief statements settle? If there are any objections inside you, notice what they are so you can deal with them shortly (step 6).

3) Step into this experience fully and feel it as you gesture it.

Feel it in your muscles. Let it become part of your muscle memory.

Invent awesome and memorable phrases for expressing this basic principle. The ones that work for me are the following. Use them as they are or to prime the pump of your own creativity as you invent ones that work best for you.

> *"If it doesn't come out of my mind, my mouth, my heart, my body . . . it's not mine!"*
>
> *"I will not insult others by treating them as fragile, weak, and unable to claim their personality powers."*
>
> *"I have my own full time job being responsible for myself."*
>
> *"I refuse to act in a co-dependent way by thinking I need to rescue others."*
>
> *"I will only invite others to contract with me for assistance, I refuse to be seduced into fixing them or cramming it down their throats."*
>
> *"I don't have to or need to rescue anyone. Others have the right to choose to be as unsane as they want to be! Especially family members!"*

4) Apply to one of your relationships.

Imagine a training group or an individual person who has contracted for you to do something (coach, train, lead, manage, be a partner, be a colleague, etc.). Now apply the responsibility to/for distinction to that relationship.

"I am responsible *to* you *for* what we have agreed that I will give *to* you."
"You are responsible *for* yourself, *for* your thinking, feelings, speaking, and behaving and *to* me for what we've agreed that you would give *to* me."

5) Elicit supporting frames.

What do you need to believe in order for this to become fully integrated?
Who do you need to be to complete the embodiment?
What other resources would empower you to make the *to/for* distinction?

6) Troubleshoot if there are any objections.

Objections to these distinctions will consist of beliefs that either do not allow you this power or some convoluted mis-belief that somehow tries to make you responsible for the *responses* you are not actually *able* to generate and so represents a false map about that.
If the first, give yourself permission to be responsible *only* for yourself. How many times do you need to repeat this until it fully settles?
If the second, give yourself permission to *not* assume god-like powers over others.

7) Future pace.

Would distinguishing responsibility to and for empower you?
Do you like this?
Will you remember it?
As you imagine using it as you relate, how does that feel?
How aligned are you with it right now?

INTENTIONALITY

As knowing what to do in a given performance is a critical success factor, so is having *a strong intention to do it.* Having the capacity to perform without the will and the intention severely undermines the performance. Yet how intense is your intention to engage in a given performance? Do you have a big enough intention? Do you have a robust and powerful intention that will carry you through in spite of obstacles?

This brings up a problem in many performances and explains *under*-performance. While often you "intend" to do something, your intention may be so weak that it is easily distracted.

> "Oh, yes, I intended to do that, I just never got around to it!"
> "Well, as you know, as they say, 'the road to hell is paved with good intentions.'"

Intentionality enables you to use your power to rise up to the higher and highest levels of your mind so you can begin to embody your highest purposes, intentions, and dreams. In Neuro-Semantics we distinguish "thought" in terms of *intention* and *attention.* These are different levels and dimensions.

Attention: What you *represent* on the screen of your mind and what's in your immediate perception is what is *on your mind.* This describes our *attention.* What are you *attending to?* What is getting your attention? What grabs your attention when you are attempting to attend to something else? The attention and content of thought creates your primary level focus and it answers such questions as:

> "What's on your mind? What are you thinking about? What are you representing? In what way?"

Intention: Yet above and beyond that you have other thoughts, thoughts *in the back of your mind,* your higher thoughts about things. This describes your *intention.* First you have *content*—what's on your mind, what is before you. Then you have other thoughts, the thoughts in the back of your mind *about* the first—these are your meta-state levels. Your intentions and higher frames generate your drive and higher level purpose. This answers such questions as:

> "Why are you thinking that? What's your motivation, agenda, or intention behind that thought? What thought lurks back there in the shadows of your mind about X?"

Thinking involves both attentions and intentions. Thinking involves the thoughts in the front of your mind (attentions) and the thoughts in the back of your mind (higher level intentions). You have thoughts layered behind or above your thoughts. Precisely because every thought has an agenda, motivation, or intention you can discern this two-layered nature of thought.

If you live only at the level of attention, *you will be full of attentions.* Yet you can only experience so many attentions before you reach a threshold and can't take anymore. Then, as attentions come and go, you will find yourself easily distracted. Then some doctor will label you ADD and try to medicate you!

If you live *from* a higher intentional level, then what you set as your goal, objective, outcome, purpose, and value will direct and guide your attentions. It is in strengthening and empowering your intentions that enable you to set your highest intentions as an attractor frame so that they can govern your daily attentions.

How does this work? How can you learn to do this? First, move up to your higher intentions and amplify these higher motives for "why" as your higher intentional states. This will enable you to take *an intention stance.* By giving yourself permission to create and live in the higher intention, you commission your highest intentions as attractors in your mind-body-emotion system. Then you can give your attentions to do service to your highest intentions. We describe the principle that governs this in this way:

Energy flows where attention goes as determined by intention.

Your mental, emotional, and somatic energies go to where your attention goes. Notice anything—and you will start thinking about it and experiencing it. In this, you will be sending signals to your body to respond to it. This describes your *attentional life.* As goes your attentions, so goes your energies. No wonder advertizers and marketers work so hard to get your attention. They know that without attention, nothing will happen. There will be no market and no sales.

This also is life in the world of reactivity. Stimulus occurs, gets your attention, and so you react. The prize goes to whoever creates the biggest stimulus that generates the most compelling attention. Such is certainly the life of animals and small children. And sadly also it is all too often the life of many adults. Today, it is in vogue to call it ADD (Attention Deficit Disorder). Yet here is the irony—there's no *deficit* of attention in Attention Deficit Disorder. The deficit is at the level of intention (IDD, Intention Deficit Disorder). If this was the end of the story, human possibilities would be severely limited, would they not?

The good news is that this is not the end of the story. Above and beyond attention is *intention.* Yet the intention has to be set and energized. And not infrequently it has to be refreshed or it will fade and you will forget as the world of attentions will keep calling to you. What is the solution? Identify and strengthen your intentions so that you can take an intentional stance and coach your body to feel your most robust intentions and then align your attentions to them. That's what the next pattern, the Taking an Intentional Stance Pattern, facilitates.

When you run the following pattern—the key to success will be your ability to hold the intention frames that emerge and by holding them for the client, to facilitate the person to access each next level.

* TAKING AN INTENTIONAL STANCE

The Pattern:

1) Identify an important behavioral task with which you have a lot of energy, focus, and motivation.

Identify an activity to use as a reference point to explore your higher intentions.
What are some of the coaching tasks (leadership, business activities, health and fitness activities) that you engage in?
What do you need to do in order to succeed?

1b) Or, identify an important task that's hard to focus on.

What are some of the tasks that you engage in as part of your performance that just as soon as you begin, you have a multitude of other thoughts interrupting your attention and preventing focus?
What task, routine, chore do you need to do in order to succeed which induces a state of ADD in you?
Good, let's use that activity as a reference point to explore

your higher intentions.

2) How is that activity important to you?

I take it that that activity is significant, right? *How* is it significant? *How* is it valuable? Meaningful?
In what way?
What else is important about that?
How many other answers can you identify about this activity?

3) Move up the meta-levels . . . one at a time.

So this activity is important to you because of these things. And how is this important to you? What's important by having this?
What is important about that outcome?
And what's even more important than that?
And when you get that fully and completely and in just the way you want it, what's even more important?

[Continue to reiterate these questions over and over until you flush out and detect all of the higher values. Write down on paper the levels of higher and higher intentions.]

4) Step into the higher states of importance to feel them fully.

That must be important to you? [Yes.] So just welcome in the good feelings that these meanings and significances invite, and just be with those higher level feelings for a bit.
Do you like that? [Yes.]
Let those feelings grow and intensify as you recognize that this is your *highest intentional stance*, this is what you are all about . . . isn't it? Now take a moment to fully enjoy this awareness.

5) Bring the higher states/ frames of mind down and out.

Now experiencing these higher feelings in mind . . . and letting them amplify so that you experience them fully . . . imagine this highest intention getting into your eyes and as you now *close your eyes*, just be with the feelings and in a moment I will ask you to open your eyes and to look at that activity with these eyes. Are you ready? Okay, open your eyes and with all of this emotion in your body, look at that activity ... and notice how *this* [fire anchor] changes *that*. And as you imagine that this becomes your way of being in the world and imagine moving out into life tomorrow with them . . . and as you do . . . and as you engage in that work-related activity that's part of your life, health, wealth building plan, etc., notice how the higher frames transforms it . . . and take all of this into tomorrow and into all of your tomorrows

6) Commission your executive mind to take ownership of this.

There's a part of your mind that makes decisions, that chooses the pathway that you want to go, will that highest executive part of your mind take full responsibility to "be of this mind" about this activity and to remind you to see the world this way?

Imagine using this as *the basis of your inner life,* your way of being in the world. Do you like that?

7) Invite other resources.

Would you like to bring any other resource to this intentional stance?

Would playfulness enrich it? Persistent? Passion? Etc.

Afterwords

Sometimes when I run this pattern with someone, we will go up several levels and suddenly the person will realize something.

> "It's not important. I thought it was, but it really is not. There's nothing I get that's more important. Actually, I'm only doing it, or trying to get myself to do it because it's important to someone else or least they say it is. I have accepted it only because I've been taught that it *should* be important to me. But it is not."

When this happens, consider it a success. You have just discovered some behavior or performance that you can eliminate from your "to do" list. Now you no longer need to force yourself to attend to it. Now you'll have more mental and emotional energy to devote to attending to the things that truly are important to you.

* META-STATING DECISIVENESS

Regarding a performance that you want to take to the next level, you know *what* to do, you have a strategy for pulling it off, you have created a clear set of representations, you have set your intentions around it. Great. Is that it? Is that sufficient?

Yes, if you have also made a decision that you are going to do it. So, are you? Have you made a clear-cut decisive decision that you will do it? When we access and use our power to decide, we experience the state of being *decisive.* In deciding, you literally *de-cide*, that is, you cut off alternatives and push away options as you focus on a singular pathway. To say *"Yes!"* to one thing necessitates saying *"No!"* to other things. It's that simple and it's that challenging.

Decision also involves aligning and empowering your highest intentions to drive and govern your everyday attentions. In this way, you engage in pathfinding and pathmaking. When you "make up" your mind, you solidify your frame of mind as you "hold" a meaning in mind. This is what empowers you to be decisive.

Thresholding: If objections emerge, it is almost always that the person doesn't have permission to decide. To check, ask the person to go inside and check. Say the words, "I give myself permission to decide and to be decisive." As you say those words, what happens? What do you become aware of? How well does it settle? Any objections? If so, what is the objection? What stops you from allowing the permission?

The Pattern:

1) Access the feeling of a "decision"

Step in and experience a great decision you made that worked out wonderfully, and which you made with the qualities of — decisiveness, resolve, without a question, firm, confident, etc. Cut off the alternatives with your *"No!"* as you affirm your preferred choice with your *"Yes!"*

Have you ever made a decision that you absolutely knew and felt was a great one?

Have you ever made a decision that you had to spend some time clarifying your values and visions and when you did, you then took effective action?

2) Amplify the feeling of "decisiveness" and apply to your desired frame or game.

What does it feel like when you juice up this state until it sizzles with a sense of power and control?
How does it influence and affect your body, eyes, breathing, and posture?
How much more empowering can you make it now?

3) Make an empowering decision about your decision.

What kind of qualities would you like to embed your decision strategy within?
What about balance between values/visions, others, health, etc.
What about thoughtfulness, permission to say *"No!"* to good choices, delight and pleasure, proactivity, willingness to take a risk, the wisdom of consultation?
What other qualities?

4) Access your higher executive.

Because there's a part of your mind that makes decisions, go inside and recall a time when you made an executive decision in your life to go in a certain direction, make a major commitment to another person, to a job, a company, etc., can you not?
As you recall it fully so that you step into it again and notice it, how does that feel?
When you finally made your decision, what was that like?
How do you know when you finally experienced the sense of decisiveness? What lets you know?

5) Amplify and anchor.

Notice the meta-state frame of mind of "making up your mind" in a powerfully decisive way and set an anchor for that meta-state. Now apply this to your decision.
Do you like it?
How would you describe this frame of mind?
What did you eat for breakfast last Monday? (Break state question).
Now notice what this brings to your mind (fire anchor). Did that bring back the state?

6) Identify supportive frames.

What belief supports you being decisive?
What intention would be highly supportive?
What identity, permission, or other resource?

Qualify with the higher frames that you choose:
— Confidence
— Quality Control
— Flexibility
— Open feedback loop
— Compassion

7) Step in and experience it fully and imagine it as a resource for all of your tomorrows.

What is it like when you imagine going in to all your tomorrows with this power to make up your mind and be decisive about the things of importance to you, your values, and what you want to do?
Will you keep this?
Really?

* FEEDBACK: RIDING SYSTEM LOOPS

How are you doing? Whatever your answer, *how do you know that?* Do you know how you're doing? How frustrating to be engaged in something that's critically important to you and not have a clue as to how you're doing or where you stand. Suppose you went bowling and had to bowl without being able to see the pins, how satisfying would that game be? Take feedback away and the joy of the game, as well as the magic of improvement, is taken away.

In taking your performance to the next level, after you have your strategy, clarity, intentionality, and decision, then what? What else do you need? The answer is that you need feedback. You need feedback to see if what you are *doing* is actually succeeding. Is it working? Is it moving you to that peak performance that you want to create? How quickly are you making improvement?

You severely impair your learning efficiency without feedback. Without feedback you are working in the dark about the results you're getting and whether what you are doing works or not or what you can do to improve. As you learn to truly welcome feedback, you have to really know that it's not about you as a person, but about the results that you are getting from your actions. It's just feedback—just information about actions.

In the human neuro-semantic system, there are several feed*back* and feed *forward* loops. These loops describe the flow of information through the system and give you insight about what happens (mentally, emotionally, and personally) along the way. In the Neuro-Semantic Matrix model we learn to follow the energy of a human mind-body system in the following loops:

1) The primary loop of stimulus — response.
2) The meta-stating loop system of meaning making.
3) The multiple meta-stating loops within the seven matrices.

All of this means that the more open and playful your attitude about feedback, the more you can learn, can accelerate your learning, use everything for improvement, for becoming smarter in your learnings, and install the ideas, knowledge, and skills that you want for yourself. Are you game? Then let's go for it.

The Pattern:

1) Identify the feed forward loops.

What expertise or skill do you want to perform?
What belief, value, understanding, expectation, frame, identity, etc.?
How do you represent it and encode it on the screen of your mind as a movie?
Where and when would you like to employ this frame?
As you feed forward your ideas, beliefs, emotions, and behaviors, what happens?

2) Identify the feedback loops.

What feedback do you anticipate that you will receive?
When will the feedback come?
From what source will the feedback come?
Will the feedback come naturally or will you have to inquire about it?
Who will notice your performance?

How will you know that they notice?
What results and effects are you expecting?
What other feedback can you anticipate?
How open are you to that feedback?
When you receive that feedback, what will you do with it?
How will you test it?

3) Imagine activating the loops at the primary level first, then add the meta-levels.

As you imagine feed forwarding your belief frame out into the world and then the responses return, notice how this affects the mental movie that you play on the inside. How does that feel?

Now notice how you then feed your new ideas and conclusion back to the higher levels of your mind to new and higher frames.

Then how that feeds forward down through the levels of mind . . . and then out into the world.

4) Enrich your feedback and feed forward loops.

What resources would open up your feedback and feed forward loops?
What beliefs would more fully support you in this process?
What would be the most empowering thought to feel about feedback?

5) Future pace and test.

As you think about all of this and add these resources, how does that settle within you?
Are you aligned with this new attitude and orientation?
So, will you keep it?

* ACCOUNTABILITY SHAPING

If you want to develop and move your performance to mastery, you *need* lots of feedback. You will need good, accurate, useful, and reflective feedback that truly assists you in tuning up your skills and integrating new patterns. Only through accurate and timely feedback can you most effectively install the ideas and skills that you desire. Doing so allows you to be shaped and to shape others. Via making yourself accountable to one or more for what you say you want, you are enabled and empowered to shape your responses most effectively.

- Have you a process for being held accountable for your performance on a daily basis?
- What evaluation process have you set up?
- What and how do you want to measure your progress?

Follow-through is all about executing the required tasks and activities that you want and to move away from non-execution. You need a process whereby you allow others to hold you accountable.

- Who will you invite into the accountability process with you?
- Regarding what will you make yourself accountable? According to what criteria?
- How will you measure it?
- How often will you engage in this evaluation process?
- What will cue you that it's time for a check-up?
- When will you practice or exercise this skill or idea? How often?

Are you ready to step up to a new level of development and receive feedback like a professional coach? Is your "receiving feedback" Matrix well formed and ready to go? What do you need to work on?

The Pattern:

1) Intention: Set a high and transformative Intention for receiving feedback positively.

Why do you want to receive feedback? How will it help you? For what purpose?

Have you decided to refuse to let another's incompetence or sloppiness in giving feedback deprive you of the feedback?

2) Meaning: Identify your current frame (meta-state/s) about feedback (correction, error detection, etc.).

When you think about someone informing you (telling you)

that you made a mistake, error, messed up, did something wrong, etc., what thoughts and feelings come to mind?
What state does that put you in?
What do you believe about that?

Deframe the old frames of meaning to slay or tame any and every old dragon state:
Do these states enhance your learning abilities?
Do these states, frames, meaning serve your creativity, growth, understandings, etc.?
How do they represent ill-formed maps?

Set new frame that powerfully reframe feedback.
What do you now want to think about feedback so you find it acceptable and even valued?
Have you the frames set to texture your state for receiving feedback with the most robust Matrix?

3) State: Separate feedback from the person and even the style.

Most people really do not know how to give sensory-based feed back. Instead, they give judgments, evaluations, mind-reading statements, and hallucinations. When they do that to you, it's critical that you *refuse* to let their incompetence or sloppiness to deprive you of useful feedback. How do you do that? By conversationally coaching them to translate their judgments into sensory-based referents so that you can receive it and experience it as "just information." To do that use indexing questions (when, where, what, how, who, etc.) to squeeze out the specific details hidden inside the criticism.

4) Power: Texture your state with the qualities and resources for a robust feedback state.

What qualities do you want to texture your feedback state with?
Do you need more patience, acceptance, appreciation, recognition of positive intention, commitment to yourself, to your learning, to your budding genius, etc.?
How hungry are you for feedback? Enough?
Are you able to invite another to specifu the feedback in precise sensory-based behavioral terms?
Will you make the sensory-based/evaluative distinction when someone communicates in judgments?

Will you help the speaker translate from judgment into feedback?
Will you also stubbornly refuse to buy into feedback that doesn't fit for you?
Does your feedback Matrix feel powerful enough yet?

5) Visit the other Matrices. [See appendix D on Matrix Questions]
What frames about Others?
What frames of meaning about the World?
What frames of reference about Time?

6) Future Pace
Now, imagine moving forward with this way of operating with your feedback matrix fully robust and powerful in this way—do you like this?
How well will it enhance your interactions and relationships?

* FIRST STEP APPROXIMATIONS

You can shape any behavior, frame of mind, habit, or response if you *reinforce* it with pleasure and especially with massive pleasure at meta-levels. You only need to attach intense pleasure both to the frame (the inner game) and the game (the outer game).

You never start out in any new knowledge or skill at the top with refined expertise or with an expert performance. Your first step is just that—a beginning, a first approximation. From there, you learn how to use your approximations, along with feedback, to learn how to move closer and closer to your goals. Every step then become one step closer. Every step enables you to embody the knowledge and skill as you make it yours. This is the nature and value of using first step approximations as part of your development toward mastery. There is power and momentum in being able to move in the right direction. There is a building momentum that you can then use for building up more energy and focus.

The key for development in this is to add massive pleasure to your first approximations. There's a reason for this: *Pleasure reinforces every movement and every step forward in the right direction.* To do this, make a list of pleasurable things that you would find "rewarding." What would you like to use to reward movement in the right direction? The design of this pattern is to use every approximation to put us in the right direction and to begin moving.

The Pattern:

1) Identify a skill or knowledge that you want to develop.

What is the knowledge, concept, or skill that you want to develop?
What would a first step, a baby-step, moving toward that look, sound, or feel like?
What would be some of the first steps?

2) Establish an anchored reward.

How will you or could you reward it?
What for you is fun, rewarding, and delightful?
What pleasurable activity makes you feel more resourceful?
Access fully and set an anchor for two or more of the pleasures.
Do you now have a pleasure anchor for these?

3) Practice rewarding the early approximations.

Imagine seeing that first step and *feel* this [fire anchor].
How will you reward yourself?
Who else will reward you?
Who could you invite into a supporting role to provide rewards like a high five or a meta-high five?

4) Check for alignment and support.

What processes support the change or implementation?
Is your mind-body aligned in support of the new behavior?
Do all of the higher frames in your mind support implementing this?

5) Add kaizen to the mix.

If *kai* means "change" and *zen* "for the better," then what changes for the better are you planning?
What if you were to *continuously improve* (kaizen) in this day after day, week after week, and month after month?
Would you like that?
How much would you like that?
As you imagine the kaizen of continuous improvement that follows with that, do you like that?
How much openness to feedback do you now experience?

* PROPULSION SYSTEM

To achieve peak performance, you have to have a never-die, never-quit motivation—a passion that will enable you to see things through. In this, you are pushed and pulled into your desired outcome. And when you have both pushes and pulls in your motivation, you have a *propulsion system.* Aversions and pains kick you in the butt while attractions and pleasures simultaneously allure you forward. As a system for enabling you to become more skilled in implementing your knowledge and skills, a propulsion system facilitates you to embody what you know in your skill development.

Where there is non-performance or under-performance, you can count on there being either the lack of attractions or the lack of consequences. You establish one side of a propulsion system when you use the Meta-*Yes-ing* and the Meta-*No-ing* pattern (Chapter 4). You de-commission disabling beliefs as you reduce them once again to mere thoughts as you say,

> "*Hell No!* I will not tolerate or put up with or allow those old toxic ideas, understandings, feelings, etc. to run my life anymore."

You then transform other thoughts into empowering beliefs as you say,

> "*Yes! Yes! YES!* I will welcome and embrace those empowering and enhancing ideas, understandings, feelings, and response patterns so that they become my way of being in the world."

A propulsion system accesses and utilizes the twin-feelings of *aversion and attraction.* So as you identify what you want and why you want it, you build up your feelings of attraction to a compelling future. Every empowering concept, belief, decision, feeling, state, and action that you identify . . . increases the *pull of the attraction.*

- How strong is the attraction?
- How much stronger would you want the attraction?
- Do you feel compelled?
- Would you like to wake up every day of your life with that frame of mind?
- What consequence will you set for non-performance?

A propulsion system also accesses and utilizes the feelings of *aversion* in order to get the booster effect. As you look at the ideas, beliefs, situations, experiences, memories, fears, etc. that hold you back, that get in your way, that sabotage your best, you identify the things that you can now turn into powerful aversions. You can then use them to kick yourself in the butt.

- How strong is your aversion to move away from those interferences?
- How much stronger would you like to have the feeling of those aversions?
- Which do you need to sequence first in your awareness, *away from* or *toward?*

If you're interested in propulsion systems, see the spiral book *Propulsion Systems in NLP and Neuro-Semantics* (2002). That work has a list of eight different propulsion systems.

The Pattern:

1) Prepare for the propulsion.

Identify the meta-program filters of direction and time. Do you first move toward or away from things? Does either direction style drive your internal experiences? Where do you store your time-line in space: to your right, left, immediately in front, etc.?

Direction sort: Away from — — Toward; balanced.

"Time" spatial sort: left — right — side — other.

Up/Down for "More/ Less" — up for more, down or out for more.

2) Identify your current motivation.

In what area or about what performance do you want to create a propulsion system?

How are you motivated about that right now?

When you think about it, do you move toward it, away from it, or do you feel stuck somewhere in the middle?

Do you need more push or pull?

3) Emotionalize your frame of mind.

What best "emotionalizes" something for you? How do you activate your emotions?

What would it be like if you sang this frame?

What would the music and dance of this frame be like?

Suppose you wrote a pledge of allegiance to this frame?
Suppose you put it to poetry?

4) Elicit the twin states of aversion and attraction.

Fully elicit the person's "states" of attraction and aversion. Identify three answers to the following elicitation question: What do you feel strongly compelled toward in your life? As you think of it— identify what you simultaneously strongly move away from as you move toward your desired outcome.

- I want you to pick one of those experiences and fully access the attraction state [or the aversion state]. [This depends upon the person's meta-program, toward or away from.]
- *Feel* this state fully . . . how much do you have this state? Imagine having it all the way to a 10 . . . Let it double.
- As I anchor this state, I will be sliding this touch anchor up (and down) your arm as you sense experience it more or less.

  [Slide the anchor up or down depending on what seems to indicate "more" or "less" to the individual.]
- We are going to keep *amplifying* both of these states until you experience the attraction and the aversion states at a 8 to 10 on a scale from 0-to-10. ("I really, really want to get away from this!")

5) Establish pain and pleasure leverages.

How would you add massive pain and/or pleasure to this subject?
What would be massive pain for you if you don't install this new frame? What will happen? What price will you pay— personally, interpersonally, financially, in your health, etc.?
What would comprise massive pleasure if you do install this new frame? How will this make your life more enriched?
What would kick you in the butt?
How much massive pain and distress do you need to add so that you will feel it as a red hot poker in the rear end and move?

6) What "must" you do or avoid?

A "must" frame-of-reference can empower you to get things done. You then act because you *have to.* So, are you willing to refuse to leave yourself any other choice by leveraging your old frame as you set a *must* frame?

Access a compelling *must* in your life. What *must* you do? What *must* you not do? What do you absolutely *have to* do? When you find a strong and empowering *must* that's positive, access it fully in terms of how you picture it, the sounds and words you use to encode it, and then step into it so fully that you begin to experience it bodily. As you do, notice *the physiology of must.* Once there, then begin exploring why you must do this.

Accessing a positive and enhancing "must" in this way gives you a clear pathway to this neurological state of power. Think of it as *must power.* With it, you now have a way to set a *must frame* on other things.

> [If you experience *must* or *have to* as negative, I recommend that you spend some time de-energizing those words. Unload them semantically so you do not merely react to them to your own detriment.]

7) Identify and develop a pleasure anchor.

What is an exquisite pleasure for you?

As you access this state of exquisite pleasure, intensify it to the point of drool— and then apply it to the new performance. How's that?

8) Use the pain / pleasure structure for the propulsion.

Identify the content of the desired propulsion system.

- What do you want to become compulsively attracted to . . . the converse of which you will feel increasingly revolted from so that you feel increasing pleasure as you move toward the attraction and more and more pain as you stop moving toward it?
- Just imagine getting more and more of this compelling and attractive outcome . . . as I slide this anchor in this way and joyfully imagine the ever-increasing of these values, beliefs, representations, etc.
- Just imagine getting more and more of these things that you *do not want, that you hate, that undermine your success . . . . and feel this* until you say inside, or outside, 'Enough!" "No more!" I will slide this aversion anchor more and more so that you can feel the increasing of this pain when you hesitate or stop moving toward your goals and you can feel this as much as you want to until you say, "Hell no!"

- Now imagine experiencing these feelings . . . attraction and aversion as you move into your future . . . [Slide the anchors . . . as you describe the two directions.]

Establish several loops: "The more— the less . . . " and *"the less--- the more . . . "*

- *The more aversion you feel— the more aversion you will feel until you can't stand it anymore and you will get the hell out of there!*
- *The less aversion you experience— the more attraction you get to enjoy.*
- *The more attractions you feel — the less aversions you will feel or need.*
- *The less attractions you experience— the more aversion you will experience.*

9) Check Ecology.

- Do you like this? Does this combination of toward and away from directions serve to enhance your life and give you a propulsion away from everything that undermines your success and toward those things that make your life richer and fuller?
- Does it make your life more balanced, tempered, and productive?

  [Keep recycling through the Aversions/ Attractions by eliciting and solidifying meta-level frames that support each: beliefs, values, principles, decisions.]

10) Symbolize the new direction as your life orientation.

- Let some i*con,* symbol, word, color, metaphor, etc. *to stand for this toward/ away from propulsion system . . .* Just let something *come to mind*, and notice how you can use it as you imagine moving into your future.
- Is every part of you fully aligned with this?

11) Meta-Yes the propulsion system

Do you like this?
Do you want to keep this?
Would this be valuable?

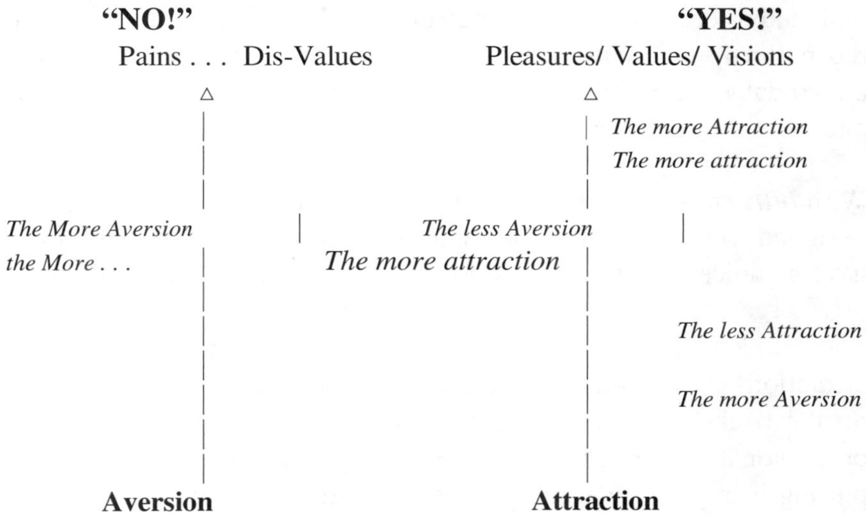

* ELIMINATING WIGGLE ROOM

How much room do you have to wiggle around with your commitments and maybe even to wiggle out of them? Do you ever wiggle out of commitments? As you now realize this phenomenon, you can now set things up so as to leave yourself no room. Now you will have to go after excellence and make your dreams come true. Actually, doing this is part and parcel of every great peak performer. They burn their boats behind them leaving them without a way to return so that they have to go forward and make it work. As they confront their reality, look it in the face, they get their back up so that they stubbornly refuse to sell themselves short from their goals and visions. Are you ready to do that?

This kind of dramatic confrontation involves the idea of putting something so much in your face that you make the attractions and the aversions completely un-avoidable. Then the subject becomes inescapable so that you, or another person, have to respond to it. You have no room to wiggle out of it. It leaves you without excuse. Would you like to become excuseless?

With *aversions,* this becomes a threshold pattern that's designed to find an aversion that you *say* you don't want, but which you put up with and tolerate to your own detriment. Upon finding the aversion, the pattern essentially *puts the aversion in your face* so that it's unavoidable, and continues to do so until you reach a threshold of pain.

With *attractions,* this becomes a compulsion or fetish pattern that's designed to turn the attraction into a compulsion so that you don't have a choice. You now have to respond to it and move toward it.

The problem with many failures-to-implement is that you push the attractions or aversions off to the side and forget them. You put them on the back-burner and ignore them. This pattern eliminates the procrastination, or ignoring of something that you ought to do by putting it in your face in a compelling and memorable way. The design of this pattern is to prevent any wiggle-room from not living up to your highest values and visions.

Once you start this process of thresholding, you need to finish it. Don't stop until the aversion bursts. The design here is to move the person to the place where every fiber of his or her body is totally disgusted with the idea or feeling of wiggling out of a commitment. To not finish it is to inoculate the person against it and will make things worse for the person.

For the coach as the facilitator of this process, you will need to prepare yourself with the right state in order to "put the idea in the person's face." So, what state, or states, do you need to access so that you can do this in a way that makes it effective? A menu list includes such states as the following: playful, respectful, teasing, mischievous, confrontative, provocative, caring, etc. You will need to be in the right state to facilitate this, so make sure you are.

The Pattern:

1) Identify the idea that you want or need to put "in your face" and make it inescapable.

What great idea, wonderful pattern, tremendous empowering belief, etc. would you like to have before you so that you can remember it and act on it?

What horrible aversion do you want to keep with you to remind yourself to avoid?

Are you absolutely committed to this? [If not then use Meta-Stating Decisiveness Pattern.]

2) Put the idea / representation in the person's face.

Do you have a great and inspiring idea —an idea that really excites you, one that you'd like to wake up every day for the rest of your life?

What if you miss that completely? What would that feel like? And why would you miss it?

What would cause you to miss out of the most important thing in your life? [Elicit the excuse or the barrier, the X.]

Provocative questions:

So X will stop you, you wimp?!

Are you going to let X rob you of this?

So it must not really be all that important to you!

3) Exaggerate until it thresholds.

Imagine the thing which you most dislike continuing and growing worse and worse over the weeks, the months, and the years . . . As you imagine that, what do you feel?

What is the most compelling thing about your representation —in a negative way? Is it the picture —it's clear, close, bright, colorful, etc.? Is it the sounds—it's loud, close, the tone, its location, etc.? Take the cinematic features of the representation and amplify the experience by exaggerating it more and more until it thresholds.

4) Check the ecology at the end and future pace.

So where are you now? How does the idea of wiggling out on a commitment or a decision now strike you?

How does this now settle with your health, relationships, career, etc.?

As you imagine going into your future, what does your time-line seem like now?

* APPLY TO SELF

The nice thing about using the Meta-States model in all of these processes is it has the *apply-to-self* mechanism built in. And no wonder, Meta-States is a model of reflexivity—a model about reflecting back onto yourself time and again. As a result of this reflexivity, you are always able to *step back* from a thought, emotion, belief, etc. and apply to yourself.

You can also step back at any and all levels of your experience to notice what you are thinking-and-feeling at that level. This enables you to recognize the frames that you are setting at that level and what frames or states you could apply to yourself at that level. This puts you at choice point and increases your ability to apply great truths and processes to yourself.

Getting used to working with your self-reflexive consciousness requires that you don't go into a spiral and get lost in the process. This is a matter of practice as well as setting frames.

The Pattern:

1) Identify a positive experience.

What state or experience do you want or want more of?

Menu list: assertiveness, calm reflection, patience, kindness when upset, strength of character, time to pace and attentively listen.

What principle, idea, belief, or practice do you want to have more self-application in?
Are you willing to apply this to yourself?
Do you have permission to apply this to yourself?
Are you going to apply this to yourself? When?

2) Step back from it to begin noticing your reflections.

As you try it on, in your mind, with a permission statement, what happens? What comes to you?
What thoughts, emotions, memories, imaginations arise when you try it on?
Have you traced out the layers of frames upward and gotten to the end of the matrix of frames? [This is a task of using meta-questions, see Appendix B.]

3) Design a new inner game for yourself.

Are you clear about what the experience would be like?
How clear is your inner movie of it?
What else do you need to edit into that movie to make it clear and compelling?
How complete is it? How important is it to you?

4) Design supportive frames for it.
What do you need to believe, understand, value, decide, etc.?
What higher frame would support that?
Do you now feel that you have a supporting matrix of frames?

5) Apply to self.
How many times do you need to do this until it stays?
After ten or more self-reflexive moves, how do you feel?

6) Accountability check.
Who will you appoint to check in with you about this?

* TAKING PERFORMANCE TO THE NEXT LEVEL

Pick a behavior, any behavior, that you actually engage in as a performance during the days of your life in any given area. What do you actually engage in and do that's important, and even critical for your personal sense of success?

Health:

Eating right. Planning and cooking a healthy meal. Exercising daily.

Relationships:

Spending time with your loved ones, being firmly caring in discipline. Investing emotionally in friends and colleagues.

Personal Development:

Studying, taking time to reflect, planning and following through on development.

Professionally:

Writing a report, memo, article, book proposal, sales letter, etc., working on a long-term project. Managing the details of your business.

Financially:

Creating and following a budget. Tracking receipts.

What kind of a *performer* are you?

- Are you mostly and primarily a *top* performer? In what areas?
- Are there areas in which you are an *under*-performer?
- Where in life would you like to take your performance to the next level?
- Are you crystal clear about where to invest your mental and emotional energies?
- Is there any area wherein you could become outstanding, where you could turn in an outstanding performance?

As you know, the bottom line of success in any realm is *behavioral performance*. So what are you doing to get the results you want? Success of any particular behavior is to get the results you want and the quality of the performance you want. To that end, are you able to discern between those areas that require *top* performance and those that do not.

With some things (i.e., getting to work on time, picking the kids up from school, brushing our teeth, opening bills and paying them), there's no need to refine and hone until you are devoting all of your mental and emotional resources and becoming the best in the world. In fact, aiming for peak performance in some areas would be a waste of your resources and energy. Ultimately, you could work out the optimum speed and time of day for hitting every traffic light so it is "green" on your way to work or school, but to what end?

The Pattern:

1) Identify an area where you want to enhance your performance.

In what realm of life do you want to improve your performance?
What is the performance specifically?
What are the critical success talents, skills, competencies, and behaviors?
How simple or complex is the performance?
What are the sub-strategies or sub-routines involved in the performance?
Which sub-strategies or capacities have to be in place to be able to pull off the performance at the most basic level?
What is your current level of competence at that level?
What strategies and capacities take one from basic competence to highly skilled?
What is your current level of competence at that level?
What strategies and capacities will take you to the highest level?
What is your current level of competence at that level?
What are the actions that are required for this?

2) Identify the critical success factors.

What are the critical success factors that determines whether you turn in an under-performance, a mediocre performance, or a superior performance?
Do you know anyone who is excellent, superior, or outstanding in it?
What are the distinctions that make a difference in them?
At the primary level of talent and skill, what's required?
At the meta-level, what attitudes, beliefs, passion, etc. give the performance its best spirit and feel?
Do you know the qualities of those who are outstanding?
Are you willing to study, interview, model, and explore to find

out? How will you do that?

3) Identify the best matrix of frames that support a top performance.

What are the best states for this performance?
What are the best meanings and intentions?
What are the best belief frames about yourself?
What are the best belief frames about your skills, resources and powers?
What are the best belief frames about others?
What are the best belief frames about time?
What are the best belief frames about that domain or area?

4) Identify the best perceptual filters for a top performance.

What perceptual filters or meta-programs do the best performers have?
How do they see things, sort for information, and make distinctions?
How much flexibility do they have with their meta-programs?
Are there any meta-programs that have to dominate in the performance? [See Appendix A for more about Meta-Programs.]

5) Identify the learning and development curve for a top performance.

What is the order or sequence of development from the capacities and sub-routines of a beginner to a top performance?
What is the best order of learning in order to master the overall performance?
What time frame can this occur in?
What factors can accelerate this process?
What skills have to become habitual and intuitive for mastery?

6) What higher level frames add the magic touch so that a top performance becomes truly masterful?

What is the inner "attitude" or "spirit" that gives a top performance that extra special touch?

7) Evaluate your behavioral development.

What *new* performance does this now open you up to?

What are the actions that fall out of this performance?
Are you now fully ready to do this?
How aligned are you about this?

* PERFORMANCE REVIEWING

Suppose when you come to the end of a day, a month, and a project, you regularly take a few moments to review what went well and what did not? Suppose you bring ruthless honesty to such reviews for the passionate purpose of learning to take your performance to the next level? You can use the following pattern as an end-of-the-day review or as an end-of-a-project review.

The Pattern:

1) Run a movie of your activities and of the performance.

Run a mental movie of all of the activities, events, conversations, and people that were involved in the performance.
What stands out? What are you aware of?

2) Freeze frame the movie at places of difficulty or challenge.

Was there anything in the performance that didn't go as planned or up to standard?
Was there anything not as smooth, elegant, powerful, effective, etc.?
Stop the movie whenever you find places where you didn't like the response you got from others or where you didn't like your own behavior.
What are the problem contexts for you?
How did you do compared to what you forecasted?
What adjustments will you make to improve the performance?
How did you grow personally through the process?

3) Identify resources to apply.

What worked very well?
What actions, feelings, ideas, responses and ways of being worked well during the performance?
What other resources could you have used and applied from other contexts?
How could you have made your performance even better?

4) Identify difficulties to address.

What did not work as well as you would have wished?

When you have identified something, use the levels of beliefs to ask the following:

Intention: How would you have wanted to affected others?

What do you deem of the most importance in this situation?

Self: What kind of a person do you want to be in this situation?

Power: What do you want to feel certain about?

What are you able to do or would like to be able to do?

What feeling or action would you like to have taken?

Chapter 4

THE ART OF IMPLEMENTATION

Everything that you do to install and embody what you know falls into a special area—the science and art of implementation. And this is the subject of this chapter.

Defining Implementation

Yet what does it mean to "implement" something? The idea of implementation is pretty simple. Implementation essentially refers to the following actions:

- To put into action, to act on knowledge
- To bring information down the levels of mind into body
- To integrate and align the information in the system
- To risk experimentation, involvement, engagement
- To learn experientially
- To get knowledge into muscle memory
- To involve the complete mind-body-emotion system
- To coach the body how to feel concepts
- To execute ideas and plans
- To make a concept a part of our way of being in the world, our *modus operandi.*
- To move competence from unconscious to conscious awareness and then to unconscious competence by practice and habituation until the information — *in forms* us and becomes intuitive, natural, and our new default program.

Merely performing and taking action is one thing, having that performance so well integrated within you so that it is fully and congruently yours is quite another. Now that you have identified and developed a new performance, the next step is to install it within you so that it is fully embodied. That's what implementation is all about.

From Knowing to Doing

In Chapter 2 we began with the Mind-to-Muscle pattern as the solution to the knowing-doing gap and as a central pattern for getting to performance. We now return to this pattern to think about it in terms of embodiment or installation.

As I mentioned earlier, I stumbled onto the *Mind-to-Muscle Pattern* while researching and during the early trainings after I had modeled the strategy of Wealth Creation. I was particularly interested in this because I found that most of the information in the field of wealth building is encoded in terms of principles. Writers and presenters in that field have the habit of presenting their information in the form of principles—"the seven laws for building wealth." Yet hardly any of them ever provide actual techniques for doing so—technologies in the form of patterns, processes, step-by-step coaching, etc. They provide the great ideas, but not the *know how* that allows a person to take on those principles and embody them.

Actually, this is true for most fields. In most fields of endeavor, you can find some truly great generalizations, beliefs, ideas, etc. for how a person needs to think to succeed in that field. Writers, trainers, and researchers typically think in terms of the guiding principles and conceptual frameworks.

> "What are the basic understandings you have to know to function effectively in this domain?"

Taking the approach of identifying principles takes you a long way down the road to understanding a field (i.e., mathematics, architecture, chemistry, sales, customer service, psychotherapy, leadership, entrepreneuring, etc.) and even becoming competent in that field. Yet it will not take you all the way. It will not because it does not provide a specific map for navigating the field in terms of informing you *how to learn to think as the experts think.*

Into this gap, Neuro-Semantics offer a way to translate the great ideas into the action of effective behaviors. As a meta-discipline, we shift from *content* to *structure*, from *details* to *form.* We move above the facts and details of *what* to think to the higher level structural elements of *how* to think. Using the levels of mind model known as the Meta-States Model, you learn how to work with the dynamic structure of your higher levels of awareness to get yourself to top performance.

> *Where there is thought, there let there be muscle.*

The idea behind the patterning of mind-to-muscle in Meta-States is that you can take a conceptual level frame-of-reference—some great idea, understanding, concept, etc., and literally incorporate it into your neurology and your muscles. Then, once it gets into your neurology, you can embody it in your *eyes* (your way of seeing the world, your meta-programs), your *voice* (your way of talking), and your *muscles* (your way of being in the world). This puts the "knowledge" into a form that allows you to have ready access to it. When you get to this level, the idea operates as your frame of reference—as your mental-and-emotional frameworks or *Matrix.*

Most of us who have worked with computers and with various software programs have so incorporated the conceptual understandings and processes like function keys, commands, etc. that now we can make a keyboard sing. Can you? In fact, you may be able to do so to such an extent, that like typing, you no longer "know" what specific keys you're using to center, set off a macro command and the like. Yet, your fingers know.

Of course, in saying that *your fingers know,* we have identified a very powerful, and almost magical, process. It indicates that now a neuro-semantic program is running the show. When your muscles know things, we call this "muscle memory." Muscle memory drives and governs such complex activities as skating, driving, skiing, reading, tying a shoe, etc. This means that you have incorporated ideas and concepts so that they have become embodied at the primary level of experience as procedural knowledge. Now they hardly seem like concepts at all; they no longer seem to be things of the mind. You now "intuitively" know. The knowing is "inside" of you. Somehow.

Well, *if* you can get higher level concepts and ideas that seem non-corporal (body, *corpus*) to become corporal experiences—actual neurological patterns in the muscles, *if* you can encode them at that level, then this gives us something truly worth modeling, does it not? And that's precisely what I have been doing with the Meta-State recognition that we have *levels* within our mind. We have been using this discovery in all of our modeling projects and subsequent trainings.

Suppose you wanted to model Wealth Creation. You could read a book like *The Millionaire Mind* (2000) and find all kinds of wonderful and insightful principles. What you will *not* find are specific processes for incorporating the ideas into your body as physiological states. That explains why most people read and feel inspired and captivated by the vision that the programs offer, but are unable to replicate it. Conceptual knowledge and inspiration are insufficient. To achieve success we have to use specific embodying patterns.

Installing Patterns

[A *gestalt state* describes what happens when you meta-state several layers or levels of mind upon mind. Then out of that mixture, the entire system of interactive parts creates "something more than the sum of the parts." This allows higher levels of states to emerge. There's more about gestalt states and gestalting in *Chapter 6*.]

You have already learned and experienced several mind-to-muscle patterns to create your own personal power of congruence as you have activated what you "know" at the higher levels. Owning your "power zone" is one such pattern. There you accessed a neurological primary state (i.e., ownership) and applied it to yourself to activate your executive powers. This describes a critical secret of personal mastery. Doing this also endows you with the ability to create other meta-states at will as well as gestalt states.

To achieve this we model both from *the top down* and from *the bottom up* to catch, unpack, and sequence the structure of a subjective state like "courage," "seeing opportunities," and even something as simple as "optimism." These are not primary states, nor even simple meta-states. They emerge from our consciousness operating in a systemic way so that our meta-stating has the effect of texturing and coloring our states as it sets higher frames. We refer to this as *the texturing* of our states.

This mind-to-muscle process works because your mind-body system inevitably works to integrate what you know conceptually so that you know it in your body as well. That's why mental, intellectual, and conceptual states do not remain abstract. They keep *coalescing* into the primary states. This is not to be confused with the collapsing of anchors. Coalescing of higher states into lower describes an entirely different phenomenon. This is the mechanism that turns meta-states into meta-programs. When you run this process linguistically, you are able to *translate down into your body* the things of your mind—the higher principles that you want to live by.[1]

That you all *know* more than you *do* speaks of the glory of being human. It highlights the possibility that you can expand to become even more than you are, that you can take your performance to the next level. Yet if you lack a neuro-semantic program for implementing knowledge, learning more and more and being unable to act effectively on that knowledge will be a tormenting distress. It will torment you with all that you cannot do.

The Design of the Pattern

The design of *the Mind-to-Muscle Pattern* is to translate insightful and valued principles into neurological patterns in the body. It is to encode the program into your muscle memory so that it can then run from that level of experience. The knowledge will be no longer "heady," "up in your mind," or merely "conceptual," but felt as "intuitive" and so operate automatically in your behavior. It will be fully integrated into who you are. Your muscles will "remember" how to perform the corresponding actions.

Mind-to-muscle is a coaching pattern par excellence. *In this process you essentially coach your body how to feel an idea.* This lets your muscles "know" and "remember" the operation of the principle so that your muscles "feel" it. You activate your neuro-pathways that fire the motor programs in the muscles so the idea becomes your way of being in the world.

Actually this describes a natural process that occurs all the time. Consider typing on a typewriter or computer keyboard. The original learning takes a considerable amount of time and trouble. It demands rote learning and lots of repetition. To get the muscle patterns and coordination deeply imprinted and encoded into the muscles, you have to engage in abundant practice. Yet, once you have practiced and trained your neurological pathways, then *the learnings become incorporated into the very fabric of the muscles themselves.* You then lose conscious awareness of the learnings as your muscles run the operation. At that point, you have translated principle into muscle. What you know conceptually is now in muscle memory.

The same holds true for expertise, excellence, and mastery in all other fields, from sports, mathematics, teaching, to surgery, selling, and public relations. Begin with *principles*—concepts, understandings, awarenesses, beliefs, etc., and translate that level of thought so that it "comes down" to another level and eventually into muscle itself. I have found this especially true in modeling resilience, leadership, wealth building, selling excellence, learning, etc.

The pattern creates this kind of *transformation* by taking you up and down the various levels of mind so that you map from your understandings about something from the lowest descriptive levels to the highest conceptual levels and back down again. This is best accomplished as you let someone coach you through the process. It typically takes five to ten experiences with this pattern before it becomes "second nature." When that happens, then you will be able to run it on yourself and after that it will eventually happen automatically. When that happens, it becomes a meta-pattern for how you think and operate. It enables you to move through life implementing your ideas. You become that kind of a person—a person who acts on what you know. And you do that as a matter of principle.

Figure 4:1

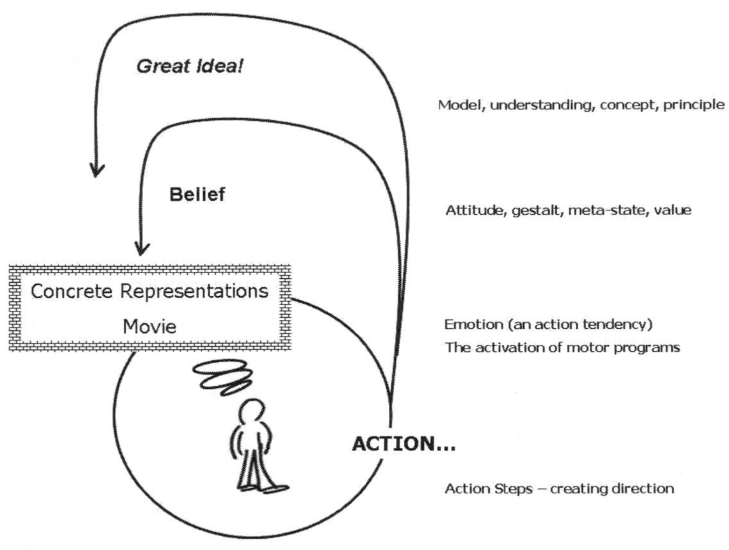

Mind-to-Muscle as Feed Back and Feed Forward Loops

It really doesn't matter if you use *the top down* approach or the *bottom up* approach. In fact, by the last step, we engage both directions.

1) *From the Top Down.*

> Mind-to-Muscle starts at the top with a principle or idea and brings it down into muscle—*this is a feed forward loop.* Feed forward an idea, belief, understanding, knowledge, concept, inspiration, etc. into your actions. This infuses the output channel of your talk and behavior with a higher level form of "energy." You "energize" your talking and acting with the idea. For example, what would it be like for you to energize your tone of voice and gesturing with the idea of confidence?

2) From the Bottom Up.

> Open your eyes, ears, skin, etc. and as you use your sensory systems, take what you notice about the effect of your talk and behavior and bring it back inside and back up to the idea or principle to check it out in terms of how successful were you in speaking and acting confidently. Did it work to your satisfaction? *This is the feed back loop.* Monitor the effect of your actions on the outside world and compare it against the higher level of mind to see how it fits and to what extent.

The *feed forward loop* of Mind-to-Muscle enables you to control your destiny and to run your own life according to your values and beliefs. Now when you get an idea in your head, you can begin to translate it down into neurology and outward into proactive action as we encounter various contexts. That's the first step of the dance.

The second step involves monitoring things and checking them out *in terms of the idea.* Use the feed back loop for running a quality control of the performance.

> Do I like the way I sound? Does my speech convey the care, compassion, and assertiveness I believe in?

Together the two loops translate information up and down the levels of mind-and-body and creates a sensitive, responsive neuro-semantic structure. It creates an ongoing system of mutual influence that keeps on enriching each other, a network of frames nested inside of yet higher frames. This re-structures you in mind-and-body so that you use feedback and creative thinking as complements to each other.

The Question of Ecology

With this pattern, we check the *ecology* both before and afterwards, but do *not* check ecology *during* the process. There are several reasons for this.

First, it is critical that you do *not* pick a stupid or toxic principle when you use this pattern. Is the principle ecological? Is the concept realistic? Is it universally true? Would it make life richer and fuller? Begin by identifying a great idea, concept, principle, "secret," "law," etc. in your field of endeavor—a principle that has been long tested and has proven itself as an essential principle for wealth, health and fitness, learning, selling, influence, etc. When you do this, begin with an idea that has ecology already built into it because it has long been tested.

Next, integrate and install that principle into *your neurology*. This may cause other conflicting ideas, feelings, principles, etc. to emerge. Let them. In fact, you want them to arise. If a conflict between the new frame and some old embodied frame emerges and you feel uncomfortable about it, *just welcome it graciously into your awareness and begin to explore it.* Oftentimes, the "sense of conflict" is only that, a sense of conflict and no actual conflict at all. You are only feeling uncomfortable, "weird," "strange," because you are experiencing something unfamiliar. For most people, the sense of being uncomfortable and *not* in your "comfort zone" is judged and evaluated as "bad," as "wrong," and the coping response kicks in—"Stop everything; go no further."

Of course, a program like that in this context will only undermine your ongoing learning and development. It can effectively con you from stretching and moving into new territory. So just for the moment, and just for the purposes of this exercise, welcome the discomfort, unfamiliarity, etc. and continue to put the principle into your muscle. By doing this, you are giving yourself a chance to try on the principle.

Then, at the end of the pattern, check the ecology. I have used this pattern to coach people in putting the basic NLP Presuppositions into their muscles. And oftentimes, perhaps most of the time, people feel uncomfortable and want to "check the ecology" at the point of feeling discomfort. Yet when they do, it messes things up.

There's a reason for that. The reason is because *any time you check the ecology while **inside** of a system, the old system itself will not want to change.* What is at work at that moment is the principle of self-organizing systems. Don't ask an alcoholic while intoxicated about the ecology of drinking "one more." Don't ask a woman suffering from the pattern of anorexia if it's ecological to avoid eating while she's still thinking and feeling that way. Don't ask about the ecology of public speaking when a person is experiencing anxiety about public speaking.

A new behavior *inside an old system of frames* will feel un-ecological. Even though it is the most effective and healing thing for you it will feel wrong. So when you use the Mind-to-Muscle pattern keep adding more resources until the system itself changes. Choose some great principles, proven principles in the field of your interest, and give yourself permission to feel a little weird until the new mapping reorganizes your mind-body at all of its levels. As you do, you will be embodying your highest principles and setting up self-organizing frames that will allow your mind-body-emotion system to learn a new way to feel and to operate.

The Implementation Process

The design of *implementation* is to weave a concept, idea, model, principle, etc. into the very fabric of your life so that it becomes fully embodied and integrated into your physiology and nervous system. The design is to transfer the ideas, concepts, principles, and mental mapping out of the head so that they become part and parcel of how you live your life, talk, relate, feel, and move through the world. In this, *implementation* is what enables you to use conceptual or abstract information and make it effective for changing your life and unleashing your potentials.

An Implementation Model

Now a fully-fledge and formal model involves four things: a foundational theory, critical success variables, guidelines for using, and patterns as human technology for taking performance to the next level. The following makes these explicit as we embody the ideas and principles.

1) Theoretical Framework

> **A Complete Model**
>
> 1. A theory or theoretical framework
> 2. Critical variables
> 3. Guidelines for using
> 4. Patterns for using

Implementation is actually your natural default program until or unless you learn otherwise. Your mind-body-emotion system works as a whole so that *what you think, you feel,* and *what you feel, you act upon.* The movement from concept to action is natural and normal. As you reason and contemplate something in your cerebral cortex, you send messages to the lower centers of your brain that creates emotions —*e-motions* which highlight the action tendency in every emotion you feel. The *motion* that is then created in your body motivates you to act on, and move out (*ex*, out) from where you were. This is how it normally works and yet you can interfere with this process.

Interference with implementation and embodiment may happen in a number of ways. Among the most common are:

- By painful experiences so that you become traumatized by attempting to implement.
- By prohibitions against acting.
- By ignorance of how to implement something, lacking the specific steps or knowledge, having insufficient knowledge so we don't know how to proceed.
- By the difficulty of the implementation and the inability to overcome that difficulty.
- By being in a state that contradicts or undermines the implementation.
- By failure to follow-through or to consistently persist at a task.
- By negative thinking patterns that create disbelief, skepticism, and doubt.

Without implementation your greatest of ideas, theories, concepts, and principles become *impotent.* You neuter them. It is implementation that makes ideas truly powerful in changing reality. After all, plans have to be executed to effectively make a difference. Planning without implementation is just a mental exercise and one that actually creates frustration and disappointment.

When you implement you translate from a concept into your neurology into your entire nervous system. Your nervous systems are designed for both excitation and inhibition. Implementation involves incorporating the "intelligence" or "knowledge" of the concepts into the entire network so that you do not just "know" it intellectually, but in all of the other ways that you can know things.

It works this way because we are holistic beings. The structure of our mind-body system shows that *we are made to integrate our energies.* When we are not aligned, integrated, then inner conflict occurs and we feel incongruous, conflicted, and inwardly torn. Studies in cognitive dissonance reveal the degree to which we need to be able to use and experience what we know and not just talk about it. When we become aware of the difference between what we know, what we seek to do, what we believe in and what we actually do or achieve, the dissonance creates a human kind of "pain," a psychological pain that we need to reduce and eliminate.

Regarding implementation, we also differ from each other in our different styles and degrees of implementation activity. The *Activity Meta-Program* runs along a continuum from inactive to active, proactive, and then to reactive. Where do you typically experience yourself on this continuum?

Inactive — Reactive — Active — Proactive

2) Components: elements, processes

What are the component elements of the implementation process by which you embody great ideas? What are all of the variables and contributing factors?

- *Concepts,* principles, premises, visions, values, understandings.
- *Nervous systems:* neurology, physiology, network levels.
    - *Exciting:* inciting, provoking, induction of positive emotions, amplifying.
    - *Inhibiting:* dampening, prohibiting, induction of negative emotions, mis-alignments that impede progress.
- *Motor cortex:* signals, commands to the body
- *Habituation:* habits, repetition, learning —> over-learning, "installation."

- *Practice:* practical action, experimentation, trial and error, play.
- *Linkages:* mind signals body, higher levels command nervous system, frames-by-implication (FBI) set invisible frames outside-of-awareness, consciousness governs control, systemic processes, clusters of processes that work together with a synergetic effect.

3) Guidelines:
What are the guidelines of implementation? What rules of thumb, heuristics, etc. govern the embodiment processes?

- Act on what you learn as soon as possible.
- Never leave the scene of a learning, discovery, feeling without doing something about it.
- Start small and simple and build up to greater complexity. Take baby steps. The small details count.
- Reinforce what works, what moves in the right direction.
- Celebrate small successes, count everything as significant that moves you in the right direction.
- Detect and interrupt discounting.
- Translate through the levels of the neuro-semantic network so the concept becomes incorporated into the fabric of the body or business.
- Align all the levels to create focus so that all of the elements work in concert within a meta-framework.
- Because implementation involves both an up-and-down process you can start anywhere. So start where you are and enter the system.
- Create sufficient energy and enthusiasm for the implementation.
- Coach the body to feel an idea by activating every facet of your physiology.
- Because it's the feeling that counts, access states with sufficient intensity as you meta-state new frames.

4) Patterns for Implementation:
What processes as patterns, rituals, and exercises will take a concept to the gut level so that it becomes incorporated in the body and in muscle memory? What mechanisms do you have with teeth in them to translate the great ideas into practice?

Mind-to-Muscle
Meta Yes and No

Excuse Blow-Out
Coaching the Body
Meta-Alignment
Audaciously bold well-formed outcomes
Commitment pattern
Executive decision making
Follow up and follow through
Meta-Kaizen
Tasking
Recording exercises (journaling)

From theory to guidelines to patterns, all of these factors come together to give us a strategy of implementation. As a result, this leads to such qualities as the following:

1) Style of implementation:

Inactively, actively, reactively, proactively
Necessity / desire / possibility
Positive / Negative
Options / procedures
Self / other referent
Internal / external locus of authority

2) Speed of implementation:

How quickly / how slowly
As a whole / piece by piece

3) *Beliefs of implementation*:

Beliefs that support and enhance or beliefs that sabotage, interfere and inhibit.

4) *Identity of implementation*:

Who you are as an implementer, whether your identity allows you to be a person who execute plans and decisions and make things happen.

5) *Decision making style*:

Away from / Toward
Avoidance / Approach

6) *Risk style:*

Approach / Avoidance
Fast and active / slow and reflective

Opportunity for advantage / safe and careful

Installation Process Factor

As a trainer, I want to create an impact. That's also true when I coach, consult, and write— I want to make a difference and have a positive impactful effect upon people. Isn't that true for you as well? Isn't that what all of us are after? You want to have a strong and lasting impact on the people who participate in your trainings and the people with whom you communicate, you consult, lead, manage, coach, even love and care for. We want to have an impact that makes a difference in their minds, hearts, and lives. And you want this impact to endure so that the benefits continue into everyday life at work, home, and in other contexts.

On the other side of the coin, when you train, coach, manage, and lead, the people who you work with similarly want to know that investing their time, effort, and money will be worth it. In the final analysis, they are buying *the impact* and *the difference* that it will make in their lives.

- What difference will this make?
- Will the inspiration, knowledge, and skills I learn last?
- Will the skills transfer back to the real world where I live?
- Will the ideas and skills be available when I need them?
- Will I be able to implement the skills at the critical contexts and times?
- Will I acquire the necessary knowledge and skills offered so that they become mine?
- In Neuro-Semantics our specific aim is to provide training, coaching, and consulting so that participants will learn new ways to run their own brains and manage their lives. To achieve that, it's necessary to know how you can get knowledge into a person's life deep enough so that it will stick. If the learnings, insights, and skills come and go, if they fade away with time, then you have missed something from truly making them yours.
- How do we take new learnings, insights, processes, patterns, and models and get them inside us so that they make a difference in how we think, feel, talk, behave, and relate?
- How do we translate new skills into everyday action?
- How do we transfer them to our workplace, home, recreation, etc.?

Our focus here is on installing the performance so it becomes fully embodied. It is important to know as much as possible about the installation process. To that end we ask:

- What factors play a critical role in the learning process that so thoroughly installs new skills so they become fully embodied?
- What are the components, elements, and contributing factors for incorporating expertise so you have it within you at the level of unconscious competence?

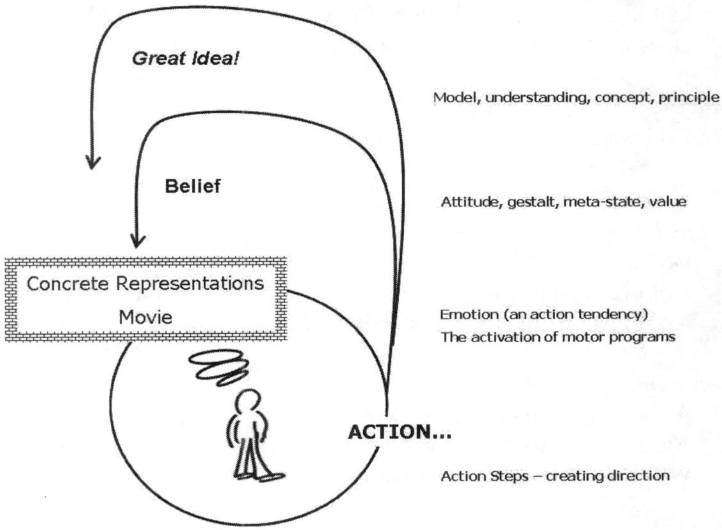

As we work with the mind-body connection, we are working to translate mind to body, conscious awareness to unconscious knowledge, explicit awareness into implicit intuition.

Components and Elements and Questions	**Patterns**
1) Strategy	
Do you have a strategy for engaging in the performance or expertise?	Strategy Elicitation Strategy design New Behavior Generator
2) Clarity	
Have I represented it vividly? Do I have representational clarity? Am I crystal clear about what to do?	Representational Clarity Sensory sizzling Index Questions

3) Emotional intensity	
Does the thought of it make me drool?	Anchoring
Am I in the best emotional state in order to do this?	Propulsion Motivation
4) Motivational energy	
Do I feel a need for it?	Amplification
Do I feel excited about it?	Meta-Stating
5) Fittingness	
Does it fit my life situation?	Meta-Alignment
Is it aligned with my highest values?	Intentionality
Does it fit my meta-programs?	Meta-Program Extension
6) Identity	
Do I want this as part of my identity?	Swish
	Self-Definition
7) Responsibility	
Do I accept responsibility for this?	Owning Powers
Am I responsible for learning it?	Responsibility To / For
Am I responsible for transferring it?	Accountability
8) Experimenting and playing	
Am I willing to play around with it?	Repetition
Am I willing to experiment with it?	Spiraling Matrix
Will I play around with it with others?	
9) Repetition	
Am I willing to repeat it until it becomes second-nature to me?	Rehearsal
	First step Approximations
Will I work with this often enough to make it habitual?	
10) Future pacing.	
Have I put it out into my future?	Time Lines
	Ecology Checks
	Quality Controlling
11) Feedback	
Will I receive sensory feedback?	Receiving Feedback
Will I look for immediate feedback?	
12) Decision	
Am I going to do this?	Decisiveness
Am I committed to doing this?	Commissioning Executive

The Levels of Competency

If installation makes unconscious what you know consciously, then *the embodiment process* is one that starts in conscious awareness and ends in intuitive response. It begins with clumsy self-consciousness of incompetence and ends in the gracious smoothness of unconscious competence.

In this process the unconscious is not good nor is consciousness bad as some have concluded. There are just different levels of "mind." To train your "instincts" in a particular excellence, you move through the levels of conscious and unconscious competency. These conscious and unconscious levels are the development or stages that we typically

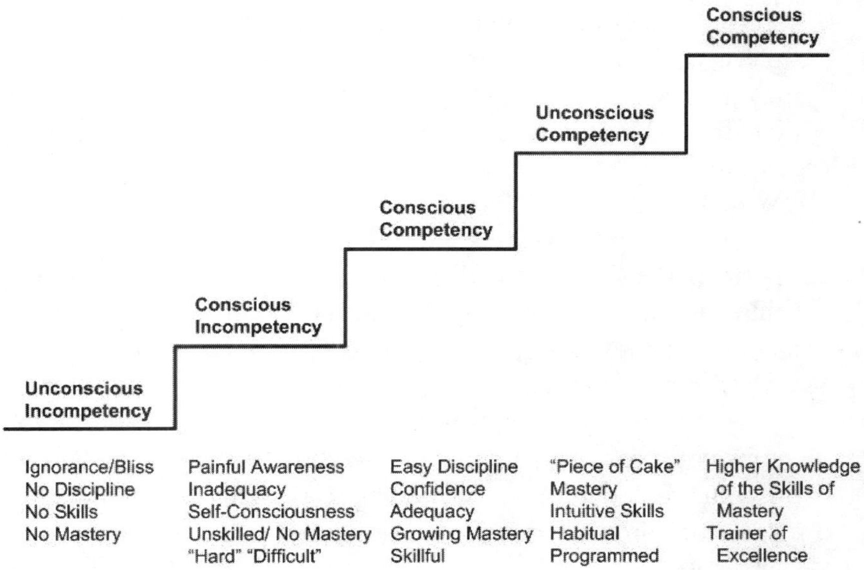

move through as we learn and develop new skills.

Figure 4:3
Up the Competency Levels

Levels of Competency

1) Unconscious Incompetence	*5) Conscious Competence of unconscious competence*
2) Conscious Incompetence	*4) Unconscious Competence*
3) Conscious Competence	*3) Conscious Competence*
4) Unconscious Competence	*2) Conscious Incompetence*
5) Conscious Competence of unconscious competence	*1) Unconscious Incompetence*

1) Unconscious Incompetence

This is where we all begin. Here you are incompetent *and* ignorant of your incompetence. So you feel just fine. You don't know, and you don't know that you don't know. This is the innocence of infancy and childhood.

2) Conscious Incompetence

Then you become *aware* of your incompetence. Here you develop awareness and intelligence about skills and competencies and begin to learn the basics and yet are also aware that you are currently clumsy and incompetent. Generally most of us dislike this stage and find the awareness of our incompetence distressful, even painful.

3) Conscious Competence

Through learning, growth, and development you move to the place where you are able to operate competently and to pull off the performance. In this stage, you are aware of what you can do and how.

4) Unconscious Competence

With habituation of the skills eventually your competency drops out of conscious awareness so that you begin to perform the skill automatically so that you don't even have to think about it. Your competence is now completely intuitive.

5) Conscious Competence of Unconscious Competence

After you have integrated a performance so it is unconscious and intuitive you can bring those intuitions back into consciousness so that you can talk about what you are doing as you are doing it thereby moving to yet a higher level where you can provide conscious training for the unconscious expertise.

Moving Through the Competence Stages

In apprenticing yourself to any discipline, you move through the developmental stages of competence. As such, you always begin with incompetence. At first, you have no skill and you don't even know that you don't. In this blissful state of ignorance you are *unconsciously incompetent.* Here there is no discipline, no learning, no skill development, no challenge. Here you live in your Garden of Eden—blissful, happy, and nakedly ignorant. You are unskilled, unchallenged, and unable to perform in a domain of excellence.

Then you become conscious. Light appears and you realize that a whole new world of excitement, skill, expertise, and knowledge exists.

You bite into the forbidden fruit of the "Tree of the Knowledge of Good and Evil." Yet this creates a certain amount of anxiety, pressure, distress, and unpleasantness. You now become *consciously incompetent.* Here you face for the first time some of the reality constraints about what it would take to become competent, the work, the process, the struggle, and the challenge. Here you feel confused, inadequate, incomplete, "dumb," and incapable of handling this domain. And so you are.

In the stage of *conscious incompetence* you will strongly feel tempted to run back to the Garden of Innocence. That's because you don't like knowing or feeling your incompetence. None of us do. And if you run programs of comparison, perfectionism, impatience, etc., you may get into a state of self-judgment.

> "I hate being put down like this." "What's wrong with me that I can't get this?" "Why does it have to be so hard?" "I'll never get this."

In conscious incompetence the "discipline" of apprenticing yourself to the new domain seems hard, overwhelming, uncomfortable, and rigorous. Many people turn back at this point. They refuse to go on because they don't have a good relationship with learning itself, with unsuccessful attempts, with using so-called "failure" and "mistakes" as just feedback. They don't seem to know how to give themselves a chance—an opportunity to grow, develop, and get better. They don't embrace and accept the incompetence as just one stage along the way. They judge and evaluate themselves harshly. If only they would take a kinder and gentler approach, validating and celebrating every little step of progress.

Yet if you do the "work" in the second stage, you find yourself eventually in the marvelous and wonderful place of the third stage. In *conscious competence* you feel great. Here the discipline seems easy and delightful. You have attained a level of competence and so enjoy it as a skill, confidence and continual development. You have become a practitioner in the science or art. You know your business, and you do it well. And though you know that you have many more things that you can develop, you delight in the level of mastery that you have attained.

Eventually, this habituates so that you *lose awareness* regarding how you do what you do. You forget where the keys are on the keyboard.

Yet your fingers know. As it drops outside of awareness, you have stepped into the next level of development—*unconscious competence.* The discipline now seems like "a piece of cake." You experience it as "No problem." You can do it without your conscious mind. The programs for the competencies have become installed in your very neurology. Now you do it "intuitively." There is literally an "in-knowing" (in-tuition) about the skills. Here the mastery has become quite pronounced.

We find experts at the level of *unconscious competence.* Yet this also means that the expert, typically, will *not* be able to explain his or her expertise. They just *do* it. They have lost awareness of how they do it.

What's beyond that? Moving up to a newer and more complex level of *conscious competence of unconscious competence.* Here you bring your competence back into awareness and become aware of its structure, form, and process. You do that so that you can teach others how to do this. This is the level of masters.

We all have walked this pathway of competence and have done so many times in our lives. We have walked it with regard to learning to talk, walk, meet and greet people, tie our shoes, drive a car, enter a profession, and a thousand other things. This explains how we can know something so intuitively. We just know how to type, drive, hit a ball, etc. The knowing is inside our mind-body system at an unconscious level. It got in through intentions, attention, and practice because we put it in as we moved it through the levels of competence.

The Myth of Unconscious Installation

It is precisely because you can and do put things into your "unconscious mind," as you habituate and integrate knowledge that the question of unconscious installation arises. One question on the mind of many people is, "Can we just bypass consciousness and install unconsciously?"

Other factors also encourage this question: *impatience* with the competency levels, *unwillingness* to embrace the conscious incompetence level, and *unwillingness* to accept the discipline of practice and habituation. There are also the old myths about subliminal programming from the old 1950s studies. Once upon a time when our knowledge was more naive about human psychology, we thought that we could subliminally install or program in messages. By the 1960s in the USA there were even laws forbidding such(!).

Some of this came from an unfounded conclusion that arose when Penfield began the early explorations into the neuro-sciences. When he began opening up brains and stimulating parts of the brain with a tiny electrode, he found that it would at times trigger such vivid memories that the person would report being there again, seeing, hearing, feeling, smelling, and tasting what was there originally. Then some people draw an unfounded and fallacious conclusion from this, "We remember everything we have ever encountered."

Today we know better. Our nervous system and neurology does *not* work like a photographic plate or computer chip in recording information. As we take data in and process it, we model it by deleting, generalizing, and distorting the information in the encoding. And that information will degrade if we don't keep refreshing it. We can and do forget things.

So can we bypass the conscious mind and install things in our "unconscious mind?" The answer is yes and no.

Yes, we can but the content of what we put into the unconscious mind is not complex content information or competencies. What we can install are feelings, response potentials, and moods. Accordingly, most "unconscious" or other-than-conscious training creates *response potential* and *motivational states.* By using various hypnotic processes you can set a person up to notice, to be motivated, and to be occupied with something. You can use sentence fragments, non-closure (not finishing statements), fail to close loops and in these ways evoke a response of interest, curiosity, or discontent. That's what we can install unconsciously. We can do this using post hypnotic suggestions, embedded commands, and therapeutic metaphors.

But *no,* you cannot bypass the conscious mind and install complete skills or complex knowledge in the unconscious. It doesn't work like that. In spite of people sleeping with tape-recorders under their pillows, listening to subliminal tapes, and trying various DHE (Design Human Engineering)[2] processes, for transferring any skill or knowledge into the unconscious mind, it doesn't work.

The idea that you can *bypass* the conscious mind and install directly into the unconscious level is a troubling assumption that has numerous problems. First it assumes that there are some complex skills that have been so installed. But what are they? Can you install the knowledge and skills for flying a plane *unconsciously*? Can you hypnotize a person and install that? What about running a printing press? How about trading on the stock market? What about surgery, dentistry, surveying, architecture, speaking foreign languages, etc.? Well, what about something as simple as driving a car? Could you by-pass the rebellious mind of a teenager and install good driving skills in the unconscious? Find out a way to do that or any of these other things and you'll become a mutli-millionaire!

Even people highly gifted and talented in these areas have to invest years of study and practice to become skilled. No one has yet found a short-cut to apprenticeship in such disciplines. *Mastery comes through consciousness.*

The fact is that when it comes to installing high level concepts and principles into muscle, *every expert in every field has to go through the learning process of apprenticing him or herself to the discipline* and using the neurological mechanisms of repetition, rehearsal, and patterning of the muscles. We do that with typing, skating, riding a bicycle, playing basketball or tennis, driving a car, piloting a plane. This muscle memory later results as our well trained intuitions. Then we "intuitively" know how to perform the task and the actions and that moves us to the level of unconscious competence.

Where is there any evidence that complex skills can be installed in a person without going through the conscious learning process? Sure we can install a fleeting feeling, but complex skills? Yet what are the patterns for bypassing the apprenticeship-mastery process? It is precisely because we do not have "instincts" for how-to-do things as animals do that we have to learn. We have to use our minds to figure things out. What we lose in the lack of instincts we gain in openness, learning, flexibility, and choice.

Howard Gardner's extensive studies into the biographies of many geniuses of the twentieth century (*Creating Minds*) led him to conclude that mastery in any field, mastery that leads to actual breakthroughs in those fields almost always takes the genius ten years— this is now recognized as the famous "Ten Year Rule."

The very idea of bypassing the conscious mind and engaging "unconscious installation" directly is a very questionable process because it confuses a predisposition and an aptitude with content knowledge; it confuses content knowledge with actual competency. It ignores the fact that domains of background knowledge support skills. In so rejecting theory, conscious understanding, and working with the higher structures of mind, the so-called "unconscious installation" actually works to prevent one from learning the skills.

There's another problem with all of this: It create a false split in the mind, a war between the conscious and unconscious part of the mind. When we over-emphasize the *unconscious* part of mind to the neglect of the *conscious* part, we split mind so that we value one part over the other. As *mind* is a holistic phenomena it never helps to put it at odds with itself.

Therefore any attempt to train the unconscious without involving consciousness distorts our understanding of how each part interfaces with the other. Sure we can use hypnotic language patterns of embedded commands, isomorphic metaphors, etc., and get some "unconscious" responses from people. We can get them scratching their noses, feeling the need to empty their bladder, and even not noticing pain as we engage them with something entrancingly compelling. Yet these are hardly the high quality skills that we seek to model from experts.

There is finally the problem that *if* we could install something *unconsciously* so that we could just intuitively and naturally perform some skill without knowing how it happens. Suppose we could, we would then *not* have the ability to recover our conscious learning because we were not conscious in the first place.

When my daughter Jessica turned sixteen and wanted to learn to drive, I found that I had to bring my unconscious and intuitive way of driving a standard shift transmission back into consciousness. At first I felt clumsy and it felt awkward trying to become aware again of how I was releasing the accelerator as my left foot was engaging the clutch and my hand was shifting the gears and so on. Yet as I began talking out loud about what I was doing, *as I was doing it,* I became conscious again of the processes. And because I could, I could then show my daughter what I was doing and coach her to do the same. If this skill had been installed unconsciously, I would not have been able to recover it consciously.

So if by-passing the conscious mind is *not* the way to go in order to fully embody and integrate a great idea, principle, or insightful learning, we are now sent back to our original focus. Now we can return to discover how to work effectively with our mind-body system.

* META-YES-ING

In terms of installing, a know-how knowledge or principle, there's nothing more powerful than the innocent *Yes.* With *Yes* you can induce *a state of confirmation and validation.* And because of this, you are thereby able to install or embody ideas and understandings at all levels of your mind. Saying *Yes!* Has the possibility of validating an idea, emotion, event, person, etc.

This reveals the meaning value of a *Yes* and the special nature of a *Yes state.* It's a very special and powerful state for incorporating things. That's why you have to be careful what you say *Yes* to. Because it validates and confirms, it welcomes and invites things into your minds and life. This is how you install most of the things that you have inside your mind-and-emotion system.

> *It is through saying a great big, bold, and passionate "Yes!" that you welcome things into your world.*

The design of this pattern is to validate inspiring *thoughts* and understandings so that you can transform them into *beliefs.* Once you do that and have a belief, it becomes a command to the nervous system and initiates a self-organizing process.

The Pattern:

1) Access a strong and robust "Yes!"

Is there anything that you can think about to which every fiber of your being can say **"Yes!"** and can say *Yes* without any question or doubt?

Do you have anything like that?

Be with that sense of *Yes!* and let it grow and double, and what does that feel like? Do you like that?

What is the breath of *Yes*?

How do you express *Yes* with your eyes, face, and voice?

2) Amplify that "Yes!"

As you experience the **"Yes!"** notice the neurology and feeling of your **"Yes!"** and how it feels, what feelings does that create in you? How does it feel?

Notice the voice of **"Yes!"** Gesture the **"Yes!"** with your hands and body.

As you amplify this **"Yes!"** until it radiates your entire body, what is the most powerful facet of this state?

How fully do you have the *Yes state?*

3) Apply this "Yes!" to the thought you want to believe or to a feeling you want to commission to be yours

And feeling that **"Yes!"** even more fully, utter it repeatedly to the empowering thought that you want to turn into a belief.

Do you want this? Really?

How many more times do you need to say **"Yes!"** right now in order to feel that you have fully welcomed it into your presence?

4) YES the "Yes!" repeatedly and put into your future

This is only an exercise and so you can't keep this!

You really want this?

Would this improve your life?

Would it be valuable to you?

Afterwords

The power of confirmation, of saying *Yes*, is powerful beyond what most people dare imagine. Perhaps because it is such a small word or such a common experience. After all we say *yes* hundreds of times a day.

> "Yes, that's right." "Yes, that's true." "Yes, that's the way it is." "Yes, that's real." "Yes, I like that." "Yes, I want that." "Yes, that would be good."

Yet it is in saying *yes* that you confirm things, that you validate what's real to you or not, valued by you or not, recognized as part of your understanding of reality or not. The word *yes* is your verbal expression of welcoming ideas, understandings, beliefs, decisions, feelings, and experiences into your world . By *Yes* you are able to fill up the inner space of your life.

Yes also transforms a mere *thought* or awareness into a nervous-system-commanding *belief.* This begins to explain the near-magical power of *yes* and the state of confirmation. Say *yes* to a thought or idea, no matter how stupid, dysfunctional, toxic, or hurtful often enough and you will come to "believe" it. That is, you will come to consider it and respond to it as if it were true and real. Then you will not only think it, but believe it. It will feel real to you. You will feel sure and confident about it. And this is when damage, semantic damage, can occur. *Yes* is your power of creating reality, by it you "make things real" to yourself.

Have you ever validated and confirmed an idea that's toxic, limiting, and hurtful? Your *Yes* brought it in and confirmed it as a frame. And if you have confirmed your confirmation and closed off any possibility of it not being true to you, you have set up a self-organizing process with that belief, a process that will *make that idea real to you* as much as it can.

Yes expresses the confirmation state and it is by confirmation that we validate and so make a thought or emotion real to us. So before you say *yes* to something, consider if you really want to *make it real* inside yourself.

* WILD EXPERIMENTING

The sooner after you learn, feel, or decide something, and the sooner you act on it, the more likely you will take your learning, feeling, or decision and *embody* it. If that's a principle of closing the knowing-doing gap, then you should choose to never leave the scene of a learning, decision, or feeling without doing something. This principle goes back to William James who argued that the way to integrate something is to act on it as soon as possible. Taking action in this manner also enables you to develop a bias for action.

William James wrote the following at the beginning of the twentieth century in *Psychology: A Briefer Course.*

> "Never should we suffer ourselves to have an emotion at a play, concert, or upon reading a book, without expressing it afterward in some active way. Let the expression be the least thing in the world—speaking genially to one's grandmother . . . but let it not fail to take place. ... If we let our emotions

evaporate, they get into a way of evaporating."

The key is the timing—acting on what you learn as quickly as possible. Quickly applying a conceptual understanding to a real life situation helps with the translation while the knowing or feeling is hot.

The Pattern:

1) Identify a learning or feeling you immediately acted on.

Have you ever learned or felt something and immediately did something about it?

What did you decide that you immediately translated into action?

When, where, with whom, and how did you do this?

As you go back into state, what were the factors that empowered you to do this?

2) Give yourself permission to do something no matter how small.

Do you have permission to *take immediate action* on something?

If not, then give yourself permission and notice what arises within you. How well does it settle? How long will you need to repeat the permission until it fully takes?

Do you need to qualify the permission with keeping the response small, for a short time frame, etc.?

3) Set a belief system (matrix) of supporting frames.

What would you need to believe to take some small action of response whenever you learn, feel, or decide on something?

How much do you believe that?

What belief would support that first belief?

[Repeat this several times until you elicit a matrix of supportive belief frames.]

* PERSONALIZING

The process and experience that we call *personalizing* is another installation pattern par excellence. It is a way to *identify with* something in such a way as to make the object of your identification yours. That same is true of any identity frame. By identifying with something you define it as your own and bring it into yourself. Yet you have to be very careful what and how you identify yourself with things.

Within General Semantics, Korzybski (1933/1994) emphasized the absolute danger of un-mindfully *identifying,* which he said inevitably leads to unsanity and if unchecked, to insanity. As a semantic class of life you have the ability to create the experience of identification, that is, to take something outside of yourself and to *identify* it as part of yourself.

In identifying or personalizing, we use the tiniest of words, we use the "to be" verbs. "He *is* an idiot!" "You *are* wonderful!" In English, we language identity frames with the "to be" verbs (is, am, are, was, were, be, being, etc.). This creates the "is" of identity. Now identifying things sends commands to your neurology to consider the two "the same," and "real."

In Neuro-Semantics we say that which saves us from the unsanity of identifying is mindfulness and choice about what and how we identify. Suppose you began to personalize what you *do* to make a living. That would lead to: "I *am* a coach." "I *am* a manager." "I *am* an employee." If you mindfully identify with something as a matter of choice and know what and why you are doing it, and doing so as a construct, then you can use identification to intentionally personalize in a healthy way that will do no semantic damage.

The Pattern:

1) Choose a frame (idea, state, emotion, etc.) that you want to identify with.

If you were to consciously choose something that you would like to identify with, what would it be?
What frame would you welcome as part of your self-defining?
What happens when you personalize it by saying, "This is about me!"?
How much more do you need to suck it in fully to make it

yours?

2) Quality control the identification frame.

As you check the ecology of identifying yourself in this way, does it truly serve you well?

Once you set this, violation of this frame will generate one of the greatest pains we humans experience—the pain of being untrue to ourselves. It leads to feelings of being incongruent, inconsistency, inauthentic, false to self, hypocritical, guilty, wrong, etc.

Does this identification or personalizing have the kind of quality that you want?

3) Say and link "mine!" with your identifying.

Access the state of "mine" (or ownership) and claim it fully.

Will you *own* this?

Is it yours?

4) Identify yourself with the frame.

Recall a time when you positively identified with something and you had the experience of being so connected to it that you *personalized* it.

[Menu list: a pet dog or cat, a girlfriend, school, etc.]

Is this who you *"are?"*

Is this who you'd like to be?

Define, describe, and vividly represent the frame you desire and value as part of your identity. See yourself in terms of the frame.

Use dramatic vividness to spice up this new self-definition so that it begins to really pull on you. "The me with this frame of mind."

5) Quality control it into your future.

Now notice what it's like as you imagine moving into the days and weeks and years to come with this self-definition . . . do you like this?

Is it ecological for all your relationships?

* REHEARSAL

One of the most dependable and predictable ways to install something inside your mind-body system so it becomes completely embodied is by using repetition. *Repetition* gives you a direct, simple, and very reliable installation tool. In rehearsal you "burn a circuit," as it were, in your nervous system as you repeatedly use your neuro-pathways so that you are much more likely to think that way, emote that way, and act that way again. This explains the proverb, "Repetition is the mother of all learning."

> *"No one makes the jump the first time."*
> The Matrix

The Pattern:

1) Embrace the process of repetition.

What kind of a relationship do you have with the idea or the experience of *repetition?*

Do you like the idea? To test your relationship with rehearsal, think about and declare to yourself, "I will rehearse the idea, state, or frame of . . ." Now notice what happens.

Do you have permission to rehearse?

Are you willing to rehearse?

Does anything stop you from rehearsing?

Do you have a good relationship with the *idea* of rehearsal?

Will you rehearse? When? How often?

How much spirit will you put into your rehearsal?

2) Make an empowering decision to repeat the frame.

Whenever you discover a great frame, never leave the scene of that discovery without making a decision to set it as your frame, and never leave without taking some action to shape and reinforce it.

Have you made a decision about this idea?

Will you, from this day forward, use this as your frame of reference and your frame of mind?

What can you do that will act out and embody with all of your body this frame?

What state does this frame initiate?

How does it show up in your posture, face, tone of voice?

3) Anchor a looping state of mind for installation.

Recall a time when you had something going round and round and round in your mind that you couldn't shake. Then anchor and use that feeling and experience as a template for the new frame. [Set anchor]

What is the new idea, emotion, state, or frame that you want to keep repeating until it becomes yours?

Really, that's what you want? [Amplifying state]

And it's strong? [Fire anchor]

4) Put it into your future by connecting to various times and places in your everyday life.

What are the context markers in your everyday that will cue the new frame?

What will you see or hear?

As you imagine that now, just *feel* [fire anchor] it continuing . . . looping until you know it is yours . . . how does that feel?

* SWISHING TO AN IMPLEMENTING IDENTITY

If you personalize the implementation process and completely identify with it, you might then think-and-feel, "I *am* an implementor." "I embody my beliefs and decisions." Doing this would then make implementation even more natural as it simply becomes a part of you who are.

- Do you have an implementation identity?
- Would you like to?

The *Swish Pattern* offers an identity or self-definition approach to installation. It enables you to directionalize your mind-body system to move toward the kind of person you want to be. Do you have a clear, vivid, and compelling internal image of *the you* for whom implementing and taking effective action is no problem?

This pattern focuses on creating an imaginative *me* for whom implementing knowledge in appropriate and ecological ways is no problem. This pattern facilitates you to see, hear, and feel the "resourceful me" fully and completely. The only questions now are: Where would you like to use this creative image? With whom? When?

The Pattern:

1) Identify an unresourceful trigger.

What trigger sets off some old response that you don't like and which does not serve to enhance your personal excellence in life?
When does this occur?
Where? With whom?
What is the trigger?
Do you have an image of the trigger that elicits the unresourceful response?
What does it look like?
What does it sound like?
If I could peak into the theater of your mind and see and hear what triggers the unresourceful feelings, what would I see?

2) Create a new resourceful trigger.

What would *the masterful you* for whom it would be no problem or challenge to put your knowledge into action be like?
Are you able to describe this fully and completely so that it's compelling and exciting? Are you willing to do that?
Have you imagined it so vividly that it feels compelling to you yet?
As you design the compelling image of *the masterful you* as someone who knows and can handle the everyday tasks involved in a given area, how does that feel?
What else can you do to juice it up so that it becomes more and more compelling and attractive?

3) Link the two images.

Clear the screen of your mind of the images and beginning with the old cue image that evokes the old unenhancing response, are you ready to link the new image to it?
Good, then in the middle of the picture, shrink down the picture of *the You who is an implementation pro* until you see it as a tiny dot in the middle of the other picture. Do you have that?

In just a moment, you will let the cue picture fade out and move back *and as it does*, let *the masterful you* picture quickly and immediately swish in to fill the screen of your mind. Do this in the time it takes you to say, *"Swish!"* Are you ready? Then, *go!*

4) Swish repeatedly to this new self-image.

As you repeat this process five times, what are you noticing? Make sure that you *clear your internal "screen"* after each swish. Direct the images so that you go only *from* the problem *to* the resourceful image. This will directionalize your brain and allow you to install the new image of yourself as an implementor.

Have you repeated the process five times being careful to clear the screen each time?

5) Test this by thinking about the old trigger.

What happens?

Do you naturally and automatically swish to *the resourceful and masterful you* image of you as an implementation pro?

* META-STATING PROACTIVITY

There's a difference between taking action in the moment and proactively planning ahead of time for a chosen response or plan of action that supports your effectiveness. *Proactivity* is about your readiness and ability to act ahead of time when there is no pressure or urgency to act. Proactivity refers to taking action in anticipation of things yet to come. Proactivity goes beyond simply being active. And because it refers to being active prior to when the action is called for or needed by the external events, it has to be internally driven—driven by our values and visions. Do you have a proactive sense of self? Would you like to think of yourself in that way?

The Pattern:

1) Access a proactive identity.

Imagine *the you* who thinks and acts and responds to the things of importance to you *proactively*.

Is this already part of your self-definition and self-identity?

Would you like it to be?
How would that be valuable to you?
Would there be any other benefits?

2) Create a vivid and compelling movie in your mind of *the proactive you.*

What does the proactive you look like?
Sound like?
How does he or she move and interact?
As you step into that movie and try it on, what is that like?
Are there any changes that you'd like to make in editing this new sense of self?

3) Edit your movie to make it incredibly compelling.

How else could you enrich this movie?
Is it compelling enough so that it's unforgettable?
What would endow it with that quality?
Have you edited *a sense of the future* into your movie so that the proactive you is able to track activities to initiate now for the days, weeks, and months to come? How does that change things?

4) Commission it as part of your identity.

Rise up in your mind to your executive level where you make decisions.
Are you ready to commission this as part of your way of being in the world?
Would you like to do that now?

5) Extend your time perspective

Research has shown that the higher a person rises in a society, the longer that person's time perspective into the future. Those with longer time perspectives are willing to pay the price of success for a long, long time before they achieve it.
How far out does your time-line go?
How far does it go out around a specific performance?
What happens if you extend your time-line for a longer perspective?

6) Leverage your productivity by prioritizing

What are the most important things you need to do every day, that if you did, would give you more leverage over your

productivity?
What are the activities that you do that are of highest priority?
What activities contribute most to your success?
What activities or skills make (or could make) the most difference?
Where in your life would *timeliness* enrich your productivity?

7) Leverage your time management via focus concentration.
Access a concentrated single-minded state to use to do that one thing at a time and to finish it.
Are you willing to discipline yourself to concentrate single-mindedly on the most important thing you have to do?
Would task completion give you a surge of energy, enthusiasm, and/or self-confidence?

* TIME FOR A CHANGE

How you choose to allocate time to something is an important message about what matters to you. When what you say matters to you and the time you devote to the activities that manifest your dreams are congruent, then you have integrity. How do we create *time* for the changes that we want? This pattern answers that question as it enables you to create the time for the changes that you choose to enhance your life.

The Pattern:

1) Identify an important goal. **(Meaning)**
What's important to you that you want to do and know it's important, but don't seem to get around to doing?
What change do you want to make?
What goal do you want to create time for in your life, even one which may be hard or challenging?
What goal do you want to create for yourself as a coach?
What goal do you want to create for what you *do* as a coach?
What goal do you want to create for your coaching as a business practice?

2) Index the Change **(Intention about Time)**
How much time would you ideally like to devote to this goal?
How often? Daily or weekly? Minimally? Maximally?
How long of a time? How short? Are you doing it now? To

what extent?
How much time do you actually devote to it? What are the numbers?
How much time would you typically allocate to it?

3) Identify your Intentions. **(Intention)**

Why do you want to make this change? What will this give you?
How important is it?
Do you have a big enough *"Why"* to do it?

4) Access Resources. **(Power)**

Do you know how to do this? Do you have a strategy? The skills?
What are the three most critical resources you need to be able to pull this off?
What is the one or two other resources that may not be critical but would flavor the quality of your experience in a new and unique way?
What frames would you have to have in order to experience the integrity to do this?
Have you made a commitment?

5) Access Self Frames. **(Self)**

Who do you need to be to make this happen? What shifts in your self-definition do you need to make?
What resources for your self-definition, self-esteem, identity, and so on?

6) Access Intentionality and Time.

Do you really want this? How much do you?
Do you want this enough to devote the minimum time?
Can anything now stop you?

7) Confirm and Solidify.

What is it like when you put this into your immediate future?
Are you aligned with this? Do you like this?
Will you do this?
Will your executive mind take charge to make this happen?

End of Chapter References

1. For more about the *coalescing* of the higher levels, see *Meta-States* (2000), *NLP Going Meta* (2004). For more about meta-states being the source of most meta-programs see Chapter Four about that in *Figuring Out People* (2005).

2. DHE stands for *Design Human Engineering,* a model developed by Richard Bandler in the early 1990s. He had hoped that it would complement, perhaps even replace, the NLP model that he had co-created with Dr. John Grinder. It was based upon the assumption that instead of modeling experts and expertise, why not start with the idea of simply *designing* skills and performances, whether there's anyone who has ever yet achieved such, and installing it. If we had a cyborg and put simply install a "program" or set of instructions that would create a certain performance, what programs would we want to create and engineer for humans? The model and trainings were playful and creative, mostly a function of trance and how we inwardly represent information in the sensory-systems. Yet it went nowhere. See my critique on DHE on www.neurosemantics.com *Ten Years and Still No Beef.*

Chapter 5

ELIMINATING PERFORMANCE BLOCKS AND INTERFERENCES

If you know what to do, if you have a plan for how to do it, if you have the capability to carry out the strategy, if you have a robust intention to execute your strategy, along with supporting beliefs and decisions— you are well along on your way to achieving peak performance. With all of that in place, the time has now come to ask some other critical questions:

- Can anything stop you?
- Could anything interfere with your progress and success?
- Do you have the resilience to bounce back if you experience a set-back?
- Are you unstoppable?

If you take time to answer these questions around an activity or performance that you have been working on, then they will enable you to identify *any interference* or barrier that's internal or external which might undermine your performance. What are the things that can block and interfere with your best performances? Here's a checklist of some possibilities:

- Negative emotions that you don't handle adequately
- "Dragon" states (unresourceful states, negative states turned against you)
- Fear and the fear emotions: timidity, apprehensiveness, worry, etc.
- Excuses, "reasons," explanations
- Procrastination / Perfectionism
- Habits

- Indecisiveness, lack of decisiveness
- Refusal to give up "options."

Because numerous things can get in your way and interfere with your best intentions, I have included the following patterns as part of the strategy of clearing your pathway and eliminating any and everything that blocks your way. Precisely because various thoughts, emotions, memories, fears, frames, beliefs, etc. can get in your way and prevent the implementation of a great idea, sometimes you have to clear space before you can even begin with the installation.[1]

* META-STATING EMOTIONS

More often than not, the problems you have with emotions are with what we call the *negative* emotions. Yet it is possible that you also may have problems with positive ones (tenderness, vulnerability, openness, spirituality, etc.). Yet to be emotionally intelligent, you need to develop a strong and powerful relationship to both positive and negative emotions.

Neuro-Semantics distinguishes *feelings* from *emotions.* Feelings are just kinesthetic sensations and your body are designed to register and recognize thousands of sensations: cold, hot, tense, relaxed, rough, smooth, etc. Sensations or feelings are part and parcel of an emotion, but are not sufficient to be considered a full fledged "emotion." For that you also need a piece of cognition—some awareness of the meaning, value, and evaluation which you give to something. And when you have this, you have a meta-state. So an "emotion" structurally is actually a meta-state. We like or dislike (the higher level interpretation) the smoothness or roughness (the pure sensation or feeling). We are disgusted or delighted (a meta-level belief) by the taste being sweet or sour (the sensation).

An emotion is therefore *the difference* between what you have mapped in your mind about something and what you are experiencing in the world due to that map. It's like a balancing set of scales. On one side are your inner maps of understandings and beliefs. On the other side are your experiences in reality. If they balance out, no emotion, no "urge to move or move (*motion*) out (*ex*)." That's what an emotion is, *a somatic urge activated by our motor cortex to move out from where we are to somewhere else.*

This creates either *inhibitory* or *excitatory* impulses in your neuro-pathways as the message of the emotion is either stop or go. The *stop* emotions are what we experience as "negative" because like the brakes of a car, they *move* you to stop, look, listen for danger to our maps—to your meanings and values. In some way the scale is shifted downward so that you are *not* getting in the world what you had mapped so you feel upset, frustrated, anger, fearful, scared, sad, disgusted, etc.

The *go* emotions are like the accelerator in a car in that they give you the message of "everything is right on target, keep going." So you feel pleased, contented, delighted, passionate, joyful, fun, playful, curious, relaxed, caring, compassionate, etc. The scale has shifted upward so that your mapping results in success in navigating the territory.

The first insight from this is a pretty radical realization for many people. Namely, *all emotions are right.* They are right to the maps from which they come and the experiences that they create. Consider that. They are always right. You cannot be *wrong* in what you feel. You can be miserable or ecstatic, that whatever you feel *makes sense* given how you have mapped things. What you feel may be the result of some really screwed up maps or some really incompetent skills, but they are still right given *that map* in relation to that *experience.*

If you have a map that people should never use a strained tone in speaking, then every time someone feels stress and tenses the vocal chords and strains his or her voice, you will feel upset, attacked, insulted, or whatever meanings you give to that experience. You will be sensitive to the other person's tone of voice. Your emotion makes sense and is right. It is right to your map.

Consequently, if every emotion is always right, then you can fully and completely *accept all of your emotions.* Indeed this is the first step to emotional intelligence. Emotions are just emotions. Now you can meta-state yourself with that idea—they are *just* emotions. They are not commands from heaven, they are not infallible messages. They are not urges that you have to act on, they are just a bodily feeling of "moving out" energy.

With acceptance and acknowledgment of emotions as emotions, you are now at a place of decision. You can choose:

- Shall I listen to this emotion or not?
- Shall I take counsel from this emotion?
- Is it wise to act on this feeling?

You can also explore:

- Where does this emotion come from?
- When I trace it back to the mental map out of which it came, is that map realistic, accurate, useful, appropriate in this context, etc.?

All of this enables you to meta-state or frame your emotions with acceptance, appreciation, curiosity, exploration, acknowledgment, testing, etc. And when you do that, you generate a higher emotional intelligence. Now you can *have* your emotions rather than them having you.

But if you meta-state your emotions with "negative" emotions, if you *hate, despise, reject, contempt, fear, anger at, guilt, shame, etc.* your basic emotions, you thereby set a frame that will create a war inside of you when you have the tabooed and prohibited emotion. "Boys shouldn't cry!" is a message that has caused many of us guys to bring *shame* and *rejection* to our sadness. And when we do that, we are no longer free to feel sad. Now we *attack ourselves, our experiences, and our emotion.* This creates what we call a dragon state.

This also leads to a basic Neuro-Semantic principle for emotional intelligence and mastery:

> Whenever you bring *negative emotional energies* (negative thinking and feeling) **against** yourself (or against any conceptual facet of yourself) you put yourself at odds with yourself. This turns your psychological energies **against** yourself in unuseful, non-productive, and typically toxic ways. It creates "dragon" or highly unresourceful states.

The Pattern:

1) Identify an emotional state with which you have difficulties handling.

What negative emotional state of thought-or-emotion do you not like, can't stand, hate, wish you didn't experience?

What negative states do you feel as "taboo" or prohibit?

Menu List: Anger, fear, disgust, regret, bitterness, sexual, sensitivity, tenderness, vulnerability, etc.

2) Check and give yourself permission.

As you go inside, quiet yourself, and utter a new permission, "I give myself permission to feel X," notice any and all internal responses that might arise as you say this, and what happens?

How well does that settle inside?

What objections, if any, may arise to this?

What resources would you need to access in order to more fully accept this?

How do you need to reframe the meaning of the emotion?

How well do things settle when you give yourself permission congruently with a strong and resourceful voice?

"I give myself permission to feel anger because it allows me to recognize things that violate my values and to take appropriate action early."

"I give myself permission to feel the tender emotions because it makes me more fully human."

3) Meta-State the negative emotion with a powerful resource.

What resources do you need?

What frames do you want to set about the emotion?

Menu List: acceptance, appreciation, calmness, thoughtfulness, fallibility, playfulness, etc.

How does it transform things when you access and amplify each resource?

4) Quality control the permission and add needed reframes.

Imagine fully and completely moving into your tomorrows with this outframe on the negative emotion . . . does any part of you object to letting this operate as your orientation style?

What other resources do you need to add?

5) Put into your future and install with Meta-Yes-ing.

Would you like this to be how you move through the world as your new orientation?
Would this empower you as a person?
Would it enhance your life?
Are you aligned with this? Any objections?

* DANCING WITH DRAGONS

Sometimes things get in your way and prevent or stop you from effectively implementing what you know. These negative and impoverishing states fall into two broad categories, those that need *taming and transforming* and those that need *slaying*. So here we will tame our "dragons" that involve legitimate emotions in their own right, emotions which simply need to be contextualized, tempered, understood, and qualified. And we will slay the "dragons" that are comprised of thought viruses and that are sick and toxic through and through.

"Dragons" here is a metaphor to describe non-enhancing, non-productive, problematic, un-useful, and toxic states. Obviously, all states do not serve us equally well. Some can make life a living hell. Some feel like "dragon" states; some turn us into dragons! Effective state-management skills enable us to shrink down the dragons, tame them (put their energies to positive uses), or to slay them.

Since you cannot fully succeed until you take care of your internal "dragons," you need to deal with these internal conflicts that tear you up, sabotage your best efforts, turn your energies against yourself, or that prevent you from becoming congruent and aligned, you can't move on. The design in this is to eliminate self-sabotaging states and to tame energies that seem out of control, to put a stop to all interferences so that you can more fully unleash your inner genius.

There are five basic steps for dealing with and dancing with dragons. These are not necessarily in the order or sequence you will use. Start by attempting to name the dragon and then do whatever seems most appropriate as you *chase the dragon* and circle his cave. You may have to do that many times before you get the real dragon.

1) Name the Dragon
2) Embrace the Dragon: Kiss the Dragon

3) Analyze the Dragon with precision questions
4) Starve or Interrupt the Dragon
5) Outframe or meta-state the Dragon

The Pattern:

1) Identify and explore the primary state reference.

What works as a "dragon" to you?
Is it an emotion, behavior, tone, or volume?
What belief, memory, concept, etc. serves as a meta-level dragon?
How do you represent this?
What lets you know to call this a "dragon?"

2) Identify the meta-level meanings that frame the external behavior.

Is there a belief, value, or understanding that drives this "dragon?"
What meaning frames and higher level understandings govern the experience?
How does this work as a "dragon?"
What is the thought virus? What's sick and poisonous about it?

3) Explore the meta-level meanings that drive you.

What causes or contributes this? How does that work?

> [This elicits meanings about causation, that is, how you map out the Cause—>Effect relationship in your understanding.]

What meanings do you give to this?
How do you know to call it that?
What do you believe about this?
What do you understand about this?

> [This elicits your meanings about meaning, that is, how you map out what is equivalent to what, your Complex Equivalences about things.]

What does this mean about you?
How do you use it for self-definition?

> [This elicits your meanings about identity, that is, how you map out how you identify yourself, with what you identify yourself, etc. hence, your Identifications.]

What is this like? If this was a metaphor, what would it be?

4) Identify the frames-by-implication about those meanings.

What has to be true in order for that meaning to exist and to operate so powerfully in your mind-body?
What other frames have you just assumed?
What conceptual universe is presumed by this?

5) Quality control the ecology of the entire semantic system.

Does this enhance your life?
Does it empower you as a person?
Do you want or need this?
What resources would enable you to handle this with more power and grace?
As you identify and apply these processes to your primary state and put into your future, how does that feel?
Where's the dragon now?

THE EXCUSE DRAGON

I developed *The Excuse Blow-Out Pattern* in this chapter after encountering three people in a row during the same month who complained, "But I just can't apply NLP to myself." Talk about an excuse!

> "Yeah, this is great stuff. And I'm a wizard at doing *NLP* with others. I can run the patterns like a charm and help them get the results they want. But I just can't do it on myself."

I didn't even have to ask about the secondary gains regarding that excuse. The payoff of that excuse is pretty obvious—the person doesn't have to be congruent, walk the talk, invest the time, trouble, and energy to change, be held accountable, *and* the person gets to be really special. "Maybe I'm just more intelligent, quick, sharp, etc. I see what you're trying to do to me when I play the role of being the client."

Yeah, right! Is that just an excuse?

The Nature of Excuses

While some excuses are really stupid, many, if not most excuses are actually pretty seductive. When someone loads up an excuse with sophisticated sounding reasons, they can seem so legitimate, so reasonable, and so right. And for anyone working with others (which actually is all of us), whether we manage, sell, do therapy, teach, parent, relate to loved ones, practice law, etc., *dealing with excuses* (our own and others) *is an important part of performing at our best.*

Since developing *the Excuse Blow-Out Pattern,* I've had lots of opportunities to get even more acquainted with the realm of excuses than ever before. It has surprised me at the range of kinds, forms, and qualities of excuses. And given the sparse amount of research and study on excuses, this has become a fascinating area of exploration.

It has also made me more conscious of my own skills in excuse making. Like any area of endeavor, our very interest makes us more conscious of its presence. It has alerted me to some of the really sneaking ways I excuse-make that I had not even recognized. Over the years, it has been funny catching myself looking around, as it were, for something that I can use to *excuse* me from some task, obligation, requirement, request, etc. The strange thing about excuse-making, the greater and more sophisticated your skills at reasoning, explaining, and intellectualizing, the more *subtle and invisible (to you)* your powers of rationalization. You can come up with more and more sophisticated B.S. for getting away with things.

Excuse-making in your life becomes political intrigue, courtroom analysis of strategies, and even high comedy (if you don't take yourself too seriously). Most of us snickered when we heard President Clinton inventing reasons, explanations, and justifications for why he did not, and could not, have had "sex with that woman," and then later began explaining why he did have sex with her, but really didn't mean it. My favorite was his retort regarding what is oral sex, "It depends on what the meaning of *is* is."

Level One of Excuse Making

The first level of excuse-making involves simply *finding or inventing a reason* that explains *why* something is out of the question, inappropriate, not useful or binding, etc. as you look for some excuse.

"But I'm too tired to exercise."
"But I'm not the kind of person who goes to those kinds of events."
"But I don't know enough."
"But I'm afraid."
"But I've never done it that way before."

> The best day of your life
> is when you give up making excuses
> and start creating results.

> "But the traffic was too heavy."
> "But I lost my watch."
> "But my wife would never let me . . ."
> "But I'd get dirty and sweaty."
> "It's too hard."
> "It's too cold outside." ("It's too hot!")
> "It takes too long."
> "What if I make a fool of myself and people laugh at me?"

Structurally, all of these "reasons" occur at a meta-level to the primary state of some activity. To the primary experience and all the thoughts, feelings, physiologies that would be involved if you engaged in it, you have *other thoughts and feelings*, usually negative thoughts and feelings that you use to let yourself off the hook. You don't want to be bothered. You dislike the experience. So excuses generally involve an unpleasant meta-state about some primary experience.

By way of contrast, consider times when you took on the activity. Or consider someone else who already seems to be *turned on* by that activity. In these instances, there is a different frame of mind about the activity. We or they did *not* see it as a bother, trouble, boring, or challenging. We or they had taken a positive mental attitude (e.g., a meta-state) *about* the activity. This made excuse-making irrelevant. We just got right to it, took effective action, and moved ourselves a little closer to fulfilling our goals.

An excuse is a frame about the proposed experience that induces you to feel put off or bothered in some way. You don't feel up to it. You don't see the value of it. So you attempt to *excuse* yourself from the engagement by making up some "reason" that seems to allow you or another person to grant an excuse. For this reason, *excuses* generally operate as a form of persuasion. You essentially say (to yourself or another),

> "Please have me excused from X activity *because* of this or that reason . . ."

> "Man is not a rational creature,
> he is a rationalizing creature."
> *Socrates*

Excuses that occur in an inter-personal context involve relationships, expectations, hopes, agreements, and the like. The excuses you use with yourself involve your intra-personal relationship to yourself, and to your goals, outcomes, hopes, dreams, etc. You want to be fit and thin, but then (here comes the excuses) you're tired, it takes time and trouble, it takes a lot of effort, is it really all that profitable, etc.

The Cognitive Content of an Excuse

As goes the quality of thinking and reasoning, so goes the quality of your excuses. This means that excuses can be discerned into two categories: *legitimate and illegitimate.* In fact, you can analyze excuses as you can analyze thinking, cognition, and reasoning. When you do, you can discern the quality and sophistication of an excuse in terms of:

- Legitimate and illegitimate excuses
- Logical and illogical excuses
- Good and bad excuses
- Intelligent and stupid excuses
- Rational and irrational excuses

In the literature on *persuasion*, we know that to use the linguistic term, "because" helps to sell an excuse and to positively influence others in our favor. Experimental research has played with people attempting to cut in line. Those who do try to do so *without an explanation* are much less likely to get a positive response than those who provide a reason. Those who only made the simple request, "Would you let me cut in line?" were denied more often than not. But when they add the word *because*, the results were nearly magical. And what's even more surprisingly magical about it was that it really didn't matter too much what the persons said after the word "because." You'd think that only legitimate, intelligent, rational, meaningful, and acceptable would work. But not so. Just about any excuse tends to work regardless of the quality of the excuse.

> "Would you let me cut in line because I'm late for an appointment?"
>
> Because I'm pregnant . . .
> Because my wife will be mad at me.
> Because my kid is sick.
> Because I can't stand this heat.

The Positive Intentions and Payoffs in Inventing Reasons "Why"

Most people, do not like to think that they are "just making excuses." How does that phrase strike you? Do you experience it as a positive thing or as a negative thing? "Just making excuses." Do you do that?

No! Not you. Not me.

We don't "make excuses," we only asked to be excused from a task or obligation if we have a legitimate reason. Ah, the beauty and music of that word — "reason."

> "I had my *reasons* for doing (or not doing) X."
> "If you only understood *why* I did that (or failed to do that), then you'd appreciate . . . "
> "They don't understand, I had to do X because of . . . "

Notice how soothing, comforting, securing, and "right" these phrases feel. What is there about human being that we need and want "reasons," "whys," and "becauses?" It seems to be part of our nature to always need to come up with a reason by which we can explain things. It's everywhere because it's built into our need to *make sense of things* and to live in an intelligent world that we can figure out. And this need or drive seems to begin very early.
"Why did you make that mess?"

> "Because . . ."

"Because why?"

> "Just because. That's why!"

It is our need for structure, order, an intelligent world—*meaning and meaningful structures* that moves us to become very skilled at finding, inventing, and creating explanations, understandings, reasons, etc. And from this drive, we create models of the world, theories, postulates, etc. This gives birth to science. With an "explanation" about how something works, what leads to solution, what causes something else, etc., we develop scientific theories and hypothesis, test them, refine them, and so develop our knowledge base. I knew there was a positive intention and payoff for the use of human reason!

Then We Become Devious

Of course, when you have such an incredible power as human reasoning that can invent new things, expand knowledge, create civilizations, etc., you know it is liable to abuse. Enter, *"The Excuse."* This has been known for a long time. Socrates was the philosopher who quipped that—

> "Man is not a rational creature, he is a rationalizing creature."

All you need is a little motivation. Add a little dislike, unpleasant task, frustration, sense of being bothered, etc., and you have the perfect context wherein excuses will be generated. It's predictable. Most people seem to operate from frames of comfort and ease ("Is it easy? Will it be fun?), the path of least resistance ("But this is hard?), and overload ("I have enough to do"). In the context of those frames, it is easy to grow a whole crop of excuses in no time!

Do you have excuse-generator states? No, that's the wrong question, of course, you do. The real question is:

> What are your excuse-generator states? When do you seem to access the exquisite ability to create a multitude of excuses? When does your excuse-creativity turn on full blast? When you are tired, frustrated, angry, overwhelmed, upset, hurt, down, etc.?

Most of us also have the ability to become devious about the way we try to excuse ourselves from doing the things necessary, essential, and even critical to achieving our goals. The gestalt that emerges from this mixture is "self-sabotage." We sabotage our own best interests. Talk about irrational. Why would we do that? What would get us to undermine our own success, fitness, health, relationships, etc.? There must be something else going on here. And yes, there is.

Meta-stating the Excuse-Making State

If "excuses" do not exist at the primary level, but as the meta-state level of *the reasons* you feed your mind, and try to feed the minds of others, regarding why you should be excused from doing something, then what's your meta-level thought or feeling about that? How have you meta-stated the experience of excuse making?

- Do you like the awareness that you're "just making an excuse?"
- Does that awareness make you feel anxious or uncomfortable?
- Do you fear it?
- Do you reject it and refuse to know that about any particular "reason?"

These questions begin the exploration of how have you *framed* the subjective experience of excuse making. To turn "negative" thoughts and feelings *against* yourself and your own experiences banishes awareness and so reduces the level of your own interpersonal mindfulness. And that makes you more unconscious about what you're doing and how you're living, which reduces your freedom of actual choices, which reduces your power to run your own brain. And, if continued, it can create a dragon state.

Not a pretty picture. The solution? *Accept* that you are an inveterate excuse maker and develop an open willingness to not only recognize your propensity for excuse-making, but to reality test the excuses, and hold yourself to a higher standard.

Above and Beyond Excuses

In making excuses, there's lots of things going on, but not only at the same level of the *primary event* or the first meta-level of our excuse making. More crucial things are happening at even higher levels. To discover what's really going on you have to go higher to the frames about your excuse-making. You have to move *up* to yet another level, and usually several other levels. Only then can you flush out and discover the higher frames that are actually driving the show. Discover these higher levels for yourself.

The Pattern:

1) Identify a desired outcome.

Think about some activity that, at some level, you *want* to do, *know* that you *should* do, and know that it would *benefit* you if you did do it. For example, perhaps you think these kinds of thoughts about eating right and exercising, or devoting more quality time to family and loved ones. Think about doing those things that awaken the best in you: reading, listening, dialoguing, investing yourself in new discoveries, etc.

Got it? Good. Vividly represent and then step into that representation so that you can sense that goal, outcome, desire . . . And just feel it. Feel the pull.

2) Let your excuses emerge.

Now as you feel the pull, imagine taking a step to doing something about that goal. As you do notice if any excuse arises. Imagine moving out to your goal and noting all of the ways that you *excuse yourself* from taking effective action in fulfilling your goals.

- What stops you?
- What do you let get in your way?
- What ideas, reasons, explanations do you give to let yourself off the hook?

3) Observe your excuse system.
Now step back, in your mind, from the desired activity and the excuses so that you can observe the whole dynamic structure of your thoughts-and-feelings and just notice what comes to mind and heart as you do.

- How do you feel about your skills in excuse making?
- How do you feel about yourself excusing yourself from being more fully engaged in life?
- What thoughts bounce around the edge of your consciousness as you think about this?

You may get things like:

"I don't know . . ." is the most common answer I get from these questions.
"I don't know . . . I know I don't like it."
"I feel bad that I don't push myself."

The Meta-State Frame of Disliking Excuse-Making
These responses indicate some of the first *default responses* that you generate to your excuses which is common to all of us. Welcome to the club! Commonly few of us do not even want to look at or face the fact that we let ourselves down, don't go for the gusto, excuse ourselves, etc. Yet all of this is part of the human experience.

And because we have a default awareness that we *should not* "make excuses" and because we feel bad about doing so, we naturally *seek to avoid awareness* of doing so. We try to *not know* this about ourselves. Why? Typically because "making excuses" has been anchored with negative feelings (shame, guilt, being bad, being a slacker, etc.), so now we are all well trained and conditioned to avoid that awareness. Isn't that true of you?

The impact of this desire to avoid awareness of our excuses then leads us to do something that makes the problem even worse, although on the surface, we think it will make the problem go away. What do we do? We *set non-awareness (unawareness) as our basic frame about this facet of our journey through life.*

By *not* wanting to know your weakness, fallibility, etc. in excuse making, you frame things so that you become mindless. Then, you begin to fall into habits (unthinking ways of acting) so that you don't maintain awareness of what you're doing. Obviously to achieve peak performance, you will have to break through this meta-level barrier and create a new level of mindfulness.

For many this is not easy. It is not easy because it's so painful. As they have tabooed and rejected awareness of their excuse making (did you notice that there are three meta-levels of frames in that statement?), they now operate from that frame as their map. It creates the frame game of *"Hey, don't ask me; I don't know. It's just my Mind!"* Of course, this creates psychic danger within.

Un-Awareness Becomes our Inner Game

When you taboo *awareness of excuse making* and refuse to know it, because you judge it and hate it (the level above the unawareness), you set up an executive frame that values "not knowing." Out of that then comes the gestalt known as "denial." This isn't conscious denial, but unconscious denial. You're denying and don't even know that you're denying. You deny that you're denying! In fact, the whole structure of these dynamic frames embedded in frames generates a general sense of being unconscious of your higher motivations and desires.

This leaves you living at the lower frames *only aware* of what you consciously know that you want—your goals and outcomes.

> I want to be fit and thin.
> I want to make lots of money and become financially successful.
> I want to expand my career.
> I want to have a loving and close family.

Yet, above these immediate and conscious goals, you have another set of goals that you have lost awareness of frames that war and conflict against your goals.

> I want the easy path.
> I want a hassle free life.
> I don't want to have to work too hard or struggle too much.
> I don't want to do unpleasant and boring things.
> I want to do only stimulating and exciting things. Etc.

At the conscious level, I really do think that I want the goals that I talk about, plan for, etc., and yet at a higher level, I have programmed in another whole set of goals. And because these goals are "higher" in terms of logical levels, operationally they are my *real* goals. That's because, structurally, higher frames govern and determine lower levels.

These higher (or more operational) goals are not only different from, but opposed to and contradictory to my conscious goals. These higher *unconscious goals* arise from my higher frames. Yet because I have forbidden awareness of them, I can't own them. I can't accept them.

Welcome to the Meta-Muddle Dimension

All of this describes the meta-muddles that we create for ourselves when we do not handle the higher levels of our mind well. To complicate matters at this point, every little clue of insight that I might experience about my higher "real" frames, only sends me into anxiety, fear, and stress. This is the self-organizing nature of the "not willing to know" frame. What then results? I push awareness away even further and harder. Of course, due to the paradoxical nature of logical levels, this increases the strength of the higher frames.

From the Meta-States perceptive, "refusing to know . . ." locks you more into a position of blindness about your own thinking and feeling. And that operates from a "fear of discovering my true thoughts." Eventually this leads to a self-alienation, a lack of psychological awareness of yourself, and a self-hatred or contempt. And so the problem gets worse and worse with this "attempted solution."

> Excuses must be uncovered
> and exposed
> as the termites of performance.

So how in the world can we solve this mess—this meta-mess? The solution lies in a direction that, at first, seems paradoxical and counter-intuitive. Namely, full acceptance of our "excuse making," stupid explanations, and skill at being devious. The solution lies first in the direction of *refusing to identify* yourself with your thoughts and feelings. When you do that you can then easily and graciously realize that this is just the way mind operates and welcome your excuses into awareness. When you do that, then you can discern between valid and invalid excuses and refuse the stupid ones—which brings us to the next step.

The Pattern:

4) Welcome your awareness of your skill in excuse-making.

Access the state of acceptance and even appreciation and set these thoughts and feelings about your excuse making. It's just the use of your powers of "reason." That's all. Just notice the tremendous skill you have at lying to yourself, trying to get out of things, inventing preposterous excuses, misusing your rational mind, etc. No judgment.

5) Honestly evaluate the quality and sophistication of your excuse-making.

From acceptance and appreciation, you can now honestly evaluate, run an ecology check, reality test, and quality control the frames that you're setting via your "reasons." This higher level honesty is your friend and your power.

How you Relate to Your Excuse-Making

If you want to create a personal structuring for self-sabotaging in your children, attach psychic pain to "making excuses" by calling them bad, lazy, selfish, etc. This will motivate your kids to feel bad *about* making excuses so that they will then use their creative imagination for inventing reasons. As they taboo and reject excuses, they will eventually lose awareness of the excuses they create and truly believe that they have legitimate reasons. They will become increasingly skilled in debating about this which will set self-alienation in motion.

If you want to allow them to own and accept this power, then play with their "excuses" by validating them as the use of reason and help them to reality test them. This will enable them to recognize the difference between legitimate and illegitimate reasoning and teach them critical thinking skills. It will also help them to avoid developing fears about themselves or the fallibility of their thinking.

Welcoming your excuses allows you to then sort through the valid and invalid ones, to distinguish a legitimate reason from a mere excuse. Then you can clearly decide, "No!" I don't need that stupid excuse, and "Yes, the reasoning that leads me to put this activity off is legitimate at this point in time."

Because *excuses are terrorists to your highest potentials* to deal with them effectively—recognize their source and nature. The Excuse Blow-Out pattern that follows is designed to enable you to sort out excuses from legitimate explanations and to eliminate them from sabotaging your highest and best.

* EXCUSE BLOW-OUT

While some "excuses" are legitimate and useful, most are illegitimate, stupid, and useless. Most only waste your time, sabotage your goals, and sell you short. This pattern is designed to go after and transform silly, wimpy, stupid, and unuseful excuses with this pattern, not legitimate reasons.

To the extent that you *refuse* to let excuses dominate our lives, you access more of your own mastery and so become increasingly emotionally intelligent. When excuses do dominate your lives, you essentially choose your excuses over your values and visions. When you do that, you sell the greatness of your values and potentials short. Knowing that, you can now develop the mindfulness and capacity to refuse that kind of self-sabotage.

The Pattern:

1) Access an outcome that you want.

What do you want that's very important to you?
What outcome do you want to achieve or go for that you know is well-formed and ecological?
What is something that would really improve the quality of your life?

2) Let the excuse or excuses emerge in your awareness.

When you think about carrying it out, do you find that numerous excuses come to mind and stop you from acting on your desired outcome?
Take a moment to imagine going ahead with taking action . . . and notice what happens. How do you excuse yourself from it? Listen to your internal voice.
Feel the excuse. Notice where you feel it in your body. What does it feel like. In your body? How do you know to call it an excuse?

3) Quality control the excuse.

Is it just an excuse? Do you want this excuse? Do you need it?
Does it serve your life at all? Does it enhance you or empower you?
If there is some part or facet of the excuse that you might need

or want to preserve, what is it?
What facets of the excuse may serve a positive purpose for you?

4) Preserve the values and benefits of the excuse.

Go inside and preserve any part of the excuse that might prove useful to you in some way at some time. Suck out of the excuse any element (a value, belief, understanding) that could be useful. Delete and remove all of the value that you can from the excuse so that all that remains is an empty shell of an excuse, devoid of any usefulness at all. Notice the value of the reason— an understanding, belief, or state that you want to keep with you. Note it and store it as something you can have apart from this particular stupid excuse.
Is there anything valuable in the excuse? If so, what?
Anything else that you want to take out of the excuse?
How do you think of this value?
How will you hold it in mind as a value?
Is it now just an excuse? Just an empty shell of an excuse?
If not, repeat until you just have an empty shell of an excuse left.

5) Reject the empty shell of the old worn out excuse.

Access a strong *"NO!"* state, a *"Hell, No!"* state. Amplify that state of "Rejection, Refusal, or Disgust" that comes out as a *"No"* fully until you feel it very strongly. Anchor it spatially in a spot and feel it in your hands and in your feet. Let it radiate throughout your body. When you have it accessed strongly, imagine the empty excuse immediately in front of you and step into that excuse with the NO!" state. Stomp on the excuse—stomp it to the ground—with the power of your "Hell, No!"
Are you going to let this excuse stop you?
Does this serve your highest values and purposes?
Have you blown out all of the old excuse?
Are you free to move forward now?

6) Test the effect of the blow-out.

Now imagine the desired activity that's ecological and notice what happens as you think about moving toward it . . .
What do you feel? What comes to mind?
Do you have any excuse lurking that you might use to excuse

yourself from life, love, and commitment?

7) Access your executive decision state.

Will you now give yourself to this goal?
Will you allow it to become an attractor in your mind so that as you think of this activity, you feel pulled toward it?
Are you now willing to build the resources so that you can go after your goal?
The part of your mind that makes decisions, will it now set the goal as your future and pathway of actions?

* META- "NO!" FOR CREATIVE STUBBORNNESS

As *Yes* induces and accesses a state of confirmation, *No* accesses a state of disconfirmation and refusal. The "no" state empowers you to set boundaries, establish limits, and use your stubbornness in a positive way. If there is a barrier or block, sometimes you just need to stand up to it and refuse it any reality in your mind-body system. Sometimes you just need to say no.

Of course, the problem that many people have is that they can't say *No*. They can't say *No* to many of the demands and pressures of life, and they can't say *No* to things that limit and sabotage their own success. At least, they can't say a *No* that counts. The design of this pattern is to provide a way to take a strong stubborn refusal to such things. It is to access your creative and powerful *stubbornness* by which you make up your mind and set boundaries.

The Pattern:

1) Access a good strong "No!"

What threat, danger, or disgusting thing evokes every fiber in your body to say *"No!"*?
What gets you to say "No!" in a strong and fully congruent way?
When you think about something that you can say "No!" or "Enough!" with every fiber of your being, what comes to mind?
Say that **"No!"** again and again until you notice and snapshot it on the inside.

Menu of elicitations:

Would you push a little child in front of a speeding bus just for the hell of it?

Would you eat a bowl of dirty filthy worms when you have delicious food available?

Would you let someone molest your child?

2) Amplify and Anchor.

Anchor the state of *"No!"* with your hand gestures. When you do that, how does that feel?

As you listen to your own voice saying *"No!"* in a strong and definitive way, how strong is it?

How much stronger can you make it?

3) Apply your meta "*No!*" to an old limiting belief.

Feeling all of this powerful *"No!",* even *"Hell No!"* feel this fully as you think about that stupid, useless, limiting belief . . . now.

And you can keep on saying *No!* to that limiting belief until you begin to feel that it no longer has any power to run your programs, that it has no more room in your presence, in your mind . . .

4) Future pace and confirm.

How many more times and with what voice, tone, gesturing, do you need to totally disconfirm that old belief so that you know —deep inside yourself—that it will no longer run your programs?

ELIMINATING FEAR FROM DOMINATING YOUR LIFE

> ***"Drive out all fear."***
> Edwards Deming

If there's anything that sabotages a person from achieving peak performance, it is fear. The frame and feeling of fear and all of its related emotions does not facilitate self-actualization or peak performances.

Edwards Deming revolutionized the business world and established many, many business experts frames. As he did this, he initiated the Quality Control movement that empowered Japanese businesses to move to the top in terms of quality in the second half of the twentieth century. In doing this, he created a list of fourteen principles for business and at the top of them was, *"Eliminate all fear."*

This was, and continues to be, revolutionary and even surprising in the field of business. Many managers, leaders, business owners, corporate CEOs, experts, and authors still preach the old theory of fear motivation that Douglas McGregor designated the Theory X of Management:

> "People will not work, will not be motivated, will not do their best if fear isn't driving them. That's why you have to motivate people with fear."

This theory of human nature proposes the following:

> "People won't work unless they *have to*. People won't want to contribute or cooperate unless there is a terrible consequence if they don't. People are basically lazy, undependable, and don't want challenges. So put terrifying fear in them."

McGregory called this Theory X which sets the frame of fear as a necessity of human motivation. Some managers and bosses and others even think that they will be more successful in business if they are rough, tough, hard, mean, threatening, demanding, and frightful. So they adopt a tough-guy role which involves intimidating, power trips, ego rushes, and the ability to make people jump.

The Problem with Fear as a Frame

While the fear frames will work in the short run, they do not work in the long run. They do not support or enable the development of a truly human business. What's wrong with a leader creating a fear atmosphere? There are lots of problems with setting frames of fear, dread, apprehension, worry, etc.

1) Avoidance: When we feel fear, we *move away from* things. It creates avoidance and freezing behaviors. This is valuable for true dangers and threats, but not for a strategy for creating a workplace culture of high performance, not for texturing and qualifying our style of leadership or management.

Setting up a frame of fear for those who deal with you, or for yourself in your responses, creates a focus on what to avoid and to move away from. This particular focus of avoidance then trains your mind to be oriented to dangers, threats, things that could go wrong, and problems. As a result, you have less consciousness and focus on what you want, on solutions, on possibilities, on opportunities. This does not make for excellence in business or in most areas of life.

Further, in groups, this undermines team work, cooperation, collaboration, and community. Fear puts people at odds with each other. Fear causes us to look at each other as enemies, opponents, and competitors. And as fear reduces creativity, it increases defensiveness.

2) Deception and falsehood. Given the states that fear creates in yourself and others (i.e., worry, apprehension, anxiety, paranoia, etc.), fear motivates you to keep things from others, to not share, to not communicate openly, and to not believe or trust in others. Fear of making mistakes, fear of not measuring up, fear of not getting as big piece of the pie, fear of being defeated, etc. causes you to put on airs, create impressions, hold your cards close to your chest, falsely represent yourself, not offer your problems or failures to others for help, and hide your mistakes.

It doesn't take much imagination to contemplate the kind of atmosphere that this creates in a group of people whether a company, corporation, community, or nation. It creates a fear culture, an environment where it is not safe to be real, to be open, to authentically share and to cooperate. It invites a culture of deceit and falsehood where people actually fear being open, truthful, authentic, etc.

3) Avoidance of feedback and truth. If feedback enables you to keep improving, to make good use of *kaizen* (small incremental improvements) and to honestly face what is not working so that you can design with better solutions, then fear sabotages all of that. When you use fear as your frame, you feel apprehensive and hold back from welcoming feedback. You label feedback as "failures" and fear it. You play the game of avoiding owning your problems or mistakes because you feel threatened as you think that this puts you one "down" in the competitive game.

When you fear mistakes, you attach negative emotional states to feedback. You then develop a bad relationship to feedback. And that makes it so that you cannot use it in a straight forward way for improving and developing. You then fear being open, real, or an honest sharing of your problems and mistakes. This leads to all kinds of avoidance behavior: denial, cover-up, posturing, worrying about image, etc.

4) Short-term individualistic thinking. Because fear focuses on dangers and threats, it orients you to *yourself.* Yet focusing exclusively on yourself—and specifically to your safety, status, image, etc.—consumes energy we could otherwise have devoted to attending to the things and people that actually support career success. This creates a focus away from long-term solutions and proactive thinking. *Fear makes you more reactive.* To think long-term and systemically means that you take into consideration other factors than just your own safety. You think about the systems and systems within systems that you live and move and do business.

Operating from fear disturbs your vision to see others as competitors rather than collaborators. You think in individualistic terms rather than cooperative and community terms. You want to win even if others have to lose because you think that when others win, you lose.

5) Blaming. Given all this focus on threat, problems, and avoidance, given this structure of fear about mistakes, fear seduces you into playing the blame game. After all, who blames? Is it not those who feel insecure, anxious, and threatened? Also, those who don't want or can't accept their own responsibility and straightforwardly look at mistakes. They have to blame. They have to accuse and insult and shift the responsibility.

6) Undermines creativity. As fear moves you away from risk taking, adventure, and fun, it moves you away from creativity. Fearful people timidly cower because they focus on problems, they look for things to go wrong. This is not the state of mind that encourages innovation in business or life.

Driving Out Fear

Fear as a frame and way of looking at the world, and the games that it initiates, cannot and will not serve you well in the long run if you want to be successful, achieve peak performance, and make a difference in the world. No wonder Edwards Deming recognized the importance of driving out all fear. He was adamant about it being destructive personally, physically, and psychologically. But how do you do that? How do you drive fear out?

1) Create a sense of security for yourself and others.
Security provides a great antidote for fear. Insecurity and threat initiates fear. Conversely, feeling safe and secure inoculates you against unreasonable, irrational, and groundless fears.

- How secure are you within yourself?
- How secure is your sense of self-value and self-worth?

Esteeming yourself as valuable, worthwhile, and having innate unconditional dignity provides a great grounding and securing that makes you immune to the majority of fears. And, when you can and do esteem yourself unconditionally just because you are a human being, it is easy (very easy) to esteem others unconditionally.

Base your esteeming, valuing, and giving worth to yourself and others for no other reason than the fact that we are all human beings. Then you can stop playing the *One Upmanship Game* with yourself and others. Making esteem (self-esteem, other-esteem) *conditional* will seduces you to rank people as more or less valuable. This is a major mistake. People are people. Each and every human being is a mysterious wonder—fallible, liable to error, and yet incredibly sacred.

2) Create safety nets for yourself and others.
With an internal and unshakable (unearned) value and worth, you can then make the distinction between person and behavior. *People are more than what they do.* You are more than what you do. What you

do is an expression of your*self*, it is not the totality of you. What you *are* is unconditionally valuable; what you *do* is always and only fallible. What you *are* describes yourself as a human being—your self-esteem. What you *do* describes you as a human *doing*— your self-confidence to do things.

Person	——	**Behavior**
Who you are	——	What you do
Human *being*	——	Human *doing*
Unconditional	——	Conditional
No conditions	——	Many conditions

Knowing that you and others *are* more than what we *do* allows us to create safety nets for all of us so that when we fail, mess up, and blow it (which we will), our fallibility will not undermine our sense of personal value or our learning. Only when you can thoroughly learn what does not work are you free to try something new. Discovering what does not work can be taken as something to feel bad about or as an occasion to celebrate learning a better approach.

This realization creates a safety net for failures. How? By refusing to connect failure, mistakes, errors, etc. with catastrophe you drive out fear. You set a safety net—they are just mistakes. They are just part of learning. How can you make it safe to make mistakes? What safety nets can you, or should you, create so that you can take the risks to experiment, play, discover, and learn?

3) Recognize and then refuse to over-value fear.

Fear has value as a primary state when it is in reference to a true danger or threat that's "out there." Any other use of fear is not useful or legitimate and should not be tolerated. To take fear as an emotion or danger and threat as a concept and over-value it as if it were a key secret of life only sets you up for paranoid living. It creates a personality structure of timidity and indecisiveness. Then you might even be seduced to think that people work at their best when driven by fear, that you manage best by being tough and threatening. This is not a wise direction.

4) Refuse to be governed by fear.

When you load fear with too much meaning, fear begins to drive how you think, perceive, evaluate, sort, reason, etc. This lets it become too pervasive in your life. Accessing a state of fear and then applying that fear to many other things—to ideas, people, experiences, anticipations, etc. sets up a fearful and dreadful approach that results in over-cautiousness. It puts you into a place where you become timid, apprehensive, worried, anxious, etc.

5) Think about what you want in the long-term.
If fear orients you in an away-from and avoidance mode, you can turn this around by developing a vision of what you want to go *toward*. "Great! If you don't want that, what do you want?" This question re-orients you to a compelling vision and dream as it re-focuses your attention and it chases out fears. Eliminate fear as your motivation and orientation by thinking of long-term effects and legacies, about what you can do to move in that direction, and about the solutions that will move you there.

6) Value mistakes, failures, and feedback.
If fear mis-represents and mis-codes "failures" and "mistakes," then you can also chase out fears as you reframe failures and mistakes as valuable learning processes. The more you know how to creatively use and embrace mistakes as experiments in learning and creativity, the more you will eliminate fear from becoming a meta-level fear and a frame of mind. And doing that will change the games you play in life.

Given all of this, are you ready to blow-out all of your fears which are unrealistic and non-productive? Are you ready to rid yourself of a fearful mentality that creates timidity and hesitation where it is not needed? Then the Fear Blow-Out pattern that follows will give you the ability to do precisely that.

* FEAR BLOW-OUT

Because you can give your fears too much meaning and significance and develop a habit of listening to them far too much, the emotion of fear can get in the way of performing at your best. You can access states of fear too often and too intensely and so stop yourself from taking action on those things that you value as well as the vision you set. You can give way to fear so often that fear can be set as a higher frame of mind darkening your perspective and interfering with achieving peak performances. To counteract these toxic effects, use the following pattern.

The Pattern:

1) Access your inspiring knowledge or goal.

What do you know, understand, or believe that's meaningful and important in living a full life?
Do you know how to represent it so fully so that you feel a growing excitement from it?
How do you do that?
How much more energy can you put into it to make it even more compelling?
What do you want to do to actualize this?
What actions and performances are needed to make this real for you?

2) Now think about acting on that knowledge or goal.

As you now think about acting on it, what do you notice in terms of fears, apprehensions, and worries?
What fears do you need to welcome in your awareness?
How intense are these fears?
Where do you feel the fear in your body? Where else?
How do you feel it as fear? What's occurring?
How do you know to call these sensations fear?
What are your thoughts and meanings of danger or threat?

3) Consult with the fear.

What is the fear about? What are the thoughts behind the fear?
How accurate or inaccurate is the message of that fear?
Is it truly dangerous?
Dangerous to what? In what way? To what degree?
How useful is the fear?

Do you need to take counsel from this fear? To what degree? What learnings and insights do you want to take from this fear?

4) Decide on the limits of the fear.

Where do you want to put the border and boundaries of the fear?
How much power do you want to give to this fear?
Where do you want to put the line between fears-to-face and fears-to-heed?

5) Access resources with which to temper the fear.

What resources would you like to access to temper your fear?
What about calmness, confidence, a stronger appreciation of your outcome?
What other resources would you like to access?

6) Executively decide about how to respond.

What fear will you listen to? To what extent? In what contexts?
How will you listen to it?
What questioning and explorations will you make in response to it?
Where will you draw the limit on the fear?

7) Blow-out any residue of the fear with your resources.

When you meta-state the fear with your resources, when does the fear blow-out, so that you feel a sense of courage and boldness to face things?
How many times do you need to loop back to texture yourself with more resources?
Are you feeling courageous now?

> *"Those who want to become wealthy have to learn to manage their fears and especially their fear of risk. We have to move beyond playing it safe to playing it smart."*
> Robert Kiyosaki

* COURAGE

Achieving peak performance takes courage. It takes courage to think big, courage to look beyond problems to see and invent solutions, courage to believe in oneself, courage to take effective actions, to learn a discipline, to invest years of study and patience, to speak up, to risk disapproval, to risk looking foolish, etc.

We have many ways by which we can build *the courage gestalt.* It all depends on the specific state-on-state arrangement you put together. So to design engineer the meta-state of courage, what are the components that you need in a given context?

- Playful risk-taking danger
- Joyous excitement of fear (or in spite of fear)
- Boldness to take risks in reaching objectives
- Overwhelming sense of one's desired outcome or value
- Not-caring what others say or think while moving forward
- Rejecting concern about embarrassment as irrelevant

The Pattern:

1) Identify the referent experience in which you want "courage" to emerge.

What activity, situation, context, etc. would you want or need "courage?"
Where do you need courage? When? In what context?
What is fearful? What is intimidating? What triggers hesitation?
What is the degree of fear or hesitation that you face?

2) Matrix detection: Flush out current frames and meta-states.

What's fearful, threatening, dangerous, etc. about this situation?
What do you think-and-feel about your fear?
How well does the fear serve you?
Does your thoughts-and-feelings about the fear serve you?
Have you had enough of this old fear dominating your life?
How realistic is the fear?
What is realistic about the fear that you need to deal with?
What is not realistic about the fear that needs to be released?

3) Meta-state the resources to elicit the gestalt.

As you experiment with boldness, passion, compelling

outcome, excitement, curiosity, playfulness, and other resources, access and bring each resource state, one at a time, so that you apply it to the primary state of fear.
After each application of another resource, step back and access how much courage has now emerged within you.
How much more do you need?
How much more would you prefer and desire?
What else do you need in effectively handling this situation?

4) Confirm and consolidate?
With all of this in mind, how does *this* [fire anchor for the gestalt state) affect this (the referent experience]?
How does it transform the situation for you?
Do you like this?
Are you fully aligned with this? Any objections?
Will you keep this? How?

* META-STATING PROCRASTINATION

Have you ever let procrastination stop you from implementing what you know to do and want to do? Procrastination can and does interfere to keep you from fully installing new learnings or embodying a new performance. You can give in to numerous voices and feelings so that you put off what you want to do that would enable you to achieve peak performance.

The Pattern:
1) Access a trigger for procrastination
Do you ever procrastinate on things? Really? When? Where? With what?
Do you even put off doing something that you ought to do and that you know would enrich the quality of your life?
How do you know to put it off? What triggers you to do that?
Is the trigger —
An unpleasant feeling, discomfort, tension, emotionally painful?
The idea of the effort or work that it would take?
Boring, menial, trivial, insignificant, like a tiresome chore, tedious paperwork or housecleaning?

Fear that it won't be good enough, that there are flaws, that you will be judged inadequate?

2) Acceptance: noticing the sense of procrastination, welcome it.

What do you easily accept?

What happens when you apply *acceptance* to just acknowledge, notice, and welcome X into your awareness.

What happens when you just welcome in the uncomfortable feelings?

What happens to the procrastination when you just let the negative feelings come in?

3) Identify the map/ territory distinction that creates the emotion.

What map are you using to evaluate the experience which then leads to the feeling of procrastination?

What standards are you using to evaluate the activity and/or the emotion?

What expectations? What does the feeling of procrastination mean?

4) Permission: check and/or give the permission for feelings.

Do you have permission to experience the X feelings that urge you to procrastinate?

Do you have permission to engage in this activity that you're putting off?

Do you have permission to be imperfect, fallible, to take risks, to not know everything?

Give yourself permission and notice what happens to the sense of "putting off." What happens?

5) Identify the importance and value of the task or activity.

Is this activity important? How? Why? In what way? How does it benefit you? Your life?

What is important about that value?

Step into the state of positive intention for the activity, and on up several levels to the highest value of the activity . . . and amplify . . . now, with *that* in mind . . . think about this activity . . . and notice what happens. How do you now think or feel about it?

6) Additional resources for meta-stating.

What other resource would you like to bring to the

procrastination state to blow it out?

What if you put off the putting off?

What if you felt fully passionate about the activity?

What if you refuse to be a person who sells yourself short?

7) Test and future pace.

As you now orient yourself to what has evoked procrastination in the past and step fully into that experience, what happens now?

Do you now have enough resources so that procrastination will no longer be a problem to you?

Do you like this?

End Notes:

1. "Clearing the path" is the theme of Day 2 of APG (Accessing Personal Genius) training when we run the Dancing with Dragons pattern and also Day 2 of the Ultimate Self-Actualization Workshop when we create and use the Crucible change pattern.

Chapter 6

THE EXPERIENCE OF PEAK PERFORMANCES

From Good to Great

If your ultimate objective is to take your performances to the next level and do so until you can reach the peak of what's possible for you, *what is a peak experience like*? How will you know when you reach it? Are there any signs or indicators?

The exciting answer is, "Yes there are." From the work of Mihaly Csikszentmihalyi on *Flow* to Maslow's work on self-actualizers to my own work on using the Meta-State model of *accessing personal genius,* today we know a lot about the peak performance state, experience, and the peak performances that result.

In this chapter, you will discover how to use the accessing personal genius pattern to step into the flow state at will, the self-actualization quadrants wherein you create the flow state by synergizing your meta-programs and optimize your performances. In these ways you will be able to reach the meta-levels of performance.

In addition, I have included several patterns here that will assist you in reaching peak performance: gestalting, super-charging your attitude, meta-alignment, meta-stating efficiency, stretching, leveraging high return behaviors, and persistence.

In a peak experience, you become *so fully engaged* with what you are doing that you feel almost as if you have "become one" with that activity. Then, being engaged so fully, you find yourself completely engrossed with no room for double-tracking in your mind. As you enter fully into the moment, you lose your sense of time. The movement feels timeless; being in that eternal moment, time stands still for you as the external world rushes on. You also lose your sense of the world, of others, even of yourself. Yet with the loss of awareness of these features of regular consciousness, something else happens.

When you step into this total engagement state, you experience yourself as being *all there*. And that enables you to have more access to all of your knowledge, skills, and abilities. It seems that you are "in the zone" of your best where you are optimally effective. In this peak experience, it feels to you that things just flow and so we call it the flow state.

Now most of us experience this state from time to time. We enter into it when we are fully engaged in a game, or at the movies, or at a party, or when engaged in an enthralling story, or when deep in an intimate conversation. The problem, however, is that the state seems to come and go without rhyme or reason. It appears when we least expect it and it vanishes when we most need it! The question then is how can you develop and work with the flow state so that you can *step into "the zone" at will*.

> *"Do what you can,*
> *with what you have, right where you are."*
> Theodore Roosevelt
>
> *Knowing* what's right isn't the hard thing;
> *Doing* the right things
> —that's the hard thing.

Because a peak experience involves a laser-beam focus of your mental, emotional, personal, physical, and spiritual energies—there is a loss of consciousness in it, and especially self-consciousness. And because of that you are hardly ever aware of being in a peak performance state *at the time* when you are in it. It is only afterwards when you reflect upon the experience that you become aware that you were in it. When you are in the experience, you are not aware of it because you are so present *to the experience* that you're engaged in.

There's something else about peak experiences. When you are in a peak experience, you typically do not experience the peak experience as a happy, ecstatic, or pleasurable experience. In fact, it is more typical that when you are extending all of your energies and straining your capacities to their limits as you stretch forward to do your very best in the engagement you experience it as effort. It is only afterwards as you review the performance that you experience it as a sense of joy, happiness, and pleasure at having performed as you did. And that joy is more typically focused, not on the outward achievement, but mostly on what the experience did to you personally.

It is from multiple peak experiences over a number of months or even years that you are able to take your performance to the next level and eventually create consistently top or *peak performances*—even world-class performances. This is where persistence, resilience, and the kaizen of continuous improvement come into play.

So, given all of that, how ready are you to learn the distinctions and skills for stepping into a peak experience at your choice whenever you so desire?

* ACCESSING PERSONAL GENIUS

The term *genius* in Neuro-Semantics means that you are "in the zone," in a totally committed and passionate state in which you become so totally engaged that the world goes away, your sense of self goes away, time vanishes, and your focus becomes highly intentional as if it is a laser beam. To access a personal genius state, you will establish a set of frames that protect your focused state so that you can get lost in the experience and trust yourself so that you can step out when you so choose.

The design of this pattern is to give you the ability to create and access various "genius" states of engagement. Then you will be able to choose when and where to step in and out of a "flow" state at will.

The qualities of a "genius" state involve focus, clarity, commitment, engagement, being lost in the moment, at your best with all of your resources available, "in the zone," experiencing "flow," etc. Because such states are very focused, you will need to protect them so that you don't contaminate them, dilute them, or reduce them. Finding your own template for how you get lost in a state enables you to recognize that personal genius is fully possible for you, that you've been there before, and that you can now mindfully control the process.

Stepping in and out of the genius state allows you to find and experience the differences that make a difference and to use those distinctions for creating ecological boundaries. These distinctions inform your neurology for when and where to cue the state. By stepping cleanly out of the state, and shifting the focus of your mind and body system, you learn to separate from this intense flow state so that you can leave it cleanly. Do this repeatedly until you can do so impeccably . . . with no residue left over.

The practice of interrupting further enables you to learn to trust yourself, to trust that you will not lose the state and to trust that you can always get it back. This then changes your relationship to the experience and to the idea of "interruption" as interruptions become less and less jarring.

The pattern involves inviting a person to be interrupted and to handle that interruption effectively by stepping out of state, handling whatever is interrupting, and then matter-of-factly stepping back into state. Begin by practicing how to best respond to an interruption. Then take charge of it by interrupting yourself so that you step out of state with a minimum overlap, and then back into the state in a moment's notice.

The brain/ nervous system will learn this pattern quickly and achieve the desire level of competency of state shifting. When the person carries over no mental or emotional residue from one state to the other, but cleanly separates and breaks between them and can then step back in and re-access that state with a strong intensity, you have achieved the goal of this exercise.

Finding a Template for your Genius State

First we access a naturally occurring "genius" state and use it as a template for the process. Doing this does several things. It creates an awareness that you already can and do access focused states of "flow" in which you get lost in an experience. It also refreshes and enriches the natural genius state. It creates a sense of self-confidence about this process and a self-efficacy for running your own brain in this way.

The Pattern:

1) Access a state of innocent witnessing and/or observing.

- What is it like for you to access a pure and discreet state of "just observing?"
- As you step into this position, just notice some of the colors and sounds, etc. of this room. How is that?
- Is there anything you need to release in order to be here fully?
- Have you ever stepped back from something and just observed things?
- As you relax all of your muscles, just observe and enjoy.

2) Identify a fully committed state wherein you can "get lost" in the state.

- Take a moment to think back over your history of special moments, has there ever been a time when you were "in the zone," in a state committed to only one thing? What was that like?
- Have you ever been committed to something else?
- As you find a specific state that you have fairly easy access to and which you can elicit fully, choose a state that comes as close to a full 100% commitment as possible.

3) Access the focus state fully.

- What do you call this commitment state?
- As you recall a time when you were really into this state, step into it fully, seeing what you saw, hearing what you heard, and feeling what you felt. Just be there fully and completely. Describe it until you refresh it and it amplifies. How much are you experiencing it now?
- When you have fully accessed this state to a level of 8 or 9 on a scale of 10, nod to let me know or say so.

4) Practice stepping in and out of the state for impeccable state shifts.

- In just a moment I want you to step out of this state fully and cleanly, leaving this state intact and as you step out, taking as little of it as possible. Okay? So ready, go. Step out to your observer position.
- Would you like to imagine a bubble that protects and secures this genius state?

5) Access an executive level of mind wherein you make decisions.

- There's a part of your mind that makes decisions, that decides when and where to have this genius state. As you now allow a part of your awareness to rise up from the focused state to this executive level state that it can take charge of things while you get lost in this state. Would you like that?
- Would you like this executive level of mind to run the choices you make so that you can be cued about when it is appropriate for staying in this state or coming out? Would you like your executive mind to determine when to make the switch in and out of the genius states and to determine the contexts for the "cage" or boundaries of your genius state?
- Good. Now, just inside your mind, allow your executive level of awareness to answer the following questions:
  Time: When should you have this state? When should you not?
  Place: Where should you have this state? Where not?
  Style: How should you? In what way, with what style? How should you not?
  Criteria: According to what other criteria and qualities?
  Contexts: In what context or contexts? In what contexts should you not?
  Intention: Why should you? Your reasons, agendas, motivations? Why should you not?
  Relational: With whom? With whom not?
  Meaning: For what significance or meaning? What meanings to not give it?
  Resources: What other characteristics and features could you add to this state that would even more fully express the quality and efficiency that you want? Any other resources to add to the genius state? Love, respect, daring, fallibility, balance, etc.?
  Emergencies, Interruptions: For what emergencies or concerns will you step out and interrupt this genius state?
  Other: Any other considerations that you would like to determine the boundaries of this genius state?

6) Commission the executive meta-state and future pace.

- Are you willing to take full responsibility for setting these parameters for this commitment state so that you can fully experience this commitment state? [Yes!]
- Are you willing to take responsibility for letting yourself fully

experience this intense and passionate state? For knowing the limits and boundaries, when to have it and when not, how to have it and how not, will you signal X when to step out?

- As you imagine moving out into your future, are you fully aligned with this? Any objections?

Building a New Genius State

Now that you have a template for how you create and experience one flow state of focus, we are ready to create additional states.

The Pattern:

1) Access the new desired focus state

What focus state of engagement would you like to build? What do you call that state?

Have you ever had a little bit of it? Good. Access what you can, seeing what you saw, hearing what you heard, and feeling what you felt. Go there and *be with it* fully. Amplify. Use your imagination and the "What If . . ." frame to assist.

2) Access a simple state of just observing

Step in and out of this new genius state, practicing a clean state shift, in order to make the distinctions that allow you to know how to have it upon cue.

3) Use your executive mind to further develop the genius state

Re-access the state and then rise up in your mind to the part of your mind that makes decisions so that you, in that facet of your awareness, can answer the following questions.

- ***World:***
  Place: Where should you have this state? Where not?
  Contexts: In what context or contexts? In what contexts should you not?
- ***Time:*** When should you have this state? When should you not?
- ***Intention:***
  Criteria: According to what other criteria and qualities?
  Value: Why should you have this state? How would it be valuable to you?
  Emergencies: For what will you be interrupted? What emergencies will bring you out?
- ***Power:***
  Style: How should you? In what way, with what style? How

should you not?
Resources: What other resources would you like to add to this state that would even more fully express the quality and efficiency that you want? Any other resources to add to the genius state? Love, respect, daring, fallibility, balance, etc.?

- ***Others:***
  Relationship: With whom? With whom not?
- **Self:** Who will you become as you engage in this focus state? How will this affect your self-definition and sense of self?
- ***Meaning:***
  For what significance or meaning? What meanings to not give it?
  Why should you? Your reasons, agendas, motivations? Why should you not?

4) Commission the executive meta-state and future pace

- Are you willing to take full responsibility for setting these parameters for this commitment state so that you can fully experience this commitment state? [Yes!]
- Are you willing to take responsibility for letting yourself fully experience this intense and passionate state? For knowing the limits and boundaries, when to have it and when not, how to have it and how not, will you signal X when to step out?
- As you imagine moving out into your future, are you fully aligned with this? Any objections?

THE META-LEVELS OF PEAK PERFORMANCE

Think about something that you do. Any activity will work. Think about any activity, behavior, and set of actions that make up and defines a performance of any sort. You can think about various skills and competencies that you have at work or in your profession—delegating, leading, creating a product, innovating a new process, customer service, researching, marketing, selling, etc. Or you can think of some personal competency that's more in your personal and private life —golfing, tennis, skiing, exercising regularly, handling family finances, parenting, woodworking, enjoying movies, etc.

At first glance, a *performance* seems about as simple and direct a phenomenon as we could imagine. At first thought, a performance seems like *just a set of actions.* It seems that way, yet it is not. It seems like it is just a primary state experience, that what you see in it is what you get. Again, it is not.

Above and beyond the primary actions that go into making up a performance, *there are many higher level frameworks.* In fact, to take performance to the level of expertise, to take your performance to the highest level so that it becomes a peak performance, you have to *move up* to detect and be able to work with the meta-levels that actually govern and manage the performance.

Why do you need to do that? You need to so that you can embed the performance inside of rich and significant meaning. This is critical if you want your performances to be textured with motivation, passion, and commitment.

Consider the opposite. If you engage in a performance without meaning, it will feel empty, trivial, even futile. Not only will it lack passion and commitment, it will feel positively awful. It is the sense of meaningfulness in your ideas, understandings, and beliefs which you bring to your actions that transform those actions into highly significant performances. *Meaningfulness that enables you to take your performances to ever new levels of skill and passion.* And you do that by framing your actions with meaning and value.

What else does this mean? It means that you actually *manage and govern performance at the higher levels of your mind and consciousness.* It means that without moving up to those meta-state levels, those levels which are full of meanings and frames and beliefs about the lower levels, you will never find the leverage points for enhancing improvement, creating transformation, and becoming world-class in what you do. World-class performance depends upon higher level frame of mind (attitudes) and meanings (passions and intentions).[1]

So, are you ready for an *uplifting* challenge? Then let's move up to the meta-levels of performance so that you can enrich even the most mundane and everyday activity so that it is richly robust in meaning for you.

Detecting the Meta-Levels

As an example of learning how to detect and see the higher levels above and beyond an activity, let's use a simple performance. One of the simplest is that of spelling. How simple is that?

In fact, the developers of the field of NLP modeled what the best spellers do and came up with "the spelling strategy." Basically they discovered that when the best spellers hear a word, as in a spelling context, they immediately make a picture of the letters. For them, it is a *picture.* So they *see* the letters. Some make the letters very big, others use color (bright red, orange, blue and yellow), others see them in special fonts, maybe even in handwriting style, etc.

They also discovered that there's no sounds in their mind about the words, especially no phonetics, and no trying to sound out the words. This means there is no sub-vocalizing, but just a picture of the word. Then they read the letters. They can just as easily read the letters backwards as forwards.

As they do this, they run a kinesthetic test, typically a feeling sensation in the stomach that cues them that the picture they create fits or doesn't fit with a remembered picture of the word. This gives them a "right" or a "wrong" cue. If wrong, they look at the picture again and compare it with remembered images. If right, they call out the letters or write them down.

We call these representational steps a *strategy* and with micro-behaviors like spelling, we model the form or structure of the behavior. In Figure 6:1 I have put the structure of that performance using the representational steps which we use in NLP to model a strategy.

Figure 6:1
The Spelling Strategy

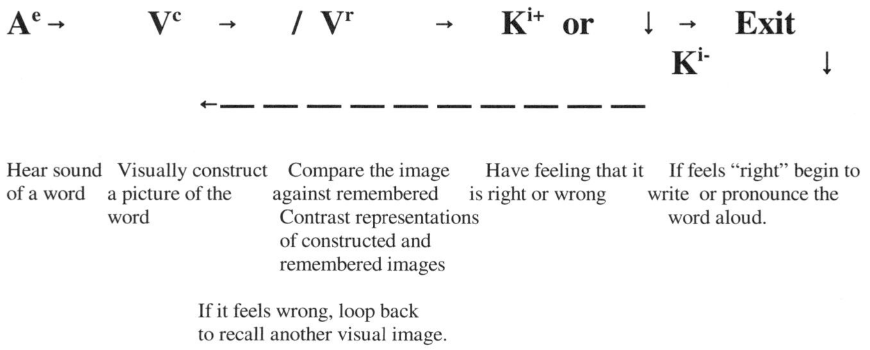

Simple and straight forward, right? Well, not exactly. Years ago when I wrote *NLP Going Meta*, I used the spelling strategy to reveal that there's a lot more to it. *In fact, there's an entire invisible meta-domain of many levels above it.* That book is about the power and importance of adding the meta-levels, or meta-states, to the modeling process. The problem is that above and beyond the specific how-to information about spelling are all of our *beliefs* about spelling, the *meanings* we give to spelling, the *reasons, intentions,* and *expectations* we have about the importance or unimportance of spelling, how we think about ourselves as spellers (identity), and dozens of other meta-frames.

- Do we like spelling?
- What emotions and emotional associations do we have to the activity of spelling?
- What memories from school or home do we have about spelling words, spelling contests, grades, etc.?
- What does spelling a word wrong mean to you?
- What does it say about you?

All of these awarenesses and feelings are the meta-states in the back of our mind about the experience and activity and they dramatically affect and influence our performance of spelling.

Figure 6:2

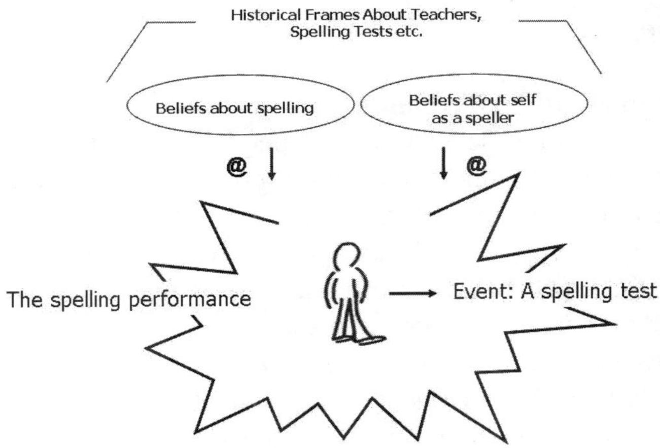

Meta-Levels Governing Spelling

Performance Questions

Obviously, there's a lot more going on *behind the scenes* in any and every performance that you engage in than meets the eye.

- What does this mean for those who regularly experience performance reviews?
- What does this mean for those who want to take their performance to the next level?
- What does this mean for those who coach, train, or consult with high performers who want to excel in their field?
- What does this mean for those who trouble-shoot poor performances or those who under-perform?

In a word it means that you have to look not only at performance's flow through its various steps and stages (its horizontal strategy), you also have to move upward to the meta-frameworks that involve the performer's inward mental contexts (its meta-strategy). These contexts within the performer's mind determine the beliefs, feelings, identities, expectations, and scores of other frames which cannot but help to influence the performance.

Four Dimensions of Performance
1) Behaviors with strategies
2) Feedback on the behaviors
3) Interferences to the strategy
4) Reward structures

The Base Levels of Performance

At the base or primary level with any performance there are almost always numerous steps and stages in the process. These involve the how-to steps that we can analyze a behavior and break it down into a flow-chart. In this way we can explore where a person begins, what happens next, and where does that go and so on until the performance is completed. Almost everything *at the base level* is behavioral, and so governed by the principles of behaviorism or what's called "learning theory," including reinforcements, pain and pleasure, feedback, etc. This gives us four key dimensions of any performance. Now we can explore these four dimensions.

Figure 6:3

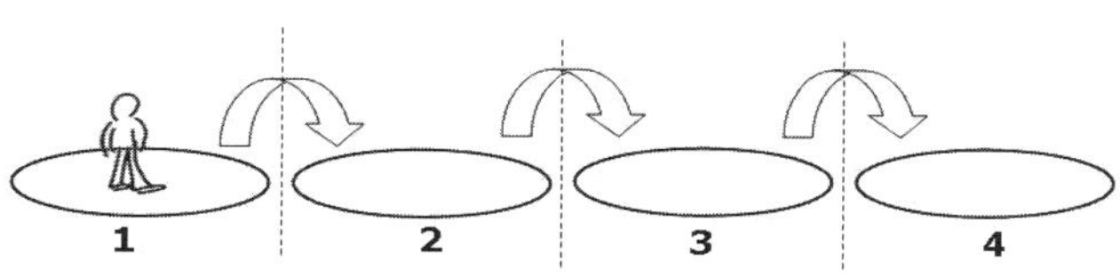

1) Behaviors with strategies
2) Feedback on the behaviors
3) Interferences to the strategy
4) Reward structures

1) Behaviors with strategies:
We begin with the capacities and talents which enable you to engage in the behavior and your personal strategies for understanding how to carry the actions out. *Strategy questions* explore what to do, how to do it, when, where, etc. Above and beyond those explorations are the *belief questions*—all of your thoughts, ideas, understandings, concepts, expectations, frames or in a word, *meanings*, about the performance. What does it mean? What else?

2) Feedback with behaviors:
Performance only has value and meaning depending on its effects and results. This is where feedback comes in giving you a mirror so you can see what happens as a result of the performance. Here we ask,

- Is it working? How is it working?
- How well is it working?
- How do you know?
- How do you measure it?
- How do others perceive it? What's happening?

The feedback that you receive (in terms of effects, results, and responses in the environment and from others) gives you corrective information about the next step and about ongoing adjustments. Of course using feedback as a mechanism for peak performance depends upon your openness to feedback and flexible adaptability in terms of making adjustments. Without such, performance stays mediocre and you are unable to reach the next level or peak of your performance.

3) Interferences to the strategy:
This dimension of a performance refers to all of the possible interferences that can arise to constrain or sabotage a performance. When interferences come from *inside*—they are personal limitations and inabilities. When they arise from *outside*—there are environmental constraints and social influences. Here we ask:

- Are you staying with it?
- Is anything stopping you? If so, what?
- Do you start well?
- Do you persist?

- Do you bounce back from set-backs?
- Do you complete what you start?
- How do you handle obstacles?
- How much resilience do you have?

4) Reward Structures:
Learning Theory (Behaviorism) teaches that what is rewarded grows and solidifies, and what is not rewarded extinguishes. The theory also warns about the inhibiting influence that pain, consequences, and negative results will have on stopping or preventing performance. This dimension of the reward structures which *reinforce* what you are doing, validating and supporting some actions and dis-validating and punishing other actions plays a crucial role if you want to take performances to new levels of expertise. That is, you need a structure that supports the ongoing development of the competency. So we ask:

- What keeps it going?
- Is it well supported? By what?
- How?
- Are there any secondary gains in avoiding it or not developing further?

The Meta-Levels of Performance
So, over and above the base level are all of the frames that make up the mental context. In contrast to the external things of the base level, these things are inside. As internal factors they move you into the cognitive and the conative dimensions, that is, the dimension of thought and choice. The leader, manager, coach, consultant, or parent who does not know how to elicit and work with these higher levels of performance will miss most of what drives behavior and will not know the leverage points of change.

How do we detect and explore these meta-levels? In the following diagrams (Figures 6:3 and 6:4), I have made a list of the basic meta-questions for both the primary and sensory level and for the meta-levels above the four dimensions of a performance.[2]

With this we can now engage in a *Meta-Performance Analysis* in working with any performance—business, personal, athletic, etc.

igure 6:4

PERFORMANCE DIMENSIONS AND LEVELS

A Cognitive Behavioral (Neuro-Semantic) Checklist

Belief Questions #12—24

Who are you in this?
Permission to do without believing in it?
Value doing it?

Decided to do it?

Believe it will work?

Other priorities?

Got better way?

an follow procedures?

Why do it?
How does it fit?

Ecological?

Believe in?

Value Feedback?

Is it possible to do?

Permission to do?

Resources to handle it?

Aligned to do it?

Believable?

Don't believe can handle the interference?

Pains for not doing?

Pleasures for not doing?

Negative consequences for doing?
Support in doing?

Pleasures for doing?

Permission?

Discipline to handle?

1
ACTION–PROCESS
Strategy questions #1-6

What? How?

Who? When? where? With whom? Complete it?

2
FEEDBACK
Questions #7-11

How are you doing?
How do you know? Do you think you are already succeeding?
How do measure it? KPIs?
Know how others perceive

3
INTERFERENCE
Questions #25-31

Able and free to do it?
Incapable? Obstacles?

Personal limitations
Interferences–
Internal?
External?

Anything stop you?
What?

4
REWARD STRUCTURES
Questions #32-35

Pain? (Punishment)	Pleasure? (Reward)
- for doing it	+ for doing it?
+ for *not* doing it	- for *not* doing it?

Restraining forces? Driving forces?
- pain for doing - pleasure avoiding

Figure 6:5

META-PERFORMANCE ANALYSIS

Neuro-Semantic Questions and Meta-Questions for Exploration

STAGE 1: The Actions and Process

1. Do you know *what* to do? *Targe*
2. Do you know *how* to do it? *Strateg*
3. Are you fully *capable* of doing it?
4. Do you know *when* and *where* to do it? *Specific*
5. Do you know how to *complete* it? *Completio*
6. Are you willing to complete it? Do you know how to improve your performance?

Strategy	Feedback	Performance Beliefs	Interferences	Reward Structures
1	2	3	4	5

STAGE 2: Feedback

7. Are you open to feedback about your performance? How much? *Feedbac*
8. Do you think or assume that you are already doing it?
9. How are you doing? How do you know?
10. How are you measuring it? What are your KPIs?
11. What do other perspectives see? (Mine, your bosses, customers, colleagues, employees, etc.)

STAGE 3: Performance Beliefs *Back of the mind consideration*
Motivation

12. Do you know *why* to do it?
13. Why do you do it? How does it fit into this business?
14. Is this reason strong enough motivation for you?
15. Do you think it will not work?
16. Do you think your way is better? Do you think you have a better way?
17. Do you think something else is more important?
18. Do you have other priorities?
19. Are you *aligned* in doing it?
20. Have you *decided* to do it?

1. Do you *believe* it will work?
2. Do you *want* it to work? Do you *value* doing it?
3. Are you *willing* to do it even if you don't want to?
4. Do you have permission within yourself to do this?

TAGE 4: Troubleshooting Interferences

5. Is there anything that stops you or could stop you?
6. Are there obstacles in the way beyond your control? *External Blockages*
7. How is it beyond your control?
8. What is within your control?
9. Are there any personal limitations creating incapacity? *Internal block: Limitations*
0. Are there any personal problems creating incapacity? *Internal block: Problems*
1. Could anyone do it? *External block: Impossible*

TAGE 5: Reward Structures *Secondary benefits*

2. Are there any positive consequences for doing it?
   What do you get from doing it?
   Do you feel supported in doing this?
3. Are there any negative consequences for doing it?
   Are you afraid of negative consequences? *Internal block: Fear*
   What do you get from *not* doing it?
   Do you feel punished in some way for doing this?
4. Is there a positive consequence for *not* doing it?
   What do you get from under-performing and procrastinating?
5. Is there a negative consequence for *not* doing it?
   What price do you pay when you under-perform?

* GESTALTING HIGHER STATES

A "gestalt" refers to some *configuration* of mind-and-emotion that emerges from many interactive parts in a system so that the result is "a whole which is greater than the sum of the parts." In a gestalt state we have one or more levels of meta-states outframing a primary state so that as a result something new and higher arises. To create this, meta-state one resource after another to texture or laminate a primary state. Keep doing so until a new gestalt emerges. This allows you to create higher and more complex states. We call these more complex states, *gestalt* states.

The Pattern:

1) Identify the state or experience and the component elements needed to make up a rich and vibrant gestalt.

What state do you want to design?

Menu list: optimism, seeing opportunities, courage, etc.

What stops you from this rich experience?

What state would counter-act that interference and enable you to experience the gestalt state?

What elements do you need in order to create this customized state of mind/body for yourself?

(Calm, empowered, centered, focused, connected, wonder, grateful, appreciation, excited, passion, mischievousness, humor, playfulness, etc.)

What else do you need so that this higher state will emerge? As you access each resource and apply it to yourself, keep checking to see when the state emerges. Has it emerged yet?

2) Experiment until you identify a gestalt structure.

The gestalt structure will involve a particular syntax, order, and sequence of the parts that allow the "mix" of thoughts, feelings, beliefs to work for you in eliciting the higher state. As you use your discoveries and begin to design engineer the new state, how playful and experimental do you feel yourself being as you do this? How much more would you need to be? As you try on *passion*, notice how that influences and effects your primary state . . .

3) Identify your reference primary state then access and amplify each resource as you relate it to that referent.

Use small and simple examples until you access the state, then keep layering it with more of the resources.
Where would you want this higher resource state of . . . (i.e., courage, seeing opportunities, etc.)?
Just notice that situation, reference, person, etc. . . . and we'll use that as our reference point.
Have you ever fully felt X (first resource)? Be there again . . . fully . . .
Now as you feel that, notice how it transforms your experience of the primary state reference . . .
Is that enough? Need more?
Have you ever fully felt Y (second resource)? Be there in that . . . fully . . . and as you feel X, you can feel Y also about that primary state reference . . .
Keep repeating until the gestalt emerges.

4) ***Apply the gestalt state into your future.***

Imagine moving through life in the weeks and months to come with this higher state of mind . . .
Imagine operating from this frame at work, at home, in your relationships, etc. Notice how it changes things.

5) ***Embody it by making an empowering decision as you confirm it.***

Do you like this?
Does this enhance your life? Empower you as a person?
Would you like to have this as your program for how to operate in this area of life?
Is the executive part of your mind willing to take full responsibly to elicit this when you need it?

* SUPER-CHARGING ATTITUDES

What is a performance without attitude? It's nothing. Merely being able to *do* something, even doing it with excellence will not lead to a peak experience and will not guarantee *peak* performance. Once you reach a certain level of expertise, attitude increasingly becomes a critical factor.

An *attitude* is a gestalt state that you can now install as a frame of mind. Attitude, as a holistic term, refers to your full mind-body-emotion stance toward something. It includes your mental and emotional stance. It includes your physiology. Can attitudes be taught? You bet. Components of attitude are the components of state.

What attitudes do you need to eliminate?
What attitudes do you need to build, develop, and install?
What attitudes do you need to juice up or super-charge?

The Pattern:

1) Identify the attitudes that you want to juice up.

Is there any attitude that you'd like to have that would make your life better?
How would you describe that attitude? What is it like? What would you call it?
Who else has that attitude?
How is it valuable?
What would it allow you to do or to experience?

2) Specify how you want to super-charge the attitude to make it more powerful or profound.

In what way would you like to super-charge that attitude?
With what new qualities or properties?
How compelling and memorable would that be for you?
How would that affect you in mind-and-body?
What would you be feeling if you had that attitude fully installed?

3) Access, amplify, and apply to the primary state.

Where, when, and with whom are you in a state of mind with an attitude that needs charging up?
As you access each resource, amplify it until it has sufficient charge, and apply it and then notice how it changes things for

you.

4) Install it within you for your tomorrows.

So you'd like this attitude as part of the way you go into tomorrow?
When you future pace it into the weeks and months to come, how do you like that?
Are you fully aligned with them?
Does any part of you object to it?

* META-ALIGNMENT

Patterns that structure a new way of thinking, feeling, talking, and acting will not be fully installed until you are fully aligned with it. That's why we end most processes by asking:

"Are all of your higher levels of thinking and emoting fully aligned with this? Are there any parts that object to using this?"

This pattern provides a way to align with your highest levels and meta-states to give us an overall sense of integration, congruency, wholeness, and well-being. The design is to refine and enhance a behavior for greater pose, power, elegance, or focus, to juice up your performance to make it more exquisite. I developed this pattern from the distinctions that Robert Dilts used in creating his "neuro-logical levels" of behavior, capacity, belief, value, identity, and mission or spirit.

The Pattern:

1) Identify a primary state sensory-based behavior that you want more alignment with.

What do you do that you consider very important, but which sometimes lacks the full range of congruency, power, and focus that you would like?
What behavior would you like to do with more personal alignment, congruency, and integrity?
Begin by describing this behavior in sensory-based terms. If we used a video camera what would we see or hear or feel? (Behavior)
Where do you do this? (Environment) Where not? When?

When not?

2) Identify the mental-emotional skills and abilities which enable you to do this (Capability).

How do you use your thinking-and-feeling to pull this off?
What strategy do you deploy in doing this?
How do you know *how to* do this?

3) Identify the meta-levels of beliefs and values that support and empower this. (Beliefs/ Values)

Why do you engage in this?
What beliefs guide this behavior?
What importance does this hold for you?

4) Identify identities which emerges from this (Identity).

Who are you that you engage in this behavior?
What does engaging in this behavior say about your identity?
Who does this make you?

5) Identify the purpose that arises (Vision, Mission, Spirit).

How does this fit into your overall sense of destiny and purpose?
When you step into this, fully and completely, what do you experience?

6) Identify the decision that supports this (Decision).

Have you decided to do this? You will?
This is your intention? How have you formatted this decision?

7) Describe these meta-levels of meaning with a metaphor or story (Metaphor).

What metaphor or story encapsulates this meta-state?
Let it emerge . . . notice also other things that might emerge: sounds, colors, shapes, music, light, etc.

8) Integrate fully by applying the higher levels to the lower levels.

As you even more fully step into this awareness and experience it completely, snapshot it and honor it and let it enrich all of your levels . . . and now imagine bringing this back down the levels, letting it coalesce into the lower levels thereby enriching them. How do you now experience the behavior, environment, etc. when you bring this higher level

> with you? And as you bring each of these levels, in turn, to bear upon your everyday states, how well do you like that?

* META-STATING EFFICIENCY

Our first consideration of a performance concerns effectiveness: "Is this performance effective?" We ask that to discover if you are doing the right thing. Is what you're doing moving you in the direction of your goals, values, and higher intentions? No behavior, no matter how skillful, is *effective* if it doesn't contribute to your ultimate objectives. Making good time (efficiency) in the wrong direction doesn't help you get to your destination. That efficiency would be ineffective.

So after you establish your effective direction, we ask *the efficiency question.* "Is this performance efficient?" While efficiency follows effectiveness, we ask it to check the quality of your execution. In this effectiveness is an aspect of strategy and strategic thinking to make sure that you are on the right path whereas *efficiency* is about your tactics ensuring that you are efficient in what you are doing.

Installing a new effective response pattern that works to enrich your experience makes you effective, yet are we efficient? Are you making the most of your effort? It is the lack of efficiency that often prevents you from the top performance that you aspire to.

> "*Efficiency* is one of the most important components of wealth accumulation. People who become wealthy *allocate* their time, energy, and money in ways consistent with enhancing their net worth." (*The Millionaire Next Door*, p. 71).

The design of this pattern is to develop your efficiency so it is exquisite and smooth.

Primer for the Pattern:
Think of something that you have learned do very efficiently, but which you did not always do efficiently. Think of that behavior when you did it inefficiently and now when you do it efficiently. What's the difference?

What saps your energy and focus?

Menu list: Indecisive, bored, unfocused, fear, at cross-

Inefficiently	Efficiently
Wasted time and energy	Used time and energy wisely
Didn't plan . . . scattered, unfocused	Planned, focused, making notes
Disoriented	Thinking strategically, on purpose
Inactive, procrastinating	Sorting out Important things
Back & forth indecisively	Making a decision and acting
Slow: unskilled, laborious	Effective in organizing
Failure to delegate	Effective in delegating tasks
Unimportant activities	Eliminate unimportant activities
Clutter	Eliminate clutter
Excessive socializing	Balance between activities
Failure to say "No."	Good Boundaries
Standards too high	Optimizing

purposes, too many choices, overwhelmed, regret, status quo, self-judgment, meaninglessness.

What puts energy into your step?

Menu list: Meaning, focus, purpose, challenge, courage, commitment, humor, connection, love, contribution.

The Pattern:

1) Access and fully represent "personal efficiency."

Think of something that you have done with efficiency. When you did not waste time, effort, energy, or resources doing it. Has there ever been a time like that in your entire life?
What does personal efficiency, effectiveness, productivity, mean to you?
What does it look, sound, and feel like for you?
How would that enhance your life?

[Keep asking about how you represent personal efficiency. Do this until you get a fully described map about it.]

What key skills or core competencies do you need to continually practice to increase your output and productivity?

Do you know that you can increase your efficiency and your effectiveness by becoming better and better at your key tasks? Are you willing to become better at the most important things you do?

2) Check neuro-semantic frames about personal efficiency.

What do you think/ feel *about* this concept of personal efficiency?

What comes to mind when you think about personal efficiency?

Do you access a positive or negative state?

What's your frame of mind about it?

Does it improve the quality of your life?

3) Check and give permission to take orders.

Do you have permission to "take orders?"

What comes to mind when you think about being "under" orders? When you have to do something? What's your attitude about the things you "have to do?"

Can you give yourself instructions and positively just follow those instructions?

Give yourself permission if you need to.

4) Amplify the personal efficiency state.

How much do you feel and sense this feeling of personal efficiency from 0 to 10?

Allow your feelings and awareness to double. Let it grow and increase.

What else can you do to step even more fully into this state?

5) Apply this state to your tasks and activities.

Holding this state . . . notice how it begins to transform the tasks and core competencies of the personal efficiency that you want.

6) Neutralize and integrate the neuro-semantics of "work," self-discipline.

As you feel this fully . . . and let it grow . . . You can recall how that others call this state of personal efficiency *"work."* And you can too . . . know that it's not really work, but fun and efficiency.

And experiencing this in this positive way, you can recognize that others may look at this and call it *self-discipline,* and so can you. But when you exercise your personal power to get yourself to do what you want to do, should do, when you need to do it, regardless of whether you feel like it or not, you know it's just being efficient!

Do you yet have the habit of just doing the things that need to be done?

7) Connect and align your everyday activities with your highest intentions.

Are you clear about your goals and objectives in your performance? Since your efficiency arises from clarity of intention, are you now clear about your goals in this performance?

What are your top 10 goals for this year about this performance? If you were to accomplish one of these goals, which one would have the greatest positive impact on your life? What is your most important goal? Second? Third?

Is every part of your mind full aligned with this efficiency in the area?

Any objections to being resourceful in this way?

8) Loop back to identity and other higher frames.

If you moved out into your future with this . . . day after day, week after week, etc. would this affect your self-definition? Your identity?

Would you like that?

This is who you would become more and more?

9) Future pace and symbolize.

Imagine doing this into your future . . .

What is this like? What symbol or metaphor . . . a color, song, whatever comes to mind that you can use as a symbol for this way of being.

* STRETCHING

What's involved in creating a lifestyle wherein you consistently produce peak performances? It requires that you continually push and stretch yourself. There's a reason for this—success is dangerous! With success and with living longer and longer with success and great accomplishments, the more comfortable you will become. And with comfort, the less able you will rally yourself to something new that might induce discomfort. With comfort, you get into a rut and your performance becomes too easy. You may think you have "hit a plateau" when in reality, you have just gotten comfortable with your current level.

The fact is, no person or business is at its best when life is too safe or too comfortable. You can't afford to live too long in a status quo mode. To open the door of opportunity for innovation, you have to drive out complacency. Explore your own situation:

- Am I just maintaining or am I stretching?
- Am I raising the bar of performance?
- What are my performance standards?
- What's the next level that I could take them to?
- Are my goals challenging or do they elicit a yawn and put me to sleep?
- What am I doing to differentiate myself so that I stand out?
- What am I doing to reach my full potential?
- What mile markers have I set to measure ongoing progress?

The Pattern:

1) Identify a stretch goal.

What goal have you set or will you set that is a *stretch* for you?
How do you know this is a *stretch* for you?
Would others describe this as a stretch for you?

2) Expand and enrich the stretch goal.

How safe or dangerous is this goal?
How do you determine the safety or risk of the goal?
Can you clearly see all of the steps necessary to reach the goal?
If so, how it is a stretch?
What is realistic in the goal?
What is the likelihood that you will reach the goal?

What is a stretch for you? How is it a stretch?
What will stretch in you in order to reach this goal?
How exciting and compelling is this goal?

3) Stretch the stretch goal some more.

How would you measure the size of this goal from being a small goal to a big goal?
What is a big goal for you?
Have you ever set a big goal and went for it?

4) Develop resources for setting a good stretch goal.

What resources will you need to be able to pull this off?
What success will you have with going after this goal even if you fall short of completely reaching it?
What mile marker will indicate that you've achieved more by setting this stretch goal?

* LEVERAGING HIGH RETURN BEHAVIORS

To get the results you want, you have to get the right things done. Doing the wrong things *well*, while an act of competence, will not make the performance difference that you desire. To get substantial results, you need to find the high leverage actions, actions that bring a high return on your performances.

> "Give me a single place to stand,
> and a lever, and I will move the Earth."
> *Archimedes*

The *Pareto Principle* describes the 80/20 rule which says that 20 percent of your effort creates 80% of your results, or that 20% of people in any organization will be doing 80% of the work. This arose from Italian economist Vilfredo Pareto who discovered that a small minority of the top earners always accounted for a large majority of the total wealth in a country. The principle of the vital few or a "tipping point" (Gladwell Maxwell) orients you to finding leverages so that you can concentrate on the key variables by which you can multiply your effectiveness.

The Pattern:

1) Identify your 80/20 activities and variables.

What 20% of your activities delivers 80% of your best results?
What are your high return activities for you as a person?
What are your high return activities in your performance?
By way of contrast, what are some of your low-return activities?
What takes you out of your strengths?
If there are a few key variables that lead to the great majority of the results, what are those variables?
Where are you outstanding?
Where do you *spike* (a distinctive strength wherein you are unusually powerful)? (Koch, 2003, p. 32)

2) Identify your stop-doing list.

What low-return tasks do you need to *stop* doing?
What low-return tasks can you outsource or delegate?
How much time and energy will this free up for you?
How habitual are these low-return tasks?
What seduces you into doing them?
What will you need to do to stop them?

3) Outsource your other 80%.

Is there any area where you're working hard to become mediocre?
What do you need to outsource through partners or delegating?

4) Develop your top 20%.

What strength do you need to develop and hone and bring to excellence?
What daily practice can you set up to do that?
What books do you need to read, experts interview, and trainings take to develop your 20%?

5) Develop a performance plan from your 80/20.

What high-leverage activities in your greatest strengths will you use to develop into a business or business idea?
What 20% of your people create 80% of the results?
How much time and energy will you devote to them?
What 20% demographic creates 80% of your sales or business?

What are you doing with these high-potential sales demographics?
How will you breathe life into these 20% high leverage variables?
What will create the most wealth for the least effort and capital?
How will you keep tweaking and embellishing the 20% to keep innovation continuing?

4) Commission and future pace.
Will the part of your mind that makes decisions take full responsibility to give up the low-return behaviors and to initiate the high-return activities?
As you imagine doing that in the coming days, are you fully aligned with this?

PERSISTENCE

> "Success seems to be largely a matter of hanging on after others have let go."
> *William Feather*
>
> "Every adversity has the seed of an equivalent or greater benefit."
> *W. Clement Stone*

Finally, you need persistence. The state of persistence enriches us with the power to persevere, hang-in, and bounce back from set-backs. Things will happen, challenges will arise, there will be set-backs, but with resilience and persistence you will not be defeated. To persist at a task, job, or work you need to let it become absorbing, you need to find value in it, and you need to manage your own states.

In terms of wealth creation, the self-made, first-generation rich millionaires stayed with their vision and persisted in learning, growing, and becoming more skilled and competent. Tenacity depends on intensity and purity of vision. Then you can stick to your vision and passion. The self-made, first-generation rich millionaires were *not* weak of heart, but strong, resilient, and dedicated.
When Andrew Carnegie modeled the secret of wealth accumulation

of Napoleon Hill, he wrote the following that highlights the importance of this frame of mind.

> "A twenty-year research of hundreds of well-known men, many of whom admitted that they had accumulated their vast fortunes through the aid of the Carnegie secret." (pp. 16-17)
>
> "I had the happy privilege of analyzing both Mr. Edison and Mr. Ford, year by year, over a long period of years and therefore, the opportunity to study them at close range, so I speak from actual knowledge when I say that *I found no quality save persistence,* in either of them, that even remotely suggested the major source of their stupendous achievements. . . . persistence, concentration of effort, and definiteness of purpose were the major sources of their achievements." (p. 164)

Thomas Stanley and William Danko (*1996*): researched the wealth in America and came up with some *Surprising Secrets.*

> *"How do you become wealthy?* Here, too, most people have it wrong. It is seldom luck or inheritance or advanced degrees or even intelligence that enables people to amass fortunes. Wealth is more often the result of a lifestyle of hard work, *perseverance, planning,* and most of all, *self-discipline.*" (pp. 1-2)

Persistence, as the ability to sustain effort in pursuing your aims and desires in the face of opposition or difficulty, is obviously critical.

> "Those who have cultivated the habit of persistence seem to enjoy insurance against failure. No matter how many times they are defeated, they finally arrive up toward the top of the ladder." (Napoleon Hill, p. 154)

So what makes up this state of mind of persistence? It is based upon definiteness of purpose, desire, self-reliance, definite plans, accurate knowledge, cooperation, and habit. These are the elements or variables that make up the state and this explains that you can cultivate it as a meta-state or as a gestalt state.

End of Chapter References

1. This means that there's an entire invisible domain of meta-frames—made up what we call in NLP and Neuro-Semantics as *meta-states* and meta-programs which exist *above and beyond any and every performance.* So if you want to take your performances to new levels of expertise, you have to become a meta-detective and a meta-coach of these higher levels.

2. The source that stimulated me to develop this was *Coaching for Improved Work Performance* (2000), Ferdinand F. Fournies, (p. 94). Chapter 7: A Practical Approach to Managing People in Business. He created 16 questions to explore the question, "Why don't employees do what they are supposed to do?" generated from the responses of 25,000 supervisors and managers.

Chapter 7

LIFE IN THE ZONE

OF PEAK PERFORMANCE

Self-actualization is the center focus of Neuro-Semantics because our aim is to embody meaning as we perform our highest and best meanings. This is Neuro-Semantics' practical focus—actualizing your highest visions to make them real in your life as you develop your best potentials. Given this, we focus our energy on such questions as:

- How do you actualize your potentials?
- How do you identify, find, and develop your potential abilities, skills, identity, dreams, values, and meanings?
- How do you move from being a novice to developing true expertise in the areas that you love and are passionate about?
- How do you make real in actual life your highest meanings and principles?

Because the term *neuro-semantics* refers to these two facets of human experience, meaning and performance, it is about two worlds. First, it is about *the internal world of your meanings* (semantics). This relates to all of your ideas, beliefs, decisions, sense of self, etc. Second, it is about *the external world of pragmatic performances* (neurology) which you engage in using your nervous systems and physiology. And with this we now have three facets that govern the unleashing process.

If self-actualization emerges through synthesizing meaning and performance then together these facets of experience make up your mind-body or neuro-semantic states and directs attention to three activities of Neuro-Semantics:

1) *Performing meaning:* taking the meaningful ideas and beliefs that you know, closing the know-doing gap, and robustly acting on your highest and best meanings.

2) *Giving rich and vibrant meaning to performances:* endowing your everyday activities with the richest and most robust meanings as you frame and reframe. This enriches your performances making them more significant and valuable.

3) *Suspending meanings:* undoing and unmaking any meaning that leads to non-resourceful performances. It is *interrupting* any performances that are driven by limiting and non-robust meanings. It is releasing old and/or toxic meanings which may have become embodied creating sabotaging or non-useful behaviors.

Self-Actualization Quadrants

When you combine your meanings and performances you create a personal synergy of power and congruency. In Neuro-Semantics we have designed the Self-Actualization Quadrants to facilitate this. In terms of performance (and especially peak performance), you can profile and plot where you are along these two axes.

Because self-actualization is a function of meaning and performance, these make up the heart of self-actualization and the *Self-Actualization Quadrants.* Self-actualization is ultimately based on these two variables: *meaning* and *performance.*

Meaning:

This refers to what you find significant, important, valuable, and challenging. Find or create what's *meaningful* in what you do so that your experiences and your actions are significant, valuable, and important. This is where dreaming, imagining, anticipating and using your mind invests value, worth, and life into what you are engaged in.

Performance:

This refers to how you are able to actually do your actions and behaviors. Now take action to make something happen about what you believe in as important. You have to translate the great ideas in your head into behaviors in your body so they become your way of being in the world.

Figure 7:1

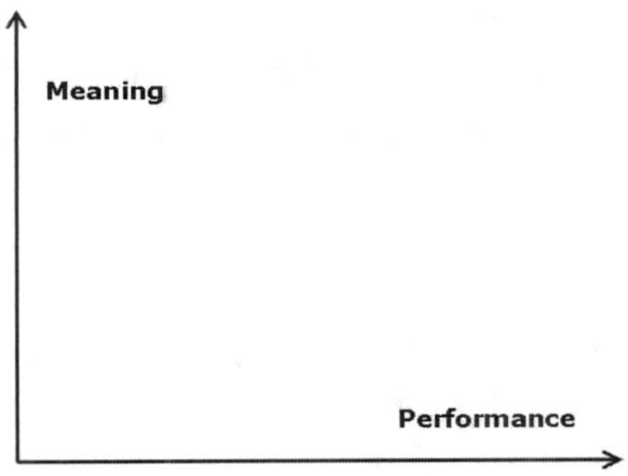

In the Self-Actualization Psychology that Abraham Maslow pioneered and developed, self-actualization does not refer to an ordinary person with something added. It is rather the ordinary person with nothing taken away. The self-actualizing person is not a super-human, but a regular person who has transcended most of the limitations that inhibit and diminish most people. This enables the self-actualizer to be a "fully functional person" (Carl Rogers).

When we format these two phenomena as two axes, they create four quadrants. When you put these together you integrate these two key facets of human nature that many have falsely separated and treated as polar opposites, *being* and *doing.*

These two variables now give us of *the Self-Actualization Quadrants.* Based on meaning and performance, these quadrants show how developing your mind (e.g., your meanings, understandings, knowledge, beliefs, dreams, etc.) and your body (e.g., your talents, capabilities, skills, competencies, and expertise), actualizes your potential self. You can now make what is only potential, actual. As you map your potentials and latent possibilities, you can then work out how to integrate and embody your highest meanings.

Abraham Maslow described this integration as a synthesis or synergy. The synergy of the whole arises from integrating the opposites that are typically viewed as a dichotomy. This integration creates a wholeness that enables you to actualize your whole self to *be* and *do* your best in all of your life. It facilitates a psychological wholeness and health.

The Quadrants

These quadrants map human development along the meaning and the performance axes. As noted in previous writings,[1] you can use the Quadrants to identify or profile where you are in terms of these factors and what you need to do to move fully into the Fourth Quadrant—*the pathway of self-actualization.*

When I first developed *the Self-Actualization Quadrants,* I diagramed the Quadrants using the X and Y axes as 90 degree axes. You can also use the Axes in a different way. While the Axes maps meaning and performance as if they are radically different phenomena, *we can also map them as facets of the same thing.* I did this originally by opening up the Axes from being pictured as a ninety-degree angle that the two axes form a line or a continuum. From the X and Y axes that create the Self-Actualization Quadrants I diagrammed the two axes forming a single 180-degree line with each at the polar ends. This created a new picture. The apparent dichotomy of the polar opposites with its dynamic tension becomes a continuum.

Figure 7:2

Meaning **Performance**

Highly Abstract Concepts	Metaphorical Knowledge	Practical Knowl.	Felt Knowl.	Habit Ritual	Competence	Mastery

Historically, in Western countries we have viewed mind and body as opposites, as polarities. Using either/or Aristotelian thinking, we interpret reflecting and acting, being and doing, meaning and performance as opposites. But now we can make them facets of the same thing.

Figure 7:3
The Self-Actualization Quadrants

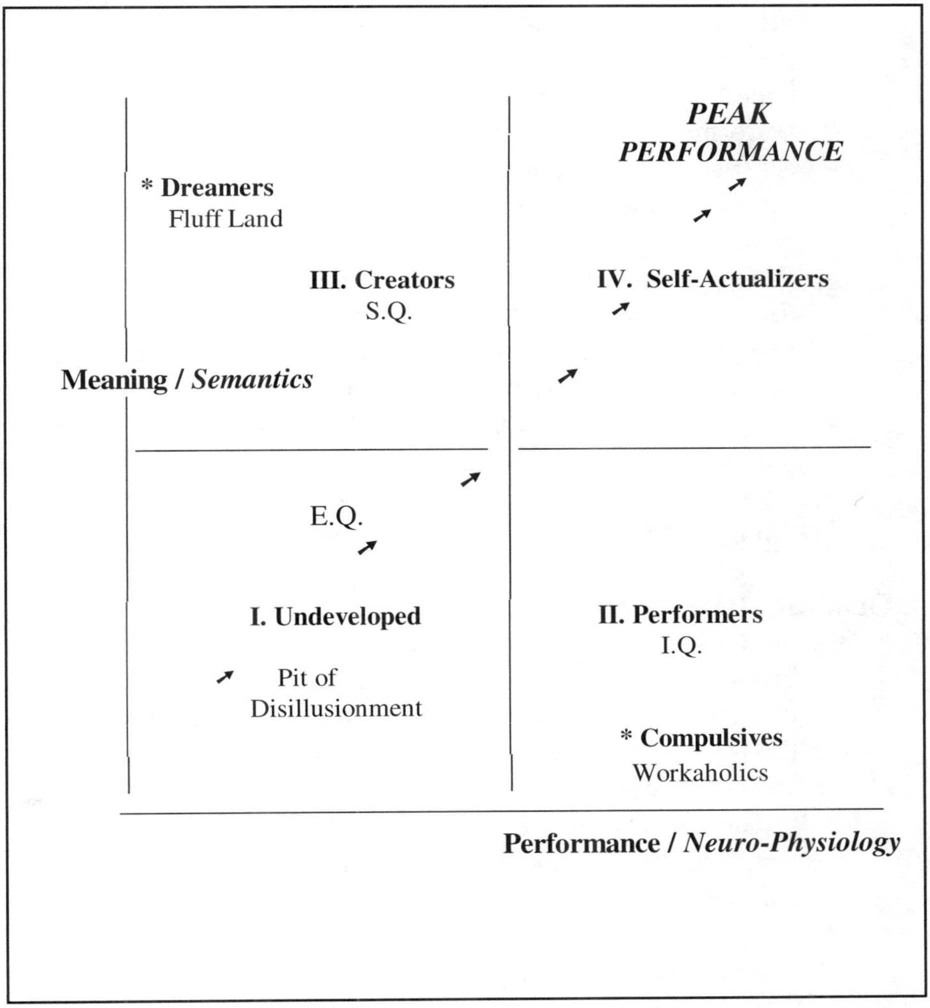

Quadrant I: Undeveloped

We all begin here. We are born undeveloped—we don't know what anything *means* and we are unable to *do* anything! We begin completely ignorant and incompetent. But there's good news: it is all uphill from there. From there you experience an inescapable development of mind (for meaning, understanding, believing, etc.) and body (for activities, emotions, skills, and performance). It is there in your cognitive and behavioral development that you move out on the two axes.

Quadrant II: Performers

You act, you behave, you speak, you take action, you react, you learn to respond. It is in these ways that you learn the behaviors and the strategies that work for succeeding in various domains of life. If your style, disposition, and/or conditioning facilitates this, you increasingly become a skilled performer. You become the kind of person who finds ways to act that increase your competency. In this way, you learn a response pattern to the world of things, events, and people as being *active.*

When over-done, however, you will act so quickly and decisively that you will step forward often and regularly and may even become compulsive about acting. As this continues, you give less and less time to reflecting until you become almost entirely reactive. Do this long enough, however, and you can burn-out and fall back into the pit of disillusionment. To create a holistic synergy, you will need an equal mix of thought and reflection.

Quadrant III: Creators

You also dream, imagine, go off on flights of fantasy. You invent, you create, you have a million, no, a zillion ideas! It is in these ways that you spend your time and use your mind. If this is your primary style, disposition, and/or conditioning then you increasingly become a skilled creator. That is, you are brilliant in thinking up ideas and schemes. This is your strength. You are the kind of person who is forever thinking and imagining and talking.

Your primary response patterns is that of *reflective* rather than active. When you over-do this, however, you become so addicted to dreams, options, alternatives, ideas, creativity, inspiration, etc. and it becomes so much of a rush you spend less and less time and have less patience with dealing with the reality of doing something about your dreams. Do this long enough, and you can become so frustrated that for all of your good ideas, you aren't experiencing the success you believe you should, and so you also fall back into the pit of disillusionment. So while exciting and positive ideas are important, you also need an equal mix of acting on your thoughts to see what works and what does not, and to what degree.

Quadrant IV: Self-Actualizers

It is in the fourth quadrant that we create a synergy from balancing meaning and activity. Here you *synthesize* meaning and performance by mixing dreaming and imagining with pragmatically making things happen as you test and experiment. Here the dreaming and the daring come together in a synthesis that allows the emergence of things that are more than the sum of the parts. Here you create *meaningful* activity and *actively* actualize your most enriching meanings.

So where are you?

Meaning —

How much of a meaning-maker, of a dreamer, of a creator and creative person are you?
How much of your time do you spend dreaming up great ideas? Researching books or reflectively thinking through ideas?

Performance —

How much of a performer are you, a mover-and-shaker, a person who makes things happen?
How much of your time are you busy with activities, with actually doing things, with expending all of that nervous energy in various projects or socializing?

Figure 7:4

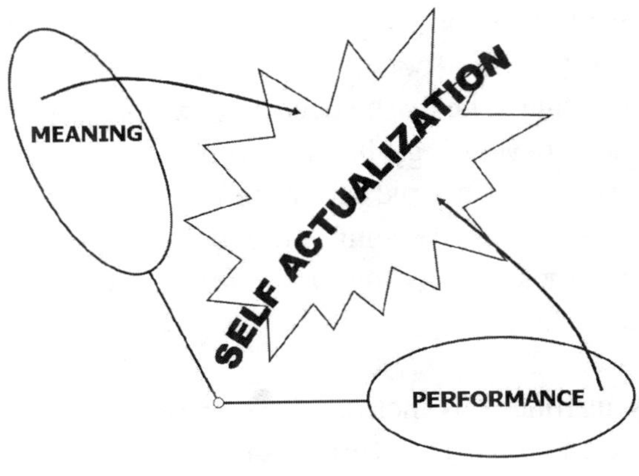

The Meta-Programs of the Self-Actualization Quadrants

Up to this point I have talked about the two axes of self-actualization in very broad terms, simply as "meaning" and "performance."

> *Question:* Is it possible for us to analyze these two phenomena in more detail and identify finer component variables within them?
>
> *Answer:* "Yes we can." Within these two axes are *meta-programs* as perceptual filters or frames of mind that make up distinctions within the meaning—performance continuum.

Now the Meta-Programs Model from NLP is a model about human perceptual filters that we use to see, perceive, and interpret things. The simplest one and the one most familiar is the perceptual filter of optimism—pessimism. "Is the glass half full (optimism) or half empty (pessimism)?" "How do you see it, interpret it, feel about it?" Whatever your answer, you are right. And wrong. It is both. It is not a dichotomy of opposites, not really. It is actually a continuum of perceptions so that the fact of a glass with some water in it is *both* half full and half empty.

Perceiving it from one side of the continuum or the other leads to different interpretations and different feelings. Yet both frames of mind are right and useful. These meta-programs are for the most part meta-states that have solidified to become the filters or frames that we use to perceive things. And when a person regularly uses one of the perceptual choices, that begins to form, influence, and govern the person's "personality."

This explains the close relationship between meta-programs and what we call "personality." If a person uses optimism or pessimism to regularly interpret things, he or she becomes an optimist or pessimist. At least that's how psychology has traditionally classified people. "She's an optimist." Yet people are more than this. These are just ways of operating— ways of seeing, perceiving, and framing things. So in Neuro-Semantics, we say that *personality is something that we* ***do****, it is not what we* ***are****.*[1]

Meta-programs as finer distinctions in our thinking and emoting patterns describe the lens that we use—our perceptual lens. Now regarding meta-programs, some of them we use everywhere—in all contexts. When we do we call that a "driving" meta-program. And yet with most of them, we have a wide range of flexibility so that we can easily move from one side of the continuum to the other. And with flexibility of consciousness, these meta-programs are not driving meta-programs. So range of flexibility in different contexts determine whether we have the meta-program or it has us. And if the meta-program has you, then you don't have a choice. You have no flexibility of consciousness or perception.

Figure 7:5

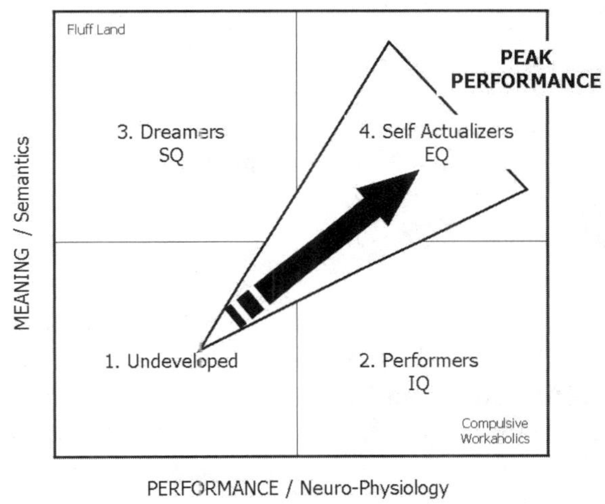

If you have a particular style of interpretation and it strongly governs your responses in most contexts, that *driving meta-program creates both your strengths and your weaknesses.* It creates your best skills as well as blind spots that identify a limitation and inability. If you are prone to optimism, you can see possdibilities. That's your strength; your temptation will be to become over-optimistic. It also creates a blind spot for seeing the pessimistic side of things.

When I realized that I could relate *the meaning—performance continuum* to the NLP Meta-Programs, this became the next step of development in the Self-Actualization Quadrants model. Next I went through the list of 60 meta-programs in the book *Figuring Out People.*[2] Recognizing that some of the meta-programs deal with the same processes of meaning and performance, I looked for those that could provide additional descriptions of these axes. Eventually I was able to identify twelve meta-programs that relate to the continuum.

Figure 7:6

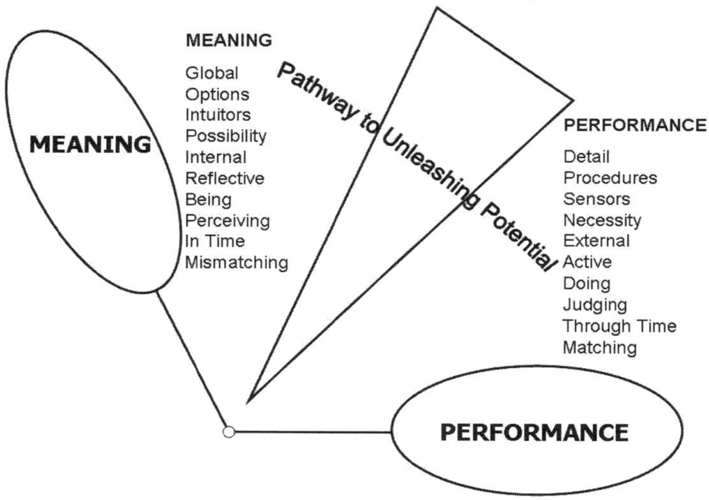

This enables you to profile your strengths using the 12 meta-programs that correspond to the Meaning—Performance continuum. They identify what you need to synthesize in order to move more fully into the fourth quadrant of self-actualization—into the zone of the flow state.

These perceptual filters indicate which axes you specialize in, which you prefer and live most of your mental-and-emotional life in. You can therefore use them to profile your meta-program style of meaning-making and performing. Yes these do influence and form what we call "personality," and yet they are fluid enough so that you can alter them and expand them if you so choose. This identifies the ideal choice—to expand each perceptual filter so you have complete flexibility in using both of the axes, so that you have complete choice about using the full range of the meta-program.

How does all of this relate to self-actualization? If self-actualization is a function of meaning and performance, if it emerges by synthesizing your highest meanings with your best performances, then the detailed analysis of meaning and performance in the meta-program gives you more distinctions that you can use for gaining leverage for change and transformation, for expanding your perceptual range.

Meaning		**Performance**
1) Global	————	Detail
2) Options	————	Procedures
3) Intuitors	————	Sensors
4) Possibility	————	Necessity
5) Internal	————	External
6) Reflective	————	Active
7) Being	————	Doing
8) Perceiving	————	Judging
9) In Time	————	Through Time
10) Mis-matching	————	Matching
11) Qualitative	————	Quantitative
12) Why	————	How

The solution to being stuck on one or the other polar ends of a meta-program distinction is simple: *expand the range of your perceptions*—expand your meta-program range. Doing this will give you a greater range along *the meaning—performance continuum* so that you can do either or both. And when you do this, you thereby unleash potentials that have been hidden from you at the opposite end of the continuum.[2]

In terms of self-actualization, you can also use the axes to profile and diagnose where you are and where you need to expand your range for unleashing potentials.

The Meanings within Performance

If you only explore the first surface level of a performance you will miss most of what informs, governs, and drives your performances. You will then only superficially understand your behaviors. And in the surface view, you will completely miss the inner drive and engine that gives any performance its quality, feel, and spirit. Since it is *meaning* that drives and empowers performances, you have to explore the meaning side of the Quadrants.

This is true of your everyday performances. It is even more true if you want to explore and model the expertise of peak performances. In high performance lies higher or meta-frames of meaning in which the performance is embedded. That's why exploring the meta-levels and frames of meaning enables you to find *the critical leverage points* whereby you can transform a mediocre performance or behavior into one of passion, commitment, and focus which thereby enables it to become a top-notch performance. And when you do that you enter into the place of mastery, the "flow" state where you are fully engaged with all of your resources.

I hope this explains the critical importance of viewing your performance neuro-semantically. While the neurology comes first and is what you see externally in behavior, above and beyond the performance are all of the inner semantics that informs and drives it with rich meanings. This is what creates passion and commitment. This meaning-making is what actually makes the performance what it is.

The Main Points

- You can now work neuro-semantically with your mind-body system to empower and enrich both the inner meanings of your frames (the inner game) and the outer expression or performance of those meanings (the outer game).

- Aim to align, synergize, and integrate your meta-programs to develop the full range of your perceptual frames. Do that and you can thereby unleash many hidden potentials.

- This will enable you to be at your best, expressing your uniqueness in ways that enrich yourself and others. And because this self-actualizing process is highly generative, you go from level to level, always taking your performances to new levels.

End of the Chapter References

1. See *The Structure of Personality* (2002).
2. There are patterns for expanding meta-programs, see *Figuring Out People* (2006) for an entire chapter on this. Also see the Unleashing Possibilities pattern in *Unleashed* (2007).

Chapter 8

WHO WANTS TO BE AN EXPERT?

THE ULTIMATE SECRET BEHIND EXPERT PERFORMANCES

Expertise does not just happen. Expertise is the result of years of commitment, practice, and dedication. This is the expertise that we admire, and often stand in awe of in those who are experts in their field. While it might be nice to go to bed one evening and wake up to discover that you have suddenly become an expert—it just doesn't work that way. There are no instantaneous miraculous experts. To become an expert in any field requires effort, work, study, learning, coaching, feedback, more effort, discipline, practice, more effort.

Ericsson who has himself become an expert about expertise writes:

> "All the paths to expert performance appear to require substantial extended effortful practice. Effortless mastery of expertise, magical bullets involving training machines, and dramatic shortcuts, are just myths." (2006, p. 61)

This means that there is rhyme and reason behind how top performances are achieved and how expertise develops over time. If then you want to discover how they do it so that you too can acquire the ability to produce peak performances, you have to find the structure and strategy that experts use in developing, acquiring, and maintaining their expertise.

- Would you like to know the secrets of experts and their expert performances?
- Would you like to discover the very heart and soul of the pathway to excellence?

As we explicate the secrets of the experts and the geniuses who amaze us with their incredible abilities, let's begin with a series of questions to orient our focus.

- How do we explain the expertise of a true expert?
- How did they get that way?
- Were they born with innate talent that made their expertise inevitable?
- Or did they have some special nurturing, education, and training that allowed them to develop their skillful competency?
- What combination of nature and nurture explains the top performances of those who consistently produced peak performances?

This subject of human excellence and expertise is the very heart of NLP and Neuro-Semantics—*meta-disciplines that model the structure of world-class experiences.* And as meta-disciplines, these fields use the study of subjective experiences to create models and patterns that allow us to replicate the expertise that we find in top performers.

Yet we are not alone in this pursuit. Four decades before NLP appeared on the scene in 1972, Abraham Maslow created the paradigm shift in psychology as he turned from studying sick and dysfunctional people and turned to studying healthy and highly functional people. That launched the Third Force in psychology and the human potential movement and many, many other disciplines seeking to create expert systems.

Among those other disciplines is the explicit study of experts and expert performances. In this field K. Anders Ericsson is one of the leading researchers. Since the early 1990s, Ericsson has been publishing his research about superior expert performances. Among his key works are these:

Toward a General Theory of Expertise: Prospects and Limits. (1991)
The Road to Excellence: The Acquisition of Expert Performance in the Arts and Sciences, Sports, and Games. (1996)

More recently Ericsson edited the massive 800-plus page book, *The Cambridge Handbook of Expertise and Expert Performance* (2006) to present and summarize the latest research in studying, understanding and modeling expertise. There are several chapters in this book by Ericsson about the research regarding the secrets of expert performances. From this we learn that expertise is a long-term developmental process, resulting from rich instrumental experiences in the world as well as extensive practice. Yet there has surfaced *one secret* that explains what takes a highly talented person beyond others. And it is this secret that almost nobody incorporates in training programs, seminars, or education. And there are reasons for that which I'll get to later.

The authors in the book have studied and modeled experts in various games and sports such as chess players, figure skaters, tennis players, swimmers, etc. They have studied people with expertise in chemistry, surgery, dancers, actors, teams, software design, medical diagnosis, political science, pilots, physicists, mathematicians, etc. They have studied musicians from violinists to concert pianists.

What's involved in the acquisition of expertise? The answer is—many things. In fact, this is one of the confounding factors, there are many variables in becoming an expert in your field of interest.

- *There is the time factor*— the period of time over which learning the skills and taking them to a level of mastery occurs.
- *There is the psychological factors of personality development*—the frame basic aptitude that's required, the persistence, adaptability, self-monitoring, handling one's emotions.
- *There are the general competency skills*—a problem-solving attitude to handle the problems and challenges within any given expertise, pattern detection, ability to experience the flow state, and deliberate practice.
- *There are the social factors*—the social support for the opportunity to develop the expertise, the interpersonal

environment, the culture.

- *There is the domain knowledge* that has to be learned, the heuristic knowledge and the procedural knowledge.

The 10-Year Rule

The first psychologist who explored this area was Galton (1869) who asserted that exceptional achievement is born rather than made. Today Ericsson and other researches have demonstrated that this is plain wrong. The literature on expertise acquisition suggests that for everybody, expertise requires approximately a decade of committed training and practice to attain world-class expertise (Ericsson, 1996, p. 327).

Regarding the time factor for expertise, all of the research on experts, expertise development, and the acquisition of superior skills in almost every area shows that for people to reach the highest levels of competence after approximately ten-years of study, training, and apprenticeship in the field. This is even true of those who seem to be born with an abundance of innate talent and naturally gifted. Still, it takes nearly ten years before that talent can be turned into actual expert performance (p. 266).

> "It is well established that to be successful in competition at the international level, experts need to have engaged in at least ten years of intensive training." (Ericsson, Krame, and Tesch-Roner, 1993; Simon and Chase, 1973). P. 235.
>
> "A generally accepted rule is that a minimum of ten years of deliberate practice is required to attain expert performance in many domains." (Ericsson and Smith, 1991). 266
>
> "A minimum of ten years of preparation is required to develop and organize the necessary repertoire of domain-specific information to attain an international level of chess skill." (Chase and Simon, 1973, p. 305)
>
> "The 10-year rule applies to composers in classical music including Mozart. It took the Beatles approximately a decade to acquire international reputation." (462)
>
> "The 10-year rule represents a very rough estimate, and most researchers regard it as a minimum, not an average." (601)

This ten-year rule has actually been around for a long time. In 1897 Bryan and Harter claimed that over ten years are necessary for becoming an expert (*Psychological Review,* 4, 27-53). Since then, researcher after researcher has repeatedly confirmed this. For classical pianists, violinists, chest master, etc. it generally takes ten years before the person wins at an international level. This is also true in the domains of sports, science, and the arts.

Even highly talented people, those who seem to have genius level abilities or intelligence, it still takes a decade. In other words, there is no magic pill that will make you an "instant expert." We certainly have ways of accelerating our learning, accessing the best states, etc., but expertise like good wine takes time.

What else is Involved in Acquiring Expertise?
There are many things that we can identify as involved in acquiring expertise. Among the most important are the following:

1) A supportive social environment.

Research has show that genius and talent are not randomly distributed across space and time, but rather tend to cluster into particular geographical locations (p. 327). What explains this? Talent development requires support of one's socio-cultural context. The number of great achievers in one generation is a positive function of the number in the preceding generation. Exceptional creators are less likely to develop during times of political anarchy, but are more likely to develop during periods of political fragmentation, when a civilization is divided into numerous independent states (p. 328).

To an amazing degree, high achievement results from the value that a given culture assigns to an activity at a given point in time. If it is important culturally, then people explore it, take interest, give themselves to it, seek out mentors. In this way, expertise is a cultural phenomenon, and so requires the right kind of cultural environment.

2) Adaptability.

Another critical success factor for the acquisition of expertise is adaptability. Ericsson and Lehmann (1996) suggest that experts show a better adaptation to task constraints. They are less bothered by unfavorable situations and they develop better ways of coping with them. They become professionals precisely because they learn to manage to tolerate negative emotional states as well as enjoying the positive experience of flow. This adaptability is obviously a function of the flexibility to adapt.

Rather than being defensive in their reactions, experts are more adaptive. They prefer to adjust their strategy rather than to avoid the task. In this they learn to solve problems— both the routine problems of their field and non-routine problems.

> "One becomes an expert by making routine what to the novice requires creative problem-solving ability." J. R. Anderson (1980, *Cognitive Psychology and Its Implications*).

This adaptability most powerfully influences the way we handle mistakes, errors, and failures.

> "Experts fail gracefully; novices crash." (Feltovich, Prietula, Ericsson, p. 56)
>
> "Experts certainly know more, but they also know differently. Expertise is appropriately viewed not as simple (and often short-term) matter of fact or skill acquisition, but rather as a complex *construct* of adaptations of mind and body..." (p. 57).

3) Creating Meaningful patterns

Expertise further involves the ability to chunk information into meaningful wholes or patterns of tactical significance. Experts learn to do this by developing detailed and extensive task-specific memory structures. Researchers have found that this is what creates accurate decision-making performance in sports. What arises and develops over the years is a greater nuanced awareness of the performance—finer distinctions and more meaningful wholes by which to sort and categorize experience.

In this, the researchers discovered that nested structures are vital for the control of behavior. Such meaningful elements, or "chunks," enables a person to organize his or her understandings, choices, and responses. This explains how the expert seems to know so much and to be able to work with so much data.

> "With increased experience and practice, most people cognitively organize the perceptually available information in their working environment into larger units. ... The experts' superior ability to encode representative information from their domain of expertise and store it in long-term memory, such that they can efficiently retrieve meaningful relations..." (pp. 49-50)

For highly skilled chess players, the best players are able to rapidly perceive the structure of the presented chess positions. This allows them to identify weaknesses and associated lines of attack. The highly skilled players are able to rapidly perceive meaningful relations between most chess pieces within presented positions.

> "After a brief exposure of a chess position, often in the 5-second range, the world-class chess players have virtually perfect recall of the location of pieces, and the ability to reproduce positions from regular chess games increases as a function of chess skill." (2003, p. 55).

For expertise, *content counts.* "Knowledge and content matter are important to expertise." (p. 47). Research now shows that knowledge is no longer seen as a nuisance variable, but a dominant source of variance.

4) Automizing the Basics

It's not only important but critical that we use *automaticity* in the acquiring of expertise. Research on the effects of practice has shown that a person's cognitive operations actually change after just a few hours of practice. As operations begin, they are slow, serial, and they demand conscious attention. Eventually, however, our operations become fast, less deliberate, and can run in parallel with other processes.

> "With enough practice, one can learn how to do several tasks at the same time. Behavioral studies of skill acquisition have demonstrated that automaticity is central to the development of expertise, and practice is the means to automaticity." (p. 53)

5) Relevance

Expertise doesn't merely involve more and more information, instead it involves selective access of relevant information. That is, it involves learning which information is most useful and which is tangential and even superfluous. So in any field, the expert is the one who can sort through lots of the details and quickly identify the relevant details, the details that make a difference, the details indicating critical leverage points for performance.

6) Meta-Cognitive Skills

Finally, expertise involves reflection. Experts do not just perform effectively, but they can and do reflect on their thought processes and methods, on what works well and what does not, and make adjustments. This is a meta-cognitive skill. It is knowledge about one's own knowledge and the ability to reflect on the quality of one's knowledge.

> "It is what an individual knows about his or her own cognitive processes. Its relevance to expertise is derived, in part, from the observation that experts are graceful in their reasoning process. As Barlett notes, 'Experts have all the time in the world.' There is an element of unencumbered elegance in expert performance..." (p. 55)

From Practice to Meta-Practice

One of the discoveries of Ericsson and colleagues involves the relationship between the amount of hours of practice to expertise. As you might suspect, they found a correlation between the number of hours a person devotes to learning and practice and one's level of expertise. One thing that distinguishes novices from experts, and then from masters, *is the amount of time devoted to practicing one's skills.*

Here's something that I found fascinating. As the researchers began exploring this, they noted that for most everyday activities such as typing, playing tennis, driving a car, etc., there's a common number of hours required to get a person up to an acceptable level. They found that it generally takes about 50 hours to reach a level where one has the basic skills for performing at an acceptable level of competence. After that, people then adapt to the domain and their performance skills become automated. At this point they can execute the skills smoothly and with minimal effort.

Fifty hours! Imagine that. In only 50 hours a great many skills can be learned, developed, and acquired! If you give yourself to *one intensive week* of study, practice, and feedback, you can perform a great many things at an acceptable level of competence. Isn't that amazing?!

Now with skills that may not be in this category of everyday skills it takes more—it requires 200 to 500 hours get you to a basic level of competence. So at that point, how far will you be from the level of an expert? How far would you guess?

If you've been through driver's education and have driven for several years, you probably are pretty good at driving and may be able to handle freeway traffic, urban traffic at rush hour, perhaps you can even drive safely in snow storms, handle black ice, etc. Yet how far are you from the expertise of the driver of a formula race car? And how much more learning, practice, and development would it take to get you there?

There's a quantum jump between these levels, isn't there? From competent, even highly competent to "expert" there is *a tremendous jump in skill.* A quantum jump. If you play chess, it probably didn't take you long to learn to play chess, and perhaps you've played enough at this point to be decent at chess. But how many more hours, how much practice, what learnings, books, studies, coaching do you need to be able to compete at world-class level?

Or consider the top violinists that Ericsson (1993) researched. He looked into the background, training, studies, and practices of those who rose to the top of their profession, of those who consistently produce superior performances. What he discovered was that those who are highly competent, but who did not move to the top had only practiced 2,500 hours (that's 62 weeks full time at 40 hours a week; so that is more than a year full-time or perhaps 3 years part-time). Those who were even more highly skilled, but not at the international level had devoted 5,000 hours of practice. And those who as with the others, by the age of 20, had reached international acknowledgment, had practiced over 10,000 hours.

This correlation between the number of hours and the level of mastery caught Ericsson's attention. But this is a correlation, not a cause, and it is not without exceptions. There are exceptions. But the exceptions are about those who do not achieve peak performance. In fact, the research showed that many people can practice 10,000 hours *without* their skills moving to the level of the top performances. So, there must be something else. There must be another distinction, another factor. And there is.

Practice alone an Expert does not Make

While most skills can be learned to an acceptable level of competent performance pretty quickly, most of us do not become experts in them. This is true for reading and studying, driving, typing, playing chess, etc. Why not? We primarily don't become experts because *we do not have the interest, motivation, or commitment.* We don't even want to become experts in these areas. So we do not attempt to. And that sufficiently explains why we stop. And yet there are some additional reasons.

Primarily there is the Competence—Expertise Gap. This refers to what happens to us neurologically on the pathway to mastery. While most skills develop quickly especially at first, which in itself can deceive us about the speed of development, something dangerous then happens to our skills. What? Habituation. This is both a blessings and a curse. A blessing because now the skill is automatic, smooth, and unconscious. Yet in another way it is a curse.

When your skills become automated you then lose the ability to control the execution of your skills. And when that happens, it makes intentional modifications and adjustments to the skills thereafter very difficult. Once you reach a stable plateau, further improvement slows down. You settle in for being unconscious at your performance level. Because you can perform adequately enough, you leave it at that.

No wonder most people become generalists rather than specialists! When they enter into a new domain, at first they learn quickly and experience a rush of excitement in that early development of their skills that takes their performance to an adequate level. This is true of learning such things as playing tennis, golf, basketball, and many sports, chess, typing, etc. Other skills take a bit longer, yet within a few months they generally reach a level of competency.

Three Problems

At this point three problems arise that powerfully influence whether you will continue to move to becoming an expert. One is the loss of excitement, another is enjoyment, and the third is unconsciousness.

> Yet one of the things that experts seem to have in common is the ability to identify next steps and mindfully work against the unconsciousness that comes from automaticity.

First, there is the loss of excitement. From competence onward the original thrill of learning something new, of entering into a new domain, of making all kinds of new distinctions— these begin to diminish rapidly and significantly. As you learn and know the field, as you discover most of the key distinctions for competence, you enter into the slower stage where the focus shifts to not developing, but refining your skills. To stay with development now requires a very different mindset and attitude—one of a dedicated persistence, patience, and the ability to count the smallest refinements.

Second, there is the seduction of enjoyment. Ericsson says that, at this point in skill development, many people shift their practice from learning to enjoying. Now they practice the performance of their skills for the sake of their own personal enjoyment. And why not? Because, after all, when you can do something well—you can now relax your efforts and enjoy the delight and pleasure of the skill. Now you can sit back and just enjoy your current level of performance. If you were to stretch forward to the next level that would mean leaving your pleasure state and pushing forward. And then you would experience a discomfort, even an unpleasant state. And why not? At this level, you are decently skilled and competent and can enjoy the experience.

At this point automaticity kicks in. You can now perform without the mental stress and strain of paying intense detailed attention to things. You can relax your consciousness and just float along. Isn't this how most of us drive, read, type, play music, etc.? We do so with an automaticity that allows us to go unconscious.

To proceed beyond this point you will have to mindfully work against this. You have to bring back to your tasks and skills the mental stress and strain of focused attention. And this is effort, struggle, and even "work." Yet one of the things that experts seem to have in common is the ability to identify next steps and mindfully work against the unconsciousness that comes from automaticity. One of the most crucial challenges for an aspiring expert is to avoid the arrested development associated with the automaticity of performance and the seduction of enjoyment.

To do this, you must acquire the cognitive skills to support your continued learning and improvement. What are these cognitive skills? Here's what Ericsson wrote:

> "By actively seeking out demanding tasks that force the performers to engage in problem solving and stretch their performance, the expert performers overcome the detrimental effects of automaticity and actively acquire and refine cognitive mechanisms to support continued learning and improvement." (2006, p. 694)

I mentioned this to a friend who plays drums, the guitar, and several other instruments. He is a true lover of music. And I didn't know just how much until recently I asked him about it and it turns out that he has spent one to two hours every single night for the past two or three decades playing(!). Yet when I told him about this research and the distinction that makes for true expertise, he slapped his forehead, "That's it! No wonder. I play purely for the enjoyment of it." So I asked, "Are there finer distinctions about playing that you know about that you could push yourself to get better?"

> "Sure, but then it would be so much fun! I think it would feel like work, and after a full day of work at the shop, I need to relax and that's where the drums or the guitar or the piano is so relaxing for me."

So to counteract arresting development associated with the skills becoming automatic requires that *you deliberately acquire and refine your meta-cognitive mechanisms:* to set stretch goals, to monitor our progress, to evaluate your performance and to get solid feedback.

> "The performers will gradually acquire mechanisms that increase their ability to control, self-monitor, and evaluate their performance in representative situations from the domain and thus gain independence from the feedback of their teachers." (2006, p. 694)

In this, Ericsson argues that expert performance improves only with what he calls "deliberate practice."

> "One distinctive characteristic of future expert performers is that they intentionally avoid the natural tendency toward automatization, with its associated loss of control of many relevant aspects. They typically seek out instruction by teachers and they regularly engage in problem solving in the form of deliberate practice. They seek out situations in which they strive to reach higher levels of performance. They strain their current performance and seek to find ways to make improvements without altering the desirable characteristics of the current performance." ("The Acquisition of Expert Performance as Problem Solving: Construction and Modification of Mediating Mechanisms through Deliberate Practice," in *The Psychology of Problem Solving,* p. 74)

Did you get that? Did you underline or highlight some of the lines in that paragraph? That's *the secret.* If you want to know the innermost secret of the success of those who become experts —you just heard it. That's it.

The Magic Challenge of Deliberate Practice

Ah, deliberate practice! Meta-practice! If that's the key to continually developing true expertise, then what is deliberate practice and what are the factors that define and characterize this special form of practice? And how can we incorporate it into our lives as trainers and coaches? Ericsson writes:

> "The core assumption of deliberate practice is that expert performance is acquired gradually and that effective improvement of performance requires the opportunity to find suitable training tasks that the performer can master sequentially—typically the design of training tasks and monitoring of the attained performance is done by a teacher or a coach. Deliberate practice presents performers with tasks that are initially outside their current realm of reliable performance, yet can be mastered within hours of practice by concentrating on critical aspects and gradually refining performance through repetition after feedback. Hence the requirement for *concentration* sets deliberate practice apart from both mindless, routine performance and playful engagement, as the latter two types of activities would, if anything, merely strengthen the current mediating cognitive mechanisms, rather than modify them to allow increases in the level of performance." (2006, p. 692)

In examining *deliberate meta-practice,* as defined by Ericsson, I have identified five factors within this very special form of "practice." And here they are:

1) Structured set of activities for improving performance.

Deliberate practice first of all involves *a highly structured set of activities* with the explicit goal of improving performance. This is the central factor in the determination of acquired performance.

> "The specific tasks rated very high on relevance for performance, high on effort and comparatively low on inherent enjoyment." (2006, p. 306)

Regarding these high effort and high relevance activities, you have to plan for them. You have to target them specifically and then focus on them exclusively. If expertise abilities are not used, they decline. That's why regular quality practice is required.

> "Improvements are caused by changes in cognitive mechanisms mediating how the brain and nervous system control performance and in the degree of adaptation of physiological systems of the body. The principal challenge to attaining expert level performance is to induce stable specific changes that allows performance to be incrementally improved." (2006, p. 698)

All of this puts the focus on *the stages of practice.* Practice is a systematic activity with predictable stages and activities. These include practicing to get the big picture or the feel of the performance, the technical practice to master it, trying out in public as a stage performance, the maintenance stage, the refining, and the stretching to new heights, and the continual re-processing through. In the Axes of Change model, these stages occur in the co-creation, actualization, reinforcement, testing and then continually repeating this process.

Making it personal:

- Have you set out a structured set of activities for improving your performance in a given area?
- When will you do that? What are the set of activities that you will set forth?

- Are these activities specific enough?
- How focused are you? Regular in your practice? Can you now call your practice *deliberate*?

2) An effortful stretch.

Deliberate practice next involves *an effortful stretch beyond your skills.* It involves a push, a struggle, a strain. In this kind of practice, you intentionally set a goal and then isolate some activity to practice with a focused concentration that will add to the overall performance. Deliberate practice enables the acquisition of expert performance as you move from one state of active practice to another state. Doing this requires physiological, mental, and emotional straining.

> "Elite performers search continually for optimal training activities, with the most effective duration and intensity, that will appropriately strain the targeted physiological system to induce further adaptation without causing overuse or injury." (2006, p. 696)

So deliberate practice is a set of structured activities that experts in the domain consider important for improving performance. It typically is so strenuous that it can only be maintained for limited amounts of time a day without danger of psychological or physiological burnout. This is what requires the mindfulness in practicing the effortful activity and the conscious monitoring of the skill to be learned. And if you've experienced some of the advanced Neuro-Semantics trainings, you may now recognize why we have structured the competency development in module three of *Coaching Mastery* and in Trainers Training as we have.

Making it personal:

- Are you straining, pushing yourself, and stretching in your practices?
- If so, how, when, where, with what, and in what way are you straining?
- What is the level of stretching, straining, and pushing that you do?
- How do you record or monitor this?

3) *Self-Monitoring and Measuring of progress.*

Because *deliberate* practice involves mindful self-monitoring and measurement, it requires that you use your meta-consciousness and awareness. It requires self-observation and meta-cognitive monitoring so we mentally track and record our performances.

Research shows that meta-cognitive self-monitoring is difficult for novices because the amount of information involved in complex performances. The large amount of information easily overwhelms them leading to inconsistent or superficial tracking. Experts are selective in their cognitive self-monitoring during practice because of the specificity of their learning, practice, and performance goals.

In self-monitoring, we consciously guide our attention, evaluate our current level of expertise, identify our errors, and set up procedures for eliminating our errors. We seek objective feedback to help us learn and refine our awareness of the standards of expertise, internalize how to identify and correct errors, set new goals, focus on over-coming weaknesses, and monitor progress. Again, this explains the value of the meta-position in Meta-Coaching and many of the trainings we conduct.

In this self-regulatory process of goal setting we specify intended actions or outcomes, and set highly specific process goals. We set not only outcome goals, but process goals which enable us to improve our strategy or technique.

Making it personal:

- Do you engage regularly in self-monitoring about your performance during and after a practice?
- How do you monitor your progress and choose the next stretch?
- What meta-cognitive observation do you engage in?

4) A focused concentration.

As you undoubtedly can tell, *deliberate practice* involves an intense focus that activates and utilizes your powers of concentration so that you truly concentrate on what you are doing as you do it. The central technique in deliberate practice involves being able to access your full mental engagement as you orient yourself to a goal so you overcome your current performance boundaries. This level of intensity of your concentration and effort during deliberate practice separates it from what we usually think of and call "practice."

In Neuro-Semantics we call this *the genius state.* We use layers of meta-states to set the frames so that we can step in and out of being "in the zone" at will. So deliberate practice is a performance that occurs in *a state of flow.*

By way of contrast, Ericsson noted that amateur singers practice for the enjoyment, for the release of tension. Expert musicians, however, practice with a different motivation —to increase their concentration and focus on improving their performance during the lesson (p. 693). The research discovered the role of the "flow" state in deliberate practice:

> "Writers as with surgeons, musicians, and athletes, perform best in a flow state of consciousness. They all try to shape their surroundings, work schedules, and rituals in ways that foster flow. (2006, p. 399)

Making it personal:

- Do you practice deliberately by first entering a state of flow?
- Are you able and skilled in stepping into "the zone" at will?
- In your practice are you so focused in your engagement that you are in flow?

***5) Mindful practice*.**

In describing *deliberate practice,* all this requires fighting against what naturally happens with competence—*we slip into unconsciousness!* Now although the skill development entails automaticity, this does not ensure an expert's level of performance will be attained, automaticity does provide a necessary foundation.

> "Deliberate practice is designed to improve specific aspects of performance in a manner that assures that attained changes can be successfully measured and integrated into representative performance."

> "Practice aimed at improving integrated performance cannot be performed mindlessly, nor independently of the representative context for the target performance."

And why is it important to do this? In order to handle the natural plateaus that occur in skill development. When you reach a plateau, you are generally feeling comfortable and confident. To acquire expertise, and to avoid experiencing an arrest in your development, you have to avoid automatization. To deliberately refine the cognitive skills required for any experience demands that you maintain conscious effort.

Typically, "practice" substantially reduces the amount of attention and effort that must be devoted to task performance. That's why we all typically go unconscious as our skills become neurologically conditioned and automatic. Various theorists have described the benefit of practice by attributing it to strengthening, chunking, or efficiency of retrieval. Yet regardless of the explanation, practice that is not *mindfully deliberate* involves a shift from attention-demanding control processing to a much more automatic mode.

Making it personal:

- Do you mindfully practice and strive to remain conscious in your practices?
- When your consciousness slips into unconsciousness, are you able to catch yourself and return to being mindful?
- How do you do that?

Deliberately Practicing

In the winter of 2007-8 I returned to Colorado after having spent the four previous winters in Sydney Australia. What I didn't know as I scheduled that, was that we would have one of the most intense winter in many decades as we experienced one snow storm after another. So instead of running in the snow and ice, I decided to join a gym and use the running machines there.

Normally I run a trail near my home, a trail I've run for so many years that I can now imaginatively run that trail in my mind and see and hear things clearly and vividly. Also, I can and do run it automatically. In fact, that's what I typically do. I get running and thinking about things other then the run, the exercise, the effort, etc.

Now in the gym, with the running machines and the stair-steppers, the dozens of television sets and people on other machines, and machines flashing all kinds of data— watts, calories burned, distance covered, time, levels, etc. So when I first began working out there, I found it difficult to get lost in my thoughts and write articles on the run. I was painfully conscious of everything— especially how I felt in every part of my body.

At first I didn't like it. That's when I started looking around at others there and discovered that 95 percent of the people there wore head-phones and listened to music or watched TV. Talk about avoiding consciousness of what they were doing! I decided I would not do that. But since I found it difficult to go into my normal "writing zone" on the run, I began watching the data and computing my time, distance, etc. When I started the speed that felt normal and right was between an 8 and an 8½ mile pace. But then I set a goal: 8 minute pace. When I reached that, I push it to a 7½ minute pace. I did that for a month and then slowly would run a half mile at 7 minute pace, then a mile at that pace, week by week I deliberately targeted and focused on the next increment of improvement.

I also began watching my heart-rate scores. When I started my heart-rate was between 110 and 120, not very much of a push. Yet as I increased speed it would range from 120 to 160. Then I discovered that if I squeeze the bars of the heart-rate gauge I could spike my heart-rate to 175 or 180. That would increase my breathing and demand much more consciousness in what I was doing. After two months I found that I could eventually run my daily 4 miles in less than 30 minutes and that by stretching my heart-rate, I'd be in a pretty intense state.

On one occasion, there was a young guy on the machine next to me just jogging along (not running) and when I finished, he looked over and said, "Hey, what a workout! Boy, you really worked it!" That jarred me out of my state because I was inside my head calculating my speed, rate, etc. I think that was a deliberate and mindful practice.

A very similar thing happens for a lot of people, and I hope most people, at Module Three of Meta-Coaching. Every day in the coaching bootcamp that we call *Coaching Mastery* we have the coaching *practice* sessions in which every coach is benchmarked by the criteria of the core coaching skills. Almost everybody, at first, finds this challenging, intimating, stressful, anxiety-producing, and a big stretch. They not only are being watched in the forty-five minute process, but given immediate feedback both in the session and afterwards.

Here a person not only has to be conscious and mindful of what they are doing, but why, and also able to use their meta-cognitive skills of self-monitoring. Here a person has to not only monitor what he or she is doing with their actual coaching conversation, but also monitor their state, the thoughts in the back of their mind, their knowledge competency with the coaching models, and monitor what they think they look like to the meta-person and the benchmarker. Talk about racheting up the challenge for multiple levels of self-monitoring!

Summary — The Expertise Secret Par Excellent Exposes

- Now you know *the secret,* the secret of those who become internationally known and recognized experts in their respected field. That secret is *deliberate practice.* As self-actualizing persons, experts are generally not satisfied where they are, believing that there's more to be achieved and experienced. Believing that they can become more, do more, and express more experts are dedicated to the principle of *kaizen— continuous improvement.*

- They are forever students, forever striving, forever restless. For them school is never out and perfection a cognitive distortion. For them, the fun is in the process—the process of becoming more, learning more, giving more. So they are process oriented, rather than outcome oriented.

Chapter 9

EVALUATING AND MEASURING PERFORMANCE

- How do we evaluate your performances?
- How do you evaluate peak performances?
- How can we measure performances that have to do with subjective states like "being in the zone" and in "flow?"
- How do we measure an expert performance of listening, learning, leading, etc.?
- What numbers can we put on such experiences?
- How can we operationalize the performances that we want to excel at?

A Problem of Language

Much of the problem in measuring and evaluating intangible, subjective, and psychological responses is ultimately a problem of language. How can we describe and define a peak performance in a language with sufficient precision and specificity? This is the most critical issue— the million-dollar question.

When it comes to empirical objects that are true things that we can see, hear, touch, handle, smell, and taste, it is fairly easy to describe things and to put numbers to them. We can*quantify* their dimensions in terms of size, weight, volume, vibration, temperature, etc.

However, we enter an entirely different domain when it comes to subjective experiences. How do we talk about things that are not seen or heard externally, but which exists *on the inside* of someone's thinking, emoting, and experiencing? How do we quantify "lost in an experience," "in the zone," "totally engaged in a laser-beam focus," and so forth? How do we even talk about such? How do we define and describe such?

Our language naturally becomes less specific and more abstract as we move into this area. At first we use generalized terms, terms that are categories of behaviors rather than behaviors: parenting, managing, communicating, being empathetic, etc. Within each of these words we can put lots of more specific terms: under managing we can put delegating, giving instructions, writing memos, holding meetings, etc. Within "holding meetings" we can identify the sub-actions within it, "getting people's attention, saying, "Let's start the meeting," presenting an agenda, asking for old business," etc.

The Language of Precision

Specifying actual behaviors with such categories makes our generalized language more specific and precise. To do this we simply ask repeatedly, "Specifically what would we be doing? When, where, with whom, in what way, how, etc.?" In the Meta-Model of language for precision, we use these indexing questions to specify the time, space, person, and action details. This helps with unspecified nouns and verbs.

Next we work with and use terms that look like and sound like *nouns* for designating "a person, place, or thing" but which do not refer to such, and are actually verbs-masquerading-as nouns. These terms take a process and treat it as if it were a *thing* by encoding it as a noun. We call them *nominalizations* because they "name" (nominalize) a verb and so treat the process and action as if it were a noun. As a result, processes are frozen and made static so that you can easily forget *what* you are actually talking about. What results from turning a process into a *thing* is a severe mis-mapping of things.

We often talk about "communication" and its effect upon our "relationship," especially by those exerting "leadership." Yet what are we talking about? What do you picture in your mind with such words? Do you see processes? Do you see one person "communicating" (in some way, at some place, at some time) to another person?

A real noun can be put on a table, in a refrigerator, or in a wheelbarrow. A nominalization cannot. You can put Fred in the wheelbarrow even though it may take a fight, but you cannot put "communication" or "leadership" there. You can now use this as a limtus test for true nouns versus the pseudo-nouns that make up nominalizations.

Because nominalizations create fluff for the mind, it's imperative that you *de-nominalize* them. You need to recover the verbs and processes for clarity about what you're talking about. This is the beginning of evaluating performances. Otherwise you only make evaluations based on the hallucinations you have in your mind about such. "That was good." "Great job." "What's wrong with you; that was terrible."

Since none of us can see these judgments or evaluations and cannot put "good," "great," or "terrible" on a table, these nominalizations prevent us from being able to measure the performance. They prevent you from specifying the standards by which you are making these evaluations.

The solution is to make your language as specific as possible. To do that you will need to index what you are referring to (your referents) until you create such explicit word pictures that you can see and hear them in the theater of your mind. When you can take a term and directly track it in sensory terms into your mental theater, you have sufficient sensory specific referents for precision. We call this skill, *representational tracking*.[1]

Benchmarking: The Art of Measuring Excellence

The term *benchmarking* was coined in the early days of carpentry and cabinet making. Carpenters would mark out certain lengths and dimensions on a bench against which they would measure all their pieces of timber. Different marks were made on the bench to represent different criteria for elements of the cabinets they were making. Cabinet-makers would lay their pieces of timber on the bench and measure them against the markings. This gave them a standard against which they could cut the pieces of lumber. In this way the bench-marks became the standard for all cabinet-makers to measure their excellence against.

If we use this as a metaphor for measuring behavioral performance, then we can ask the following questions:

- What benchmarks have you set for yourself and others?

- How do you know when you have hit the mark?
- How will you measure "being at your best?"
- What standards are you working toward as you move to peak performances?

Benchmarking for Accountability

Without clear expectations, standards, and behavioral criteria, accountability is not possible. To hold yourself or someone else accountable, there must be a clear set of measures. Clarity of specific indicators enable you to create an accountability template.

- How will you know that you are achieving the results you want?
- What will you hold yourself accountable for?
- What will you hold another accountable for?

In terms of achieving peak performance, you owe to yourself and others *accountability* because it brings out your best and activates your best efforts. Without accountability, things naturally slide. Generally speaking, all of us do what we are held accountable for.

Benchmarking Skills

Today we use benchmarking to establish a behavioral *value* for intangible concepts like listening, questioning, etc. Doing this, in turn, allows us to have a point of reference for assessment. As such, benchmarking enables us to measure what otherwise would be an intangible skill or experience (like "success," "growth," etc.). For change agents working with the "soft" sciences and skills, benchmarking provides a way to gauge both present and desired states around a value that's typically described as a *nominalization* (i.e., love, support, framing, reframing, honor, etc.).

Given this, you can now use *benchmarking*, as an essential skill for measuring your skill development against a set standard and for supporting others in measuring their skill development. The bottom line is that the skill of *benchmarking* enables you to operationalize your terms, de-nominalize verbs-turned-into-nouns and treated like things, and generate a set of see-hear-feel variables that you can use to determine and measure skill level.

In Neuro-semantics we have benchmarked a great many competencies: platform skills for public speakers, training skills, leadership skills, selling skills, and in the Meta-Coach Certification

Training, we have benchmarked twenty-six coaching skills including the *seven core coaching skills.*
1) Active Attentive Listening.
2) Support: Rapport, Presence.
3) Quality Questioning.
4) Meta-Questioning.
5) Inducing States.
6) Giving Feedback.
7) Receiving Feedback

> *"Count what is countable, measure what is measurable, and what is not measurable, make measurable."*
> Galileo

To do that *we use a scaling measure* from 0-5 to identify behaviors for various stages of development. The Benchmarks begin at 0 and move up the scale. With each ascending number, the skill quality increases and the behaviors become richer. This scale is based on the natural development from incompetency through the stages to competency.

0	*Unconscious Incompetence* Skill completely lacking, no evidence of the skill, behaviors indicating the lack or the opposite of the skill.
1	*Consciously Incompetent* Beginning signs of the skill, but mostly incompetent.
2	*Almost Competent* Expressions of the skill but weak and clumsy; some interference by opposite behaviors in executing the skill.
3	*Consciously Competent* Demonstrates basic skill competency. Effective.
4	*Unconsciously Competent* Expert level of the skill, very elegant.
5	*Conscious of Unconscious Competence* Consciously aware of unconscious competence: level of a *master* of this skill.

The Benchmarking Model

How does benchmarking work with an intangible state? As a model, the Neuro-Semantic Benchmarking Model is based upon the ability to use the Meta-Model to create a precise and specific language especially in de-nominalizing the terms that have been nominalized.

One of the complicating problems with nominalizations is that you can use nominalization about other nominalizations. When you do, you multiply vagueness by fluffiness! "Relationship communications enhance facilitation of leadership efficiency." (That's not only five nominalizations in a row, but nominalizations working on other nominalizations.)

When you do this, you now have a *multi-ordinal* nominalization—nominationalizations at multiple levels. Korzybski described the power of multi-ordinal terms for increasing the confusion and vagueness of terms. If a term is reflexive, and can apply to itself and still have meaning, it is multi-ordinal. Can you *love* love? What is it like to *fear* fear? If you became *angry* at anger, what would that create? Here your first level "love" is loved at the higher level. And you could $love^3$ your $love^2$ of your $love^1$.

When you deal with a multi-ordinal nominalization you not only have to get back down to sensory-based verbs, but you also have to identify *at what level* you are using the process terms. Why do you have to do that? *Because at each level, the term has a different reference and so means something different.* This basic distinction of the Meta-States Model works specifically with the challenges that reflexivity creates.

As an example, take the word "love." Generally "love" refers to a positive attraction that shows up in desire, care, concern, etc. When you *love* someone or something, you are attracted to it, you see its value, and you care for it. At the sensory level, your love reaches out to its object investing time and energy in it. If you move up a level, can you *love* the experience of love? Yes. So to be succinct, let's call that infatuation—*love* of love. Can you reflexively move up yet another level and *love* infatuation (love the love of love)? Again, yes you can! So let's call that romanticism. Can we do that yet again and *love* romanticism (love the love of love of love)? This reflexive use of "love" at different levels is what we call multi-ordinality.

To effectively benchmark you will therefore first specify the levels and then *drill down* from abstract to concrete, from conceptual to sensory. Via benchmarking you will be able to identify the KPIs (key performance indicators) of an activity.

The Benchmarking Process of something Intangible:
1) Name the concept or skill.

What idea, concept, or experience do you want to benchmark?
How do you describe it as precisely and clearly as possible?
What do you mean by this term or work?
At what level of abstraction are you using the term?
What parameters and criteria are you using as you speak about this term?
What is the *verb* or *verbs* that hide inside the nominalized term?
What processes lie underneath the nominalized term?

2) Define the word in behavioral terms.

What are the see, hear, feel components (the sensory-based elements)?
What are you speaking about that we could video-tape, record on a tape-recorder?
What is the process that you're speaking about?
Are there any sub-processes within the process?
What are the sub-skills within this competency?
How many sub-skills are required?
How many sub-skills are minimally required?
How are the sub-skills related to each other?

3) List the behaviors that indicate the presence of the concept or skill.

As you brainstorm about all of the signs and cues of the concept, have you made as complete a list as you can? What other indicators can you imagine?
What are the signs and cues that indicate the lack of the skill or concept?
If the skill is *not* present, what is present?
What behaviors indicate the *lack* of the skill or concept?
What would you see or hear if the skill or experience was elegant or even masterful? What new distinctions now arise?

4) Arrange the set of behaviors, actions, gestures, tones, etc. along a continuum.

Have you scaled the list of behaviors along a continuum?
What behaviors indicate the opposite or lack? Give them a 0.
What behaviors indicate an extremely low level? Give them a 1.
What behaviors indicate beginning level of the skill? Give them a 2.

What behaviors indicate a basic competency? Give them a 3.
What behaviors indicate expertise of the competency? Give them a 4.
What behaviors indicate absolute mastery? Give them a 5.

5) Put the distinctions in a 0 to 5 arrangement.

Have you scaled the list of behaviors along a continuum?

Once you have a continuum of behaviors for none (0) to some (1-3) to sufficient (3) to complete (5) and from clumsy and awkward (2) to adequate and on to elegant and masterful (4 and 5), test it.

Criteria for a Benchmarking Project

Do you have a project in which you want to create a set of sensory-based benchmarks? Do you want to create a high quality set of benchmarks? First, have you established an operational definition? Have you created a set of competency levels for the skill, idea, or concept? Do you have specific behaviors for each level? Here are the criteria we use in the Meta-Coach Training system when we have groups work together on a benchmarking project to learn these skills.

1) Operational definition:

Is there a clear operational definition?
Is there a definition that tells a person *what to do*?

2) Sub-skills:

Are there sub-skills, behaviors, and actions within the skill?
Are there three or more sub-behaviors or skills?

3) Levels identified and integrated into one form.

Are the degrees and levels of the skill distinguished?
Were the behaviors described as developing and progressing from 0 to 5?
Can the behaviors be seen, heard, and felt?

4) Specificity:

Were there sensory based behaviors?
Were there precise behaviors describing the process?
Were there any nominalizations left in the descriptions?
Have all of the metaphors been eliminated and make sensory-specific?

5) Completion:

Is the project completed?

Are the levels of competency on that particular benchmark complete?
If not fully complete, to what degree is it complete?
To what extent? How much?

Examples of Benchmarking

Definition: **Listening:** *Being actively present to a client, collecting and synthesizing the sensory information (visual, auditory, and kinesthetic) as well as non-sensory specific terms so as to accurately reflect back the content as well as process information.*

5 Speaking less than 30% of the time, ideally 5% to 10%. Turning body to client to be fully physically present to the client, acknowledging the communication by maintaining eye contact, using soft "sparkling eyes," head nodding, and encouragers. Asking about what is *not* being said. Asking questions that invite client to co-create more questions or awareness of mental and emotional structures and resources, client talking extensively and then saying, "I never thought of any of this before you asked about it."

4 Asking questions that probe for more details about client's view of things, inviting client to self-listen ("Did you hear what you just said?") to increase awareness of what's "in the back of the mind," giving space and time for person to be with those thoughts and feelings, being silent as the client speaks 60% or more of the time, supporting client (See *Supporting*). Asking lots of awareness questions about patterns, "How aware are you that you have said lots of things about X, but nothing about Y?"

3 Actively exploring the structure and content by using questions that ask about form, using more body language of head nodding to encourage client to speak, using "encouragers" such as sounds, "hmmm," "ahhh," "yes, go ahead," "say more." Using extended silences and pauses so client speaks at least 50% of the time.

2 Eye contact regular, repeating back specific words and some paraphrasing that matches client's content, speaking 60% or more of the time and quiet only 40% of time, giving little time for client to speak.

1 Making some eye contact, paraphrasing the client's sentences, only partially keeping general track of the content. "Where are we?" Taking notes on other things than client's statements and eyes internally processing while client speaks. [If eye contact *means* something other than listening and respect in a given culture, then turning body toward client or equivalent.]

0 No evidence of being present to client as indicated by no eye

Definition: Supporting: *Providing a sense of safety to client through questioning, listening, celebrating, expressing affirmations of belief in and trust in the client, through managing environment, and the conversation.*

5 Stating one's own concerns and emotions of support with a client, expressing a willingness to invest in the other's well-being and resourcefulness in support of the client's outcomes and agendas, "I'm here for you," "Use the coaching call between sessions when you need to."

4 Responding to client's emotion with one's own that pace, respectfully exploring, inviting the client to access and apply own resources to situation, offering statements of affirmation that conveys belief in the person's potentials, celebrating and cheer-leading client's successes, pacing meta-programs, meta-states, concepts, and values.

3 Actively and intently listening, asking about emotions, investing energy into conversation and managing the environment so that it enables client to stay focused, summarizing, offering some physical response such as putting hand on shoulder, "That must have been challenging." **Matching & Mirroring:** pacing posture, breath, gesture, etc. Words, sounds that encourage to continue: "yes, and then?" "Hmmm," "ahhhh!"

2 Partially matching client's words, posture, breathing, etc., listening for facts, details, ideas, failure to fully match output of other's gestures and non-verbal expressions.

1 Listening with no or little eye-contact, fiddling with other things, failing to follow up statements expressing emotion, seemingly preoccupied with other things. Little or no attention to context and atmosphere to deal with noises, distractions, etc.

0 Indicates little interest: failing to track the content, repeatedly asking "What did you just say?", firing off questions without time to respond. Interrupting. Making statements of judgment, evaluation, blame and interpretations.

* MONITORING IMPLEMENTATION

It's not enough to create a plan for achieving a peak performance or a desired outcome, you have to implement that plan. To implement, you start with an ambitious goal regarding something that you want to put into action. Do this to improve your performance and gain strategic advantage in making a dream come true. Overall planning and working your plan increases your ability to deliver on your outcomes. Yet this does not end the process. There's also the process of monitoring and reviewing the plan to ensure continual implementation.

An implementation plan, as a plan for action, results from strategic thinking. While a well-designed plan sets forth both a strategy and lots of tactical plans, you have to treat it as something dynamic, rather than static. While some plans fail due to poor design, lack of quality thinking and research, lack of ability, *most fail due to failure to implement over the period of the plan.* Plans typically fail, and are vulnerable to being incomplete, due to memory lapses, over-trusting the good will of others, or operating "from the seat of your pants." They also often fail because you do not effectively monitor them as you go along.

To effectively monitor your plans you will need to continue to review the results you're getting to see if you are on or off course. Doing this allows you to harvest critical learnings for the next level while things are small and manageable. *Effective monitoring and reviewing enables you to keep following up and following through.* It gives you a way to consistently attend to what you are doing and how things are going. It gives you the ability to detect early failures and correct them while they are small enough to be easily managed.

Effective reviews also enhance accountability. By reviewing your performance regularly you can plan for a self-correcting progress. This allows you to adjust in a timely manner to an ever-changing environment. When you do this, then deviations from your plans become valuable information.

> *Planning is a focusing process.*
> "Facts often kill a good argument."
> Brian L. Joiner

What will you review? First and foremost review the critical success factors that contribute to the performance. What are the critical factors for your success? Second, focus on early warning signals that indicate a deviation from plan or best practice. What early warning signals shall you focus on?

In the book, *On Target: How to Conduct Effective Business Reviews* (2002), Michele Bechtell writes about the importance of "deviation" as critical information for improving performance. Her following comments offer several new ways to think about deviations so that you access a positive state that allows you to squeeze all the value you can out of them.

> "Positive and negative deviations demand equal attention. This is because every deviation provides a valuable opportunity to uncover the assumptions that cause faulty predictions. Even when we achieve our desired results, it is important to verify that we achieved our results *because* of our plan. The purpose of a plan is to get *planned* results." (p. 74)
>
> "*[Wise leaders] see failure information as leading-edge information* to a find a way to make things work. They routinely identify and study the predictions that did not come true." (p. 73)
>
> "When we ignore problems, we avoid solutions." (p. 131)
>
> "The more quickly we can elicit failure information, the more easily we can diagnose and eliminate root barriers to progress." (p. 132)
>
> "Blame is never part of the solution. We achieve far better results when we analyze and improve the *process*—the methods, protocols, or procedures that got us into trouble in the first place." (p. 133)

> *"One accurate measurement*
> *is worth a thousand expert opinions."*
> Grace Hopper

Figure 9:1

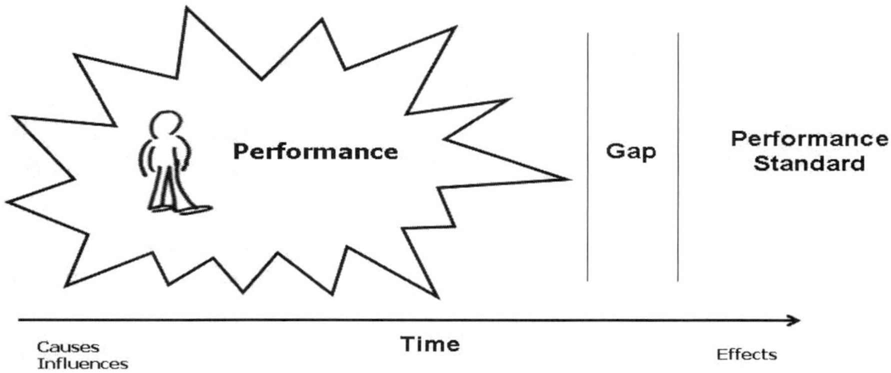

The Pattern:

1) Create a written implementation plan.

What do you want?
What is your plan for obtaining that result?
How long will it take?
What are your priorities? [If everything matters, then nothing matters.]
What are the steps and stages involved?
What must occur first, second, third, etc.? In what sequence?
How much flexibility is there in the task sequences?
How will you measure your progress? [Verification]
How will you know that you're doing a good job?
Is your plan process oriented?
How have you mapped the process?
What will you focus on? What will give you a strategic focus?
What are a few of the most important opportunities that offer the greatest advantage to you? Your core competencies?
Are you mobilized to fulfill your vision?
What must you accomplish this year, this month, this week, and today to ensure your outcome?

2) Identify the critical factors of performance.

What are the critical factors of performance that will make your plan work?
What are the critical factors for break-through to your vision?
What are the rules of the game?
What operational knowledge is required?
How are cause-effect structures related to the outcome?
What are the performance drivers?
How do you know?
How do you differentiate the critical factors from the trivial?
How do they relate to your strategy for the results you want?
How does this fit into your strategic plan?
Are there any gaps in your performance? Where?

3) Tie to your daily schedule.

Have you divided your desired outcome into 12 monthly increments? Bi-monthly increments?
How are you using your calendar?
Have you detailed the critical factors of performance to your daily schedule?
What are 2 to 5 things you will do everyday to make the critical factors of performance real and activated?
How will these tactical pieces make a difference?
Are you just talking about change or have you made structural changes to achieve it?

4) Regularly monitor and track the critical factors of performance.

What will you monitor? How will you monitor it?
How often?
Have you zeroed in on your own critical factors of performance?
What are you learning?
How are your learnings being fed back into the plan?
Are there any gaps between plan and performance?
Do you have some tools for tracking?
Will your tracking catch the needed "failure information?"
Will you catch critical deviations for timely corrective action?

Verification:

How will you know that you are implementing your strategies?
How will you know when you are on plan or off plan?

Figure 9:2

Implementation Plan of Critical Factors of Performance

Objective:

Strategy	*Action Items*	*Calendar*	
1st Quarter	2nd Quarter	3rd Quarter	4th Quarter

1.
2.
3.
4.
5.

5) Study the deviations for critical "failure information."
Because deviations alone do not explain, you have to use them to explore and examine your assumptions and strategy to find the pattern behind the gap.

Have you installed a timely corrective action?
Do you know why you are off plan?
What are the causes and contributing factors?
What false assumptions, non-adherence to the plan, weak strategies, etc. contributed?
What has been the impact of your actions on your goals?
How do you quantify it?
To what extent is the strategy working?
Does your tracking method indicate the speed of your progress?
What is your reporting protocol?
What are the important trends and patterns?
Are you satisfied with your gap analysis?
What are the inhibiting factors?

Is there a delay between any of the cause-effect circuits?
What are the hidden factors (stress, overload, lack of motivation, reactivity, procrastination, excuses, forgetting, etc.)?
What are the sources of the deviation?

6) Develop action plans that are corrective.

Do you have a Plan B or a Plan C in worst-case scenario?
If something goes wrong, what will you do?
What are your alternative plans for failure in the critical factors of performance?
What counter-measures are you planning?
What are your priority objectives?
Do you have a self-corrective plan in place?
Will this solution address the fundamental problems?
Are you focusing on the process or on the goal?
Are you thinking structurally or in terms of a quick-fix?
Is your process *capable* of meeting your goals?
Is it legitimate?
What is the nature of the variation:

An unpredictable outside event?
A bottleneck in the system?
Poor execution: lack of a best practice?
Too much busywork?
Excessive paperwork?
Poor state management?

Deployment: when, where, how?
Have you applied creativity to bridge the gap?
What is the speed of your adaptability?
Do you have a field manual of best practices?

* KEY PERFORMANCE INDICATORS

Benchmarking Personal KPI for Success

- How do you know if you are succeeding in a particular goal?
- What are the key performance indicators at the behavioral level that you are successfully reaching and experiencing the goals and objectives that you've set?

The Pattern:

1) Identify a general goal, objective, or outcome/s that you want.

I want to experience X.
I want to achieve Y.

2) Use funneling questions to drill down to specific criteria (variables) that will become your personal KPIs.

Taking one outcome at a time use the following questioning models to drill down to the necessary specifics:

The precise questions of the Meta-Model.
The indexing questions of who, what, how, where, when, and which?
The scaling questions of how much, to what degree, what percentage?
The realistic questions: what's the probability, how likely is that, is that realistic within the limits of X?, etc.

3) Co-create with your client or colleague a KPI statement that summarizes in sensory-specific terms.

What statement summarizes for you the criteria by which you will measure your outcome?
How can you make that statement even more succinct and compelling?
In reading the statement, does it put you in state and give you a clear mental representation?

4) Evaluate the statement against the crucial criteria of a well-formed outcome.

Sensory-based
Positive statement
Context specific
Time frame
Self-initiated and maintained

Realistic
Compelling
Ecological

5) Record the KPI statement/s for future review and evaluation.

What is the KPI statement that you want to write down that we can use to measure your success in reaching this particular goal?

Example of a personal KPI:

Self: I know I'm confident when I hear myself speaking with a measured and even tempo as I breath fully and deeply from my stomach, and feel the muscles in my shoulders and neck relax as I address the concerns that I want to bring up to my friend (e.g., lover, board, etc.).

Business: I hold my business plan in hand ready to take to the bank. It is a business plan that specifies my market, the budget I have planned, marketing plans, description of the business, how I will do the business, the forecast of expenses and income, etc.

Skill: I feel the phone on my shoulder as I pick it up and my finger runs down the list of numbers of potential clients. And as I dial the number, I feel a growing excitement indicated by faster breath and a slight increase in the muscle tension in my arms and legs. I express this energy in my tone of voice so I speak 10% quicker than my normal tone and speed. This gives "warmth" to my voice as I use lower tones and ask people about their needs, wants, and desires. As I hear these as well as their words about value, I feed them back as I invite them to my introductory coaching session.

Benchmarking the KPI Process

The following is a process that we use in Meta-Coaching for a coach to obtain a KPI with a client in the beginning part of a coaching session. Getting a KPI means assessing a client's needs and wants or doing a needs analysis prior to jumping in and coaching. The sub-skills within this include the following:

1. Directly asking a client what he or she wants.
2. Asking repeatedly about that *want* (4 to 10 times of iteration).
3. Asking about the want while indexing it in the following ways:
   Behavior: Doing what?
   Space: Where?
   Time: When?
   Relation: With whom?
   Process: How?
   Context: In what context?

4. Checking the response with criteria:
   Realism: Is it realistic? Can we do that in this time frame?
   Resources: Do you have the required and necessary resources to reach your outcome? What resources do you need?
   Motivation: Is it compelling? Does it excite you? Would it be worth your time and energy?
   Responsibility: Are you willing to begin and sustain the actions needed to reach your goal?
   Ecology: Is this fitting and appropriate for all of the systems of your life— health, energy, relationships, etc.?

5. Specify the evidence for recording awareness and recognition.
   Is it stated in sensory based terms?
   Can you quantify it? Can you measure it? (Amount, degree, how many times, etc.)

6. Cut through distractions and irrelevancies to the goal.

What are the frames of mind (beliefs) for getting a KPI? Among the key ones are the following:

- I can only coach when I have a specifically stated objective to coach to, and preferably one that is written down.
- To move forward in a new direction and create a desired change begins with a small step.
- Goals have to be grounded in a specific instance with a

specific behavior.

- I will not allow the client to fluff around, but facilitate him or her to get to the point.
- I first gather information; I gather high quality information.
- The presenting problem, need, and want is *the presenting* problem, need, and want (P/N/W).
- There are always things in the back of the mind about problems, needs, and wants (P/N/W).
- There is available information within every person if I only ask enough questions.
- There is always information that is not yet available, but which can be obtained.

The process of getting a KPI for and with a client is essentially conducting a needs analysis with a client. It is asking the central question, "What do you need? You need what to fulfill what desire, fear, hope, etc.?"

Benchmarks:

5: Obtains a statement from the client about what really matters most with less than 10 questions, get the question written down as a sensory-based written statement.

4: Quickly cuts through stories, details, and statements that distract from a sensory-based goal statement. Listens to the client's intent behind the words and stories of the client by asking "What is your intention behind this desire?" "When you get that fully, what will you get?"

3: Asks "What do you want?" repeatedly (4 to 10) to get sensory based statement specifying where, when, with whom, how, and in what contexts. Checks the statement against 3 criteria: realistic, motivation, ecology. Forms the statement to quantify it in terms of amount, degree, times. Sign off with client.

2: Asks, "What do you want?" and repeats the question two or three times, then begins a coaching conversation without co-creating a highly specific goal (sensory-based, indexed to coordinates, stated succinctly) for the coaching conversation.

1: Begins a conversation with the client ("the coaching conversation") without checking what the client wants for that conversation. Probes into global and value desires rather than drilling down to a specific goal for the session.

0: No asking about what the client wants. Telling the client what he or she should want. Ignoring client's statements about goals. Talks about problems and complaints. Starts by suggesting a pattern to use with the client.

Examples:

I want to develop expertise in asking meta-questions so by the end of this session, I will have written 6 meta-questions on a paper. I will hold the paper, see the words cuing me of the meta-question, and run a scenario in my mind of taking the paper with me and using it in my next coaching session.

By the end of this session, I will have 3 ideas about how to facilitate a client to esteem him or herself as having "unconditional value." I will write them down on a paper, and I will know that I have them by recalling the 3 ideas as I verbalizing them out loud.

End of Chapter References

1. See the book *Communication Magic* (2001) for a full description of the Meta-Model of Language model of NLP.

Chapter 10

MEASURING THE SYNERGY OF SELF-ACTUALIZATION

Measurements Scales For Meaning and Performance

Measuring Self-Actualization Potentials and Reality
In this approach to self-actualization the next step is to develop a way *to measure where you are along the meaning and performance axes.* By setting up a scale for each, we can then set behavioral benchmarks for them. Now we can profile our position and range along both the meaning and performance axes.

This is where Geoff Dowell took the development to the next level and created the foundation of *a Self-Actualization Measuring Tool.* He began by designating the 180 degree continuum and creating a scale from -5 to +5, with 0 at the middle. On the left side of the scale we have *meaning* and on the right side we have *performance*. The meaning side of the continuum relates to responding and processing *internally* whereas the performance side relates to responding and processing *externally.* This structure enables us to use the sum of each scale and the difference between the scales to get numeric indicators. This will give us two measurements. First *a range* along the meaning—performance line, and second, *a bias* or preference for where we typically live.

The Meaning—Performance Scale

-5	Meaning	0	Performance	+5

The self-actualization of a fully functioning person means that for the greatest rapport and influence in communicating and relating and for the greatest use of our full potentials as human beings, *we need full range and maximum flexibility in our meanings and performances.* Conceptually, the less range we have and the more our bias is off to one or the other side, the less we can fully actualize our potentials.

How does this work? Geoff describes using it as a measurement tool by illustrating it in the following way:

> Suppose a person has a preference for more meaning (say -4) than for performance (say +2). That person's *range* would be 6 (-4 to +2) out of a possible 10. And that person's *bias* for those numbers would be a -2 (-4 + +2 = -2) indicating a bias for internal processing and the balance is off by 2 units (the "units" here are the 0 to 5 measurements).

This tool for measuring *range* and *bias* also gives us a way to check for agreement with a person regarding how one prefers to operate. When we get the measurement right, people tend to readily relate to it, when we don't, they let us know that it doesn't fit for them. Once we have agreement about the ratings on each scale, we have a rationale for drilling down into the meta-program biases and stretching the range on the limiting side first. Doing this enables the person to move from their comfort zone to the new ground for growth and unleashing new potentials. Ths will give them more alignment and balance.

This zero-centered continuum now gives us a tool that we can use to diagnose the limits or leashes of a person's growth in self-actualization as well as a predictive tool to help us assess what to do to unleash limitations. With this tool, we can use it to determine the interventions for change and development such as coaching *the inner game for the meaning leashes* and training for *the outer game for the performance leashes.*

Testing the Measurement Tool

Geoff tested this with some managers in the UK Health Service to see how they would use it and what they could do with it. The result was encouraging, even exciting because he worked with an organization that didn't relish change.

> "The managers that I worked with immediately understood what I was assessing: 'Is my bias for thinking and reflecting or for active or proactive taking action and doing something?' The managers also immediately recognized the need and value of having full access to the full range of each of the meta-programs as well as the meaning and performance areas of the continuum. While they were a bit suspicious, they were excited about the possibilities."
>
> "There was a difference from how I presented it and how they talked about it. They tended to describe the meaning —performance continuum in terms of *inside versus outside* or the *inner game versus the outer game."*

Geoff said that these particular managers had a strong bias for reflection, even to the point of procrastination. So the discussions turned to "what might happen" (options), if they were really able to be assessed in these terms, how valid would they be, what could they be taken to mean, and if they were mis-interpreted, how might these ratings be used?

From all of that, Geoff reflected on the significance of their lengthy discussions.

> "Could this be the generic "away from" (meaning) bias that I had mapped as the greatest leash within this industry? What these managers chose to do with this tool was to identify the "misfits and mavericks" they knew by their rating at the extremes of the scales. We rated these extreme behaviours as three on the scale of 5, knowing that there would be even more extremes. In fact, these managers would prefer to do anything rather than assess themselves and each other. Could this be why they were managers, and not leaders. I found that they experienced self-assessment and feedback as demeaning and threatening. For self-actualisers this limitation has usually been resolved.
>
> "A few managers were brave enough to develop a couple of

leadership benchmarks to assess themselves and each other. They found that when they had extended their range on the continuum and balanced their bias to around zero, a shift in their *way of being* seemed to take place. Something changed as they stepped back and rose above their patterns and preferences. So they discovered that they were just patterns and preferences, they no longer felt attached to their biases or needed to defend or apologize for them. They found themselves more accepting of themselves and they were given feedback that they were more understanding of others.

This occurred because we had used relevant meta-programs for their roles as well as their improved flexibility. Yet they also seemed to get the meaning / performance synergy at a feeling level of whole body-mind as they transcended the dichotomy. As a result the black-or-white, with us or against us, like me / unlike me, co-operative / disruptive splits faded. Then, in response to the unexpected or unexplained they would ask, 'Is this a meaning issue or a performance issue?'"

Reflections about this Measurement Tool

One of Geoff's conclusions from this was that it appears that, at least for some people, when we achieve a high rating (over 3) on each end of the continuum, a point comes when people seem able to transcend the dichotomy. They can then see both halves of the scale as facets of the same continuum. Meaning and performance may then be considered facets of a meta-category of "potential" or "experience."

Perhaps this is what Maslow referred to when he considered self-actualisation as the opposite of the need for safety.

> "Let us think of life as a process of choices, one after another. At each point there is a progression choice and a regression choice. There may be a movement toward defense, toward safety, toward being afraid; but over on the other side, there is the growth choice. To make the growth choice instead of the fear choice . . . is to move toward self-actualisation." (1993, p. 44)

The bottom line is that the more we *extend* our skills in the opposite direction to our habitual pattern, the more we move from the safety need of our bias. Simultaneously, we move nearer to our true self our potential self, without the limitation.

Scaling the Meaning and Performance Axes — Preliminary Benchmarks

The next step in creating a measurement tool is to identify the key sub-skills of "meaning-making" and "performing" and set up a 0-to-5 scaling. So what follows is a benchmarking the skills within both the meaning and performance axes.

- How do we measure a person's development of "meaning?"
- What's entailed in this ability to create meaning, to quality control the meaning, to suspend meaning, etc.?

These questions raise the subject of sub-skills. So the *sub-skills* within the Meaning Axis involve not only the ability to create meaning, but the quality of those meanings, and those meanings about specific areas such as our psychological health, self, needs, time, problems, knowledge, etc.

1) Quality of Meaning
2) Psychologically Healthy Meaning
3) Power to Create Meaning
4) Self Meaning
5) Meaning about Needs
6) Meaning about Time
7) Meaning about Problems / Difficulties
8) Domain Knowledge Meaning: procedures, strategies, heuristics

Once we have the different sub-skills, we need a scaling format for the meaning axis. The following is what I came up with for the Self-Actualization Workshop:

0: Meaningless	No awareness that meaning can be created. Negative competence
1: Futile	Incompetent, creates sick meanings Unconscious Incompetence
2: Trivial	Creates meanings that are weak, uninspiring Conscious incompetence
3: Conventional	Creates meanings that motivate sufficiently Conscious competent
4: Unique	Creates rich, robust meanings Expert level
5: Legacy or mission	Creates long-term meanings Master level

Scaling the Meaning Axis and its Sub-skills

1) The Quality, Levels, and Meaningfulness of Meaning:

What is the quality of the meanings that you create? Are your meanings inspiring, compelling, exciting, and enlivening? Do they get you up in the morning and excite you through the day? Or, are the meanings that you give to things conventional, "average," okay, but nothing special? To what degree can you *sacrilize* anything? This refers to looking at things in terms of them being special, delightful, wonderful, sacred, full of wonder, seen through the lens of eternity? Or, to what extent is your view of life, people, work, relationships, exercise, etc. full of *de-sacrilizing* and *discounting*? How accurate are your meanings in terms of being "maps" of the territory? How precise are they? How useful? How effective?

0-1: *Futile:* Feeling apathy about life, feeling empty, anhedonia so you receive no pleasure from basic pleasures. Inaccurate, fallacious mapping with lots of distortions, deletions.
2: *Trivial:* Meanings that are "bland" leading to a sneering attitude about almost everything, language that debunks and discounts things. Many meanings contaminated by distortions, cognitive distortions.
3: *Conventional:* A focus on adjusting to culture. Wanting to be "normal," to fit in and "be like everyone else," reading papers and journals about what's "in," and "cool." Meanings mapped fairly accurate to the territory.
4: *Unique:* Meanings that are idiosyncratic to the person; want to "be my own person," meanings that are precise, clear, and accurate.
5: *Legacy / Mission:* Seeing things as if precious, special ("sacrilizing") and re-sacrilizing of meaning, sense of ecstasy, peak experiences. Able to accurately perceive reality, continuously updating maps and increasing precision and clarity.

2) Psychologically Healthy Meanings:

The meanings about yourself as a person, as a living, breathing human being and your development through life, your self-actualization, the health and vitality of your mind, your emotions, your memories, your imaginations, etc. How healthy or unhealthy are the meanings that you create in this area? To what extent have you developed an awareness of your own typical cognitive distortions? To what extent have you eliminated them?

0-1: *Toxic:* The meaning of life, self, work, others, etc. feel hopeless, leading one to be emotionally unwell (or sick) and despairing.
2: *Shallow:* The meanings code life and self in a superficial way leading to debunking actions and sneering attitudes, saying "What's the use?" "Why bother?" Person has lots of "buttons" that can be pushed to trigger a defensive reactiveness.
3: *Culturalized:* The aim is to be "normal," to conform, which requires hiding one's real self behind persona, roles, and masks; and to not allow others to know what one really feels, wants, thinks, or believes.
4: *Personal:* Focus in life is on discovering one's real self; developing a healthy and vigorous sense of self as evidenced by meaningful work, relationships, sense of significance, an unconditional sense of value and worth.
5: *Transpersonal:* Focus in life goes beyond oneself to living by an inspiration about contributing to others, making a difference in the world, leaving a long-term legacy.

3) The Power to Create Meanings:

The meaning you give to your *power* or ability to create meaning in the first place. Do you view yourself as powerful to do so or do you view meaning as given, fated, controlled, and out of your hands? Do you know your powers of constructing meaning? Do you use these powers? To what extent? How much more could you take charge of these powers, develop them? How flexible are you in your creation of meaning? Can you give anything 3 other meanings, 7, 20? How flexible is your creativity in this?

0-1: *Dis-empowerment:* Feeling helpless and hopeless in creating meanings, passive about merely receiving meanings created by others, believe that "meanings are never created," using desacrilizing (discounting, cynicism) as defense mechanism.

2: *Cynicism:* Attitude of "why try," living like a passive receiver of meanings. Viewing meaning as "given, fated, and controlled." Showing little flexibility in identifying alternative meanings when asked.
3: *Normal:* Having some choice in creating meaning, but little to no ability to suspend the meanings one has lived with. Some flexibility in inventing additional meanings, able to create 3 to 5 alternative meanings.
4: *Enlivening:* Able to create uniquely individual and idiosyncratic meanings for oneself; generally able to suspend meaning. Able to create 10 alternative meanings.
5: *Robust:* A sense of empowerment in creating meaning at will, a sense of the fluidity of meaning, able to immediately suspend any meaning that doesn't serve one. Able to create 20 to 30 alternative meanings.

4) Self Meaning:

The meanings that you give to yourself. Do you love yourself, adore and appreciate yourself, see yourself as lovable, precious, sacred, etc. Or do you view yourself as nothing special, okay, average, or do you de-value yourself with judgments, contempt, hatred? The meanings you give about yourself enable you to either get over yourself and on with life or stuck so that you become your biggest problem. Do you separate self-esteem from self-confidence? What meanings do you give to your fallibility, character flaws, and errors? How well do you maintain your dignity when you make a mistake?

0-1: *Worthless:* Speaks with contempt about self, shows self-hatred and despair about oneself by not treating oneself well, letting appearance go, saying one does not care what happens to self.
2: *Nothing special:* A striving to become "okay," but speak often with self-judgments, one is easily threatened about one's "self-value," questioning ones right to be and to deserve good things in life.
3: *Okay:* A sense of being normal and average, speaks about having made a good adjustment to life, but speaks about one's self-value in conditional terms, dependent on doing okay.
4: *Uniqueness:* Embracing one's unique self, and unconditionally self-esteeming and valuing, able to give of self, extend oneself, become self-forgetful.

5: *Sacrilizing:* Quickly acknowledge love for oneself, shows appreciation for one's self and life, acts and speaks about being lovable and precious, at times feeling ecstatic about being human, embrace all of oneself.

5) Meaning of Needs and Impulses:

The meanings you give to your biological, physiological, and animal nature. Do you view your nature and human nature as good or bad; sacred or evil and depraved? What meaning do you give to your basic drives? What are these needs? How do you gratify these needs with accurate and effective gratifications? What meanings do you give when you have a basic needs that's frustrated?

0-1: *Depraved:* Says that human nature is bad, evil, corrupt, and depraved. Represses one's awareness of needs, inability to adequately satisfy needs. May reject needs, drives, and condemn them as evil, and part of depraved human nature.
2: Bad: Says that human nature is mostly bad; tries to avoid awareness of human drives; only minimally attempts to gratify needs; speaks in ways that show a non-acceptance. Rejection of some drives as evil (sex, anger, etc.). Over-load need with too much meaning (psycho-sexing, psycho-eating, etc.)
3: *Good and bad:* Human nature is both good and bad; basic gratification. Accepts human drives, needs, passions, emotions as simply drives.
4: *Is and Inspiring:* Speaks about human nature as just *is*, needs are valid and important, gratify for self. Able to achieve good gratification with appropriate meanings.
5: *Awesome:* Speaks of human nature as the foundation for sacrilizing, for standing in awe of the human experience; sees and describes needs as valid and important, gratify needs in order to reach for a transpersonal vision about contribution of self in life.

6) Meaning about Time:

The meanings you give to the concept of recognizing that our lives begin at a certain time and end at a certain time. Do you construct positive meanings about time so that you enjoy and appreciate each day or do you create interpretations that make you impatient about time, skeptical, regretful, living in the past, fearful of the future? What meanings do you give to scheduling? Prioritizing? Making time for things?

0-1: *Toxic and dis-empowering time:* Impatient about things, refusing to spend and invest time in learning, practice; skeptical about future. No planning or scheduling.
2: *Time as a bother:* Mostly impatient, constantly asking, "How long will this take?" Looking for short-cuts, "get rich quick" schemes (get smart quick, get thin quick, etc.).
3: *Understands value of time:* Recognizes and values that one must devote time to developing a skill; off and on about scheduling.
4: *Values time:* Says, "I know expertise takes a decade of devotion." Prioritizing one's scheduling; recognizes importance of being in the now, using past for learnings, and has a future direction.
5: *Sacrilizes time:* Expresses the attitude, "No matter how long this takes me, I will stay with it." Makes time for all of the important things in life, never feels sense of wasting time; able to fully step into this moment.

7) Meaning about Problems / Difficulties:

The meanings you give to the gap between your present state and your desired state. How do you think of that difference? What meanings do you give to the tasks required to move you to your goal state? Do you love the effort to reduce the difference? Is it fun? Does it mean the activation of your problem-solving skills? Or is it a bother, a nuisance, unpleasant, etc.?

0-1: *Toxic attitude about problems:* Says that one hates problems; denies and resists the presence of problems; refuses to deal with life's problems.
2: *Escape from problems:* Mostly wants a no-problem and no-hassle life, speaks about escaping and avoiding problems. Looks and asks about ways for path of least resistance.
3: *Deals with problems:* Recognizes and says, "Problems are inevitable, make life interesting." "I can learn problem-solving skills." Faces problems head-on without defenses.
4: *Loves problems:* Says and expresses attitude, "I love problems; bring them on." Well developed set of problem-solving skills. Openness to problems.
5: *Sacrilizes problems:* Recognizes and speaks about

problems as the source of growth and opportunity for success. Expansive set of problem-solving skills, skills for creative solving problem. Loves and looks for problems.

8) Domain Knowledge Meaning: procedures, strategies, heuristics:
The meanings about knowledge, about learning, developing strategies, figuring out how to do something, developing procedures and heuristics. What do you think about investing time, energy, effort to understand things? What meanings do you give to learning, unlearning, and re-learning? Is learning fun, delightful, the purpose of life? Or is drudgery, hateful, boring? What do you think about not-knowing or confusion? Are these valuable or dreadful states?

0-1: *Arrogantly ignorant:* Speaks and acts like a know-it-all, invests no time or energy in studying, reading.
2: *Hides ignorance:* Shows interest in studying domain knowledge, but one's recording of information is incorrect or inconsistent, no reference to sources; often pretends one knows more than one really does, admits ashamed to not know.
3: *Openly learning:* Recognizes the domain knowledge of each area, speaks about wanting to study and learn, invests energy in learning, openly admits what one does not know.
4: *Humbly knowledgeable:* Reads widely, demonstrates knowledge about a domain, refers to sources, can compare authors, models, ideas, philosophies; passionately seeking to learn more, modest about what one does not know.
5: *Kaizen learner:* Seeks out everything to read, interview, understand about the domain, able to identify new and creative input to field.

9) Consciously self-reflective about one's meaning-making:
It is only when you step back and reflect with a mindful state that you are able to truly choose. Choosing arises from that higher level awareness of the possibilities. And to reflect on your meanings and your skills of meaning-making puts you in the architect's chair.
0-1: *Totally unaware of creating meaning:* Denies one's role in creating meaning; uses the "is" of identity ("this is that;" "that's what it means").
2: *Stuck in meanings:* When aware of meanings, feels trapped

or limited in altering the meaning, says, "What else could it mean?" "It means what it means."

3: *Meaning awareness:* Speaks about the meanings created and attributed, questions the ecology and quality of them, considers ways to improve extent and flexibility of meaning-making.

4: *Mindful meaning making:* The amount of self-aware conversation about meaning increases (30%); often reflects on one's ability and quality of meaning-making.

5: *Sacrilizes meaning making:* Has a specific plan about increasing reflections on meaning making power, takes time daily to reflect on meanings created or offered; asks about new possible meanings.

Scaling the Performance Axes and its Sub-skills

How do we measure performance? How do we determine the quality and quantity of actual performances that makes things happen in the world? Again, we begin by creating a list of sub-skills. The *sub-skills* within the Performance Axis include how we speak, plan, get along with others, cope with our needs and impulses, put forth effort, practice, follow procedures, persist, keep refining our performances, and bounce back when we experience a set-back. Again, here is the list that I came up with in the Self-Actualization Workshop to make explicit what's involved in "performance."

1) Verbally expressive and precise
2) Planning
3) Social, interpersonal
4) Coping
5) Effort, discipline
6) Practice
7) Procedures
8) Persistence
9) Refining
10) Resilience

In creating a scale for the performance axis we use the following as levels of proficiency in terms of our competency in performing and in presenting a poor, medium, to top performance:

0: Incompetent and unaware.

1: Inexperienced and incapable.

2: Almost competent, the first steps toward competency as an initiate, consciously incompetent, skill in the rough, trainee,

first learner, novice.
3: Competency, able to cope effectively, apprentice, and then a journeyman.
4: Expertise, elegant and efficient in demonstrating the skill, skill well integrated into personality, consistent across contexts.
5: Masterful, consistent and dependable in demonstrating the skill, extending the skill to new areas.

1) Verbally expressive and precise: inquiry, requesting.

This concerns your verbal behavior, your ability to put into words and effectively articulate the meaningfulness and significance of the skill or experience. Are you clear or fuzzy? Can you effectively describe the skill? Can you effectively communicate your passion of it and excite others about it? Does your self-communications induce you into the required states? Your best states of the skill? How precise are your words? How expressive?

0-1: *Inarticulate:* one can't find the words, acts in shy and hesitant way and shuts down even trying to find the words. Says one feels stupid.

2: *Vague expressions:* Speaks one's ideas and meanings but often tongue-tied, or engages in irrelevant chatting, words and articulations are vague and imprecise so that others are constantly asking. "What do you mean?" "What are you talking about?"

3: *Articulate:* Able to express one's thoughts and feelings sufficiently to keep a conversation going without stopping to ask about meanings, able to describe goals and objectives to mean the criteria of a well-formed outcome.

4: *Precisely focused:* Able to articulate the how-to of the skill, or to describe something in a sensory-specific terms, effect of the words leaves others not only understanding, but impressed as they say, "That was great. Now I understand and am excited."

5: *Precision in vision:* Able to articulates an idea, skill, dream, plan, etc. and to induce listeners into state of appreciation of its meaningfulness as others say, "Sign me up." "I want some." Influences others inspiring with a vision of the value of the skill; able to put goals in specific KPIs.

2) Planning: fits well-formed criteria, scheduled, time allocated for the plan:

To embody meaning, it is almost always a matter of efficiency and effectiveness to create an action plan that details what you're going to do, when, where, with whom, using what resources, for what objectives, etc. In designing a desired future, planning is typically one of the first actions that we take to embody our highest meanings. Do you have a written plan? How clear, detailed, relevant, compelling, etc. is your action plan? How often do you look at it and use it? How do you use it?

0-1: *Planless:* Responding spontaneously in off-the-cuff activity, showing no structure or plan for actions, reactive rather than thinking ahead and planning an action (proactive).
2: *Some planning:* Showing or expressing a rough outline of a plan, a sketch, a "to do" list.
3: *Well-formed plan:* Showing or expressing a reflective plan for what to do that includes specifics about when, where, with whom, why, etc. The plan written or diagramed.
4: *Comprehensive plan:* A plan presented in some form that's been reviewed and refined, discussed and agreed with peers, then used or consulted 2 or 3 times a week [monthly/ weekly].
5: *Enticing plan:* A comprehensive plan that is continuously reviewed and improved, used daily as personal checklist and guide for prioritizing activities; a plan that entices those who hear to sign up for it.

3) Inter-personal effectiveness, social, relating to others:

This refers to the social dimension of performance, the actions that we take that involve others as we work *with* and *through* people. How are you at the social interactions of contacting, networking, informing, communicating, supporting, listening, delegating, leading, managing, etc.? What do you do to facilitate the resources of others? Who do you have to work with? What do you do to win that person's heart? How are you at conflict resolution, forgiveness, starting over, holding accountable, etc.? Do you have a support group?

0-1: *Completely individualistic:* Person ignores other people, judges them, mismatches what they say and do. Fails to contact others, speak to them, when in their presence, does not listen, but lectures and gives advice.

2: *Awkward contacts:* Mismatches what others say and do as much of the time as matches; shows little awareness of others as evidence by saying things about them that they then correct; often continues to lecture and gives advice.
3: *Connecting:* Matches others in how they speak, tempo, gestures, words ("pacing"), expresses compassion and concern in words and gestures, gives others time and energy as one actively listens (with eye contact, able to repeat words), supports, delegates tasks as part of leading.
4: *Higher level contact:* Matches the person's values, beliefs, etc. by using the other's words and gestures, extends self with and for others as indicated by amount of time. Leads by going first, inducing sense of support in others.
5: *Devoted connections:* Matches the person's thinking style or "meta-programs" in a way that leads to win-win relationships that the other says, "This is good; I like this."

4) Coping with needs:

This dimension of performance involves how we cope with our basic needs as well as cope with the demands and requirements of the environment. How are you at coping with the challenges, problems, and difficulties involved as you unleash this potential? What's holding you back, keeping your down, or interfering? What coping skills do you have? What coping skills will you need to learn and develop? What are the satisfiers that you use to gratify your needs? Do they satisfy your lower needs so they vanish and the self-actualization needs emerge? Do you take care of your physical needs for exercise, fitness, and energy?

0-1: *Dependency:* Dependent on others for have basic "needs" met (as per Maslow's hierarchy of needs), needs often not met, presence of pathologies and meta-pathologies (as per Maslow's list); reactive and aggressive (in "survival" mode).
2: *Growing independence:* Able to independently meet many of one's own needs yet often falls back into a neediness that can lead to being reactive when frustrated; most of the time thinks and speaks about one's own needs (70%).
3: *Independence:* Meets one's own needs without remorse or regret, being a "healthy animal" (Maslow) in valuing and appreciating needs as expressed in language.
4: *Interdependence:* Living for the *Being*-needs (order,

justice, truth, contribution, meaning, music, math, etc.) as expressed in words and seen in actions, little attention or comments about the lower or deficiency needs.

5: *Transcendence of needs:* "Transcends" B-needs by not speaking about them at all or very little, focus entirely on the higher needs, conversation, energy, time, devoted almost entirely on such.

5) Activity level: Discipline, effort, energy

The dimension of effort explores how much effort, work, discipline, struggle, etc. are required in developing and unleashing the potential. What is the effort that you have to expend to learn or further develop your competency? What area is this effort in? How long will you be required to put forth the effort? How consistent are you in the discipline of learning, apprenticing yourself, etc.? What percentage of effort do you put out in your daily actions? Do you have a disciplined approach? How well can you get yourself to follow through?

0-1: *Inactive*: Level of activity, movement, task engagement too low to succeed at the skill. Language full of excuses, complaints, grumbles.

2: *Inconsistent activity*: One's efforts on, then off, others cannot depend on the activities or exertion, need encouragement and motivation of others as expressed by statements, "I need someone to motivate me or get me going."

3: *Consistent activity*: One exerts actions constantly which lead to new skills, results desired from exertion.

4: *Intense activity*: One's actions of effort sustained over course of developing skill, learning new domain, getting the results that indicate "success" in a given area. Effort extends beyond what's necessary.

5: *Planned intensity:* The effort exerted is not only consistent, regular, that others can depend on, but motivated from an inner passion of a vision or mission, and carried out as a planned for developing.

6) Practice:

The dimension of practicing our skills involves rehearsing what we know to do until our skills habituate as our daily ritual. Within your rituals will be the regularity of your practice, the quality of the coaching, consulting, training, etc. you receive. Do you practice your skills? How much practice do you give yourself to? How structured is the practice? Do you set stretch goals? How often? Do you engage in "deliberate practice?"

0-1: *Lack:* One resists the need for practice by missing opportunities, failing to plan for time, making excuses, no carrying through.
2: *Inconsistent*: One's efforts and attendance at showing up for scheduled practices on and off, others cannot depend on whether one does or does not carry through.
3: *Consistent:* Person believes in the value of learning as evidenced by showing up, carrying out required number of repetitions, learns and uses the details about the practice in exerting effort.
4: *Consistent learning*: One engages in activities ("practices") constantly asking about what it means, what it will do, looking for results, and in this way being "mindful" in the practice.
5: *Mindfully active*: Engages in rehearsing times with an intense that is consistent and devoted to success as evidenced by speaking about improvement and asking for hints for further improvement.

7) Following Procedures: sequencing efficiency

Within the actions that make up a skill that we want to unleash are often specific procedures that have to be followed in a stepwise way. What procedures are required for developing your skills? To what degree do you follow through on the procedures? How do you handle your own excuses?

0-1: *Rebels to procedures*: One may try to follow required procedures, but gets distracted, makes excuses, says that one "feels controlled," and has "lost his freedom."
2: *Inconsistent*: One sometimes follows procedures, then one does not; practice of following is on and off, constantly trying to amend or improve the process.
3: *Consistent*: One speaks about importance of correct

procedures in appropriate areas and follows the steps to get results in as short a time as possible ("efficient").

4: *Efficiently consistent:* Repeats procedural steps until the steps streamline as if a single efficient response that's automatic as evidenced by the behavior occurs whenever person decides to act.

5: *Flexible follow-through*: One "efficiently" follows through and embodies the procedures so they are "natural" as evidence by no words indicating conscious awareness; one is able to change the procedure and perform the new one "efficiently."

8) Follow-up: persistence

Within practice, discipline, and effort is the activity of persisting in our action plan. Are you persistent? Do you keep focused on developing competency and expertise? How consistent are you in persisting over time? What interrupts or interferes with your persistence? What would increase or improve your persistence?

0-1: *Lack of follow-up*: One makes excuses, blames, judges, fails to act on the required task.

2: *Inconsistent follow-up*: One makes attempts at returning to an incomplete task to complete it, but often gets side-tracked, or makes excuses.

3: *Consistent:* One keeps at a task until one completes it, doesn't let external circumstances to get in the way; others can depend on the person doing what he or she says.

4: *Facilitative consistency:* As one stays with a task, the activities seem so natural, easy, and inevitable that others comment using these terms; one shows no struggle or stress in acting on tasks.

5: *Powerful consistency*: One's consistent activity in returning to the task until it is complete carries with it a determination and "never-say-die" attitude evidenced in person say, "I just have to do this; and I will!"

9) Refining: Kaizen, Feedback, Celebration, acknowledgment

Inside of practice and persistence is the refining process of *kaizen*—continuous improvement. This occurs through the receiving and using of feedback. How open are you to receiving feedback and shaping on your skills? From whom do you look for feedback? What kind of feedback? How often do you receive feedback? How do you use the feedback? What do you do with it? Do you ask for feedback? How often?

0-1: *Repeated mistakes and failures:* One forgets about feedback, about refining skill, makes excuses, blames; one says, "Why keep learning; it's good enough as it is."
2: *Inconsistent:* One sometimes hears and acts on feedback and at other times does not; can quickly fall back onto making excuses and offering judgments.
3: *Consistently improving:* One receives feedback as part of learning process for improvement and uses mirroring information and suggestions for taking actions that correct things ("corrective actions").
4: *Dedicated improvement:* One looks for and invites feedback for refining improvements and immediate acts on such ("integrate") into next performance.
5: *Passionate improvement:* One invites feedback from everyone, friend and foe, integrates as soon as possible and does giving thanks to those who provide it.

10) Resilience

In the development of any skill there will be set-backs—set-backs in our schedule, to our health and well-being, to succeeding or failing, etc. Resilience is the dimension of embodying the skill through getting back up when we have been knocked down, shaking off the dust, and going for it again. What do you do to "bounce back" with resilience when you have experienced a set back? When you are knocked down, what do you do? How long do you stay down? What resilience-building things do you do? What puts "bounce" into your spirit and attitude?

0-1: *Defeated:* When one is defeated, person lies down, quits, uses excuses to explain why he can't achieve success, says he or she is "Doomed to failure." Uses lots of deterministic language expressions: fate, predestinated, etc.
2: *Inconsistent resilience:* One experiences high levels of stress, depression, frustration, anger, fear, etc. when suffers a set-back; long periods of time used for getting over the emotional roller-coaster of the set-back (months or years).
3: *Consistently bouncing-back:* One returns to life, the skill,

an activity, etc. after being knocked down by a defeat or failure; time frame much shorter (weeks or months).
4: *Quick bounce:* One quickly faces the fact of the set-back, looks for understanding and returns to the task.
5: *Unstopable:* One keeps on learning, getting and integrating feedback even in the set-back so no time away from the task, gives the impression of being "unknock-down-able."

Scaling Meaning and Performance Synergy

1) *Identify a specific item.*

Start with a specific item that you want to see where you are in terms of the meaning you give to it and the level of performance you have developed with it. It could be writing a business plan, running a marathon, delegating, exercising, writing a book, etc.

2) *Scale the item for meaning.*

Go through each of the sub-skills for creating meaning and identify a number for each, locating each on the left side of the continuum (between -5 and 0).

3) *Scale the item for performance.*

Go through each of the sub-skills for gauging where you are on the performance scale and put those numbers on the right side of the continuum (between 0 and +5).

4) *Average the numbers.*

Get an average on each of the sub-skills for your meaning scale and your performance scale. This will give you your *range*. For example, you may have a -4 as your average on the meaning side, and +1 on performance. That would put you in the Self-Actualization Quadrant III —you're a dreamer. If you have -2 on meaning and +4 on performance, you may be a workaholic in Quadrant II.

5) *Merge the numbers.*

Take the meaning and performance numbers and merge them and you will find your *bias* in terms of how well you are or are not creating synergy with both your inner and outer games. The aim is to *center* your bias so that it is equally balanced with high meaning and performance.

6) *Review the 12 key meta-programs in terms of unleashing greater potential.*

Review the dozen meta-programs as meaning-performance continua looking for "driving" meta-programs that may be given too much meaning to the point of making it rigid. Use the expanding meta-programs process for any driving meta-programs.

Summary

- Self-actualization is a function of meanings and performance. So we actualize our highest and best unique expertise through creating a synergy of these two variables.

- On the *meaning* side, a self-actualizing person who develops expertise has extensive domain knowledge about an area that comes from extensive reading, exploring, experimenting. The expert finds the domain fascinating, interesting, highly significant, and valuable—all expressions of meaningfulness. And the expert has practical how-to knowledge involving strategies, formulas, methods, and heuristics that enables the expert to know the domain practically.

- On the *performance* side, a self-actualizing person who develops expertise develops a practical how-to or procedural knowledge in practical skills for negotiating the territory of the domain. The expert also has a repertoire of skills that are far more wide-ranging than a novice as the development moves through being an apprentice through practice and persistence, a journeyman, to an expert in following-through, and executing with elegance.

- With this measurement tool we can now begin to measure and profile where we are in our development. This process of measuring inevitably raises our cognitive and physiological awareness about our limits and potentials. By expanding our range and balancing our bias with both meaning and performance creates a new synergy. Now we can constantly evaluate and calibrate how we think about our meanings and actions. This measuring process also enables us to more effectively quality control our development making sure it is healthy and ecological.

End of the Chapter References

1. *Geoff Dowell,* is qualified Manager, Teacher, and Therapist. After 25 years in industry with a wealth of experience in working with people, he is now pursuing his passion for actualising human potential. As a NLP and Neuro-Semantic Trainer, and a certified Meta-Coach, he specialises in Coaching Senior Executives, "Transforming organizations by working with individuals" in the UK.

1. See *Unleashed: A Guide to Your Ultimate Self-Actualization* (2007) and the articles on the websites www.neurosemantics.com and the Self-Actualization Reflections on www.self-actualizing.org.

APPENDIX A

NLP models

1) The Meta-Model. A model about language and the linguistics that make up the structure of our mental mappings about the world and how we conceptualize the worlds that we seek to navigate. Originally a set of 12 linguistic distinctions (and now 21, in *Communication Magic, 2001*) from which you can ask great questions. Meta-model questions invite a person to re-access an experience and re-map it more accurately, usefully, and empoweringly. These "down" questions ground conversation in specific references which then creates greater precision and clarity.

2) The Meta-Modalities. A model about the cinematic features of your inner "movies." Discovering the cinematic features and how to use them to edit your representations enables you to often create comprehensive change of a perception or frame of mind. Altering cinematic features, or creating new ones, can change the way a person processes information and therefore the meaning it holds for that person. See *Sub-Modalities Going Meta* (2005).

3) Meta-Programs. This is a model of perceptual filters—the lens you use that governs what you sort for and attend to. Meta-Programs are also the thinking patterns you use to create how you create your "personality." *Figuring Out People* (2006) presents 60 key meta-programs.

Neuro-Semantic Models

1) The Meta-States Model. A model of self-reflexive consciousness that maps the way you create levels of awareness and embed them in yet higher levels of frames. This model details how you create meaning at multiple levels and then perform those meanings. See *Meta-States* (2008 third edition).

2) The Matrix Model. A systemic model for being able to follow information as it enters into a mind-body-emotion system and then leaves as energy for responding to your world. The Matrix model combines the cognitive psychology of NLP with developmental psychology. The result is three processes and five contents of self that make up the Matrix of meaning frames that determine the world you live in and operate from. See *The Matrix Model* (2003).

3) The Self-Actualization Quadrants. The quadrants are based on the two axes of meaning and performance. This model maps the relationship between your values and visions for challenge and meaning and your skills and competencies for performance. Synergizing them facilitates the unleashing of potentials and results in a state of flow. Using the meaning and performance scales, the quadrants gives you a way to create a synergy for personal transformation. And based on twelve meta-programs, the Quadrants provides a way to identify hidden areas for the unleashing of potentials. See *Unleashed* (2007) and *Self-Actualization Psychology* (2008).

4) The Axes of Change Model. A model based on four meta-programs that govern how psychologically healthy people change, distinguishing it from models of therapeutic and remedial change. The model provides eight roles for a coach or change agent in facilitating the generative and adaptive change process. See *Coaching Change, Meta-Coaching Volume I* (2004).

5) The Matrix embedded Pyramid. A model that transforms Abraham Maslow's Hierarchy of Prepotent Needs model making it dynamic. It does so by incorporating the neuro-semantic mechanism of creating meaning within the pyramid (using the Meta-States and Matrix models). This transform the Pyramid into a Volcano and thereby makes it possible to use it for facilitating the actualizing of potentials. See *Self-Actualization Psychology* (2008).

APPENDIX B

META-QUESTIONS

The *meta-questions* are based on the fact that all of the higher or meta-levels of our mind are made up of the same "stuff." What is that *stuff*? They are made out of see-hear-feel representations, words, and physiology. These are the components by which we build up meanings in all of the matrices of our mind.

To explore and elicit the higher level structures that govern our lives, use the meta-questions.[2] This will enable you to view a "meaning" as a "belief," a "value," an "identity," an "understanding," or any of the more than 70 categories. The secret about all of these words is this: *Every term as a frame or facet of mind contains within all of the other categories.*

The metaphor I like using to think about this involves imagining a *diamond.* Then I can imagine the many facets of the diamond of my consciousness as simply different *facets* of my perception and focus. Here is a list of the first fifty meta-level distinctions with their meta-questions.

1. Meaning / Significance	What does this mean to you? What meanings are you holding in mind?
2. Belief / Believe / Confirm as real	What do you believe about this? What do you believe about that belief?
3. Frame / Reference	What is your frame of mind about this? What's your frame of reference for this? How are you framing this experience?
4. Generalization / Abstraction	What's your conclusion about this? What have you generalized from that? What do you abstract from this?
5. Realize / Realization	What are you now realizing about this? What realization do you have about this? Realizing that, how do you feel? (Denis Bridoux)
6. Permission /Allow /Permit /Embrace	Do you have permission for this? Who took permission away from you? Are you ready to allow this for yourself?
7. Prohibition /Taboo /Censor /Dis-allow	Is this experience prohibited in you? Does it enhance things to taboo this? Who has tabooed this for you?
8. Feeling (i.e., love, hate, care, joy, etc.)	What do you feel about this? What if you could enjoy this? What feeling would enhance this most?
9. Thought / Notion / Idea	What do you think about this? What thoughts come to mind about this?

What's your notion about this?

10. Appreciate /Appreciation /Celebrate What do you appreciate about this?
What could you appreciate?
Do you appreciate this too much?

11. Value /Importance /Count /Honor What do you value about this?
What's important about this that counts?
Do you honor this in yourself or others?

12. Interest / Fascination What do you find of interest in this?
What's fascinating about this?
How curious are you about this?

13. Decision /Choice /Will /Pros-Cons What's your decision about this?
What choice would you like to make?
What pros and cons are you weighing?

14. Intention / Want / Desire What's your highest intention about this?
What do you really desire about this?
What intention is driving your response?

15. Outcome / Goal / Agenda What outcome do you have about this?
What goal do you have beyond this?
What's your higher agenda behind this?

16. Strategy / Game Plan What's your strategy for this happen?
What's your game plan for this?
What strategy could you develop?

17. Expectation / Anticipation What's your expectation about this?
What do you anticipate will happen?
What do you expect about this idea?

18. Connection / Connect What connection do you see about this?
What's the connection between these ideas?
How do you connect this with . . . ?

19. Cause / Causation What causes this experience?
What's the causation at the heart of this?
Who or what do you hold accountable for this?
What are other contributing factors?

20. Culture /Family /School /Religion What cultural context taught this?
Was this part of your culture?
What will you pass on as a legacy?

21. Presupposition /Assumption /Implication What is the implication of that?
What are you assuming about this?
What premises are you operating from?

22. History / Memory / Referent What does this remind you of?
What examples relate to this?
What memories do you link to this?
How does your history affect this?

23. Rules /Demand /Should /Must /Shall What *should* you do about this?
Authorize / Injunctions / Policy What do you *have to* do about this?
What rule governs these thoughts?
Who authorizes this policy for you?
What injunctions are you acting out?

24. Judgments / Conscience What is your judgment about this?
How do you evaluate this?
By what criteria?
How does this affect your conscience?

25. Definition /Class /Categorize /Category What your definition for this?

How do you categorize this?
What other definition could you use?

26. *Understand / Understanding / Comprehension* What do you understanding about this?
What background knowledge informs this?
How do you comprehend this?

27. *Identity /Identify /Self /Self-definition* What identity are you using in this?
What does this say about you?
Are you personalizing this?

28. *Paradigm /Model /Map /Schema* What paradigm governs these ideas?
How have you mapped your thoughts?
What schema would you like to use?

29. *Metaphor /Symbol /Poem /Story* To use a metaphor, what is this like?
What poem or story enriches your ideas?
Who storied you? Do you like that story?

30. *Principle /Concept /Abstraction* What concept governs this?
What is the principle that's directing your thoughts?
What abstraction would enhance you?

31. *Insight /Contemplation /Scrutinize Think Through* What insights do you have about this?
What's your highest contemplation?
What are you now reflecting in this?

32. *Construct / Computation* What constructs are you making about this?
How are you computing this?
What computations guide these feelings?

33. *Myth / Archetype* What myth is in the background?
How aware are you of this archetype?
What archetype would you like to use?

34. *Hypothesis / Proposal* What's your hypothesis about this?
What proposal would you like to make?
What's your best guess will happen?

35. *Know /Knowledge /Epistemology* What knowledge informs this thought?
What's your epistemology regarding how you know that you know this?

36. *Consequences /Implications* What consequences do you see coming?
What will inaction lead to?
What are you implying in this?

37. *Difference /Comparison /Exception* What's the difference you want?
How are you making comparisons?
When do you not think that way?

38. *Inspiration /Inspires /Moves* What's most inspiring about this?
What moves you most in all of this?
Is this inspiration in your best interests?

39. *Theme / Thematic* What's theme above this?
How thematic are these ideas?
What theme will you bring to this?

40. *Opens up / Emerges* What's now opening up about this?
What emergent thoughts are arising in your mind?
What feelings are about to emerge?

41. *Reason /Rationale / Excuse* What is your rationale for this?
Is this a rationalization for what you want?
Will you let this excuse stop you?

42. Reputation	What reputation is governing this? Who are you in the mind of your loved ones as you say this?
43. Ascribe /Ascription /Affix	What are you ascribing to this? What blame or responsibility are you affixing? What ascriptions govern your thoughts?
44. Transcend / Transcendence	What transcends your thoughts about this? If you were to transcend this, what would you feel? What's the highest way to transcend this?
45. Validate / Approve / Sanction	What validation are you bringing to this? As you hear yourself say that, do you approve of it? How have you sanctioned this?
46. Dis-validate /Disapprove /Taboo	How are you disapproving this? What dis-validation are you experiencing? Would you like to dis-validate this?
47. Higher level of consciousness /Meta	What would happen if you brought an expanded higher level of consciousness to this? What's meta to even this?
48. Step back /Witness /Just observe	What are you aware of as you step back? What happens when you just observe this? As you witness this as a spectator, what happens?
49. Possibility	What possibilities lie behind and above this? What possibility in this are you aware of? What possibility would you like to explore?
50. Probability / Degree / Extent / Percentage	What's the probability this will happen? To what degree are you sure about this? How much are you now experiencing this?

APPENDIX C

Welcome to the Matrix

All of us were born in a Matrix. We didn't create it. We didn't particularly want it, and none of us recognize it at first, yet we were born in *a matrix of frames* within frames within frames. We call that Matrix by numerous terms, "culture," "civilization," "the human condition," our mind-body system, "reality," etc.

The Matrix had been coming together for thousands upon thousands of years as the human race engaged in *time-binding* activities and encoding their learnings in symbolic form (language, mathematics, the sciences, the arts) and enabling those who came later the possibility of beginning where they left off. In this way, the belief frames, value frames, understanding and knowledge frames, the identity and religious frames, and a hundreds of other kinds of frames came together to offer a whole set of filters, constraints, and maps about self, others, and life. In this way the Matrix is given birth or more accurately, evolves. And to the degree we're unaware of it, *the Matrix has us.*

The Matrix comes to us not only as all of the see-hear-feel-smell-taste-balance sensory information from the outside world, but also all of the internal sensory information—remembered and imagined—and all of the conceptual frames that sets mental contexts around that information. So like Neo in the Movie, *The Matrix*, we live in a mind-body Matrix comprised of multiple embedded frames. It is made up of belief frames, value frames, understanding frames, meaning frames, and many more. Our Matrix is our internal model of the world made up of multiple belief frames about many things.

The Matrix Model

The Matrix is made up of multiple sub-matrices that are made up of multiple sets of embedded frames about all kinds of things. Together it gives us our *model of the world*—the internal map that we use to navigate life. Unlike animals who operate in the world with genetically encoded programs for what to do, how to be, and what to pay attention to, we experience a freedom and responsibility to construct those meanings ourselves. It is precisely from constructing meanings as we develop and move through life that we construct the matrices in which we now live. And with that, the adventure begins.

Yet before the full Matrix develops, it all begins with a state—just a simple mind-body state of awareness.

States and the Matrix

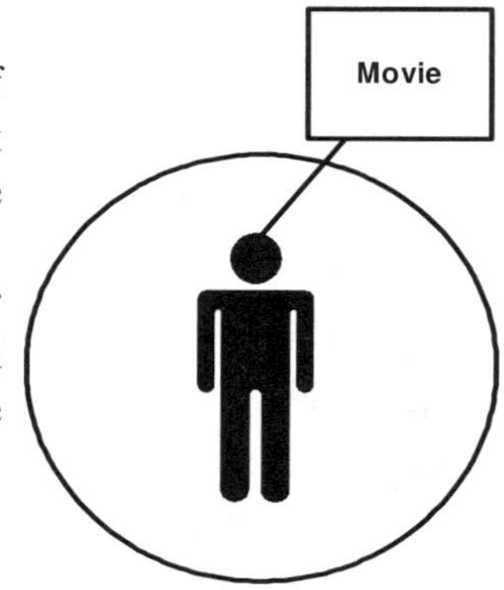

It all starts with our everyday *states* of consciousness. We never leave home without These are mind-body-emotion states. After all, we are always in some state of mind or emotion. These neurological energy fields govern our perception, communication, behavior, memory, and learning and so color our world. These states are also driven by frames of meaning.

Matrix Grounding

The Matrix is grounded in a neuro-semantic *state.*
Without this grounding, we lose our sense of reality and our ability to effectively adjust ourselves to the world as we find it. This reduces "sanity," making us "unsane." Each of the matrices in-forms and influences the cinema playing in our mind. You could think of your mental movie as the work station of your mind where you present and represent things to yourself again and again. As states rise up to a higher level, or as we say, "go meta," they *stay* and they stay as the matrices of our mind to become the higher level frames that establish our internal contexts of meanings.

First Encounter with the Matrix

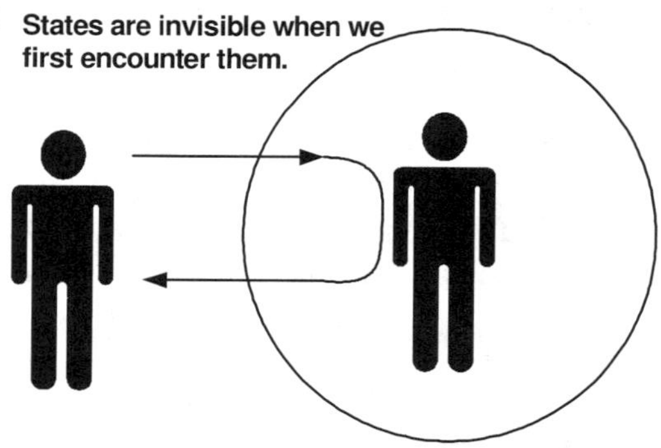

When we first encounter a person, we don't see the Matrix. We don't even see the person's state. It's all invisible to us.

The Matrix "Within"

As we learn how to recognize the meanings and the framings that create our internal world we are enabled to see the invisible matrices of our mind. In that way, they become visible to us.

Our Matrix is our internal world of frames embedded within frames of frames. This makes them layered and complex and our assumed reality. The Matrix of our mind is made up of the thoughts, feelings, and physiology that we use to map the world we live in—the "stuff" that makes up our states.

Our Matrix Movie

We map the World inside as we *re-present* mental movies inside our mind. These maps or movies create our states. The particular content that plays out on the theater of our mind puts us into state by sending signals to our body.

Movie Frames

Above and beyond our internal Cinema are our frames of meaning that influence them. We never just "think"—we think about our thinking. We observe our thinking, direct our thinking, etc. This describes the higher levels of our mind. In this, we think in more ways than just *representation*. We also think in terms of *editing* the Cinema, and the camera shots we use. We think in terms of *directing* the focus of our mind. We think in terms of the Cinema that we *produce*.

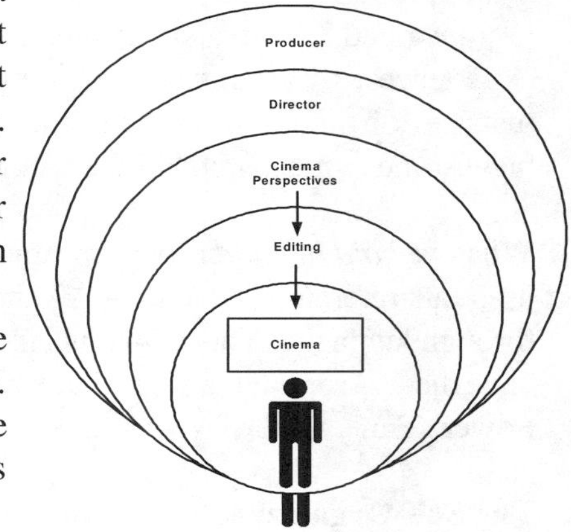

The Funnel of Meaning-Making

As we map things, we generate meanings that we encode into our movies which in turn create our states. This is the foundation or core or *funnel* of our neuro-semantic system. With regard to our states, it is the *meanings* that count. They drive and create the layered nature of our consciousness. When a stimulus occurs, we frame things which activate our state and that in turn evokes our feelings and behaviors. And with that, *the game begins*.

Meanings drive States to create Multi-level Meaning

We make meanings at many levels and though we use different words to describe these different meanings, each of these processes are involved at each level of meaning-making. We first create meanings through associations, then through classifications, framings, and evaluations. At the primary state it begins by making associations—we link our emotional states to our experiences in the world. Then from there we make a meta-move to frame, classify, and evaluate the experience. And while these are different terms and each describes a little different facet of the structure, they all refer to the same process. Our reflexivity creates our meaning making "funnel."

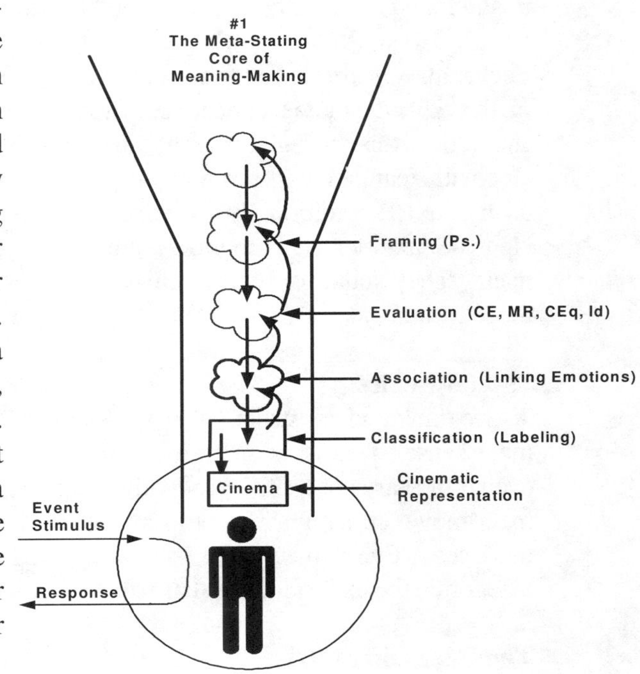

Meta-Stating the Meaning Making Funnel
Via the central and core Meaning matrix we create all of the other matrices in our mind. We give meaning to things by associating states with experiences, by framing, classifying, evaluating, etc. and this calls other matrices of the mind into existence. It is in this way that we stabilize our highest meta-states making them our frames-of-mind or *attitudes*.

What we *hold in mind* is our "meaning" precisely because we hold it and use it as our reference structure. We hold such meanings in our mind mostly through language. This explains language as "the structure of magic." We have these essential matrices that we almost never leave home without: Self, Power, Time, Other, World, and Intention.

The Self-Organizing Nature of the Matrix
The core Meaning matrix creates frames upon frames that make up the other matrices. These provide us understandings, definitions, values, beliefs, decisions, expectations, etc. about a given domain like "Self." These embedded frames also work as self-organizing attractors so that each and every matrix attracts and organizes itself according to the meanings incorporated in its highest frames. An attractor frame dynamically stabilizes a matrix and can put it in conflict with another matrix.

Levels of our Movie-Mind
We experience our awareness of things in terms of the Movie that plays in the Cinema of our mind. What's "on your mind?" Take a look at the movie that's playing inside. These movies typically are two-second movies that flash on and off very quickly, so you have to be fast at catching them.

Each matrix *in-forms* and *frames* the Movies that we watch through how that matrix edits the movie, chooses camera perspectives, directs the production, etc. It does this through using the various belief frames in the matrix. These cinematic features work semantically to encode the meaning in sensory-based terms. NLP traditionally called these features "sub-modalities," but in Neuro-Semantics we recognize them as meta-frames governing the Movie itself. They stand for higher semantic frames and incorporate within them those meanings.

Psycho-Logics:
As we think and construct our maps—our frames and embedded frames all make sense. That is, from the inside they make perfect psycho-logical sense even if they are not useful, productive, or logical to the outside world. Every meta-move sets a higher frame as a "logical" level and so creates our internal matrices. Every meta-state is another "logical" level as it classifies or categories the experience in that way.

The Intention Matrix
The idea of having an intention and wanting to do something about whatever

we're thinking and feeling creates the *Intention* matrix and this leads to the intentional matrix emerging in every matrix. These sets of frames arise from how we map our goals, objectives, outcomes, and purposes. It creates our sense of motivation which we experience as our agendas.

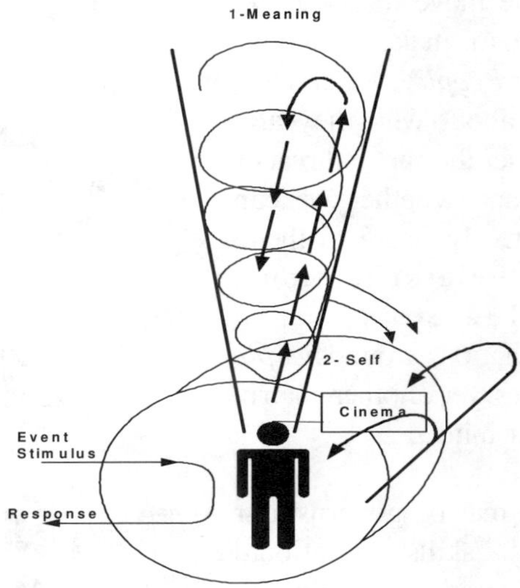

So within every matrix we generate motives and intentions about what to do and what we need to do. Sometimes these conflict with each other. We experience or feel this Intention matrix in terms of what our motor programs create an urge within us to do.

Making Meaning About the "Self" Matrix

We never leave home without our "Self." This set of frames-within-frames influences nearly every experience and is nearly always ready to be activated. How have you meta-stated your "self?" What frames of beliefs, understandings, concepts, classifications, etc. have you set that creates your Self matrix about the following?

- Worth or Self-esteem: Conditional or Unconditional.
- Competence in a skill: Self-Confidence to do that.
- Social Self: Self as seen in the eyes of others.
- Self-Definition: Self-image.
- Conscience: Self- as super-ego.
- Ego-Strength: Self that faces reality.

There are many facets of our "self" as a concept. How this most intimate map is constructed and what it allows us to do or not do fundamentally influences all of our thoughts and feelings.

The Power Matrix

We also make meanings as we meta-state ourselves about our sense of power and resourcefulness. This matrix governs our core mapping about what we can or cannot do as we move through the world. Can I handle the world? Do I have the skills and ability to cope with things? What things can I do with competence and confidence? Am I helpless or can I do something? Can I grow and develop more skills and become empowered? This matrix governs whether we will approach or avoid events.

The Others or People Matrix

As we move through life, we also make meanings about *People*. We create a map about who they are, whether they are a threat or not, and whether we can effectively relate to them. The classifications, evaluations, and associations around *people* creates yet another matrix of our mind.

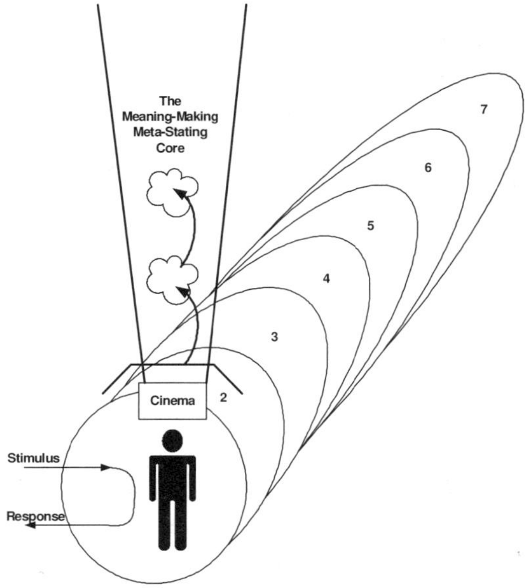

This matrix governs our social skills, relational skills, and our ability to work with and through other people. It determines whether we approach or avoid, whether we like or dislike, whether we fear or desire or in what combination. This matrix also reflects our meanings about ethnic and cultural groups, communities, politics, and persuasion.

If we never leave home without our audience, who is in your social panorama? How do you structure and categorize all of the people that play a role in your life?

The Time Matrix

As we move through the world, we map our understanding of events that *have happened, are happening,* and that *will happen.* It is this identification and comparing of events that allow us to conceptualize the idea of "time."

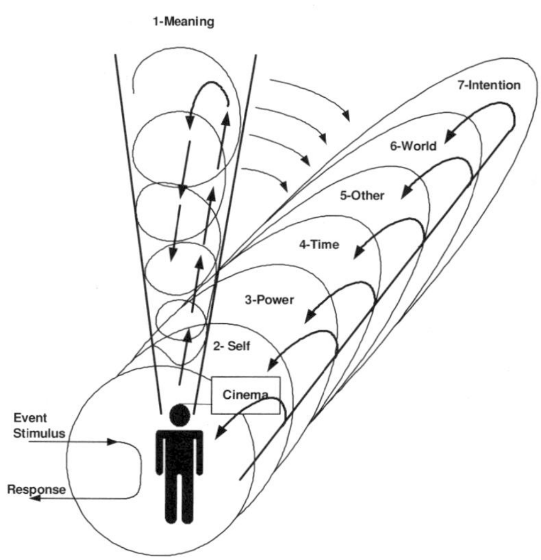

This allows us to live in various time zones: the past, present and future. It enables us to relate to Time as a friend or as an enemy, as a resource or a limitation, sequentially (through-time) or all at once (in-time).

The World Matrix

In this matrix we map how we have created meaning regarding all of the worlds we live in: the various physical environments, the world of work and business, culture, physics, family, and every other universe of meaning. In this matrix we answer such questions as: What's out there? Is the world friendly or unfriendly? Then, when we put all of this together, we create our world-view.

When the Invisible Becomes Visible

The Matrix becomes visible to us as we recognize the various frames of the sub-matrices activated. We can see this in neurology and physiology as a person goes into a state and we can hear it when a person uses the language that activates a given matrix. Think of the Matrix as a hologram in space . . . with the individual matrices flashing on and off as they are activated.

When the internal semantics are activated, the Matrix becomes visible as it is activated by an event or by information. Via the Meaning matrix we construct the other matrices which together becomes our intention model of the world.

The System Loops of the Matrix

There are multiple feedback—feed forward loops in the neuro-semantic system. At the primary state we have input-output that we recognize as Stimulus–Response. This is the most obvious and overt of them. A situation occurs and we respond. At the core meta-state loop of meaning making, we feed information to the higher levels of our mind which in turn, informs the matrices. Then each matrix offers a system loop as information and energy enters each one and activates the frames within it . . . and then that matrix responding and feeding forward its information.

The Matrices in the Back of the Mind

The matrices are always ready to be activated according to current conditions and stimuli. These matrices lie in the back of our mind—outside of conscious awareness and make up our "unconscious" mind. They all influence the cinema of the mind.

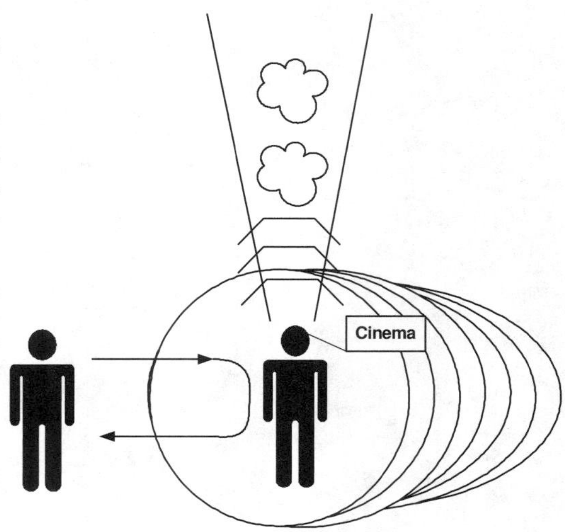

Matrix Analysis

Matrix analysis allows us to understand the neuro-semantic system as a system: how it works, what drives it, the spiraling loops within it, and the leverage points for transformation. *Matrix analysis* allows us to identify the driving and critical matrix within and behind every experience.

Matrix Holarchy

Holons (a part in a whole within a larger whole, etc.) enables us to understand the system as a system. The Matrix is a holarchy. The levels of the mind do not operate as a hierarchy with steps and ladders, but as a holarchy. We can find in every part of the cinema the whole. The whole shows up in the cinema as the cinematic features of the movie.

BIBLIOGRAPHY

Bechtell, Michele L.(2002). *On target: How to conduct effective business reviews.* San Francisco: Barrett-Koehler Publishers

Bossidy, Larry; Charan, Ram. (2002). *Execution: The discipline of getting things done.* NY: Random House, Crown Business.

Cooper, Michael; Goodenough, Tim. (2007). *In the Zone with South Africa's Sports Heroes: How to Achieve Top Performance in Sport and Life.* Cape Town, South Africa: Zebra Press.

Dilts, Robert; Grinder, John; Bandler, Richard; DeLozier, Judith. (1980). *Neuro-linguistic programming, Volume I: The study of the structure of subjective experience.* Cupertino. CA.: Meta Publications.

Ericsson, K. Anders; Charness, Neil; Feltovich, Paul; Hoffman, Robert. (2006 Ed.). *The Cambridge Handbook of Expertise and Expert Performance.* New York, NY: Cambridge University Press.

Fournies, Ferdinand F. (2000). *Coaching for improved work performance.* New York: McGraw-Hill Publishers.

Hall, L. Michael. (2000). *Meta-States: Mastering your higher states of mind.* Grand Jct. CO: Neuro-Semantics.

Hall, L. Michael. (2000). *Frame Games: Persuasion elegance.* Grand Jct. CO: Neuro-Semantics.

Hall. L. Michael. (2000). *Secrets of personal mastery.* Wales, UK: Crown House Publications.

Hall, L. Michael. (1999 / 2006). *Inside-out Wealth: Training Manual.* Clifton, CO: Neuro-Semantic Publications.

Hall, L. Michael. (2003). *NLP going meta: Meta-levels of modeling.* Clifton, CO: Neuro-Semantic Publications.

Hall, L. Michael. (1997 /2005). *Figuring out people: Reading people using meta-programs.* Clifton, CO: Neuro-Semantic Publications.

Herron, Timothy; Bohan, George; Meyer, Robert. (1997). *People make the difference: Prescriptions and profiles of high performance.* NY: Oakhill Press.

Koch, Richard. (2003). *The 80/20 Individual: How to accomplish more by doing less—The nine essentials of 80/20 Success at work.* New York: Currency, Doubleday.

Korzybski, Alfred. (1941 / 1994). *Science and sanity: An introduction to non-Aristotelian systems and general semantics,* (4th. ed. & 5th. ed.). Lakeville, CN: International Non-Aristotelian Library Publishing Co.

Levinson, Steve; Greider, Peter. (1998). *Following through.* NY: Kensington books.

Marsh, Henry. (1997). *The breakthrough factor: Creating a life of value for success and happiness.* New York: Simon and Schuster.

Pfeffer, Jeffrey; Sutton, Robert. (2000). *The knowing-doing gap: How smart companies turn knowledge into action.*

Pryor, Karen. (1984). *Don't shoot the dog! The new art of teaching and training.* New York: Bantam Books.

Rostron, Sunny Stout. (2002). *Accelerating performance: Powerful new techniques to develop people.* London: Kogan Page Limited.

Scott, Susan. (2002). *Fierce Conversations: Achieving success at work and in life, one conversation at a time.* New York: Viking: Penguin Press.

Stanley, Thomas J.; Danko, William D. (1996). *The millionaire next door: The surprising secrets of America's wealthy.* Atlanta, GA: Longstreet Press.

Stanley, Thomas J.; (2000). *The millionaire mind.* Kansas City, MO: Andrews McMeel Publishing.

Thomas, Dan. (1993). *Business sense: Exercise management's five freedoms.* NY: The Free Press, Simon and Schuster.

Ziglar, Zig. (1986 / 2003). *Top Performance: How to develop excellence in yourself and others.* Grand Rapids: MI. Revell.

L. Michael Hall, Ph.D.

Neuro-Semantics®
P.O. Box 8
Clifton, Colorado 81520 USA
(970) 523-7877

www.self-actualizing.com
www.neuro-semantics-training.com
www.neurosemantics.com
www.meta-coaching.org

L. Michael Hall is a visionary leader in the area of personal development, empowerment, and self-actualization. Founding the field of Neuro-Semantics with the Meta-States model in 1994, Dr. Hall has created numerous models and hundreds of patterns—all designed to enable people to facilitate their own self-actualization.

Michael is a modeler of excellence and self-actualization; he is also an entrepreneur, author, researcher, and international trainer. His doctorate is in the Cognitive-Behavioral sciences from Union Institute University. For almost two decades he had a private practice as a psychotherapist and was licensed as a professional counselor (LPC) in the state of Colorado.

Dr. Hall found NLP in 1986 and studied it in trainings with Richard Bandler, afterwards writing several books for him. Later when modeling resilience, he developed the Meta-States model (1994). That led to the beginning of his international trainings. In 1996 he co-created the first Society of Neuro-Semantics with Dr. Bob Bodenhamer, now *The International Society of Neuro-Semantics* (ISNS).

As a prolific writer, Michael has written more than 35 books, many best sellers in the field of NLP. While Dr. Hall first applied NLP to coaching in 1991, it wasn't until 2001 that he began creating the beginnings of Neuro-Semantic Coaching, then with Michelle Duval, they co-created Meta-Coaching Training System.

Dr. Hall is primarily a modeler of positive psychological experiences. He has modeled resilience, meta-cognition, leadership, coaching, accelerated learning, and so on.

ISNS: International Society of Neuro-Semantics. L. Michael Hall and Bobby G., Bodenhamer trademarked both Meta-States and Neuro-Semantics in 1996 and began the first *Institute of Neuro-Semantics*.